Diagnostic Essentials of Psychopathology: A Case-Based Approach

This book is dedicated to my husband, Scott Hammond, and my two children, Adriana and Neil Hammond, the loves of my life.

Diagnostic Essentials of Psychopathology: A Case-Based Approach

Cheree Hammond

Eastern Mennonite University

Los Angeles | London | New Delhi
Singapore | Washington DC | Melbourne

FOR INFORMATION:

SAGE Publications, Inc.
2455 Teller Road
Thousand Oaks, California 91320
E-mail: order@sagepub.com

SAGE Publications Ltd.
1 Oliver's Yard
55 City Road
London, EC1Y 1SP
United Kingdom

SAGE Publications India Pvt. Ltd.
B 1/I 1 Mohan Cooperative Industrial Area
Mathura Road, New Delhi 110 044
India

SAGE Publications Asia-Pacific Pte. Ltd.
18 Cross Street #10-10/11/12
China Square Central
Singapore 048423

ISBN: 9781506338101

Acquisitions Editor: Abbie Rickard

Editorial Assistant: Elizabeth Cruz

Production Editor: Megha Negi

Copy Editor: Diacritech

Typesetter: Diacritech

Proofreader: Eleni-Maria Georgiou

Indexer: Diacritech

Cover Designer: Dally Verghese

Marketing Manager: Katherine Hepburn

21 22 23 24 25 10 9 8 7 6 5 4 3 2 1

Brief Contents

Acknowledgements xv

About the Author xix

1 Making Sense of the DSM 5 1

2 Eight Steps to Diagnosis 23

3 The Justification Process 49

4 Case Conceptualization and Treatment Planning 65

5 Neurodevelopmental Disorders 87

6 Schizophrenia Spectrum and Other Psychotic Disorders 119

7 Disorders of Mood: The Bipolar and Unipolar Disorders 151

8 Anxiety Disorders 203

9 Obsessive Compulsive and Related Disorders 239

10	Sleep-Wake Disorders	269
11	Trauma and Stressor-Related Disorders	299
12	Dissociative Disorders	333
13	Somatic Symptom and Related Disorders	355
14	Feeding and Eating Disorders	383
15	Sexual Dysfunctions	415
16	Disruptive, Impulse and Control Disorders	435
17	Substance-Related and Addictive Disorders	461
18	Personality and Related Disorders	503
19	Paraphilia	537
20	File Length Cases	561
Appendix		**583**
Index		**597**

Detailed Contents

Acknowledgements xv

About the Author xix

1 Making Sense of the DSM 5 1

The Purpose of the DSM 1
The Constructivist Nature of Mental Health and Mental Illness 2
Alternative Frameworks for Understanding Mental Illness 3
Criticisms of the DSM 5 4
Poor Inter-Rater Reliability 6
Validity Questions 7
Other Criticisms 10
Social Trends and Diagnostics 11
Minimizing Risk 12
Importance of Mastering the DSM 5 12
The Changing Structure of the DSM 12
The DSM 5 Structure and Its Revisions 15
Conclusion 18
References 19

2 Eight Steps to Diagnosis 23

Step One: Identify Presenting Problems, Symptoms and Observations 23
Step Two: Cluster Related Symptoms, Observations and Presenting Problems 24
Step Three: Identify Potential Diagnoses 25
Step Four: Locate the Diagnosis and Its Criteria Table in the DSM 28
Step Five: Apply Relevant Diagnostic Principles 28
Diagnostic Steps Six, Seven and Eight 30
Step Eight: The Diagnostic Notation 30
Diagnostic Principles and Considerations 37
Clinical Significance 37

Conclusion 47
References 47

3 **The Justification Process** **49**

A Review of the First Five Steps in the Diagnostic Process 51
The Justification Process, Step Six 51
Step Seven, Writing Your Justification 54
Conclusion 62
References 63

4 **Case Conceptualization and Treatment Planning** **65**

Clinical Hypothesis and Case Conceptualization 65
A Contemplative Approach to Conceptualizing Client Difficulties and Strengths 70
The Treatment Plan 73
Nita 79
Justification and Diagnosis 80
A Conceptualization of Nita's Case Through a Cognitive-Behavioral Lens 81
Nita's Cognitive-Behavioral Treatment Plan 81
A Conceptualization of Nita's Case Through an Existential Lens 82
Nita's Existential Treatment Plan 83
A Conceptualization of Nita's Case Through a Narrative Therapy Lens 83
Narrative Treatment Plan 84
A Conceptualization of Nita's Case Through an Integrated Interpersonal Lens 84
Nita's Integrated Interpersonal Treatment Plan 85
References 86

5 **Neurodevelopmental Disorders** **87**

A Glimpse at the Neurodevelopmental Dimension 88
The Autism Spectrum 91
Autism's Tragic History: Nazis, Refrigerator Mothers, Parent-ectomies and the Anti-Vaccination Movement 96

Attention Deficit Hyperactivity Disorder 101
Evidence-Based Practices for Treating ADHD 103
Treatment Interventions for ASD 105
Definitional Cases in Neurodevelopmental Disorders 106
Narrative Cases in Neurodevelopmental Disorders 108
References 110

6 Schizophrenia Spectrum and Other Psychotic Disorders 119

Features of the Schizophrenia Spectrum 120
The Schizophrenia Continuum 122
History and Theories of Etiology 128
Competing Diagnostic Nosologies 131
Skilled Diagnostician: Differential Diagnosis 132
Treatment Interventions for the Schizophrenia Spectrum 137
Cases in Schizophrenia Spectrum and Other Psychotic Disorders 138
References 144

7 Disorders of Mood: The Bipolar and Unipolar Disorders 151

Changes Reflected in the DSM 5 151
Mood Episodes and Their Specifiers: The Building Blocks of the Mood Disorders 152
Non-pathological Mood States 157
The Bipolar and Unipolar Dimensions 160
Bipolarity in Children and Adolescents 164
Diagnosis of Depression in Children and Adolescents 166
The Skilled Diagnostician and Bipolar and Unipolar Mood Disorders 170
Treatment of Mood Disorders 175
Psychotherapy and the Treatment of Mood Disorders 177
The Mood Disorders: Definitional Cases 180
Episodes of Mood and Their Specifiers: Cases 180
Mood Disorders: Definitional Cases 184
Narrative Cases in Mood Disorders 186
References 193

8 Anxiety Disorders 203

Theoretical Approaches to Anxiety 204
Disorders of the Anxiety Continuum 206
Generalized Anxiety Disorder (GAD) 211
Theories and Models Explaining GAD 214
The Skilled Diagnostician: Differential Diagnosis 217
The Treatment of Anxiety 220
Definitional Cases 223
Narrative Cases in Anxiety 224
References 232

9 Obsessive Compulsive and Related Disorders 239

The Obsessive Compulsive Related Disorders 240
Obsessive Compulsive Disorder 242
Etiological Theories of OCD and How OCD Is Sustained 248
The Skilled Diagnostician 251
A Brief Note on the Treatment of OCD and OCRD 255
Definitional Cases in OCD and OCRD 257
Narrative Cases in OCD and OCRD 259
References 262

10 Sleep-Wake Disorders 269

Key Disorders of the Sleep-Wake Dimension 270
Treating Sleep-Wake Disorders 279
Differential Diagnosis of Insomnia: Birgitta 282
Birgitta's Treatment Plan 283
Birgitta: Treatment Plan 285
Definitional Cases 286
Cases in Sleep-Wake Disorders: Narrative Cases 288
References 294

11 Trauma and Stressor-Related Disorders 299

Stress, Trauma and The Trauma Continuum 300
Disorders of the Trauma Continuum 300
PTSD and Its Evolution 304
The Future of the PTSD Diagnosis 306
Populations and PTSD 308
The Skilled Diagnostician 314
Treatments 316
Definitional Cases in Dissociative Disorders 318
Narrative Cases in Dissociative, Trauma and Stressor-Related Disorders 320
References 324

12 Dissociative Disorders 333

Disorders of the Dissociative Continuum 338
DID/MPD and Its History: A Cautionary Tale 340
The Skilled Diagnostician: Differential Diagnosis 344
Treatment Interventions for Dissociative Disorders 346
Definitional Cases in Dissociative Disorders 348
Narrative Cases in Dissociative, Trauma and Stressor-Related Disorders 349
References 350

13 Somatic Symptom and Related Disorders 355

Changes to the SSDs in the DSM 5 357
The Somatic Symptom Continuum of Disorders 358
Theories of Somatic Manifestation 364
SSD in Childhood and Adolescence 365
The Skilled Diagnostician: Differential Diagnosis 366
Treatment 371
Somatic Symptom and Related Disorders Cases for Diagnosis 372

Definitional Cases in Somatic Symptom and Related Disorders 373
Narrative Cases in Somatic Symptom and Related Disorders 375
References 378

14 Feeding and Eating Disorders 383

The ED Continuum 385
An ED Spectrum: Anorexia, Bulimia, Binge Eating and Purging Disorder 386
Newly Identified Disorders: The ED Horizon 389
Theories of Etiology and Factors that Sustain EDs 394
Skilled Diagnostician 398
Treatments for EDs 401
Definitional Cases 402
Narrative Cases 403
References 407

15 Sexual Dysfunctions 415

The Disorders of the Sexual Dysfunction Continuum 416
Changes in The DSM 5 and Their Implications 416
The Biopsychosocial Model for Understanding Sexual Disorders 417
The Skilled Diagnostician 423
Differential Diagnosis: Beatriz 426
Treatment for Sexual Dysfunction 427
Definitional Cases in Sexual Dysfunctions 428
Narrative Cases in Sexual Dysfunctions 429
References 431

16 Disruptive, Impulse and Control Disorders 435

The Disorders of the Continuum 436
Developmental Psychopathology and the Disruptive, Impulse Control and CDs 442
The Skilled Diagnostician 444
Treatment for CDs 450

Definitional Cases in Disruptive, Impulse Control and CDs 451
Narrative Cases in Disruptive, Impulse Control and CDs 453
References 456

17 Substance-Related and Addictive Disorders 461

Substance Use and Cultural and Theoretical Shifts: Implications for the New Diagnostic Paradigm 462
The Diagnostic Process 469
Substance Use and Special Populations 472
Diagnostic Complexity: Dual Diagnosis 477
The Skilled Diagnostician 478
Substance and Addiction Treatment: A Brief Overview 479
Definitional Cases in Substance-Related and Addictive Disorders 486
Narrative Cases in Substance-Related and Addictive Disorders 488
References 493

18 Personality and Related Disorders 503

The Personality Disorders Continuum 504
Winds of Change: The Alternative Framework 507
Three Points of Controversy Regarding the Personality Disorder Construct 512
Borderline Personality Disorder 516
The Skilled Diagnostician 519
Etiology Theories of Borderline Personality 522
Treatment Approaches for Personality Disorders 526
Definitional Cases 527
Narrative Cases 529
References 532

19 Paraphilia 537

The Disorders of the Paraphilic Dimension 538
Conceptualizing “Normal” Sexual Fantasies 544

The Skilled Diagnostician 545
Treating Paraphilias 548
Definitional Cases in Paraphilic Disorders 550
Narrative Cases in Paraphilic Disorders 552
References 558

20 File Length Cases **561**

Adult Intake Form: Case 1: John King 561
Adult Intake Form: Case 2: Seo-Yeon 572

Appendix **583**

Index **597**

Acknowledgements

Perhaps there is no page in this book more important than this one, the page in which I have an opportunity to pause and reflect with profound gratitude on all those who supported me in bringing this project to fruition. I am sure I can't fully do justice to the gratitude I feel, but I will try.

First among these, I want to thank my husband, Dr. Scott Hammond, who supported me through late nights, computer fiascos and all manner of challenges, and even read drafts of the manuscript right up to the 11th hour. For your humor, unending generosity, kindness and love through our decades together, I am deeply grateful.

A host of colleagues, whom I am also blessed to count among my cherished friends, also offered unending support, encouragement and expertise. Dr. Teresa Haase offered a most valuable listening ear in moments of discouragement, commentary and advice on several chapters, and repeated reminders to make room for life, despite the work that still needed to be completed. Dr. Jennifer Cline collected literature on substance use disorders, recommended books and read the chapter manuscript. She was the source of encouragement and shared celebration. Dr. Greg Czyszczon provided consultation on the trauma and stress-related disorders, offering insightful recommendations and support. Dr. Michael Horst contributed case conceptualizations and treatment plans to Chapter 4, identified wonderful quotes from fictional literature, which are scattered throughout the text and co-authored the chapter discussing schizophrenia. Amanda Williams, another generous source of support, contributed the intake format for the final chapter and provided a steady stream of shared laughter. Teresa, Michael, Jenny, Greg and Amanda, thank you so much. Your support and faith through this process has been absolutely priceless.

I want to extend a special thank you to Rebecca Peifer, MA, Tre Harris III, MA, and Garrett Serrels, MA, each of whom contributed to this project in their roles as graduate students. Rebecca has been invaluable in her ability to organize the many, many tasks required when putting together a project of this magnitude. A gifted student with a curiosity for the subject, Rebecca also contributed tables, notably the comprehensive insomnia table in Chapter 10, which is the best part of that chapter, as well as several cases. She continued to provide support and ideas well after graduating. Rebecca is now an outstanding clinician in her own right and a friend. Tre and Garrett each contributed countless hours compiling literature reviews and reading drafted chapters. Both Tre and Garrett have also graduated and have begun their counseling careers. I want to extend my gratitude to each of you and to say how proud I am to include you among my colleagues.

I also want to thank the people who have taught me and made it possible for me to write this book. Dr. Eric Cowan, James Madison University, taught my first psychopathology course, and it is through him that I first became interested in the process of diagnosis. Thank you Eric, for modeling a great classroom experience and for the many intriguing conversations in the intervening years. Dr. Ed Neukrug gave me my first opportunity to contribute to a textbook back when I was still an untested doc student. That experience was inspiring and informative but also gave me the courage to attempt this work. Thank you Ed for giving me that chance. I also need to thank the countless researchers and diagnosticians upon whom I have relied to fill the pages of this book. Finally, my students are probably my best teachers. I want to extend my gratitude to all of my students at the Master of Arts in Counseling Program at Eastern Mennonite University, past and present, for making the teaching experience so meaningful and engaging.

As I come to the end of this text, I want to thank my dear friends, Mert Brubaker, MA, and Mary Pargas, MA. The two of you have been tireless heart companions and champions. Thank you for the support I have felt so deeply. And thank you for the powerful healing each of you brings to the world through your own skillful work with clients.

Finally, a third of this text was written while on sabbatical, at which time I was able to take a 6-month retreat. I want to thank Eastern Mennonite University (EMU) for awarding the sabbatical, which made that work possible. I also want to extend my gratitude to Jetsun Khandro Rinpoche, Barbara Ryan, and Helen Berliner. A most sincere thank you to Jetsun Khandro Rinpoche for granting me to the opportunity for retreat while working on this project at the same time. Barbara and Helen, thank you for the support, care and friendship during my retreat and for helping me to bring important balance between work and practice.

And finally-finally, a very special thank you to Abbie Rickard and to Elizabeth Cruz, editors for SAGE. What can I say? The two of you are amazing. Both of you need a raise, immediately.

Reviewer Acknowledgements

James W. Bartee, West Virginia University

Orly Calderon, Long Island University

Melinda Parisi Cummings, Holy Family University

William D. Ellison, Trinity University

Sherrie Foster, Tennessee Tech University

Christopher C. Garland, Northeastern State University

Mark Giesler, Saginaw Valley State University

Jerry Gold, Adelphi University

Sha-Rhonda Green, The University of Alabama

Carolyn Hester, Grambling State University

Robin J. Lewis, Old Dominion University
Michael J. Lyman, Shippensburg University of Pennsylvania
Amy Mezulis, Seattle Pacific University
Donna Nesbit-Veltri, University of Texas- El Paso
Claudia Porras Pyland, Texas Woman's University
Eric A. Seemann, The University of Alabama in Huntsville
Molly K. Tschopp, Ball State University
Jessica S. Waesche, University of Central Florida
Nikki R. Wooten, University of South Carolina

About the Author

Cheree Hammond received a PhD in Counselor Education and Supervision from the University of Virginia and an MA and EdS in Counseling Psychology from James Madison University. A faculty member of Eastern Mennonite University's Master of Arts in Counseling program for over a decade, Cheree specializes in psychopathology, counseling theories and mindfulness, and psychotherapy, with a focus on Buddhist contemplative theory. When not in the classroom you can find her in the garden, with her husband Scott, adult children, Adriana and Neil, and treasured friends, listening to bird songs and deciding where to plant that next hydrangea.

1 Making Sense of the DSM 5

The Diagnostic and Statistical Manual of Mental Disorders, commonly known as the DSM 5, is the dominant model for diagnosing mental health concerns in the United States. The fifth edition marks the most dramatic, and most highly contested, revision of the manual since its earliest conception in 1844, when the American Psychiatric Association (APA) first attempted to classify institutionalized persons. The APA published the first edition with this name in 1952 (American Psychological Association, 2013/1952). The DSM in all its iterations has been both widely embraced but also deeply criticized. This chapter will describe the purpose of the DSM 5, explore some of the key concerns about the book and the medical model it represents, and will offer guidance into how to navigate the DSM 5 and its current format.

The Purpose of the DSM

The purpose of the DSM is to describe and classify mental health disorders. A classification system is important in order to create a common language for communicating with other helping professionals about client concerns. Without a reliable and valid classification system, it is difficult to conduct research to understand how common a disorder is, which population may be most likely to experience a disorder, and most importantly, how a disorder might best be treated. If the classification system isn't trustworthy, then we can't know if different researchers are describing the same concerns, making it difficult to arrive at a place of confidence that recommendations born out of research can be expected to be helpful with the clients we see in clinical settings. The APA's stated aim in developing and continuing to revise the DSM is to best reflect current research about mental disorders, their symptoms and prevalence, and to clarify and refine diagnostic criteria. Consequently, the manual has been revised several times since its first printing to reflect current research and to respond to changing understandings around what constitutes disorder (American Psychological Association, 2013).

The Constructivist Nature of Mental Health and Mental Illness

When a person's body has difficulty producing insulin and responds to sugars in such a way as to threaten that person's life, this process is described as diabetes. We can apply more specific language to the term "diabetes"depending upon when signs of illness first began, in childhood or later in life. The word diabetes serves as a helpful shorthand to doctors in conveying to one another that a patient presents with a particular cluster of symptoms, physical and sometimes cognitive in nature, as well as to the physiological obstacles, such as a failure to produce sufficient amounts of needed insulin or to properly make use of insulin. This very brief communication through the diagnosis of diabetes also helps to lead doctors quickly to a set of potentially life-saving interventions.

The DSM also represents an attempt to create both a framework and a shorthand for communicating clients' experiences of emotional and cognitive difficulties. However, unlike the example of a person with diabetes, there are no dependable blood tests for commonly diagnosed mental health concerns such as depression, anxiety, or psychotic processes. Mental health concerns, such as depression, arise out of a variety of causes that aren't easily traced to biological markers. What's more, states of experiencing, such as deep and unrelenting feelings of sadness, are individual, subjective, and given to differences in cultural interpretation and expression, and are not as easily quantified as a blood sugar level. Consequently, the process of categorizing, describing, and quantifying mental health concerns is much more complicated than illnesses that arise from the physical body.

As a vastly diverse society, it is difficult to describe any single behavior or experience as "normal" for all groups and more difficult still to create a shorthand for a subjective experience that makes sense within the context of every culture, every age group, gender or sexual orientation, further complicating the already challenging task of cataloguing mental health concerns. While diabetes is a process that can be identified tangibly and acts and reacts in more or less predictable ways, depression and other mental health concerns can't be understood in the same way. For these reasons, what we have come to call a major depressive disorder (MDD), for example, is something more along the lines of a social construction than a disorder of the same quality of a medical disorder, such as diabetes.

A social construction, for these purposes, simply refers to the practice of developing a shared understanding of an idea or, in this case, an experience. Experiences of debilitating and lasting sadness are as varied as the people who experience them. However, for the sake of communication and in order to better facilitate our intervention, mental health professionals have agreed, for example, to describe a particular cluster of experiences of sadness as MDD and to discern that cluster from another subset of experiences that also includes sadness as persistent depressive disorder.

It is important to remember that our understanding of mental health disorders is evolving and the DSM is under constant review. Shifts in the mental health profession's understanding of any given disorder or continuum are prompted by innovations in neuroscience, gains in the understanding of cultural influences and differences in both presentation and intervention that exist between groups. Shifting attitudes within Western culture have also influenced how mental disorders are conceptualized and fundamentally shape what is understood to fall within normal experiencing or behavior and what is understood to be problematic enough to be described as disordered. A key example of shifting cultural beliefs that have shaped diagnosis is illustrated in the changes in the way that the DSM has treated sexual orientation. With the publication of the DSM III homosexuality was dropped as a diagnosable disorder except in those cases when same-sex attractions were the source of distress, which was described as ego dystonic homosexuality. However, in the DSM III-R, this diagnosis was dropped and the distress a person felt arising from same-sex attractions was diagnosed as a sexual disorder not otherwise specified. This disorder was maintained in each edition that followed until the DSM 5, where mention of same-sex attractions and distress are no longer included. It stands to reason, then, that as we make use of the DSM 5, we keep in mind that this manual is a reflection of the APA's best understanding of the current research literature. The descriptions included within the DSM 5 are not uncontested.

Alternative Frameworks for Understanding Mental Illness

Alternative approaches to the DSM 5 are currently in use but don't enjoy the same kind of attention and popular application. For example, a system of understanding mental health concerns can be found in the Psychodynamic Diagnostic Manual (PDM-2), a manual that is embedded in psychodynamic models of understanding the manifestations of mental disorders. The PDM-2 features a much greater focus on personality structure than does the DSM 5. The PDM-2 offers attention to dimensions of functioning as well as insights into the use of defense mechanisms. The PDM-2 also offers typical belief structures about self and others within each of the outlined personality structures (Lingiardi & McWilliams, 2017).

While the DSM is the most widely used classification system in the United States, the International Classification of Diagnoses (ICD) enjoys the most use worldwide and is currently in its 11th edition. The ICD is published in collaboration with the World Health Organization and is used in collecting data and in research on physical and mental disorders across the globe. The ICD coding system works to capture not only the nature of physical illnesses and mental health disorders but also their etiology (Goodheart, 2014), something the DSM classification system has attempted to avoid.

Many mental health clinicians, however, see mental health concerns as directly tied to the workings of the brain, and embrace a more biologically based system (psychophysiological) of understanding mental disorders than the DSM describes. For these clinicians, the Research Domain Criteria (RDoC) offers a science-based classification. Sponsored by the National Institutes of Health, the RDoC attempts to map diagnostic domains and syndromes around neurological dysfunction. This system is still in its infancy (Cuthbert & Insel, 2012; Insel et al., 2010).

Another relatively new initiative to create an alternative diagnostic framework comes out of the Global Summit on Diagnostic Alternatives. This group aims to create a system that meets the following criteria: (1) to give equal attention to sociocultural contributions to mental health concerns as is given to biological causes; (2) to give attention to categories of problems, rather than categorizing people; (3) to give equal consideration to the science related to sociocultural etiologies as is given to biological etiologies; (4) to emphasize collaboration between the client and the clinician in the diagnostic process and (5) developing a system that can be used across theoretical domains (Raskin, 2014).

Non-Western approaches have worked to organize mental health concerns as well. For instance, contemplative psychotherapy, an approach based in Tibetan Buddhist psychology, organizes disorders by their resemblance to samsaric preoccupations known as the six realms and includes the realm of the gods, the realm of the jealous gods, the human realm, the animal realm, the realm of the hungry ghosts, and the hell realm. Within this conceptualization of mental health concerns, addictions, for example, are described as being rooted within the hungry ghost realm, a state of being in which desires are many but the capacity for feeling satisfied is impaired (Trungpa, 2010; Wegela, 2014). Similar to the PDM-2, this system focuses on ways of seeing and engaging the world and the ways in which each perspective causes suffering.

Any framework for understanding mental illness will be constructed within a cultural frame and worldview and will be built on a theory describing the etiology of disorder. Sometimes the grounding theory of the model is readily apparent and sometimes it is much more subtle, as with the DSM 5. A quick internet search of these alternative approaches or of the DSM 5 itself reveals that clinicians tend to hold strong opinions about the utility and validity of these systems. Perhaps as you read through this discussion, you found yourself drawn to or curious about one system or noticed an instant distaste for another?

Criticisms of the DSM 5

The draft of the DSM 5 was much anticipated. Many clinicians had expressed concerns about the gaps between the disorders represented in the DSM IV-TR and available research. However, soon after the draft was posted for commentary from the mental health community, criticisms and concerns were raised. The Society of Humanistic Psychology, a division of the American Psychological Association, in partnership with the British Psychological Society penned an open letter to the DSM 5 task force and was joined by 11 other APA divisions endorsing the statement. These divisions included but were not exclusive to the following: The Division of Developmental Psychology; The Division of Psychotherapy; The Society for the Psychology of Women; The Society for the Psychological Study of Ethnic Minority Issues and The Society for

BOX 1.01 CONSIDER THIS: REFLECTING ON YOUR BELIEFS AND PREFERENCES

As you consider your responses to each of the alternative approaches to the DSM 5, what might your response reveal about your own beliefs and worldviews? What do your preferences suggest about the ways you may come to understand your clients and their difficulties? How might your preferences suggest something to you about how you may go about selecting interventions with and for your clients?

the Psychological Study of Lesbian, Gay, Bisexual and Transgender (LGBT) Issues. These divisions were soon joined by professional organizations within the counseling field as well as notable international organizations, including but not exclusive to The Association of Black Psychologists, Counselors for Social Justice; The Association of LGBT Issues in Counseling; National Latina/o Psychological Association; the UK Council for Psychotherapy and so on (Coalition for DSM-5 Reform, 2012). In addition to key professional organizations, the DSM 5 draft received strong criticism from notable leaders in the field, including Dr. Allen Frances, Task Force Chair of the DSM IV-TR, and Dr. Robert Spitzer, Chair of the DSM III.

Contained within the concerns outlined in the open letter coauthored by the American Psychological Association and the British Psychological Society and mirrored in an open letter from the American Counseling Association (2014b), are concerns that remain after the DSM 5's publication, though other concerns not listed here were addressed. These concerns seem to fall into three overarching categories: (1) a lowering of diagnostic thresholds that may have the effect of pathologizing normal human experiencing, such as bereavement, and unfairly targeting vulnerable populations; (2) the inclusion of new diagnoses with little empirical support and (3) a theoretical orientation embedded in biology and neuroscience that is not well supported with scientific evidence, ignores social and relational causes of mental health concerns, and may result in unnecessary and dangerous pharmacological treatment of mental health concerns (Society for Humanistic Society, 2011; Coalition for DSM-5 Reform, 2012).

Another criticism arose around the language in the draft defining mental disorder. Concern was raised that the wording in the draft made it possible to diagnose differences in political or religious views that contrasted enough from the mainstream to place the client in conflict with society at large (Coalition for DSM-5 Reform, 2012). The language on page 20 of the DSM 5 now reads this way:

> A mental disorder is a syndrome characterized by clinically significant disturbance in an individual's cognition, emotion regulation, or behavior that reflects a dysfunction in the psychological, biological, or developmental processes underlying mental functioning. Mental disorders are usually associated with significant distress or disability in social, occupational, or other important activities. An expectable or culturally approved response to a common stressor or loss, such as the death of a loved one, is not a mental disorder. Socially deviant behavior (i.e., political, religious, or sexual) and conflicts that are primarily between the individual and society are not mental disorders unless the deviance or conflict results from a dysfunction in the individual, as described above.

Here, the phrase "socially deviant behavior" refers to behavior or beliefs that depart from the mainstream, such as political or religious beliefs, or sexual practices. The stance taken in the DSM 5 is that while some religious or political views may stand in conflict with the broader social perspective, such as White supremacist views, these views by themselves do not constitute a mental disorder. However, these views may be symptomatic of disorder when the beliefs are born out of cognitive or emotional disturbances, such as paranoid processes.

Poor Inter-Rater Reliability

Decades old research demonstrates that diagnosticians have had difficulty arriving at the same diagnosis when given case scenarios to diagnose, often described as inter-rater reliability (Beck, 1962; Spitzer & Fleiss, 1974). Freedman et al. (2013) and his colleagues conducted a field study of the DSM 5, which resulted in disappointing inter-rater reliability rates even for commonly diagnosed disorders such as MDD (kappa.28) and generalized anxiety disorder (kappa.20). These studies suggest three key points: (1) mental health practitioners, and diagnosticians in particular, need a more reliable structure for arriving at an appropriate diagnosis; (2) a format is needed for conveying the reasoning behind a particular diagnosis or diagnoses and (3) this research supports concerns expressed about a lack of clarity within the wording of the DSM 5 itself. The justification process (Hammond, 2015), described in Chapter 3, is a procedure that provides the students new to diagnosis with an avenue for arriving at and supporting a particular diagnosis. Research is needed to explore whether using this structure increases inter-rater reliability, however. Low inter-rater reliability due to ambiguous language, differences in the ways clinicians interpret client complaints and symptoms, and those born out of structural bias within the DSM itself, however, will be harder for clinicians to work around. Careful use of key diagnostic principles may support more accurate diagnosis.

Validity Questions

A significant portion of the criticisms of the DSM 5 and its previous editions centers around the question of validity. Recall that when we are discussing the validity of an assessment measure or tool, we are describing how well a tool does what it claims to do. We can explore this question more deeply by looking at construct validity, which assesses whether or not a tool measures the underlying psychological construct that it aims to measure. When clinicians evaluate the question of the validity of the DSM 5, we are asking at least four questions:

1. "Does this tool measure what it claims to measure?"
2. "Does the manual reflect the data available in the research?"
3. "Does the DSM 5 reflect what I see in my practice with clients?"
4. "Does the DSM 5 provide useful predictive value in describing the course of my client's disorder?"

Measuring what it claims to measure and reflecting current research. Unlike most other assessment tools, the DSM 5 attempts to describe a great number of psychological constructs: dimensions, disorders and indeed the symptoms outlined within each. Consequently, in order to answer the construct validity question, we are challenged to evaluate the manual dimension by dimension and disorder by disorder. Since its publication, a steady stream of research has been undertaken to determine the manual's validity; for example, in the areas of autism spectrum disorder (Mandy et al., 2012), borderline personality disorder (Anderson & Sellbom, 2015), on the somatic symptom disorders (Häuser et al., 2015) and for the DSM's personality assessment tool, the PID-5-BF, for use in older adults (Debast et al., 2017), to name a few. It is validity research that will continue to inform the future changes to the DSM.

Does the DSM 5 reflect what we see in the clinical setting? The American Psychological Association and the National Council on Measurement in Education offer another way to think about validity, "the extent to which inferences made from [the tool] are appropriate, meaningful, and useful," (Salkind, 2019, p. 64). Considering whether or not inferences made from using the DSM 5 are appropriate, meaningful or useful to our work with clients may depend a bit on who is asked. While many agree that the DSM 5's symptom checklist format is useful for research purposes, others question its usefulness in clinical work, and many go so far as to question whether the DSM 5 is, in fact, unhelpful (Pies, 2012). Perhaps more telling, Zimmerman and Galione (2010) conducted a study of psychiatrists and non-psychiatrists in mental health professions and found that a quarter of psychiatrists and two-thirds of non-psychiatrists surveyed used the DSM IV-TR less than half of the time when diagnosing MDD, citing the over-simplification of the disorder as it is represented in the manual. This suggests that professional diagnosticians have not always found the DSM to be useful.

Racism and other forms of bias. Concerns regarding bias in the diagnostic process can be discussed within two primary categories: problems that are built into the structure of the DSM itself and problems that arise within the person doing the diagnosing. The DSM is based upon a medical model of disorder that assumes that the illness arises from within the individual and consequently gives little attention to those stress reactions that arise out of the context in which the individual is living. Volumes have been written connecting racism, sexism, homophobia and socioeconomic stressors to mental health concerns. Take for instance experiences of microaggressions, subtle, brief and sometimes unintended forms of discrimination. Microaggressions have been tied to cultural mistrust and decreased well-being in Asian Americans (Kim et al., 2017). Similarly, daily microaggressions have been positively correlated with depression and suicidality in bisexual women (Salim et al., 2019); depressive symptoms and negative affect in African Americans (Nadal et al., 2014) and somatic symptoms, externalizing symptoms and aggressive behavior in homeless youth (Sisselman-Borgia et al., 2018). Many object to the notion that an individual who experiences sadness, anger, sleeplessness, hopelessness, loss of interest and restlessness as a result of daily experiences of racism or other forms of oppression would be pathologized rather than naming and addressing the source of the problem.

Another long-standing concern about the medical model of the DSM is that it assumes that the presentations of each disorder are universal and reflect the experiences of all cultural groups. Research studies on the presentation and treatment of mental disorders have long been criticized for poorly representing minority groups and assert that the bulk of published research more accurately describes White, middle class clients. Further, the manual and its conceptualization of what is normal and what is abnormal is essentially embedded in dominant cultural values and rarely on biomedical markers (Jun, 2010).

The authors of the DSM IV-TR and of the DSM 5 have worked to include culture-related diagnostic issues within the discussion sections of many of the disorders; however, these are frequently brief notations and require first that the diagnostician consult the discussion sections of the DSM and not just the criterion tables, and often require the clinician to explore further into cultural norms specific to their clients. For example, the culture-related diagnostic issues for separation anxiety disorder correctly notes that cultures vary widely in their expectations for relative interdependence or independence. The discussion does not offer examples, making it necessary for the clinician to do some research about a particular client's cultural expectations and to consider how closely a client falls within those expectations. Consequently, ethical use of the DSM 5 presupposes clinical multicultural competencies.

Added to this edition of the DSM is a chapter dedicated to the exploration of cultural context and mental health. The chapter, *Cultural Formulation,* provides a caution about the importance of considering cultural identity, cultural conceptualizations of distress, features of vulnerability and resilience and therapeutic relational dynamics and their intersection with culture. Provided within this chapter is the *Cultural*

Formulation Interview that offers a structure and guide for diagnosticians for use at intake. This edition also retains the *Glossary of Cultural Concepts of Distress* (American Psychological Association, 2013). However, Thornton (2017) argues that while the DSM does seem to strive to achieve both validity and cultural sensitivity, the glossary of cultural concepts remains a mere afterthought.

Today we are still grappling with the consequences of racist practices in medicine and psychology. A deep stream of distrust of the psychology profession is still present within marginalized populations. Racism and other forms of bias still threaten the diagnostic and treatment process and consequently the DSM 5 can also be used in ways that reinforce these abuses. It is the streams of personal bias that individual diagnosticians have the most immediate power over in their day-to-day work. Consequently, understanding how individual bias can manifest in our work and being attuned to these issues can help to reduce the impact of individual bias on our clients. Poland and Caplan (2004) offer several examples in which bias finds its way into the diagnostic process:

1. Clinicians often focus on some types of information and exclude others or privilege certain sources of information over others.
2. Clinicians frequently make judgments about whether or not a client's feelings or behavior are pathological without having spent adequate time with the client to make an informed assessment.
3. Clinicians may more readily judge women, people of color or the poor to be mentally ill than men, White people or the middle class or the wealthy.
4. Clinicians may be prone to taking at face value the statements made by male clients over those made by women, by White clients in contrast to clients of minority statuses, or of wealthy or middle-class clients over those that struggle with poverty.

Caplan and Cosgrove (2004) also offer a helpful reminder about sources of bias that arise out of unhelpful dynamics or emerge from the personal psychology of the clinician. Some of these processes that impact diagnosis include unchallenged stereotypes about others, or encountering a client who is reminiscent of someone who is disliked. Cognitive processes that can generate bias might include giving greater attention to information gathered early in the diagnostic process over information gathered later, known as anchoring bias. The workings of confirmation bias, in which a diagnostician forgets or minimizes information that conflicts with an original hunch, also figures into diagnostic bias. Availability bias, another source of skewed diagnosis, is a tendency for the mind to lend importance to information that is easier to remember and to disregard other pieces of relevant data. Finally, a "stereotyped memory" bias is a process in which the mind creates inaccurate memories that fit stereotypes of a group but not the actual person being evaluated (Caplan & Cosgrove, 2004).

Lack of clarity and poor wording choices. In addition to the problems listed above, Frances (2013) has mirrored concerns offered by divisions of the American Counseling Association and American Psychological Association related to the reconceptualization of the book as well as about a lack of clarity in the writing itself that he feels will lead to increased inaccuracies in diagnosis and lowered inter-rater reliability.

By way of example, Frances (2013) drew attention to a lack of clarity about how many of the "A" sub-criterion must be met in Autistic Spectrum Disorder, leaving it up to the clinician to decide if only one or all three of the sub-criteria should be met in order to diagnose. Frances also voiced concerns about phrasing within the DSM 5 that may dramatically lower the threshold for what is a diagnosable disorder, as with MDD and Mild Neurocognitive Disorder. In fact, since the publication of the DSM 5 in 2013, the APA has published two supplements that offer revisions that clarify ambiguities, including the criterion requirements for a diagnosis of autism. A discussion of the DSM 5 Supplements can be found at the end of this chapter and instructions for their use are described in Chapter 2, *Eight Steps to Diagnosis.*

Frances, 2013, also points to an example of poor judgment in language illustrated in the attempt to clarify the difference between a pedophilic disorder from a sexual preference for children that has never been acted upon and does not cause any functional or emotional distress. The DSM 5 describes the latter as a "pedophilic sexual orientation but not a pedophilic disorder." The importance of separating disturbing thoughts and urges that result in functional, behavioral or emotional impairment (disorder) is a key diagnostic principle. However, the implications of using the wording "pedophilic sexual orientation" rather than "pedophilic sexual preference/inclination/compulsion" lends pedophilic thoughts the same kind of languaging as is used to describe LGBT sexual orientations. The scientific community is in agreement that homosexuality is not a disorder, though it had been included within the DSM until 1974 (Drescher, 2010). It seems both unwise and inappropriate to employ similar language to describe such a destructive sexual compulsion (pedophilia) with what is understood to be one end of the normal continuum of human sexuality (homosexuality).

Other Criticisms

A variety of additional concerns swirl around the latest edition of the DSM. Many organizations, including the American Counseling Association, have pointed to what seems to be a conflict of interest between those who serve as task force members while also maintaining financial or research relationships with pharmacology companies. Seventy percent of the task force members also have ties with pharmaceutical companies who stand to gain from lowered diagnostic thresholds of disorders (Moisse, 2012).

Finally, a criticism of the DSM as a whole is that when diagnosticians embrace this nosology as a diagnostic model, they place the DSM in a position of power within the clinical relationship and distance the clinician from the client:

BOX 1.02 CONSIDER THIS

Multicultural competence is essential to the ethical use of the DSM and the diagnostic process.

"Meanwhile, we have lost sight of one of the most important motivations of the anti-psychiatric movement, namely, to address the typically authoritarian relation between the expert and the patient. So, the final question is: Has the DSM diagnostic changed anything in the relationship between diagnosticians and patients? The answer is an unqualified no. From such a perspective, the expert remains an objective observer who inspects an object of study . . ." (Verhaeghe, 2019, p. 31).

Social Trends and Diagnostics

While societal attitudes about most physical health issues tend to hold less stigma than they did at one time in our history, societal attitudes about mental health concerns are still heavily burdened by social stigma and misunderstanding. Consequently, many mental health professionals are reluctant to use the DSM (Kress et al., 2010). Other clinicians are averse to using the DSM because it is seen as equating difficult emotional states or phenomena with physiological states of illness, an approach described as a medical model for mental health diagnoses. Many of the concerns about the DSM and its structure are embedded in philosophical questions that pertain to the practitioner's theory related to the connection or disconnection between mind and body and particularly to the relative centrality of the physical brain or the complex phenomena of mind in the manifestation of suffering.

It is also important to note that our understanding of what it means to be mentally fit is both a social construction and is informed by the clinician's individual theoretical perspective. By way of example, some, such as those who embrace cognitive therapy, would view anxiety as a consequence of faulty thinking that, with support, could be remedied. Other theoretical approaches, however, view anxiety as part and parcel of the human condition, such as psychodynamic, existential or contemplative frameworks, although each of these three would differ in their understanding of the source of this anxiety and would differ significantly in how to go about working with a client presenting with anxiety.

Minimizing Risk

The Table 1.01 Criticisms of the DSM 5 and Recommended Actions outlines the key criticisms of the DSM 5 and offers recommended actions or safeguards that may help support clinicians in avoiding the pitfalls embedded within the DSM 5.

Importance of Mastering the DSM 5

The reader might reasonably ask, "When faced with these criticisms what is the utility of learning the DSM in my training program or in using it in my practice?" The DSM 5 is currently the language of the field. If you hope to navigate the research and literature related to intervention, you must be able to understand what is being described. As clinicians, we must be able to communicate client concerns in a way that other mental health professionals can understand. And if we hope to contribute to the process of shaping and clarifying diagnostic processes, then we must be able to work effectively within the DSM system. A comprehensive understanding of concerns related to this model of diagnostics strengthens our ability to use it ethically (American Counseling Association, 2014b; American Psychological Association, 2013). Further, a decision to use an alternative diagnostic system is arguably made more sound when clinicians understand the DSM as well as their preferred diagnostic model. And, finally, the RDoC and the PDM-2, two western approaches that contrast with the DSM, which reflect different ends of the philosophical continuum, each share language that overlaps considerably with the DSM, and presuppose fluency with the DSM nosology. Further, both the RDoC model and the PDM-2 are also subject to criticisms, many of which are similar to criticisms levied against the DSM. In short, the DSM 5, like all diagnostic modalities, is an imperfect but necessary tool for training, practice, and professional fluency.

The Changing Structure of the DSM

In this section, you will be introduced briefly to the history of the DSM and then to the structure of the manual. This section will outline the structure of the diagnostic criteria tables as well as the DSM's coding system.

Early Editions of the DSM. The first edition of the DSM, published in 1952, was written in a historical context in which psychoanalysis was the dominant therapeutic framework. Consequently, the first edition reflects this theoretical approach within its structure and language. Symptoms and diagnoses were divided into two primary categories: *Disorders Caused by or Associated with Impairment of Brain Tissue Function* (e.g., brain trauma or intoxication) and *Disorders of Psychogenic Origin or without Clearly Defined Physical Cause or Structural Change in the Brain*. Presentations of psychogenic origin were then divided into two subcategories: those that were described as "reactions" and those determined to be personality disorders. A personality disorder was

BOX 1.03 CONSIDER THIS: REFLECTION QUESTIONS

Professional ethics are built on a fabric of respect for clients and a prizing for cultural competency. At the same time, mental healthcare providers must be skilled in diagnostics.

- How will you maintain an awareness of these demands as you grow your knowledge and skills?
- What is your opinion of the role of diagnosis in the therapeutic relationship?
- Can clinicians diagnose without objectifying their clients?
- Do you see dangers in unconscious thought processes and cognitive bias, as Caplan and Cosgrove (2004) caution?
- What steps can you take to maintain a humanistic and multiculturally competent ethic in your practice while mastering diagnostic skills?

described as a life-long, "deeply ingrained maladaptive pattern of behavior" (p. 41). Reactions, on the other hand, described responses of the personality to any factor (biological, social or psychological). Put more simply, patients/clients were assigned a personality disorder when the presenting difficulties seemed to originate in the personality structure of the individual, were persistent and unlikely to change, while a reaction was attributed when the difficulty seemed to be a response to a stressor that was then expressed uniquely thanks to an individual's own personality structure. The DSM II, published in 1968, began what would eventually end in a complete departure from the psychodynamic language, dropping terms like "reaction." The structure of the manual remained largely the same.

A second distinction of the early editions of the DSM was their brevity. For example, the DSM II describes paranoid personality in a pithy 55 words while the DSM 5 discusses the same disorder in four pages. However, this brevity lent itself to wide variations in interpretation and misdiagnosis. For example, the only guidance offered in the DSM II for the diagnosis "occupational maladjustment" read as follows: "This category is for psychiatrically normal individuals who are grossly maladjusted in their work" (APA, 1968/2009, p. 52). Besides offering little guidance in what it means to be "psychiatrically normal," the language offered in this description leaves a great deal of ambiguity around what one would describe as "maladjusted in their work" nor is guidance offered for how to differentiate maladjustment from "gross maladjustment." Each successive edition of the DSM has worked to clarify ambiguous language within its definitions and criteria.

TABLE 1.01 Criticisms of the DSM 5 and Recommended Actions

Criticism	Recommended Action or Safeguard
The lowering of diagnostic thresholds:	• Do not diagnose thoughts, feelings or behavior that appear to be normal responses to difficult situations: consider culture, gender and the range of typical behaviors (American Psychological Association, 2013) • Defer diagnosis if symptoms have not been persistent or are in response to a crisis (American Psychological Association, 2013) • Avoid diagnosis of developmentally expected behavior or responses (American Psychological Association, 2013)
The inclusion of new diagnoses with little empirical support	• Use extreme caution with diagnoses newly added to the DSM 5 • Consider alternative, better researched, and more common diagnoses where appropriate
Theoretical orientation: embedded in biology: (medical model)	• Maintain a conceptual framework that takes into account sociocultural and relational influences on thoughts, feelings and behavior (Hays, 2008)
Racism and Other Biases:	• When considering a diagnosis, be aware of vulnerable populations that may be susceptible to over or under diagnosis within each diagnostic dimension • Consider your client's unique cultural context and its relationship to your client's complaints and symptoms (Hays, 2008) • Consider areas of bias or lack of knowledge you may have as it relates to your client's cultural identities (Hays, 2008) • Develop an awareness of one's own culture, worldview, blind spots, and biases (Hays, 2008) • Carefully consider power differences between you and your client and work to level these power differences (Hays, 2008)
Lack of clarity in diagnostic criteria:	• Use a conservative interpretation of the diagnostic criteria table when wording is unclear

Source: Adapted from American Psychiatric Association (2013) and Hays (2008).

DSM III-DSM IV-TR. The publication of the DSM III in 1980 marked a revision of both the structure of the manual as well as the framework on which it rests. Robert Spitzer led the DSM III and its task force in a movement that would ultimately lead to broader appeal of the DSM. The task force aimed to restructure the classification system so that it maintained compatibility with the ICD-9 and reflected the current knowledge of the field (a data focus) so that it might be "clinically useful" and also serve as a basis for research (APA, 1980, p. 2). In shifting emphasis to data and available research, the DSM III completed a shift from a psychodynamic theoretical foundation, which had begun in the second edition, into an attempt to become atheoretical in its attribution of etiology. It is with the third edition that the DSM took on a medical model for understanding mental health concerns.

The organizational structure of the DSM also shifted so that disorders were placed in categories that contained disorders which shared symptoms (e.g., Schizophrenic Disorders, Affective Disorders, Somatic Disorders, Personality Disorders and so on). The definitions and criteria for each disorder were expanded and an effort was made to clarify what kind and how many symptoms were needed to diagnose a particular disorder in the hopes to increase inter-rater reliability and to provide a stronger foundation for research.

The DSM III-R, DSM IV and DSM IV-TR each made revisions to language and information with the continued aim of maintaining pace with the knowledge of the field but also adding diagnoses with each edition. While the DSM III fell just short of 500 pages, the DSM IV-TR had ballooned to well over 900 pages. The fifth edition of the DSM, however, is thought to mark the most significant revision of the model since its first printing. What follows are key features of the DSM 5.

The DSM 5 Structure and Its Revisions

The Dimensional System. The DSM 5 has shifted from a categorical framework to a dimensional system for organizing mental health concerns. Previous editions organized distinct disorders into distinct categories while the current DSM 5 takes the perspective that related disorders occupy a space along a dimension of difficulties that share signs and symptoms. Closely related dimensions are placed close together within the manual.

Chronological organization. Within each dimension, diagnoses are organized roughly in line with human lifespan development so that first to appear within a dimension are more typically observed earlier in life. Thus, a disorder like separation anxiety is listed before generalized anxiety since we are more likely to see separation anxiety disorder in children than in adults. Reflecting the developmental organization of the text, the neurodevelopmental disorders are listed at the opening of the manual, since these are evidenced in early childhood, and the neurocognitive disorders are listed at the back, as we typically see these closer to the end of life.

Diagnostic tables and their elements. Each chapter describing a diagnostic dimension opens with a list and brief description of the disorders contained within a given section. A diagnostic table is provided for each diagnosis that describes the criteria that must be met in order to make a diagnosis. The table often begins with a description of the disorder, and is followed by the *major criteria* marked with capital letters beginning with the letter "A" and varies from table to table as to how many major criteria follow. However, all diagnoses share descriptive criteria, generally the A criteria, an impairment criteria, since no diagnosis can be made if impairment is not present, and a rule out criteria that cautions the reader to consider other mental health disorders, and medical health concerns or substances that might cause the symptoms described or observed. Most tables also include a duration criteria. Sub-criteria, are listed numerically under the A criteria, and less often the B and C major criteria. Tables vary a great deal in the number of major and sub-criteria listed within the table. For example, post-traumatic stress disorder lists major criteria A-H and contains a total of 24 sub-criteria, while circadian rhythm disorder lists only A-C and has no sub-criteria at all.

Specifiers. A specifier is a description that captures the distinct manifestations of a given disorder. Specifiers provide an avenue for noting severity, whether or not the current manifestation is the first occurrence of the disorder or a reemergence as well as the nature of symptoms that are present. Specifiers are unique to each disorder; some criteria tables contain many specifiers while others have none. When noting your diagnosis, include all specifiers that apply. It is important to note that for some disorders

BOX 1.04 WHEN SPECIFIERS INFLUENCE CODING

Joan and Antonio have each been diagnosed with a mild major depression. While this is Joan's first depressive episode, Antonio has a history of three episodes in the past 5 years. Note below how the coding of their disorders differs.

Joan: F32.0 Major depressive disorder, single episode, mild

Antonio: F33.0 Major depressive disorder, recurrent episode, mild

Try this: Using the table on page 162 of your DSM, recode Joan and Antonio's diagnoses assuming that Joan's episode is severe and Antonio's current episode is moderate.

BOX 1.05 CONSIDER THIS

Remember that the bolded codes in the DSM 5 criteria tables expired in October of 2015 and are no longer used. All F codes should be checked against the current DSM supplements available online.

the specifier determines the diagnostic code. For example, consider two clients with a mild MDD, one client experiencing a first episode and the other experiencing a recurrence of his depression. In the following example, you will note that while each is experiencing the same disorder, the episode specifier has created a coding difference (find the specifier table for MDD on page 162 of the DSM 5):

The steps to coding and notation of a diagnosis as well as opportunities to practice this skill will be explained in Chapter 2, *Eight Steps to Diagnosis.*

Discussion. Each table is followed by a discussion of the presentation of the featured disorder in a section titled *Diagnostic Features.* This section is followed by a brief description outlining prevalence, a discussion of the development and course of the disorder, risks and prognostic factors, culture-related issues to be attuned to, gender concerns, functional impacts of the disorder, a list and discussion of alternate diagnoses, and, finally, the comorbidity rates. These sections often clarify vague or ambiguous descriptions within the diagnostic table and should be consulted carefully before diagnosis.

Coordination with the ICD-10 CM. In thumbing through the DSM 5, you will notice that each diagnostic table contains within it a code, and sometimes more than one code for each disorder. For example, on page 345 of the DSM 5, you will find the diagnostic table for Bulimia Nervosa. Beneath the name of the disorder, you will note a bolded code, **307.51**, and in a light grey font, within parentheses, F50.2. The bolded code in each table reflects the ICD-9 CM code and the grey code in parentheses, F50.2, reflects the ICD-10 CM code. The ICD-9 codes were to be used between the publication of the DSM 5 in 2013 and October 1, 2015, and should no longer be used in your coding or notation of disorders. The grey codes in parentheses reflect the revised ICD 10 CM codes. Since the publication of the ICD 11 in 2018 a sizable number of the ICD 10 codes have been updated and are now found in supplements to the DSM available as free downloads. It is worth noting that nearly all of the diagnoses contained in the DSM 5 begin with the letter F. In the current ICD structure,

BOX 1.06 THE USE OF Z CODES

Penny, 37, is homeless, unemployed and is currently sharing a space under a large overpass with her boyfriend, Mick. Mick has sometimes been violent with Penny and, since she has started counseling, has twice knocked her unconscious.

T74.11XD Partner violence, physical, confirmed, subsequent encounter

Z59.0 Inadequate housing

Z59.4 Lack of adequate food or safe drinking water

Z59.5 Extreme poverty

"F" signifies a disorder that is mental, behavioral or neurodevelopmental in nature. Disorders are then further organized within number groupings.

Updates and Supplements to the DSM 5. The fifth edition of the DSM has been described as a "living document" and, in this spirit, periodic supplements are published on the American Psychiatric Association's (APA) website. Though early revisions were offered in 2014, which went into effect in 2015, the first full supplement was published in September of 2016 and went into effect in October of the same year. Readers will want to remain aware that the DSM 5 will continue to undergo review and will incorporate changes to maintain alignment with future editions of the ICD. Consequently, further revisions will be forthcoming on the APA's website at http://dsm.psychiatryonline.org. A benefit of these regular updates is the potential to create a document that is responsive to research and to clarifications from within the field. The drawback of this approach is the potential for clinicians to be working from different versions of the DSM 5, undermining one of the stated purposes of the DSM, which is to create a shared language and shorthand for disorders and to increase inter-rater reliability. Checking the APA website regularly for these updates and subscribing to APA announcements is advised.

Z codes. Often clients bring difficulties to psychotherapy that are not themselves disorders but are the focus of a client's work. For example, a client who is rebuilding her life after leaving an abusive relationship will likely want to focus on the experience of the abuse as a part of her therapeutic process. Concerns that are the focus of clinical work but are not disorders are categorized and coded within the "Z codes" (previously "V codes") located in the back of the DSM 5, pages 715-727, in a section titled *Other Conditions that May be a Focus of Clinical Attention*.

In Box 1.06 note that the clinician is working with a client who has come to a local free clinic where she can receive counseling and other services. Note how the clinician has made use of Z codes to convey her client's current struggles more fully.

Conclusion

In this chapter, we have explored together the purpose of diagnostic nosology and the DSM 5 in particular. We have been briefly introduced to a few alternative approaches including the widely used ICD and emergent models, such as the RDoC, and have even touched upon a non-Western approach to conceptualizing mental health concerns. We have explored the basic structure of the DSM and its major criticisms and have explored some avenues for reducing the risks posed by the shortcomings of the manual.

Unfortunately, it is not enough to be able to find one's way around the DSM 5, indeed, a great deal of work and thought must be undertaken between the time when a clinician meets with a client for the first time and is ready to make a note of a diagnosis. In Chapter 2, you will be introduced to eight steps to arriving at a sound clinical diagnosis as well as 10 guiding diagnostic principles. Together, the eight steps and 10 principles will offer structure and guidance through the often challenging and complex process of clinical diagnosis.

References

American Counseling Association. (2014a). *ACA code of ethics*. Author. https://www.counseling.org/resources/aca-code-of-ethics.pdf

American Counseling Association. (2014b). *Open letter to the American Psychiatric Association regarding the draft of the DSM 5*. http://www.counseling.org/Resources/pdfs/ACA_DSM-5_letter_11-11.pdf

American Psychiatric Association. (1968/2009). *Diagnostic and statistical manual of mental disorders DSM 2* (Reprint ed.). Author.

American Psychiatric Association. (1980). *Diagnostic and statistical manual of mental disorders* (3rd ed.). Author.

American Psychological Association. (2013). *Diagnostic manual of mental disorders*. Author.

Anderson, J. L., & Sellbom, M. (2015). Construct validity of the DSM–5 section III personality trait profile for borderline personality disorder. *Journal of Personality Assessment*, *97*(5), 478–486. https://doi.org/10.1080/00223891.2015.1051226

Beck, A. T. (1962). Reliability of psychiatric diagnoses: A critique of systematic studies. *American Journal of Psychiatry*, *119*, 210–216. https://doi.org/10.1176/ajp.119.3.210

Caplan, P. J., & Cosgrove, L. (2004). Is this really necessary? In *Bias in Psychiatric Diagnosis* (pp. 55–59). Jason Aronson.

Coalition for DSM-5 Reform. (2012, October). *Copy posted in Society for Humanistic Psychology Newsletter*. https://www.apadivisions.org/division-32/publications/newsletters/humanistic/2012/10/dsm-5-reform

Cuthbert, B. N., & Insel, T. R. (2012). Research domain criteria: Cognitive systems, neural circuits, and dimensions of behavior. *Dialogues in Clinical Neuroscience*, *14*(1), 29–37. PMCID: PMC3341647.

Debast, I., Rossi, G., & Van Alphen, S. P. J. (2017). Construct validity of the DSM-5 section III maladaptive trait domains in older adults. *Journal of Personality Disorders*, *31*(5), 671–688. https://doi.org/10.1521/pedi_2017_31_274

Drescher, J. (2010). Parallels and contrast in the history of homosexuality, gender variance, and the diagnostic and statistical manual. *Archives of Sexual Behavior*, *39*, 427–460. https://doi.org/10.1007/s10508-009-9531-5

Frances, A. (2013). *Essentials of psychiatric diagnosis: Responding to the challenge of the DSM 5*. Guilford Press.

Freedman, R., Lewis, D. A., Michels, R., Pine, D. S., Schultz, S. K., Tamminga, C. A., & Shrout, P. E. (2013). The initial field trials of DSM-5: New blooms and old thorns. *American Journal of Psychiatry, 170*, 1. https://doi.org/10.1176/appi.ajp.2012.12091189

Goodheart, C. (2014). *Primer for ICD-10-CM users: Psychological and behavioral conditions.* American Psychological Association.

Hammond, C. (2015). The justification process: A teaching tool for diagnosis using the DSM 5. *Virginia Counseling Journal, 34*, 48–53.

Häuser, W., Bialas, P., Welsch, K., & Wolfe, F. (2015). Construct validity and clinical utility of current research criteria of DSM-5 somatic symptom disorder diagnosis in patients with fibromyalgia syndrome. *Journal of Psychosomatic Research, 78*(6), 546–552. https://doi.org/10.1016/j.jpsychores.2015.03.151

Hays, P. (2008). *Addressing cultural complexities in practice: Assessment, diagnosis, and therapy* (2nd ed.). American Psychological Association.

Insel, T., Cuthbert, B., Garvey, M., Heinssen, R., Pine, D., Quinn, K., & Wang, P. (2010). Research domain criteria (RDoC): Toward a new classification framework for research on mental disorders. *American Journal of Psychiatry, 167*(7), 748–751. https://doi.org/10.1176/appi.ajp.2010.09091379

Jun, H. (2010). *Social Justice, multicultural counseling and practice: Beyond a conventional approach.* SAGE.

Kim, P. Y., Kendall, D. L., & Cheon, H. S. (2017). Racial microaggressions, cultural mistrust, and mental health outcomes among Asian American college students. *American Journal of Orthopsychiatry, 87*(6), 663. https://doi.org/10.1037/ort0000203

Kress, V. E., Hoffman, R. M., & Eriksen, K. (2010). Ethical dimensions of diagnosing: Considerations for clinical mental health counselors. *Counseling and Values, 55*(1), 101–112. https://doi.org/10.1002/j.2161-007X.2010.tb00024.x

Lingiardi, V., & McWilliams, N. (2017). *Psychodynamic diagnostic manual* (2nd ed.). PDM-2. Guilford Press.

Mandy, W. P., Charman, T., & Skuse, D. H. (2012). Testing the construct validity of proposed criteria for DSM-5 autism spectrum disorder. *Journal of the American Academy of Child & Adolescent Psychiatry, 51*(1), 41–50. https://doi.org/10.1016/j.jaac.2011.10.013

Moisse, K. (2012). *DSM 5 criticised for financial conflicts of interest.* ABCnews.go.com. http://abcnews.go.com/Health/MindMoodNews/dsm-fire-financial-conflicts/story?id=15909673

Nadal, K. L., Griffin, K. E., Wong, Y., Hamit, S., & Rasmus, M. (2014). The impact of racial microaggressions on mental health: Counseling implications for clients of color. *Journal of Counseling & Development, 92*(1), 57–66. https://doi.org/10.1002/j.1556-6676.2014.00130.x

Pies, R. W. (2012, February 8). *Beyond DSM-5, psychiatry needs a "third way."* Psychiatric Times. http://www.psychiatrictimes.com/print/article/10168/2029546

Poland, J., & Caplan, P. (2004). The deep structure of bias in psychiatric diagnosis. In M. McHugh (Ed.), *Bias in psychiatric diagnosis.* Jason Aronson Press.

Raskin, J. D. (2014). *How about a diagnostic alternative for talk therapy? Global summit on diagnostic alternatives.* http://dxsummit.org/archives/2190

Salim, S., Robinson, M., & Flanders, C. E. (2019). Bisexual women's experiences of microaggressions and microaffirmations and their relation to mental health. *Psychology of Sexual Orientation and Gender Diversity, 6*(3), 336. https://doi.org/10.1037/sgd0000329

Salkind, N. J. (2019). *Statistics for people who (think they) hate statistics.* SAGE.

Sisselman-Borgia, A., Budescu, M., & Torino, G. (2018). The association of racial and homelessness microaggressions and physical and mental health in a sample of homeless youth. *Urban Social Work, 2*(2), 139–158. https://doi.org/10.1891/2474-8684.2.2.139

Society for Humanistic Society. (2011). *Open letter to the American psychiatric association regarding the draft of the DSM 5.* http://www.ipetitions.com/petition/dsm5

Spitzer, R. L., & Fleiss, J. L. (1974). A re-analysis of the reliability of psychiatric diagnosis. *British Journal of Psychiatry, 125,* 341–347. https://doi.org/10.1192/bjp.125.4.341

Thornton, T. (2017). Cross-cultural psychiatry and validity in DSM-5. In R. White, S. Jain, D. Orr, & U. Read (Eds.), *The Palgrave handbook of sociocultural perspectives on global mental health.* Palgrave Macmillan.

Trungpa, C. (2010). *The sanity we are born with: A Buddhist approach to psychology.* Shambhala Press.

Verhaeghe, P. (2019). *On being normal and other disorders: A manual for clinical psychodiagnostics.* Routledge.

Wegela, K. K. (2014). *Contemplative psychotherapy essentials: Enriching your practice with Buddhist psychology.* WW Norton & Company.

Zimmerman, M., & Galione, J. (2010). Psychiatrists' and nonpsychiatrist physicians' reported use of the DSM-IV criteria for major depressive disorder. *The Journal of Clinical Psychiatry, 71*(3), 235–238. https://doi.org/10.4088/JCP.08m04940blu

2 Eight Steps to Diagnosis

Providing your client with a sound diagnosis requires an intentional and thoughtful engagement with a formal diagnostic process. While it can be tempting to turn directly to your DSM and quickly identify a diagnosis that resembles what your client is describing, taking the time to carefully map out your client's symptoms, walking through the steps and arriving at an accurate diagnosis will greatly increase the likelihood that your interventions will be effective. While the process may seem cumbersome in the beginning of your diagnostic career, over time you will find the steps come naturally and will flow easily. It may be helpful to know that after teaching this course for more than 10 years, I have found that students new to the DSM find the manual overwhelming and the diagnostic process daunting. However, with the practice that comes with working weekly with cases, almost without exception, students begin to feel confident about their growing skills and many even find that they enjoy diagnosis, approaching the process like a challenging puzzle to be solved.

In this chapter, we will consider eight basic steps to arriving at a diagnosis as well as 10 essential diagnostic principles. Within this chapter, you will be provided with a discussion of each of these steps as well as illustrative case examples to support your understanding of each step and principle. You will also be given the opportunity to practice steps as you move along through each section. Table 2.01 outlines the eight steps.

Step One: Identify Presenting Problems, Symptoms, and Observations. Symptoms are subjective physical, cognitive, or emotional experiences noticed by the client that cause disturbances in their well-being. Observations, also referred to as signs, may or may not be noticed by the client but are noted by the clinician or intake worker. A client's dress, demeanor, state of mental clarity or confusion and so on are all important observations or signs to be noted by the clinician (Morrison, 2007). The presenting problem is the reason your client has decided to come in for counseling, and usually describes the impact your client's symptoms have on their well-being. The line between presenting problems, symptoms, and clinician observations can be blurry, for instance feelings of depression may

TABLE 2.01 Eight Steps to Diagnosis

Step	Action
Step One	Identify complaints, symptoms, and observations
Step Two	Cluster related symptoms and observations
Step Three	Identify a potential diagnosis or diagnoses
Step Four	Locate the potential diagnoses and their criteria table in the DSM 5
Step Five	Apply relevant diagnostic principles
Step Six	Use the Justification Process (outlined in Chapter 3) to affirm or disconfirm the diagnosis
Step Seven	Write your justification for your diagnosis (outlined in Chapter 3)
Step Eight	Write your coded diagnosis

be the client's primary complaint, included within the symptoms your client describes. Perhaps more important than being able to discern these is cultivating a practice of considering all three and how they relate to one another.

Step Two: Cluster Related Symptoms, Observations, and Presenting Problems. The second step is to cluster the client's symptoms together. When clients present with a lot of symptoms, it is especially important to gain a picture of how these symptoms are related. This is an especially important task in helping you to determine if your client is experiencing more than one disorder. In this way you may ask yourself, "Are all of these symptoms connected or are they somehow arising from different sources or dynamics?" One of the best sources for linking symptoms is your client. Often clients imply or directly state that symptoms are connected or that some symptoms seem unrelated to the others.

Example: For the past several months, Dottie, 82, has not been herself. She explains, "I can't remember the last time I felt this tired. I try to rest but I toss and turn and just

BOX 2.01 CONSIDER THIS

How are you feeling now about this process? What do you anticipate will be challenging? What strengths do you bring to this process?

can't drop into a good sleep. I've been feeling pretty down, too. Throughout the day I spend a lot of time thinking about losing someone close to me. I think of my husband dying or losing my sister and it really bothers me. Sometimes I can't stop thinking about my own death. My daughter says I've been cranky, too." Dottie also notes, "I've lost my appetite completely, but I think that is because of all these damn medications they've got me on. They give me a stomach ache."

Note in Table 2.02 Dottie's counselor has clustered Dottie's symptoms.

TABLE 2.02 Dottie's Concerns and Symptoms Clustered

Dottie's Concerns	Symptoms/Observations
Cluster 1 Concern: Mood: Depression	• Feeling down • Thoughts of death (others) • Thoughts of death (self) • Irritability
Cluster 2 Concern: Bodily Function: Sleep	• Fatigue • Difficulty getting to sleep
Cluster 3 Concern: Stomach Upset (client suspects it is a reaction to medication)	• Loss of appetite

Step Three: Identify Potential Diagnoses. The third step is to identify a list of potential diagnoses for each cluster of symptoms. In order to arrive at potential diagnoses, you will want to first consider the diagnostic dimensions that seem to capture some or all of your client's symptoms. Past editions of the DSM have included decision trees, flow charts that served to guide the decision-making process in identifying potential diagnoses; however, these have been dropped from the current edition of the DSM. With time you will gain a familiarity with the DSM and you will be able to readily identify the dimensions of the manual that are most relevant to your client. If this is your first introduction, however, you may find Tables 2.03 and 2.04 to be helpful.

In Table 2.03, Dimensional Table of Diagnoses, the dimensions have been organized for you. You will notice that the left-hand column offers a question about your client's primary concern and the right-hand column matches that concern with diagnostic dimensions of the DSM. Table 2.04 lists the Dimensions and a brief description of select disorders.

For example, Trent, 15, has been trying to stop picking at his many moles for about a year. But when he finishes his shower each evening and begins to dry off, he notices the moles and begins again to pick at them, often causing them to bleed. This habit has sometimes led to an infection. His body is now covered with small scars that have

BOX 2.02 TRY THIS: IDENTIFY SYMPTOMS, OBSERVATIONS, AND PRESENTING PROBLEMS

Read through the following example and identify the information that you would describe as a symptom, those which are observations and those that are complaints/presenting problems.

Joel. Upon entering the counselor's office, the clinician noticed immediately that Joel, age 34, was dressed for warm weather despite the snow falling outside the clinic's office window. Joel's long hair fell in greasy strands over his shoulders. He seemed unaware that his baggy shorts were unzipped. Joel, nearly 20 minutes late, explained he had a lot of difficulty getting out of bed that morning and had thought of skipping the appointment since he had been unable to sleep much in the past several weeks; he complained of feeling foggy and tired. He described being constantly bothered by a voice narrating his actions. Joel was recently laid off of his part-time job and shared that he was "desperate" to get some work.

- What are Joel's presenting problems/ complaints?
- What are Joel's symptoms?
- What key observations has the clinician made about Joel's presentation?

resulted from his tendency to pick at his moles. Trent notes, "I try and try to stop but something keeps driving me to pick and pick."

Using Table 2.03, we can quickly identify a potential diagnosis for Trent. First, looking in the left-hand column, we note that Trent's problem is not one of cognition or of mood; it is a behavior that he would like to stop. Turning to the column to the right, we can further narrow his potential diagnosis by noting that his difficulty is not one of disruptive or impulsive behavior but instead it is a compulsive one, since he feels compelled and admits he can't stop without help.

Again, narrowing your diagnosis further, move to Table 2.04, and use the left-hand column to locate "compulsive behavior," and note that in the column on the right three potential diagnoses are offered: obsessive compulsive disorder (OCD), trichotillomania and excoriation disorder. Were you to try to diagnose Trent, you would then look at each of these diagnoses in the DSM to discover which of these is the more appropriate for Trent.

Once you have identified your client's primary concern or concerns and a potential diagnostic dimension for each concern, Table 2.03 will help you in narrowing your search to one or more potential diagnoses. In examining our example of Sarah, using the table above, it seems her primary concern is one of mood. In examining the potential diagnostic dimensions, in the right-hand column, the best fit seems to be the bipolar dimension, since her concern is not anxiety related nor one primarily of low mood

TABLE 2.03 Primary Concern and Potential Diagnostic Dimensions

Primary Concern	Potential Diagnostic Dimensions
Cognitive Is your client's primary concern one that pertains to the way your client thinks or learns?	• *Neurodevelopmental*: began in early childhood and affects learning • *Dissociative:* leaves your client feeling out of touch with him or herself or as if in a dream • *Schizophrenia and Related:* client experiences odd beliefs that are distressing to him or her • *Obsessive Compulsive:* thoughts are intrusive/unwelcome and cause distress • *Neurodegenerative:* thinking, learning or memory are impaired due to injury or illness
Mood Is your client's primary concern related to emotional states?	• *Anxiety:* worries, fears and phobias • *Depression:* low mood and melancholy • *Bipolar:* extremes of mood; mania or hypomania have been present
Behavior Is your client's primary concern related to behavior?	• *Disruptive, Impulse Control and Conduct*: the behavior is disruptive to others, impulsive, does not match developmental expectations, harms others or violates their rights • *Compulsive Behavior:* behavior is compulsive, sometimes used to stave off some feared event • *Substance and Addiction*: Behavior is compulsive and involves a substance or addictive interaction • *Eating:* eating is restricted, excessive or consumption causes harm or distress • *Neurodevelopmental:* Behavior is stereotyped, self-soothing or self-harming (Autism) or impulsive, non-rhythmic and repetitive • *Paraphilic:* sexual behaviors with children, or sexual behaviors harmful or distressing to self or others or that violates the rights of others
Bodily Function Is your client's primary concern related to the body or basic functions such as eating, sleeping or sexual function?	• *Eating:* eating is restricted or excessive, or causes harm or distress • *Elimination:* difficulties with control of elimination functions • *Sexual:* Difficulties obtaining satisfaction in sexual experiences • *Sleep:* difficulty obtaining or maintaining satisfactory sleep states
Identity/Personality Is your client's primary concern related to gender or patterned ways of relating to themselves and others?	• *Gender:* a sense that one's physical body is not in harmony with one's identified gender • *Personality:* patterns and ways of being in the world create predictable difficulties for self and other in interpersonal and intrapersonal experiencing

BOX 2.03 TRY THIS: IDENTIFYING A POTENTIAL DIAGNOSIS FOR SARAH

In the following case example, use Tables 2.03 and 2.04 to identify a potential diagnosis or diagnoses for Sarah.

Example: Sarah, age 25, has experienced significant mood swings over the past 4 years, including prolonged low mood and shorter periods of elevated mood. She was recently hospitalized after attempting suicide, and is now attending a partial hospitalization program.

1. What are Sarah's primary concerns?
2. Consult Table 2.03. Is Sarah's concern primarily cognitive, mood, behavior, bodily function or identity?
3. In consulting Table 2.04, what potential disorders might Sarah be grappling with?

but of fluctuations in mood. Our next step is to identify one or more specific diagnoses that might be a good fit for Sarah and then to turn to those diagnostic tables in the DSM 5. In consulting Table 2.04, and using the left-hand column, finding Mood and skipping down to Bipolar, thanks to our previous step, we can now look to the right and see three potential diagnoses for Sarah: Bipolar I, Bipolar II and Cyclothymic disorder.

Step Four: Locate the Diagnosis and Its Criteria Table in the DSM. After using Table 2.04 to locate potential diagnoses, using the DSM 5's index locate the diagnostic criteria table and discussion of that disorder. For additional support in narrowing potential diagnoses within a dimension, you may want to use the pivot tables located in this book. Pivot tables contain questions (pivot points) that will help you to turn your attention to potential diagnostic options. A pivot table has been provided for you for each diagnostic dimension in the DSM, a sample, the OCDs pivot table, is provided in Table 2.05.

Step Five: Apply Relevant Diagnostic Principles. Once you have identified a diagnosis or diagnoses that seem to be a good fit, you will want to refer to key diagnostic principles. Diagnostic principles are guidelines and best practices that support strong diagnostic decision-making. You will find 10 diagnostic principles discussed at the end of this chapter.

TABLE 2.04 Diagnostic Concerns and Matching Diagnoses

Concerns: Diagnostic Dimensions	Potential Diagnoses
Cognitive	
• *Neurodevelopmental:* began in early childhood and affects learning	• Learning Disorders; Intellectual Disability; Attention-deficit/hyperactivity disorder (ADHD); Autism
• *Dissociative:* leaves your client feeling disconnected from self or as if in a dream	• Dissociative Identity Disorder; Dissociative Amnesia; Depersonalization/Derealization
• *Schizophrenia and Related:* client experiences odd beliefs that your client finds distressing	• Schizophrenia; Delusional Disorder; Brief Psychotic Disorder; Schizophreniform Disorder; Schizoaffective Disorder
• *Obsessive Compulsive:* thoughts are intrusive/unwelcome, compulsive and cause distress	• Obsessive compulsive disorder (OCD); Body Dysmorphic Disorder; Hoarding
• *Neurodegenerative*: thinking, learning or memory are impaired due to injury or illness	• Major and Minor Neurocognitive Disorders, such as Alzheimer's, Parkinson's, Huntington's, etc.
Mood	
• *Anxiety:* worries, fears and phobias	• Separation Anxiety, Social Anxiety, Selective Mutism, Specific Phobia, Panic Disorder, Agoraphobia
• *Depression:* low mood and melancholy	• Disruptive mood dysregulation disorder, major depressive disorder, persistent depressive disorder, premenstrual dysphoric disorder
• *Bipolar:* extremes of mood; mania or hypomania have been present	• Bipolar I, Bipolar II and Cyclothymic Disorder
Behavior	
• *Disruptive, Impulse Control and Conduct:* the behavior is disruptive to others, impulsive, does not match developmental expectations, harms others or violates other's rights	• Oppositional Defiant Disorder; Intermittent Explosive Disorder; Conduct Disorder; Pyromania; Kleptomania
• *Compulsive Behavior*: behavior is compulsive often used to stave off some feared event	• OCD; Trichotillomania; Excoriation
• *Substance and Addiction:* Behavior is compulsive and involves a substance or addictive interaction	• Variety of substance disorders
• *Eating:* eating is restricted, excessive or consumption causes harm or distress	• Anorexia Nervosa; Bulimia Nervosa; Pica; Avoidant/Restrictive Intake
• *Autism:* Behavior is stereotyped, self-soothing or self-harming	• Autism Spectrum Disorder
• *Motor Tics:* involuntary motor or vocal experiences	• Tourette's Disorder; Persistent Motor or Vocal Tic Disorder
• *Paraphilic:* sexual behaviors with children, or is harmful or distressing to self or others or that violates the rights of others	• Voyeuristic Disorder; Exhibitionistic Disorder; Frotteuristic Disorder; Sexual Sadism; Pedophilic Disorder; Fetishistic Disorder; Transvestic Disorder

Concerns: Diagnostic Dimensions	Potential Diagnoses
Bodily Function	
• *Eating:* eating is restricted or excessive or causes harm or distress	• Pica; Rumination Disorder; Avoidant/Restrictive Food Intake Disorder; Anorexia Nervosa; Bulimia Nervosa; Binge-Eating Disorder
• *Elimination:* difficulties with control of elimination functions	• Enuresis; Encopresis
• *Sexual:* Difficulties attaining satisfaction in sexual experiences	• Delayed Ejaculation; Erectile Dysfunction; Female Orgasmic Disorder; Female Interest/Arousal Disorder; Geno-Pelvic Pain/Penetration Disorder; Male Hyposexual Desire Disorder; Premature Ejaculation
• *Sleep:* difficulty attaining or maintaining	• Insomnia Disorder; Hypersomnolence Disorder; Narcolepsy; Obstructive Sleep Apnea Hypopnea; Central Sleep Apnea; Sleep-Related Hypoventilation; Circadian Rhythm Sleep–Wake Disorders; Non-Rapid Eye Movement Sleep Arousal Disorders; Nightmare Disorder; Rapid Eye Movement Sleep Behavior Disorder; Restless Leg Syndrome
Identity/Personality	
• Gender Dysphoria: distress that arises from the mismatch between one's assigned gender and one's own self-identified gender	• Gender Dysphoria in Children; Gender Dysphoria in Adolescents and Adults
• Personality Disorders: entrenched patterns of relating to self and others that differ markedly from the expectations of that individual's cultural contexts	• Paranoid Personality; Schizoid Personality; Schizotypal Personality; Antisocial Personality; Borderline Personality; Histrionic Personality; Narcissistic Personality; Avoidant Personality; Dependent Personality; Obsessive Compulsive Personality

Diagnostic Steps Six, Seven and Eight

Steps six and seven make use of the Justification Process, which is outlined more fully in Chapter 3. This process and the written format of your justification will support the expression of clear diagnostic rationale for each diagnosis that you give. The justification process may also serve as documentation in your clinical notes or support clear communication with other healthcare professionals working with your client. Using this process may also serve to interrupt some forms of bias by encouraging clinicians to carefully consider all information presented and to reduce diagnoses based on assumptions (Hammond, 2015).

Step Eight: The Diagnostic Notation. The final step is to make your diagnostic notation. The notation is made up of the code, name of the diagnosis and any relevant specifiers. Recall that the codes located in the DSM 5 reflect the International Classification of Diagnoses (ICD) coding system used by the World Health

Organization. The ICD has historically been updated more frequently than the DSM so the print edition of the DSM 5 contains some outdated codes. The bolded code, reflecting the ICD 9, is no longer in use. Refer instead to the code within the parenthesis, shown in grey font in the DSM criteria tables; this reflects the ICD 10 code. Some of the codes, but not all, have been updated with the publication of the ICD 11; always check the most recent DSM 5 Supplement, available on the American Psychiatric Association (APA) website for any updated coding or changes in criteria. New supplements seem to be released in October each year.

When noting a diagnosis with its code, use the following format:

1. First list the most recent ICD code, being sure to check supplements for updates.
2. Next, list the name of the diagnosis, capitalizing only the first word of its name.

TABLE 2.05 Sample Pivot Points Table: Obsessive Compulsive Disorders

	Consider
Pivot Point One: Does your client's suffering arise from intrusive, repetitive and distressing thoughts or from irresistible and unwelcome rituals?	*Obsessive Compulsive Disorder*
Pivot Point Two: Does your client's suffering arise out of grossly distorted or incongruent perceptions of the body?	
• Is your client's distorted body image related to an exaggerated or perceived physical flaw?	*Body Dysmorphic Disorder*
• Is your client's distorted body image related primarily to weight?	*Anorexia Nervosa*
• Is your client's distress about the body? Are they embedded in a feeling of incongruence between gender identity and the physical body?	*Gender Dysphoria*
Pivot Point Three: Do your client's distressing thoughts and compulsions manifest in an inability to let go of objects that have lost their functional value and create a cluttered and unsafe environment?	*Hoarding Disorder*
Pivot Point Four: Do your client's compulsions manifest in sounds or movements that your client can't control (tics)?	*Tic Disorders*
Pivot Point Five: Does your client experience distress as a result of an irresistible urge to pull out their hair?	*Trichotillomania*
Pivot Point Six: Does your client experience distress as a result of an irresistible urge to pick their skin?	*Excoriation Disorder*

Using the pivot table above, which diagnosis or diagnoses would you like to explore further in order to reach a diagnosis for Spencer?

BOX 2.04 TRY THIS: SPENCER

Read through the following case then refer to the pivot table above. As you consider each question in the pivot table, ask yourself, whether or not the question fits the case description well. When you can answer positively, look to the right-hand column for a possible diagnosis. Once you have identified one or more potential diagnoses, explore each for a possible fit with Spencer's concerns and symptoms by turning to its diagnostic criteria table in the DSM 5. Once you have read through the related diagnostic criteria table or tables, remember to turn to the alternative diagnoses section that follow the criteria table in the DSM and consider other similar diagnoses that may be a better fit.

Spencer. Spenser, age 36, has been struggling for years with feelings of low self-worth and isolation. He works from home for a tech company. While he describes himself as an introvert and once appreciated the low social demands that came with this job, he now feels isolated from others and longs for social connection. While Spencer believes he is talented in his work and could find a position easily, he is held back from applying for a position by his "looks." Spencer believes that his nose and chin are "grotesque." Though his friends and family members have tried to convince him that there is nothing unusual in either the size or the shape of his nose or chin, Spencer has had three plastic surgeries to try to correct the problems he perceives. Spencer estimates that he spends several hours a day distracted by the "ugliness" of his nose and feels sure it will prevent him from finding a partner.

3. Finally, list all relevant specifiers, using all lower-case letters. Separate each specifier with a comma.

Example: F50.2 Bulimia nervosa, in partial remission, mild

When No Diagnosis Fits Comfortably. Frequently our client's concerns and symptoms do not fit neatly into the descriptions provided with the diagnostic tables, but our client is clearly suffering and is in need of support. The DSM 5 provides two options for situations in which diagnosis seems appropriate or necessary but the client's symptoms are atypical: specified or unspecified categories. Within each dimension are criteria tables for unspecified manifestations. This designation is used when the general dimension of suffering is known but very little additional information is available, or the clinician has chosen not to describe the symptoms at the time of diagnosis. The second option is to use the other specified criterion table located at the end of each dimension chapter. These offer atypical presentations of the dimension. For example, on page 353 of the DSM 5, other specified feeding or eating disorder, offers five atypical presentations, such as atypical anorexia.

Coding Deferral, Provisional and Rule-Outs. Often, we are faced with situations in which the diagnostic picture is unclear for one reason or another and despite following the eight steps, we cannot give a diagnosis with any real certainty, and the specified and unspecified tables are not a good fit. In these situations, we have several options.

The first to consider is a diagnostic deferral. Defer the diagnosis when it seems that diagnostic criteria are not met for a diagnosis; for instance, when the duration of your client's depression is too short to describe a major depressive episode. For situations in which symptoms strongly suggest a particular diagnosis but more information is needed to confirm the diagnosis, use a provisional diagnosis (APA, 2014). This is generally done by writing out the code and then the name of the diagnosis followed by the word *provisional.*

In situations in which you are discerning between two diagnoses, consider using the term *rule out* to note an alternate, but perhaps less likely, diagnosis that is still under consideration. Though it may be counter-intuitive, *rule out* indicates that the clinician

BOX 2.05 TRY THIS: IDENTIFY THE UPDATED DIAGNOSTIC CODE

Using the DSM 5 Supplement, identify the updated code for the following:

- F63.3 Kleptomania
- F64.1 Gender dysphoria
- F 42 Hoarding disorder

BOX 2.06 TRY THIS: IDENTIFY THE CORRECTLY FORMATTED DIAGNOSES

Box 2.06 Below find five examples. Identify which of the following is written in the correct format and change those that are incorrect into its correct notation:

- Nightmare Disorder (F51.5), During Sleep Onset, Severe
- 307.53 (F98.21) Rumination Disorder, in remission
- F44.81 dissociative identity disorder
- F45.22 Body dysmorphic disorder, with poor insight
- 312.81 Conduct Disorder, (F91.1) Childhood-onset type, unconcerned about performance

needs more information and is still in the process of considering a diagnosis and not that the clinician is sure that this diagnosis is not at play. It is worth noting that the DSM has dropped the term rule out from the manual, though it retains the term provisional (APA, 2014).

The Use of Questions. In the three examples above, diagnosticians should consider listing the specific questions that will lead them to either solidify a diagnosis, as in example 2, or to clearly distinguish between two competing diagnoses, as in example 3

BOX 2.07 NOTATION OF DEFERRED AND PROVISIONAL DIAGNOSES: EXAMPLES

Example 1: In the following example, the clinician does not have enough information to offer a diagnosis and has judged that listing a provisional diagnosis is inappropriate due to significant gaps in information.

F84.0 Autism spectrum disorder, without accompanying intellectual impairment, without accompanying language impairment, diagnosis deferred

Example 2: In the following example, the clinician's notation indicates that she intends to gather more data to support her strong suspicion that her client is struggling with autism and anticipates confirming this diagnosis after formal testing:

F84.0 Autism spectrum disorder, without accompanying intellectual impairment, without accompanying language impairment, provisional

BOX 2.08 THE RULE OUT NOTATION: EXAMPLE

In the following example, the clinician has only enough information to diagnose a communication disorder but is concerned that the problem may in fact be an autistic spectrum disorder:

F80.89 Social (pragmatic) communication disorder; Rule out F84.0 Autism spectrum disorder, without accompanying intellectual impairment, mild or to determine that no diagnosis is needed. Listing these questions serves two important purposes. First it provides prompts or reminders for clinicians in their follow up sessions. Second, and as importantly, listing these questions and, later, their answers, adds clarity, transparency and documentation to your diagnostic process. These questions should be maintained in your clinical notes.

The following process and format may be helpful in structuring the inclusion of questions in your notes. First, document any diagnostic questions that remain. Then note how the answer to that question will influence your decision. Box 2.12 on page 40 offers an example of how a clinician has used questions to support and document her diagnostic decision-making process.

When no diagnosis is being made. When through your careful clinical judgment, it is not necessary or appropriate to give a diagnosis, the APA website, 2013, recommends that you note this in the following way: V71.09 No diagnosis given.

The preceding eight steps help to create a strong practice in diagnostics. However, some outside pressures can intrude on the diagnostic process and impinge on ethical diagnostic practices. First among these problems are pressures to document a diagnosis early in the therapeutic relationship. Systems of managed care, for example, can require that a diagnosis be given before a client's treatment can be reimbursed. Similarly, some agency settings require a diagnosis be given in the first session. These outside demands can hinder diagnosticians in their efforts to take the time needed to diagnose complex presentations carefully and accurately. Another impediment to strong and ethical diagnostic practice is fostered by insurance policies that limit the types of disorders that are covered, tempting clinicians to misdiagnose in order to assure that a client's treatment is covered. When clinician's give clients a diagnosis that is not warranted by the client's symptoms, this is known as "up-coding." Up-coding sometimes happens when clinicians want to assure that a client receives needed services but their symptoms don't fully meet the diagnostic criteria, a presentation described as "sub-threshold,"when the presentation blends two or more diagnoses but fits neither well, or when symptoms fluctuate, sometimes meeting and sometimes not meeting criteria, but still requiring intervention (Cartwright et al., 2017). Up-coding can have a number of consequences for clients, for instance, it may shift how clients understand themselves and is but one of many contributions to diagnostic inflation (Frances, 2013b).

When More than One Diagnosis Is Needed. It is not uncommon for a client to carry two or more diagnoses at the same time. A number of diagnoses tend to appear together. For example, 75% of people struggling with depression also experience sleep difficulties, 40% experience hypersomnia (Nutt et al., 2008). Similarly, in one 2008 study, 84% of participants diagnosed with autism also carried at least one other diagnosis; 29.2% of study participants also carried a diagnosis of social anxiety disorder, and 28.1% held an oppositional defiant diagnosis (Simonoff et al., 2008). How do you diagnose and code more than one diagnosis?

Four terms are used to describe situations in which more than one diagnosis is needed or used: comorbid, co-occurring, multiple diagnosis and dual diagnosis. For

BOX 2.09 THE USE OF QUESTIONS IN DOCUMENTATION OF THE DIAGNOSTIC PROCESS

Example 1: It is unclear if Adam's interests fully meet criteria for B3 of the autism diagnosis or are simply a topic of captivation about which he holds a great deal of knowledge.

If his interests rise to the level of a restricted and fixated interest: *DX F84.0 Autism spectrum disorder, without accompanying intellectual impairment*

If his interests don't rise to the level of restricted interest: *DX F80.89 Social (pragmatic) communication disorder*

many clinicians, but not all, the term dual-diagnosis is used to describe a situation in which a client has been diagnosed with both a substance use disorder as well as a companion mental health disorder. For other clinicians, this term is simply used to describe two or more diagnoses that exist at the same time. Co-occurring disorders are those disorders that arise at the same time but are happenstantial to one another and not causal or directly linked. For example, when a client has chicken pox and also a broken arm, this situation is very unfortunate but the two are not causal to one another. Similarly, an eating disorder and depression may exist independently of one another in the same client. Comorbid disorders, on the other hand, imply that there is a relationship between the two distinct disorders, for instance, a client who has developed agoraphobia and has been unable to leave the house as a result, and gradually develops all the symptoms of a major depressive disorder thanks to feelings of helplessness and isolation. The problem of determining what mental health disorders are co-occurring and which are comorbid can be very difficult to parse, and some have argued that when describing mental health disorders, the difference may be specious at its base (Kaplan et al., 2006). I've noticed that many clinicians and researchers use these terms interchangeably; as language evolves, these terms may eventually come to refer to the same dynamic.

In the following section, you will be introduced to diagnostic principles that will serve to guide you in making diagnostic decisions when complexities arise, as they are bound to.

BOX 2.10 DOCUMENTATION OF "NO DIAGNOSIS"

When no diagnosis is being given, code in this way:
V71.09 No diagnosis given

Diagnostic Principles and Considerations

Morrison (2007) in his now classic text *Diagnosis Made Easier* outlines a number of guiding principles that work to provide direction in the process of identifying an appropriate diagnosis. Allen Frances (2013a), in *Essentials of Psychiatric Diagnosis*, also provides principles for arriving at a sound diagnosis, which he describes as "steps."In the following pages, I have consolidated Morrison's and Frances' principles and reorganized them into two primary themes: clinical significance, and differential diagnosis.

Clinical Significance

At times, we are faced with a decision about whether or not a diagnosis is appropriate or needed. Ethically, clinicians are bound to avoid applying a diagnosis when one is not necessary or when a diagnosis might be harmful to the client. In instances in which a clinician is discerning whether or not a diagnosis should be applied, principles one, two and three can be helpful.

Principle 1: The Warranted Concern. This principle is one that guides us to offer a diagnosis only when thinking, emotional distress or behavior significantly impairs functioning, or impinges on the rights or welfare of others, and is outside of the client's cultural expectations. This principle is so important that each diagnostic table in the DSM 5 contains a reminder to examine the symptoms or behavior and to confirm that they result in clinical levels of distress or impairment in social or occupational functioning before diagnosing. This criterion is designed to prevent unnecessary diagnoses and the diagnosis of culturally sanctioned responses to stress, trauma or grief. Frances (2013a) offers an additional recommendation and advises clinicians to be patient in assessing signs and symptoms and to avoid diagnosing early in the therapeutic process where possible, as symptoms may be at their most intense when your client decides to seek help but may quickly soften or ease afterward. Signs and symptoms that are considered for diagnosis should be significant and persistent. It is helpful to remember that being unhappy or dissatisfied with one's life is not the same as having a mental illness.

Battling Diagnostic Inflation and Misdiagnosis. Diagnostic inflation describes the trend to fold normal feeling states and behaviors into diagnostic categories and generally refers to a pattern of treating normal or expected responses with psychiatric medications, but also includes diagnostic trends or fad diagnoses. For example, prior to 1979 only 76 people had been documented to display more than one personality; however, in the decade following the inclusion of the multiple personality diagnosis in the DSM III and two popular movies featuring the disorder, more than 40,000 cases were diagnosed (Acocella, 1999; Piper & Merskey, 2004). Similarly, when the DSM IV-TR was published, the incidence of autism was estimated to be one in 250 births; however, in a 2018 survey of more than 50,000 participants, one in 40 parents reported having a child diagnosed with the disorder (Kogan et al., 2018). Our diligence in diagnosing only those concerns that are not typical responses to the stressors that come with living, and carefully applying appropriate and well-reasoned diagnoses serve an essential function in quelling trends toward inflating diagnostic numbers (Batstra & Frances, 2012; Frances, 2013b).

Principle 2: Life span Development. A second key diagnostic consideration is the principle of life span development. When applying this principle, we consider the fact that certain expressions of feelings, thoughts and behaviors may be expected and even appropriate at one stage of the life span but infringe on functioning at another. We see an example of this in the early stages of toddler development in which separation anxiety is a typical and expected part of cognitive and emotional development as well as a positive signal of secure attachment. During this stage, children show tremendous reluctance and even fear when leaving their mother's sight and may cry and cling when separation is anticipated. However, in a child age 7, for instance, this type of responding is not typical and may seriously impair a client's ability to go to school or to feel comfortable and safe when away from parents. In the case of the 7 year old, if the response is prolonged, pervasive and causes difficulties in the child's ability to socialize or go to school, a clinician will want to consider whether or not the child is experiencing a separation anxiety disorder (APA, 2014; Ehrenreich et al., 2008). When making use of this principle, it is important to remember to consider the client's approximate developmental stage rather than chronological age. For clients with a cognitive impairment, for example, certain behaviors may be developmentally appropriate after accounting for delays in development (APA, 2014; Frances, 2013a; Morrison, 2007).

Principle 3: Culturally Informed Responding. We live in a diverse world where our unique beliefs and experiences frame our thoughts, feelings and behavior as well as our understanding of and relationship to those thoughts, feelings and behaviors. Consequently, in determining whether or not a set of symptoms meet the level of clinical significance, we must also take into consideration the intersection of the client's cultural identities (ethnicity, race, gender, sexual orientation, socioeconomic class,

TABLE 2.06 **10 Diagnostic Principles**

Clinical Significance	
	The Warranted Concern
	Life span Development
	Culturally Informed Responding
Differential Diagnosis	
	Horses and Zebras
	The Principle of Predominance
	Occam's Razor or the Law of Parsimony
	Caution in Crisis
	Unaccounted for Symptoms
	Contributing Factors
	Client Resonance

Source: Adapted from Morrison, J. (2007) and Frances, A. (2013).

first language etc.) with the problem itself (APA, 2014; Frances, 2013a; Hays, 2008). Asking ourselves the following questions helps prevent misdiagnosis based in bias or lack of information:

- "How does my client's cultural background inform the way that they are experiencing this problem?"
- "Is this response typical and expected given this set of beliefs, cultural experiences or practices?"

The answers to these questions will take time and constitute an investment in your cultural competence when working with clients different from yourself. We will explore cultural considerations for each dimension throughout this text.

Differential Diagnosis. Often, we are faced with clients who present with symptom sets that are complex, layered or don't fit well into the descriptions outlined in the diagnostic tables. When reflecting on your own life experiences, you may be able to recall times when you have experienced feelings that seemed to conflict, feelings of relief, regret and sadness all mixed in together, for instance. Our human capacity

BOX 2.11 DEFINITION BOX: PRINCIPLE 1: THE WARRANTED CONCERN

The concern must cause distress and impairment to be diagnosed.

BOX 2.12 PRINCIPLE 2: LIFE SPAN DEVELOPMENT

Consider your client's social and cognitive development. Do not diagnose difficulties that might be expected thanks to typical developmental conflicts or challenges.

for feeling, thinking and behavior is nearly limitless, and so are the possibilities for client presentations and symptom sets. The physical structure of the human brain is extremely complex, and disruptions, injury and illness can result in a vast combination of potential difficulties within the organ of the brain itself. Very often, we will be able to find a shorthand for our clients' concerns within the DSM 5, but for some clients, these descriptions will not be an easy or tidy fit. Principles 4, 5 and 6 can be helpful in finding a more comfortable diagnosis for these clients.

Principle 4: Horses and Zebras or the Principle of Commonality. Imagine you were sitting in a café in downtown Manhattan enjoying a cup of coffee with a friend when you heard the sound of hooves clopping in the street. As you glance out the window, would you expect to see a horse or a zebra? Morrison (2007) points out that with a few exceptions, most of us expect to find a horse or horses trotting down the street and expect to see a zebra only in the zoo or on safari. When faced with a choice between

BOX 2.13 PRINCIPLE 3: CULTURALLY INFORMED RESPONDING

Give careful consideration to your client's culture and identities. Do not diagnose culturally sanctioned thoughts, feelings or behavior. Maintain awareness of trends in diagnosis that either exclude or overdiagnose populations.

BOX 2.14 PRINCIPLE 4: HORSES AND ZEBRAS OR THE PRINCIPLE OF COMMONALITY

This principle cautions clinicians to take care when considering rarely seen diagnoses or when diagnosing very uncommon presentations of a disorder.

BOX 2.15 PRINCIPLE 5: THE PRINCIPLE OF PREDOMINANCE

The principle of predominance reminds us that some disorders hold within them all the criteria for other less pervasive disorders; in these cases, diagnose only the predominant diagnosis.

two diagnoses, one common and one relatively uncommon, this principle advises that the safer diagnosis is the more common of the two. This principle can be applied by asking which of the two diagnoses is more common, and thus more likely, but can also be applied in examining the client's presentation by asking, "Does this case reflect a more common presentation of one diagnosis than another?" In other words, occasionally, a presentation may look like two disorders but reflects a more typical presentation of one disorder than another.

By way of example, children with attention-deficit/hyperactivity disorder (ADHD) struggle with attention and with high activity levels. However, the consequence of this distraction and frenetic activity frequently results in difficulties noticing cues in the social environment which, in turn, prevents them from responding to those cues. Children with autism share these difficulties in seeing, interpreting and responding to social cues. While both children with ADHD and children with autism spectrum disorder (ASD) struggle with social cues, they struggle for different reasons. A child with high functioning autism and a child significantly impacted by ADHD can have very similar presentations. ADHD, however, is five times more common than autism (APA, 2014), and may be the more appropriate choice if the child's presentation is very cloudy, particularly if given with a rule out for ASD.

Principle 5: The Principle of Predominance. The principle of predominance helps to reduce the potential for multiple and unnecessary diagnoses. A number of diagnoses are pervasive in their nature, affecting thought, emotion and behavior. Schizophrenia and autism are classic examples of disorders that come with far-reaching consequences. Diagnosticians who fail to observe the principle of predominance may find themselves offering a veritable submarine sandwich of diagnoses to persons suffering from Schizophrenia, for example, ranging from Delusional Disorder, Brief Psychotic Disorder, Major Depressive Disorder, Generalized Anxiety Disorder, Derealization/Depersonalization Disorder and so on. The principle of predominance reminds us that some disorders hold within them all the criteria for other less pervasive disorders. It is only necessary to diagnose those additional disorders that are not adequately described by the primary or predominant diagnosis and those that may not resolve with the treatment of the primary concern (Morrison, 2007).

Often, however, it is necessary to diagnose more than one disorder at a time. This process can be a bit complicated; however, as it is not always immediately evident whether two disorders are working independently, such as with a person struggling with schizophrenia also abuses substances as a way of responding to the symptoms of the psychotic disorder, or if a single disorder is generating symptoms that also mimic a second disorder, such as when a client in the end stages of an alcohol use disorder exhibits symptoms consistent with a psychotic disorder. When trying to determine whether or not to diagnose two disorders at the same time, the following principles will be supportive in your diagnostic process.

Principle 6: Occam's Razor or the Law of Parsimony. The principle of Occam's Razor states that when we must choose between two competing answers it is best to choose

BOX 2.16 PRINCIPLE 6: OCCAM'S RAZOR OR THE LAW OF PARSIMONY

Choose the diagnosis that requires the fewest assumptions.

the answer that requires the fewest assumptions (Morrison, 2007). When applying this principle to a case, take note of what information you can verify and what information is reliant upon inference or assumption. Keeping this distinction in mind will also help support you in avoiding diagnoses based heavily on assumption or, worse, bias.

Principle 7: Principle of Caution in Crisis, Transition and Personality Concerns. There are moments in a person's life that naturally bring about elevated states of anxiety, distressed behavior or thinking. Many readers can attest to experiences like this during the early weeks of the pandemic and the quarantines that were mandated across the country, for example. Difficult situations often require a bit of time before people feel they have their legs under them again, and can return to their baseline state. A diagnosis will be more accurate when the crisis has begun to settle and the clinician is better able to gauge the client's functioning and well-being (Frances, 2013a; Morrison, 2007). Clinicians are ill advised, for example, to diagnose a child shortly after a parent's military deployment. This period of adjustment can cause very high levels of stress and foster or elevate behaviors that make diagnosis difficult at best. Other critical situations, such as immediately following a catastrophic loss or a natural disaster, are not good times for accurately assessing and diagnosing client concerns at any age. Clients with an untreated primary diagnosis can display symptoms consistent with a personality disorder but do not display those symptoms once treated successfully for the primary diagnosis. Best practices advise extreme caution when diagnosing clients with a personality disorder during a time of significant crisis since very stressful moments can escalate symptoms and may then resemble a personality disorder (Morrison, 2007).

Principle 8: Unaccounted for Symptoms. This principle reminds us to examine the client's concerns for symptoms that have not been captured within the primary diagnosis (Morrison, 2007). For instance, consider a client diagnosed with separation anxiety who also complains of regular nightmares over the past year. While anxiety may underlie these dreams, the separation anxiety disorder likely does not adequately account for

BOX 2.17 PRINCIPLE 7: PRINCIPLE OF CAUTION IN CRISIS, TRANSITION AND PERSONALITY CONCERNS

This principle reminds us to use caution and allow sufficient time before applying a personality disorder diagnosis.

the nightmares. What's more, the nightmares may continue without separate intervention. In this case, careful consideration of an additional diagnosis of a nightmare disorder should be made if the nightmares do not seem to respond to treatment of the anxiety.

Principle 9: Contributing Factors. This principle reminds us to keep in mind the possibility of an underlying medical condition, particularly in the elderly. Also essential is to consider the possibility that substance use may be creating or exacerbating mental health symptoms. Include within your consideration any prescribed medications, many of which have side effects that mimic mental health concerns (Atkins, 2014; Frances, 2013a; Morrison, 2007).

Principle 10: Client Resonance. At times, it may be unclear if a set of symptoms is entirely accounted for by a primary diagnosis or should be considered to be part of a diagnosis of their own. For instance, sleep disturbances are very common in major depressive disorder. It is important for a clinician to consider whether or not the sleep disturbance is a concern that requires separate treatment. This principle suggests that we can turn to our clients for these answers by asking clients how they experience the relationship between their symptoms. For example, you might ask:

- "Do these sleep difficulties feel like they are part of the depression you describe, or do they feel separate to you?"
- "Do you have a sense that if the depression resolved that your sleep would stabilize or is this something we should work on independently of the depression?"

BOX 2.18 PRINCIPLE 8: UNACCOUNTED FOR SYMPTOMS

If after diagnosing a client with a disorder, symptoms remain that are not accounted for in this diagnosis, consider a second diagnosis.

BOX 2.19 PRINCIPLE 9: CONTRIBUTING FACTORS

Remain mindful of potential medical conditions that may be responsible for your client's symptoms.

BOX 2.20 PRINCIPLE 10: CLIENT RESONANCE

This principle reminds us that our clients are our own best resource for understanding the quality of symptoms.

This principle forwards the idea that our clients are a key resource in arriving at an appropriate diagnosis.

Consultation. Remember the adage *pride goeth before the fall.* Don't allow a busy schedule or personal pressures to have mastered diagnosis to prevent you from asking for a consultation with a trusted colleague when you are left feeling less than confident with a diagnosis. Where possible establish an ongoing relationship with a trusted and seasoned professional with whom you can consult regularly. Talk through your diagnostic decision-making processes being sure to make note of your colleague's ideas, and to document questions that may have arisen thanks to your consultation. Include these notes with your case notes in order to document your effort to provide excellent care. Diagnosis is a complicated process and is all too often riddled with ambiguities; however, the stakes for your clients are high. The extra time you give to consultation with another thoughtful practitioner will pay dividends in increased accuracy and peace of mind.

Creating a symptom timeline. While clients may find it difficult to recall clearly when symptoms first began, you may find a symptom timeline to be supportive in your diagnostic process. Morrison (2007) suggests a symptom timeline can be drawn from a well-designed client intake form, provided this form outlines symptoms and provides an opportunity to describe when the symptom emerged as well as its duration, and provided the client is a good historian for their own symptoms. A symptom timeline can provide invaluable information in differentiating a diagnosis or determining if dual diagnoses is more appropriate. For example, a client, Jared, has been seeing his counselor for major depression for about a month. He reports that he is unable to sleep and would like to look into medication for this concern. Jared's counselor would like to do a symptom timeline and explore whether the sleep disturbance has been present at any time outside of his current depression or during the depression Jared experienced 5 years ago. His counselor believes this will help her to understand better if the sleep disturbance is a manifestation of depression or if it represents an independent difficulty.

Creating a diagnostic genogram. A number of disorders have a tendency to run in families, either because they have a genetic component, as with autism, or because they are learned through family systems. Sometimes both dynamics are at play. Morrison (2007) recommends creating a genogram of documented diagnoses. This process may help you to get a sense for the psychological environment in which your client grew up or currently lives within.

However, drawing conclusions about your client's diagnosis based on the diagnoses of family members is not appropriate. First, you will not be able to count on the accuracy or completeness of the diagnoses that are reported to you and placed in the genogram. Any reporting of undiagnosed mental health concerns will be highly biased and not fully informed. Remember, too, that a number of diagnostic terms are used in common parlance but may not represent an accurate reflection of diagnostic criteria. For instance, a client may report, "My mother is totally OCD, she freaks out if I miss my curfew or I forget to do my chores. It is so annoying." In this case, it is less likely that the client's mother meets criteria for OCD and more likely that she is a bigger stickler for the rules than the client appreciates. Second, using the genogram to diagnose your client is at best a significant use of inference; used in addition to careful diagnostic processes; however, the genogram can provide supportive evidence when working with a cloudy diagnostic picture. A genogram is also useful in understanding better your client's perceptions and understanding of their own psychological environment and may potentially reveal family patterns for particular mental health concerns. Should you decide to make use of this tool, be sure to include physical disorders as well, since physical health has a significant impact on mental health and vice versa.

Conclusion

In this chapter, we have looked carefully at eight steps for arriving at a diagnosis. We have discussed the importance of carefully organizing presenting problems, symptoms and clinician observations and considering their relationship to one another. We looked at the structure of the formal diagnostic notation. We also explored 10 guiding principles for use in the diagnostic process. Finally, we explored the importance of cultivating relationships with other diagnosticians with whom you can confer about your conclusions and share questions. In Chapter 3 we will explore in depth the function and structure of the justification process, which constitutes the steps six and seven of the diagnostic process.

References

Acocella, J. (1999). *Creating hysteria: Women and multiple personality disorder.* Jossey-Bass.

American Psychiatric Association. (2013). *Diagnostic and statistical manual of mental disorders (DSM-5®).* Author.

American Psychiatric Association. (2014). *Frequently asked questions about DSM-5 implementation- for clinicians.* http://www.dsm5.org/Documents/FINAL%20FAQ%20for%20Clinicians%20PDF%2010-7-14.pdf

Atkins, C. (2014). *Co-occurring disorders: Integrated assessment and treatment of substance use and mental disorders.* PESI Publishing & Media.

Batstra, L., & Frances, A. (2012). Holding the line against diagnostic inflation in psychiatry. *Psychotherapy and Psychosomatics, 81*(1), 5–10. https://doi.org/10.1159/000331565

Cartwright, J., Lasser, J., & Gottlieb, M. C. (2017). To code or not to code: Some ethical conflicts in diagnosing children. *Practice Innovations, 2*(4), 195. https://doi.org/10.1037/pri0000053

Ehrenreich, J. T., Santucci, L. C., & Weiner, C. L. (2008). Separation anxiety disorder in youth: Phenomenology, assessment, and treatment. *Psicologia Conductual, 16*(3), 389.

Frances, A. (2013a). *Essentials of psychiatric diagnosis: Responding to the challenge of DSM-5*. Guilford Publications.

Frances, A. (2013b). *Saving normal: An insider's revolt against out-of-control psychiatric diagnosis, DSM 5, big pharma, and the medicalization of ordinary life*. William Morrow.

Hammond, C. (2015). The justification process: A teaching tool for diagnosis using the DSM 5. *Virginia Counselors Journal, 34*, 48–53.

Hays, P. A. (2008). *Addressing cultural complexities in practice: Assessment, diagnosis, and therapy* (pp. 7–275). American Psychological Association.

Ingram, B. L. (2011). *Clinical case formulations: Matching the integrative treatment plan to the client*. John Wiley & Sons.

Kaplan, B., Crawford, S., Cantell, M., Kooistra, L., & Dewey, D. (2006). Comorbidity, co-occurrence, continuum: What's in a name? *Child Care Health Development, 32*(6), 723–731. https://doi.org/10.1111/j.1365-2214.2006.00689.x

Kogan, M. D., Vladutiu, C. J., Schieve, L. A., Ghandour, R. M., Blumberg, S. J., Zablotsky, B., Perrin, J. M., Shattuck, P., Kuhlthau, K. A., Harwood, R. L., & Lu, M. C. (2018). The prevalence of parent-reported autism spectrum disorder among US children. *Pediatrics, 142*(6), e20174161.

Morrison, J. (2007). *Diagnosis made easier: Principles and techniques for mental health clinicians*. Guilford Press.

Nutt, D., Wilson, S., & Paterson, L. (2008). Sleep disorders as core symptoms of depression. *Dialogues in Clinical Neuroscience, 10*(3), 329–336. PMCID: PMC3181883.

Piper, A., & Merskey, H. (2004). The persistence of folly: A critical examination of dissociative identity disorder. Part I. The excesses of an improbable concept. *The Canadian Journal of Psychiatry, 49*(9), 592–600. https://doi.org/10.1177/070674370404900904

Simonoff, E., Pickles, A., Charman, T., Chendler, S., Loucas, T., & Baird, G. (2008). Psychiatric disorder in children with autism spectrum disorders: Prevalence, comorbidity, and associated factors in a population-derived sample. *Journal of the American Academy of Child & Adolescent Psychiatry, 47*(8), 921–929. https://doi.org/10.1097/CHI.0b013e318179964f

3 The Justification Process

Undertaking the diagnostic process marks a significant step in our professional and ethical responsibilities as mental healthcare professionals. However, diagnostics seem to present marked challenges to both the individual professional and the mental health profession as a whole. As discussed in Chapter 1, diagnosis has been marred by two primary difficulties: first, practitioner bias and the use of diagnosis in systemic oppression of marginalized groups coupled with bias built into the manual itself, and second, poor inter-rater reliability in the application of the DSM.

The justification process encompasses the sixth and seventh steps in the eight steps of the diagnostic process discussed in Chapter 2, and was developed to do four things: create structure, provide transparency, to bring unconscious processes into conscious thought and increase diagnostic accuracy.

The first purpose of the justification process was to provide a structure for students in approaching diagnosis and a sense of clarity and confidence about their diagnostic decision-making. Justifications can provide instructors with insight into their student's thought processes, and, if used in clinical work, can support clear communication with team members who work with your client about how you've arrived at your diagnosis. The structure and clarity of the justification are also aimed at supporting more accurate diagnosis and at disrupting some of the unconscious processes that can result in biased diagnosis (Hammond, 2015).

In developing our personal diagnostic skill, we can make significant inroads into reducing diagnostic bias by being intentional about the thought processes that might otherwise fall outside of our awareness. Again, one way that bias manifests itself in the diagnostic process happens when we give attention to some kinds of information and less to others, latching onto unsupported assumptions, or when we don't give a critical eye to the information related to our client that has been gathered by others (Caplan & Cosgrove, 2004).

When reviewing a file, talking with a client or reading a case study, it is as important to understand the source of the information as it is to understand the context that frames that information. Only then should you begin checking to see how well that information fits into a diagnostic criterion set and, of course, looking for disconfirming information or evidence.

Since bias can arise out of unconscious processing of available data, using the justification process provides an opportunity to work to transform unconscious processes into more deliberate steps; for example, by listing all information available and applying an objective structure for considering each piece of data. However, unconscious processes may still lead a clinician to glean some pieces of information and not others or to remember incorrectly, making the need for careful attention and intention throughout the process essential to reducing bias.

The second purpose of the justification process is to support a more accurate diagnosis by limiting the application of a diagnosis to those situations in which a justification can be written that fully supports it. This process may limit instances in which a diagnosis is given based on intuition or a subjective interpretation of criteria, and increase the consistency with which clinicians diagnose, which may in turn improve inter-rater reliability rates. However, research is needed to investigate whether or not the use of the justification process results in measurable differences in inter-rater reliability.

This chapter will use a single case example, Kelly, to guide you through the eight steps of making a diagnosis. We will first review steps one through five, move through steps six and seven, which include the justification process, and then conclude with step eight, writing your coded diagnosis.

A Review of the First Five Steps in the Diagnostic Process

As we discussed in Chapter 1, **the first step** in diagnosing a case study or a client's difficulty is to carefully read through the scenario or intake and session notes for key information. Again, key information includes any details that describe the individual's suffering; for example, symptoms of anxiety or changes in eating or sleep patterns, the duration of those symptoms, and indications of intensity, such as frequency and the age at which the symptoms began. It is often important to note areas of strength or well-being as these areas of our clients' lives help us to differentiate between two diagnoses and ultimately point us toward a more appropriate therapeutic intervention.

The second step in the diagnostic process is to cluster complaints and their related symptoms. In this case, Kelly's chief complaint, a fear of the dentist and all of her symptoms are related to that fear, suggesting that we are looking for a single diagnosis.

In deciding that a diagnosis is needed, **the third step** is to identify potential diagnoses. Using Table 2.03, Diagnostic Dimensions, to match Kelly's most prominent symptoms and key information to an appropriate diagnostic dimension, we note that Kelly's primary concern is related to mood states, anxiety in particular. Moving to Table 2.04, Matching Diagnoses, located in Chapter 2, we note that Kelly's primary symptom is anxiety, which leads us to consider the anxiety disorders; however, some of her fear is related to becoming ill, which suggests that we should give some consideration to the

BOX 3.01 PURPOSES OF THE JUSTIFICATION PROCESS

- Add structure and consistency to the diagnostic process
- Lend transparency and additional documentation to the diagnostic decision-making process
- Support more objective diagnostic decision-making in an effort to reduce bias in diagnostic decision-making
- Increase the accuracy of diagnoses

somatic symptom disorders as well. After reviewing the basic elements of the anxiety and somatic symptom disorders, two plausible disorders emerge, specific phobia and illness anxiety disorder (IAD).

Step four is a simple step; locate your potential diagnoses in the DSM 5. In this case, you will find these tables on pages 197 and 315, respectively. At step four, you should also review the differential diagnosis section for each of the diagnoses you are considering and read those criteria as well. When diagnosing Kelly, as you refer to specific phobia, for example, the differential diagnosis section notes the following disorders share overlapping presentations that should also be considered: agoraphobia, social anxiety, separation anxiety, panic, obsessive-compulsive, trauma and stressor-related disorders, eating disorders and the schizophrenia spectrum. IAD shares features with several disorders as well. Turn to each and consider which diagnosis or diagnoses best fit Kelly's presentation. Finally, check your DSM 5 Supplement for any changes in criteria or differential diagnosis recommendations.

In **step five,** we pause for a moment and consider any relevant diagnostic principles.

The Justification Process, Step Six

The sixth step in the diagnostic process is the use of the justification process that begins with coding the case study. A case study is coded by using each of the relevant DSM tables identified in step four. Coding the data requires that you read through the case study, or intake when diagnosing a client, and match the DSM 5 table criterion connected to plausible diagnosis or diagnoses with the symptoms and concerns reflected in your case.

Below, Kelly's case has been offered again exactly as written earlier; however, this time, it has been coded for you using both the specific phobia table (first example) and the IAD table (second example).

In these examples, you will notice that the end of each relevant complaint or symptom has been matched with the major criterion letter associated with the relevant criterion table, and placed inside parentheses. For the purposes of this example, a brief explanation is offered as to why I chose to code in the way that I have (these explanations are not part of the final justification). Please open your DSM 5 and locate each of the criteria identified in the examples below.

Kelly's case coded using the Specific Phobia Criterion Table (page 197 of the DSM 5):

Now look at Kelly's situation with coding for criteria found in the IAD criteria table.

IAD coded (page 315 of the DSM 5):

Differential diagnosis of Kelly's fears. Differential diagnosis is a process in which we pull apart the details of a case and rearrange them, like pieces of a puzzle, until we arrive at a clear picture of what is unfolding diagnostically. Generally, the process of differential diagnosis is one in which the clinician is working to differentiate between two or more potential diagnoses, as with Kelly.

Kelly's case is a bit complicated. Her fear of the dentist is nuanced because it includes within it a fear that she might be exposed to human immunodeficiency virus (HIV) while in the dentist's chair. In looking at the diagnostic criteria for each disorder, Kelly meets all the criteria for specific phobia but meets only a few of the criteria for IAD (criterion A and E). Kelly's anxiety about contracting HIV or acquired immunodeficiency syndrome (AIDS) while at the dentist begs the question, "Is she afraid of getting AIDS or afraid of the potential for the dentist to transmit the virus?" However, Kelly has said she is not afraid of contracting HIV in other circumstances, suggesting that her concern is specific to some aspect of the dentist appointment itself.

Criteria B of IAD implies that the client is not ill but worries about illness; however, Kelly does have a broken tooth and is in a great deal of pain, contradicting this criterion. The B criterion is also describing a situation in which a person's fears about illness are out of proportion with the likelihood of illness. Kelly does match this portion of the B criterion description, since it is unlikely that she would be infected with HIV at the dentist's office. Finally, her case description contradicts criterion C of that diagnosis since she has said she is not worried about illness generally. So, while Kelly's situation has components in common with IAD, the better fit here is specific phobia. After arriving at a diagnosis, the next step is to clearly support this diagnosis with a written paragraph in the justification format.

Looking for Disconfirming Evidence. A misdiagnosis can easily be made if you search your case for information that confirms the suspected diagnosis without actively looking for evidence that contradicts your hunch. As you examine your criteria, it is essential that you consider not only how your client fits the description, but also the ways in which your client's presentation does not fit the spirit or the detail of the criteria. For example, finding disconfirming evidence for IAD was central to our diagnosis of Kelly's specific phobia. This is a natural step in differential diagnosis, but

BOX 3.02 TRY THIS: IDENTIFY COMPLAINTS AND SYMPTOMS

In the following case, Kelly will serve as an example of the entire diagnostic process. Read through Kelly's case and identify her symptoms and complaints.

Kelly. Kelly, age 25, has struggled since childhood with extreme discomfort when faced with the prospect of going to the dentist and consequently has not been to the dentist for 10 years. Kelly has shared that she is afraid that if she goes to the dentist, she might be exposed to acquired immunodeficiency syndrome (AIDS) and become very ill, though she does not worry about contracting AIDS in other situations nor does she worry about being exposed to illness in general. For the past year, Kelly has experienced intense pain in her mouth and jaw related to a broken tooth. She has gone so far as to make dental appointments but worries and loses sleep about meeting with the dentist until she finds herself canceling her appointments at the last moment.

Key Complaints:
Key Symptoms:
Areas of Strength:

BOX 3.03 CHECK YOUR THINKING: KELLY

Symptoms that you might have highlighted in Kelly's experience include the following:

- Fear of the dentist beginning in her teens
- Avoidance of the dentist despite a threat to her dental health and experiencing pain
- Fear of becoming ill (limited to exposure by the dentist)
- Loss of sleep over the prospect of seeing the dentist

Kelly's chief complaints:

- Fear of the dentist
- Chronic pain resulting from a broken tooth

Kelly's strength:

- Kelly does not fear infection or illness in all situations, instead this fear is limited to dentistry
- Kelly has made dental appointments (a sign of strength and courage) but has not yet been able to keep these appointments

GRAPHIC 3.01 **Matching Symptoms to a Potential Diagnosis**

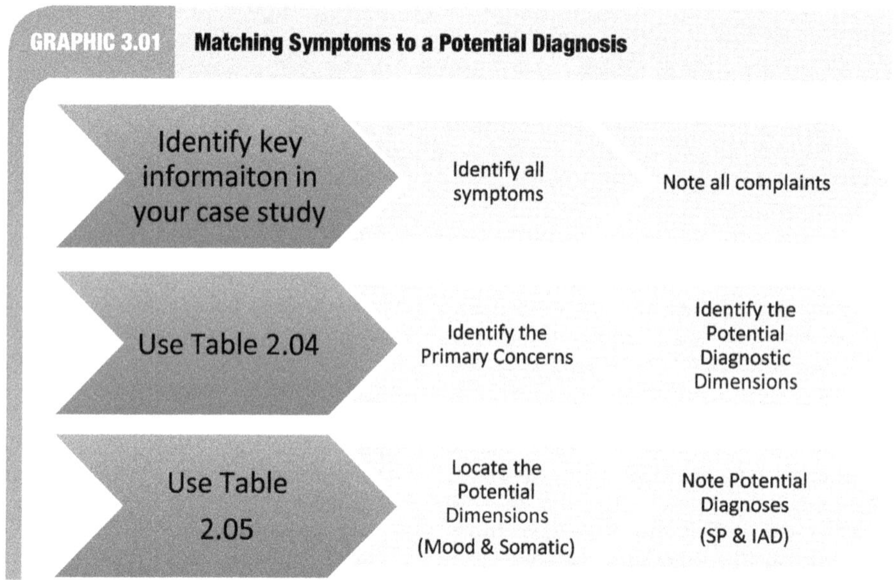

should be included in your thought process even when you are only considering a single diagnosis.

Kelly meets all criteria for social phobia but only a few for IAD.

Step Seven, Writing Your Justification

The seventh step is the documentation of your diagnostic process and comes in the form of a structured paragraph, described as the justification format. The justification is a paragraph formulated around the structure of DSM 5 diagnostic tables and makes use of the criteria table format to code symptoms. The paragraph is written to reflect the alphabetical and numerical order of the relevant table so that the "A" criterion is described first and then the "B" criterion until all major criteria are addressed including exclusion and impairment criteria. (See discussion in Chapter 2 for review of criteria and DSM 5 format.) When diagnosing a case, if the case has been coded as illustrated in step six, the format can be written up quickly and easily by re-organizing the information so that it is presented alphanumerically.

It is important to note that the justification paragraph can make use of some of the same language and phrasing as is found in the case study itself without concerns about plagiarism. In much the same way as we use similar language and phrasing to reflect client experiences in the therapy setting, using similar language offered by a client or in a case study to convey the ways in which a client meets a particular diagnosis helps to develop a habit of drawing from our client's words and experiences (Hammond, 2015).

BOX 3.04 TRY THIS: USING THE DIAGNOSTIC PRINCIPLES

Review the diagnostic principles outlined in Chapter 1. Which principles might apply to this case? How would you apply these principles?

Principles:

BOX 3.05 CHECK YOUR THINKING: PRINCIPLES THAT MAY APPLY TO KELLY

Principle 3: Culturally Responsive Responding: Are we in danger of pathologizing normal fears thanks to stereotypes of women as fearful?

Caution is called for. A diagnostician's perspective may be swayed by social perceptions of women as fearful or overly emotional. However, by seeing Kelly's strengths, such as the fact that her fear of becoming ill is situational and acknowledging that these are not related to character, personality or gender, the diagnostician reduces the chance of offering a biased diagnosis. The clinician does not seem to be overlooking information that suggests Kelly's fears are culturally sanctioned beliefs, lending further confidence that the diagnosis is accurate and appropriate.

The first step in writing up a justification is to identify each of the major criteria in the relevant diagnostic table. The major criterion that *must* be addressed are marked with a capital letter in the diagnostic table. For example, in the diagnostic table located on page 197, the capital letter "A" is followed by a statement describing "marked fear or anxiety about a specific object or situation." Again, each diagnostic table differs in how many criteria must be met; however, in order to diagnose, the client or subject of the case study must meet all of the major criteria as well as the specified sub-criteria for that table. Each diagnosis varies in the number of sub-criteria that are listed and in

GRAPHIC 3.02 **Including Diagnostic Principles**

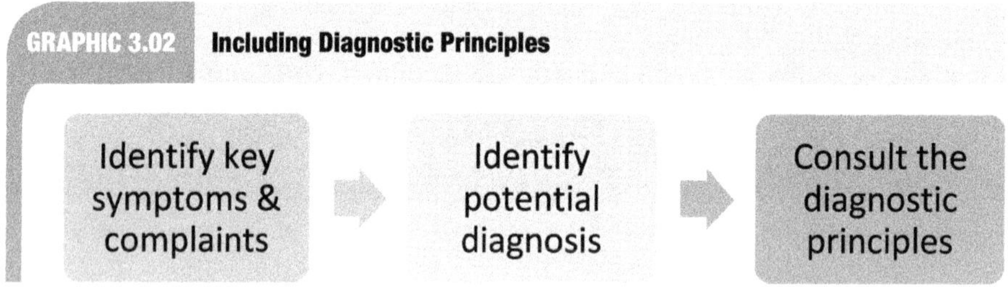

the number of possible sub-criteria that must be met. The criteria for specific phobia are made up only of major criteria.

In writing your justification, you will develop a sentence for each of the major criterion that explains how that criterion was met, followed by parentheses containing the letter and sometimes the number associated with the criterion or sub-criteria, for example "(A)" or "(A1)."

Specifiers are justified at the end of the justification paragraph in the order they appear in the criteria table. When noting your specifier, include the justification statement for the specifier, noting the symptom or circumstance, and then the specifier, within parenthesis. An example follows:

Occasionally, an inference must be made rather than noting direct evidence from your client or a case study. In these instances, it is helpful to qualify these statements with phrases like "it seems" or "it appears" in order to remind yourself to check these less concretely supported points with your client in order to confirm your diagnosis. However, if you don't have information that supports or strongly suggests your client meets a major criterion, then you can't justify making a particular diagnosis. For example, we did not have enough information to suggest that Kelly met more than the A and E criteria of IAD, and we had evidence that she did not experience high levels of anxiety related to her health in general (the C criteria); consequently, it would not have been appropriate to diagnose Kelly with IAD in addition to or instead of a specific phobia. Here you will find a sample justification has been provided for Kelly's diagnosis. Give careful attention to the alphanumerical format given in the example paragraph.

Why write a justification? Why write a justification when it seems to simply reiterate information already available to us? The benefits of writing a justification are many. First, when we are learning the diagnostic process, we typically lack confidence in our diagnoses. Taking the time to write a justification sheds light on your thought processes and makes it possible for your instructor to give you helpful, direct and individualized feedback. Writing up a justification can work to lend you an additional level of certainty that you have considered all aspects of the diagnosis you've identified and that your thinking has been sound. Taking this step supports you in looking for evidence that might contradict a diagnosis, an important step in accurate diagnosis. Another benefit of writing a justification is that the more complex or nuanced a case, the more potential for the diagnostician to see the case differently from other mental

BOX 3.06 KELLY'S CASE CODED USING THE SPECIFIC PHOBIA CRITERION TABLE

Kelly, age 25, has struggled since childhood (*E. persistent*) with extreme discomfort (*D. the fear is out of proportion*) when faced with the prospect of going to the dentist (*A. fear of a specific situation*) and has not been to the dentist for 10 years (*B. suggests she has a sustained fear that keeps her from the dentist*). Kelly has shared that she is afraid that if she goes to the dentist she might be exposed to acquired immunodeficiency syndrome (AIDS) and become very ill, though she does not worry about contracting AIDS in other situations nor does she worry about being exposed to illness in general. For the past year, Kelly has experienced intense pain in her mouth and jaw related to a broken tooth (*F. the fear causes clinically significant distress and health impairment*). She has gone so far as to make dental appointments but worries and loses sleep about meeting with the dentist until she finds herself canceling at the last moment (*C. the phobic situation is avoided*)

BOX 3.07 KELLY'S CASE CODED USING THE ILLNESS ANXIETY DISORDER CRITERION TABLE

Kelly, age 25, has struggled since childhood with extreme discomfort when faced with the prospect of going to the dentist. Kelly has shared that she is afraid that if she goes to the dentist she might be exposed to acquired immunodeficiency syndrome (AIDS) and become very ill (*A, preoccupation with getting ill*), though she does not worry about contracting AIDS in other situations nor does she worry about being exposed to illness in general (*contradicts criterion C, which describes high levels of health anxiety*). For the past year (*E, fear has lasted for more than 6 months*), Kelly has experienced intense pain in her mouth and jaw related to a broken tooth. She has gone so far as to make dental appointments but worries and loses sleep about meeting with the dentist until she finds herself canceling at the last moment.

GRAPHIC 3.03 Graphic: Weighing Kelly's Differential Diagnosis

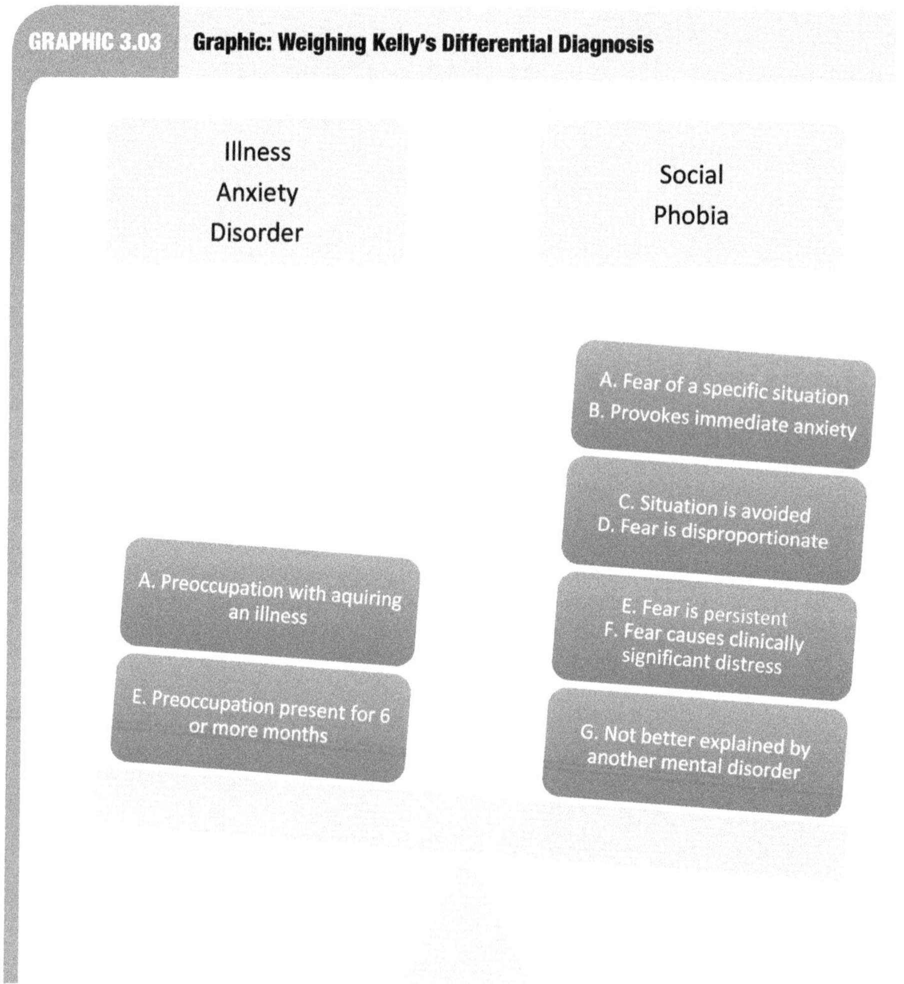

health professionals. Taking this step to outline exactly how you arrived at your diagnosis offers insight and clarity to those who might work with your client later. A justification also provides you and others who might work with your client with a concise description of symptom presentation at the time of diagnosis that can be referenced later. Again, when diagnosing many cases over time, clinicians can fall into habits or succumb to bias; for example, looking for certain diagnostic features and repeatedly diagnosing the same few disorders without giving careful consideration to each client and their unique presentation. The justification process offers the clinician an opportunity to pause and take careful account of the full scope of the clinical presentation and to bring to light outstanding or unanswered questions that may, in turn, hone the diagnosis (Hammond, 2015).

BOX 3.08 EXAMPLE: JUSTIFICATION OF THE A CRITERION IN SPECIFIC PHOBIA

Kelly experiences a marked fear of dental appointments (A).

BOX 3.09 EXAMPLE: JUSTIFICATION OF THE BLOOD–INJECTION–INJURY SPECIFIER IN SPECIFIC PHOBIA

Kelly's fear is related to a medical procedure (blood–injection–injury).

Box 3.10 offers another example of a diagnostic justification. As you read through the justification, consider whether or not the paragraph provides a clear diagnostic picture and clarifies how the clinician arrived at the diagnosis.

Notice here that a number of the listed sub-criteria in the Bulimia Nervosa table are not addressed in the justification. For example, criteria B2 and B4 are not included in the justification because the clinician did not have evidence to support the idea that Tess ate until she was uncomfortably full (B2) or that she sometimes eats alone because she is ashamed of how much she eats (B4); consequently, these are not "met." When writing up your justification, address all major criteria (marked by capital letters) and include only the sub-criteria that are met within the case study or by your

BOX 3.10 JUSTIFICATION FOR KELLY'S DIAGNOSIS OF SPECIFIC PHOBIA

Kelly experiences a marked fear of dental appointments (A). Kelly appears to react with marked fear at the prospect of seeing the dentist every time she needs to make a dental appointment (B). Kelly has not seen a dentist despite having lived with intense tooth pain and risking infection for the past year (C). Her fear seems to be out of proportion with the threat posed by visiting the dentist, particularly because her fear lies in being infected with human immunodeficiency virus (HIV) by the dentist or (D). Kelly's fear has persisted since adolescence (E). Kelly's inability to go to the dentist places her health at risk, she experiences significant dental pain and her fear causes clinically significant anxiety (F). Kelly's difficulty does not seem to be better explained by illness anxiety disorder since she denies fears of illness generally and denies fears of contracting HIV in other situations, nor are her fears better explained by panic, agoraphobia, trauma or other mental health concerns (G). Kelly's fear is related to a medical procedure (blood–injection–injury).

BOX 3.11 EXAMPLE, F50.81* BINGE EATING DISORDER, MODERATE

Locate the diagnostic table on page 350 of your DSM 5 and follow the table as you read through the following example. Note that the code for this disorder was updated from F50.8 to F50.81 effective October 1, 2016; the updated code is found in the DSM 5 Supplement.

Tess, age 22, experiences episodes in which she eats very large quantities of food (A1) during which she reports feeling "completely out of control" (A2). Tess reports that during these episodes she eats "as if the food might disappear from my plate" (B1). She frequently experiences these episodes when she does not feel hungry (B3), and generally feels ashamed and depressed following these episodes (B5). Tess describes being both distressed by and ashamed of these incidents (C). She reports that these binge eating episodes occur 4 to 5 times a week (D). Tess does not meet criteria for bulimia or anorexia nervosa (E). Tess experiences episodes of binge eating 4-5 times a week (moderate).

BOX 3.12 CLEARLY CODING YOUR JUSTIFICATION

Yes: Tess, age 22, experiences episodes in which she eats very large quantities of food (A1) during which she reports feeling "completely out of control" (A2).

No: Tess, age 22, experiences episodes in which she eats very large quantities of food during which she reports feeling "completely out of control" (A1, A2).

BOX 3.13 TRY THIS: WRITE A JUSTIFICATION FOR DENNIS

Dennis. Dennis, age 7, has been in the hospital for the past 6 weeks recovering from life threatening injuries sustained following an automobile accident in which his father and the driver of another automobile were killed. During his stay in the hospital, he has frequent intrusive memories of the accident. Dennis resists talking about the accident and has become angry and tearful when approached about the subject. He describes distressing and vivid memories of the sounds and smells that followed but few of the accident itself. He has revealed that he believes that the accident is his fault since he was talking to his father when their car swerved into oncoming traffic and he believes he distracted his father. He has refused to have pictures of his father in his room. Dennis also wakes up from distressing dreams of the accident and is difficult to console at these times. The nurses and attending physicians have noted that his mood is largely characterized by anxiety and depression. He has difficulty getting to sleep and his concentration seems to be impacted.

client. Again, a criterion is met when the information in the case study or provided by your client affirms the criteria. Addressing only the sub-criteria that are met by the case will reduce the total length of the justification paragraph, which is meant to be a concise communication.

Box 3.13 offers another case study example, Dennis. Use the post-traumatic stress disorder (PTSD) diagnostic criteria table on page 271 of your DSM 5 to practice coding data and writing a justification. Remember to order your justification sentences

BOX 3.14 STEP EIGHT, DIAGNOSTIC NOTATION: EXAMPLES

DX: Kelly: *F40.232 Specific phobia, blood-injection-injury**

*Note that the specifiers in specific phobia determine the code in specific phobia

DX: Tess: F50.81 Binge eating disorder, moderate*

*The code for this disorder was updated from F50.8 to F50.81 effective October 1, 2016.

DX: Dennis: F43.10 Post-traumatic stress disorder

alphabetically and numerically and to place your criterion codes within parenthesis at the end of each sentence. Avoid clustering several criterion codes after a single sentence or you will leave room for confusion.

The final step, **step eight**, in the diagnostic work with Kelly is to write up her coded diagnosis, being sure to check for any updates to coding in the latest DSM 5 Supplement. In the following table, note the notation format for Kelly and for other chapter case examples:

As can be seen in Kelly's case example, the justification is written in such a way that the symptoms can be easily referenced in the DSM, and clearly articulates the diagnostician's decision-making process.

Conclusion

Final Thoughts. As you use the case studies in this book, you will find that all cases, with the exception of the definitional cases, lend themselves well to writing a justification. In order to support your decision-making process and, later, as you work with clients, you may also find this process adds important detail to your clinical case notes.

In this chapter, we discussed the Justification Process and its place within the eight diagnostic steps. We explored both the structure and function of the justification process and used case examples to illustrate its uses. In Chapter 4, we will touch briefly on how the diagnostic justification process and the diagnosis itself contribute to conceptualizing your client's case and creating an appropriate treatment plan.

References

Caplan, P. J., & Cosgrove, L. (Eds). (2004). The deep structure of bias in psychiatric diagnosis. In *Bias in psychiatric diagnosis*. Jason Aronson.

Hammond, C. (2015). The justification process: A teaching tool for diagnosis using the DSM 5. *Virginia Counseling Journal*, *34*, 48–52.

4 Case Conceptualization and Treatment Planning

Before you and your client can begin your work together, you will first need to develop a rich understanding of your client, the presenting difficulty and the contexts, both internal and external, in which the difficulty arose and has persisted. This process of developing a complete understanding of your client, and the written product that results, is known as a case conceptualization. Once a case conceptualization has been created, a well-conceived treatment plan can be developed.

This chapter will briefly introduce the purpose and structure of case conceptualizations and treatment plans. In this chapter, you will also be provided with several cases, one of which will be accompanied by four conceptualizations, each written from a different theoretical lens and each accompanied by a sample treatment plan. The chapter will end with a case example that will follow the diagnostic process from step one to its completion, a treatment plan. This chapter, however, serves as only an introduction to this complex process and aims to serve as a necessary conceptual bridge between the diagnostic process and treatment intervention.

Clinical Hypothesis and Case Conceptualization

Defining the Problem. Clients seek out counseling when their problems become more than what they can address on their own. Ingram (2011) notes "The term problem refers to difficulties, dysfunctions, complaints, and impairments that are identified by the client, others with whom the client interacts (e.g., family members, course, or school systems), or by the professionals who evaluate the client's functioning," (p. 10). Generally, when we think of problems, we consider the presenting problem (the problem that brought the client to counseling) and the additional areas of concern, such as those noted by others or observed by the counselor.

How are client problems different from a diagnosis? A diagnosis is a formal notation that captures a collection of symptoms and features agreed upon criteria. A diagnosis is given only by a qualified clinician and may involve formal assessment. A problem statement, on the other hand, generally describes a subjective experience of a difficulty, and can be raised by the client, those concerned about the client, or may emerge from the clinician's direct observations. Not every presenting problem leads to or even contributes to a diagnosis, though many will. For example:

- Diagnosis: F34.1 Persistent depressive disorder, early onset, moderate
  - Presenting Problem: Levi has struggled with feelings of depression for most of his adult life.
- Diagnosis: Z64.0 Problems related to unwanted pregnancy
  - Presenting Problem: Eva is concerned that her unexpected pregnancy will cause financial and emotional strain and is considering adoption.
- V71.09 No diagnosis given
  - Presenting Problem: Adelle is having difficulty identifying a career choice.

Ingram (2011) recommends beginning your conceptualization and treatment planning process by making a comprehensive list of your client's problems. The problems should include all the difficulties described and observed, and should be listed in order of their priority. Prioritize problems first by the level of risk to your client or those around them, such as active suicidal or homicidal thinking, substance abuse, psychosis, mania and so on. When no serious risk is present, prioritize problems with the most far-reaching consequences, such as depressive thinking styles or problematic relational patterns. Problem statements will be more helpful to you if they are free of theory or etiology, as this will lend you more freedom in selecting theories later in the process, and are non-judgmental in nature, since this stance will support stronger client relationships and will be more likely to garner client collaboration.

In the following example, Sasha is struggling to develop healthy relational patterns and complains of frequent conflict and unhappiness in his relationship with his wife. Sasha grew up in a conservative home in which his father and mother held very traditional roles and expectations. He remembers that both of his parents were distracted and unavailable to him and, as a child, he often worried they would leave him. Sasha has grown to believe that a healthy marriage is one in which there is little to no conflict, consequently, he experiences his wife's changing political views and growing desire for independence as evidence that their relationship is unstable. Sasha is worried his wife will leave the marriage. He feels hopeless, angry and blames his wife for their troubles. Prioritize the following problem statements:

- Sasha's Presenting Problem #1: Sasha is concerned about growing discord in his marriage.
- Sasha's Presenting Problem #2: Sasha is feeling hopeless and angry.

- Additional Area of Concern/Problem: Sasha has a relational pattern of abandonment fears.

Clinical Hypothesis. In research, a hypothesis is something of a supposition, or a best explanation of a phenomenon. A hypothesis is always based on the information currently available to us and serves as a starting point for further exploration. In clinical work, a hypothesis consists of the clinician's understanding of the cause or source of a client's difficulty, often referred to as the presenting problem, and an assumption about what sustains the problem. The hypothesis lends structure and direction to the case conceptualization (Ingram, 2011). The clinician draws on two kinds of information in forming the hypothesis, first the information conveyed by the client and other informants, such as parents, teachers, doctors, previous counselors and so on. The second source of information is the clinician's own theoretical orientation. What follows are four hypotheses each describing a different origin for Sasha's difficulties, each derived from different theoretical orientations. Of the hypotheses listed in the example below, which theory or theories resonate with your own theoretical leanings as you consider Sasha's difficulties?

When building your hypothesis of your client's difficulty, you may find that your explanation leans toward an integrative approach, embracing more than one theoretical orientation. The benefit of an integrative approach to conceptualization and treatment planning is, of course, that it is more comprehensive and takes a broader view of the client's difficulty. An intentional integrative approach considers carefully all of the following hypotheses and their contribution to either the development or continuation of the problem: cognition, behavior, medical conditions or other biological contributors, psychodynamic patterns, sociocultural influences, existential concerns and the stressors of crisis and life transitions. The challenge of the integrative approach is to elegantly and effectively weave all of your theories into your treatment approach in a way that is cohesive and complementary (Ingram, 2011).

Case Conceptualization. A case conceptualization is a brief discussion, usually a page or two in length, that works to bring a greater depth of understanding of your client, their problem and the meaning they make of their difficulties. A strong case conceptualization has three key elements. First, it delves into the complexity of the client's identities, their intersections with one another (Hays, 2008). Second, a strong case conceptualization provides a hypothesis that explains the source of the client's difficulty and what sustains the problem (Ingram, 2011) and finally, it is grounded in one or more theories that lend clarity to the dynamic relationship between the client and the presenting problem (Ingram, 2011; Schwitzer & Rubin, 2012; Seligman & Reichenberg, 2007). Consequently, the case conceptualization is foundational to building an effective and cohesive treatment plan.

Client Identities. As we discussed in Chapters 1 and 2, our clients' cultural identities are an important part of who they are, how they experience and make sense of the world and how they understand and deal with problems as they emerge. Recall that

BOX 4.01 TRY THIS: WRITE A STRONG PROBLEM STATEMENT FOR DASHA

Dasha has come to counseling to gain some skills and strategies for supporting and guiding her children when their behavior is challenging. Dasha's own parents tended to be harsh and often physically and verbally abused her when she misbehaved. Dasha recognizes that while she does not physically abuse her children, she is often too harsh and sometimes demeaning when her children don't comply. Read through the following examples of flawed problem statements. Then, create your own non-theoretical, non-judgmental problem statement or statements.

Etiology is implied: Dasha was physically abused as a child and now verbally abuses her own children.

Judgmental: Dasha is not a loving mother to her children.

Your Problem Statement:

when we are discussing client identities, we are referring to at least seven dimensions of the Self: ethnicity and race, gender, sexual orientation, socioeconomic status, spiritual or religious orientation, age and ability status. Also important to identity are educational achievement and first language and other aspects of your client's understanding of themselves and position in society may also play an important role. Exploring these dimensions of your client's identity, particularly in relationship to the difficulty a client brings, is essential to understanding your client in a rich and full way (Hays, 2001). These dimensions can be integrated into a case conceptualization in a number of ways, including but not exclusive to the Body, Speech, and Mind model discussed later in this chapter.

Theoretical grounding. A strong conceptualization offers one or more theories that provide the structure for making sense of both the client's own development and the development of the client's difficulty. Theories also help to frame the relationship between the client and their struggles and then act as a compass guiding the clinician toward an intervention. Theory and worldview are always present in our work with our clients; however, some clinicians are intentional in their use of theory and others are less clear about the theory implied in their work. Problems in our work can arise when we are not intentional and clear about the theory we are using or we are not careful about the integration of two or more theories together. A lack of intentionality can lead to work that is directionless and haphazard (Prochaska & Norcross, 1999).

TABLE 4.01 Relational Troubles Framed Through Four Theoretical Perspectives

Theory	Example Hypothesis
Attachment-Based Hypothesis	Sasha's experience of an insecure attachment in his early childhood has resulted in patterns that prevent healthy attachment in his adult romantic relationships.
Cognitive Behavioral-Based Hypothesis	Sasha has developed false beliefs and expectations in his relationships that lead him to respond with demandingness and criticism in his personal relationships.
Existential-Based Hypothesis	Sasha's difficulty accepting choice and responsibility in personal relationships has led to a pattern of blaming others and inevitable feelings of disappointment.
Feminist Theory-Based Hypothesis	Sasha's conservative religious and cultural expectations for a spousal relationship presume obedience from his partner, an expectation that has strongly conflicted with his wife's upbringing and worldview, and consequently results in ongoing conflict.

It is important to pause and remember that many approaches can be useful in supporting clients through difficult times. Decades old research strongly suggests that the curative power of therapy arises from within the therapeutic alliance and not from any particular approach or set of techniques (Roth & Fonagy, 2005). Theory and technique are not unimportant, however. Theories provide clinicians with a framework for understanding and making meaning of a client's difficulties, and often provide tools for guiding and supporting clients. When we embrace a particular theory, we consider our clients through a lens that focuses our attention on an aspect or aspects of human nature, we describe the source of human suffering in a particularized way, and prescribe a specific route to relieving that suffering (Corey, 2012). Most theories, then, leave unexplored some aspects of the client's experience, and neglect some dynamics that may contribute to or support a problem while giving attention to others. In your own work with clients, it is important to be mindful of the kinds of information that you are giving attention/preference to, and to pause and ask yourself what might be falling outside of your conceptual frame.

Approaches to Conceptualization. A variety of approaches are available to clinicians that will provide structure for your conceptualization. A theory-based approach is guided by the assumptions of the particular theoretical approach that you have chosen to explain your client's situation. If you are working from a cognitive theory, your conceptualization would be largely guided by themes related to your client's thoughts, and how those thought patterns create and sustain their difficulty. If you are working from one of the psychodynamic perspectives, your conceptualization may be focused on themes of unconscious dynamics and so on (Berman, 2018). As described above, an integrative approach depicts a multifaceted problem and considers contributions from cognition, learned behavior, sociocultural influences, crisis and transition, medical

BOX 4.02 KEY TERMS: CASE CONCEPTUALIZATION AND TREATMENT PLANNING

Case Conceptualization. A case conceptualization is a descriptive, theory-based discussion of the origin of your client's difficulties and how these problems function within your client's life. A thorough case conceptualization offers a holistic picture of your client, their cultural identities, relational patterns and personal strengths.

Hypothesis. Your hypothesis is a brief statement, a sentence or two, describing the source of your client's primary concern or concerns and functions to lend direction and structure to the case conceptualization.

Outcome Goal. An outcome goal presents a snapshot of the client's functioning or status when your client is ready to end therapy.

Problem-Based Approach to Treatment Planning. In a problem-based approach, clinicians list all presenting problems and match each problem with an outcome goal.

Subgoals/Milestones. Subgoals represent milestones along the way to achieving the outcome goal.

conditions and medications, existential concerns, as well as psychodynamics (Ingram, 2011).

Symptom-based and diagnosis-based approaches organize ideas and information within the conceptualization according to either the symptoms or the diagnoses your client carries (Berman, 2018). In contrast, a historical approach to case conceptualization considers developmental periods and their relationship to your client's problems. A historical approach is individualized to your client and may trace only relevant developmental stages rather than detailing stages beginning in early childhood (Berman, 2018). A contemplative approach, like the integrative approach, considers a broad range of facets of your client's life. The contemplative approach to conceptualization is unique in that it takes a non-western perspective informed by Buddhist Psychology, and is discussed at greater depth in the following pages.

A Contemplative Approach to Conceptualizing Client Difficulties and Strengths

In my own work as a counselor and as a counselor educator, the conceptual frameworks I reach for most often are Ingram's integrative (2011) and the contemplative approaches described by Walker (2008), also known as the body, speech and mind approach. I appreciate the contemplative approach for a number of reasons, first among them is that it provides a natural format for considering a broad range of aspects of identity and culture that supports my efforts, and those of my students, to develop a culturally competent practice. I also appreciate this conceptualization format because it serves as an excellent complement to the integrative case formulation approach to conceptualization, helping to fill in gaps left by other approaches. Finally, the contemplative approach does not emphasize faults, problems or struggles over strengths, but gives equal consideration to each, making it much more balanced in the way that clients are understood. This approach considers three primary domains: body, speech and mind.

Body. In this approach the concept of body is a broad category that captures both body type as well as demographic information. Physical aspects of your client such as skin tone, hair type and style, how closely your client fits expectations for their assigned gender, your client's health and ability status are all integrated aspects of a comprehensive culturally inclusive conceptualization; however, these details about your client are sometimes neglected. Any of these aspects may reveal important components of your client's life experiences and may help to frame the presenting problem (Walker, 2008). For instance, imagine meeting with Arla, a client who identifies as African American, who presents with concerns that she has been unable to secure a job since graduating with an engineering degree a year ago. A culturally competent conceptualization would include Arla's experience of bias during her education experience and in the workplace. The contemplative approach would invite you to explore more deeply the types of bias she might be experiencing, by noting her light skin tone, making her the subject of bias based on colorism and her large and muscular frame that may also be subject to judgment and bias.

The second aspect of the body category to consider is the way your clients use their bodies to communicate with the world. You might ask yourself and take note of the ways that your clients sit while talking with you, what they do with their hands and how your clients move. Does your client move gracefully, as if at peace with his body, or move with some difficulty as if there were an invisible force holding him back? Maybe your client moves awkwardly, as if she didn't quite have a sense of her own presence in the room, or perhaps she moves only painfully, cautiously and with some difficulty. All of these ways of movement can be important sources of information about your client's experiences and about how others may experience your client (Walker, 2008).

Finally, when considering the body aspect, we also consider the physical contexts in which our clients live and work. If you use this approach to better understand your client, you will want to know whether your client experiences his home and work as peaceful or chaotic, tidy or cluttered, welcoming or hostile and so on. Are these spaces reflective of the way your client would like them to be or are there things your client would like to change?

Speech. The speech domain captures four main dimensions of being in the world: (1) energy, (2) use of language, (3) style of communication and (4) the quality of your client's relationships. Energy, in this context, refers to how much energy your client

GRAPHIC 4.01 **From Diagnosis to Treatment Planning**

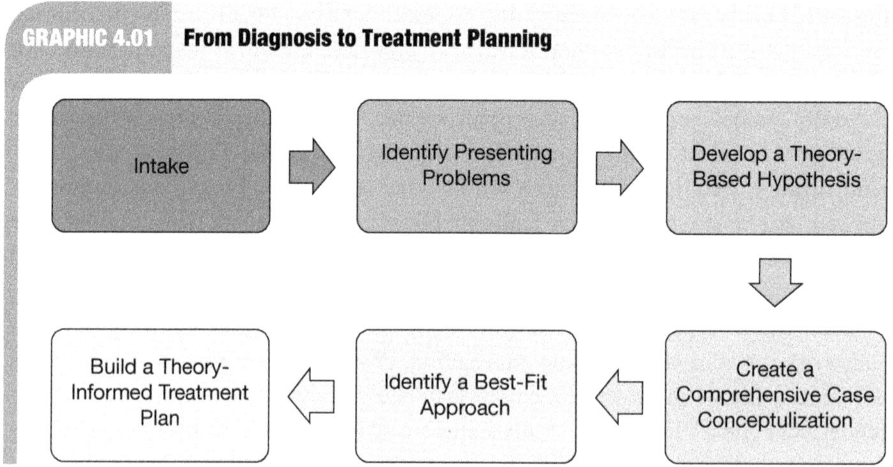

feels in the body, but also to how much energy is evident in the client's speech. For instance, does your client speak quickly and with a great deal of animation or slowly and deliberately? In exploring this aspect you might ask yourself, "Does my client seem agitated or calm and serene?" for example (Walker, 2008).

The speech domain also includes your client's communication style. For instance, many clients are direct and come straight to the point when asked a question, while others use allegory or metaphor to make a point. When considering this aspect of speech, it is important to note whether or not your client describes events in a linear or non-linear way. Does your client prefer to be indirect, or prefer to speak plainly. Your client's use of language is also important. You will want to consider whether or not your client is more comfortable in a language other than the one you are speaking together, for instance, and if your client speaks with an accent, which can impact how your client is received in the community. Your client's word choice is also important. You may want to ask yourself what words or gestures your client uses often. Are there words that your client uses in an odd way? What words or phrases do your clients use to describe themselves? Each of these offer clues into your client's self-perception and, again, into how others may perceive your client (Walker, 2008). Again, the purpose in noting these distinctive traits is not so that you can change them, influence them or even evaluate the traits but rather to gain a greater clarity into what it is like to be your client and to gain a better sense for how others might be responding to them, positively, negatively or in a neutral way.

Finally, the speech domain also includes the types of relationships that your client has and the patterns that unfold within those relationships. You will want to note not only what strong relationships your client maintains but also relational difficulties, particularly where patterns of relational problems seem to be present (Walker, 2008).

Mind. Mind is the third domain of this case conceptualization. In this domain, we consider three key dimensions: (1) your clients' relationship to their thoughts, (2) their mental speed and (3) horizons of possibility. In considering your clients' relationship to their thoughts, you will want to know if your clients are curious about their own thoughts and how much stock they place in the thoughts that emerge.

Consider the difference between three clients who sometimes worry that others don't appreciate them. A client who accepts these worries as truth will experience those thoughts differently than the client who wonders, "Where is this feeling coming from?" and also differently from the client who dismisses the concern as ridiculous. Each of these clients will need to be approached in different ways.

The final aspect of mind includes the *horizons of possibility*. In this domain, the clinician listens for the ways the client thinks about the future and their role in it. In considering this domain, you will want to reflect upon whether or not your client feels limited by internal or external forces. Does your client see possibilities for growth and change, for new relationships, possibilities to learn new things and so on, or does your client feel stuck, stifled and locked-in? (Walker, 2008).

Together these three dimensions, body, speech and mind, will add to the richness of any theoretical frame you use to better understand your client and the problems that they bring.

As you read through the theoretical conceptualizations of Nita, our first case example found near the end of this chapter, note the differences in focus of attention and the privileging of certain kinds of information or ways of understanding. As you read, you may want to ask yourself the following questions:

- What are the strengths of this approach?
- What does this approach miss?
- Which of these conceptualizations is the best fit for Nita and her difficulty? Might another approach fit aspects of Nita's concern better than those presented here?
- Which is the most comfortable fit in understanding what causes people to suffer?
- How might I combine selected elements of these approaches to make the strongest treatment plan for Nita?

The Treatment Plan

Treatment plans are documents that map out the goals that you and your client have formulated together, though occasionally they are developed by the therapist alone. The treatment plan describes the steps that will be taken to reach those goals and establishes milestones that let the client and therapist know that progress toward their goals is being made. In this way, the treatment plan serves to clarify and give structure

BOX 4.03 CONSIDER THIS: RELATIONSHIPS WITH OUR THOUGHTS

Sarah, Paulo and Mamta all experience worries that others don't like them and that they won't ever fit in with others; however, each has a different relationship with those thoughts. Note the relationship each has with these worrisome thoughts. How might your work differ with each?

Sarah: When self-doubt crosses Sarah's mind, she rarely questions whether they might be true, she feels certain these perceptions are accurate.

Paulo: When self-doubt and concerns about how others feel about him cross Paulo's mind, he quickly dismisses them as ridiculous and does not give them another thought.

Mamta: Mamta's reaction to these thoughts is to ask, "Where is this feeling coming from?" and approaches her thoughts with curiosity.

to the therapy, assuring that both client and therapist are working toward the same end and have a shared vision of what each would describe as successful therapy. As importantly, the treatment plan provides a picture of the beginning, middle and end of the therapeutic process.

Careful planning is important to an ethical practice. Knowledge, skill and intervention planning are what separate a counseling session from a chat with an understanding friend.

Treatment Plan Structure. Treatment plans are made up of outcome goals, which are supported by subgoals. Outcome goals paint a picture of what we hope the client will achieve by the end of therapy. Pairing outcome goals with the problem statements that you have compiled will help to assure that you have created a comprehensive plan (Ingram, 2011).

Subgoals serve as both milestones, and are sometimes referred to as such, and provide a map for reaching the outcome goals. It is often helpful, and sometimes mandatory depending upon insurance provider or agency policy, to provide a timeline for meeting goals within the structure of the treatment plan. It is good practice to include some avenue for measuring how the client has met a particular goal.

Best practices encourage practitioners to list goals in order of urgency; those that must be addressed first are also listed first. Subgoals are generally written so that one subgoal leads logically to the next. Call to mind an image of a staircase in which you are climbing from one stair step to the next until you reach the top. Subgoals are outlined in much the same way, describing the first, second and third steps (more when necessary) to reaching the outcome goal. However, rather than describing the avenue for achieving the goal, subgoals describe the small successes your client will demonstrate in the journey toward the outcome goal. When subgoals build logically, one upon the next, these goals are described as step-wise goals.

Both example one and example two share the same basic strategy for supporting Ben in dealing with his angry feelings. Example two, however, is not only more detailed but more clearly outlines the milestones that Ben will achieve along the way, and by implication, the steps that will be taken by the counselor. It is clear from the treatment plan that his counselor intends to educate Ben about how angry feelings manifest in the body, then about different ways of handling those feelings, and finally, the counselor will support him in replacing negative responses with responses that are more conducive to success at school. You will notice, too, that in writing goals in this fashion, the clinician has created subgoals that are accomplished "with support" and subgoals for accomplishing these independently. Because his counselor is working within the school setting or in conjunction with teachers, her inclusion of the "with support" subgoals reassures everyone that progress is being made, even if Ben needs a lot of support in the early stages of the therapy. Adding a timeline for each sub goal will further strengthen the treatment plan.

Timelines. The treatment plan serves two key ethical imperatives as well. First, the treatment plan creates transparency, making it clear to your client what you are doing and why, and, consequently, leaves space for your clients to ask questions about their treatment. Second, the treatment plan establishes accountability for one's work and helps to avoid some of the abuses of the past in which clients engaged in prolonged therapy with little to no effect. Accountability is supported by writing goals that are measurable and provide clear timeframes for achieving those goals.

Many agency policies require that a treatment plan include timeframes for reaching milestones and goals. When progress is slower than hoped for, the therapist and client can revisit the treatment plan and consider making changes to the therapeutic approach. This provides the additional benefit of bringing attention to the therapeutic process and provides a natural opportunity for you to talk together about the therapy's progress.

A timeframe may be written into the treatment plan by creating an expectation for quarterly review, and developing goals that can be reached within that time frame. Alternatively, goals can be given timeframes that take into consideration the typical time needed to complete treatment, often 18-22 weeks, and adding time if the client's constellation or severity of difficulties will likely complicate their resolution. For instance, a moderate depression with a typical presentation will likely respond more quickly than a moderate depression that is accompanied by eating and substance use disorders.

BOX 4.04 TRY THIS: IDENTIFYING STEP-WISE GOALS

Two examples of outcome goals followed by subgoals are outlined below. Identify the example that illustrates step-wise subgoals.

Example 1:

Goal: Within 12 weeks of therapy, Ben will refrain from hitting other children when he is angry, in 9 of 10 opportunities.

Subgoal 1: Ben will understand his angry feelings are not his "boss."

Subgoal 2: Ben will go to the office when he is angry.

Subgoal 3: Ben will tell his teacher when he is being bullied in class.

Example 2: Within 12 weeks of therapy, Ben will refrain from hitting other children when he is angry, in 9 of 10 opportunities.

Subgoal 1: Ben will be able to articulate what happens in his body when he is angry (heart pounding, teeth clenching, "mad" thoughts).

Subgoal 2: Ben will be able to articulate positive and negative responses to anger with counselor support (Positive: talk to a teacher, go to the principal's office to cool off, take deep breaths, etc.; Negative: hitting, yelling, biting).

Subgoal 3: Ben will be able to independently articulate positive and negative responses to anger.

Subgoal 4: With support, Ben will be able to identify his angry feelings as they arise, as evidenced by his teacher's report.

Subgoal 5: Ben will be able to identify his angry feelings as they arise independently, as evidenced by counselor and teacher report.

Subgoal 6: With support, Ben will be able to replace negative responses to anger with positive responses, as evidenced by his teacher's report.

Subgoal 7: Ben will be able to replace negative responses to anger with positive responses independently, as evidenced by his teacher's report.

Phrasing can be added to goals that cues the reader to the expected time in which the client and therapist hope to attain these goals, as in the following examples:

- By October 20, 2018, Elliot will be able to tolerate a 3-hour flight (standard air travel) with only minimal discomfort, as evidenced by client self-report.
- Within 20 weeks of the opening of therapy, Elliot will be able to tolerate a 3-hour flight (standard air travel) with only minimal discomfort, as evidenced by client self-report.

Measurable Goals. As you and your client begin to develop your goals, you will want to ask yourselves, "How will we know that this goal has been met?" Strong treatment plans are written so that the goals have a measurable quality to them. A measurable goal contributes to accountability and clarity, which in turn may support your client in achieving the goal. A goal can be described as measurable when it is expressed in a way that makes it clear what will be happening when the goal is met. A measurable goal should also indicate who or by what tool the assessment will be made. These assessments of whether or not a goal has been met can be made by the clinician, the client, a parent, a teacher or even an assessment tool, such as the Beck Depression Inventory. In the second example, provided above, it is clear how his counselor will judge whether or not Ben's subgoals have been met. In this example, Ben's counselor will be evaluating Ben's knowledge and behavior in session and will check in with Ben's teacher about how well Ben is meeting these goals in the classroom. Likely, Ben's teacher will be collecting data to assess whether or not the hitting behavior is decreasing and by how much. When using goals that are not behavioral in nature, a client's subjective experiencing can serve as a measure for your goal.

The first example in Box 4.05 is easily measured and will have a certain appeal to insurance companies or within a research context. The second example, on the other hand, is vague, and offers little insight into how the counselor or client will determine that this goal is met. What does it mean for her to be "caught up"? If panic feelings are present, how will she be responding? However, the first goal has a decidedly behavioral flavor, requires data collection, and may not fit well within every theoretical orientation. For some therapists, the first example is an uncomfortable fit in part because it lacks a sense of humanism and reduces the counseling process to behaviors and outcomes. The third example represents a kind of compromise in which Jill is entrusted with the measurement of the success of the goal to feel relatively comfortable most of the time while in class. With some finesse, it is possible to write measurable goals to fit many different theoretical orientations. In the examples below, the articulation to the counselor serves as the means of measurement:

- Jill will be able to describe to the counselor a sense of meaning and personal freedom in her life (Existential therapy)
- Jill will develop a rich and full narrative of strength and resiliency, as evidenced through Jill's own report and through her representations in art, prose and poetry produced within the therapy setting and at home (Narrative Therapy)
- Jill will develop techniques for extending compassion toward herself in moments of difficulty, as measured by self-report and through expressions of self-compassion within the counseling setting (Compassion-Focused Therapy)
- Jill will be able to describe the cultural and socioeconomic forces that support and sustain the oppressions she experiences in the workplace (Feminist Therapy)

Writing Achievable Goals. Importantly, goals should be ones that can be accomplished. Clinicians sometimes write goals that are nearly impossible to meet. Someone

TABLE 4.02 Elements of a Strong Goal

Achievable aim	The goal can be accomplished and represents satisfactory, but not perfect, functioning
Individualized	The goal is created with your client's specific needs and uniquenesses in mind
Measurable	Readers can easily discern if the goal is met; clear, not vague; indicates who will measure the goal
Timeframe	Offers a timeframe in which the goal will be achieved

once told me, "Never write a goal that a dead man can accomplish more easily than a client." (I wish I was able to remember who shared this wisdom so I could offer credit for this piece of advice.) Listed below are three examples of goals that a corpse could accomplish more easily than a client:

- Jill will no longer be troubled by anxiety.
- Ben will not hit his sister.
- JoAnne will no longer experience sleep disturbance.

As we create goals with our clients, it is important to remember that we are working with human beings, and humans are given to making mistakes, such as when small children hit others when frustrated or tired. We are also living in a world fraught with stressors and challenges. It is very difficult to live a life in which no anxiety, anger or sadness creeps in, or to live a life where these experiences don't bother us at all. Therapeutic goals are aimed at making it possible to encounter difficult experiences, acknowledge, hold and feel them, without having our work or relational functioning impaired by these experiences for extended periods of time.

It can be helpful to ask, what would be "good enough" responding? While it would be ideal, for example, if Ben would stop hitting his sister when he was angry, and it is our hope that he will, one might wonder if it is more realistic and if his therapy would be successful if he hit no more than one time in any 3-week period. This kind of goal reminds the therapist and his parents that Ben is still growing and that he will never be perfect—none of us are—and that his dramatic improvements can be celebrated.

Here are the three goals listed above rewritten so that they are achievable:

- No: Jill will no longer be troubled by anxiety.
  - Yes: Jill will report making successful use of strategies to deal with anxiety as it arises, in 8 of 10 opportunities.
- No: Ben will stop hitting his sister.

    - Yes: Ben will hit others no more than one time in any 3-week period.
- No: JoAnne will no longer experience sleep disturbance.
    - Yes: JoAnne will experience restful sleep in six of seven nights for a period of at least 1 month.

In the following pages, we will provide Nita with a diagnosis and consider her difficulties from the perspective of four different theories. Each conceptualization will then be followed by a treatment plan. Please note that in order to best illustrate the contrasts in theory-based conceptualization, the case conceptualizations have been written from a pure theory perspective, and as a result cultural considerations are absent from all but the integrative approach. It is important to remember, however, that best practice integrates cultural understanding with theory rather than separating them or choosing either culture or theory for conceptualization.

Nita

Nita, age 20, lives with her boyfriend, Adam, in a small apartment in the center of a neighborhood known for violence, drug use and drug trafficking. Nita and Adam have a daughter, Evangeline, 26 months, who was recently removed from the home by Child Protective Services when the toddler was found to be dirty, hungry and dehydrated

BOX 4.05 TRY THIS: CREATING MEASURABLE GOALS

Jill, 14, has come to counseling with her mother to talk about her mounting anxiety at school and in social settings. She would like strategies to deal effectively with her anxiety and hopes that the anxiety will lessen enough that she can be more comfortable throughout the day. Below you are provided with three sample goals. Decide whether or not each goal is measurable. If the goal is not measurable, revise it:

- Jill will make use of four-point breathing techniques in five of six stressful situations.
- Jill will no longer find herself getting “caught up” in panic feelings.
- Jill will experience a lifting of performance anxiety in the classroom, as measured by Jill’s report of relative comfort for most of her class time, for a period of at least 1 month.

during a home visit. Nita has been mandated to counseling as part of a reunification plan.

As a girl, Nita's mother was addicted to heroin. As a result, her mother was often absent, on the streets looking for drugs or in prison for drug related crimes. Consequently, Nita and her sister were often alone and sometimes were without heat or food. During this time, her church was a key resource for Nita and her sister. Together with a neighbor, Nita went to a local Catholic church and was often given food by the church's food charity. However, Nita explains, "Thanks to the Church my sister and I were able to get by, but I didn't ever have the chance to learn how to be a mother. We tried our best but sometimes things didn't go so well, like the time I tried to cook something on the stove and my sister got a bad burn. We didn't have anyone to help her and we didn't know what to do. We were both scared and we cried for a long time when that happened. I never learned what I needed to know to be a good mom to my baby and now all I can ever do is let her down."

While her sister dropped out of school, Nita managed to finish high school just before her baby was born. Nita reports, "I was so happy when Evangeline was born and I vowed I would be a good mother to her. But then these thoughts started, just once in a while at first and then all the time."

Nita confides that she has been bothered by "constant thoughts" that she might accidentally hurt her baby. She reports that she has fears that if she fills the tub with water to bathe Evangeline that "something might happen" and the baby will be scalded or might drown. "I'm really afraid to give her a bath, that's why she was dirty when the social worker came. I know it doesn't make sense, but I am terrified that somehow I will hurt her like when my sister was burned when I was cooking. Sometimes I am afraid to fix food for Evangeline because I am afraid I will make some mistake and she will get really sick. These thoughts are going through my head all the time and I can't make them stop! I've tried everything. I've even tried to get Adam to bathe her or to fix her dinner, but he says this is the mother's job and that I need to get my head on straight."

Nita reports that these thoughts started shortly after she brought the baby home from the hospital and that she has been praying that the baby would be safe every day since. Nita reports that she spends a great deal of time praying and "asking God not to let anything happen to the baby." Nita reports that she sometimes prays for 2 hours in one sitting trying to get the prayer "just right," but that when she makes a mistake in her prayer, she feels she has to start again from the beginning. Nita would like to get help with these fears so the state will return her baby to her.

Justification and Diagnosis

Justification. What follows is a justification written for Nita, followed by a diagnosis using the diagnostic table found in the DSM 5 on page 237.

Nita complains of obsessive thoughts that her child will come to some harm (A1, obsessions) and describes making use of compulsive prayer to stave off these concerns (A1, compulsions). Nita prays for several hours a day (B). There is no evidence that Nita's symptoms are a consequence of substance use or medications (C), nor are they better explained by generalized anxiety disorder, or other mental health disorder (D). Nita understands that her fears "don't make sense," (with fair insight).

(Note: Because there are two A1 and two A2 criteria in the diagnostic table for obsessive compulsive disorder (OCD) in the DSM 5 it necessary to add the tag *obsession,* or *compulsion*, as in the example above, in order to create greater clarity to your justification of your diagnosis.)

DX: F42 OCD, with fair insight

In the following pages you will find four case conceptualizations as well as a companion treatment plan.

A Conceptualization of Nita's Case Through a Cognitive-Behavioral Lens

Nita is plagued by fears that she is inadequate to the task of caring for her daughter. She *catastrophizes* these fears, thinking that she could badly hurt her daughter while trying to complete simple but necessary tasks such as bathing or feeding. Nita seems to be holding the *false belief* that in order for her to have the needed parenting skills to care for her daughter, she must first have had them modeled for her by her own mother. Additionally, she seems to have developed a worldview that she can't look for help outside the home. Consequently, she has not reached out for help or gained these skills elsewhere.

Thoughts that some harm might come to her daughter thanks to an accident or her own insufficient care are based in *faulty information processing*, as is the ritualized prayer that she uses to prevent the harm she fears will come to Evangeline. Together, Nita's intrusive thoughts and false beliefs coupled with faulty information processing converge in a way to create an obsessive compulsive disorder. Nita would benefit from interventions that interrupt intrusive and faulty thinking. Nita also needs support in developing alternative and supportive behaviors to replace rituals. Finally, Nita would benefit from psychoeducation about basic care for children in order to provide her with both essential skills and to restore her confidence in her ability to care for the daughter she clearly loves.

Nita's Cognitive-Behavioral Treatment Plan

Outcome Goal 1: Within 15 weeks from the opening of therapy, Nita will recognize intrusive thoughts as OCD and respond to these thoughts in a way that supports her mental health.

Subgoal 1: Within 2 weeks of the opening of therapy, Nita will understand and articulate OCD processes.

Subgoal 2: Within 3 weeks of the opening of therapy, Nita will articulate her recognition that her ritualized prayer is part of an OCD process.

Subgoal 3: Within 4 weeks of the opening of therapy, Nita will be able to identify her own obsessive thoughts with support.

Subgoal 4: Within 4 weeks of the opening of therapy, Nita will create, with the therapist, alternative responses to obsessive thoughts.

Subgoal 5: Within 5 weeks of the opening of therapy, Nita will be able to identify her own obsessive thoughts independently.

Subgoal 6: Within 6 weeks of the opening of therapy, with support, Nita will be able to enact alternative behaviors after noticing obsessive thoughts.

Subgoal 7: Within 10 weeks of the opening of therapy, Nita will be able to enact alternative behaviors when experiencing obsessive thoughts, independently in 5 of 10 opportunities.

Subgoal 8: Within 15 weeks of the opening of therapy, Nita will be able to enact alternative behaviors when experiencing obsessive thoughts independently, in 9 of 10 opportunities.

Outcome Goal 2: Within 6 weeks of the start of therapy, Nita will be able to provide basic childcare skills with confidence such as feeding, bathing and attending to medical needs.

Subgoal 1: Within 3 weeks of the start of therapy, Nita will be able to articulate how to execute basic childcare skills.

Subgoal 2: Within 4 weeks of the start of therapy, Nita will be able to demonstrate childcare skills with supervision and support.

Subgoal 3: Within 6 weeks of the start of therapy, Nita will be able to demonstrate childcare skills independently and with confidence.

A Conceptualization of Nita's Case Through an Existential Lens

Contributed by Michael Horst, Ph.D.

Nita is struggling to suppress neurotic anxiety resulting from the four existential givens: death, freedom, responsibility and meaninglessness. For Nita, her daughter Evangeline, has become a source of personal meaning, as we see in her sincere desire to be a good mother. Her desire to be a good mother seems to arise from her childhood experiences of neglect. Intense fears of hurting Evangeline have their roots in her early traumatic experience in which her sister was accidentally burned while Nita was cooking. Constructing personal meaning around her love for Evangeline and a sense of self that includes being a good mother is an excellent first step for Nita, but it also demands that Nita take responsibility for the freedom she has to choose and work for this meaning. The anxiety resulting from this freedom and responsibility may seem unbearable for Nita, so she has identified authority figures, such as God and to her partner, Adam, to whom she can transfer her responsibility and allow her to suppress her anxiety. Nita's surrendering of her personal freedom and responsibility, in an effort to suppress her anxiety, is resulting in obsessive thoughts of hurting Evangeline because she is not yet fully accepting control of the situation. Further, Nita's surrendering personal freedom and responsibility to God is resulting in compulsive praying. If she prays correctly, then she is free of her responsibility and experiences relief from her anxiety. Nita needs to encounter a safe, healing relationship that explores her responses to anxiety and empowers her to choose to live the life that is most meaningful for her.

Nita's Existential Treatment Plan

Outcome Goal 1: Nita will begin to accept the freedom and personal responsibility inherent in her pursuit of the meaningful life of being a good mother, as evidenced by her ability to articulate her desires (meaning) and create action plans that empower her to take responsibility for her behaviors.

> Subgoal 1: Nita will articulate what is most meaningful for her in her life.
>
> Subgoal 2: Nita will articulate how her intrusive thoughts and compulsive praying are related to her meaningful desire to be a good mother, and how they are preventing her from pursuing that meaningful desire.
>
> Subgoal 3: Nita will explore the ways she has accepted freedom and personal responsibility in her past (e.g., caring for her sister, graduating high school) to aid in empowering her to act in the present.
>
> Subgoal 4: Nita will create an action plan that empowers her to pursue that which is most meaningful for her (e.g., attend parenting class at the community center).
>
> Subgoal 5: Nita will be able to act in accordance with her meaningful desire to be a good mother, as evidenced by completing items on her action plan.

A Conceptualization of Nita's Case Through a Narrative Therapy Lens

Over the course of Nita's lifetime, she has developed a dominant narrative portraying herself as a person who is not competent to parent because she was not parented well herself. Much of her story is peppered with images of incompetence and mistakes that caused harm. Nita has internalized these stories so that they have become a part of her identity rather than obstacles to be overcome. Nita would be helped by providing her with questions that help to clarify her own hopes and values in her parenting and to gain strength from her desire to be a nurturing parent and find strength and direction in her life. Nita would also benefit from placing distance between her problematic thoughts and difficulty completing parenting tasks from her identity and sense of self.

Narrative Treatment Plan

Outcome Goal 1: Nita will begin to reauthor her dominant narrative as flawed and incapable, as measured by her ability to describe her personal story more fully and richly, including within that narrative personal strengths and triumphs.

> Subgoal 1: Nita will be able to explore the dimensions of her parenting, positive and negative, with her counselor.
>
> Subgoal 2: Nita will explore and articulate her own strengths and resiliencies in her own life and as they relate to her role as a parent.
>
> Subgoal 3: Nita will be able to draw on her strengths and resilience to enact the parenting she wants to exhibit.
>
> Subgoal 4: Nita will be able to explore and articulate a comprehensive more realistic narrative of her own identity independent of her parenting.

A Conceptualization of Nita's Case Through an Integrated Interpersonal Lens

Contributed by Michael Horst, Ph.D.

Nita has lived through experiences that have made trusting others and herself difficult. Nita's mother was unreliable for her and her sister. Nita has a traumatic memory of accidentally burning her sister. Her boyfriend, Adam, will not help care for their baby. Nita is a young woman living in a neighborhood known for crime and she and Adam are a low-income family, both of which may contribute to her anxiety. Nita's cultural background and religious beliefs may both contribute to her suffering and provide resources for resilience. In order to fully relate to Nita, the counselor must work to understand Nita's cultural and religious experiences as a Catholic. Nita's relationships have been characterized by unreliability, with the exception of her experience with the Catholic Church. For this reason, her primary relational resource may be with her conception of God. However, her relationship with God also contains elements of mistrust, as evidenced by her compulsive praying behavior. If she does not get the prayer "just right," then even God may betray her. Nita needs support in repairing her ruptured experiences of relationships. Through forming a trusting relationship with a therapist, Nita may experience corrective emotional experiences that help reframe her experiences of relationships in general. Within this relationship, Nita and the therapist will explore how cognitive, emotional, and existential elements each play a part in her current relational experiences.

Nita's Integrated Interpersonal Treatment Plan

Outcome Goal 1: Nita will begin to be able to trust others and herself.

Subgoal 1: Nita will articulate her experiences of her past and present relationships.

Subgoal 2: Nita will articulate what she needs in a relationship to feel like she can trust the other person.

Subgoal 3: Nita and the therapist will work to illuminate the ways she may unwittingly elicit mistrust if she is expecting others to betray her.

Subgoal 4: Nita will be able to openly discuss relational dynamics occurring between her and the therapist.

Outcome Goal 2: Nita will feel empowered to trust herself to care for Evangeline.

Subgoal 1: Nita will recognize that some of her thoughts are not rational and articulate possible origins and functions of her intrusive thoughts.

Subgoal 2: Nita will articulate her emotional responses to caring for Evangeline.

Subgoal 3: Nita will create an action plan to build confidence in her ability to care for Evangeline (e.g., enroll in a parenting class at the community center).

Outcome Goal 3: Nita and Adam will form a trusting and collaborative relationship.

Subgoal 1: After the initial phase of therapy (about 8 weeks), Adam and Evangeline will attend couples counseling for at least 4 weeks.

Subgoal 2: Nita and Adam will be able to articulate their relational dynamics (including personal values, such as caring for children is "women's work").

Subgoal 3: Nita and Adam will be able to identify primary and secondary emotional responses to relational situations.

Subgoal 4: Nita and Adam will create an action plan for caring for Evangeline.

Cognitive Behavioral, Existential, Narrative, and Integrative theories each contribute something unique to our understanding of Nita and her difficulty, but none of them alone paints a full picture of how the painful thoughts unfolded for her or began to take hold as they have. Other unexplored theories might lend an even richer understanding of Nita and her difficulties. For instance, a multicultural perspective would lend insight to the ways that socioeconomic and racial dynamics have created a context for these problems to develop and to escalate into the removal of her child by the state. The most effective approach would likely acknowledge the cognitive, biological, cultural, relational, existential and narrative components that support Nita's difficulty and would result in a treatment plan that incorporated all of these elements together.

References

Berman, P. S. (2018). *Case conceptualization and treatment planning: Integrating theory with clinical practice*. SAGE.

Corey, G. (2012). *Theory and practice of counseling and psychotherapy* (9th ed.). Brooks Cole.

Hays, P. A. (2001). *Addressing cultural complexities in practice*. American Psychological Association.

Hays, P. A. (2008). *Addressing cultural complexities in practice*. American Psychological Association.

Ingram, B. L. (2011). *Clinical case formulations: Matching the integrative treatment plan to the client*. John Wiley & Sons.

Prochaska, J. O., & Norcross, J. C. (1999). *Systems of psychotherapy: A transtheoretical analysis* (8th ed.). Brooks Cole.

Roth, A., & Fonagy, P. (2005). *The contributions of therapists and patients to outcome, in what works for whom: A critical review of psychotherapy research*. Guilford Press.

Schwitzer, A. M., & Rubin, L. C. (2012). *Diagnosis and treatment planning skills for mental health professionals: A popular culture casebook approach*. SAGE.

Seligman, L., & Reichenberg, L. W. (2007). *Selecting effective treatments: A comprehensive, systematic guide to treating mental disorders*. John Wiley & Sons.

Walker, R. (2008). The discipline of inquisitiveness: The body-speech-mind approach to contemplative supervision. In F. L. Kaklauskas, S. Nimanheminda, L. Hoffman, & M. S. Jack (Eds.), *Brilliant sanity: Buddhist approaches to psychotherapy*. University of the Rockies Press.

5 Neurodevelopmental Disorders

Clients who present with neurodevelopmental disorders vary widely from one another. The disorders represented in this dimension are extremely broad and range from difficulties with learning, obstacles in communication, struggles in social interactions and challenges in body movement. Homogeneity seems to be the rule in this dimension of disorders since the degree to which these difficulties permeate each individual's daily functioning, impact wellbeing or influence the sense of self also varies a great deal from one disorder and one person to the next. These disorders share the fact that they are manifested and identified early in development. The disorders of the neurodevelopmental continuum impact the parent system early and, often, for the life of the family. Siblings and whole family processes and functioning can be profoundly challenged, but also enriched, when a child is diagnosed with a disorder such as autism spectrum disorder (ASD), attention deficit hyperactivity disorder (ADHD) or an intellectual disability. As Solomon (2013) notes, "Having exceptional children exaggerates parental tendencies; those who would be bad parents become awful parents, but those who would be good parents often become extraordinary," (p. 6). School and work experiences can also be significantly impacted by neurodevelopmental disorders. For some, ASD also holds the unique quality of creating a space of pride, identity and culture, which sets it apart from other disorders in the DSM 5.

It is important to note that the diagnosis of these disorders is very complex, and appropriate diagnosis has broad implications for a child's education, family and social relationships, lending additional weight to accurate diagnosis. As a rule, extensive psychological testing by those with specialized training and qualifications should accompany these diagnoses in order to assure that the difficulties are well understood and that a thorough intervention plan can be developed. This point can't be under-emphasized. It is, however, important for psychotherapists to have the ability to recognize these difficulties so that children can be referred for formal assessment when appropriate. Further pointing to the importance of referring to specialized assessment (rather than by a primary care physician) is the potential for exacerbating what appears to be a trend to over-diagnose some disorders on this continuum. For example, an astonishing 20% of boys in the

United States have been diagnosed with ADHD (Visser et al., 2014) and 1 in 40 children in the United States is diagnosed with autism (Kogan et al., 2018) suggesting the need for greater diagnostic caution and skill when providing services for these children.

In this chapter, I will touch on a select subset of disorders in this dimension that might be identified in the counseling setting and referred for further assessment and diagnosis or that might be treated by counselors. I will briefly expand on ADHD and ASD, giving the most attention to the higher end of this spectrum. Additionally, this chapter will touch upon the history of the evolution of the autism diagnosis and its strange and often tragic intersections with the social and political world. Understanding the history and impact of diagnoses provides another reminder of the importance of carefully considering how culture and theory influence our beliefs about disorder and shape intervention. Learning disorders, communication disorders and intellectual disabilities will not be discussed as they are outside the diagnostic and treatment purview of the psychotherapy office.

A Glimpse at the Neurodevelopmental Dimension

This dimension is made up of three continuum and two spectrums of disorder: intellectual disabilities, communication disorders, movement disorders, which include tic disorders, ASD and the ADHD spectrum. Again, the learning disorders, intellectual disabilities and most communication and movement disorders will not be discussed here.

Social (Pragmatic) Communication Disorder (SPCD). This disorder made its first appearance in the DSM 5; its key feature is consistent difficulties with verbal and non-verbal communication and is diagnosed in those without intellectual disabilities that would account for these problems. SPCD centers on social communication deficits in the use of appropriate communication for a given social context. Those diagnosed with SPCD evidence an inability to change communication to match the needs of the setting or listener, and show considerable difficulty following communication rules or expectations. These clients have considerable difficulty understanding communication that is not stated explicitly, as with irony (American Psychiatric Association [APA], 2013).

While SPCD is identified early in development, clinicians should withhold a diagnosis until a child's language ability has developed enough to adequately assess the strengths and deficits in communication, usually around age 4-5 (APA, 2013). This cluster of social communication deficits is also found in ASD, but unlike ASD, those with SPCD show no evidence of, and have no history of, repetitive or restrictive behaviors or interests. Consequently, SPCD and ASD would not be diagnosed together. However, SPCD can co-occur with other communication and neurodevelopmental disorders.

The inclusion of SPCD in the DSM-5 is not without its critics. Concerns about the lack of validated assessment tools for diagnosing the disorder is chief among the

BOX 5.01 KEY TERMS: NEURODEVELOPMENTAL DISORDERS

Asperger Syndrome (AS). AS was the diagnosis given to a form of autism in which no early language delay was evidenced. Clients diagnosed before 2013 may carry a diagnosis of AS, or have the diagnosis in their diagnostic history (American Psychiatric Association, 1994).

Echolalia. A pattern of speech in which a person echoes back what is said rather than responding with an original answer. For example, a mother might ask, "Would you like some milk?" and the echolalic response would be, "Would you like some milk?" rather than, "Yes," or "No, juice, please."

High Functioning Autism (HFA). This term refers to clients diagnosed with autism but do not have an intellectual disability. In previous editions of the DSM, HFA and AS were differentiated by examining early language development. The child with HFA had a documented history of early communication delays while the child with AS did not (Attwood, 2001).

Mentalization. Mentalization is the capacity to think about thinking, and includes our ability to conceptualize how we and others come to understand ideas and events and draw conclusions. Mentalization shapes how we communicate with others and how we make and support arguments.

Neurodiversity: This term acknowledges a broad spectrum of diversity in human neurological expression and is forwarded in efforts by autism self-advocates to secure the rights and dignity of autistic persons (Kapp et al., 2013; Owren & Stenhammer, 2013).

Neurotypical: This term describes those whose neurological expression is reflective of norms and expectations; also used as a synonym for "non-autistic."

Premonitory Urge. This phenomenon describes the mounting tension that accompanies an intense urge to enact a tic behavior, such as lip smacking, vocalizations or facial grimacing. These urges, and the accompanying tension, are relieved only briefly by enacting the behavior before the urge returns (Spect et al., 2013).

Perseveration. Perseveration is a phenomenon in which a thought, action or commentary is repeated or prolonged long after the stimulus has passed. In perseveration, thoughts, ideas and conversation can become stuck in a continual loop.

Prosody. This term refers to a pattern of speech that lacks emotional inflection or emphasis on words that would add meaning and depth to communication (Paul et al., 2005).

Relative Age Effects. Relative age effects describe differences observed in children at critical cut off points, such as differences in maturity and school readiness between the youngest and oldest children in kindergarten classrooms (Evans et al., 2010; Happe, 2005).

Stereotyped Movement. Stereotyped movements are patterns of movement that appear to the outside observer to be purposeless. They are often prolonged, as compared to tics, which are generally briefer, and may be sustained over long periods of time, sometimes into adulthood. A common stereotyped movement might include hand wringing, finger wiggling or hand flapping. These behaviors are generally experienced as pleasurable by the person who engages in them (Martino & Hedderly, 2019).

Theory of Mind: This developmental milestone marks a person's capacity to understand that their mind and that of another are separate. This understanding is foundational to grasping that others may have different capacities for knowing, different levels of information and different feelings, views or preferences from one's own (Pedreño et al., 2017).

Tic. A tic is a patterned behavior, frequently spasmodic in nature (such as eye blinking, grimacing, coughing etc.) but are sometimes preceded by an urge to engage the behavior, known as a premonitory urge (Martino & Hedderly, 2019; Pringsheim et al., 2019).

voiced objections (Ash et al., 2016; Brukner-Wertman et al., 2016; Jafari et al., 2019; Norbury, 2013; Swineford et al., 2014). Future research is expected to look at the overlap between ASD and SPCD, the assessment tools needed for diagnosis of SPCD, and longitudinal studies of individuals who receive the diagnosis (Norbury, 2013; Swineford et al., 2014).

Stereotypic Movement Disorder. Stereotypic movements are repetitive and seemingly purposeless movements that follow a consistent pattern (Mackenzie, 2018; Martino & Hedderly, 2019). These movements often develop by age 3 but frequently persist well into adulthood (Mackenzie, 2018). Stereotypic movement disorder is diagnosed when the movements are the source of some kind of impairment, for example, when they cause injury, or would if they were not interrupted. These movements are categorized in one of two ways, primary and secondary (APA, 2013). Stereotyped movement is described as primary when seen in children with otherwise normal development, or as secondary when observed alongside other disorders (Freeman et al., 2010; Mackenzie, 2018; Martino & Hedderly, 2019). When diagnosing this disorder, a specifier is applied to indicate whether or not the presentation includes self-injurious behavior (APA, 2013).

Tic Disorders. Tics are defined as "sudden, rapid, recurrent, nonrhythmic motor movements or vocalizations" (APA, 2013). The tic disorders include Tourette's disorder, persistent (chronic) motor or vocal tic disorder and provisional tic disorder. These disorders are first differentiated by the tic presentation, that is, motor and/or vocal, and second by the duration of symptoms. Tourette's disorder includes both motor and vocal tics that have been present for more than 1 year. Persistent (chronic) motor or vocal tic disorder accounts for those in which only one type of tic is observed, motor or vocal, but have been present for more than 1 year. Provisional tic disorder is applied when diagnosing tics that have been present for less than 1 year (APA, 2013).

Onset of tic disorders often occurs between the ages of 4 and 8 with simple motor tics (Essoe et al., 2019). Vocalizations, if they occur, will often develop a year or more after the first motor tics (Leckman et al., 2014). Tics and tic disorders appear to be closely tied to psychosocial stress. Experiences of excitement, fatigue, anxiety or even social gatherings frequently exacerbate tics. Ongoing psychosocial stress seems to predict the future severity of the tic disorder. For many, tics are preceded by a sensory phenomenon not unlike the sensation that precedes a sneeze or the urge to scratch an itch, described as a premonitory urge (Cavanna et al., 2017; Leckman et al., 2014; Specht et al., 2013). In addition to pharmacological treatment of tic disorders, tic suppression, which works with premonitory urges, has shown some promise (Specht et al., 2013). It is important to note that the tic disorders have high comorbidity rates, particularly with ADHD, obsessive compulsive disorder, movement disorders and other mental health concerns such as depression (APA, 2013; Leckman et al., 2014).

Differentiating Stereotypies and Tics. How do we differentiate stereotyped movements from tics, especially when these can easily be confused and can sometimes occur together? One helpful point of distinction comes in the way the movement is experienced; stereotypies are often experienced as pleasurable and frequently increase in response to excitement, over-stimulation or boredom (Freeman et al., 2010; Mackenzie, 2018; Martino & Hedderly, 2019). In contrast, those with tics, again, note a mounting and unwelcome tension that precedes a tic movement when the tic is resisted (Cavanna et al., 2017; Leckman et al., 2014; Specht et al., 2013). Additionally, tics develop later than stereotypic movements, with onset typically occurring between the ages of 4 and 6. Those who have tics tend to show variation in the tic movements over time, and tics frequency seem to show greater correlation with stress than do stereotypic movements (APA, 2013; Freeman et al., 2010; Mackenzie, 2018). Again, stereotypic movement can co-occur with other disorders including tic disorders (APA, 2013; Martino & Hedderly, 2019).

Attention Deficit Hyperactivity Disorder (ADHD). This disorder, which first appeared in the DSM II as hyperkinetic reaction of childhood, was later revised and renamed attention deficit disorder and again revised and renamed attention deficit hyperactivity disorder ADHD. As the name suggests, ADHD describes a collection of difficulties that cluster in the realm of inattention, impulsivity and hyperactivity. The criteria for this disorder vary slightly for those 16 and under from older clients; however, symptoms must be present for at least 6 months to be diagnosed and should be the source of impairment. Markers of impairment in attention include a failure to give close attention to one's work or schoolwork that results in careless mistakes, trouble sustaining the attention needed for the task at hand, failure to follow instructions or finish tasks and so on. Indications of difficulties with hyperactivity and impulsivity is probably best described by the DSM's use of the phrase appearing to be "driven by a motor" (p. 60) and are evidenced in behaviors such as squirming, fidgeting, aimless tapping, leaving one's seat often when staying seated is expected, feeling or displaying restlessness, such as running around or climbing in inappropriate settings, finding it difficult to remain quiet in restful activities and similar behaviors. When reflecting on these patterns, it is important to take into consideration developmental expectations and norms in discerning behaviors that will resolve naturally as the child matures, from those behaviors that might have a biological source and are in need of intervention. This disorder will be explored at greater length later in this chapter.

The Autism Spectrum

Autism Spectrum Disorder (ASD). ASD describes a highly diverse continuum of presentations that share two primary deficits, each beginning early in life: deficits in social interaction and deficits related to communication and restrictive or repetitive behaviors. New to this edition is a criterion that describes hyper- and hyposensitivity to sensory input, such as pain, temperature, sound and light, and is listed under criteria indicating social communication impairments and restricted and repetitive behaviors. As Francesca Happe (2005) notes, "People with autism show a strikingly uneven profile of abilities, and show islets of unimpaired or even superior skills . . ." (p. 53), which may contribute to what seems to be a remarkable degree of within-group differences among autistic persons.

The Specifiers. The revised organization of the DSM 5 leans heavily on specifiers for clarifying the individual presentation of diagnosed clients. Specifiers are especially important in the diagnosis of ASD. Because the symptom combination and the severity of each of the symptoms varies widely from one person to the next, the careful use of specifiers is especially important in conveying information to other practitioners.

Autism severity specifiers are first organized according to impairment in social communication and second in restricted and repetitive behaviors, each of which is placed within one of three levels of required support, ranging from very substantial (Level One) to requiring support (Level Three). Diagnosticians are also asked to specify whether or not the diagnosis comes with an intellectual impairment, and whether or not language impairment is present. Further, specifiers are provided to indicate catatonia, and, finally, associations with other medical or neurodevelopmental disorders (APA, 2013).

Early Signs and Symptoms. Most parents of autistic children note differences and raise concerns about their children in the first year. Often the first concerns raised are about vision or hearing (Bolton et al., 2012). Researchers have reviewed home movies of these first months and have been able to identify the first manifestations of autism, including gaze aversion, a lack of emotional expression and low activity levels (Adrien et al., 1991; Adrien et al., 1993). By the second year of life, parent concerns often include peculiar eating habits, differences in play and observations of repetitive behaviors (Bolton et al., 2012). Unfortunately, while most children can be reliably assessed and diagnosed by age 2, the average child is not diagnosed until age 4 (Baio et al., 2018) delaying opportunities for intervention.

Frequently Shifting Diagnostic Organization. Since its first inclusion in the DSM, the conceptualization and organization of the diagnostic nosology for autism-related disorders has shifted significantly with nearly each edition. When the DSM-III was published in 1980, a new class of disorders was introduced, the pervasive developmental disorders, which included the first mention of infantile autism in the manual (APA, 1980; Cohen et al., 1986). In 1994, Asperger's Syndrome (AS) was added to the DSM IV as a separate codable disorder. However, the revision of the DSM reflected in the fifth edition did away with the pervasive developmental disorder category altogether, leaving a single diagnosis, ASD, to represent the entire spectrum.

A Note About Asperger's Syndrome. While AS is no longer included within the DSM, it is discussed widely in the literature, literature that addresses the needs and experiences of this group, and most closely matches the clients that are likely to seek out and benefit from traditional psychotherapy. Further, it is a disorder that has been taken on as an identity by some autistic people, lending it continued importance despite its exclusion from the DSM 5.

Again, until May of 2013, AS was one of five diagnoses described as a pervasive developmental disorder. This was an apt categorization since unlike most other disorders of the DSM, a diagnosis of AS brought with it a recognition that the individual was encountering challenges on nearly every level of experiencing: social, emotional, behavioral and cognitive. Children diagnosed with AS did not display intellectual disability or functional language delays, however. Their challenges came in a failure to seek others out or to share their interests, seek help or share delight. Clients with this diagnosis tended to be rigid in their adherence to patterns and schedules and to be change averse. They frequently invested a great deal of attention and energy in a single focus of attention, such as baseball statistics, train schedules, weather patterns, the classification of dinosaurs and so on, and typically were interested in this topic to the exclusion of all else (Attwood, 2001; APA, 1994).

Questions About Cognition and ASD. The cognitive challenges faced by those with ASD range from very significant intellectual disabilities to quite subtle cognitive and perceptual differences that can be hard for the lay-person to detect. One area of nuance in cognitive development thought to be problematic for children on the spectrum is a milestone known as theory of mind. Theory of mind is the understanding that one's own mind is separate from the minds of others and that others have their own understandings, feelings and experiences (Happe, 1994; Pedreño et al., 2017). Another area of subtle cognitive difference can be seen in the capacities around mentalization, or thinking about thinking. Deficits in these skills make tasks like understanding irony and other abstract or subtle forms of communication difficult. However, research is a bit mixed on differences between those with autism and neurotypical persons and whether or not these deficits are central or peripheral to the difficulties experienced by those on the spectrum (Saban-Bezalel et al., 2019).

Relating to Others: Instrumental versus Expressive Relationship. There is a special kind of wonder and magic in early interactions with infants and toddlers, moments of experience sharing, attunement and shared curiosity. These moments create the foundation that later strengthens the bonds of attachment. These early interactions feature sustained eye gaze and attention sharing, experiences that are often uncomfortable and sometimes not possible for autistic children. When children and adults encounter relationships in a way that is designed to share and elicit emotion and extend connection, these relational exchanges are described as expressive. Interactions that are undertaken in order to fulfil a personal need and are not meant to be reciprocal are described as instrumental. Consider your interactions with a bank teller or a person at the drive through window at a fast food chain, for example. These exchanges are often pleasant but the primary aim of the interaction is to meet a personal need. All of us have both expressive and instrumental relationships, but for people on the autistic spectrum the bulk of relationships, sometimes including those with parents and siblings, fall into this category of relationship, though the degree to which this imbalance is present differs a great deal from one person to the next (Siegel, 1997).

Seeking Social Engagement: Two Subtypes. Heinrichs (2003) notes that children with Asperger syndrome tend to present as either fairly introverted or especially extroverted. She notes that introverted children and teens with AS/HFA are more comfortable tucked into a good book or absorbed in a favorite interest and are less drawn to social interaction with others the same age. However, children and adolescents described as engaging are interested in social interaction and seek others out but, unfortunately, skill deficits in social interaction make these efforts awkward and can draw the attention of bullies. She notes that these children and teens often have a hard time differentiating behavior that should be imitated from those that should be avoided, making the social world especially challenging.

Heinrichs (2003) further notes that engaging-type children tend to draw more negative attention from both teachers and peers, which can make the educational experience a painful one. When children and teens on the spectrum imitate and adopt negative behaviors, these behaviors can be very hard to extinguish, escalating negative interactions between peers and teachers. Consequently, Heinrichs advises advocacy for these students and recommends avoiding placing children on the spectrum in special education classrooms reserved for children with emotional disturbances where they are likely to adopt negative behaviors observed in class.

Communication Delays and Obstacles. Persons with low functioning autism have little language facility and often depend on the use of augmentative communication, such as picture boards, to convey their needs (Cafiero, 2001); however, a variety of communication difficulties, with varying degrees of severity, have been observed among persons on the spectrum. Echolalia, a communication pattern in which a person responds by repeating another's comments rather than offering an original response is frequently observed in autistic people (Neely et al., 2016). Overly formal language, difficulties understanding abstract speech, such as metaphor and idiom, and odd tonal qualities or prosody are also common. Prosody is a quality of speech that lacks inflection, may seem robotic, or features errors in where pauses are placed. Inflection in the tone of voice conveys intent and emotion, and assists in conveying grammatical information as well (Paul et al., 2005). People on the autistic spectrum may have difficulties knowing how and when to ask questions of others, a skill that correlates with positive prognosis later in life (Koegel et al., 2014).

Non-verbal communication may also be impacted. These clients may make limited use of gestures, body language or facial expressions. Observed differences seem to be more profound in areas of expressive language, however, when compared to deficits seen with receptive language (Grossman & Tager-Flusberg, 2012). Differences in communication not only interfere with the ability to receive and convey information, but also may tend to attract bullying behaviors from others (Heinrichs, 2003).

BOX 5.02 CONSIDER THIS

One of the ways we communicate meaning is in the way we lend emphasis to words or parts of words. Note how the meaning of the following sentence changes when emphasis is placed on a different word.

I didn't say you embarrassed me. [someone else said you embarrassed me]

I *didn't* say you embarrassed me. [you didn't embarrassed me]

I didn't *say* you embarrassed me. [I implied you embarrassed me, however]

I didn't say *you* embarrassed me. [Someone embarrassed me, but it wasn't you]

I didn't say you *embarrassed* me. [The interaction raised a feeling in me, but it wasn't embarrassment]

I didn't say you embarrassed *me*. [Someone was embarrassed but it wasn't me]

Sensory Sensitivity and Food Selectivity in ASD. A common concern among parents of children and teens with ASD is diet and "picky eating" in particular. These clients may restrict their diets to a handful of tolerated foods, leaving them at risk for poor nutrition. Some of the blame for the selectivity in food choices seems to be linked to heightened sensory sensitivities including texture, taste and smell. Consequently, bland foods, such as carbohydrates are often preferred (Attwood, 2001; Cermak et al., 2010).

Differences in Pain Sensitivity. Parents have long expressed concerns that children with ASD did not seem to show the same levels of sensitivity to pain or temperature that typically developing children do (Attwood, 2001). Few studies have examined this phenomenon, but recently Yasuda et al. (2016) found that while the body does register discomfort, for many with ASD, there is an impairment in the brain's processing and recognition of the discomfort. Consequently, people with ASD may experience, for example, a severe ear infection without registering the pain in the same way another person would. This difference in processing pain can slow responsiveness and intervention to underlying health problems.

Anxiety, obsessive-compulsive disorder (OCD) and ASD. Clinicians who work with autistic clients/clients with ASD should be aware that elevated rates of anxiety are common among this group. Meta-analytic research reveals that nearly 40% of youth with ASD met criteria for at least one other disorder; just under 30% reported a specific phobia, while 16.6% reported a social anxiety disorder. OCD was reported in 17.4% (Van Steensel et al., 2011). Large meta-analytic studies reveal that anxiety is correlated with IQ scores, consequently, the higher the client's functioning the more elevated the anxiety is likely to be. When compared to typically developing children,

children with ASD have higher rates of anxiety, which is also true in comparison to clinic referred children and children with externalizing disorders, such as oppositional defiance, and children with other developmental difficulties. These differences in levels of anxiety seem to grow as clients age (Van Steensel & Heeman, 2017). Neurological factors as well as adverse life experiences may account for a portion of the increased occurrence of anxiety in these youth. Incidences of bullying, unmet social and relational needs and limits in preferences may all contribute to elevated anxiety (Postorino et al., 2017). Ongoing assessment for anxiety is essential for clients who occupy a space on the spectrum. Preventative interventions for clients who are not yet displaying symptoms of anxiety is advised.

ASD and OCD. OCD and ASD are often seen together (Griffiths et al., 2017; Postorino et al., 2017; Van Steensel et al., 2011). OCD, like ASD, brings with it significant burden; when packaged together with the symptoms of autism, the level of suffering is amplified (Griffiths et al., 2017). Repetitive behavior is a core feature of both disorders and can be challenging to pull apart for those new to diagnosis; however, the function and experience of these behaviors differs. The stereotyped and repetitive movement that is associated with ASD is typically experienced as pleasurable or stress relieving while the repetitive behaviors of OCD are a direct response to the intrusive thoughts of OCD obsessions and are intended to hold a feared result at bay, as when intrusive fears of illness are addressed with compulsive hand washing. OCD behaviors are generally experienced as unwelcome but necessary to the person who performs them, while repetitive behaviors of ASD are experienced as pleasurable or relieving (Postorino et al., 2017).

ASD and Sleep Disturbances. In their comprehensive study of sleep disturbance in ASD, Deliens et al., (2015) found that the role of sleep disturbance in ASD was far more significant than simple comorbidity. These researchers found that sleep difficulties appeared early in life, before age two and persisted well into adulthood. Sleep disturbance in autism, they found, is likely the result of the intersection of genetic predisposition, epigenetics and their interaction with the individual's social, psychological and environmental context, making sleep issues especially complex to address. Their review of the literature revealed that more significant sleep disturbance served to amplify symptoms, leaving clients with greater difficulties with social communication, diminished emotion regulation capacities and poorer adaptive functioning. These researchers argue that treatment of sleep disturbance should be made a priority in addressing the needs of persons with ASD.

Autism's Tragic History: Nazis, Refrigerator Mothers, Parent-ectomies and the Anti-Vaccination Movement

The history of the autism diagnosis and its current place in the social and political dialogue is one that is at once fascinating and tragic. It is a story that again reminds clinicians of the importance of perspective, curiosity and healthy skepticism when approaching theories of etiology, the DSM and diagnostics generally.

Mapping the story of the autism diagnosis has not one but two starting points. The first begins in Austria with a controversial figure, Hans Asperger, the other in Maryland with Leo Kanner. Asperger served as a child psychiatrist at the Universitats-Kinderklinik in Vienna where children with disabilities were evaluated and treated. It was in this clinic where Asperger first described "autistic psychopaths," children who displayed a wide range of functionality and had little interest in the larger community. Asperger was of the view that autism was a biological disorder and rejected psychoanalytic explanations for mental health issues including autism (Slagstad, 2019). While working in Vienna, Asperger identified a subgroup of autistic children with talents and gifts who, he argued in papers and lectures, could be educated and socialized back into their communities (Silberman, 2015; Slagstad, 2019). It is the context within which Asperger worked and disputes about his relationship with it, however, that lend much of the controversy to Asperger's contributions.

Vienna was, by this time, run by the Nazi party and the policies under which Asperger worked were framed by the ideology and aims of the Third Reich. The Nazi eugenics movement had as one of its central aims to "purify" the German race; consequently, ridding itself of disabled children was one of the earliest atrocities of the holocaust. Beginning in the summer of 1940 and until the Nazi defeat, at least 789 children died or were put to death in Am Spiegelgrund, a Vienna hospital where Asperger had referred disabled children. "It is 'extremely unlikely' that Asperger with his unique position and various tasks and contacts, was unaware of what was going on at Am Spiegelgrund," (Slagstad, 2019) particularly since there was an awareness of the eugenics program at Am Spiegelgrund among the people of Vienna (Slagstad, 2019). Other authors, and Asperger himself, argue that it was his aim to save autistic children from Nazi extermination and that he had worked to provide a setting friendly to their unique needs and tailored to cultivate gifts that the Nazi regime might capitalize upon (Silberman, 2015; Slagstad, 2019).

At Johns Hopkins University in the United States, Leo Kanner, an Austrian-born psychiatrist who would later become known as the father of child psychiatry, was also researching and writing about autism. Owing to the social isolation seen in his patients and its resemblance to the social withdrawal observed in clients with schizophrenia he concluded, "Early infantile autism may therefore be looked upon as the earliest possible manifestation of childhood schizophrenia," (Kanner, 1949, p. 417).

Kanner embraced a psychoanalytic perspective around the causes of autism. Though Kanner would later reverse his opinion (Rimland, 1974), it is from his 1949 paper that the term "refrigerator mother" took hold and helped to proliferate the notion that autism was caused by cold and withholding parenting. Kanner notes:

> "Most of the patients were exposed from the beginning to parental coldness, obsessiveness, and a mechanical type of attention to material needs only. They were the objects of observation and experiment conducted with

an eye on fractional performance rather than with genuine warmth and enjoyment. They were kept neatly in refrigerators which did not defrost. Their withdrawal seems to be an act of turning away from such a situation to seek comfort in solitude" (Kanner, 1949, p. 425).

Another well-known figure in the history of the diagnosis and treatment of autism is Bruno Bettelheim, a Jewish–Austrian psychologist who had been imprisoned in both Dachau and Buchenwald concentration camps and later immigrated to the United States. Like Kanner, Bettelheim attributed the cause of autism to cold parenting, which he likened to treatment he had experienced in the concentration camps. Bettelheim recommended that autistic children be removed from their homes and placed in institutions that could support their needs, a process described as parent-ectomies (Bettelheim, 1972). After their children were removed, mothers were treated, sometimes for years, to understand the cause for their "hostility" toward their children (Silberman, 2015).

The Complicated Etiology of ASD: Genetics, Mirror Neurons and Environmental Factors. A great deal of evidence supports a biological cause for autism that begins with genetic differences that create predispositions for ASD that then interact with environmental factors to create the possibility for ASD to develop (Bai et al., 2019; Fakhoury, 2015; Grove et al., 2019). The detail of genetic involvement is far outside the scope of this chapter to describe with any satisfying depth. Similarly, a wide range of environmental factors that may create vulnerability or exacerbate vulnerabilities already present have also been described, including maternal infection, prenatal use of tobacco, prenatal exposure to alcohol and other substances, diet lacking in key nutrients, low socioeconomic status, low parental education and so on, and are also outside the scope of this chapter (Fakhoury, 2015).

Neurological differences have also been described that may account for some attributes of ASD, including a discussion of the role of mirror neurons in the development of autism, though no single explanation seems to account for all deficits and difficulties. Mirror neurons are thought to support social, emotional and cognitive tasks. When we enact a movement, for example, when we play tag football with friends, our mirror neurons fire. These same mirror neurons fire when we watch others playing football. The firing of mirror neurons in our observation of others is thought to support our capacity to engage in those activities ourselves. Researchers using neuroimaging, such as functional magnetic resonance imaging (fMRI), have found deficits in mirror neurons among people on the autistic spectrum that seem to impair their ability to make sense of other's actions (Fakhoury, 2015). A number of other neurological differences have been documented. Again, a complete discussion is outside the purview of this text but includes, for example, differences in neural density in the limbic system (Blatt et al., 2001).

The Question of the Rising Prevalence Rates of ASD. The question of the prevalence of autism, and whether or not the incidence of the disorder is actually rising, is being over-diagnosed, or perhaps both, is a complicated one. One of the complicating factors rests in the fact that since autism first made an appearance in the DSM in 1980, the organization of that spectrum has shifted significantly and often, making it hard to track incidence over time. When Kanner was writing about early infantile autism, he argued the disorder was very rare (Kanner, 1949; Rimland, 1974), while writers like Lorna Wing would later point to research suggesting that for the higher functioning manifestations of autism, the prevalence was closer to 35 in 10,000 or 1 in 286 births (Wing, 1996). However, drawing from the 2016 National Survey of Children's Health and examining the responses of a representative sample of 50,212 American participants, Kogan et al., 2018, found that an alarming one in 40 parents surveyed reported that their child had been formally diagnosed with autism; 27% of these children were reported to take medications for symptoms related to the disorder. How do we make sense of this dramatic and troublesome increase in the diagnosis of autism?

Vaccines: A False Lead. In 1998 John Wakefield and his colleagues published a paper in the Lancet drawing a link between measles, mumps and rubella (MMR) vaccines and the development of autism (Wakefield et al., 1998). The article, paired with the fact that the first symptoms of autism emerge at roughly the same time as the MMR schedule begins, left many parents fearful that the MMR vaccine was at the bottom of the apparent increase in autism diagnoses (Frances, 2013). However, years of research found no evidence for a link between the vaccine and the development of autism. In the meantime, dogged investigative reporting followed the Lancet article that ultimately revealed Wakefield's work to be both methodologically and ethically flawed and, ultimately, the fraudulent nature of the data that he and his team had reported. The Lancet formally retracted the Wakefield article 12 years after its publication (Deer, 2011; Farrington et al., 2001; Frances, 2013; Godlee et al., 2011; Rao & Andrade, 2011), but the damage was done. As fear spread about the safety of the MMR and increasing numbers of parents chose not to immunize their children, pockets of measles outbreaks were documented in the United Kingdom, Canada and across the United States, places where the disease had previously been eliminated (Hinman et al., 2011). In 2019, there were 1,282 cases of measles documented in the United States, an increase of 240% over 2018 (Centers for Disease Control [CDC], 2020).

Allen Frances, chair of the DSM IV task force, points out that before the publication of the DSM IV, one child in 2,000 was diagnosed with autism; however, by 2013 that number had jumped to 1 in 80 (again, today this number is 1 in 40). Frances argues that the proliferation of autism diagnoses is due to three convergent factors: (1) improved awareness among doctors, parents and educators; (2) the introduction of AS to the DSM IV, a subthreshold autism diagnosis and (3) incorrect diagnoses driven by the need for educational and mental health services. Frances further noted that normal differences in human expression, including normal levels of eccentricity and social awkwardness exist within any given community; however, because the demarcation between these typical differences and those that are pathological is unclear, the diagnosis has been artificially elevated. Additionally, the decrease in the stigma once carried by the autism diagnosis and the advocacy for clients, families and for services have likely also contributed to increased diagnoses (Frances, 2013).

Race and Social Class and Their Impact on ASD Diagnosis. The uneven diagnosis of marginalized children is a well-documented phenomenon that deprives children of essential early intervention (Baio et al., 2018; Christensen et al., 2018; Durkin et al., 2010; Travers & Krezmien, 2018). Substantial numbers of comprehensive research studies have shown that while the rates of diagnosis have risen across racial groups, the growth has not been proportionate. While diagnostic gaps between racial groups are closing, White children are more likely to be diagnosed than African American Children and White and Black children are far more likely to be identified and receive services than are Hispanic children (Baio et al., 2018; Christensen et al., 2018; Travers & Krezmien, 2018). Research also indicates that non-Hispanic White children are more likely to receive comprehensive evaluation for autism by 36 months (Christensen et al., 2018).

Identity, Neurodiversity and Self-Advocacy Among Autistic Persons. Not all people diagnosed with autism view ASD as a deficit to be cured and many argue that too much of the autism resources are dedicated to research invested in identifying a cause for autism rather than providing needed services. A sizable group of autistic people experience autism as an essential part of their personal identities and embrace the autism-related traits with a sense of acceptance and pride. This group has described themselves as the autism rights movement asserting that their efforts are part of a drive for inclusiveness of human neurodiversity. Several online groups and blogs have been formed around these values and views, such as the Autism Self-Advocacy Network, Neurodefiance, Neurocosmopolitanism, the Autistic Women and NonBinary Network and so on. Members of these groups tend to have a preference for identity first language (autistic person vs. person with autism) (Cascio, 2012; Kapp et al., 2013; Owren & Stenhammer, 2013), a notable contrast to the person-first language recommended by the APA.

These activists and their allies assert that the current diagnostic model places undue emphasis on deficits, which may arise out of comorbid disorders, such as intellectual disabilities, and that the diagnosis tends to pathologize behavioral differences that diverge from social preference but are not, in and of themselves, essentially pathological. By way of example, these authors assert that restricted interests, a preference to avoid direct eye contact or self-stim behaviors, such as rocking or hand flapping, are not impairments but differences. These activists argue that autism is a natural expression of human diversity and should be treated with respect while offering autistic persons needed coping mechanisms for issues such as stress or anxiety (Cascio, 2012; Kapp et al., 2013; Owren & Stenhammer, 2013).

Attention Deficit Hyperactivity Disorder

ADHD Etiology. Though genetic research into ADHD is still in its infancy, research suggests that the heritability of ADHD is somewhere in the 60%-90% range (Power et al., 2018), though no single gene has been identified that can account for ADHD or its symptoms (DuPaul et al., 2016). The interaction between environmental stressors, such as exposure to lead, pesticides and maternal smoking may all contribute to a diathesis-stress model that awakens a complex combination of inherited biological predispositions that then lead to ADHD (DuPaul et al., 2016).

Comorbidities. High comorbidity rates for children with ADHD have been documented for decades (Barkley, 2006; Jensen & Steinhausen, 2015; Reale et al., 2017; Szatmari et al., 1989). A comprehensive study published in 2017 revealed that among

BOX 5.03 EVOLUTION OF THE AUTISM DIAGNOSIS IN THE DSM

DSM I-II

What would later come to be named "autism" is described in the first two editions as childhood schizophrenia

DSM III

Addition of three disorders organized under the Pervasive Developmental Disorders category:

- Infantile Autism: Most similar to Kanner's description of autism
- Childhood Onset pervasive Developmental Disorder:
- Atypical Pervasive Developmental Disorder; prevalence for all of these disorders together 1 in 2,000

DSM IV

Asperger Syndrome is added: no prevalence data is offered

DSM IV-TR

Asperger Syndrome descriptions updated: no prevalence data is offered

Autistic Disorder descriptions updated: prevalence estimated at 2-20 cases in 10,000

DSM 5

The pervasive developmental disorders, including Asperger syndrome, are removed and replaced with autism spectrum disorder (ASD): featuring deficits in two areas: social communication and interaction and repetitive patterns of interests, behaviors and activities. The prevalence is estimated to be about 1% of the population, or 1 in 100 births

Source: Information drawn from each of the editions of the DSM APA, 1952, 1980, 1994, 2013

children diagnosed with ADHD, 66% had at least one comorbid disorder, most common among these were learning disorders (56%) and sleep disorders (23%), followed closely by oppositional defiance (20%) and anxiety disorders (12%) (Reale et al., 2017). Research suggests that male children with ADHD are more apt to develop externalizing disorders, while female children are more apt to develop internalizing disorders (Jensen & Steinhausen, 2015).

Sleep Disturbance and ADHD. Wajszilber et al., (2018) point out that the difficulties observed in children with ADHD are all potentially exacerbated by sleep deprivation and further note that, among those seen in clinical practices, between 25% and 50% report sleep difficulties. Their review of the literature examining the intersection between sleep disturbance and ADHD revealed that the consequences of restricted or interrupted sleep for this population were wide-reaching and included fatigue, changes in mood, including higher levels of symptoms of depression and anxiety, decreased capacities for attention, declines in verbal fluency and executive function, behavioral problems, negative impacts of physical health and an overall decline in personal quality of life. Consequently, evaluating clients with ADHD for sleep disorders is important to providing optimal care and may help to limit the impact of the primary ADHD. These researchers recommend evaluation through a formal sleep study where possible.

ODD and ADHD: Two Models. Why do we see such high rates of conduct disorders in children with ADHD? Researchers exploring this question believe that, by and large, ADHD precedes conduct problems, but the reverse does not seem to be true. A developmental theory suggests that the behaviors evident in ADHD cause a disruption in the family system that may lead to higher incidences of negative parenting practices that, in turn, contribute to the development of oppositional defiance. Additionally, researchers have examined whether or not a family history of ADHD and ODD/CD was predictive of early symptoms of ADHD and conduct problems. Their research suggests the interaction of both factors, family history and a developmental/transactional model between ADHD and conduct are at play in the comorbidity of ODD and ADHD (Harvey et al., 2016). Parents of children with ADHD seem to use more demands and critical feedback. Research suggests that when parents also have ADHD symptoms, family communication and interaction may be especially challenged by the child's ADHD symptoms, often resulting in communication strain that may then contribute to the development of conduct disorders (Harvey et al., 2016; Wymbs et al., 2015). More research is needed to understand these dynamics.

The Misdiagnosis of ADHD and Mania. A particularly damaging period in the history of mental health diagnostics unfolded under the watch of the National Institutes of Health in a series of studies conducted by Dr. Joseph Biederman. Biederman and his research team argued that some of the symptoms understood to be ADHD were, in fact, manifestations of a comorbid mania of bipolar disorder described as "rapid cycling" (Biederman & Jellinek, 1998). This theory was embraced by clinicians and prescribing physicians across the country and spurred a dramatic up-tick in the medication of young children. In response to rising concerns about over-medication and misdiagnosis, the members of the DSM task force decided to add a disorder, disruptive mood dysregulation disorder (DMDD) to the DSM and added explicit warnings against using the rapid cycling specifier for mood shifts in children with duration cycles that unfolded within a single day or week. A more complete discussion of the history of the rapid cycling bipolar diagnoses in children and misdiagnosis of children with ADHD can be found in Chapter 7, which discusses the mood disorders.

Overdiagnosis, Relative Age Effects and ADHD Diagnosis. While public information about ADHD has doubtlessly made it possible for more children to receive appropriate diagnosis and needed services, some researchers ask if a portion of the rise in the diagnosis of ADHD in the United States and across the globe might be due to misdiagnosis. If so, what factors might contribute to the misdiagnosis of ADHD? For over a decade, researchers have drawn attention to concerns about a phenomenon known as the relative age effect, in which age relative to classroom peers seems to play a role in diagnosis (Morrow et al., 2012). In Canada, where the school year begins in January, the youngest children in the classroom have December birthdays, while in the United States, where the school year begins in the fall, the youngest children were born in August. Research reveals that Canadian boys born in December are 30% more likely to receive an ADHD diagnosis than boys born in January, and girls are 70% more likely to be diagnosed with ADHD when born in December. In a study conducted in the United States, Evans et al., (2010) found that boys with August birthdays were more likely to be diagnosed with ADHD than their older counterparts. They note that their results suggest that younger children are inappropriately diagnosed based on maturation differences relative to older peers and not on an underlying biological disorder (Evans et al., 2010). A recent meta-analysis of relative age effects in the United States and internationally found that the countries with higher incidences of ADHD overall also had higher relative age effects. Predictably, higher diagnosis rates among younger children are reflected in higher rates of prescription stimulant drug usage (Holland & Sayal, 2018).

Evidence-Based Practices for Treating ADHD

ADHD is typically treated by employing a combination of pharmacological, educational and psychosocial interventions, which, when used together, seem to enhance the effect of one another (DuPaul et al., 2016; Power et al., 2018). Stimulants, including methylphenidate, are considered to be the front-line medications for ADHD, and are supported by numerous double-blind studies demonstrating efficacy in ADHD and the conduct symptoms that often accompany it. Stimulants are prescribed in both short- and long-acting doses (DuPaul et al., 2016; Kral et al., 2017; Power et al., 2018). Short- and long-acting medications have different efficacies for different symptoms, however. For instance, short-acting methylphenidate seems to show better efficacy in ADHD symptoms and note-taking and better client satisfaction than do long-acting formulations. In a small naturalistic study, however, long-acting pemoline showed better medication adherence. In this same study, both short- and long-acting formulas seemed to demonstrate benefits in some academic habits, in grade point average (GPA) and in ODD symptoms, though the effects were smaller than anticipated (Pelham et al., 2017). Long-acting doses seem to be more likely to interfere with sleep (Power et al., 2018). Finally, methylphenidate has been shown to be effective in improving performance in cognitive tasks in boys with developmental ADHD as well as in those with ADHD associated with epilepsy (Bechtel et al., 2012).

Stimulant Diversion. While the efficacy of stimulants has been established, sociological consequences, such as drug diversion, have also been widely documented. Stimulant diversion, also known as non-medical use, is a phenomenon in which medications prescribed for one person are used by another, a practice with obvious risks. Diversion can come in the form of selling or sharing medications for academic or recreational purposes (Faraone et al., 2019). A study of 483 college students found that nearly 36% had diverted some type of prescribed medication at some point in their lifetimes, but among those who had been prescribed ADHD medications, 61.7% admitted to diverting these medications at least once (Garnier et al., 2010). Pham et al., (2017) conducted a survey of 180 parents of youth who had been prescribed stimulants for ADHD. They found that 16% of these parents had diverted these medications to someone else in the home, the majority of whom admitted taking the medication themselves, and an additional 13% described being tempted to take the medication but denied doing so.

Stimulants, Treatment-Emergent Psychosis and Sudden Unexplained Deaths. For a very small number of children with ADHD who are treated with stimulants, such as methylphenidate or amphetamine, psychotic episodes have resulted (Cherland & Fitzpatrick, 1999; Moran et al., 2019; Shibib & Chalhoub, 2009). One study of nearly 338,000 adolescents diagnosed with ADHD and who were being treated with stimulants found that 1 in 660 experienced a psychosis that resulted in the prescription of antipsychotic medications (Moran et al., 2019), a number that does not account for those who experienced psychosis but did not require pharmacological intervention. Among the more common psychotic symptoms instigated by prescription stimulants include visual and sensory hallucinations of snakes and worms (Mosholder et al., 2009).

Though rare, sudden unexplained deaths in youths who have been prescribed stimulant medications for the treatment of ADHD have been reported. Researchers have not been able to identify a direct correlation between stimulants and these deaths. However, Gould et al. (2009) reported "a significant association or 'signal' between sudden unexplained death and the use of stimulant medication, specifically methylphenidate,"

(p. 1000). A more recent study of children and adolescents diagnosed with ADHD and ASD found no link between psychostimulants and serious cardiovascular events in either group (Houghton et al., 2020). More research is needed to bring certitude to the safety of psychostimulants in children and adolescents.

Evidence-Based Psychosocial Interventions for ADHD. A significant volume of research supports the use of behavioral interventions for ADHD (DuPaul et al., 2016). Behavioral interventions are designed by identifying a target behavior for change and assessing its antecedents and consequences. By adding support and adjustments to the context in which the target behavior arises and managing consequences, behaviors are changed. Behavioral interventions have been delivered successfully directly to youth, individually, in the context of peer interactions and in the classroom. Additionally, evidence-based behavioral intervention has been provided indirectly by providing instruction to parents in individual or group settings as well as in the home (DuPaul et al., 2016; Evans et al., 2014; Pelham & Fabiano, 2008; Power et al., 2018). School-based academic interventions are included within the list of evidence-based interventions and include direct academic support and peer tutoring (DuPaul et al., 2016; Power et al., 2018).

Treatment Interventions for ASD

Compensatory Medications. Medications are often prescribed to people with autism to address symptoms such as severe behavioral disturbances. Most common among these are risperidone and aripiprazole. However, the side effects of these medications can be quite burdensome, including nausea and abdominal discomfort, constipation, sleepiness and hostility and aggression (Subramanyam et al., 2019). Among the most significant and lasting side effects of risperidone in particular is significant weight gain. Though some research suggests that risperidone can be helpful in reducing tantrums and outbursts, the average child gains 6 pounds in the first 8 weeks of starting the medication. Risperidone can lead to shifts in insulin responses that result in body shape changes that can last the rest of the child's life (McCracken et al., 2002; Shea et al., 2004; Subramanyam et al., 2019).

Multidisciplinary Approaches to the Treatment of Autism. Because the impact of an autism diagnosis is so far-reaching, the interventions must also be multidisciplinary. Effective intervention with persons on the autistic spectrum begins early and may include occupational, physical and speech therapy together with a wide variety of behavioral, psychosocial and special education services (Subramanyam et al., 2019; Wong et al., 2015). Social communication interventions vary widely from applied behavior analysis (ABA) play-based approaches, such as floortime (Greenspan et al., 1998), or relational approaches, such as relational development intervention (RDI) (Gutstein, 2000).

Evidence-Based Interventions. In their comprehensive review of interventions designed for youth on the autistic spectrum, Wong et al., 2015, identified 27 interventions that could be described as evidence-based practices. Sifting through studies that included randomized control, quasi-experimental or regression discontinuity designs, they found the interventions that employed the foundational applied behavior analysis techniques to be most strongly supported with research evidence. Others with strong support included antecedent based intervention, differential reinforcement of behavior and video modeling.

A Note on Aversives and the ABA Backlash. Iver Lovaas is credited with developing applied behavior analysis for the treatment of children with autism (ABA). A great admirer of B.F. Skinner's work using operant conditioning with disabled children, Lovaas is also credited with integrating aversive stimuli, also known as punishment, in combination with reward in order to change behavior. An early use of aversives was evidenced in his work with his colleague, Rekers, with boys who expressed themselves in ways that fell outside typical gender roles (Rekers & Lovaas, 1974). He later implemented aversives to extinguish self-stim behaviors, self-injury and echolalia. Lovaas made use of very loud noise, painful electric shock and withholding food and water (Silberman, 2015). A call for the ban on the use of electric shock and other extreme forms of aversives first came in 1988. Two decades later these practices became the focus of a high-profile lawsuit when The Judge Rotenberg Center was sued for mistreatment of one of its residents. Ultimately, the Food and Drug Administration (FDA) banned aversive shock treatment for mentally ill clients in March of 2020. While ABA is recognized as an evidence-based intervention for autism, neurodiversity advocates criticize ABA and draw similarities between the use of ABA with autistic children and the use of conversion therapy in gay and lesbian persons (Neumeier & Brown, 2020; Silberman, 2015).

The six pivot points in Table 5.01 may help point you in the direction of a broad category of disorders within the neurodevelopmental dimension. Again, thorough testing and observation as well as a complete developmental history are necessary to make any neurodevelopmental diagnosis. If you work with children, often it can be helpful to develop a strong working relationship with local school and clinical psychologists. Together with parents and teachers, a collaborative relationship can help to support accurate diagnosis, the development of strong intervention plans and coordinated efforts between family, school and the counseling settings.

Definitional Cases in Neurodevelopmental Disorders

Austin

Since he was old enough to spend time with other children, Austin's mother has noticed that Austin has difficulty with the social give and take of play. He doesn't show an interest in what other children are doing, becomes engrossed in his own play and

TABLE 5.01 **Pivot Points: Neurodevelopmental Disorders**

	Consider Assessment for:
Pivot Point One: Do your client's difficulties arise out of struggles with attention or excessive activity?	Attention Deficit Hyperactivity Disorder
Pivot Point Two: Does your client experience unevenness in learning abilities, fairing well in some areas and much more poorly in others?	Specific Learning Disorder
Pivot Point Three: Do your client's concerns include difficulties related to cognition and learning in all or most areas?	Intellectual Disabilities
Pivot Point Four: Do your client's difficulties seem to center around verbal and/or non-verbal communication?	Communication Disorders
Pivot Point Five: Do your client's difficulties pervade social, emotional and communication difficulties and include stereotyped movement or restricted interests?	Autism Spectrum Disorder
Pivot Point Six: Do your client's difficulties stem from problematic patterns of movement?	Motor Disorders
• Do your client's difficulties stem from difficulties with mastery of coordinated movement?	Developmental Coordination Disorder
• Do your client's difficulties involve repetitive and seemingly purposeless behavior?	Stereotypic Movement Disorder
• Do your client's difficulties include irresistible urges to make sounds or movements without function?	Tic Disorders

doesn't share what he is exploring as the other children do. When stressed, Austin can become quickly overwhelmed and bite himself or pound his head into the wall. He is also easily upset by changes in schedule or diet. Austin is showing characteristics of which diagnosis?

Gurveer

Gurveer, age 6, was born with a rare genetic disorder, Lesch-Nyhan syndrome. As a result, Gurveer bites his hands and lips throughout the day and can't control the writhing motions in his body. The children in his classroom won't approach him and he is often teased by others. What diagnosis in addition to Lesch-Nyhan syndrome is appropriate?

Nakita

Nakita has been showing signs of significant difficulty with both attention and hyperactivity at home and at school for more than a year.

Mehdi

In school, Mehdi, age 8, frequently leaves his seat without permission, fidgets, seems to find playing quietly to be very challenging, has difficulty waiting his turn and answers questions before being called on. His teachers are both concerned and irritated.

Ryan

Ryan has experienced multiple motor tics since he began middle school and had his first vocal tic in high school.

Felicity

For the past 2 years, Felicity has had a vocal tic but has never experienced a motor tic.

Lina

In the past 3 weeks, Lina, age 14, has developed a motor tic. She is not currently taking a medication nor has she recently been sick.

Narrative Cases in Neurodevelopmental Disorders

Rose

Ms. Preston, a classroom teacher, has invited Mr. and Mrs. Fuller to talk with her about the concerns she has about their 10-year-old daughter, Rose. "I asked you to come so that I could share some of the concerns I've had about Rose, concerns I've had for about 8 months. I've noticed that Rose is very easily distracted by other children during the day in the classroom, when they are in the hallway, or on the playground. I've also noticed this makes it difficult for Rose to concentrate while I'm teaching. She is often coming to school without her homework, which is also a problem. I have tried a number of different things to try to support Rose so that she can remember her homework but these supports have not been as effective as I hoped they would be. Another concern that I need to share is that Rose often doesn't seem to hear directions because she is so distracted by other things. She makes errors that I really think are due more to carelessness than to difficulty with comprehension. She's definitely a smart kid and can do the work. I think it would be important to get Rose tested and see what is going on and how we can help her." Mrs. Preston shares.

"I'm sorry that this is happening but I'm not surprised. Rose can't seem to remember to do her chores without a lot of reminders. Same thing with her homework. We try to stay on top of the homework but we aren't always sure what homework is due. Rose needs a lot of reminders and a lot of redirection. She gets distracted easily," Mrs. Fuller offers. Mr. Fuller adds, "We've noticed that Rose has a tendency to interrupt a lot. She has been called a 'motor mouth' by some of her friends and she has shed some tears about it. Rose doesn't seem to understand what it means to be quiet. She plays so loudly she sometimes wakes her little brother and she has a hard time with things like waiting her turn. She's constantly wiggling in her chair. It's a source of constant nagging on our part. We love her but, boy, she can be a handful."

Jackson

Jackson, age 14, has just been released from the hospital after an event in which he tried to strangle his sister after an argument over video games. In his early development, Jackson experienced delays in language and both large and small motor skills. By age 3, he was given to significant and frequent tantrums that his parents describe as "very difficult to deal with." Jackson's parents report that he appeared to have normal receptive language skills, for example, he followed basic instructions well. However, Jackson was delayed in his use of expressive language and often used three-word phrases to communicate his needs until age 6; however, he displayed little in the way of communication of ideas, interests or feelings. Jackson also showed little interest in other children and generally occupied himself with isolated play. His play rarely seemed to include imaginary elements but featured careful examination of objects that spin, or creating sound with toys.

At age 6, after entering Kindergarten and displaying several difficulties of concern to teachers and his parents, Jackson was tested and was found to have a full-scale IQ of 115. The psychologist noted in her assessment report that Jackson struggled with both large and small motor skills, such as throwing and catching a ball. Jackson was also observed to have difficulties establishing peer relationships. Thanks to the report, Jackson was found eligible for special education services as "developmentally delayed." Since that time, Jackson has received speech therapy services to encourage reciprocal communication through the school system. At age 12, Jackson was placed in an alternative school setting where ongoing behavioral problems are being addressed through behavior modification, with limited success.

Jackson continues to have considerable difficulty in making use of non-verbal communication, including inhibited eye contact and body posture. Jackson finds it difficult to offer social and emotional reciprocity, such as showing interest in others' ideas or experiences, and consequently has built few age-appropriate friendships. Jackson has well-developed language skills but shows little interest in initiating or sustaining conversation outside of his interest areas (global warming and the effects of climate change on world ecosystems; birds of North and South America; effects of global warming on bird habitats).

Jackson has had difficulty managing negative emotion, and while he is largely calm and easy-going, when angry, Jackson has become violent. Jackson was removed from the public school setting following an incident in which he became angry and knocked another student to the ground and began pounding her in the head with a toy truck. When his stress levels are growing, Jackson rocks back and forth. What diagnosis would you anticipate finding in Jackson's records?

Pierce

Pierce, age 8, is in a class for children gifted in math and science. He is intrigued by the physical sciences and explains, "When I grow up I want to work for NASA." However, Mr. Frances, Pierce's teacher, is concerned about Pierce and has decided to consult with the school psychologist before contacting Pierce's parents. Mr. Frances shares, "I like Pierce a lot. He's a smart, kind and never causes any trouble, but he struggles a lot in the classroom and though he is a nice kid he hasn't made many friends. It seems like Pierce does not understand the basic unspoken rules of communication. He often uses a voice that is much louder than what would be expected inside, he almost shouts everything he says. And he seems to miss entirely subtle conversation cues, he doesn't seem to know when it is time for him to nod and let other kids know he's heard them, for instance, and there are times when I'm pretty sure he didn't understand me but he doesn't do anything to check. Like I said, he is a nice kid but he alienates the other kids by talking over them or changing the subject randomly. He doesn't say hello or good-bye, simple things like that. Pierce isn't able to make effective use of body language and often misses important facial expressions. So I have to be pretty direct and concrete with Pierce for him to get my meaning. I'm wondering if he needs to get tested or if I should talk to his parents."

References

Adrien, J. L., Faure, M., Perrot, A., Hameury, L., Garreau, B., Barthelemy, C., & Sauvage, D. (1991). Autism and family home movies: Preliminary findings. *Journal of Autism and Developmental Disorders, 21*(1), 43–49. https://doi.org/10.1007/BF02206996

Adrien, J. L., Lenoir, P., Martineau, J., Perrot, A., Hameury, L., Larmande, C., & Sauvage, D. (1993). Blind ratings of early symptoms of autism based upon family home movies. *Journal of the American Academy of Child & Adolescent Psychiatry, 32*(3), 617–626. https://doi.org/10.1097/00004583-199305000-00019

American Psychiatric Association. (1952). *Diagnostic and statistical manual of mental disorders.* Author.

American Psychiatric Association. (1980). *Diagnostic and statistical manual of mental disorders: DSM-III*. Author.

American Psychiatric Association. (1994). *Diagnostic and statistical manual of mental disorders: DSM IV*. Author.

American Psychiatric Association. (2013). Diagnostic and statistical manual of mental disorders: DSM 5. *BMC Medicine*, *17*, 133–137. https://doi.org/10.1176/appi.books.9780890425596

Ash, A. C., Redmond, S. M., Timler, G. R., & Kean, J. (2016). The influence of scale structure and sex on parental reports of children's social (pragmatic) communication symptoms. *Clinical Linguistics & Phonetics*, *31*(4), 293–312. https://doi.org/10.1080/02699206.2016.1257655

Attwood, T. (2001). *Asperger's syndrome: A guide for parents and professionals*. Jessica Kingsley Publishers.

Bai, D., Yip, B. H. K., Windham, G. C., Sourander, A., Francis, R., Yoffe, R., & Gissler, M. (2019). Association of genetic and environmental factors with autism in a 5-country cohort. *JAMA Psychiatry*, *76*(10), 1035–1043. https://doi.org/10.1001/jamapsychiatry.2019.1411

Baio, J., Wiggins, L., Christensen, D. L., Maenner, M. J., Daniels, J., Warren, Z., & Durkin, M. S. (2018). Prevalence of autism spectrum disorder among children aged 8 years—Autism and developmental disabilities monitoring network, 11 sites, United States, 2014. *MMWR Surveillance Summaries*, *67*(6), 1. https://doi.org/10.15585/mmwr.ss6706a1

Barkley, R. A. (Ed.). (2006). *Attention-deficit hyperactivity disorder: A handbook for diagnosis and treatment*. Guilford Publications.

Bechtel, N., Kobel, M., Penner, I. K., Specht, K., Klarhöfer, M., Scheffler, K., & Weber, P. (2012). Attention-deficit/hyperactivity disorder in childhood epilepsy: A neuropsychological and functional imaging study. *Epilepsia*, *53*(2), 325–333. https://doi.org/10.1111/j.1528-1167.2011.03377.x

Bettelheim, B. (1972). *The empty fortress: Infantile autism and the birth of the self*. Simon and Schuster.

Biederman, J., & Jellinek, M. S. (1998). Resolved: Mania is mistaken for ADHD in prepubertal children. *Journal of the American Academy of Child & Adolescent Psychiatry*, *37*(10), 1091–1099. https://doi.org/10.1097/00004583-199810000-00020

Blatt, G. J., Fitzgerald, C. M., Guptill, J. T., Booker, A. B., Kemper, T. L., & Bauman, M. L. (2001). Density and distribution of hippocampal neurotransmitter receptors in autism: An autoradiographic study. *Journal of Autism and Developmental Disorders*, *31*(6), 537–543. https://doi.org/10.1023/A:1013238809666

Bolton, P. F., Golding, J., Emond, A., & Steer, C. D. (2012). Autism spectrum disorder and autistic traits in the Avon Longitudinal study of parents and children: Precursors and early signs. *Journal of the American Academy of Child & Adolescent Psychiatry*, *51*(3), 249–260. https://doi.org/10.1016/j.jaac.2011.12.009

Brukner-Wertman, Y., Laor, N., & Golan, O. (2016). Social (Pragmatic) communication disorder and its relation to the autism spectrum: Dilemmas arising from the DSM-5 classification. *Journal of Autism and Developmental Disorders*, *46*(8), 2821–2829. https://doi.org/10.1007/s10803-016-2814-5

Cafiero, J. M. (2001). The effect of an augmentative communication intervention on the communication, behavior, and academic program of an adolescent with autism. *Focus on Autism and Other Developmental Disabilities*, *16*(3), 179–189. https://doi.org/10.1177/108835760101600306

Cascio, M. A. (2012). Neurodiversity: Autism pride among mothers of children with autism spectrum disorders. *Intellectual and Developmental Disabilities*, *50*(3), 273–283. https://doi.org/10.1352/1934-9556-50.3.273

Cavanna, A. E., Black, K. J., Hallett, M., & Voon, V. (2017). Neurobiology of the premonitory urge in Tourette's syndrome: Pathophysiology and treatment implications. *The Journal of Neuropsychiatry and Clinical Neurosciences*, *29*(2), 95–104. https://doi.org/10.1176/appi.neuropsych.16070141

Centers for Disease Control. (2020). *Measles cases and outbreaks*. https://www.cdc.gov/measles/cases-outbreaks.html

Cermak, S. A., Curtin, C., & Bandini, L. G. (2010). Food selectivity and sensory sensitivity in children with autism spectrum disorders. *Journal of the American Dietetic Association*, *110*(2), 238–246. https://doi.org/10.1016/j.jada.2009.10.032

Cherland, E., & Fitzpatrick, R. (1999). Psychotic side effects of psychostimulants: A 5-year review. *The Canadian Journal of Psychiatry*, *44*(8), 811–813. https://doi.org/10.1177/070674379904400810

Christensen, D. L., Braun, K. V. N., Baio, J., Bilder, D., Charles, J., Constantino, J. N., & Lee, L. C. (2018). Prevalence and characteristics of autism spectrum disorder among children aged 8 years—Autism and developmental disabilities monitoring network, 11 sites, United States, 2012. *MMWR Surveillance Summaries*, *65*(13), 1. https://doi.org/10.15585/mmwr.ss6513a1

Cohen, D. J., Volkmar, F. R., & Paul, R. (1986). Introduction: Issues in the classification of pervasive developmental disorders: History and current status of nosology. *Journal of the American Academy of Child Psychiatry*, *25*(2), 158–161. https://doi.org/10.1016/S0002-7138(09)60221-1

Deer, B. (2011). How the vaccine crisis was meant to make money. *BMJ*, *342*, c5258. https://doi.org/10.1136/bmj.c5258

Deliens, G., Leproult, R., Schmitz, R., Destrebecqz, A., & Peigneux, P. (2015). Sleep disturbances in autism spectrum disorders. *Review Journal of Autism and Developmental Disorders*, *2*(4), 343–356. https://doi.org/10.1007/s40489-015-0057-6

DuPaul, G. J., Belk, G. D., & Puzino, K. (2016). Evidence-based interventions for attention deficit hyperactivity disorder in children and adolescents. In L. A. Theodore (Ed.), *Handbook of evidence-based interventions for children and adolescents*. Springer Publishing Company.

Durkin, M. S., Maenner, M. J., Meaney, F. J., Levy, S. E., DiGuiseppi, C., Nicholas, J. S., & Schieve, L. A. (2010). Socioeconomic inequality in the prevalence of autism spectrum disorder: Evidence from a US cross-sectional study. *PlOS ONE*, *5*(7), e11551. https://doi.org/10.1371/journal.pone.0011551

Essoe, J. K.-Y., Grados, M. A., Singer, H. S., Myers, N. S., & Mcguire, J. F. (2019). Evidence-based treatment of Tourette's disorder and chronic tic disorders. *Expert Review of Neurotherapeutics*, *19*(11), 1103–1115. https://doi.org/10.1080/14737175.2019.1643236

Evans, S. W., Owens, J. S., & Bunford, N. (2014). Evidence-based psychosocial treatments for children and adolescents with attention-deficit/hyperactivity disorder. *Journal of Clinical Child & Adolescent Psychology*, *43*(4), 527–551. https://doi.org/10.1080/15374416.2013.850700

Evans, W. N., Morrill, M. S., & Parente, S. T. (2010). Measuring inappropriate medical diagnosis and treatment in survey data: The case of ADHD among school-age children. *Journal of Health Economics*, *29*(5), 657–673. https://doi.org/10.1016/j.jhealeco.2010.07.005

Fakhoury, M. (2015). Autistic spectrum disorders: A review of clinical features, theories and diagnosis. *International Journal of Developmental Neuroscience*, *43*, 70–77. https://doi.org/10.1016/j.ijdevneu.2015.04.003

Faraone, S. V., Rostain, A. L., Montano, C. B., Mason, O., Antshel, K. M., & Newcorn, J. H. (2019). Systematic review: Nonmedical use of prescription stimulants: Risk factors, outcomes, and risk reduction strategies. *Journal of the American Academy of Child & Adolescent Psychiatry*, *59*(1), 100–112.

Farrington, C. P., Miller, E., & Taylor, B. (2001). MMR and autism: Further evidence against a causal association. *Vaccine*, *19*(27), 3632–3635. https://doi.org/10.1016/S0264-410X(01)00097-4

Frances, A. (2013). *Saving normal: An insider's revolt against out-of-control psychiatric diagnosis, DSM-5, big pharma and the medicalization of ordinary life*. William Morrow.

Freeman, R. D., Soltanifar, A., & Baer, S. (2010). Stereotypic movement disorder: Easily missed. *Developmental Medicine & Child Neurology*, *52*(8), 733–738. https://doi.org/10.1111/j.1469-8749.2010.03627.x

Garnier, L. M., Arria, A. M., Caldeira, K. M., Vincent, K. B., O'Grady, K. E., & Wish, E. D. (2010). Sharing and selling of prescription medications in a college student sample. *The Journal of Clinical Psychiatry*, *71*(3), 262. https://doi.org/10.4088/JCP.09m05189ecr

Godlee, F., Smith, J., & Marcovitch, H. (2011, January 8). Wakefield's article linking MMR vaccine and autism was fraudulent. *British Medical Journal*, *342*(7788), 64–66. https://doi.org/10.1136/bmj.c7452

Gould, M. S., Walsh, B. T., Munfakh, J. L., Kleinman, M., Duan, N., Olfson, M., & Cooper, T. (2009). Sudden death and use of stimulant medications in youths. *American Journal of Psychiatry*, *166*(9), 992–1001. https://doi.org/10.1176/appi.ajp.2009.09040472

Greenspan, S. I., Wieder, S., & Simons, R. (1998). *The child with special needs: Encouraging intellectual and emotional growth*. Addison-Wesley/Addison Wesley Longman.

Griffiths, D. L., Farrell, L. J., Waters, A. M., & White, S. W. (2017). ASD traits among youth with obsessive–compulsive disorder. *Child Psychiatry & Human Development*, *48*(6), 911–921. https://doi.org/10.1007/s10578-017-0714-3

Grossman, R. B., & Tager-Flusberg, H. (2012). Quality matters! Differences between expressive and receptive non-verbal communication skills in adolescents with ASD. *Research in Autism Spectrum Disorders*, *6*(3), 1150–1155. https://doi.org/10.1016/j.rasd.2012.03.006

Grove, J., Ripke, S., Als, T. D., Mattheisen, M., Walters, R. K., Won, H., & Awashti, S. (2019). Identification of common genetic risk variants for autism spectrum disorder. *Nature Genetics*, *51*(3), 431–444. https://doi.org/10.1038/s41588-019-0344-8

Gutstein, S. E. (2000). *Autism Asperger's, solving the relationship puzzle: A new developmental program that opens the door to lifelong social & emotional growth*. Future Horizons.

Happé, F. (1994). *Autism: An introduction to psychological theory*. Harvard University Press.

Happé, F. (2005). *Autism: An introduction to psychological theory*. Psychology Press.

Harvey, E. A., Breaux, R. P., & Lugo-Candelas, C. I. (2016). Early development of comorbidity between symptoms of Attention-Deficit/Hyperactivity Disorder (ADHD) and Oppositional Defiant Disorder (ODD). *Journal of Abnormal Psychology*, *125*(2), 154. https://doi.org/10.1037/abn0000090

Heinrichs, R. (2003). *Perfect targets: Asperger syndrome and bullying: Practical solutions for surviving the social world*. AAPC Publishing.

Hinman, A. R., Orenstein, W. A., Schuchat, A., & Centers for Disease Control and Prevention. (2011). Vaccine-preventable diseases, immunizations, and MMWR: 1961–2011. *MMWR Surveillance Summaries*, *60*(Suppl 4), 49–57.

Holland, J., & Sayal, K. (2018). Relative age and ADHD symptoms, diagnosis and medication: A systematic review. *European Child & Adolescent Psychiatry*, *28*(11), 1–13. https://doi.org/10.1007/s00787-018-1229-6

Houghton, R., de Vries, F., & Loss, G. (2020). Psychostimulants/atomoxetine and serious cardiovascular events in children with ADHD or Autism spectrum disorder. *CNS Drugs*, *34*(1), 93–101. https://doi.org/10.1007/s40263-019-00686-4

Jafari, P. J., Younesi, S. D., Asgary, A., & Kazemi, M. (2019). Pragmatic abilities in children with neurodevelopmental disorders: Development of pragmatic abilities questionnaire based on the Rasch rating scale model. *Psychology Research and Behavior Management*, *12*, 629–639. https://doi.org/10.2147/prbm.s209345

Jensen, C. M., & Steinhausen, H. C. (2015). Comorbid mental disorders in children and adolescents with attention-deficit/hyperactivity disorder in a large nationwide study. *ADHD Attention Deficit and Hyperactivity Disorders*, *7*(1), 27–38. https://doi.org/10.1007/s12402-014-0142-1

Kanner, L. (1949). Problems of nosology and psychodynamics of early infantile autism. *American Journal of Orthopsychiatry*, *19*(3), 416. https://doi.org/10.1111/j.1939-0025.1949.tb05441.x

Kapp, S. K., Gillespie-Lynch, K., Sherman, L. E., & Hutman, T. (2013). Deficit, difference, or both? Autism and neurodiversity. *Developmental Psychology*, *49*(1), 59. https://doi.org/10.1037/a0028353

Koegel, R. L., Bradshaw, J. L., Ashbaugh, K., & Koegel, L. K. (2014). Improving question-asking initiations in young children with autism using pivotal response treatment. *Journal of Autism and Developmental Disorders*, *44*(4), 816–827. https://doi.org/10.1007/s10803-013-1932-6

Kogan, M. D., Vladutiu, C. J., Schieve, L. A., Ghandour, R. M., Blumberg, S. J., Zablotsky, B., & Lu, M. C. (2018). The prevalence of parent-reported autism spectrum disorder among US children. *Pediatrics, 142*(6), e20174161. https://doi.org/10.1542/peds.2017-4161

Kral, M. C., Lally, M. D., & Boan, A. D. (2017). Effectiveness and side effect profile of stimulant medication for the treatment of attention-deficit/hyperactivity disorder in youth with epilepsy. *Journal of Child and Adolescent Psychopharmacology, 27*(8), 735–740.

Leckman, J. F., King, R. A., & Bloch, M. H. (2014). Clinical features of Tourette syndrome and tic disorders. *Journal of Obsessive-Compulsive and Related Disorders, 3*(4), 372–379. https://doi.org/10.1016/j.jocrd.2014.03.004

Mackenzie, K. (2018). Stereotypic movement disorders. *Seminars in Pediatric Neurology, 25*, 19–24. https://doi.org/10.1016/j.spen.2017.12.004

Martino, D., & Hedderly, T. (2019). Tics and stereotypies: A comparative clinical review. *Parkinsonism & Related Disorders, 59*, 117–124. https://doi.org/10.1016/j.parkreldis.2019.02.005

McCracken, J. T., McGough, J., Shah, B., Cronin, P., Hong, D., Aman, M. G., & McDougle, C. J. (2002). Risperidone in children with autism and serious behavioral problems. *New England Journal of Medicine, 347*(5), 314–321. https://doi.org/10.1056/NEJMoa013171

Moran, L. V., Ongur, D., Hsu, J., Castro, V. M., Perlis, R. H., & Schneeweiss, S. (2019). Psychosis with methylphenidate or amphetamine in patients with ADHD. *New England Journal of Medicine, 380*(12), 1128–1138. https://doi.org/10.1056/NEJMoa1813751

Morrow, R. L., Garland, E. J., Wright, J. M., Maclure, M., Taylor, S., & Dormuth, C. R. (2012). Influence of relative age on diagnosis and treatment of attention-deficit/hyperactivity disorder in children. *Canadian Medical Association Journal 184*(7), 755–762. https://doi.org/10.1503/cmaj.111619

Mosholder, A. D., Gelperin, K., Hammad, T. A., Phelan, K., & Johann-Liang, R. (2009). Hallucinations and other psychotic symptoms associated with the use of attention-deficit/hyperactivity disorder drugs in children. *Pediatrics, 123*(2), 611–616. https://doi.org/10.1542/peds.2008-0185

Neely, L., Gerow, S., Rispoli, M., Lang, R., & Pullen, N. (2016). Treatment of echolalia in individuals with autism spectrum disorder: A systematic review. *Review Journal of Autism and Developmental Disorders, 3*(1), 82–91. https://doi.org/10.1007/s40489-015-0067-4

Neumeier, S. M., & Brown, L. X. (2020). Torture in the name of treatment: The mission to stop the shocks in the age of deinstitutionalization. In S. K. Kapp (Ed.), *Autistic community and the neurodiversity movement* (pp. 195–210). Palgrave Macmillan.

Norbury, C. F. (2013). Practitioner review: Social (pragmatic) communication disorder conceptualization, evidence and clinical implications. *Journal of Child Psychology and Psychiatry, 55*(3), 204–216. https://doi.org/10.1111/jcpp.12154

Owren, T., & Stenhammer, T. (2013). Neurodiversity: Accepting autistic difference. *Learning Disability Practice, 16*(4), 32–37. https://doi.org/10.7748/ldp2013.05.16.4.32.e681

Paul, R., Augustyn, A., Klin, A., & Volkmar, F. R. (2005). Perception and production of prosody by speakers with autism spectrum disorders. *Journal of Autism and Developmental Disorders, 35*(2), 205–220. https://doi.org/10.1007/s10803-004-1999-1

Pedreño, C., Pousa, E., Navarro, J. B., Pàmias, M., & Obiols, J. E. (2017). Exploring the components of advanced theory of mind in autism spectrum disorder. *Journal of Autism and Developmental Disorders, 47*(8), 2401–2409. https://doi.org/10.1007/s10803-017-3156-7

Pelham, W. E., Jr., & Fabiano, G. A. (2008). Evidence-based psychosocial treatments for attention-deficit/hyperactivity disorder. *Journal of Clinical Child & Adolescent Psychology, 37*(1), 184–214. https://doi.org/10.1080/15374410701818681

Pelham, W. E., Smith, B. H., Evans, S. W., Bukstein, O., Gnagy, E. M., Greiner, A. R., & Sibley, M. H. (2017). The effectiveness of short- and long-acting stimulant medications for adolescents with ADHD in a naturalistic secondary school setting. *Journal of Attention Disorders, 21*(1), 40–45. https://doi.org/10.1177/1087054712474688

Pham, T., Milanaik, R., Kaplan, A., Papaioannou, H., & Adesman, A. (2017). Household diversion of prescription stimulants: Medication misuse by parents of children with attention-deficit/hyperactivity disorder. *Journal of Child and Adolescent Psychopharmacology, 27*(8), 741–746. https://doi.org/10.1089/cap.2016.0058

Postorino, V., Kerns, C. M., Vivanti, G., Bradshaw, J., Siracusano, M., & Mazzone, L. (2017). Anxiety disorders and obsessive-compulsive disorder in individuals with autism spectrum disorder. *Current Psychiatry Reports, 19*(12), 92. https://doi.org/10.1007/s11920-017-0846-y

Power, T. J., Hom, J., & Huang, P. (2018). Current best practices for assessing and treating children and adolescents with attention-deficit/hyperactivity disorder. *Current Treatment Options in Pediatrics, 4*(1), 94–107. https://doi.org/10.1007/s40746-018-0111-6

Pringsheim, T., Okun, M. S., Müller-Vahl, K., Martino, D., Jankovic, J., Cavanna, A. E., & Piacentini, J. (2019). Practice guideline recommendations summary: Treatment of tics in people with Tourette syndrome and chronic tic disorders. *Neurology, 92*(19), 896–906. https://doi.org/10.1212/WNL.0000000000007466

Rao, T. S., & Andrade, C. (2011). The MMR vaccine and autism: Sensation, refutation, retraction, and fraud. *Indian Journal of Psychiatry, 53*(2), 95. https://doi.org/10.4103/0019-5545.82529

Reale, L., Bartoli, B., Cartabia, M., Zanetti, M., Costantino, M. A., Canevini, M. P., & Group, Lombardy ADHD. (2017). Comorbidity prevalence and treatment outcome in children and adolescents with ADHD. *European Child & Adolescent Psychiatry, 26*(12), 1443–1457. https://doi.org/10.1007/s00787-017-1005-z

Rekers, G. A., & Lovaas, O. I. (1974). Behavioral treatment of deviant sex-role behaviors in a male child. *Journal of Applied Behavior Analysis, 7*(2), 173–190. https://doi.org/10.1901/jaba.1974.7-173

Rimland, B. (1974). Infantile autism: Status of research. *Child Personality & Psychopathology*, (19), 130–133. https://doi.org/10.1177/070674377401900203

Saban-Bezalel, R., Dolfin, D., Laor, N., & Mashal, N. (2019). Irony comprehension and mentalizing ability in children with and without autism spectrum disorder. *Research in Autism Spectrum Disorders, 58*, 30–38.

Shea, S., Turgay, A., Carroll, A., Schulz, M., Orlik, H., Smith, I., & Dunbar, F. (2004). Risperidone in the treatment of disruptive behavioral symptoms in children with autistic and other pervasive developmental disorders. *Pediatrics, 114*(5), e634–e641. https://doi.org/10.1542/peds.2003-0264-F

Shibib, S., & Chalhoub, N. (2009). Stimulant induced psychosis. *Child and Adolescent Mental Health, 14*(1), 20–23. https://doi.org/10.1111/j.1475-3588.2008.00490.x

Siegel, B. (1997). *The world of the autistic child: Understanding and treating autistic spectrum disorders.* Oxford University Press.

Silberman, S. (2015). *Neurotribes: The legacy of autism and the future of neurodiversity.* Penguin.

Slagstad, K. (2019). Asperger, the Nazis and the children-the history of the birth of a diagnosis. *Tidsskrift for den Norske laegeforening: Tidsskrift for praktisk medicin, ny raekke, 139*(9).

Solomon, A. (2013). *Far from the tree: Parents, children, and the search for identity.* Simon & Schuster.

Specht, M. W., Woods, D. W., Nicotra, C. M., Kelly, L. M., Ricketts, E. J., Conelea, C. A., & Walkup, J. T. (2013). Effects of tic suppression: Ability to suppress, rebound, negative reinforcement, and habituation to the premonitory urge. *Behaviour Research and Therapy, 51*(1), 24–30. https://doi.org/10.1016/j.brat.2012.09.009

Subramanyam, A. A., Mukherjee, A., Dave, M., & Chavda, K. (2019). Clinical practice guidelines for autism spectrum disorders. *Indian Journal of Psychiatry, 61*(Suppl. 2), 254.

Swineford, L. B., Thurm, A., Baird, G., Wetherby, A. M., & Swedo, S. (2014). Social (pragmatic) communication disorder: A research review of this new DSM-5 diagnostic category. *Journal of Neurodevelopmental Disorders, 6*(1), 1–8. https://doi.org/10.1186/1866-1955-6-41

Szatmari, P., Offord, D. R., & Boyle, M. H. (1989). Ontario child health study: Prevalence of attention deficit disorder with hyperactivity. *Journal of Child Psychology and Psychiatry, 30*(2), 219–223. https://doi.org/10.1111/j.1469-7610.1989.tb00236.x

Travers, J., & Krezmien, M. (2018). Racial disparities in autism identification in the United States during 2014. *Exceptional Children, 84*(4), 403–419. https://doi.org/10.1177/0014402918771337

Van Steensel, F. J., Bögels, S. M., & Perrin, S. (2011). Anxiety disorders in children and adolescents with autistic spectrum disorders: A meta-analysis. *Clinical Child and Family Psychology Review, 14*(3), 302. https://doi.org/10.1007/s10567-011-0097-0

Van Steensel, F. J., & Heeman, E. J. (2017). Anxiety levels in children with autism spectrum disorder: A meta-analysis. *Journal of Child and Family Studies, 26*(7), 1753–1767. https://doi.org/10.1007/s10826-017-0687-7

Visser, S. N., Danielson, M. L., Bitsko, R. H., Holbrook, J. R., Kogan, M. D., Ghandour, R. M., & Blumberg, S. J. (2014). Trends in the parent-report of health care provider-diagnosed and medicated attention-deficit/hyperactivity disorder: United States, 2003–2011. *Journal of the American Academy of Child & Adolescent Psychiatry*, *53*(1), 34–46.

Wajszilber, D., Santiseban, J. A., & Gruber, R. (2018). Sleep disorders in patients with ADHD: Impact and management challenges. *Nature and Science of Sleep*, *10*, 453. https://doi.org/10.2147/NSS.S163074

Wakefield, A. J., Murch, S. H., Anthony, A., Linnell, J., Casson, D. M., Malik, M., & Valentine, A. (1998). RETRACTED: Ileal-lymphoid-nodular hyperplasia, non-specific colitis, and pervasive developmental disorder in children. *Lancet*, *351*(9103), 637–641. https://doi.org/10.1016/S0140-6736(97)11096-0

Wing, L. (1996). Autism spectrum disorders: No evidence for or against an increase in prevalence. *BMJ*, *312*, 327–328. https://doi.org/10.1136/bmj.312.7027.327

Wong, C., Odom, S. L., Hume, K. A., Cox, A. W., Fettig, A., Kucharczyk, S., & Schultz, T. R. (2015). Evidence-based practices for children, youth, and young adults with autism spectrum disorder: A comprehensive review. *Journal of Autism and Developmental Disorders*, *45*(7), 1951–1966. https://doi.org/10.1007/s10803-014-2351-z

Wymbs, B. T., Wymbs, F. A., & Dawson, A. E. (2015). Child ADHD and ODD behavior interacts with parent ADHD symptoms to worsen parenting and interparental communication. *Journal of Abnormal Child Psychology*, *43*(1), 107–119. https://doi.org/10.1007/s10802-014-9887-4

Yasuda, Y., Hashimoto, R., Nakae, A., Kang, H., Ohi, K., Yamamori, H., & Takeda, M. (2016). Sensory cognitive abnormalities of pain in autism spectrum disorder: A case–control study. *Annals of General Psychiatry*, *15*(1), 8. https://doi.org/10.1186/s12991-016-0095-1

6 Schizophrenia Spectrum and Other Psychotic Disorders

CHEREE HAMMOND AND MICHAEL HORST

Not so long ago after, a long sleepless layover in a Chinese airport, I (Cheree) had settled in for an equally long flight from Beijing to Toronto. The flight had been delayed due to bad weather and had started with a lot of turbulence that didn't seem to be changing much as time went on. I placed my earbuds in my ears, selected a movie that looked interesting and resigned myself to the rocking and shaking of the plane. I was about 2 hours into my flight when I was suddenly jolted awake by screaming and loud thuds. The body of the plane rocked violently. The overhead lights had a strange amber glow and I saw that smoke was pouring out of the overhead compartments. The oxygen masks dropped from overhead and people were fumbling to place them on their faces. I turned to the woman sitting next to me, my heart pounding. She was sleeping soundly, as was her son next to her. Then, just as suddenly, I realized the screaming was coming from my earbuds. I took them out and looked around again. The light was indeed an unusual color, and the plane was moving like a ship in a storm, but there was no smoke, and no oxygen masks. My fellow passengers were either dozing, watching movies or chatting with the person next to them. I realized my sleep-deprived mind had filled in the details of my unconscious fear, aided by the sounds of the audio of the movie in my headphones.

The half-dream-half-hallucination I had experienced had been startling, at least for a moment. My whole body had responded to the reality my mind had formed around the disconcerting rocking of the plane and the screams coming from the film that my exhausted mind had tried to process into a cohesive whole. The experience offered me a window into what it must be like to experience a psychosis, one of the more distressing and striking manifestations of mental illness. This chapter will briefly describe each of the disorders along the schizophrenia continuum and will touch on treatments for these disorders. However, the chapter will focus on two topics important to a clinician's diagnostic process; first, we will explore points that will support clinicians in recognizing prodromal symptoms and identifying clients at ultra high risk (UHR) for developing a schizophrenia spectrum disorder. Second, we will give some attention to the current conversation around the proposed transdiagnostic spectrum approach to the affective and non-affective psychotic disorders (Reininghaus et al., 2016). At the end of this chapter, you will find a number of cases that can be diagnosed.

Features of the Schizophrenia Spectrum

The DSM 5 identifies five primary domains shared by the schizophrenia spectrum and other psychotic disorders, hallucinations, delusions, grossly disorganized behavior, disorganized thinking and speech (described as positive symptoms) and a collection of negative symptoms. A simple way to remember the difference between positive and negative symptoms is that positive symptoms are those that we would normally not anticipate seeing in a person, such as very odd ideas (delusions) or strange and disturbing perceptual experiences (hallucinations). In contrast, negative symptoms are characteristics we would anticipate seeing in a healthy person but are absent or noticeably dampened, as with a flattened affect or catatonic behavior (American Psychiatric Association [APA], 2013; Foussias & Remington, 2008). Both positive and negative symptoms can be expressed in a great variety of ways.

Positive Symptoms: Hallucinations and Delusions. Positive symptoms are those that immediately raise concern and are probably most often associated with the schizophrenia spectrum. These symptoms include hallucinations and delusions. Hallucinations are perceptual disruptions that can involve any of the sensory perceptions and are without basis in outside stimuli, for instance hearing another's voice while alone in a silent room. The most commonly occurring hallucinations are either visual or auditory. The more complex and well formed the auditory or visual material and the more impaired the insight about these experiences, the poorer the prognosis (APA, 2013). Consequently, a great deal of research has been conducted and assessment tools developed to measure the severity of positive symptoms, such as the Revised Beliefs About Voices Questionnaire (BAVQ-R) (Chadwick et al., 2000) or the Psychotic Symptom Rating Scales (PSYRATS) (Haddock et al., 1999) and so on, as well as for negative symptoms, such as the Four-Item Negative Symptom Assessment (NSA-4) (Alphs et al., 2010).

Delusions, on the other hand, are unusual or implausible thoughts that don't shift even in the face of disconfirming evidence. Delusions tend to fall within one of five general themes: grandiose, referential, persecutory, nihilistic or somatic. When a person experiences grandiose delusions, their view of themselves is one in which their talents, wealth or fame is perceived to be much more positive than it is in reality. The person experiencing a grandiose delusion is not simply boasting or puffing up their own capabilities but fully believes themselves to be greatly superior in some way. A referential delusion, on the other hand, is one in which a person believes that unrelated cues in the environment have some message or meaning for them alone, such as a secret coded message in billboard advertisements meant just for them. A persecutory delusion is one in which a person is convinced that another person or organization

TABLE 6.01 Domains and Positive and Negative Symptoms of the Schizophrenia Spectrum

Five Domains of the Schizophrenia Spectrum	Positive Symptoms	Negative Symptoms
Delusions	*Delusions*	*Flattened Affect*
Hallucinations	*Hallucinations*	*Poverty of Speech*
Disorganized Thinking/speech	*Disorganized Thinking/speech*	*Catatonia*
Grossly Disorganized Behavior	*Grossly Disorganized Behavior*	*Avolition*
Negative Symptoms		*Prosody*

Source: American Psychiatric Association (2013).

wants to hurt or control them in some way. Delusions of persecution can range in how plausible they might be, for example, imagining that the dean of the college wants you to fail out of school as opposed to imagining that the Pentagon is plotting one's demise. Nihilistic delusions are composed of implausible fears that something terrible is about to befall the person or those around them; for instance, carrying the conviction that an asteroid is sure to hit the earth and destroy life on the planet. Finally, somatic delusions are those related to the body, such as a strong belief that insects are moving underneath the skin.

While some delusions are focused on the body, others are related to the mind and thought. Thought insertion is the delusion that some other force or entity is placing thoughts into one's mind, while thought withdrawal is the belief that someone or some organization is removing one's thoughts without permission. Finally, thought broadcasting is the delusion that others can hear one's thoughts, almost as if they were being projected by a radio (APA, 2013).

Context is Everything: Cultural and Normative Beliefs and Experiences. Beliefs influence our experiences as do cultural norms. Culture is also what shapes our ideas about how to interact with one another. Cultural norms set the boundaries for what gets included within the outer reaches of "normal" and what falls just inside the vessel of what is described as "abnormal." This boundary, then, is a shifting one and varies from one community or group to another. Ideas that are embraced by one group can be rejected as bizaare in another. When we consider beliefs and perceptual experiences, clinicians should always consider the context in which the individual who experiences them lives and learns. Ideas that are culturally sanctioned, even if very strange to the clinician, should not be viewed as psychotic symptomatology.

Grossly disorganized behavior. Most of us can point to an area of our lives that could be described as disorganized, evidenced by, for example, by a "chairdrobe" in the corner of the bedroom of not quite dirty and not quite clean laundry, appointments missed often enough to irritate others or an unsightly cluttered desk. This type of disorganization is born out of differences in preference, priority and focus and are not what is being described here. The behaviors that are considered for diagnosis of psychosis are given the label "grossly disorganized" and describe behavior that has an odd, unpredictable or purposeless quality and can be expressed in a number of ways. Catatonic behavior occupies the extreme end of this collection of behaviors and may include rigidity or extreme flexibility in the limbs, unusual body postures or extraordinarily slow movement, facial grimacing and so on (APA, 2013).

Disorganized thoughts. Additionally, persons with disorders on this continuum frequently find it difficult to organize their thoughts and, as a result, are often unable to care for their basic health and hygiene. Evidence of disorganized thinking is seen in disorganized speech, which plays out on a continuum of severity. At one end, clients may find that they easily lose track of their train of thought and can be tangential, others have such difficulty that their communication becomes very confusing or impossible to understand, a word salad, and may even contain words or phrases that are idiosyncratic to the individual, known as neologisms. Needless to say, these difficulties interfere with social and occupational functioning, often leaving clients at risk for homelessness and social isolation (APA, 2013).

Negative Symptoms. Typically, when a person is faced with a difficult or painful situation, for instance, when a beloved childhood friend is lost unexpectedly to illness, we expect to see the emotional residue of that experience wash across the person's face. Similarly, when something surprising and delightful happens, we anticipate a smile or laughter. But when these responses are absent or somehow less evident than is typical, we describe this as a flattened affect, just one of several of the negative symptoms of the schizophrenia spectrum. Other negative symptoms include an inability to feel pleasure, difficulty identifying or experiencing one's own emotions, a lack of volition, and impoverished speech (APA, 2013; Foussias & Remington, 2008; Kane, 2013).

The Schizophrenia Continuum

Five disorders sit on the schizophrenia spectrum continuum: delusional disorder (DD), brief psychotic disorder, schizophreniform disorder, schizophrenia and schizoaffective disorder. One syndrome, attenuated psychosis syndrome (APS), is described in the section of the DSM reserved for research. Finally, schizotypal personality disorder is mentioned but not included within this continuum and will be discussed in the personality disorders chapter. The disorders of the schizophrenia continuum are very similar in that they share psychotic symptoms but differ in intensity, duration and in the individual's capacity for functioning independently. Each of these will be described briefly below; however, as always, you should consult your DSM 5 for the full criteria for each.

Delusional Disorder. The mildest of the schizophrenia spectrum is DD. Persons experiencing a DD are unique to the spectrum in that their symptoms are limited to delusions, though these delusions persist for at least 1 month. Delusions experienced

BOX 6.01 TRY THIS: IDENTIFYING DELUSIONS

Read through the following case scenarios: Chad, Akihito, Eleni and Daisy and determine the type of delusion being experienced, either referential, persecutory, nihilistic or somatic.

Eleni. Eleni is aware that some of her neighbors are supporters of the Black Lives Matter movement. She has been terribly disturbed by the belief that the local neighborhood association has been plotting a violent socialist uprising. Eleni has confronted members of the association who have assured her that their primary goal is to plan the 4th of July block party, but Eleni is frightened by their "secret meetings" and is considering getting a gun to protect herself.

Akihito. Though Akihito has been to several specialists and has even had functional magnetic resonance imaging (fMRI) testing on three separate occasions and he has been reassured that he is in good health, he has a strong and unshakable belief that he has a brain tumor. He believes he can feel the tumor tingling at night before he goes to sleep.

Chad. Each morning Chad scours the paper for coded messages that provide instruction for his day. Chad believes he has been receiving these messages from the angel Gabriel for about 5 months.

Daisy. Since Daisy was in 6th grade and learned that the universe expands and contracts, she has been burdened with the feeling that something "devastating and irreversible will happen to the universe." This years-long worry has tainted most days with a feeling of dread and sadness despite being reassured that the progress of change in the universe is very slow and will not play out dramatically in her lifetime.

by persons with this disorder fall into one of six general categories that should be indicated with a specifier: erotomanic, grandiose, jealous, persecutory, somatic, mixed (for those in whom no one theme predominates). DD is unique in that persons diagnosed with DD don't experience impairment as a result of their delusion, apart from the residue of the delusion itself, and does not result in odd or bizarre behavior (APA, 2013).

Peralta and Cuesta, 2016, conducted a study of just over 500 participants comparing the symptoms and histories of those with DD with those with schizophrenia. They found that these two populations differed in a number of key ways. First, the study participants diagnosed with DD were more likely to have used substances than the group diagnosed with schizophrenia and had a later age of onset. While those in the DD group demonstrated stronger personal care skills, more robust histories of paid work and better social functioning, they also endorsed more affective symptoms than those with schizophrenia. Importantly, those in the DD group had "fewer but more severe delusions," (p. 2829) as well as more conviction in those delusions than the other group. In this study, only those in the DD group experienced delusions of jealousy or somatically themed delusions.

BOX 6.02 TRY THIS: DISCERNING PSYCHOSIS FROM CULTURALLY SANCTIONED BELIEFS AND EXPERIENCES

Read the two cases, Ray and Martin. Is your first impression one of a psychotic episode or a culturally sanctioned belief? Why? What questions do you have for them that would clarify this for you?

Ray. Though Ray, a 22-year-old architecture student, was raised in a traditional Methodist church he has spent the last 4 years studying and practicing Reiki, a form of energy healing. Ray now believes that he is able to use his skills to heal others by placing his hands on them and using Reiki technology to free their energy field of illness. Ray feels that his future is in Reiki rather than architecture as his parents had hoped.

Martin. Six months ago, Martin, a 22-year-old business student, suddenly had the idea that he had "the healing touch of the Phoenix." Feeling that perhaps this new development was not something he should tell anyone, he kept this new power to himself until one day, on the subway, he noticed a woman with a bandaged leg sitting in the seat next to him. He surreptitiously reached his hand over and laid it on her leg, and then directed a "beam of healing fire" into her injury. The woman immediately became angry, pulled away from him, protesting loudly. Martin believed that her anger was an energetic product of the healing fire and immediately felt affirmed that his healing powers were working. Since that time, Martin has repeatedly touched strangers in an effort to heal them and has several times met with wrath from the recipient. He describes having an irresistible urge to heal others, "like a call from the spirit world."

Brief Psychotic Disorder. Brief psychotic disorder and schizophreniform disorder share features with schizophrenia but differ in their duration. A person diagnosed with brief psychotic disorder will have experienced delusions, hallucinations, disorganized speech, grossly disorganized or catatonic behavior for more than 1 day but for less than 1 month. Sometimes a large stressor alone, or combined with others, can overwhelm a person and bring on these symptoms. When exploring this diagnosis, it is important to specify if the symptoms occurred with marked stressor(s) or without. Additionally, brief psychotic disorder can have its onset during pregnancy or up to 4 weeks post-partum and should be indicated with the appropriate specifier (APA, 2013).

Schizophreniform Disorder. Experiences related to schizophreniform disorder last between 1 and 6 months and include at least two of the following: delusions, hallucinations, disorganized speech, grossly disorganized or catatonic behavior and/or negative symptoms. The DSM-5 notes that if this diagnosis is made before the person has recovered from their symptoms, then it must be made as a provisional diagnosis in

BOX 6.03 KEY DEFINITIONS: SCHIZOPHRENIA SPECTRUM DISORDERS

BLIPS. This acronym for brief limited intermittent psychotic symptoms, represent symptoms that don't rise to the level of diagnosis for a formal schizophrenia spectrum disorder but place the experiencer at ultra-high risk (UHR) for developing a disorder on this continuum (Fusar-Poli et al., 2017).

Command Hallucinations. Command hallucinations are auditory hallucinations that feature a voice directing the individual to act in one way or another.

Delusions. Delusions are odd beliefs or idiosyncratic beliefs that are contradicted by logic, reason or common understanding of reality. These beliefs rise to the level of delusion when despite evidence to the contrary the belief is firmly maintained. However, for a belief to be delusional, it must fall outside of the commonly accepted belief of the individual's community (APA, 2013).

Disorganized Speech. Disorganized speech is a category of communication that can include derailing or loose associations (jumping from one topic to another unrelated topic without transition or cue), word salad (incoherent strings of unrelated words or phrases), neologisms (words created by the speaker with meaning known only to that person), echolalia (echoing their conversation partners rather than conversing with them) and so on (APA, 2013).

Disorganized Thinking. Disorganized thinking, usually in evidence in a person's speech, describes an inability to maintain a coherent stream of thought. Thoughts may become quickly derailed and jump from one idea or topic to another, sometimes making it impossible to respond to another's questions or ideas (APA, 2013).

Echolalia. Echolalia is a pattern in which a person simply repeats what has been said by another person rather than responding with original meaningful content (APA, 2013).

Echopraxia. Echopraxia is a type of grossly disorganized behavior in which a person mimics the body movements of another.

Grossly Disorganized Behavior. This category of observable behaviors, sometimes referred to as catatonia, describes a wide range of responses from rigid or limp limbs, stupor, non-responsiveness and so on, but may also include purposeless movements, unusual mannerisms or echopraxia.

Hallucinations. Hallucinations are spontaneous perceptual experiences that are not triggered by outside stimuli and can involve any of the five senses but are most frequently experienced in visual or auditory senses (Howes & Murray, 2014).

Narrative Auditory Hallucinations. Narrative auditory hallucinations are unique in that they feature a voice or voices that describe the experiencer's every action. This type of hallucination is associated with especially poor outcomes.

Negative Symptoms. Sometimes described as residual symptoms, reflect deficits such as social withdrawal and impairment in social role function as well as flattened affect, a lack of motivation and poverty of speech (Howes & Murray, 2014).

Positive Symptoms. Positive psychotic symptoms denote the presence of hallucinations and/or delusions (Howes & Murray, 2014).

Prosody. Prosody describes speech that lacks natural inflection that lends meaning and emphasis to communication (APA, 2013).

Thought Broadcasting. This type of delusion is the belief that others can hear one's thoughts.

Thought Insertion. This delusion is the belief that unwanted thoughts have been put into one's head by an external force.

Thought Withdrawal. This delusion describes the belief that one's thoughts have been removed by an external force or entity.

case a person's symptoms persist beyond 6 months. Specifiers for this diagnosis include with or without good prognostic features, with catatonia, and a rating of each primary symptom of psychosis on a 5-point scale (APA, 2013).

Schizophrenia. Readers of the DSM-5 may notice that the traditional subtypes, paranoid, disorganized, catatonic, undifferentiated and residual have been removed for a diagnosis of schizophrenia; these were removed because these subtypes were seen to be both unreliably diagnosed and unstable in the client's presentation (Nemeroff et al., 2013). Currently, the DSM-5 relies instead on rating the severity of core symptoms (APA, 2013; Nemeroff et al., 2013). Persons diagnosed with schizophrenia experience impairment in their functioning at school or work, socially, and often in caring for themselves. This diagnosis requires two or more of the following "active phase" symptoms to be present for a large majority of a 1-month period. If a client is successfully treated before that time a diagnosis can still be made, since it is assumed the symptom would have continued if left untreated. Again, schizophrenia is set apart in that the client also evidences persistent signs of disturbance related to schizophrenia for 6 months or more. Note that in determining the duration that these symptoms can span the prodromal (the period leading up to the active symptoms) or residual periods (the period following the active symptoms). In other words, look carefully at the timeline of symptoms leading up to the psychotic episode and the period that follows in establishing the duration (APA, 2013).

Both childhood and late onset of schizophrenia are very rare, less than 1% for each group; early onset, before age 18, constitutes about 5% of all schizophrenia cases (Teigset et al., 2018). In their meta-analysis of 35 studies of early-onset schizophrenia, conducted between 1990 and 2014, Stentebjerg-Olesen et al., (2016) found that the vast majority of the psychotic symptoms observed were auditory hallucinations, followed by persecutory and grandiose delusions. Also frequent were thought disorder, disorganized behavior and negative symptoms such as blunted affect. Their analysis concluded that while early onset is less common the impairment and burden is quite high. They also noted a number of comorbidities among this group, including post-traumatic stress disorder (PTSD), attention deficit hyperactivity disorder (ADHD) and substance use disorders.

Other research has investigated late-onset schizophrenia. These clients are more often female, who begin to present with symptoms of diagnosable schizophrenia after the age of 35-40 (Convert et al., 2006; Greenfield et al., 2018; Harris & Jeste, 1988; Reinhardt & Cohen, 2015). Those who are diagnosed with late-onset schizophrenia, typically have been married and have a history of work; however, when psychotic symptoms arise, these clients have often already begun to experience social isolation and unemployment as well as social skills deficits. When symptoms begin late in life, they are less likely to include negative symptoms and more likely to include auditory and visual hallucinations (Convert et al., 2006).

Schizoaffective Disorder. A diagnosis of Schizoaffective Disorder combines experiences of delusions, hallucinations, disorganized speech, grossly disorganized or catatonic behavior and/or negative symptoms with a major mood episode (i.e., manic or major depressive). Persons with a diagnosis of Schizoaffective Disorder experience symptoms that meet criteria for a major mood episode for the majority of the duration of their illness (APA, 2013). Since major mood episodes are a defining feature of the schizoaffective disorder, the DSM-5 provides specifiers for a bipolar type or depressive type, as well as specifiers for catatonia and specifiers used to indicate whether the person is experiencing an episode for the first time or has suffered multiple episodes (APA, 2013).

Some researchers argue that the conceptualization of schizoaffective disorder as a separate disorder is a false construct and that these clients should be understood to have schizophrenia or bipolar disorder with psychotic features, or in some rare situations, to have both disorders (Coryell, 2016). Still other researchers place schizoaffective disorder in the center of a continuum with schizophrenia and bipolar I (BPI) with psychotic features holding the spaces at either end (Reininghaus et al., 2016), a theory that will be discussed at greater length later in the chapter. However one conceptualizes this disorder, it is clear that the burden of schizoaffective disorder is quite significant since the difficulties that come with schizophrenia are compounded by cycling moods.

Attenuated Psychosis Syndrome(APS), a Condition for Further Study. (p. 783 of the DSM) In addition to the five schizophrenia spectrum diagnoses discussed above, the considerations for further study section of the DSM-5 outlines APS, previously known as psychosis risk syndrome. This syndrome captures a phenomenon that is sometimes described as ultra-high risk (UHR), clinical high risk (CHR) or the prodromal phase. As the name implies, psychotic symptoms (i.e., delusions, hallucinations, disorganized speech) in this proposed diagnosis are attenuated, or less severe. Researchers and clinicians lobbied for the inclusion of APS within the schizophrenia continuum arguing that early detection and early treatment intervention are correlated with better outcomes for disorders on the schizophrenia spectrum, that the vast majority of those who later develop schizophrenia first exhibit these types of symptoms and that early detection may prevent conversion to more serious disorders (Fusar-Poli et al., 2014; Tsuang et al., 2013; Yung et al., 2012; Reddy, 2014). Yung et al., note that the decision to exclude APS followed a great deal of concern that to include the syndrome within the continuum would result in unwarranted diagnoses, which would then lead to increased and unnecessary prescribing. In the end, however, APS was not included because it did not show high diagnostic reliability. Researchers continue to work to fine-tune the diagnostic criteria in the hope that it might be included within a later edition (Fusar-Poli et al., 2014).

Schizotypal Personality Disorder. This disorder is given a brief mention in the DSM's schizophrenia continuum but is organized with the personality disorders. This disorder shares features with this continuum in that clients with this personality disorder experience significant social discomfort, odd, often magical thinking and unusual perceptions, odd speech patterns and so on. However, unlike those on the schizophrenia spectrum, these clients don't manifest persistent periods of psychotic symptoms but instead are experienced by others as eccentric and having few friends. While they frequently hold odd beliefs, those beliefs are not held as strongly as those with schizophrenia, for example, and can be dissuaded from them if provided with evidence contradicting their belief (APA, 2013).

History and Theories of Etiology

Conceptualization of the origins of psychosis may be among the most varied of all dimensions of the DSM 5. Psychoanalytic conceptualizations place these events somewhere in the realm of a complete break with parts of the Self, an inability to recognize thoughts, feelings and urges as one's own because to do so would be too threatening. From the psychoanalytic perspective, psychosis results from a defensive externalizing of one's own intolerable thoughts, feelings or desires (Leader, 2011). In contrast, much of the contemporary conventional wisdom embraces biological causes for disorders along the schizophrenia spectrum ranging from differences in immunological function (Müller et al., 1999) and neurological and genetic causes and connections (Farrell et al., 2015; Henriksen et al., 2017) and their interactions with the environment. In this section, we will explore three historical models of the etiology of schizophrenia and other psychotic disorders that have, at one time or another, enjoyed some popularity: the schizophrenogenic mother, Bateson's double-bind and the contemporary sociobiological approach, the diathesis stress model.

Schizophrenogenic Mother: A Discounted Theory. Theories related to the etiology of mental disorders have often placed the origin of mental health disorders squarely at the feet of parents, particularly mothers, and the term "schizophrenogenic mother" follows this unfortunate trend (Harrington, 2016; Johnston, 2013; Seeman, 2016). Thought to be coined by Frieda Fromm-Reichmann in the late 1940s and then fading in popularity by the late 1970s, the term "schizophrenogenic mother" postulated that a mother could cause schizophrenia in her children through her inability to form a healthy, stable relationship with her children (Johnston, 2013; Seeman, 2016). In particular, Fromm-Reichmann (1948) suggested that a mother who is at once overprotective and rejecting could cause a psychological conflict for her child so confounding as to serve as the genesis for schizophrenia. If placed on the continuum of the nature–nurture debate, the schizophrenogenic mother hypothesis rests on the side of nurture, theorizing that a mother could give birth to a healthy child and then, through her own psychological distress, drive the child to develop schizophrenia, or another disorder (Dolnick, 2007 as cited in Johnston, 2013). Like the idea of the schizophrenogenic mother, Bateson et al., (1956) double-bind hypothesis regarding the origin of schizophrenia placed its origin as emerging from a relational double-bind with a caregiver.

Bateson and the Double Bind: A Discounted Process. The schizophrenogenic mother hypothesis was most popular from the late 1940s into the 1970s (Seeman, 2009). During this time, a similar hypothesis, Bateson's "double bind," gained attention and enjoyed some popularity. Most of us have experienced a situation in which we felt "in a bind" because we were forced to choose between two not very attractive options. For instance, having to choose between missing an essential work-related event or disappointing your child by missing an award ceremony, concert or game. A double bind, however, involves repeated experiences between two or more people in which the communication and demand has three levels of uncomfortable challenge embedded, described as primary, secondary and tertiary negative injunctions. The primary negative injunction involves the threat of punishment if the person, often a child, does not act, or sometimes refrain from acting, in some way. The punishment in this case is typically received as the withdrawal of love or an expression of dislike or, worse yet, abandonment. The secondary injunction primarily involves non-verbal communication that contradicts the verbal communication of the primary injunction. Often this may come in the form of imploring children not to see the punishment as punishment, for example, "Don't think of this as a punishment, think of this as my way of showing you how much I love you." Similar to the schizophrenogenic mother, a parent might say they love the child while simultaneously conveying disgust through a non-verbal behavior. The tertiary injunction, the final component of the double bind, describes the feeling the child is left with, a feeling that there is no way to escape the double bind they've been placed in and are doomed to disappoint the parent, and ultimately, will be rejected. Finally, Bateson et al. asserted that if experienced often enough, these injunctions would become internalized by the child and, as a result, they would begin to see the world in double-bind patterns, even experiencing double binds from auditory hallucinations (1956). Double-bind communication was purported to create a habit of thinking literally about metaphorical speech (a defensive move) and to avoid inquiring about the meaning of communications, due to a perceived threat to their relationship. Bateson asserts that doubt about one's own thoughts combined with the metaphorical nature of thought results in mismatched thought processes and "odd" connections between ideas.

Genetic Factors and the Role of Dopamine. While poor parenting styles can certainly have a damaging effect on a person's mental health, researchers today don't draw a clear causal link between parenting and the etiology of schizophrenia (Javitt, 2015; Johnston, 2013). Much of the current research assumes a diathesis–stress model and focuses on biological factors, such as genetics and brain-based phenomena (Howes et al., 2017). For example, the dopamine and glutamate hypotheses, which were originally established through studies on medications to treat schizophrenia, have been explored with more sophisticated measures to establish how the risk factors for schizophrenia affect the dopamine and glutamate systems (Howes et al., 2015).

Extensive research reveals brain-based differences and genetic uniquenesses in those on the schizophrenia spectrum, though definitive causal forces for the neurological difficulties are still speculative and include maternal exposure to viruses (Kneeland & Fatemi, 2013), for example. Extensive genetic research has identified genetic candidates for schizophrenia etiology, but these studies have suffered from less than robust statistical data and methodological difficulties that make exact etiological ties difficult to discern. However, researchers are still hopeful that genetics will uncover causal sources (Farrell et al., 2015; Henriksen et al., 2017). Despite the challenges still evident in genetic research of the schizophrenia spectrum, in 2012, researchers Mark Brennan and Kay Phillips secured a patent for a method of using genetic markers for determining an elevated risk for developing schizophrenia, schizoaffective disorder and schizotypal personality disorder.

Diathesis Stress Model. A more recent perspective on the etiology of schizophrenia puts forward the idea that some people are more vulnerable to schizophrenia due to genetic predispositions. These predispositions (the diathesis) are triggered by environmental factors, such as trauma, illness, poverty and so on (stress) and result in the emergence of psychotic symptoms. On the nature–nurture continuum, the diathesis–stress model for the etiology of schizophrenia posits the likelihood that schizophrenia is a result of both nature and nurture. Assuming a diathesis–stress model for the etiology of schizophrenia involves the understanding that part of what "stresses" the individual are core deficits that emerge from genetic brain-based difficulty that is not, itself, schizophrenia, but contributes to its fruition. For example, cognitive deficits, affective symptoms (e.g., depression), social isolation due to brain-based tendencies and school failure may play a part in contributing to the emergence of schizophrenia in a person (Cornblatt et al., 2003). Seeman (2016) points out in her exploration of the shifting spotlight on mothers, that contrast with models like the schizophrenogenic mother and Bateson's double-bind, assuming a diathesis–stress model moves parents to a position of burdened caregiver, who, along with their child, benefit most from support and psychoeducation.

Sociocultural Considerations. People who experience schizophrenia and other psychotic disorders live in the same reality, world, socioeconomic system and multicultural landscape as everyone else in their communities, though they are simultaneously vulnerable to breaks in that reality. Different cultures and historical perspectives have treated psychotic experiences differently, ranging from ridiculing such experiences as madness or demonic possession to exalting it as prophecy and a path of insight to deeper truth (APA, 2013; Bhugra & Bhui, 1997). As described earlier, the DSM-5 reminds us that these diagnoses have strong culture-related diagnostic issues. For example, "Ideas that appear to be delusional in one culture (e.g., witchcraft) may be commonly held in another. In some cultures, visual or auditory hallucinations with religious content (e.g., hearing God's voice) are a normal part of religious experience" (APA, 2013, p. 103). As clinicians, it is vital that we understand our own cultural context and that of our clients when drawing diagnostic conclusions.

Along with differing intercultural perspectives, there are also various intracultural perspectives to consider. For example, some discussion exists about the utility of drug-induced psychoses (e.g., psychedelic drugs, lysergic acid diethylamide [LSD], N, N-Dimethyltryptamine [DMT]) to bring greater self-awareness, personal insight and spiritual growth (Sessa, 2012). On the other hand, when viewed from a contemporary western, post-positivist perspective, psychotic experiences are most typically viewed as a medical problem and destructive if left untreated.

While considering cultural differences in perspectives and perceptions of schizophrenia and psychosis generally, it is also important not to mythologize cultural experiences. For example, Stephen and Suryani (2000) conducted a study in Bali and Indonesia looking at the experiences and mental health histories of Balian healers who often use trance and sometimes trance possession as an avenue for treating their clients. These researchers explored the historical idea of "shaman as self-healed psychotic." They first assert, "We consider that the prominence given in the anthropological literature to the self-cure of the shaman may be more the creation of Western myths (Florsheim, 1990) than an accurate reflection of the varying cultural practices within which traditional healers operate," (p. 6). They found that 19% of the healers reported mental health concerns prior to becoming a healer, a number they point out is much lower than might be expected if the shaman-as-psychotic construct were accurate. So, while some shamans and healers likely do experience psychosis, there is evidence to suggest this may not always, or even usually, be the case.

Competing Diagnostic Nosologies

The disorders in this dimension can be difficult to diagnose in part because the key features of schizophrenia and other psychotic disorders are not unique to this dimension. Symptoms of psychosis can be seen in depressive, bipolar disorders and, less often, in those suffering from severe anxiety (APA, 2013; Varghese et al., 2009). Additionally, psychosis can be triggered by substance use as well as by some medical conditions. The treatment and prognosis for a depressive disorder with peripartum psychosis, for example, is very different from the treatment of and prognosis for schizoaffective disorder, making an accurate diagnosis extremely important to clinical outcomes.

For the better part of a decade, the National Institutes of Mental Health (NIMH) has been funding work aimed at identifying neurological underpinnings for mental health disorders, including those that involve psychotic processes, and developing a diagnostic model that they believe more closely matches functional differences in clients who present with psychosis. Challenging the current DSM nosology, much of the work related to schizophrenia coming from the NIMH supports the conceptualization of a continuum of biotypes roughly matching pure schizophrenia at one end and BPI disorder with psychotic features-type presentations at the other. These biotypes, however, don't map directly to these DSM disorders. Their research suggests that the continuum as outlined in the DSM does not accurately depict the overlap in symptoms and functioning between these three constructs and instead argue for a transdiagnostic spectrum approach to the affective and non-affective psychotic disorders organized by the biotypes they've identified (Esterberg & Compton, 2009; Keshavan et al., 2011; Phelps, 2016; Reininghaus et al., 2018; Reininghaus et al., 2019). Dubbed Bipolar-Schizophrenia Network on Intermediate Phenotypes (B-SNIP), this consortium of researchers is working to construct just such a continuum and diagnostic nosology (Reininghaus et al., 2018; Reininghaus et al., 2019). However, until such a time as a new model would be adopted by the APA, differentiating between disorders that include psychotic features will be challenging.

Skilled Diagnostician: Differential Diagnosis

Identifying Prodromal Stage Symptom Sets: Recognizing the Emergence of Schizophrenia/UHR. A strong predictor of successful management of schizophrenia spectrum and other psychotic disorders, like most mental health concerns, is early diagnosis and intervention. Early diagnosis and treatment are particularly pivotal for persons who may fall into the category, UHR. Factors that have been found to contribute to elevated risk first include those who have experienced psychotic symptoms that don't rise to the level of diagnosis, either because of their low intensity, brief duration or both, but are frequent enough to raise concern. These types of psychotic events have been variously described as BLIPS (brief limited intermittent psychotic symptoms), transient psychosis or attenuated psychosis. Other characteristics that place a person in the UHR category include a decline in psychological functioning, comorbid depression and/or anxiety, frequent social isolation, poor school performance and a family history of schizophrenia (Fusar-Poli et al., 2013; Fusar-Poli et al., 2017; Yung et al., 2005). Cornblatt et al. (2003) offer the acronym CASIS to help clinicians remember traits that set adolescents up for vulnerability to schizophrenia: cognitive deficits, affective disturbances, social isolation and school failure. Haroun, Dunn, Haroun and Cadenhead, 2005, followed a group of adolescents in the UHR group and found that at follow-up 1 year later the conversion to a psychotic disorder was about 13%; half of these developed an affective-type psychosis. Notably, adolescents who did not use substances were less likely to convert to a schizophrenia diagnosis. Clinicians working with adolescents who meet these criteria should monitor these clients closely and refer when appropriate for medication evaluation.

Differentiating Schizoaffective Disorder and BPI with Psychotic Features. The key difference between a BPI disorder with psychotic features and schizoaffective disorder lies in the timing of the symptoms of psychosis. If a client experiences psychotic symptoms for 2 weeks or more outside of mood symptoms, then the client is diagnosed with schizoaffective disorder. If, on the other hand, the client only experiences psychosis during a mood episode, then the DSM diagnosis is BPI (APA, 2013). In theory, this is a straightforward diagnostic decision; however, in the field, the combination of mood

BOX 6.04 EARLY EXPERIENCES OF PSYCHOSIS: LIFE CHANGING EVENTS

People with schizophrenia and other psychotic disorders inhabit an experience of reality that is at once convergent and divergent from that of those who do not live with these disorders. It is convergent in the ways that they too are thrust into being and experience the needs that each of us does as human beings. Their experience of reality is also divergent from that of those who have never experienced a psychotic episode or the social and interpersonal struggles that come with such diagnoses. Clients may notice startling moments of strange thoughts, disturbing ideas or hearing an internal voice that doesn't feel like their own. Persons who experience schizophrenia and other psychotic disorders may also begin noticing changes in the ways they experience the world through their senses. For example, colors may appear exceptionally vivid, they may become sensitive to sounds and react as if they've heard an explosion, or feel sensations against their skin with no apparent cause. In some cases, objects might appear that no one else can see (positive symptoms). These sensory experiences can sometimes make the world resemble a dream-like state, and as these experiences become stronger and the person's behavior becomes more eccentric, they may attempt to compensate for them, hide them and withdraw from social interaction where others might admonish their behavior, beliefs and disorganized thinking (Bollas, 2015). These experiences are isolating, but so is living in a social world full of people who insist your experiences are not real.

In his book, *When the Sun Bursts: The Enigma of Schizophrenia*, Bollas, 2015, describes a former client, who describes a memory from when he was 10 years old. One day during a break at school, his client walked outside, felt something strange, looked up into the sky and watched as the sun burst. Justifiably terrified, he sprinted indoors and hid in a closet for hours. When he was finally found by his upset teachers, he screamed that they were in danger and fled from them when they tried to calm him. This client was never able to fully trust others, who seemed somehow in league with those who burst the sun.

Bollas (2015) writes that these early experiences are critical and are rarely forgotten as they constitute a landmark change in the person's perception of the world and of others. When others seem oblivious to the changes in the world the person is experiencing, she or he often must construct a secret logic for what is happening, a logic that can prevent the trust necessary to seek treatment.

*Contributed by Michael Horst, Ph.D.

episodes and psychosis in the client's history is very challenging to pull apart, because it is timeline dependent, and, as discussed earlier, accurate timelines are notoriously difficult to construct. Further, diagnostic shifts can occur over time; for example, from schizoaffective disorder to schizophrenia, or from bipolar disorder to schizoaffective disorder. Note in the following example how Tim's diagnosis would change from BPI, with psychotic features to schizoaffective disorder, bipolar type

Example: Tim has a years-long history of cycles of mood episodes. During a number of manic episodes, Tim also experienced auditory hallucinations that led to brief

BOX 6.05 ULTRA HIGH RISK: A COLLECTION OF RED FLAG SYMPTOMS AND TRAITS

- Adolescence/Early Adulthood (ages 15–29)
- Attenuated Psychosis Syndrome/BLIPS (brief limited intermittent psychotic symptoms)
- Decline in psychological functioning
- Family history of schizophrenia
- Significant symptoms of depression or anxiety
- Social isolation
- Poor school performance
- Substance use

Source: Cornblatt et al. (2003), Fular-Poli et al. (2017) and Yung et al. (2005).

hospitalizations. However, Tim was recently hospitalized after a month-long period in which he experienced both visual hallucinations and delusional fears about a Bulgarian plot to overturn the American government. During this period, Tim did not experience symptoms of mania or depression but did display moderately tangential speech.

Some researchers have worked to identify differences in the psychotic symptoms experienced by those in different diagnostic groups. For example, Baethge et al. (2005) conducted a study of all patients admitted with psychosis over a 20-year period in a hospital in Germany, producing a cohort of 4,972 patient records. In their review, they examined differences in the type of hallucinations evidenced in those with schizophrenia, bipolar disorder and major depression. They found that for those with BPI, their hallucinations were judged to be less severe (judged in part based upon the intensity, anxiety provoked and degree of insight retained), were more often visual and less often auditory, and further, their delusions were more often accompanied by persecutory delusions. Since, no single symptom was experienced exclusively by a single diagnostic group, it is not possible to use studies like this one to differentiate with confidence a schizoaffective or bipolar disorder. However, as with the initial differentiation between substance-induced psychosis (SIP) and schizophrenia, auditory hallucinations, particularly those that are quite distressing and accompanied by a history of poor functioning, *may* point to schizoaffective disorder. However, some studies have found no differences in specific types of delusions and hallucinations between those thought to be on the schizophrenia spectrum and those with bipolar psychosis (Pini et al., 2004). As Schöttle et al. (2012) point out that at the point of first presentation with psychosis and in the early stages of illness, statistical points of differentiation between BPI and Social Anxiety Disorder (SAD) are, unfortunately, of little usefulness in diagnosis.

Differentiation of Schizoaffective Disorder, Depressive Type and Depressive Disorders with Psychotic Features. Researchers examining the features of schizoaffective disorder, schizophrenia and major depression with psychotic features have also challenged the current DSM nosology that places these symptomologically similar disorders on different continuums. These researchers assert that SAD represents the middle ground between a continuum with schizophrenia at one end and major depression at the other (Cheniaux et al., 2008). Currently, however, diagnosticians are challenged to disentangle client symptoms and place them within a best-fit continuum and diagnosis. When a client's psychotic symptoms persist outside of mood episodes for at least 2 weeks, the client should be diagnosed with schizoaffective disorder. When the client experiences exclusively depressive symptoms and has never had a manic episode, code this diagnosis with the specifier "depressive type." However, if your client's psychotic features appear only during depressive mood episodes, diagnose the appropriate depressive disorder using the psychotic features specifier. Again, this diagnostic process will be complicated by incomplete or inaccurate symptom reporting or difficulties constructing an accurate timeline.

Psychosis and Perinatal Depression. Pregnancy and new motherhood are significant risk factors for depressive disorders; estimates place perinatal depression prevalence numbers between 5% and 25% of mothers. However, peripartum/post-partum psychosis is believed to occur more rarely, between 1 and 4 in 1,000 births. Distinguishing peripartum psychosis from schizophreniform or schizoaffective disorder is aided by the fact that the onset of peripartum psychosis nearly always manifests within 2 weeks of delivery (Gaynes et al., 2005; Jones & Craddock, 2001). Frequently, but not always, the delusional thoughts that are sometimes experienced in perinatal depression concern the baby, for example, a belief that the baby is already dead or in some danger (Hamed & Attiah, 2019). Consequently, psychotic symptoms that are new to the client's history, follow closely on the heels of pregnancy and those that have infant-related themes point to peripartum depression rather than SAD.

When Substance Use Is Part of the Clinical Picture. The rate of co-occurrence between the schizophrenia spectrum and substance use disorders is extremely high; as many as 50% experience a comorbid substance use disorder. What's more, a number of substances can provoke symptoms of psychosis, a phenomenon described as substance induced psychosis (SIP). These include alcohol, amphetamines, cannabis and cocaine (DeLisi, 2008; Caton et al., 2000; Fiorentini et al., 2011). Alarmingly, among heavy cannabis users the risk of developing schizophrenia is as much as six times as high as for those who don't use the drug at all (Fiorentini et al., 2011).

Niemi-Pynttäri et al., (2013) conducted a study of over 18,000 discharge records of Finnish patients who had been diagnosed with a substance-induced psychosis (SIP) and were followed until the first diagnosis of schizophrenia, until death, or until the end of the study period in 2003, whichever came first. They found that the overall risk of conversion from SIP to primary schizophrenia was higher than anticipated, 46%. Kirkbride (2013) used the same data to conduct further analysis and noted that the bulk of the SIPs were instigated by alcohol use, followed by amphetamines; however, those with the highest conversion rate to schizophrenia were those initially diagnosed with a cannabis-induced schizophrenia, followed by amphetamine and then by alcohol-induced psychosis conversion. The rate of conversion did not seem to be affected by gender. On the whole, these authors assert that substance use constitutes a significant risk to client mental health with regard to the eventual development of psychosis and schizophrenia in particular.

For decades, clinicians and researchers have looked for markers that would successfully differentiate between primary (PP) and SIPs. In their 1997 article, Rosenthal and Miner (1997), noted that one of the biggest challenges to arriving at the correct differential diagnosis is simply getting an accurate timeline for symptoms and for the onset of substance use. Caton et al. (2007) conducted a 1-year follow-up study of more than 300 people who had been admitted to the hospital emergency department for comorbid psychosis and substance use. Their results may help diagnosticians in making stronger differential diagnoses between substance-induced and primary psychosis, which may, in turn, lead to stronger treatment and better outcomes. They found that those with primary psychosis had poorer functioning prior to the psychotic symptoms than did those with SIP. Those with primary psychosis also demonstrated poorer insight and had stronger family histories of mental health concerns. In their research, Fiorentini et al. (2011) found that patterns in the psychotic symptoms themselves may help to differentiate primary and substance-induced psychosis. In their examination of 130 participants those believed to have a SIP were more apt to experience persecutory delirium and visual hallucinations, while those believed to have a primary psychosis presented with first rank psychotic symptoms such as thought insertion, thought broadcasting, thought withdrawal, delusional perceptions or auditory hallucinations.

Similarly, among heavy cocaine users presenting with psychosis, differences were observed between those thought to have a primary psychosis and one that was substance induced. Vergara-Moragues et al. (2016) found that the SIP group had more visual hallucinations as well as a greater history of arrest. Their study revealed that the independent psychosis (IPD) group displayed more of the classic psychotic symptoms, such as delusions of grandeur, disorganized speech, somatic or bizarre delusions, catatonic and negative symptoms. These studies suggest that recruiting assistance from family and consulting medical records to construct an accurate symptom timeline, evaluating pre-substance use functioning and correctly identifying the type of delusions or hallucinations your client is experiencing may greatly support an accurate differential diagnosis of primary or SIP.

Schizophrenia and Autism Spectrum Disorder. At first glance, one might not immediately connect the autism and schizophrenia spectrums; however, until the late 1970s these disorders were thought to be closely linked. On closer inspection, it becomes clear that these two continuums share a number of overlapping symptoms, and, at times, can be complicated to sort out, particularly at the mild end of each of these spectrums. For example, the "A" criterion for the autism spectrum describes social interaction and communication deficits, such as poor social reciprocity, odd or absent non-verbal communication skills, language deficits, lack of facial expressiveness and difficulties in developing social relationships. All of these signs and symptoms resemble negative symptoms of schizophrenia. Both spectrums feature odd and sometimes idiosyncratic speech and motor abnormalities (Esterberg et al., 2008; Konstantareas & Hewitt, 2001).

Growing awareness of the autism spectrum and its early detection has likely helped considerably in preventing confusion between the two. In differentiating autism disorder from schizophrenia, the age of symptom onset offers a first point of distinction. For children on the autism spectrum, a period of developmental regression of social skills and language development, between 24 and 30 months, is frequently observed, while this is not a trend seen in those with early-onset schizophrenia. Further, childhood onset schizophrenia is quite rare and early-onset type is uncommon (APA, 2013; Esterberg et al., 2008; Konstantareas & Hewitt, 2001). Finally, psychotic symptoms are not a feature of the autistic spectrum criteria and their presence should shift the diagnostician's attention to the schizophrenia spectrum diagnoses. These disorders can co-occur, however, and when symptoms are met for both, each diagnosis will be given. Referral for appropriate testing is essential here.

Synesthesia. Synesthesia is a sensory difference experienced by a small segment of the population, perhaps 1 person in 2,000, in which two senses become entwined. For the person with synesthesia, when one sensory pathway is stimulated, there is a simultaneous activation of a second unstimulated sensory pathway. For most who experience this phenomenon, the visual and auditory perceptions are linked, sometimes described as colored hearing, but it is possible for any of the five senses to combine. For these people, one sense, for example sound, also triggers visual stimuli, such as color, that others do not see (Cytowic, 1989; Hubbard & Ramachandran, 2005). These differences in perception are not the same as psychosis and are not accompanied by functional impairments as hallucinations or delusions are. Consequently, perceptual differences of this kind should not be confused with psychosis and are not diagnosed.

Treatment Interventions for the Schizophrenia Spectrum

Grover et al., (2017) published updated guidelines for the treatment of schizophrenia, tailored to the poverty and lack of resources typical to regions of India. Their guidelines offer helpful insights to clinicians serving clients who come from well-resourced as well as under-resourced communities alike. First, they recommend that clients displaying psychotic symptoms undergo a complete evaluation covering all areas of disturbance, including comorbid symptomatology, such as substance and mood, in order to establish an accurate and complete diagnosis. Next, placement decisions should be made regarding whether a client is best served in a hospital, group home, with family or in independent living. Third, they recommend interventions first include medications, followed by assessment for the use of electroconvulsive shock treatment where appropriate, and finally, consideration of psychotherapy, psychoeducation or both. Clients who fair the best, however, are those with combined treatments that include both medication and psychosocial intervention (Pfammatter et al., 2006).

Pharmacological Interventions. Medication is a central pillar in the treatment of schizophrenia spectrum and other psychotic disorders. When working with someone experiencing psychotic symptoms, refer to a psychiatrist or another qualified physician to explore appropriate diagnoses, prescriptions and management of medication. The first line treatment for the schizophrenia spectrum are antipsychotics. Among the most commonly used antipsychotics are Thorazine (chlorpromazine), Seroquel (quetiapine), Risperdal (risperidone), Haldol (haloperidol) and Abilify (aripiprazole). Adjunctive medications include anticholinergics, antidepressants, benzodiazepines, anticonvulsants and lithium (Grover et al., 2017).

Psychotherapy. Though individual psychotherapy alone is unlikely to reveal practical value in treating florid psychosis, a meta-analysis of psychological treatments used in intervention with schizophrenia has shown that family therapy has some value in relapse prevention of psychotic symptoms as well as reductions in readmission to the hospital. Meta-analysis suggests that family therapy can reduce relapse by as much as 20% (Pitschel-Walz et al., 2001). Cognitive Behavioral Therapy (CBT) seems to help clients attain improvements in mood states (Pilling et al., 2002). Similarly, in their meta-analysis, Zimmermann et al., (2005) found that those with acute psychosis treated with CBT evidenced reductions in positive symptoms, but this effect was not as strong in those with chronic conditions.

Psychoeducation. Finally, psychoeducation is thought to be helpful for families both in educating them about the symptoms and course of the disorder (Cassidy et al., 2001; Pfammatter et al., 2006) but also in reducing the burden of the illness on the family (Gutiérrez-Maldonado & Caqueo-Urízar, 2007). There is some evidence that these programs reduce hospitalization (Cassidy et al., 2001).

Cases in Schizophrenia Spectrum and Other Psychotic Disorders

The following five pivot points may help you to narrow your diagnosis. Remember, however, that you must carefully examine the full diagnostic criteria before offering a diagnosis. Using the pivot points to assign a diagnosis would not reflect ethical diagnostic practice. After reading the diagnostic criteria, be certain to consider the diagnoses listed in the differential diagnosis section of your DSM 5. As you consider assigning a diagnosis, keep in mind that when one diagnosis contains all of the symptoms of a second diagnosis, the first predominates. This is called the principle of predominance.

Sunil

Sunil lost his business a month ago when his business partner and childhood friend disappeared with their business savings and left him in debt. Sunil describes feeling "betrayed, heartbroken, and hopeless." Though Sunil is generally described as "level-headed" by his friends and family and has enjoyed good physical and mental health, he recently developed the belief that there was a cobra in his bedroom "lurking and ready to strike as I sleep." Though Sunil understood that cobras don't live in Chicago where he currently keeps his apartment, he hired an exterminator to find and kill the snake. The exterminator found no evidence of a snake, but Sunil maintained this strong belief and fear for nearly 2 weeks. However, 1 week ago Sunil had a realization, "It dawned on me how foolish my fear had been and I was ashamed I could let myself get so caught up in such a belief."

Oliver

Oliver, age 17, is a successful student in a local high school who holds an internship at a local television station doing work with video editing as part of a work–study program. Oliver has several friends that he spends time with regularly and enjoys playing Magic: The Gathering© late into the night. In the last 2 months however, Oliver has developed a secret fear that if he uses his voice during the game "with just the right tonality and volume" he can "destroy any human mind." Consequently, Oliver is reluctant to speak without using extreme caution and deliberate care in order to avoid hurting others. Oliver has no history of any unusual thinking, depression or other mental health concerns.

Elias

Elias, 45, works at a regional branch of a large multinational computer firm. About 3 months ago, he had an opportunity to meet Mr. Roberts, the head of his division, whose office is located in another state. Though he has only met his boss in passing, Elias has been convinced since shaking Mr. Roberts' hand, that his boss is infatuated with him and that eventually Mr. Roberts will approach Elias for a sexual relationship. Elias has been very upset and distracted about this possibility. He is concerned that he might lose his job should he refuse the advances that he feels sure will come from Mr. Roberts. This is Elias's first experience with implausible thoughts.

Donald

Donald, 62, has been living successfully in a state-funded group home for the past 3 years where he gets support with self care and social skills as well as some occupational skills. Before living in the group home, Donald had been a long-term resident

TABLE 6.02 Pivot Points Schizophrenia Spectrum

	Consider this Diagnosis
Pivot Point One: Does your client experience mood symptoms together with symptoms of psychosis?	
• Does your client experience depressive symptoms but only when symptoms of psychosis are present?	Schizoaffective Disorder, Depressive Type
• Does your client experience mood symptoms, both depressive or manic, but only when symptoms of psychosis are present?	Schizoaffective Disorder, Bipolar Type
• Does your client experience psychotic symptoms only during a major depressive episode?	Major Depressive Disorder, Severe, With Psychotic Features
• Does your client experience psychotic symptoms only during a major depressive episode during or following a pregnancy?	Major Depressive Disorder, Severe, With Psychotic Features, With Peripartum Onset
• Does your client experience psychotic symptoms but only during either a manic or depressive episode?	Bipolar I Disorder, Severe, With Psychotic Features
Pivot Point Two: Have your client's psychotic symptoms lasted less than a month before resolving?	Brief Psychotic Disorder
Pivot Point Three: Are your client's psychotic symptoms restricted to delusional thoughts?	Delusional Disorder
Pivot Point Four: Have your client's psychotic symptoms lasted more than a month but resolved before 6 months have passed?	Schizophreniform Disorder
Pivot Point Five: Are your client's delusional thoughts shared with another person?	Shared Psychotic Disorder

of a state hospital, interspersed with periods in which he lived with his parents, now deceased. In different periods Donald has struggled against command hallucinations, voices directing him to hurt himself and sometimes others. At other times Donald has been captivated by the belief that he was "occupying a space that belonged to someone else" and that he was "in the wrong dimensional reality." He would often try to convince his parents that "he was not their Donald" and that "their Donald was stuck in another reality."

More recently however, Donald's group home supervisors have noted "odd, directionless behaviors, such as a strumming motion across his left leg when he is becoming upset, as well as the emergence of rocking." Supervisors have also noted that Donald's affect has gradually shifted from a typical animation, to a somewhat blunted affect and, later, to a nearly flat representation of emotion. Donald denies symptoms of depression, however. Though he has experienced depressive symptoms in the past, these have been fleeting.

Julius

Julius is a 35-year-old married father of three who has worked for several years as an electrical engineer. Last year he and his wife sought help from a psychiatrist. At that time, they reported that Julius had undergone a dramatic shift in his behavior and thinking in the 5 weeks prior to their visit, which had led Julius to feel confused and upset. Julius reported at the time that he "caught glimpses" of spies and evidence of government spy equipment "just out of the corner of my eye and then it would be gone." Julius reported that when he saw these things it was very upsetting, and that he was confused about why the government would be interested in him. "This just doesn't seem plausible to me," he reported at the time. In an interview with Julius and his wife, she reported at the time that there had been several occasions in which he had started to talk about something and "Julius just seemed to jump topics or something. He would get really hard to follow and a little touchy when I would ask about it or if I tried to get some clarity." Julius and his wife confirm that he has no history of depressed or anxious mood, nor previous episodes of confusion or odd thinking. Julius also denies any use of substances and was not taking any medications or illegal substances when his symptoms emerged.

After meeting with the psychiatrist, Julius was prescribed antipsychotic medications and the couple was referred to counseling where they learned tools for managing Julius's delusions and how to recognize new or worsening symptoms. Within 2 months, Julius no longer embraced the belief that spies were watching him and did not experience any further unusual speech patterns. Julius has been symptom free for 10 months.

Portia

Portia, 20, has returned to the psychiatrist for a follow-up visit after being released from the hospital. Sitting in the psychiatrist's office, she seems visibly shaken and uncomfortable. Portia recalls that about 6 weeks ago she became convinced that her roommate wanted to sacrifice her at the next summer solstice. She recalls that as the days and weeks passed, she became more and more afraid to go home and was terrified to go to sleep at night when she felt sure that her roommate was "doing her witchery." She was admitted to the hospital 2 weeks ago following an incident in which she had arrived at one of her classes disheveled, agitated and making little sense. Her professor took her to the campus mental health clinic and from there she was taken to the hospital and admitted. While in the hospital, she was treated with antipsychotics and within a week began to show a resolution of her fears. Currently, Portia reports that she is no longer afraid of her roommate but is worried that "these crazy thoughts will return." Portia's psychiatrist notes that her speech is intermittently tangential and difficult to follow at times during their session, however. Portia has no history of previous mental health concerns or substance use.

Miranda

Miranda, 37, has been married for 11 years. She is the mother of three children, the president of the parent–teacher association and runs a successful wedding photography business. In the past 3 months, Miranda and her husband have had a number of arguments. Miranda is convinced that her husband, Joel, is having an affair with a woman at work. Despite Joel's attempts to reassure her, and his insistence that there are no women employed at his small firm, Miranda's belief that he is having an affair has only intensified. Recently Miranda put together a disguise and followed Joel to work each day for an entire week, often sitting outside his office with binoculars. Miranda believes that Joel was aware that she was following him and that this is why she did not catch him in his affair. Miranda does not complain of any other mental health symptoms and holds no other odd beliefs.

Heather

Heather, 21, has been struggling socially for several years, has often been socially isolated and has had a difficult time fitting in with her peers since middle school. Heather dropped out of college and has been living with her parents and working part time in a flower shop. In the last 7 weeks, Heather has developed the belief that an evil spirit has taken up residence in her parent's basement and wants to harm her. She reports that she can hear the spirit communicating to the devil everything that she does, "almost like a narrator in a story." The spirit's voice is very distressing and makes it impossible for her to concentrate. Heather reports that she smells the odor that the spirit gives off. Heather also reports that she is "terrified" of the spirit and has difficulty sleeping knowing it is there. Heather's parents report that she is sometimes difficult to understand and her speech can become jumbled and peppered with "made up words."

Morgan

Morgan, 21, lives at home with her mother and grandmother where she spends much of her time painting and doing pen and ink abstract art. Morgan was admitted to the hospital 2 days ago after her parents found Morgan leaning out of her third-story bedroom window threatening to "fly across the city, over the river and into Never-Never Land." Morgan has been admitted to the hospital on two separate occasions in the past 20 months. Though always a bit withdrawn and something of a "loner," Morgan first began to struggle with observable mental health problems in her final year of high school. During that time, Morgan developed a strong belief that there was "an alien force attempting to extract [her] thoughts." Though Morgan was able to function for a time with this belief without causing herself or others difficulty, her behavior became more and more odd. Over several months, Morgan grew more concerned about the alien force and later came to believe that if she coated her hair with a great deal of coconut oil blended with tea tree oil, she would be able to protect her mind. In addition to coating her hair thickly with this solution each day, Morgan also began to wear layer upon layer of clothing, even in the hot summer months, in order to protect herself from "polluted atoms." In the past 10 months, she has complained of "a voice that has someone else's interests in mind and just won't leave [her] alone."

For the bulk of this time, Morgan has also struggled with moods that have shifted from extremes of depression to manic experiences. Her first hospitalization followed a suicide attempt during a particularly trying depressive episode. Morgan's second hospitalization followed 3 days of irritability, lack of sleep and her belief that she could fly, at which time she was diagnosed with a manic episode.

Morgan was able to finish high school with a standard diploma but her deteriorating mental health has prevented her from going to college or from keeping a job.

Winston

Winston, a 35-year-old bank teller, suddenly left work complaining of stomach pains. Winston felt badly enough that he went to the local hospital's emergency room and explained that he had "a strong sense of knowing that an animal was tearing away at [his] insides." When asked what kind of animal Winston thought he might have inside him, Winston replied, "I'm not sure but I can feel its claws cutting away at my insides trying to get free. It doesn't want to be there." Winston's attending physician did an exam, found nothing out of the ordinary, other than a slightly elevated heart rate, and decided to consult with the psychiatrist on duty, who recommended he prescribe an antipsychotic. After 3 days, Winston no longer experienced the sensation in his stomach and a day later he abandoned the belief that there was ever an animal inside of him. Winston has no history of earlier mental health concerns and appears to have returned to his previous functioning.

Maxwell

For several years, Maxwell's conversation has turned to his deeply held conviction that "the Blacks and Jews of this country are running the government and banks. Nothing happens that the Blacks and the Jews aren't keeping track of or manipulating. They are constantly watching, keeping track and waiting for the day when they can lead an open rebellion." Maxwell becomes highly agitated when he watches the domestic news, particularly related to financial fluctuations in the Dow, which Maxwell attributes to "Jewish conspiracy." Aside from these beliefs, Maxwell's behavior and thoughts can't be described as unusual. He holds a steady job and has friendships, though they are often strained by his tireless distraction with Jewish and Black people.

Deidre

Deidre, a 25-year-old graduate student studying nursing, has come to counseling complaining that her studies have been impacted and grades have suffered from her inability to concentrate. She reports that beginning 4 months ago, she began to feel very tired and a bit apathetic, having to fight to get out of bed and get to the classes she once enjoyed but now dreads. She reports she has found it increasingly difficult to sleep and finds herself staying up late, baking and eating cookies, cakes and bread. As a result, she has gained 12 pounds.

Deidre reports that for several months before she noticed a decline in her concentration she began to experience "a constant inner struggle, like an inner dialogue between my good side and a darker part of me, struggling for dominance. The voice of the evil part of me was constantly speaking to my good side, suggesting I do things I did not want to do, like steal things or to slap a stranger in line ahead of me. I think this inner struggle began to wear me down." Deidre reports that she still hears "the voice of her darker side" but that it isn't as loud or insistent as it once was. "The voice is more like far off scratching that I choose to ignore."

Deidre reports having heard a soft whispering voice that was distressing to her during her undergraduate college experience and for a brief period of time during her final year of high school. She denies any substance use and does not currently take medications.

References

Alphs, L., Morlock, R., Coon, C., van Willigenburg, A., & Panagides, J. (2010). The 4-item negative symptom assessment (NSA-4) instrument: A simple tool for evaluating negative symptoms in schizophrenia following brief training. *Psychiatry (Edgmont)*, *7*(7), 26.

American Psychiatric Association. (2013). *Diagnostic and statistical manual of mental disorders (DSM-5®)*. Author.

Baethge, C., Baldessarini, R. J., Freudenthal, K., Streeruwitz, A., Bauer, M., & Bschor, T. (2005). Hallucinations in bipolar disorder: Characteristics and comparison to unipolar depression and schizophrenia. *Bipolar Disorders*, *7*(2), 136–145. https://doi.org/10.1111/j.1399-5618.2004.00175.x

Bateson, G., Jackson, D. D., Haley, J., & Weakland, J. (1956). Toward a theory of schizophrenia. *Behavioral Science*, *1*(4), 251–264. https://doi.org/10.1002/bs.3830010402

Bhugra, D., & Bhui, K. (1997). Cross-cultural psychiatric assessment. *Advances in Psychiatric Treatment*, *3*(2), 103–110. https://doi.org/10.1192/apt.3.2.103

Bollas, C. (2015). *When the sun bursts: The enigma of schizophrenia*. Yale University Press.

Cassidy, E., Hill, S., & O'Callaghan, E. (2001). Efficacy of a psychoeducational intervention in improving relatives' knowledge about schizophrenia and reducing rehospitalization. *European Psychiatry*, *16*(8), 446–450. https://doi.org/10.1016/S0924-9338(01)00605-8

Caton, C. L., Hasin, D. S., Shrout, P. E., Drake, R. E., Dominguez, B., First, M. B., & Schanzer, B. (2007). Stability of early-phase primary psychotic disorders with concurrent substance use and substance-induced psychosis. *The British Journal of Psychiatry*, *190*(2), 105–111. https://doi.org/10.1192/bjp.bp.105.015784

Caton, C. L., Samet, S., & Hasin, D. S. (2000). When acute-stage psychosis and substance use co-occur: Differentiating substance-induced and primary psychotic disorders. *Journal of Psychiatric Practice®*, *6*(5), 256–266.

Chadwick, P., Lees, S., & Birchwood, M. A. X. (2000). The revised beliefs about voices questionnaire (BAVQ-R). *The British Journal of Psychiatry*, *177*(3), 229–232. https://doi.org/10.1192/bjp.177.3.229

Cheniaux, E., Landeira-Fernandez, J., Telles, L. L., Lessa, J. L. M., Dias, A., Duncan, T., & Versiani, M. (2008). Does schizoaffective disorder really exist? A systematic review of the studies that compared schizoaffective disorder with schizophrenia or mood disorders. *Journal of Affective Disorders*, *106*(3), 209–217. https://doi.org/10.1016/j.jad.2007.07.009

Convert, H., Vedie, C., & Paulin, P. (2006). Late-onset schizophrenia or chronic delusion. *L'Encephale*, *32*(6 Pt. 1), 957–961. https://doi.org/10.1016/S0013-7006(06)76273-X

Cornblatt, B. A., Lencz, T., Smith, C. W., Correll, C. U., Auther, A. M., & Nakayama, E. (2003). The schizophrenia prodrome revisited: A neurodevelopmental perspective. *Schizophrenia Bulletin*, *29*(4), 633–651. https://doi.org/10.1093/oxfordjournals.schbul.a007036

Coryell, W. (2016). Schizoaffective and schizophreniform disorders. In *The medical basis of psychiatry*, (PP. 121–135). Springer, New York, NY. https://link.springer.com/chapter/10.1007/978-1-4939-2528-5_7

Cytowic, R. E. (1989). Synesthesia and mapping of subjective sensory dimensions. *Neurology*, *39*(6), 849–850. https://doi.org/10.1212/WNL.39.6.849

DeLisi, L. E. (2008). The effect of cannabis on the brain: Can it cause brain anomalies that lead to increased risk for schizophrenia? *Current Opinion in Psychiatry*, *21*(2), 140. https://doi.org/10.1097/YCO.0b013e3282f51266

Dolnick, E. (2007). *Madness on the couch: Blaming the victim in the heyday of psychoanalysis*. Simon & Schuster. https://journalofethics.ama-assn.org/sites/journalofethics.ama-assn.org/files/2018-05/oped1-1309.pdf

Esterberg, M. L., & Compton, M. T. (2009). The psychosis continuum and categorical versus dimensional diagnostic approaches. *Current Psychiatry Reports*, *11*(3), 179. https://doi.org/10.1007/s11920-009-0028-7

Esterberg, M. L., Trotman, H. D., Brasfield, J. L., Compton, M. T., & Walker, E. F. (2008). Childhood and current autistic features in adolescents with schizotypal personality disorder. *Schizophrenia Research*, *104*(1–3), 265–273.

Farrell, M. S., Werge, T., Sklar, P., Owen, M. J., Ophoff, R. A., O'Donovan, M. C., & Sullivan, P. F. (2015). Evaluating historical candidate genes for schizophrenia. *Molecular Psychiatry, 20*(5), 555. https://doi.org/10.1038/mp.2015.16

Fiorentini, A., Sara Volonteri, L., Dragogna, F., Rovera, C., Maffini, M., Carlo Mauri, M., & A Altamura, C. (2011). Substance-induced psychoses: A critical review of the literature. *Current Drug Abuse Reviews, 4*(4), 228–240. https://doi.org/10.2174/1874473711104040228

Foussias, G., & Remington, G. (2008). Negative symptoms in schizophrenia: Avolition and Occam's razor. *Schizophrenia Bulletin, 36*(2), 359–369. https://doi.org/10.1093/schbul/sbn094

Fromm-Reichman, F. (1948). Notes on the development of treatment of schizophrenics by psychoanalytic psychotherapy. *Psychiatry, 11*(3), 263–273. https://doi.org/10.1080/00332747.1948.11022688

Fusar-Poli, P., Borgwardt, S., Bechdolf, A., Addington, J., Riecher-Rössler, A., Schultze-Lutter, F., & Valmaggia, L. (2013). The psychosis high-risk state: A comprehensive state-of-the-art review. *JAMA Psychiatry, 70*(1), 107–120. https://doi.org/10.1001/jamapsychiatry.2013.269

Fusar-Poli, P., Cappucciati, M., De Micheli, A., Rutigliano, G., Bonoldi, I., Tognin, S., & McGuire, P. (2017). Diagnostic and prognostic significance of Brief Limited Intermittent Psychotic Symptoms (BLIPS) in individuals at ultra high risk. *Schizophrenia Bulletin, 43*(1), 48–56. https://doi.org/10.1093/schbul/sbw151

Fusar-Poli, P., Carpenter, W. T., Woods, S. W., & McGlashan, T. H. (2014). Attenuated psychosis syndrome: Ready for DSM-5.1? *Annual Review of Clinical Psychology, 10*, 155–192. https://doi.org/10.1146/annurev-clinpsy-032813-153645

Gaynes, B. N., Gavin, N., Meltzer-Brody, S., Lohr, K. N., Swinson, T., Gartlehner, G., & Miller, W. C. (2005). Perinatal depression: Prevalence, screening accuracy, and screening outcomes: Summary. In *AHRQ evidence report summaries*. Agency for Healthcare Research and Quality (US).

Greenfield, P., Joshi, S., Christian, S., Lekkos, P., Gregorowicz, A., Fisher, H. L., & Johnson, S. (2018). First episode psychosis in those over 35: Is there a role for early intervention? *Early Intervention in Psychiatry, 12*(3), 348–354. https://doi.org/10.1111/eip.12322

Grover, S., Chakrabarti, S., Kulhara, P., & Avasthi, A. (2017). Clinical practice guidelines for management of schizophrenia. *Indian Journal of Psychiatry, 59*(Suppl. 1), S19. https://doi.org/10.4103/0019-5545.196973

Gutiérrez-Maldonado, J., & Caqueo-Urízar, A. (2007). Effectiveness of a psycho-educational intervention for reducing burden in Latin American families of patients with schizophrenia. *Quality of Life Research, 16*(5), 739–747. https://doi.org/10.1007/s11136-007-9173-9

Haddock, G., McCarron, J., Tarrier, N., & Faragher, E. B. (1999). Scales to measure dimensions of hallucinations and delusions: The Psychotic Symptom Rating Scales (PSYRATS). *Psychological Medicine, 29*(4), 879–889. https://doi.org/10.1017/S0033291799008661

Hamed, S. A., & Attiah, F. A. (2019). Peripartum psychological distress conditions and disorders: Biopsychosocial view. *Journal of Neurology and Psychiatric Disorders, 1*(1). http://www.scienceinquest.

com/open-access/pdf/jnpd/peripartum-psychological-distress-conditions-and-disorders-biopsycho-social-view.php

Haroun, N., Dunn, L., Haroun, A., & Cadenhead, K. S. (2005). Risk and protection in prodromal schizophrenia: Ethical implications for clinical practice and future research. *Schizophrenia Bulletin*, *32*(1), 166–178. https://doi.org/10.1093/schbul/sbj007

Harrington, A. (2016). Mother love and mental illness: An emotional history. *Osiris*, *31*, 94–115. https://doi.org/10.1086/687559

Harris, M. J., & Jeste, D. V. (1988). Late-onset schizophrenia: An overview. *Schizophrenia Bulletin*, *14*(1), 39–55. https://doi.org/10.1093/schbul/14.1.39

Henriksen, M. G., Nordgaard, J., & Jansson, L. B. (2017). Genetics of schizophrenia: Overview of methods, findings and limitations. *Frontiers in Human Neuroscience*, *11*, 322. https://doi.org/10.3389/fnhum.2017.00322

Howes, O. D., McCutcheon, R., Owen, M. J., & Murray, R. M. (2017). The role of genes, stress, and dopamine in the development of schizophrenia. *Biological Psychiatry*, *81*(1), 9–20. https://doi.org/10.1016/j.biopsych.2016.07.014

Howes, O. D., McCutcheon, R., & Stone, J. (2015). Glutamate and dopamine in schizophrenia: An update for the 21st century. *Journal of Psychopharmacology*, *29*(2), 97–115. https://doi.org/10.1177/0269881114563634

Howes, O. D., & Murray, R. M. (2014). Schizophrenia: An integrated sociodevelopmental-cognitive model. *Lancet*, *383*(9929), 1677–1687. https://doi.org/10.1016/S0140-6736(13)62036-X

Hubbard, E. M., & Ramachandran, V. S. (2005). Neurocognitive mechanisms of synesthesia. *Neuron*, *48*(3), 509–520. https://doi.org/10.1016/j.neuron.2005.10.012

Javitt, D. C. (2015). Meeting overview: Sensory perception and schizophrenia. Lausanne, Switzerland June 31–July 1, 2014. *Schizophrenia Research: Cognition*, *2*(2), 42–45. https://doi.org/10.1016/j.scog.2015.04.003

Johnston, J. (2013). The ghost of the schizophrenogenic mother. *AMA Journal of Ethics*, *15*(9), 801–805. https://doi.org/10.1001/virtualmentor.2013.15.9.oped1-1309

Jones, I., & Craddock, N. (2001). Familiality of the puerperal trigger in bipolar disorder: Results of a family study. *American Journal of Psychiatry*, *158*(6), 913–917. https://doi.org/10.1176/appi.ajp.158.6.913

Kane, J. M. (2013). Tools to assess negative symptoms in schizophrenia. *The Journal of Clinical Psychiatry*, *74*(6), e12. https://doi.org/10.4088/JCP.12045tx2c

Keshavan, M. S., Morris, D. W., Sweeney, J. A., Pearlson, G., Thaker, G., Seidman, L. J., & Tamminga, C. (2011). A dimensional approach to the psychosis spectrum between bipolar disorder and schizophrenia: The Schizo-Bipolar Scale. *Schizophrenia Research*, *133*(1–3), 250–254. https://doi.org/10.1016/j.schres.2011.09.005

Kirkbride, J. (2013). The risk of substance-induced psychosis converting to schizophrenia varies with substance used and patient age. *Evidence-Based Mental Health, 16*(3), 65. https://doi.org/10.1136/eb-2013-101361

Kneeland, R. E., & Fatemi, S. H. (2013). Viral infection, inflammation and schizophrenia. *Progress in Neuro-Psychopharmacology and Biological Psychiatry, 42*, 35–48. https://doi.org/10.1016/j.pnpbp.2012.02.001

Konstantareas, M. M., & Hewitt, T. (2001). Autistic disorder and schizophrenia: Diagnostic overlaps. *Journal of Autism and Developmental Disorders, 31*(1), 19–28. https://doi.org/10.1023/A:1005605528309

Leader, D. (2011). *What is madness?* Penguin Books.

Müller, N., Riedel, M., Ackenheil, M., & Schwarz, M. J. (1999). The role of immune function in schizophrenia: An overview. *European Archives of Psychiatry and Clinical Neuroscience, 249*(4), S62–S68. https://doi.org/10.1007/PL00014187

Nemeroff, C. B., Weinberger, D., Rutter, M., MacMillan, H. L., Bryant, R. A., Wessely, S., & Malhi, G. S. (2013). DSM-5: A collection of psychiatrist views on the changes, controversies, and future directions. *BMC Medicine, 11*(1), 202. https://doi.org/10.1186/1741-7015-11-202

Niemi-Pynttäri, J. A., Sund, R., Putkonen, H., Vorma, H., Wahlbeck, K., & Pirkola, S. P. (2013). Substance-induced psychoses converting into schizophrenia: A register-based study of 18,478 Finnish inpatient cases. *The Journal of Clinical Psychiatry, 74*(1), e94–e99. https://doi.org/10.4088/JCP.12m07822

Peralta, V., & Cuesta, M. J. (2016). Delusional disorder and schizophrenia: A comparative study across multiple domains. *Psychological Medicine, 46*(13), 2829–2839. https://doi.org/10.1017/S0033291716001501

Pfammatter, M., Junghan, U. M., & Brenner, H. D. (2006). Efficacy of psychological therapy in schizophrenia: Conclusions from meta-analyses. *Schizophrenia Bulletin, 32*(Suppl.1), S64–S80. https://doi.org/10.1093/schbul/sbl030

Phelps, J. (2016). *A spectrum approach to mood disorders: Not fully bipolar but not unipolar–Practical management.* WW Norton & Company.

Pilling, S., Bebbington, P., Kuipers, E., Garety, P., Geddes, J., Orbach, G., & Morgan, C. (2002). Psychological treatments in schizophrenia: I. Meta-analysis of family intervention and cognitive behaviour therapy. *Psychological Medicine, 32*(5), 763–782. https://doi.org/10.1017/S0033291702005895

Pini, S., Queiroz, de., V, Dell'Osso., L, Abelli., M, Mastrocinque., C, Saettoni., M, & Cassano, G. B. (2004). Cross-sectional similarities and differences between schizophrenia, schizoaffective disorder and mania or mixed mania with mood-incongruent psychotic features. *European Psychiatry, 19*(1), 8–14. https://doi.org/10.1016/j.eurpsy.2003.07.007

Pitschel-Walz, G., Leucht, S., Bäuml, J., Kissling, W., & Engel, R. R. (2001). The effect of family interventions on relapse and rehospitalization in schizophrenia—A meta-analysis. *Schizophrenia Bulletin, 27*(1), 73–92. https://doi.org/10.1093/oxfordjournals.schbul.a006861

Reddy, M. S. (2014). Attenuated psychosis syndrome. *Indian Journal of Psychological Medicine, 36*(1), 1. https://doi.org/10.4103/0253-7176.127239

Reinhardt, M. M., & Cohen, C. I. (2015). Late-life psychosis: Diagnosis and treatment. *Current Psychiatry Reports, 17*(2), 1. https://doi.org/10.1007/s11920-014-0542-0

Reininghaus, U., Böhnke, J., Chavez-Baldini, U., Clementz, B., Pearlson, G., Keshavan, M., & Tamminga, C. (2018). 5.3 evidence on a transdiagnostic psychosis spectrum of schizophrenia, schizoaffective and psychotic bipolar disorder in the bipolar-schizophrenia network on intermediate phenotypes (b-snip). *Schizophrenia Bulletin, 44*(Suppl. 1), S6. https://doi.org/10.1093/schbul/sby014.015

Reininghaus, U., Böhnke, J. R., Chavez-Baldini, U, Gibbons, R., Ivleva, E., Clementz, B. A., & Tamminga, C. A. (2019). Transdiagnostic dimensions of psychosis in the Bipolar-Schizophrenia Network on Intermediate Phenotypes (B-SNIP). *World Psychiatry, 18*(1), 67–76. https://doi.org/10.1002/wps.20607

Reininghaus, U., Böhnke, J. R., Hosang, G., Farmer, A., Burns, T., McGuffin, P., & Bentall, R. P. (2016). Evaluation of the validity and utility of a transdiagnostic psychosis dimension encompassing schizophrenia and bipolar disorder. *The British Journal of Psychiatry, 209*(2), 107–113. https://doi.org/10.1192/bjp.bp.115.167882

Rosenthal, R. N., & Miner, C. R. (1997). Differential diagnosis of substance-induced psychosis and schizophrenia in patients with substance use disorders. *Schizophrenia Bulletin, 23*(2), 187–193. https://doi.org/10.1093/schbul/23.2.187

Schöttle, D., Schimmelmann, B. G., Conus, P., Cotton, S. M., Michel, C., McGorry, P. D., & Lambert, M. (2012). Differentiating schizoaffective and bipolar I disorder in first-episode psychotic mania. *Schizophrenia Research, 140*(1–3), 31–36. https://doi.org/10.1016/j.schres.2012.07.010

Seeman, M. V. (2009). The changing role of mother of the mentally Ill: From schizophrenogenic mother to multigenerational caregiver. *Psychiatry, 72*(3), 284–294. https://doi.org/10.1521/psyc.2009.72.3.284

Seeman, M. V. (2016). Schizophrenogenic Mother. In J. Lebow, A. Chambers, & D. C. Breunlin (Eds.). *Encyclopedia of couple and family therapy*. Springer International. https://doi.org/10.1007/978-3-319-15877-8_482-1

Sessa, B. (2012). *The psychedelic renaissance: Reassessing the role of psychedelic drugs in 21st century psychiatry and society*. Muswell Hill Press.

Sessa, B. (2016). Schizoaffective and schizophreniform disorders. In *The medical basis of psychiatry* (pp. 121–135). Springer Publishing.

Stentebjerg-Olesen, M., Pagsberg, A. K., Fink-Jensen, A., Correll, C. U., & Jeppesen, P. (2016). Clinical characteristics and predictors of outcome of schizophrenia-spectrum psychosis in children and adolescents: A systematic review. *Journal of Child and Adolescent Psychopharmacology*, *26*(5), 410–427. https://doi.org/10.1089/cap.2015.0097

Stephen, M., & Suryani, L. K. (2000). Shamanism, psychosis and autonomous imagination. *Culture, Medicine and Psychiatry*, *24*(1), 5–38. https://doi.org/10.1023/A: 1005528028869

Teigset, C. M., Mohn, C., Brunborg, C., Juuhl-Langseth, M, Holmén, A., & Rund, B. R. (2018). Do clinical characteristics predict the cognitive course in early-onset schizophrenia-spectrum disorders? *Journal of Child Psychology and Psychiatry*, *59*(9), 1012–1023. https://doi.org/10.1111/jcpp.12896

Tsuang, M. T., Van Os, J., Tandon, R., Barch, D. M., Bustillo, J., Gaebel, W., & Schultz, S. (2013). Attenuated psychosis syndrome in DSM-5. *Schizophrenia Research*, *150*(1), 31–35. https://doi.org/10.1016/j.schres.2013.05.004

Varghese, D., Scott, J., Welham, J., Bor, W., Najman, J., O'Callaghan, M., & McGrath, J. (2009). Psychotic-like experiences in major depression and anxiety disorders: A population-based survey in young adults. *Schizophrenia Bulletin*, *sbp083*, 389–393. https://doi.org/10.1093/schbul/sbp083

Vergara-Moragues, E., Mestre-Pintó, J. I., Gómez, P. A., Rodríguez-Fonseca, F., Torrens, M., & González-Saiz, F. (2016). Can symptoms help in differential diagnosis between substance-induced vs independent psychosis in adults with a lifetime diagnosis of cocaine use disorder? *Psychiatry Research*, *242*, 94–100. https://doi.org/10.1016/j.psychres.2016.05.043

Yung, A. R., Woods, S. W., Ruhrmann, S., Addington, J., Schultze-Lutter, F., Cornblatt, B. A., & Cannon, T. D. (2012). Whither the attenuated psychosis syndrome? *Schizophrenia Bulletin*, *38*(6), 1130–1134. https://doi.org/10.1093/schbul/sbs108

Yung, A. R., Yuen, H. P., McGorry, P. D., Phillips, L. J., Kelly, D., Dell'Olio, M., & Godfrey, K. (2005). Mapping the onset of psychosis: The comprehensive assessment of at-risk mental states. *Australian and New Zealand Journal of Psychiatry*, *39*(11–12), 964–971. https://doi.org/10.1080/j.1440-1614.2005.01714.x

Zimmermann, G., Favrod, J., Trieu, V. H., & Pomini, V. (2005). The effect of cognitive behavioral treatment on the positive symptoms of schizophrenia spectrum disorders: A meta-analysis. *Schizophrenia Research*, *77*(1), 1–9. https://doi.org/10.1016/j.schres.2005.02.018

7 Disorders of Mood: The Bipolar and Unipolar Disorders

The business of living brings with it the certainty of periods of anguish, heartache, occasions of irritability, regret, sorrow and even moments of hopelessness. Perhaps this is why the words of Longfellow's poetry, "Into each life some rain must fall/Some days must be dark and dreary," (Longfellow & McClatchy, 2000, p. 18) still resonates a century after it was penned. However, for persons experiencing a diagnosis within the categories of either the bipolar and related disorders or one of the depressive disorders, regaining stability in mood can represent both hard fought battles and short-lived victories. For some, these periods of extreme moods can bring with them a feeling that their volition and agency has been taken from them, leaving them abandoned to the whims of shifting moods.

This chapter will explore disorders related to mood, both unipolar (depressive) and bipolar. The structure of this chapter, however, departs from that of the DSM 5, which splits unipolar and bipolar disorders into two continuums. Because both dimensions are organized and diagnosed around shifts in mood, known as mood episodes, and because understanding these episodes and learning to differentiate them must be tackled before diagnosing disorders within either continuum, the mood disorders have been folded together here as they were in the DSM IV-TR. The chapter will begin with a brief discussion of changes to the mood disorders in the DSM 5 and then followed by an exploration of the mood episodes and their comparison with non-pathological mood states. Depression, bipolar disorder and the problem of the diagnosis of bipolar disorder in children will be discussed in this chapter followed by an exploration of critical points for differential diagnosis. The chapter will conclude with cases for diagnosis.

Changes Reflected in the DSM 5

Splitting the Mood Disorders into Two Dimensions. The decision to break the mood disorders into two dimensions, the depressive disorders and the bipolar and related disorders, marks a significant change in the DSM 5. As discussed in Chapter 1, the recent edition of the DSM recognizes disorders within each dimension as existing on a continuum. Contrary to the current organization, however, some authors argue that all mood disorders, bipolar and unipolar, exist on a single spectrum or continuum. This argument arises out of the fact that while some clients manifest presentations that fit neatly into either the depressive or bipolar dimension alone, many other clients display symptoms and timelines that are not as readily captured by the DSM 5's current criteria tables, necessitating some additional diagnostic considerations and decision-making in order to arrive at a sound diagnosis. Some argue that the difficulty in differentiating a diagnosis for these clients is due to the false dichotomy created by the DSM itself (Fawcett, 2014; Phelps, 2016). Further, it has long been understood that a subset of clients that first present with unipolar depression eventually develop a bipolar disorder, further supporting the notion of a single continuum. Still other researchers argue that these continuums are distinct and that the DSM 5 has not done enough to accurately describe substantive differences between unipolar and bipolar processes—essentially arguing that the manifestation of depression is different in unipolar and bipolar disorders, and asserting that clarification in the DSM would make early detection of bipolar depression possible (Koukopoulos et al., 2013). While a subset of researchers are debating whether or not the mood disorders should have been split, still others believe that the bipolar disorders would be better understood if combined with the psychotic disorders, citing research that suggests these disorders are born out of similar processes and have similar detrimental impacts on clients (Phelps, 2016). Ultimately, the decision to split the mood disorders and to place the bipolar and related disorders between the schizophrenia and depressive continuums represents an attempt to acknowledge the relationship between the three (American Psychiatric Association [APA], 2013). While at first blush, these arguments may seem purely theoretical in nature, the salience of these discussions comes to life when working with clients who don't fit neatly into one diagnostic category or disorder.

Mood Episodes and Their Specifiers: The Building Blocks of the Mood Disorders

Episodes of Mood. Diagnosis of disorders within the bipolar or depressive continuum, begins with the ability to identify and diagnose "mood episodes." An episode of mood is a distinct period of time in which a person's mood has shifted from their typical affect and takes on a distinct character matching a cluster of symptoms. Practically speaking, a mood episode captures the key features of the heart of unipolar or bipolar disorder. The benefit of describing episodes separately from disorders arises out of the fact that clients experience these episodes of mood in different ways and in different combinations that has implications for treatment and prognosis. The first step in diagnosing mood disorders is to identify mood episodes and to place them on a timeline. Consequently, accurately identifying mood episodes is a pivotal diagnostic skill.

One of the most challenging steps in diagnosing the disorders on the bipolar or depression continuums is learning to differentiate one type of mood episode from another, particularly where subtleties in one experience may overlap with another. Students often ask, for example, "How does a clinician identify the difference between a person experiencing a period of absorbed creativity or protracted irritation, for instance, from a person in a hypomanic state?" "What is the differentiating point between the person experiencing a hypomania and the person experiencing a full manic episode?" and "Are there cultural differences in the ways that people present mood episodes?" The next section will address some of these questions and will offer opportunities to practice differentiating episodes through scenarios.

Mania. Manic episodes are states of elevated or agitated mood lasting four or more days, unless hospitalization is required in which case the episode is diagnosed regardless of duration (APA, 2013). Manic states can look very different from one person to the next, but all share two primary features. First, though mania may resemble either elation or irritation, the mood will be observed as exaggerated or amplified. Second, for a mood episode to be identified as manic, it must cause *social or occupational impairment*. In other words, mania always causes difficulties for the person experiencing it, either while it is unfolding, as a consequence, or both. Mania can present differently thanks to cultural distinctions. For example, African Americans seem to describe having more hallucinations and delusions than do European Americans, making them more susceptible to a misdiagnosis of schizophrenia (Perlman et al., 2016).

A person experiencing a manic episode may not have insight into changes in their mood that are obvious to friends, family or to the clinician meeting with them in the therapeutic setting. When a client is manic, the diagnostician may observe or experience the client's ideas and speech as rapid, difficult to follow, jumping quickly from one idea to the next. A person who is manic may describe having a lot of ideas and a great deal of energy for projects, for example, but will not be able to focus their attention for long enough on any one idea to bring it to full fruition. They will often speak more loudly than is typical for them and will likely be unaware of the effect they are having on others (APA, 2013; Phelps, 2016).

Mania almost always includes impulsivity. This impulsivity is at the bottom of reckless behaviors that are also a feature of manic experiences. Often these behaviors create social or financial difficulties, such as excessive spending or gambling, but may also include behaviors that are dangerous to the person, such as promiscuous sexual encounters, or irresponsible drug and alcohol use. Psychosis is sometimes a feature of manic episodes, particularly, odd or grandiose beliefs (APA, 2013; Koukopoulos, 2014; Phelps, 2016). Though there are a number of different types of typical triggers for manic episodes, chief among them are stressful life events (Koenders et al., 2014), social pressures (Owen et al., 2015) and sleep disturbance (Phelps, 2016). Mania is sometimes divided into two categories: euphoric mania, which is the typical presentation, and dysphoric mania, which was once described as a mixed state episode.

Mixed Features Specifier. In Bipolar Disorders, components of the manic state could be seen together with components of depressive symptoms, until the publication of the DSM 5. This presentation was described as a mixed episode. However, the recent edition of the DSM has done away with the mixed episode and has instead included it among the specifiers for major depressive disorder (MDD), persistent depressive disorder (PDD), bipolar I and bipolar II disorders. Research suggests that mixed state presentations bring with them both a treatment response and course of illness distinct from those with more clearly distinguished manic or depressive states. These clients tend to experience more co-occurring disorders, suffer from anxiety, are more likely to have a "severely recurrent and complicated course," greater likelihood of suicidal behavior and poorer treatment outcomes overall (McIntyre et al., 2015; Swann et al., 2013). Consequently, the importance of identifying and treating mixed state features is clear. Further, mixed states can present as predominantly depressed or predominantly manic. However, this conceptualization of the mixed specifier has been challenged by researchers. They point out that some of the symptoms listed in the specifier's criteria table are so rarely seen in clients with MDD that they are of little diagnostic value, namely euphoria and grandiosity, (Koukopoulos, 2014; Leonpacher et al., 2015). For a more comprehensive discussion of the current understanding of distinguishing features of unipolar and bipolar depressive, manic and mixed features turn to the section at the end of the chapter, titled *The Skilled Diagnostician and Bipolar and Unipolar Mood Disorders.*

When depression is the predominant presentation but the features are mixed, meaning most of the symptoms you observe are symptoms of depression with a few manic symptoms scattered within, the likelihood of attempted suicide is increased when compared to those with depression alone, particularly when hopelessness is combined with impulsivity (Balázs et al., 2006; Goldberg et al., 2009). Consequently, noting this specifier is important in your diagnostic process.

Hypomania. Descriptively, a hypomanic episode looks very much like a manic episode though the intensity of the mood is not as extreme and the consequences are not as dire. By definition, hypomania does not require hospitalization and is never accompanied by psychosis (APA, 2013). Though a hypomanic episode is not difficult to discern from a manic one, primarily because a hypomanic episode is not impairing, it may be difficult to discern from sustained periods of creative and euphoric mood states or prolonged irritation. Research demonstrates that for clients, too, this is difficult. For instance, a study conducted in the Netherlands of those with documented histories of mood episodes revealed that while 85% of respondents were able to recognize and report a history of depressive episodes, only 22.5% recognized and reported hypomanic or manic episodes, suggesting that clients either recognize depressive episodes more readily, recall them better, or are more comfortable reporting them (Regreer et al., 2015).

The Depressive Episode. Though experiences of deep sadness and feelings of being on the outside looking in are unfortunately fairly common and even, perhaps, inevitable, depressive episodes are distinct from these more typical but uncomfortable periods. Depressive episodes are pervasive experiences of mood with long fingers that reach

TABLE 7.01 Differentiating the Manic Spectrum from Flow States

	Flow* *not a pathological experience	Hypomania	Mania*
Focus and Attention	Very focused upon a single creative activity	Sustained difficulty staying on task	Inability to remain on task at all
Experience of Ideas and Information	Highly creative around a single focused endeavor	Making connections easily, excited about ideas	Many, many ideas generated at a high rate of speed, often unrelated
Functionality	Highly focused, effective and productive	Working on several projects at once, may have some difficulty completing tasks	Unable to complete work
Communication	Speaks enthusiastically about project, but not necessarily on other themes	Rapid speech that is, at times, hard to follow	Extremely rapid speech, disconnected
Sleep	May or may not experience sleep changes	May require less sleep to feel rested	Feels sufficiently rested after 3 hours of sleep; may not sleep at all for several days
Experience of Self	May temporarily lose a sense of self, becoming one with their creative venture	Enthusiastic, tends to be entertaining, center of attention	Tending toward narcissism and grandiosity
Relational Skills	Unremarkable	Enthusiastic, extroverted, center of attention	Irritating, lacking self-awareness, dominates the relational space
Risk Behaviors	Unremarkable Impulsivity or risk	Impulsive, some moderate risk-taking evident	Evident risk-taking, damaging/ potentially damaging decisions
			*Note that manic level symptoms bring impairment to full functioning in the domain

Source: *Adapted from American Psychiatric Association (2013) and Phelps (2016).

TABLE 7.02 Psychotic Presentations and Mood Congruency

Mood Congruent Psychotic Features	Mood Incongruent Psychotic Features
These delusions or hallucinations fit within the client's general beliefs and mood	These delusions and hallucinations contradict the client's beliefs and mood
Example A:	Example A:
A depressed client hears a voice whispering to her that she is a failure and taunts her when she makes small errors.	A depressed client holds the belief that she has the special ability to see cancer in complete strangers and to heal them with her mind before it is ever detected by a doctor.
Example B:	Example B:
A manic client believes his "extraordinary powers of telepathic influence" will assure success in promoting his idea to a business sponsor.	A manic client hears a voice calling him a loser and suggesting he would be better off dead.

into all aspects of daily functioning, seriously impacting wellbeing. Depressive episodes can look very different from one person to the next depending upon the severity of the episode and the combination of features that are manifested. Most prominent in the depressive episode is the sense of despair, hopelessness and worthlessness that frequently give way to avolition, a kind of paralysis of human spirit and loss of connection. Basic functions of living, such as eating and sleeping are typically disrupted. A depressive episode is identified when five of the following features are present: disruptions of sleep, disturbances in eating, suicidal or morbid thinking, decreased energy, psychomotor agitation or slowing, loss of concentration, intense and disproportionate guilt and a loss of interest or pleasure in things that once were enjoyed (APA, 2013).

Psychosis. Psychosis is not a mood episode but it can be a feature of either a manic or depressive episode. Psychotic features might include grandiose ideas, odd beliefs and auditory or visual hallucination. In the unipolar and bipolar disorders, however, these experiences of psychosis occur exclusively within mood episodes, either depressive or manic, but never during periods when the client's mood has stabilized. When a person experiences mood episodes along with symptoms of psychosis that fall outside of these mood episodes, the differential diagnosis of schizoaffective disorder must be considered (see p. 105 of the DSM 5). Psychotic features when seen in clients with mixed features of mood are more likely to be mood incongruent, than in either purely manic or purely depressive psychotic presentations. For clients with bipolar disorder who also experience psychosis, the executive function skills appear to be very similar to those on the schizophrenia spectrum, making this configuration of symptoms quite impairing (Ancín et al., 2013). These clients need specially tailored support as do their families and caregivers.

Suicide. Like psychosis, suicide and suicidal thinking are not considered episodes. When present, however, suicidal thinking is a serious concern to clinicians and represents a significant threat to those diagnosed with bipolar and unipolar depressions. According to the World Health Organization (WHO) (2018) in 2016, suicide was the second leading cause of death among those 15-29. Perhaps due to the impulsivity seen in bipolar clients, the incidence of suicidal behavior and deaths from suicides is higher among those with bipolar disorders than those with depression only. Those experiencing depressive episodes with mixed features show greatly increased rates of suicidal behavior and suicide completion, as much as 120 times as high as those not experiencing a mood episode of any kind. Some evidence suggests that among those diagnosed with bipolar I disorder (BPD I) and bipolar II disorder (BPD II), a longer durations of a major depressive episode are predictive of higher rates of attempted suicide as is a comorbid cluster C personality disorder (avoidant, dependent and obsessive-compulsive personality) (Pallaskorpi et al., 2017). Adolescents diagnosed with bipolar disorders are much more likely to attempt suicide than peers with other mental health diagnoses (De Crescenzo et al., 2017; Goldstein et al., 2005). Whether the client is suffering from a bipolar or unipolar disorder, however, the risk of attempted suicide is highest during mixed presentations and within major depressive episodes (Pallaskorpi et al., 2017). Risk is also elevated following psychiatric hospitalization (Turecki & Brent, 2016).

Across dimensions, the likelihood of suicide and attempted suicide is increased when a person describes feeling extreme hopelessness, when depression is accompanied by chronic illness, after a significant financial loss, during a period of bereavement, when there are complaints of sleep deprivation, as well as when a person is very introverted (Turecki & Brent, 2016). Risk of depression and suicidality also increase dramatically with increase in adverse childhood experiences, such as experiences of physical or sexual abuse, witnessing domestic violence or experiencing substance use in the home (Fuller-Thomson et al., 2016). The highest risk factor for suicide attempt, however, is the history of previous attempt (WHO, 2018). Chances of suicide and suicide attempts decrease when a person has a strong social network, a religious or spiritual identity, is the parent to young children or identifies other compelling reasons for living, has capacities for problem-solving and is generally more extraverted and positive (Turecki & Brent, 2016). Currently, both the Veterans Administration and social media platforms, such as Facebook, are implementing artificial intelligence programs to identify and flag those at high or imminent risk of suicide. Facebook used A.I. to contact police with concerns about suicide risk over 3,500 times by the end of 2018 (Kaste, 2018; Marks, 2018).

Non-pathological Mood States

Flow. Mihaly Csikszentmihalyi, a Hungarian psychologist, introduced the idea of flow. Flow, he explained, is a highly focused mental state that allows for freedom of

BOX 7.01 TRY THIS: DIFFERENTIATING MANIA, HYPOMANIA AND FLOW

What follows are three different experiences of high energy, lessened need for sleep and increased appreciation for creativity. Can you discern differences that point to either non-pathological experiences or those that disrupt wellbeing? As you reflect on each person's experience of painting and creativity, which of these states best fits each description: mania, hypomania or flow? What questions would you like to ask in order to verify your hunch?

Manuel. Manuel is a sophomore in college. He is currently enrolled in several courses, including a class in portraiture. Manuel has been captivated by this class and while his other courses interest him, none have captured his imagination like the painting course. He regularly paints in the art studio on campus until the building closes and he is forced to stop. He often thinks of new ideas for artwork during other classes and doodles in the margins of his class notes. When he paints, he loses a sense of time and sometimes forgets to eat. Manuel notes, "If the art studio didn't close at eleven, I would probably paint right through til dawn!" Manuel admits that his grades in his Italian Language class have suffered because his painting cuts into his homework time, so his homework is sometimes rushed. He will likely earn a "B" this semester in several of his courses.

Devin. Devin, a 58-year-old theoretical mathematics professor at a local university, describes a recent period that culminated in his being admitted to the hospital. Devin shares that he had been working at the university the previous summer on a new theory, about which he felt growing excitement. "In fact, I was completely absorbed by this idea and I remember my whole body seemed to be charged with energy as I considered its possibilities." He reports that the theory so captivated him that he felt no desire to sleep and does not remember eating at all over the three-day period. While in his office, one evening he had an idea that rather than depict his theory with numbers, which he felt was "too flat and without life," he wanted to depict it with imagery and music. Working through the night and into the next day, Devin took down shelving from the Northern facing wall and, using markers and paint he covered the surface in swirling splashes of color and texture over which he included mathematical formulas as well as lines from music, poetry and movies. Late into the second night of his painting and theorizing, a security guard noticed the light coming from Devin's office and investigated. The guard found him distracted, agitated and surrounded by piles of books, papers and the remains of the shelving. Confused, the security guard challenged Devin and the exchange quickly devolved into shouting. The local police were called. Soon after the police arrived, Devin was taken to the hospital where he was admitted. Once treated and released, Devin shared, "I was so sure I was onto something really illuminating, something that was going to create a kind of mathematical coherence between thought and movement, but looking at it now I can't remember or grasp what I was thinking. It is frightening to think about how out of touch with reality I was."

Alicia. Alicia, a 37-year-old mother of three, woke 4 days ago to a welcome and familiar feeling of renewed energy and creative impulse. After a winter-long depression, Alicia was glad to find her interests renewed and to experience restored energy for long-neglected chores. She eagerly cleared out her laundry room of months worth of towels, sweaters, jeans and dirty linens, cleared cupboards of empty and near empty cleaning products, scrubbed floors, cabinets and shelves. She then decided to "completely redo the room into something bright and cheery." Alicia painted the walls a deep chartreuse and the cabinets a brilliant violet. Working late into the night and leaving her children to fend for themselves with cereal and toast, she began tearing out the room's outdated linoleum tiles. However, just as suddenly as it appeared, Alicia's energy returned to what it had been before she had experienced her depression and her mood became more even and reflective. Alicia now reports that she wishes she had taken more time and given some thought to planning the remodel of the space. She shares, "Yikes! That color is really something awful. I'm going to have to hire someone to repaint it, the paint is not only ugly, I rushed through it and it shows. There is paint all over the ceiling. I'll also have to hire someone to finish the floor. I don't have the skill to lay flooring. It was nice having all that energy and inspiration while it lasted, though, and I'm thrilled that I got that room cleaned up."

creativity. In this state, people have described feeling unbound by a sense of self and are instead completely absorbed in the creative act. People reflecting upon experiences of flow sometimes describe losing themselves or "becoming their work," they frequently lose a sense of time and feel they have limitless energy for their creative interests. People experiencing flow can lose interest in things outside their creative focus (Csikszentmihalyi, 2014). Flow is not a pathological experience, and as such is not diagnosed but might be confused with hypomania. Flow can be differentiated from hypomania; however, in that the energy, creativity and focus of flow is centered around the person's primary interest or passion, is productive, and adds to personal wellbeing. In contrast, the person experiencing hypomania will experience a more pervasive elevation in mood and energy and will be less able to focus this energy productively than the person in a state of flow.

Charette. Charette is a term coined by Parisian students of architecture in the mid-19th century, and has come to describe a period of intense focused work that is generated in order to meet a looming deadline (Oxford English Dictionary, 2018). A period of charette, like flow, features focused intensity of work and creativity but, because it is driven by a deadline, is time-limited. A state of charette is not pathological and is not diagnosed.

Ennui. In contrast to the experience of flow or of charette, people can sometimes feel an absence of inspiration or excitement, a feeling of ennui. People experiencing ennui may have a great deal to do, such as a project at work, housework, social obligations and so on, but feel very little motivation to begin or complete these projects. A person experiencing ennui may feel listless, lacking energy and generally dissatisfied. With a bit of reflection people experiencing ennui will often describe a lack of meaning in their work, and, in this way, ennui may be existential at its core (Hollis, 2008). Though this experience may be both protracted and unpleasant, it is not itself, pervasive. A person having this experience may still enjoy the company of friends or the taste of a morning cup of coffee and a good pastry, for example, while at the same time, wonder if their work is creating meaning in their lives. This type of experience is not pathological and is not diagnosed but may be most unwelcome and inconvenient.

Protracted Irritation and Dissatisfaction. Arguably, anyone paying attention to the state of the world will find a great deal to be concerned about and anyone interested in the causes of turmoil in the world will be able to identify sources of anger and despair. Both family and work situations expose us to the failings of those in our immediate circles. Social dynamics such as racism, paternalism, homophobia and so on create chronic sources of suffering for a significant portion of our society. National and international conflicts are also sources of frustration, worry and disappointment. Mood can be impacted by these experiences in such a way that irritation, sadness and worry are sustained, but are not by themselves pathological.

The Bipolar and Unipolar Dimensions

Again, in your current edition of the DSM, the unipolar and bipolar disorders will not be presented together as they are in this chapter. As you read through the DSM 5, you will note that there are three disorders on the bipolar continuum (bipolar I, bipolar II and cyclothymic disorder) and four on the unipolar or depressive continuum (disruptive mood dysregulation, major depressive, persistent depressive and premenstrual dysphoric disorders). Each is described here briefly.

Bipolar I. The distinguishing feature of BPD I is the manic episode. Any history of one or more episodes of mania (episodes should not arise out of a medical illness, the side effects of medications or substances or are not better explained by the schizophrenia spectrum) results in a diagnosis of BPD I. Most often BPD I is accompanied by a history of depressive episodes or by subthreshold depression, but in some cases there is no history of depression at all. A history of hypomania is also likely but not necessary for diagnosis (APA, 2013). BPD I is frequently misdiagnosed in part because mania is challenging to capture in case histories (Zimmerman et al., 2008). Though the manic episode differentiates BPD I from BPD II and from major depression, most people diagnosed with BPD I experience only a third as many manic symptoms as they do depressive. It is important to keep in mind that while these depressive symptoms may manifest as full major depressive episodes or as a subthreshold syndrome, for most of those with BPD I, the bulk of the presentation is depressive (Judd & Akiskal, 2003). Consequently, for many with BPD I, the initial diagnosis is major depression and is only accurately diagnosed 5-10 years later (Phillips & Kupfer, 2013).

Bipolar II. Bipolar II is something of a bridge diagnosis. The client who is accurately diagnosed with BPD II has a history of at least one major depressive episode and at least one hypomanic episode but will never have met full criteria for mania (APA, 2013). Like those with BPD I, those with BPD II also experience significantly more depressive symptoms than hypomania, consequently, BPD II can be difficult to distinguish from major depression (Judd & Akiskal, 2003). BPD II, like BPD I, is chronic.

BOX 7.02 CONSIDER THIS: DEPRESSIVE SYMPTOMS IN BIPOLAR DISORDERS

Keep in mind that while manic and hypomanic episodes distinguish the bipolar dimension, depression symptoms are more likely to constitute the bulk of symptoms experienced by those with BPD I or BPD II (Judd & Akiskal, 2003; Phillips & Kupfer, 2013).

A longitudinal study of individuals diagnosed with bipolar disorder, spanning over a decade, revealed that participants experienced symptoms of one pole or the other just over 53% of the time, however, the vast majority of that time featured depressive symptoms, more than 50% of the year, while 1% was spent hypomanic and just over 2% in mixed states (Judd et al., 2003). In our work as diagnosticians, keeping in mind the dominant presence of depressive symptoms in both BPD I and II while remembering the distinguishing features of mania (BPD I) and hypomania (BPD II) will help to avoid misdiagnosis.

Cyclothymia. For a long time, cyclothymia was thought to be a less severe form of BPD II and little was written about the disorder beyond its potential to evolve into another of the "major bipolar disorders." However, in the last decade interest has turned to cyclothymia, its characteristics, treatment and potential for misdiagnosis. Diagnostically, cyclothymia features long-standing (at least 2 years) subthreshold cycles of depressive and hypomanic symptoms, and brings with it near constant fluctuations in mood and volatility. Predictably, the unstable moods that are the key feature of cyclothymia interfere with relationships and cause considerable disruptions to well-being (Perugi et al., 2015; Van Meter et al., 2018; Van Meter et al., 2012).

Disruptive Mood Dysregulation Disorder. Disruptive mood dysregulation disorder, DMDD, is new to the DSM 5 and was added to the depressive disorders continuum in large part to stem the destructive tsunami of the misdiagnosis of rapid cycling bipolar disorder in children. DMDD, its placement in the history of bipolar diagnosis and its differential diagnosis from oppositional defiance will be discussed at length later in this chapter. Diagnostically, this new disorder features frequent outbursts of temper (three or more per week) that are both out of sync with the child's level of development and out of proportion with the triggering event. Children accurately diagnosed with DMDD are characterized by pervasive and persistent irritability and anger. To diagnose this disorder, these symptoms must have been present for a year with no more than 3 months reprieve from these symptoms during that time (APA, 2013).

Major Depressive Disorder. In the United States, MDD is the most commonly diagnosed mental disorder. MDD is accurately diagnosed when a person reports a history of at least one major depressive episode, described earlier, and reports no history of mania or hypomania. Of course, the depressive episodes should not be the result of a medical condition or the side effect of substances or medication (APA, 2013). MDD tends to be chronic, nearly a third of those diagnosed never experience a full remission of symptoms and about 75% of those treated with first-line antidepressants will not respond (Phillips & Kupfer, 2013). Researchers have challenged the idea that the symptoms included within the construct of depression constitute a single disorder. Fried and Nesse (2015) examined the symptom presentations of more than 3,000 participants diagnosed with depression. If depression is a valid construct, they argue, they should have been able to identify a few symptom profiles populated by a large number of participants. Instead, these authors found an astounding 1,031 symptom profiles, more than 800 of which were populated by five or fewer participants. What's more, the most common presentation described less than 2% of the total study population. These differences in symptom presentation within depression, described as "covert heterogeneity" seem to suggest that depression as it is described now, is less likely to be a single consistent syndrome (Fried & Nesse, 2015). Whether a single syndrome or a large collection of closely related presentations, mounting evidence points to the genetic origins of major depression. A person with a first degree relative with depression is nearly three times as likely to develop depression in their lifetimes. (Sullivan et al., 2000, in Flint & Kendler, 2014). Though the heterogeneity of depression is not debated, attempts to differentiate depressive subtypes through the use of genetic markers have not born fruit, likely due to the fact that depression arises out of a number of causal factors, only one of which is genetic (Flint & Kendler, 2014).

Persistent Depressive Disorder (Dysthymia). This presentation is one that stands out from the other depressive disorders thanks to its duration. Adults who struggle with PDD have experienced depression for 2 or more years with no more than 8 weeks of relief from these symptoms. These clients differ from one another, however, in that some may experience full major depressive episodes for the entire duration, sometimes known as "double depression" (specify *with persistent major depressive episode)*, while others experience subthreshold depression symptoms (specify *with pure dysthymic syndrome)* and variations in between. While PDD is less broadly discussed than MDD, it would be a mistake to assume that it is a less impactful or less burdensome form of MDD. PDD tends to be resistant to psychotherapy and has poorer outcomes generally than MDD (Quitkin, 2002; Vandeleur et al., 2017). Of clients on the depressive spectrum, those with PDD with persistent major depressive episode, in contrast to those with pure dysthymia, have been shown to be the most severely impacted, followed by those with MDD with recurrent depressive episodes (Vandeleur et al., 2017).

BOX 7.03 DEPRESSION DESCRIPTORS FOUND OUTSIDE THE DSM 5

Anergic Depression. Sometimes also described as "*retarded depression,*" this describes a depression featuring a distinctive lack of mental and physical energy (Cristancho et al., 2011).

Compassion Fatigue. Also described as *vicarious trauma*, this describes feelings overlapping with depressive symptoms, such as hopelessness, powerlessness, sadness, guilt and so on, that arise from close contact with others who are suffering, and is often seen in primary care providers (Figley, 2002). Individuals who suspect they are suffering from compassion fatigue may also meet full criteria for a depressive disorder.

Double Depression. This subtype of depression includes those who meet the full criteria for major depressive disorder for 2 or more years and would be diagnosed with persistent depressive disorder (PDD), with persistent major depressive episode

Melancholia. This subtype of depression can be indicated with the specifier *with melancholic features*, and features psychomotor disturbance, weight loss, early morning waking, guilt and loss of all pleasure in life (APA, 2013).

Role Impairment. This term describes the degree to which depression interferes with an individual's capacity to function within their social role, for example as partner, parent, employee, student and so on. Role impairment is typically measured by the Sheehan Disability Scale © or the World Health Organization's Disability Scale (WHO-DAS) (APA, 2013).

Vital Exhaustion. Similar to anergic depression, this construct describes extreme fatigue and includes irritability and feelings of demoralization. Clients who suspect they might be suffering from vital exhaustion may also meet full criteria for a depressive disorder (Van Diest & Appels, 1991).

Premenstrual Dysphoric Disorder. Premenstrual dysphoric disorder, PDD, is a mood disorder tied to the fluctuations in women's reproductive hormones. PDD is diagnosed when a year or more of symptoms coinciding with menstrual cycles is documented. To be given this diagnosis a woman will experience one or more symptoms of irritability, mood swings, interpersonal conflicts, depressed mood or anxiety and at least one of decreased interest, poor concentration, fatigue, appetite changes, changes in sleep patterns, feelings of being overwhelmed or breast tenderness. These symptoms begin a week before the onset of the cycle and begin to subside as the cycle begins (APA, 2013). PDD tends to be chronic and has a similar impact on wellbeing as MDD (Halbreich et al., 2003).

Covid-19 and the Incidence of Unipolar and Bipolar Symptoms. Researchers and clinicians have noted a significant increase in reported mental health-related symptoms since the advent of the Covid-19 pandemic. Stressors that result from efforts, to curb the spread of the disease, such as sheltering in place, and the resultant job-loss,

TABLE 7.03 Mood Disorders and Their Episodes

DX	Manic Episode	Hypomanic Episode	Depressive Episode	Psychosis
Major depressive disorder (MDD)	never	never	MUST	may
Bipolar I (BPI)	MUST	may	may	may
Bipolar I (BPII)	never	MUST	MUST	never
Schizoaffective Disorder	MUST (Or Depressive Episode)	may	MUST (Or Manic Episode)	MUST
Cyclothymia	never	Subthreshold only	Subthreshold only	never
Persistent depressive disorder (PDD)	never	never	subthreshold or full	may

Source: Adapted from American Psychiatric Association (2013).

isolation, additional burden and stress of educating children from home and caring for elders without additional help, paired with isolation from family and friends, as well as financial worries have compounded stressors that might otherwise lead to depression and anxiety. Survey research reveals that negative mental health consequences were higher for those sheltering in place than for those who were not. More than half of those that suffered income loss due to the pandemic reported mental health consequences. Researchers anticipate increased rates of substance use problems as well as suicide, though data is not available at this writing to support or contradict these concerns (Panchal et al., 2020).

Bipolarity in Children and Adolescents

The recent history of the diagnosis of bipolar disorder in children serves as a cautionary tale for every student of diagnostics and is included here both to help clarify the current understanding of continuum and also to again remind ourselves of the importance of skilled and thoughtful diagnostic processes in providing mental health care. Understanding this history makes it clear that diagnosis of bipolarity in children should be undertaken only with extraordinary caution, hesitancy, consideration and consultation.

Concern, Controversy and an Evolving Understanding within the Profession. For decades, bipolar diagnoses in children were seen only rarely. For example, in 1995 the incidence of pediatric bipolar disorders (PBD) was estimated to manifest in only 25 children in 100,000. However between 1995 and 2003, the number of diagnoses rose dramatically to 1,003 in 100,000, a 40-fold jump in less than a decade, boys with comorbid attention deficit hyperactivity disorder (ADHD) making up the bulk of these (Blader & Carlson, 2007; Moreno et al., 2007; Pogge et al., 2001). The explosion of diagnoses can be traced to a series of research studies sponsored by the National Institutes of Health (NIH) and spearheaded by Dr. Joseph Biederman. He forwarded that nearly 25% of children with ADHD would also meet criteria for a bipolar diagnosis and argued for significant reconceptualization of symptom presentation in children, many of which, he argued, overlapped with criteria for ADHD and oppositional defiance (Biederman et al., 1999; Biederman et al., 2004; Biederman et al., 1996; Wozniak et al., 2005). With the growing number of diagnosed cases of PBD came a dramatic increase in prescription treatment of this population.

At about the same time, prescribers were warned about the potential for increased suicidality in teens taking selective serotonin reuptake inhibitors (SSRIs), which led prescribing physicians to turn, instead, to other classes of medications. This shift is thought to have resulted in an increase in the use of atypical antipsychotics and other medications for these children and also for children diagnosed with PBD, something that alarmed some medical professionals and is a continuing concern today (Roy et al., 2014).

When a 2 ½-year-old Massachusetts toddler was diagnosed with bipolar disorder and later, at the age of 4, died of an overdose of the prescription medication clonidine, the debate over pediatric diagnosis and medications was further inflamed (Couric, 2007). However, at this same time the NIH funded a group of studies, The Course and Outcome of Bipolar Youth (COBY). These studies were conducted using long-term naturalistic study of children and adolescents carrying a PBD diagnosis. A number of these studies challenged the traditional thinking around bipolarity and began to produce support for a presentation, or phenotype, that featured a slow and insidious onset, a much more rapid cycling of moods than described in the DSM, and featuring irritability rather than euphoria and grandiosity. As the debate became more contentious, researchers and clinicians fell into two primary camps regarding the diagnosis of PBD: narrow and broad views.

The more narrow or conservative view held that BPI should be diagnosed only when there were episodes with clear beginnings and endings representing a distinct departure from the child's typical mood and functioning and impacted the child in such a way as to be impairing (Dickstein et al., 2005; Pogge et al., 2001). The broader view, taken by most research coming out of the COBY studies, held that Bipolar disorder existed on a spectrum, and that the spectrum should include episodes with less clearly defined beginning and ending points. Those taking the broader view argued that these less discrete episodes were marked by severe irritability and explosive behavior. They further asserted that children don't usually experience elation or grandiosity and these traits should not be required to diagnose mania or hypomania (Biederman et al., 2005; Margulies et al., 2012) This very rapid cycle was described as *ultradian cycling*, when occurring in a single day, and *ultra rapid* when occurring within a week.

The State of the Debate as of the Publication of the DSM 5. The DSM 5 sides with the narrow view of the diagnosis of bipolarity and addresses this debate in two ways. First, the fifth edition added DMDD with the express purpose to reduce the number of misdiagnoses of pediatric bipolar disorder (APA, 2013). The DMDD criteria describe a tendency toward irritability and reactivity but without grandiosity or euphoria, previously described in the literature as BD-NOS and sometimes as BP II "rapid cycling"). The sustained irritability between temper outbursts characterized in DMDD also seemed to describe children who did not demonstrate clear and discrete mood episodes.

In a second effort to curb the explosion of pediatric bipolar disorder diagnoses, the DSM 5 also maintained the rapid cycling specifier that could be added to BP I or BP II. The language and description of rapid cycling remains such that it excludes the possibility of ultradian or ultra-rapid cycles. The rapid cycling specifier can only be added when the following conditions are met: (1) full criteria are met for each episode including duration and (2) there is an inter-episode return to previous function of at least 2 months, unless the second episode is of the opposite polarity. Each of these criteria make cycling between episodes within a single day or week impossible (APA, 2013).

There is currently no consensus as to whether DMDD is a manifestation of the depressive continuum, a manifestation of ADHD with dysregulated mood, or would be more appropriately placed within the bipolar continuum (Margulies Weintraub et al., 2012).

Most of the extant research on pediatric bipolar disorder predates the DSM 5; many of the conclusions and recommendations coming out of that literature for diagnosis and treatment are now challenged by researchers and practitioners. However, there are still practitioners ill-informed about recent changes in best practice approaches to diagnosing and treating children with volatile moods. Consequently, it is all the more important that we maintain strong consultative relationships with other professionals who share contact with our clients, such as physicians, psychiatrists and social workers.

Diagnosis of Depression in Children and Adolescents

When Teens and Children Experience Depression. Depression among adolescents is common, a recent NIH sponsored study places the 12-month prevalence rates at 7.5%. When Adolescents experience depression, it tends to come with high levels of role impairment and is generally accompanied by a comorbid disorder, most often anxiety, ADHD or conduct disorders (Avenevoli et al., 2015). As described earlier, suicidality is frequently reported and represents a significant threat as suicide is the second leading cause of death in this population (WHO, 2018).

TABLE 7.04 Contrasting DMDD and BPD

	Disruptive Mood Dysregulation Disorder	Bipolar Disorder
Mood	Protracted and consistent irritation, anger and tantrums across settings	Elevated, expansive or irritable mood with inter-episode return to stable state
Episodes	Tantrums of verbal and/or aggressive acting out	Manic or hypomanic with possible depressive episodes
Frequency	Three or more tantrums per week	Cycles may be infrequent or "rapid cycling"; ultradian and ultra rapid (daily or weekly cycling is not recognized in the DSM 5 and should not be diagnosed as BPD)
Duration	1 year	Varies by mood cycle combinations and inter-episode states, see pages 123-127 of the DSM 5
Exclusions	Younger than 6; older than 18 May not be diagnosed with oppositional defiant disorder, intermittent explosive disorder, bipolar disorder Causal substance use, medical or neurological disorders	When mood episodes are better explained by schizoaffective disorder, schizophrenia or schizophreniform disorder, exclude BPD When no clear distinction between mood episodes is present, inter-episode states remain irritable and/or angry, or mood shifts rapidly over the course of the day or week, diagnose DMDD
Predominance	DMDD predominates oppositional defiance History of BPD predominates DMDD	Confirmed BPD predominates DMDD

Source: Table contents sourced in APA, 2013, assembled by Rebecca Peifer, M.A.

Depression in children may show up as somatic complaints, such as stomach ache or muscular pain (Saps et al., 2009), which are then predictive of depression and generalized anxiety disorder later in life (Shanahan et al., 2015). Depression may also manifest as irritability in addition to or instead of sadness typically associated with depression (APA, 2013) and, as in adolescence, is frequently comorbid with behavioral problems. There is some evidence from differences in cognitive styles among children with depression and conduct problems and those without. For example, children with depression have a tendency to make hostile attributions to others' behavior and to respond in kind, suggesting the need to tailor treatment to address counter-productive cognitive styles (Schepman et al., 2014).

Depression in childhood and adolescence is caused by the intersection of a number of factors, which include genetics (Flint & Kendler, 2014), adverse childhood events such as domestic violence or substance use in the home that lead to poor attachment

BOX 7.04 CONSIDER THIS: CONSULTING WITH PRIMARY CARE PHYSICIANS AND PRESCRIBERS

An important part of our work in counseling children is advocacy for our clients. When our clients are children, vigilance and care are especially needed. It may be necessary to advocate for clients with parents, teachers and prescribing physicians who may not be familiar with current diagnostic practices where pediatric bipolar disorder and the differential diagnosis of DMDD is concerned. In the role of advocacy, the power differential between the counselor, parents and physician should also be considered.

Many clients get medications for bipolar disorder and other mental health concerns from primary care physicians who may not have kept pace with the current caution around the diagnosis and treatment of pediatric bipolar disorder. Strong, positive relationships with local physicians and pediatricians will be important in your work with children and adolescents generally, and with children who present with volatile moods in particular. Keep in mind that any communications with your client's doctors requires consent for release of information and documentation of that consent. In broaching a conversation about appropriate diagnosis and treatment of your client, you will want to develop some of the following habits:

- Gaining and keeping up-to-date release of information documents for each of your clients and each of their prescribing physicians.
- When a diagnosis is made and a treatment plan is developed, send the prescribing physician or primary care physician (PCP) a brief letter justifying and naming your client's diagnosis along with a short description of your intervention approach and a summary of key milestones that you will be using to measure progress.
- Update this letter if your diagnosis changes or you have concerns about progress that may relate to pharmacological interventions.
- Keep these notes very short and clear. Doctors' time, and yours, is at a premium.
- Maintain copies of these letters in your own records.

or physical or sexual abuse (Brodsky, 2016; Ivarsson et al., 2016) and so on, the full breadth of which is too numerous and complex to be captured in this very brief discussion. While adverse childhood events have long been associated with depression in childhood and adolescence, the role of peers and peer victimization in depression is the focus of a good deal of recent attention. Peer victimization has been associated with both immediate and delayed-effect depression (Stapinski et al., 2015).

Differentiating between MDD and oppositional defiant disorder (ODD). Because DMDD is a new diagnosis, very little research is available to provide direction in distinguishing DMDD from other disorders with similar features, such as intermittent explosive disorder (IED) or ODD. As is illustrated in Table 7.05, all three disorders feature tantruming that stands out as both more frequent and more intense than might otherwise be expected, and these tantrums are out of sync with expected developmental responses in children of comparable age. Children diagnosed with any of these three disorders evidence angry and defiant behavior and frequently strike out at others or break things (Dougherty et al., 2014; Freeman et al., 2016).

The DSM 5 notes that the child with DMDD will have sustained irritable and angry mood between tantrums and outbursts while the child with ODD will not, and further notes that many children with DMDD will meet criteria for ODD, but not the reverse (APA, 2013). However, the overlap of diagnostic criteria between the three disorders leaves room for bias to determine the diagnosis rather than distinguishing features. In fact, when field tested, this disorder was accurately diagnosed only half the time (Regier et al., 2013). In an effort to discover and describe differences between children diagnosed with ODD and those diagnosed with MDD, researchers compared more than 500 children carrying one or the other diagnosis and, using a number of checklists and inventories measuring behavioral problems, found that these two groups did not differ in caregiver reported symptoms, current mania symptoms or depressive symptoms. This study also revealed that these two groups were not significantly different in teacher reports of aggression, or on clinician rating scales. However, children with DMDD did show more impairment and tended to have poorer family functioning than children with ODD. Ultimately, the authors of this study called into question the utility of the mood dysregulation diagnosis since the discerning traits between these two groups were not strong (Freeman et al., 2016).

When a child is brought to counseling because of frequent tantrums, a dark and angry mood, defiance and a habit of irritating others, how will you distinguish whether or not your client has a DMDD, oppositional defiance or IED? How will your diagnosis shape the treatment you select for your client? The DSM 5 instructs clinicians to diagnose only DMDD when criteria are met for DMDD and ODD, do not diagnose both disorders together. The DSM's language discerning the two seems to hinge on whether or not the anger, irritability and outbursts are frequent (ODD) or severe (DMDD). In session, sitting with concerned parents, however, this differentiating point may offer little help. To what is the clinician meant to compare how frequent or severe the client is tantruming? A comparison with a non-clinical population in Sweden revealed that almost 58% children have stopped having any tantrums by age 5 and most often begin between ages 2 and 3. Their study revealed that the average tantrum lasted between 5 and 10 minutes and only 6% if their participants had tantrums lasting 30 minutes or longer (Österman & Björkqvist, 2010). An American study comparing the tantrums among 6-year-old children (with a variety of clinical diagnoses and those without) found that among those with a diagnosis, half displayed severe tantrums (measured using the ODD subscale of the Preschool Age Psychiatric Assessment) and 24% were described as irritable. Conversely, among those with no diagnosis, only 11% had tantrums (Carlson et al.,

2016). These studies and others like them suggest that tantruming after the age of 6 is concerning.

Whatever diagnosis you decide upon when assessing your clients, Freeman et al. (2016) recommend that in selecting your treatment, identifying an evidence-based intervention for ODD as the best treatment option, given the difference between DMDD, IED and ODD are arguable and that there has not been enough time to establish evidence for best practice treatment for DMDD.

The Skilled Diagnostician and Bipolar and Unipolar Mood Disorders

Bipolar and unipolar mood disorders can be difficult to diagnose, particularly when clients present with complicated symptoms, such as psychosis or when the use of substances is part of the clinical picture. For example, a study of over 700 participants found that bipolar disorders are especially given to misdiagnosis. Among their participants, those previously diagnosed with bipolar disorder were significantly over-diagnosed when re-evaluated using the DSM IV-TR SCID and among those who had not been previously diagnosed with a bipolar disorder there was a significant underdiagnosis (Zimmerman et al., 2008). What makes mood disorders so difficult to diagnose accurately? Bipolar disorders in particular are difficult to diagnose because the key features overlap with several other chronic disorders and because the bipolar pattern takes time to unfold fully. The following pages will explore some features and situations that complicate diagnosis and will offer recommendations for how to proceed; however, for most of these issues, there is no one-size-fits-all diagnostic rule. Taking the following issues and considerations into account, framed within the unique context of your client's presentation will increase the likelihood of finding a comfortable and appropriate diagnosis.

Obstacles to Obtaining Accurate Histories. A sound diagnosis of unipolar or bipolar mood disorders can't be made without a reliable history. However, gathering accurate information can be challenging with clients on the bipolar spectrum. People have imperfect memories of events, particularly during crises. Time span, sequence, and certain features of their experiences may not be remembered clearly or accurately. Further, clinical notes passed along to you may be incomplete; notes may include a diagnosis but may not be accompanied by a comprehensive description of symptoms, cycles or durations of episodes, which will cloud your ability to fully grasp the diagnostic picture.

Recommendations

- Despite the fact that others will undoubtedly have incomplete memories of symptoms, you will likely need to draw from family members and healthcare providers in filling in where you or the client is less than certain about symptom and timeline information (Morrison, 2014).

TABLE 7.05 Trait Overlap and Distinguishing Features of DMDD, IED and ODD

Disruptive Mood Dysregulation Disorder	Intermittent Explosive Disorder	Oppositional Defiant Disorder
Frequent, severe tantrums *Tantrums are out of proportion to the situation* *Tantrums are not developmentally appropriate* *Persistent severe irritability, anger*	*Aggressive impulses: verbal or behavioral* *Tantrums/tirades* *Strikes out/lashes out at others* *Response is out of proportion with trigger*	*Frequently loses temper* *Touchy/easily annoyed* *Argumentative/Actively defiant* *Deliberately annoys others* *Vindictive*
Distinguish: sustained negative mood and anger (severe) between temper outbursts; requires impairment in at least one setting	*Distinguish:* *Return to typical mood between temper outbursts*	*Distinguish:* *Frequently irritable and resentful; primary disposition features opposition to authority*

Source: Adapted from American Psychiatric Association (2013) and Freeman et al. (2016).

- When assessing your clients, remember that researchers have noted a tendency to report depressive and not hypomanic/manic symptoms. You will need to be deliberate in asking if symptoms related to mania and hypomania have been present and may need to educate clients about what these symptoms look like (Phelps, 2016; Regreer et al., 2015).
- Be meticulous in your own clinical notes when describing your diagnostic process. Use the justification process and depict your best understanding of your client's symptom timeline within your notes, in order to aid clinicians who may later support your client.

Discerning mood episodes. The first step in effectively diagnosing bipolar disorders is correctly identifying mood episodes; however, the DSM 5 uses vague descriptions in its discussion of the episodes, particularly in differentiating mania and hypomania or hypomania from more typical mood states. This situation may be further complicated by your own time limitations, for example, when a diagnosis is needed quickly in order to secure treatment but you don't have all of the information you would like to have to make a diagnosis with confidence. Here, again, look for impairment. If no impairment is evident but in your clinical judgment there has not been enough time for the impairment to fully become evident, delaying diagnosis until the mood event begins to resolve and you have a better picture of what is taking place, mania or hypomania, for example, may be your wisest course of action. Consultation, supervision and experience will support more accurate diagnosis of mood episodes.

How Much Sleep Constitutes Hypersomnia and Insomnia? When navigating the depressive episode criteria table, it can be difficult to know how much sleeping counts for hypersomnia (listed as criterion A4 in a major depressive episode or criterion B2 of PDD). Generally, hypersomnia is present when a client sleeps 10 or more hours per day, but because the amount of sleep necessary varies from one person to the next, hypersomnia may alternatively be considered when the client is sleeping 2 or more hours more than is typical each day. Similarly, insomnia can be identified when your client is getting 6 or less hours of sleep that is also fitful and does not leave the client feeling rested on waking, or 2 or less hours than is typically needed for restorative sleep (Phelps, 2016; Quitkin, 2002).

Clients who meet full criteria for a sleep disorder should receive an additional diagnosis for that disorder if it appears that the difficulties with sleep are present even when the client is not experiencing a mood episode or when it seems that the sleep-related symptoms will not resolve without independent treatment. Please refer to the Sleep–Wake Disorders chapter for a more in-depth exploration of sleep issues and diagnostic challenges.

Differentiating Bipolar Depression from Unipolar Depression. As mentioned earlier, Phillips and Kupfer (2013) point out that a client with a bipolar disorder who first presents with a depressive episode will typically experience a 5-10 year gap between that first episode and an appropriate diagnosis. This may be due in part to the fact that the DSM's criteria for depressive episodes are identical for BPD I and MDD and by the fact that differences between unipolar and bipolar depression are not well understood. Given that clients with BPD II spend more time depressed than they do in hypomanic or manic states, and because clients frequently don't recognize hypomanic states when they are happening, clinicians may misdiagnose MDD rather than BPD I or II (Phillips & Kupfer, 2013).

For years, researchers and clinicians have looked for markers that would clearly distinguish bipolar and unipolar depressions. We know that for half of bipolar clients, the first episode reported was depressive. Research strongly suggests that the first occurrence of depression happens earlier in those who are eventually diagnosed with bipolar disorder than in those with unipolar depression. There is also evidence that persons with bipolar disorders tend to experience more depressive episodes over time than do those with unipolar depression (Diler et al., 2017; Paris & Black, 2015; Phillips & Kupfer, 2013). In the therapy room, faced with a client presenting with depressive symptoms, however, these statistics are not immediately helpful in making a diagnosis.

Another more recent study comparing groups of youth diagnosed with bipolar and unipolar depression found that those with bipolar depression endorsed more non-suicidal self-harm, had higher mood reactivity and also scored higher on subthreshold manic markers (Diler et al., 2017). There are also several studies that suggest that, among outpatients, depressive episodes with psychotic features are more predictive of bipolar I than of MDD. For example, in a study of 4,724 participants, those with depressive episodes with psychotic features were five times as likely to have BPD I than MDD or BPD II (Goes et al., 2007). Until researchers are able to identify pathogenic markers that clearly indicate which type of depression is in evidence, however, Mitchell et al. (2008) recommend taking a "probabilistic" approach. Examining extant data describing the traits of those diagnosed with MDD who would later be diagnosed with a bipolar disorder, a group frequently described as *converters*, these authors identified key features that they believe will help clinicians identify bipolar depression earlier and more accurately. Included among the differentiating symptoms for bipolar depression are hypersomnia, an early onset of the first depressive episode, leaden feelings and slowed movement, weight gain, psychotic features and a history of five or more depressive episodes. Whether or not a probabilistic approach is taken, there does seem to be consensus among researchers and therapists who specialize in mood disorders that before diagnosing a depressive disorder, it is important to first exclude the possibility of a BPD II by educating and carefully assessing your client for a history of hypomania.

Differentiating Unipolar or Bipolar Psychosis from Schizoaffective Disorder. As described earlier, in unipolar and bipolar disorders, clients sometimes experience psychotic features; however, these experiences of psychosis occur exclusively within mood episodes, either depressive or manic. For clients appropriately diagnosed with a mood disorder, psychotic features are not in evidence during periods when the client's mood has stabilized. In situations in which your client describes a history of psychotic episodes that fall outside of mood episodes, schizoaffective disorder is diagnosed (see p. 105 of the DSM 5). It is important to note, however, that clients who are diagnosed with bipolar disorder with psychosis and those with schizoaffective disorder have very similar levels of functional difficulties and can present similarly in session. Because client histories can be murky or incomplete, these two diagnoses can be particularly difficult to discern (Mitchell et al., 2008; Morrison, 2014; Phelps, 2016).

Differentiating Borderline Personality Structures (BPS) from Bipolar Disorders. The presentation overlap between the person with BPD I, II, cyclothymia and the person with BPS is significant and can be difficult to pull apart. Both the bipolar spectrum disorders and BPS feature unstable affect; people in either group can experience transient paranoia. A person diagnosed with any of these can present with intense anger, unstable relationships, frequent suicidal overtures, transient psychotic features as well as periods of risk-taking. With such a significant number of overlapping features, these clients can be difficult to diagnose accurately (Ha, 2018; Hidalgo-Mazzei et al., 2015; Perugi et al., 2015; Phelps, 2016). Phelps, 2016, offers key points to discern borderline personality from bipolar disorder: first, he points out that for the client with borderline personality extremes are not as long-lived, usually no more than a few hours, and contrast with those of bipolar disorder, lasting 4 or more days. He also notes that the client with BPD is more likely to report emptiness and fears of abandonment while the client with bipolar disorder is more likely to have more typical attachment patterns. Finally, bipolar episodes are more independent of psychosocial triggers than are mood fluctuations in BPD. To these recommendations Ha (2018) adds the suggestion that using a psychodynamic approach to differentiating borderline from bipolar presentations may be informative. Ha notes that the identification of defense mechanisms frequently seen in those with borderline patterns, such as splitting and projective identification, may be helpful in lending confidence to your diagnosis.

When Substance Use Is Part of the Clinical Picture. Client substance use and substance use disorders will tend to cloud the source of your client's mood disturbances as well as their experience of those moods which will, in turn, complicate the diagnostic process. It is estimated that between 50% and 60% of clients with bipolar disorders (Atkins, 2014; Messer et al., 2017) and between 20% and 40% of those with depressive disorders (Atkins, 2014; Blanco et al., 2012; Grant et al., 2004) will have a co-occuring substance use disorder in their lifetimes. Substance abuse, of course, comes at a considerable cost to clients with bipolar and unipolar mood disorders, including increased rates of suicidality, more frequent and prolonged mood episodes, and higher rates of psychosis, to name a few (Atkins, 2014; Blanco et al., 2012). Further, the use of substances elevates functional impairments and decreases the chances that medications will be taken regularly and as prescribed (Atkins, 2014; Messer et al., 2017; Substance Abuse and Mental Health Services Administration [SAMHSA], 2018).

Discovering the underlying cause of your client's mood disorder and mood episodes, and whether mood symptoms are primary or secondary to substance use, presents its own difficulties and, predictably, is the subject of debate and discussion within the field (Tolliver & Anton, 2015). Traditionally, a mood disorder is considered to be substance-dependent when the mood disorder arose close to the time when the misuse of substances began, abates when the individual's substance use decreases, and when the mood symptoms resolve within a few weeks of substance abstinence (Akiskal, 1995 in Bakken et al., 2003; Tolliver & Anton, 2015). Blanco et al. (2012), however, point out that a number of studies have suggested that few cases of depression, possibly as few as 1%, may be directly attributable to substance use.

Many clients come for treatment with concerns related to depression and anxiety but are reluctant to report fully about their alcohol and substance use and misuse, making it very difficult to diagnose a concurrent or primary substance use disorder. Adding complexity to the diagnosis, it has long been understood that the affective presentation of those with depression and those with substance use disorders overlap significantly (Tolliver & Anton, 2015). Bakken et al. (2003), for example, conducted a study of almost 300 Norwegian primary and secondary substance abusers in an attempt to discern differences between the manifestation of independent mood disorder and those thought to have substance-induced mood symptoms. They found the differences between these two groups to be insignificant. Previously, best practice recommendations for suspected primary substance use disorders was to treat the substance use and wait to see if the depression resolved before prescribing medications for depression. This recommendation has been challenged by studies that suggest that depression is less commonly a direct consequence of substance use and abuse than previously believed (Blanco et al., 2012; Tolliver & Anton, 2015) and because some research suggests that those who are taking antidepressant medication have longer, more successful recovery periods than those without (Grant et al., 2004, in Tolliver & Anton, 2015). These more recent recommendations seem to suggest that when in doubt, diagnose and treat both the substance use disorder and the mood disorder.

Differentiating Grief and Other Normal Responses from Depression. Students often wonder if a person should be diagnosed with depression if the client's depressive episode follows an event that would reasonably lead to deep sadness, such as a loss of a loved one. Grief is an expected response to the loss of a cherished person, pet, job or, for example, a home lost in a natural disaster or after a financial crisis. In these cases, we avoid pathologizing normal human responses to painful experiences. However, it is important that a depressive episode be noted in your clinical notes, the events that led to the symptoms, as well as a clear timeline of their resolution. Clients who show less resilience in the face of crisis will benefit from interventions that can strengthen resolve and capacities for managing difficulties in the future. Further, when symptoms seem vastly out of proportion to the circumstances, or are unusually protracted or debilitating, a formal diagnosis should be considered despite the fact that the symptoms were prompted by bereavement. This recommendation represents a change within the DSM and diagnostic practices. A strong understanding of cultural and developmental differences in responding to loss will greatly enhance the accuracy of your diagnosis in situations where grieving is the seed for the depressive symptoms.

Screening for Sexual Dysfunction. Clients who present with mood disorders, particularly depression, frequently report sexual dissatisfaction or dysfunction. This phenomenon arises out of the intersection of a number of causal factors that include the tendency of depressed persons to lose pleasure in things that once brought satisfaction or enjoyment, including sex, the side effects of medications for medical conditions or for the depression itself, chronic illness and pain, and age-related hormonal changes, all of which are associated with depression (Atlantis & Sullivan, 2012). The intersection between sexual dysfunction and depression is so common that when your client presents with depressive symptoms, either unipolar or bipolar, assessment for sexual dysfunction is recommended. The relationship between sexual dysfunction and depression is discussed at greater length in Chapter 10.

Treatment of Mood Disorders

Medication and the Treatment of Bipolar Disorders. The consensus of the mental health field holds that medications should be the first-line approach to stabilizing and treating bipolar disorder. Medications are used for four primary purposes: (1) to stabilize mood, (2) to prevent relapse into mania and depression, (3) to stave off psychosis and (4) to support consistent and adequate sleep. However, not all medications have shown themselves to be equally efficacious in each of these four aims. Consequently, about

90% of successfully treated clients take more than one medication and a significant number of clients find that medications alone are insufficient in fully treating bipolar disorder (Miura et al., 2014). Three primary classes of medications are used to treat bipolar disorders: antipsychotics, anticonvulsants, and, less often, monoamine oxidase inhibitors (MAOIs). Taken together, the research on pharmacology used to treat bipolar disorders is vast, rapidly changing and often relies on flawed or limited trials that frequently contradict one another (Pacchiarotti, et al., 2013).

The APA notes the challenges to creating treatment guidelines: first, guidelines lag behind the research and are, by their nature, outdated by the time they are published. Further, the utility of any recommendations is always limited by the relative strength of the research that supports them. Much of the extant research contains noteworthy limitations in scope or design. Additionally, the APA notes, "Recommendations [based on opinion or consensus] may be erroneous . . . and find their way into guidelines on the basis of their popularity, which can lead to the widespread perpetuation of clinical myth and folklore," (p. 1). And finally, many trials in the literature are funded by pharmaceutical companies, rather than independent researchers, which clouds the results of the trials (APA, 2013; Pacchiarotti et al., 2013). With these cautions in mind, some key points taken from the literature, including the APA practice guidelines are summarized below.

Stabilizing mood. In the prevention of relapse, no drug has as much support for long-term outcomes as lithium (Geddes & Miklowitz, 2013). While lithium is not addictive, it is highly toxic and can be used for intentional overdose. Consequently it is used with caution in suicidal patients. The side effects of lithium can be difficult to tolerate or dangerous and may include, but are not exclusive to dry mouth, nausea, weight gain, tremor, hyperthyroidism and leukocytosis, an elevation of white blood cell counts. It is important to note that there is a narrow dosage band between what constitutes a therapeutic dose of lithium and a dose that results in toxic side effects; consequently, lithium requires careful monitoring. Anticonvulsants are also used to stabilize mood and are much less toxic but research suggests anticonvulsants are also less effective than lithium in managing symptoms (Frank, 2005; Geddes & Miklowitz, 2013; Miura et al., 2014).

Preventing Relapse and Psychotic Episodes. Prescribers face particular challenges in identifying medications for preventing mood episode relapse. Antipsychotics show evidence for their helpfulness in treating acute mania and psychotic episodes but seem to do little for depressive episodes (Geddes & Miklowitz, 2013) and while antidepressants can be helpful for those experiencing depressive episodes, their use is discouraged in clients with a rapid cycling pattern and in those with a history of mania or hypomania (Malhi et al., 2015). Similar problems have been found with some anticonvulsants. For example, while lamotrigine can be helpful with depressive symptoms, it may induce a manic or hypomanic episode and is often avoided in bipolar clients (Geddes & Miklowitz, 2013).

BOX 7.05 CONSIDER THIS: DIFFERENTIATING GRIEF AND DEPRESSION

Read Roberta's story. How do you view Roberta's response? Is Roberta more likely experiencing grief or depression? What questions do you have that would help you to clarify your hunch?

Roberta. Roberta, a 60-year-old mother of four adult children, finds her thoughts drifting frequently to her daughter, Patience, who passed away at age 6 after a protracted struggle with cancer. Roberta fell into a deep depression after the loss of her daughter and was only able to give minimal care and attention to her other children. Though Patience died nearly 25 years ago, Roberta still regularly cries over the loss of her daughter and attributes her decades-long depression to that event. She was never able to recover her bond with her surviving children and the distance felt between her children and herself is the source of additional pain and conflict.

Restoring sleep. When a client is in the midst of a manic episode, restoring sleep becomes a critical therapeutic goal. A great deal of research points to the importance of consistent sleep schedules in preventing mood episode relapses thus adding to the importance of interventions that improve the quality of sleep. A number of antipsychotic medications are used to support sleep restoration; for example, haloperidol (Haldol ©) or perphenazine (Trilafon ©). However, these medications tend to carry with them burdensome side effects. Consequently, "atypical" antipsychotics, which seem to have fewer and more mild side effects, such as risperidone (Risperdal©) or olanzapine (Zyprexa©), are often prescribed instead (Frank, 2005).

Psychotherapy and the Treatment of Mood Disorders

Circadian Rhythms and Treatments for Bipolar Disorders. Though a significant portion of the biologically based research of the bipolar spectrum is focused on the brain, researchers have also given renewed attention to chronobiology, a science that examines processes and patterns of the body that are cyclical, such as sleeping and eating, and their relationships to mood disorders. When these patterns follow a 24-hour cycle, they are described as circadian rhythms. Circadian rhythms, coded by our clock genes and controlled by the hypothalamus and pituitary glands, dictate neurological, cellular, biochemical and behavioral systems that, in turn, mark the passing of time. This science continues to expand our understanding of bipolar spectrum disorders. Researchers have found a bidirectional relationship between circadian rhythms and the bipolar continuum that link presentations to different genetic markers (Melo et al., 2017; Phelps, 2016).

Psychotherapy for Bipolar and Unipolar Disorders. Chronobiology, neuroscience and mounting efficacy research supports the use of psychotherapy in addition to pharmacological approaches to the treatment of bipolar disorders. Treatment approaches that are supported by this research include Interpersonal and Social Rhythm Therapy (IPSRT) (Asarnow et al., 2014; Frank, 2005), Light Therapy (Frank, 2005), Dark Therapy (Abreu & Bragança, 2015; Levenson & Frank, 2010; Phelps, 2016; Phelps, 2008) and sleep deprivation therapy (Asarnow et al., 2014; Abreu & Bragança, 2015; Papadimitriou et al., 2007). Asarnow et al., 2014, note in their review of the literature that, "overall, sleep deprivation has been described as the most rapid antidepressant available today. Data on hundreds of depressed patients of all diagnostic subcategories show marked improvement within hours in approximately 60% of patients" (p. 366).

Interpersonal Therapy with Social Rhythm Therapy (IPSRT). The IPSRT is a behavioral-biopsychosocial, evidence-based approach that takes a special interest in the relationship between the troublesome symptoms of bipolar disorder, difficulties with social relationships, and the client's biological rhythms, such as sleep cycles. The IPSRT therapist works to educate clients about the importance of balancing social and biological patterns in order to stabilize moods, prevent relapse and to solve relational problems. IPSRT begins with careful case conceptualization and has a central ethic that is client-centered (Frank, 2005; Frank et al., 1994). Though more commonly used to treat bipolar disorders, the efficacy of IPSRT has been demonstrated with MDD as well as BPD (Ehlers et al., 1993).

IPSRT Key Concepts and Objectives. The IPSRT therapist attributes emergent mood episodes to three primary sources: (1) failure to adhere to medication regimens, (2) role changes and stressful life events and (3) vulnerability to social rhythm disruptions, such as changes in sleep. IPSRT therapists also attend to the dynamic interplay of zeitgebers (social cues that support biological cycles, such as arriving at work at 8:30 each morning) and zeitstorers (events that disrupt regular circadian cycles, such as irregular shift work). Consequently, therapists who use the IPSRT model work to educate clients on the importance of medication adherence, help to resolve interpersonal stressors and to restore healthy lifestyle habits, such as maintaining very regular sleep patterns (Frank, 2005; Swartz et al., 2010).

Cognitive Therapy for Bipolar and Unipolar Disorders. Cognitive behavioral therapy (CBT) is founded upon the idea that mood cycles in bipolar disorder and depression in major depression are the consequence of unhelpful beliefs about the world and oneself in it and unproductive responses to difficult life events. Consequently, the CBT therapist works to help clients cultivate more productive, realistic and positive thoughts and behaviors. Many iterations of CBT, those designed to include themes such as religion (Ramos et al., 2018) and mindfulness (Teasdale et al., 2000) have been developed to address a wide range of disorders including those along the bipolar and unipolar spectrums. CBT for bipolar disorder has been shown to have some efficacy over medication alone (Lam et al., 2005) but seems to bring the same results as augmentative psychoeducation (Parikh et al., 2012). CBT in whatever form or iteration generally takes place over 12-20 sessions.

CBT and Depression. Again, a number of CBT-based approaches to addressing depression have been developed and many seem to show efficacy. For example, for those with chronic depression, cognitive-behavioral analysis system of psychotherapy (CBASP) is an approach that integrates interpersonal goals with cognitive approaches. The primary aim of this therapy is to change interpersonal behavior by exploring relationship interactions and building communication and problem-solving skills. This approach has shown efficacy when combined with medications (McCullough, 2003). For clients with a history of three or more episodes of major depression, mindfulness-based cognitive therapy (MBCT) may provide the support and skills needed to identify and counter depressogenic thinking and cultivate resilience (Teasdale et al., 2000). MBCT enjoys a growing body of evidence for its efficacy in relapse prevention among the subset of clients described as treatment resistant (Gotink et al., 2015).

Family-Focused Therapy (FFT). FFT is also an evidence-based treatment often used as adjunct therapy along with medications and other psychosocial interventions that is begun after a client has cycled through a manic or depressive episode. FFT finds its origins in behavioral management interventions focused on supporting clients with schizophrenia within the context of family relationships. In the 1980s, the therapy was adapted for bipolar clients who had been hospitalized and were being released into family care. FFT was adapted with the aim to educate clients and their families about the disorder and to improve strained communication that theorists believed was often unclear or too emotionally charged (Miklowitz & Chung, 2016; Miklowitz & Frank, 2010; Miklowitz et al., 2003; Miklowitz & Goldstein, 1990; Miklowitz et al., 2007; Rea et al., 2003).

FFT Key Concepts and Objectives. Several key concepts shape FFT, expressed emotion (EE) being chief among them. EE is primarily understood to describe two domains: critical or hostile communication and over-involvement or intrusiveness, and is generally measured using the Camberwell Family Inventory or the Family Questionnaire. Research strongly suggests a relationship between clients with high-EE family interactions and illness recurrence both for bipolar disorder and for schizophrenia (Miklowitz & Chung, 2016; Vaughn & Leff, 1976; Wiedemann et al., 2002).

FFT works on the assumption that mood episodes represent non-normative life cycle crises for the family as a whole that results in disorganization of the family system. In order for the family system to stabilize, members must develop coping strategies. Consequently, FFT aims to work with as many of the available family members as possible (Cohen, 2013). Though FFT has been evolving, today FFT focuses on assisting patients and their relatives with the following six objectives: (1) integrating negative experiences of mood episodes; (2) acceptance of the cycle of bipolarity;

(3) medication compliance; (4) early symptom recognition and distinction from personality; (5) stress identification, coping and reduction and (6) family relationship restoration (Cohen, 2013; Miklowitz et al., 2008; Miklowitz & Chung, 2016; Miklowitz & Frank, 2010; Miklowitz & Otto, 2006). While the research is promising for FFT, less consistent support exists for cultural contexts in which high EE is a value. Both familial and cultural expectations influence a family's EE. Consequently, it is therefore important to explore with clients cultural and familial norms for emotional expression before proceeding with FFT interventions (Bhugra & McKenzie, 2003).

The Mood Disorders: Definitional Cases

In the following pages you will find a number of cases to diagnose. The first cases are definitional, capturing only the key features of each disorder, but not giving enough information to fully diagnose. These cases will offer an opportunity to practice quickly narrowing disorders to a few likely candidates. The second set of cases, the narrative cases, are longer, have more information and make it possible for you to offer a diagnosis and justify it fully. These cases also provide enough information and context to consider a treatment plan. In this chapter, you have also been provided cases that describe mood episodes in order to provide you with more practice differentiating episodes. You may want to make use of the pivot table to help you narrow your diagnostic choices.

Episodes of Mood and Their Specifiers: Cases

Ximena

Ximena's mood has suddenly changed over the past week, becoming unusually talkative, jumping from one idea to the next and from one project to another. She has slept very little during this time. The shift in mood has made it impossible for her to get anything accomplished at work and her boss has asked her to stay at home until she is feeling more like herself. What type of mood episode is Ximena experiencing?

Vesna

Though Vesna and her work are widely admired, she has been experiencing delusions that her coworkers are attempting to get her fired. She has been very distracted by this belief and has slept very little, in part thanks to her distraction. Vesna has been fuming at the betrayal she feels. During this time, about a week and a half, she has been very irritable, has had difficulty maintaining a train of thought and has been talking more than is typical for her. What episode and specifier are appropriate for Vesna?

BOX 7.06 KEY TERMS: MOOD DISORDERS

Expressed Emotion: This term is used to describe the relative rates of critical or hostile communication and over-involvement or intrusiveness, and is generally measured using the Camberwell Family Inventory or the Family Questionnaire.

Zeitgebers (time giver): Social cues that support biological cycles, such as arriving at work at 8:30 each morning (Frank, 2005; Swartz et al., 2010)

Zeitstorers (time disturber): Events that disrupt regular circadian cycles, such as irregular shift work. (Frank, 2005; Swartz et al., 2010)

Zeitstorers (time disturber): Events that disrupt regular circadian cycles, such as irregular shift work.

Alejandro

Alejandro has, for the past 4 days, felt irritated, and his coworkers have noticed that while he is usually both modest, focused and a pleasure to work with, he has been grandiose, highly distracted and a bit surly, though still able to complete his work effectively.

Daniela

For the past 3 weeks, Daniela has described feeling very blue. She goes to bed early each evening but does not feel rested, even after sleeping late. She has told her partner that she feels worthless and a burden and is not sure why he stays with her. Though she normally enjoys spending a little time painting with her niece each afternoon, she feels little interest or motivation to drive across town and spend time with her.

Giada

Giada recently gave birth to twin boys. Shortly before the birth of the boys, Giada began experiencing symptoms of depression. She slept a great deal, though she never quite felt rested, she lost her appetite and ate very little, which concerned her doctors a great deal, she lost the excitement she had felt about the upcoming birth of her children and felt inadequate to the task of mothering. What episode and specifier are appropriate for Giada's situation?

TABLE 7.06 Pivot Points: Mood Disorders

	Consider
Pivot Point 1: Does your client's difficulty take the form of recurrent temper outbursts and difficulty regulating anger?	Disruptive Mood Dysregulation Disorder
Pivot Point 2: Does your client's suffering manifest as deep unrelenting depression?	Major Depressive Disorder
Pivot Point 3: Does your client experience symptoms of both depression and mania or hypomania?	
• Do your client's difficulties primarily concern depressive mood states but include subthreshold manic symptoms?	Major Depressive Disorder, With Mixed State
• Has your depressed client ever experienced a manic episode?	Bipolar I
• Has your client's history included both a hypomanic and depressive episode, but never a manic episode?	Bipolar II
Pivot Point 4: Has your client experienced a depressed mood more days than not for 2 years or more?	Persistent Depressive Disorder (Dysthymia)
Pivot Point 5: Is your client's change in mood related to her menstrual cycle?	Premenstrual Dysphoric Disorder
Pivot Point 6: Has your client experienced both symptoms of depression and psychosis?	
• Are your client's predominant symptoms depressive and accompanied by psychosis?	Major Depressive Disorder, With Mood Congruent/Incongruent Psychotic Features
• Does your client experience psychotic symptoms at times when depressed or manic mood is not present?	Schizoaffective Disorder, Depressive Type
Pivot Point 7: Has your client experienced a manic episode?	Bipolar I
Pivot Point 8: Has your client experienced at least one each of a hypomanic and depressive episode, but never a manic episode?	Bipolar II
Pivot Point 9: Does your client struggle with difficult relational patterns that feature impulsive behaviors that resemble mania, such as excessive spending or risky sexual involvement, as well as demonstrate poor emotional regulation?	Borderline Personality Disorder
Pivot Point 10: Is your client's depressed mood tied to or coincide with the use or withdrawal of a medication or substance that is capable of producing depressive-like symptoms?	Substance/Medication-Induced Depressive Disorder
Pivot Point 11: Are your client's experiences of disturbances in mood, which include either hypomanic or manic episodes, tied to the use of or withdrawal from a substance or medication?	Substance/Medication–Induced Bipolar and Related Disorder

	Consider
Pivot Point 12: Is your client's depressed mood a direct result of a physical or medical condition, such as hypothyroidism?	Depressive Disorder Due to Another Medical Condition
Pivot Point 13: Are your client's experiences of disturbances in their mood (which include either hypomanic or manic episodes) related to a physical or medical condition?	Bipolar and Related Disorder Due to Another Medical Condition
Pivot Point 14: Does your client present with symptoms of depression that don't quite rise to the level of a depressive disorder?	Other Specified Depressive Disorder
Pivot Point 15: Are your client's experiences characteristic of a bipolar and related disorder, causing significant distress or impairment, but do not meet the full criteria for any of the disorders above and you are prepared to specify why?	Other Specified Bipolar and Related Disorders
• Does your client have a history of hypomanic episodes but has never met full criteria for a major depressive episode?	Other Specified Bipolar and Related Disorders, Hypomanic episode without prior major depressive episode
Pivot Point 16: Are your client's experiences characteristic of depression, but you do not yet have enough information to fully justify a diagnosis?	Unspecified Depressive Disorder, Insufficient Symptoms
Pivot Point 17: Are your client's clinically significant depressive symptoms of too brief a duration to meet full major depressive criteria?	Unspecified Depressive Disorder, Short-Duration Depressive Episode/ Recurrent Brief Depression
Pivot Point 18: Are your client's experiences characteristic of a bipolar and related disorder, causing significant distress or impairment, but do not meet the full criteria for any of the disorders above?	Unspecified Bipolar and Related Disorder
Pivot Point 19: Has your client had subthreshold experiences of hypomanic and subthreshold depressive symptoms over the course of a few years? Has your client experienced near constant mood fluctuations over the past 2 years?	Cyclothymic Disorder
Pivot Point 20: Does your client experience psychotic symptoms as well as high and low emotional states?	
• Has your client experienced both a manic episode as well as symptoms of psychosis?	Bipolar I, With Mood Congruent/ Incongruent Psychotic Features
• Has your client experienced both a depressive episode, a hypomanic episode and symptoms of psychosis?	Bipolar II, With Mood Congruent/ Incongruent Psychotic Features
• Does your client experience symptoms of psychosis outside of mood states that tend to fluctuate between very high highs and very low lows?	Schizoaffective Disorder, Bipolar Type

Ivan

Ivan dreads the holiday season since it is at this time of year when he regularly falls into a pattern of symptoms meeting the criteria for a depressive episode. What episode and specifier best fits Ivan's situation?

Kieran

Kieran has been experiencing a major depressive episode during which time he has felt keyed up and has had a vague sense that he might lose control of himself. Which episode and specifier is appropriate to give to Kieran?

Ljubica

Ljubica has struggled with the symptoms of a major depressive episode for three and a half weeks. During this time, she has also experienced talkativeness, has been intensely driven in her schoolwork, and has been shopping to excess. Which episode and specifier are appropriate to give to Ljubica?

Aleksandar

Aleksandar has struggled with the symptoms of MDD for the past 2 weeks. During this time, he has complained of a feeling of profound despondency, has lost weight, describes experiencing intense guilt and does not feel relief from his symptoms when positive events happen. Which episode and specifier are appropriate for Aleksandar?

Elena

Elena has reported to her counselor the symptoms of MDD; however, she does report that when positive things occur, such as the birth of her nephew or while attending a play, she does feel her mood brighten some. During the period of depressed mood, she has gained 30 pounds and describes a particular heaviness in her arms and legs. Which episode and specifier are appropriate to apply to Elena's situation?

Mood Disorders: Definitional Cases

Aafreen

Aafreen has just been treated in a local hospital for his second manic episode. He has a history of depression.

Tim

Tim, age 9, has been brought into counseling by his mother who reports that Tim has experienced a depressed mood, poor sleep and irritability for more than a year.

Becky

Becky, 21, has noticed a pattern in her menstrual cycle. In the week before her period begins, she feels anxious and a bit more sensitive to others. She begins to question why she has chosen her line of work, loses sleep and feels fatigued. Once her cycle begins, however, these symptoms lift and she "feels like her old self again."

Misaki

Since moving to the United States from Japan 3 years ago, Misaki has experienced what she describes as "a highly changeable mood." On investigation, it is clear that Misaki's ups and downs have been difficult for her but never quite reach the threshold of either hypomania or depression.

Franklin

Franklin, 8, has always had a difficult time managing even small frustrations and disappointments. Franklin has frequent temper outbursts, often resulting in kicking others. Franklin generally doesn't make a full recovery from these incidents and tends to feel angry and irritable most every day.

Eva

Eva has experienced a number of major depressive episodes; however, she has also experienced two hypomanic episodes in the past 4 years. She has never had a manic episode.

Antoni

Since retiring 9 months ago, Antoni, age 67, has felt worthless, sad, restless, reports having difficulty sleeping and can't enjoy the things he once did. He describes feeling "a bit guilty" for not contributing anything and laying around like a slug.

Narrative Cases in Mood Disorders

Neerja

Neerja, a 26 year old with a master's degree in business, moved from India to the United States 3 years ago with her new husband so that he could attend medical school. Neerja has worked steadily providing consultation for a local marketing firm that does work internationally. She was well known for her sunny disposition, her generosity with her time, and the creativity and beauty of her flower gardens. Four months ago, Neerja and her husband had their first child. Since that time Neerja's health has taken a turn for the worse. She reports, "I can take delight in nothing, it seems. Even the baby cannot make me smile. As soon as my husband leaves the house, tears well up behind my eyes and I feel lost. I once had so much energy for life but now I prefer to stay in bed all day. I feel so tired sometimes it feels like an effort to take a breath. I feel so guilty because I don't have joy in my heart when I pick up my precious son. I seem to be going through the motions of caring for him."

She also reports, "My garden is now covered in weeds and vines. It was so pretty and it was such a nice way to greet people as they came to the door but now the house and yard look as dark and uncared for as I feel. I feel like things would be better if I could just get some sleep but I toss and turn until the early hours of the morning and then find myself so tired all day I can barely move."

Neerja's husband reports that she has lost a considerable amount of weight since the baby was born and that she is not caring for herself; for instance, she neglects showering. Her husband shares, "Neerja is a shadow of herself. All of her light is gone. I have hired someone to help with the baby because I'm not sure she has the energy to be responsive to him. We've had to hire a lady to come in and clean the house. She sometimes helps with dinner, too. As a result, Neerja is always talking about how worthless she is and that she has failed our family. I am very, very concerned about her."

Upon further questioning, it is clear that Neerja experienced similar feelings of low mood, fatigue, weight loss and so on in high school during her preparations for college entrance exams.

Jeremy

Jeremy, a 32-year-old African American traffic engineer, has come into counseling with concerns related to work. Jeremy explains, "About 18 months ago I met a woman that I really loved. We dated for about 7 months and I thought about her all the time. I was so sure she was the one, so two months ago I asked her to marry me. But then things started to unravel. She said she loved me too, but she said it would cause a rift with her family since her family is Korean and I am Black. She refused to talk with her parents about our relationship. She said she felt like she would have to choose between me and her family."

"The tension between us started to build and eventually we broke up. It was pretty bad. But now, I guess I feel like we shouldn't get married if she wasn't sure, but I haven't been able to bounce back from this and it has been weeks. I feel empty inside, really flat like there aren't any feelings there at all. It's like I'm walking around in a fog, I just can't concentrate on anything and I don't have any motivation to do any work. I've lost all my focus and I can't get any work done. I used to love my job and now I can barely drag myself to the office. The worst part is that I just keep kicking myself for wrecking our relationship. I keep asking myself over and over why I had to ruin a good thing by asking her to marry me. Why not just leave good enough alone? My life feels pretty pointless without her."

Jeremy also complains of difficulty sleeping and a shift in appetite leading to significant weight gain. Further, Jeremy reports feeling "pretty keyed up all day and really restless. My roommate has complained about my restlessness and says that it is bugging him." Jeremy has no previous history of low mood.

Amanda

Amanda is a 23-year-old librarian at a local university. For as long as she can remember, she has felt herself "riding the tides of [her] emotions." Amanda explains that she sometimes has much more focus and energy and is able to work long hours on little sleep. While she enjoys these periods of "productivity," she admits that her peers have sometimes complained that during this time she can be irritable and is hard to work with. At other times, Amanda experiences long periods of feeling especially blue. Though she does not experience problems with sleep or appetite, she does find herself feeling both sluggish and sad, though she is not able to identify why. "For the past 3 or 4 years these ups and downs have been pretty constant and relentless. I never feel just right." Amanda has seen counselors on and off over the course of the past several years but has never met the criteria for a full depressive episode, manic or hypomanic episode.

Lidia

Lidia, 42, has come to counseling seeking help with a long-standing feeling that "at any moment something awful might happen to me or someone in my family. It is hard to explain and I can't pin-point where it comes from, but this feeling of dread is always with me." Lidia notes that with this feeling of dread, she also has a sense of restlessness that makes it difficult to sleep. In describing herself to her counselor, Lidia shares that she is embarrassed that several weeks ago she declared to her supervisors that "If it weren't for her skills and talent, the library couldn't keep its doors open." During this same period, she felt herself talking a great deal more than is typical and found it difficult to slow or focus her thoughts. On reflection, Lidia realizes that she experiences a cycle of feelings, shifting between a more positive but driven mood and something closer to a low mood that is difficult to shake, but has never quite reached the status of a depressive episode. These turns in mood, as Lidia describes them, have been happening for several years. When asked Lidia shares, "I can't recall if there has been a period of time when I was not feeling either down-in-the-dumps or amped up and worried. I guess I felt pretty normal when I was a teen, but I haven't felt really good for a long time."

Iskandar

Iskandar, a 22-year-old office intern, recently came to his immediate supervisor insisting that he be given a full-time position and significant pay raise in recognition for his contribution to a small project given to him when one of the full-time employees took maternity leave. His supervisor reports that she recognized his hand in putting the finishing touches on the project but explains that the bulk of the work had been completed before it had come to him. She further reports, "I never would have expected this kind of response from Iskandar. He's usually so even-tempered, takes direction well and is full of curiosity but modest about his own work." Iskandar, however, told his supervisor that he was "shocked" at the company's lack of insight into the quality of his work. "It was my artistry and skill that made the project what it was!"

In talking further with Iskandar, his supervisor learned that he had gone without much sleep for the past week or more, working through the night on projects he had not been assigned but that he felt sure he was more talented and qualified to complete than others in the office. He also admitted that he was experiencing "a flood of great ideas for the company" and that these ideas were "coming faster than he could keep track of."

Dale

Dale, a 45-year-old writer who hosts his own blog but is otherwise unpublished, has experienced a series of periods in which his mood shifts from a mood that his friends would describe as "pleasant and friendly" into a mood of irritability and elevated enthusiasm for his work. During these periods, Dale has been known to stay up for a week or more without sleep, gambling and spending a great deal of money. Dale reports that during these periods, he develops an exaggerated sense of importance about his writing and his impact on "the literary world." He describes feeling both very restless and tense at these times. Dale reports he also finds it very difficult to write or do other kinds of work and reports that his thoughts race, making it impossible for him to get his thoughts into coherent statements. Several times, when in one of his "moods," as he describes them, Dale has gotten into fights and has been jailed. Currently, Dale's mood has returned to a more stable state and he is able to focus on his writing again.

Sandrine

Sandrine, 36, has returned to her counselor of several years feeling "very depressed and like a worthless piece of shit." Sandrine tells her counselor, "Well, I've done it again, I got caught up in a crazy scheme and now I've lost a lot of money . . . again." Sandrine reports that her daughter, age 4, had come to her and said, "Just because you are grown up doesn't mean you know everything," a statement that at the time had struck Sandrine as "profound, powerfully insightful and complexly layered." Sandrine reports that she had been kept up several nights consecutively thinking about the implications of the statement and ultimately decided that she wanted to "share her daughter's wisdom with the world." Sandrine went to a t-shirt shop and had 4,000 t-shirts and 300 hooded sweatshirts made with her daughter's quote printed on them with the intention of selling them online. Sandrine reports that she is embarrassed and feeling guilty and ashamed as well as very worried about how she will pay the t-shirt shop the thousands she still owes.

Though Sandrine does not have a history of substance abuse, she does have a long history of elevated mood and risky financial decisions generally followed by weeks of deep regret, shame and depressed mood that requires counseling intervention. Sandrine tends to move in and out of these cycling moods frequently and can experience as many as six mood episodes in a single year.

Arturo

Arturo, a 47-year-old Mexican-American artist has come to therapy complaining of relational problems. He and his partner, James, have been talking about moving in together and possibly of building a family. However, James has asked Arturo to seek therapy to deal with what he describes as "Arturo's shadows." Arturo explains that he is happy in his relationship with James and is looking forward to a life with him. However, for most of his adult life, he feels he has had a shadow of unhappiness at his heels. "Most of the feelings are just a vague feeling of dissatisfaction in myself and my work. It leaves me feeling wrung out, just no energy. James, though, is very positive and high energy. It's one of the things that draws me to him. But my gloominess is a problem in our relationship." Arturo adds, "I have gotten used to this feeling. I can't remember a time when it didn't follow me around. It has never gotten so bad that I couldn't work with it, never a real depression, just this persistent feeling of being exhausted and doubting myself."

Isaac

Isaac, 24, was taken to the hospital by his worried parents and ultimately admitted for treatment. Several days ago, Isaac became fascinated with the idea that the monsters and magical creatures described in folk tales were, in fact, real. Isaac researched these stories day and night, getting little to no sleep. He found it nearly impossible to convey to others all the thoughts that were racing through his head, though when he tried, his speech was rapid and difficult to follow. Two nights ago, Isaac became convinced that his neighbor was actually a werewolf and that the neighbor posed a significant threat to the neighborhood. Isaac was taken to the hospital after breaking into the neighbor's house and trying to burn it down.

Edil

Edil, a 35-year-old man of Peurto Rican descent, was recently released from the hospital following a depressive episode in which he attempted to commit suicide by hanging himself. He was discovered by his mother, who had stopped by his apartment with groceries. Edil reports that his gradual decline into depression began with a "few stray thoughts" and grew into a "relentless feeling of worthlessness, shame and guilt" at his inability to find work.

Edil has a long history of mental health concerns. He has been hospitalized twice in the past 5 years, once following a suicide attempt and the second time in the midst of a manic episode. Edil has been under a psychiatrist's care for the past 11 years and has tried a number of medications to help support mood stabilization.

Lettie

In her annual checkup with her gynecologist, Lettie, 24, has shared concerns about a distressing trend she has noticed in her menstrual cycle. Lettie explains, "I've noticed that the week before my period starts I start to feel anxious. It starts out as a weird body experience where I feel the anxiety in my body but I'm not sure why. But then it starts to grow and I start worrying about work and my friendships and then I start to worry about my relationship with my husband and in my mind I'm just picking him apart. I start to feel overwhelmed by all the work I have to do and the idea that I have to get my relationship in order. During that time I have a hard time getting to sleep and then I'm really tired all day. Before I know it I'm melting down into tears." She further explains, "The way that I figured out it was related to my period was that as soon as my period started it was like a huge weight lifted off my shoulders and suddenly the anxiety was gone for a while . . . for almost a month and then it begins again."

Amy

Amy, a 32-year-old piano teacher working at a private school for girls has been seeing a therapist for symptoms of depression for several months. She had complained of feeling that she did not make a significant contribution to the world and consequently felt "guilty for using so much of the world's resources when I'm not giving anything back."

She had recently ended a 4-year relationship with her boyfriend when he broke their engagement. "The whole thing with Tom just left me feeling completely worthless." As a result, she had slept a great deal and found herself "just feeling tired all the time and moving around the house like an old grandma." Additionally, she describes having difficulty concentrating.

Amy, however, has noticed a dramatic shift in her behavior in the past 6 days. Amy reports that for the last several days she has not felt the need for any sleep. "It is really the most remarkable change! I feel tremendous, actually, I have so, so much energy and I'm getting so much done! I've been baking, and I painted my kitchen and reorganized all the cupboards and the drawers. I guess I hadn't really realized how skilled I am at getting things organized, I should think about doing this as a side job or something. Or maybe I should write a book about it, you know? A lot of people need help with that. But anyway, I baked, painted organized and then got into my office and really started to sort through my piano music and started to build a proper organizing system there, too." Though Amy has appreciated her recent shift in need for sleep, newfound enthusiasm, very high energy and productivity, she tells her counselor that her loneliness is still a problem for her. She misses her boyfriend but can't see holding onto a relationship that "is going nowhere" and worries that her life is "ultimately purposeless."

Donna

Donna and Joseph are meeting with their obstetrician for a checkup. Joseph has been very concerned about his wife. Since entering the second trimester of her pregnancy, Joseph has felt she has not been herself. Joseph tells their doctor that she seems sad almost every day, and often cries or looks despondent. "She moves around the house strangely, like she is in a slow-motion picture show." Donna confirms that she has felt very blue for the past 3 weeks. "I've been so, so tired. I know that some fatigue is normal in pregnancy but this seems different from what my sisters experienced. I have no energy at all!" Donna reports that she has been sleeping as much as 13 hours a day. Joseph adds, "All the stuff she used to love to do, she doesn't want to do any of that now." Donna also describes having a lot of trouble keeping track of appointments, obligations and making decisions in general.

Bret

Bret, 46, is currently a resident of a state-funded group home for persons recently released from the hospital; he is receiving daily group therapy, medication management and transition skills. Bret was admitted when he became concerned that he would not be able to control his increasingly suicidal thoughts. During his hospitalization, Bret was treated with antidepressants and showed enough improvement to be released to the transition center.

For the past 4 days, staff at the group home have noticed Bret's remaining symptoms shift, and note that Bret now seems "antsy," pacing and shaking his left leg while sitting. Bret also seems to have become quite irritable with staff and fellow residents. He complains that he is unable to sleep, talks excessively and does not seem to be able to keep his attention on group activities or the tasks he has been assigned.

Bret has complained to staff, "I really don't need this shit! What I need is a car and a job. Sitting around in this place and listening to people whine about their problems isn't going to get me on my feet again! If I don't have a job I can't pay my bills and my ex-wife won't let me see my kids. That's the kind of help I need!"

Autumn

Autumn, age 42, has a long history of cycling moods. She shares, "Winter is always especially hard for me. For at least 20 years, I've had depressive episodes that made it next to impossible to get out of bed. Sometimes I can't take care of the children and they have to stay with their grandparents for several weeks until I start to feel more like myself. These low periods have caused me a lot of problems. Twice I lost a job thanks to being so depressed, either I couldn't get to work at all or I just couldn't focus and be present for the work. But then at other times I have these periods when I am very productive and have a lot of creative juices flowing. Sometimes this can lead me to be a little reckless or very grumpy. And then, of course, there are other times when things are really fine. I just feel normal, not too up and not too down. That's how I've been feeling for the past few weeks, just normal. It is a relief." Autumn has returned to counseling hoping that this time she can learn to balance her moods and "lead a more normal life."

Hannah

Hannah, age 12, has been brought to counseling by her mother. Hannah's mother shares, "My parents think I'm overreacting and that Hannah is a normal kid and just needs some discipline. But for as long as I can remember Hannah has just been, well, kind of low energy and not interested in very much of anything but social media and streaming movies on the internet. She sits in front of the computer for hours, never going out or talking with friends. But she doesn't really seem to enjoy these movies and she doesn't seem to get any pleasure out of social media either." Hannah's mother also complains, "Hannah is a real grouch at home. She can be pretty snarky with me and with her younger sister and I'm just not sure what's going on with that. I can't really put my finger on any particular trigger and there doesn't seem to be much that softens her edginess, especially in the morning."

In her intake interview, Hannah shares that she does not feel hungry and at school she often throws the entire contents of her lunchbox in the trash so her mother won't "get on her for not eating." She also reports having a difficult time falling asleep at night and sometimes watches movies under her covers on her laptop into the early morning while the rest of the family sleeps. Hannah also admits that it is difficult for her to concentrate during school and that she wishes she didn't have to go. Hannah reports, "I don't really get why I feel this way. I know I'm pretty lucky, I have everything I need and my parents are ok, I guess, but I pretty much hate school. I hate coming downstairs for dinner or going out with my family. I wish I could just be happy. I don't like being mad all the time, but I just am." Hannah denies any substance use and denies other physical or mental health symptoms.

References

Abreu, T., & Bragança, M. (2015). The bipolarity of light and dark: A review on bipolar disorder and circadian cycles. *Journal of Affective Disorders, 185*, 219–229.

American Psychiatric Association. (2013). *Highlights of changes from DSM IV-TR to DSM-5*. http://www.dsm5.org/documents/changes%20from%20dsm-iv-tr%20to%20dsm-5.pdf

Ancín, I., Cabranes, J. A., Santos, J. L., Sánchez-Morla, E., & Barabash, A. (2013). Executive deficits: A continuum schizophrenia–Bipolar disorder or specific to schizophrenia? *Journal of Psychiatric Research, 47*(11), 1564–1571. https://doi.org/10.1016/j.jpsychires.2013.07.008

Asarnow, L. D., Soehner, A. M., & Harvey, A. G. (2014). Basic sleep and circadian science as building blocks for behavioral interventions: A translational approach for mood disorders. *Behavioral Neuroscience, 128*(3), 360. https://doi.org/10.1037/a0035892

Atkins, C. (2014). *Co-occurring disorders: Integrated assessment and treatment of substance use and mental disorders*. PESI Publishing & Media.

Atlantis, E., & Sullivan, T. (2012). Bidirectional association between depression and sexual dysfunction: A systematic review and meta-analysis. *The Journal of Sexual Medicine, 9*(6), 1497–1507.

Avenevoli, S., Swendsen, J., He, J. P., Burstein, M., & Merikangas, K. R. (2015). Major depression in the national comorbidity survey–Adolescent supplement: Prevalence, correlates, and treatment. *Journal of the American Academy of Child & Adolescent Psychiatry, 54*(1), 37–44. https://doi.org/10.1016/j.jaac.2014.10.010

Bakken, K., Landheim, A. S., & Vaglum, P. (2003). Primary and secondary substance misusers: Do they differ in substance-induced and substance-independent mental disorders? *Alcohol and Alcoholism, 38*(1), 54–59. https://doi.org/10.1093/alcalc/agg012

Balázs, J., Benazzi, F., Rihmer, Z., Rihmer, A., Akiskal, K. K., & Akiskal, H. S. (2006). The close link between suicide attempts and mixed (bipolar) depression: Implications for suicide prevention. *Journal of Affective Disorders, 91*(2–3), 133–138. https://doi.org/10.1016/j.jad.2005.12.049

Bhugra, D., & McKenzie, K. (2003). Expressed emotion across cultures. *Advances in Psychiatric Treatment, 9*(5), 342–348. https://doi.org/10.1192/apt.9.5.342

Biederman, J., Faraone, S. V., Chu, M. P., & Wozniak, J. (1999). Further evidence of a bidirectional overlap between juvenile mania and conduct disorder in children. *Journal of the American Academy of Child & Adolescent Psychiatry*, *38*(4), 468–476. https://doi.org/10.1097/00004583-199904000-00021

Biederman, J., Faraone, S. V., Mick, E., Wozniak, J., Chen, L., Ouellette, C., & Lelon, E. (1996). Attention-deficit hyperactivity disorder and juvenile mania: An overlooked comorbidity? *Journal of the American Academy of Child & Adolescent Psychiatry*, *35*(8), 997–1008. https://doi.org/10.1097/00004583-199608000-00010

Biederman, J., Faraone, S. V., Wozniak, J., Mick, E., Kwon, A., Cayton, G., & Clark, S. (2004). Clinical correlates of bipolar disorder in a large, referred sample of children and adolescents. *Journal of Psychiatric Research*, *39*(6), 611–622. https://doi.org/10.1016/j.jpsychires.2004.08.003

Blader, J. C., & Carlson, G. A. (2007). Increased rates of bipolar disorder diagnoses among US child, adolescent, and adult inpatients, 1996–2004. *Biological Psychiatry*, *62*(2), 107–114.

Blanco, C., Alegría, A. A., Liu, S. M., Secades-Villa, R., Sugaya, L., Davies, C., & Nunes, E. V. (2012). Differences among major depressive disorder with and without co-occurring substance use disorders and substance-induced depressive disorder: Results from the national epidemiologic survey on alcohol and related conditions. *The Journal of Clinical Psychiatry*, *73*(6), 865–873. https://doi.org/10.4088/JCP.10m06673

Brodsky, B. S. (2016). Early childhood environment and genetic interactions: The diathesis for suicidal behavior. *Current Psychiatry Reports*, *18*(9), 86. https://doi.org/10.1007/s11920-016-0716-z

Carlson, G. A., Danzig, A. P., Dougherty, L. R., Bufferd, S. J., & Klein, D. N. (2016). Loss of temper and irritability: The relationship to tantrums in a community and clinical sample. *Journal of Child and Adolescent Psychopharmacology*, *26*(2), 114–122. https://doi.org/10.1089/cap.2015.0072

Cohen, R. B. (2013). *The family focused approach to bipolar disorder*. familyfocusedsolutions.com. www.familyfocusedsolutions.com/the-family-focused-approach-to-bipolar-disorder/

Couric, K. (host). (2007). *What Killed Rebecca Riley? 60 minutes*. Columbia Broadcasting System.

Cristancho, M. A., O'Reardon, J. P., & Thase, M. E. (2011). Atypical depression in the 21st century: Diagnostic and treatment issues. *Psychiatric Times*, *28*(1), 42–47.

Csikszentmihalyi, M. (2014). Toward a psychology of optimal experience. In *Flow and the foundations of positive psychology* (pp. 209–226). Springer Publishing.

De Crescenzo, F., Serra, G., Maisto, F., Uchida, M., Woodworth, H., Casini, M. P., & Vicari, S. (2017). Suicide attempts in juvenile bipolar versus major depressive disorders: Systematic review and meta-analysis. *Journal of the American Academy of Child & Adolescent Psychiatry*, *56*(10), 825–831.

Dickstein, D. P., Garvey, M., Pradella, A. G., Greenstein, D. K., Sharp, W. S., Castellanos, F. X., . . . & Leibenluft, E. (2005). Neurologic examination abnormalities in children with bipolar disorder or attention-deficit/hyperactivity disorder. *Biological Psychiatry*, *58*(7), 517–524.

Dictionary, O. E. (2018). *Oxford english dictionary*. http://www.oed.com/

Diler, R. S., Goldstein, T.R., Hafeman, D., Merranko, J., Liao, F., Goldstein, B.I., & Birmhamer, B. (2017). Distinguishing bipolar depression from unipolar depression in youth: Preliminary findings. *Journal of Child and Adolescent Psychopharmacology*, *27*(4), 310–319. https://doi.org/10.1089/cap.2016.0154

Dougherty, L. R., Smith, V. C., Bufferd, S. J., Carlson, G. A., Stringaris, A., Leibenluft, E., & Klein, D. N. (2014). DSM 5 disruptive mood dysregulation disorder: Correlates and predictors in young children. *Psychological Medicine*, *44*, 2339–2350. https://doi.org/10.1017/S0033291713003115

Ehlers, C. L., Kupfer, D. J., Frank, E., & Monk, T. H. (1993). Biological rhythms and depression: The role of zeitgebers and zeitstorers. *Depression*, *1*(6), 285–293. https://doi.org/10.1002/depr.3050010602

Fawcett, J. (2014). *Report of the DSM-5 mood disorders work group*. http://www.dsm5.org/progressreports/pages/0904reportofthedsm-vmooddisordersworkgroup.aspx

Figley, C. R. (2002). Compassion fatigue: Psychotherapists' chronic lack of self care. *Journal of Clinical Psychology*, *58*(11), 1433–1441.

Flint, J., & Kendler, K. S. (2014). The genetics of major depression. *Neuron*, *81*(3), 484–503. https://doi.org/10.1016/j.neuron.2014.01.027

Frank, E. (2005). *Treating bipolar disorder: A clinician's guide to interpersonal and social rhythm therapy*. Guilford Press.

Frank, E., Kupfer, D., & Ehlers, C. (1994). Interpersonal and social rhythm therapy for bipolar disorder: Outcome of the first year. *Archives of General Psychiatry*, *60*, 145–152.

Freeman, A. J., Youngstrom, E. A., Youngstrom, J. K., & Findling, R. L. (2016). Disruptive mood dysregulation disorder in a community mental health clinic: Prevalence, comorbidity and correlates. *Journal of Child and Adolescent Psychopharmacology*, *26*(2), 123–130.

Fried, E. I., & Nesse, R. M. (2015). Depression is not a consistent syndrome: An investigation of unique symptom patterns in the STAR* D study. *Journal of Affective Disorders*, *172*, 96–102. https://doi.org/10.1016/j.jad.2014.10.010

Fuller-Thomson, E, Baird, S. L., Dhrodia, R., & Brennenstuhl, S. (2016). The association between Adverse Childhood Experiences (ACEs) and suicide attempts in a population-based study. *Child: Care, Health and Development*, *42*(5), 725–734. https://doi.org/10.1111/cch.12351

Geddes, J., & Miklowitz, D. (2013). Treatment of bipolar disorder. *The Lancet*, *381*(9878), 1672–1682. https://doi.org/10.1016/S0140-6736(13)60857-0

Goes, F. S., Sadler, B., Toolan, J., Zamoiski, R. D., Mondimore, F. M., MacKinnon, D. F., & Potash, J. B. (2007). Psychotic features in bipolar and unipolar depression. *Bipolar Disorders*, *9*(8), 901–906. https://doi.org/10.1111/j.1399-5618.2007.00460.x

Goldberg, J. F., Perlis, R. H., Bowden, C. L., Thase, M. E., Miklowitz, D. J., Marangell, L. B., & Sachs, G. S. (2009). Manic symptoms during depressive episodes in 1,380 patients with bipolar disorder: Findings from the STEP-BD. *American Journal of Psychiatry*, *166*(2), 173–181. https://doi.org/10.1176/appi.ajp.2008.08050746

Goldstein, T. R., Birmaher, B., Axelson, D., Ryan, N. D., Strober, M. A., Gill, M. K., & Bridge, J. A. (2005). History of suicide attempts in pediatric bipolar disorder: Factors associated with increased risk. *Bipolar Disorders*, *7*(6), 525–535. https://doi.org/10.1111/j.1399-5618.2005.00263.x

Gotink, R. A., Chu, P., Busschbach, J. J., Benson, H., Fricchione, G. L., & Hunink, M. M. (2015). Standardised mindfulness-based interventions in healthcare: An overview of systematic reviews and meta-analyses of RCTs. *PLOS ONE*, *10*(4), e0124344. https://doi.org/10.1371/journal.pone.0124344

Grant, B. F., Stinson, F. S., Dawson, D. A., Chou, S. P., Dufour, M. C., Compton, W., & Kaplan, K. (2004). Prevalence and co-occurrence of substance use disorders and independent mood and anxiety disorders: Results from the national epidemiologic survey on alcohol and related conditions. *Archives of General Psychiatry*, *61*(8), 807–816. https://doi.org/10.1001/archpsyc.61.8.807

Halbreich, U., Borenstein, J., Pearlstein, T., & Kahn, L. S. (2003). The prevalence, impairment, impact, and burden of premenstrual dysphoric disorder (PMS/PMDD). *Psychoneuroendocrinology*, *28*, 1–23. https://doi.org/10.1016/S0306-4530(03)00098-2

Ha, T. H. (2018). The border between bipolar disorder and personality disorders. *Journal of Korean Neuropsychiatric Association*, *57*(4), 308–316. https://doi.org/10.4306/jknpa.2018.57.4.308

Hidalgo-Mazzei, D., Walsh, E., Rosenstein, L., & Zimmerman, M. (2015). Comorbid bipolar disorder and borderline personality disorder and substance use disorder. *The Journal of Nervous and Mental Disease*, *203*(1), 54–57. https://doi.org/10.1097/NMD.0000000000000235

Hollis, J. (2008). *What matters most: Living a more considered life*. Penguin.

Ivarsson, T., Saavedra, F., Granqvist, P., & Broberg, A. G. (2016). Traumatic and adverse attachment childhood experiences are not characteristic of OCD but of depression in adolescents. *Child Psychiatry & Human Development*, *47*(2), 270–280. https://doi.org/10.1007/s10578-015-0563-x

Judd, L. L., & Akiskal, H. S. (2003). Depressive episodes and symptoms dominate the longitudinal course of bipolar disorder. *Current Psychiatry Reports*, *5*(6), 417–418. https://doi.org/10.1007/s11920-003-0077-2

Judd, L. L., Akiskal, H. S., Schettler, P. J., Coryell, W., Endicott, J., Maser, J. D., & Keller, M. B. (2003). A prospective investigation of the natural history of the long-term weekly symptomatic status of bipolar II disorder. *Archives of General Psychiatry*, *60*(3), 261–269. https://doi.org/10.1001/archpsyc.60.3.261

Kaste, M. (2018, November 17). *Facebook increasingly reliant on A.I. to predict suicide risk*. National Public Radio.

Koenders, M. A., Giltay, E. J., Spijker, A. T., Hoencamp, E., Spinhoven, P., & Elzinga, B. M. (2014). Stressful life events in bipolar I and II disorder: Cause or consequence of mood symptoms? *Journal of Affective Disorders*, *161*, 55–64. https://doi.org/10.1016/j.jad.2014.02.036

Koukopoulos, A., Sani, G., & Ghaemi, S. N. (2013). Mixed features of depression: Why DSM-5 is wrong (and so was DSM-IV). *The British Journal of Psychiatry*, *203*(1), 3–5.

Koukopoulos, G. S. (2014). DSM-5 criteria for depression with mixed features: A farewell to mixed depression. *Acta Psychiatrica Scandinavica Avica*, *129*, 4–16. https://doi.org/10.1111/acps.12140

Lam, D. H., Hayward, P., Watkins, E. R., Wright, K., & Sham, P. (2005). Relapse prevention in patients with bipolar disorder: Cognitive therapy outcome after 2 years. *American Journal of Psychiatry*, *162*(2), 324–329. https://doi.org/10.1176/appi.ajp.162.2.324

Leonpacher, A. K., Liebers, D., Pirooznia, M., Jancic, D., Mackinnon, D. F., Mondimore, F. M., & NIMH Genetics Initiative Bipolar Disorder Consortium. (2015). Distinguishing bipolar from unipolar depression: The importance of clinical symptoms and illness features. *Psychological Medicine*, *45*(11), 2437–2446.

Levenson, J., & Frank, E. (2010). Sleep and circadian rhythm abnormalities in the pathophysiology of bipolar disorder. In *Behavioral neurobiology of bipolar disorder and its treatment* (pp. 247-262). Springer Publishing.

Longfellow, H. W., & McClatchy, J. D. (2000). *Poems and other writings* (Vol. 118). Library of America.

Malhi, G. S., Masson, M., & Bellivier, F. (2015). Teasing apart Bipolar III: The causes and consequences of a Treatment-Emergent Affective Switch (TEAS) into mania. *Australian & New Zealand Journal of Psychiatry*, *49*(10), 866–868. https://doi.org/10.1177/0004867415607644

Margulies, D. M., Weintraub, S., Basile, J., Grover, P. J., & Carlson, G. A. (2012). Will disruptive mood dysregulation disorder reduce false diagnosis of bipolar disorder in children? *Bipolar Disorders*, *14*(5), 488–496.

Marks, M. (2018, December 30). *Suicide prediction technology is revolutionary. It badly needs oversight.* Washington Post.

McCullough Jr, J. P. (2003). Treatment for chronic depression: Cognitive behavioral analysis system of psychotherapy (CBASP). *Educational Publishing Foundation*, *13*(3–4), 241. https://doi.org/10.1037/1053-0479.13.3-4.241

McIntyre, R. S., Soczynska, J. K., Cha, D. S., Woldeyohannes, H. O., Dale, R. S., Alsuwaidan, M. T., & Kennedy, S. H. (2015). The prevalence and illness characteristics of DSM-5-defined "mixed feature specifier" in adults with major depressive disorder and bipolar disorder: Results from the international mood disorders collaborative project. *Journal of Affective Disorders*, *172*, 259–264. https://doi.org/10.1016/j.jad.2014.09.026

Melo, M. C., Abreu, R. L., Neto, V. B. L., de Bruin, P. F., & de Bruin, V. M. (2017). Chronotype and circadian rhythm in bipolar disorder: A systematic review. *Sleep Medicine Reviews*, *34*, 46–58. https://doi.org/10.1016/j.smrv.2016.06.007

Messer, T., Lammers, G., Muller-Siecheneder, F., Schmidt, R., & Lafti, S. (2017). Substance abuse in patients with bipolar disorder: Asystematic review and meta-analysis. *Psychiatry Research*, *253*, 338–350. https://doi.org/10.1016/j.psychres.2017.02.067

Miklowitz, D. J., Axelson, D., Birmaher, B., George, E., Taylor, D., & Schneck, C. (2008). Family-focused treatment for adolescents with bipolar disorder—Results of a 2-year randomized trial. *Archives of General Psychiatry*, *65*(9), 1053–1061. https://doi.org/10.1001/archpsyc.65.9.1053

Miklowitz, D. J., & Chung, B. (2016). Family-focused therapy for bipolar disorder: Reflections on 30 years of research. *Family Process*, *55*(3), 483–499. https://doi.org/10.1111/famp.12237

Miklowitz, D. J., & Frank, E. (2010). *Bipolar disorder, second edition: A family-focused treatment approach*. Guilford Publications.

Miklowitz, D. J., George, E., Richards, J., Simoneau, T., & Suddath, R. (2003). A randomized study of family-focused psychoeducation and pharmacotherapy in the outpatient management of bipolar disorder. *Archives Of General Psychiatry*, *60*, 904–912. https://doi.org/10.1001/archpsyc.60.9.904

Miklowitz, D. J., & Goldstein, M. J. (1990). Behavioral family treatment for patients with bipolar affective-disorder. *Behavior Modification*, *14*, 457–489. https://doi.org/10.1177/01454455900144005

Miklowitz, D. J., & Otto, M. (2006). New psychosocial interventions for bipolar disorder: A review of literature and introduction of the systematic treatment enhancement program. *Journal of Cognitive Psychotherapy*, *20*(2), 215–230. https://doi.org/10.1891/jcop.20.2.215

Miklowitz, D. J., Otto, M., Frank, E., Reilly-Harrington, N., Kogan, J., & Sachs, G. (2007). Intensive psychosocial intervention enhances functioning in patients with bipolar depression: Results from a 9-month randomized controlled trial. *The American Journal of Psychiatry*, *164*, 1340–1347. https://doi.org/10.1176/appi.ajp.2007.07020311

Mitchell, P. B., Goodwin, G. M., Johnson, G. F., & Hirschfeld, R. (2008). Diagnostic guidelines for bipolar depression: A probabilistic approach. *Bipolar Disorders*, *10*, 144–152. https://doi.org/10.1111/j.1399-5618.2007.00559.x

Miura, T., Noma, H., Furukawa, T. A., Mitsuyasu, H., Tanaka, S., Stockton, S., & Cipriani, A. (2014). Comparative efficacy and tolerability of pharmacological treatments in the maintenance treatment of bipolar disorder: A systematic review and network meta-analysis. *The Lancet Psychiatry*, *1*(5), 351–359. https://doi.org/10.1016/S2215-0366(14)70314-1

Moreno, C., Laje, G., Blanco, C., Jiang, H., Schmidt, A. B., & Olfson, M. (2007). National trends in the outpatient diagnosis and treatment of bipolar disorder in youth. *Archives of general psychiatry*, *64*(9), 1032–1039.

Morrison, J. (2014). *Diagnosis made easier: Principles and techniques for mental health clinicians*. Guilford Publications.

Österman, K., & Björkqvist, K. (2010). A cross-sectional study of onset, cessation, frequency, and duration of children's temper tantrums in a nonclinical sample. *Psychological Reports*, *106*(2), 448–454. https://doi.org/10.2466/pr0.106.2.448-454

Owen, R., Gooding, P., Dempsey, R., & Jones, S. (2015). A qualitative investigation into the relationships between social factors and suicidal thoughts and acts experienced by people with a bipolar disorder diagnosis. *Journal of Affective Disorders*, *176*, 133–140. https://doi.org/10.1016/j.jad.2015.02.002

Pacchiarotti, I., Bond, D. J., Baldessarini, R. J., Nolen, W. A., Grunze, H., Licht, R. W., Post, R. M., Berk, M., Goodwin, G. M., Sachs, G. S., Tondo, L., Findling, R. L., Youngstrom, E. A., Tohen, M., Undurraga, J., González-Pinto, A., Goldberg, J. F., Yildiz, A., Altshuler, L. L., . . . Vieta, E. (2013). The International Society for Bipolar Disorders (ISBD) task force report on antidepressant use in bipolar disorders. *American Journal of Psychiatry*, *170*(11), 1249–1262. https://doi.org/10.1176/appi.ajp.2013.13020185

Pallaskorpi, S., Suominen, K., Ketokivi, M., Valtonen, H., Arvilommi, P., Mantere, O., & Isometsä, E. (2017). Incidence and predictors of suicide attempts in bipolar I and II disorders: A 5-year follow-up study. *Bipolar Disorders, 19*(1), 13–22. https://doi.org/10.1111/bdi.12464

Panchal, N., Kamal, R., Orgera, K., Cox, C., Garfield, R., Hamel, L., & Chidambaram, P. (2020). The implications of COVID-19 for mental health and substance use. *The Henry Journal. Kaiser Family Foundation, 21.*

Papadimitriou, G. N., Dikeos, D. G., Soldatos, C. R., & Calabrese, J. R. (2007). Non-pharmacological treatments in the management of rapid cycling bipolar disorder. *Journal of Affective Disorders, 98*(1-2), 1–10.

Parikh, S. V., Zaretsky, A., Beaulieu, S., Yatham, L. N., Young, L. T., Patelis-Siotis, I., & Velyvis, V. (2012). A randomized controlled trial of psychoeducation or cognitive-behavioral therapy in bipolar disorder: A Canadian Network for Mood and Anxiety Treatments (CANMAT) study [CME]. *The Journal of Clinical Psychiatry, 73*(6), 803–810. https://doi.org/10.4088/JCP.11m07343

Paris, J., & Black, D. W. (2015). Borderline personality disorder and bipolar disorder: What is the difference and why does it matter? *The Journal of Nervous and Mental Disease, 203*(1), 3–7. https://doi.org/10.1097/NMD.0000000000000225

Perlman, G., Kotov, R., Fu, J., J, Bromet. E., Fochtmann, L. J., & Medeiros, H. (2016). Symptoms of psychosis in schizophrenia, schizoaffective disorder, and bipolar disorder: A comparison of African Americans and Caucasians in the genomic psychiatry cohort. *American Journal Medical Genetics B Neuropsychiatry Genetics, 171*(4), 546–555. https://doi.org/10.1002/ajmg.b.32409

Perugi, G., Hantouche, E., Vannucchi, G., & Pinto, O. (2015). Cyclothymia reloaded: A reappraisal of the most misconceived affective disorder. *Journal of Affective Disorders, 183*, 119–133. https://doi.org/10.1016/j.jad.2015.05.004

Phelps, J. (2008). Dark therapy for bipolar disorder using amber lenses for blue light blockade. *Medical hypotheses, 70*(2), 224–229.

Phelps, J. (2016). *A spectrum approach to mood disorders: Not fully bipolar but not unipolar—Practical management.* Norton Press.

Phillips, M. L., & Kupfer, D. J. (2013). Bipolar disorder diagnosis: Challenges and future directions. *The Lancet, 381*(9878), 1663–1671. https://doi.org/10.1016/S0140-6736(13)60989-7

Pogge, D. L., Wayland-Smith, D., Zaccario, M., Borgaro, S., Stokes, J., & Harvey, P. D. (2001). Diagnosis of manic episodes in adolescent inpatients: Structured diagnostic procedures compared to clinical chart diagnoses. *Psychiatry Research, 101*(1), 47–54.

Quitkin, F. M. (2002). Depression with atypical features: Diagnostic validity, prevalence and treatment. *Primary Care Companion Journal of Clinical Psychiatry, 4*(3), 94–99. https://doi.org/10.4088/PCC.v04n0302

Ramos, K., Erkanli, A., & Koenig, H. G. (2018). Effects of religious versus conventional Cognitive–Behavioral Therapy (CBT) on suicidal thoughts in major depression and chronic medical illness. *Psychology of Religion and Spirituality, 10*(1), 79. https://doi.org/10.1037/rel0000113

Rea, M. M., Tompson, M. C., Miklowitz, D. J., Goldstein, M. J., Hwang, S., & Mintz, J. (2003). Family-focused treatment versus individual treatment for bipolar disorder: Results of a randomized clinical trial. *Journal of Consulting and Clinical Psychology*, *71*(3), 482.

Regier, D. A., Narrow, W. E., Clarke, D. E., Kraemer, H. C., Kuramoto, S. J., Kuhl, E. A., & Kupfer, D. J. (2013). DSM-5 field trials in the United States and Canada, Part II: Test-retest reliability of selected categorical diagnoses. *American Journal of Psychiatry*, *170*(1), 59–70.

Regreer, E. J., Kupka, R. W., Havc, M. T., Vollebergh, W., & Nolen, W. A. (2015). Low self-recognition and awareness of past hypomanic and manic episodes in the general population. *International Journal of BiPolar Disorder*, *3*(1), 22. https://doi.org/10.1186/s40345-015-0039-8

Roy, A., Lopes, V., & Klein, R. (2014). Disruptive mood dysregulation disorder: A new diagnostic approach to chronic irritability in youth. *The American Journal of Psychiatry*, *171*(9), 918–924. https://doi.org/10.1176/appi.ajp.2014.13101301

Saps, M., Seshadri, R., Sztainberg, M., Schaffer, G., Marshall, B. M., & Di Lorenzo, C. (2009). A prospective school-based study of abdominal pain and other common somatic complaints in children. *The Journal of Pediatrics*, *154*(3), 322–326 . https://doi.org/10.1016/j.jpeds.2008.09.047

Schepman, K., Fombonne, E., Collishaw, S., & Taylor, E. (2014). Cognitive styles in depressed children with and without comorbid conduct disorder. *Journal of Adolescence*, *37*(5), 622–631. https://doi.org/10.1016/j.adolescence.2014.04.004

Shanahan, L., Zucker, N., Copeland, W. E., Bondy, C. L., Egger, H. L., & Costello, E. J. (2015). Childhood somatic complaints predict generalized anxiety and depressive disorders during young adulthood in a community sample. *Psychological Medicine*, *45*(8), 1721–1730. https://doi.org/10.1017/S0033291714002840

Stapinski, L. A., Araya, R., Heron, J., Montgomery, A. A., & Stallard, P. (2015). Peer victimization during adolescence: Concurrent and prospective impact on symptoms of depression and anxiety. *Anxiety, Stress, & Coping*, *28*(1), 105–120. https://doi.org/10.1080/10615806.2014.962023

Substance Abuse and Mental Health Services Administration. (2018). *Key substance use and mental health indicators in the United States: Results from the 2017 national survey on drug use and health (HHS Publication No. SMA 18-5068, NSDUH Series H-53).* Center for Behavioral Health Statistics and Quality, Substance Abuse and Mental Health Services Administration. https://www.samhsa.gov/data/

Sullivan, P. F., Neale, M. C., & Kendler, K. S. (2000). Genetic epidemiology of major depression: Review and meta-analysis. *American Journal of Psychiatry*, *157*(10), 1552–1562.

Swann, A.C., Lafer, B., & Perugi, G. (2013). Bipolar mixed states: An international society for bipolar disorders task force report of symptom structure, course of illness, and diagnosis. *American Journal of Psychiatry*, *170*(1), 31–42. https://doi.org/10.1176/appi.ajp.2012.1n.d.301

Swartz, H. A., Frank, E., Zajac, L. E., Kupfer, D. J. (2010). In L. N. Yatham & M. Maj (Eds.), *Bipolar disorder: Clinical and neurobiological foundations* (pp. 430–442). John Wiley & Sons, Ltd.

Teasdale, J. D., Segal, Z. V., Williams, J. M. G., Ridgeway, V. A., Soulsby, J. M., & Lau, M. A. (2000). Prevention of relapse/recurrence in major depression by mindfulness-based cognitive therapy. *Journal of Consulting and Clinical Psychology*, *68*(4), 615. https://doi.org/10.1037/0022-006X.68.4.615

Tolliver, B. K., & Anton, R. F. (2015). Assessment and treatment of mood disorders in the context of substance abuse. *Dialogues in Clinical Neuroscience*, *17*(2), 181.

Turecki, G., & Brent, D. A. (2016). Suicide and suicidal behaviour. *The Lancet*, *387*(10024), 1227–1239. https://doi.org/10.1016/S0140-6736(15)00234-2

Vandeleur, C. L., Fassassi, S., Castelao, E., Glaus, J., Strippli, M. F., Lasserre, A. M., & Preisig, M. (2017). Prevalence and correlates of DSM-5 major depressive and related disorders in the community. *Psychiatry Research*, *250*, 50–58. https://doi.org/10.1016/j.psychres.2017.01.060

Van Diest, R., & Appels, A. (1991). Vital exhaustion and depression: A conceptual study. *Journal of Psychosomatic Research*, *35*(4-5), 535–544.

Van Meter, A. R., Goldstein, B. I., Goldstein, T. R., Yen, S., Hower, H., Strober, M., & Ryan, N. D. (2018). Parsing cyclothymic disorder and other specified bipolar spectrum disorders in youth. *Journal of Affective Disorders*, *238*, 375–382. https://doi.org/10.1016/j.jad.2018.06.023

Van Meter, A. R., Youngstrom, E. A., & Findling, R. L. (2012). Cyclothymic disorder: A critical review. *Clinical Psychology Review*, *32*(4), 229–243. https://doi.org/10.1016/j.cpr.2012.02.001

Vaughn, C. E., & Leff, J. P. (1976). The influence of family and social factors on the course of psychiatric illness: A comparison of schizophrenic and depressed neurotic patients. *The British Journal of Psychiatry*, *129*(2), 125–137.

Wiedemann, G., Rayki, O., Feinstein, E., & Hahlweg, K. (2002). The Family Questionnaire: Development and validation of a new self-report scale for assessing expressed emotion. *Psychiatry Research*, *109*(3), 265–279.

World Health Organization. (2018). *Suicide*. https://www.who.int/news-room/fact-sheets/detail/suicide

Wozniak, J., Biederman, J., & Kwon, A. (2005). How cardinal are cardinal symptoms in pediatric bipolar disorder? An examination of clinical correlates. *Biological Psychiatry*, *58*, 583–588. https://doi.org/10.1016/j.biopsych.2005.08.014

Zimmerman, M., Ruggero, C. J., Chelminski, I., & Young, D. (2008). Is bipolar disorder overdiagnosed? *Journal of Clinical Psychiatry*, *69*(6), 935–940. https://doi.org/10.4088/JCP.v69n

8 Anxiety Disorders

Anxiety seems to have captivated philosophers reaching back into the earliest writings of both the Eastern and Western hemispheres. In the 4th-century BCE Aristotle wrote of fear: "Fear is caused by whatever we feel has great power of destroying us in ways that tend to cause us great pain" (Grimaldi, 1980). Around the same time period, Hippocrates described disruptive levels of social anxiety. A century before these Greek scholars, the Buddha described the origins and solution to anxiety and other forms of suffering. Today, anxiety disorders rank among the most commonly experienced of those included within the DSM 5. Prior to the Covid-19 pandemic, estimates placed the lifetime prevalence of experiencing any anxiety disorder at nearly 34% and 12-month prevalence rates at about 25% (APA, 2013; Bandelow & Michaelis, 2015), suggesting that a third of all readers would experience an anxiety disorder within their lifetimes and that one in four would have already experienced significant and troublesome anxiety within the last year. Though these rates are quite high, as of 2015, there did not seem to be evidence that anxiety disorders were on the rise (Bandelow & Michaelis, 2015). However, the Covid-19 has had a documented impact on mental health across the globe, including increases in anxiety symptoms." (Huang & Zhao, 2020; Jungmann & Witthöft, 2020; Mertens et al., 2020)."

The disorders of the anxiety and related disorders dimension can be organized into two primary groups: one composed of difficulties that center on excessive worry or anxiety and a smaller group, those that are more accurately described as featuring amplified fear (phobias). Fear might be thought of as a response to a perceived immediate danger, and brings with it physiological, cognitive and behavioral responses. Generally, when we speak of fear we can identify a tangible trigger, for example, a fierce and angry dog snapping and growling as you pass, an oncoming car as a child toddles into the road and the sound of a tornado roaring in the distance, can all generate strong feelings of fear and with it an immediate shift in heart rate and other physiological responses. In contrast, the term anxiety has been used to describe a wide array of experiences from the unwelcome negative impact of work and life stressors to the natural consequence of living in a world of uncertainty. "Anxious" is also a word that is sometimes used to describe excited anticipation, for example, the anticipation of an upcoming wedding, graduation or travel abroad. However, in the context of this chapter we will use the terms "anxious" or "anxiety" to describe those worried and agitated states that are not clearly associated with a tangible trigger but to an abstract, existential or distant threat, such as the inevitability of failure, illness or death, and that sometimes are also accompanied by physiological symptoms (Whitley, 1994).

This chapter will offer a brief introduction to the disorders of the anxiety dimension, with a special focus on generalized anxiety disorder (GAD) and will follow with an exploration of key points of differentiation between these disorders and those outside the continuum. A brief survey of treatment interventions is included, followed by cases for diagnosis and treatment planning. Unlike in other chapters, we will begin with a brief discussion of the history of the theoretical understandings of anxiety and follow with the disorders themselves.

Theoretical Approaches to Anxiety

To form an understanding of anxiety is to develop a philosophy of angst, a belief system not only about how anxiety manifests but also of its origins. Evidence of the search to understand and describe anxiety can be found in classical writings and remains a topic that fascinates philosophers and theorists today. The experience of anxiety is so profoundly universal that there is even a popular European fairy tale describing the life of someone who had never felt anxiety at all, *The Boy Who Went Forth to Learn What Fear Was,* sometimes known as, *The Boy Who Went in Search of the Shivers* (Grimm & Grimm, 2016), which details the troubles the absence of anxiety causes him.

Kierkegaard, often credited with the birth of existential thought, famously noted, "Anxiety is the dizziness of freedom," framing anxiety as a natural and perhaps necessary consequence of living a life in which one must make choices. Paul Tillich, also an existential thinker, noted, "Anxiety is the existential awareness of nonbeing. 'Existential' [here] means that it is not the abstract knowledge of nonbeing which produces anxiety but the awareness that nonbeing is a part of one's own being" (Tillich, 1952, p. 35). Here, Tillich takes Kierkegaard's insight one step further and points to our own inevitable mortality and the shadow cast by the awareness of this truth. In contrast, Freud, born a year after Kierkegaard passed away, ultimately developed two theories of anxiety over the course of his career: first arguing that sexual repression was the seed of anxiety and later arguing that it was anxiety, in fact, that motivated sexual repression (Freud, 1936). Explaining Freud's early conceptualization, Fenichel (1944), wrote, "Freud showed that all psychoneuroses are the outcome of conflicts between infantile sexual strivings, remobilized by regression, and fears of the dangers unconsciously connected with these strivings; that neurotic symptoms are a compromise between the instinctual demands and the counterforces motivated by fears" (Fenichel, 1944, p. 313). In this way, both Freudian and existential views of anxiety would frame anxiety

BOX 8.01 KEY TERMS: ANXIETY AND RELATED DISORDERS

Anxiety. For the purposes of this chapter, anxiety is largely a diffuse emotional state marked by physiological responses, such as increased heart rate, sweating, shallow breathing, and so on, and is accompanied by troubling or worried thoughts (APA, 2013).

Cognitive-Attentional Syndrome (CAS). This term, not included within the DSM, describes a collection of symptoms, which includes cognitive self-consciousness, doubt about one's own thoughts, and includes both positive and negative meta-beliefs about the function of worry. These meta-beliefs are thought to sustain anxiety problems in children, adolescents and adults (Esbjørn et al., 2015).

Experiential Avoidance. When a feeling, thought, memory or bodily sensation becomes too uncomfortable to tolerate, experiential avoidance describes the strategies enacted in order to avoid fully engaging our anxieties (Hayes et al., 1996).

Fear. Fear, for the purposes of this chapter, describes anxious responding to a tangible threat that is perceived to present a physical or psychological danger. Common fears include objects such as snakes, spiders, heights, dentists, public speaking, and so on.

Thought Suppression. An attempt to push uncomfortable or unwelcome thoughts out of one's mind.

Metaworry. Metaworry describes worry about worry, a phenomenon believed to contribute to a number of anxiety disorders, generalized anxiety disorder in particular (Roemer & Orsillo, 2005).

Worry. For the purposes of this chapter, worry is understood to be a cognitive activity featuring concern triggered by an actual or potential external event or internal sensation, contained within a largely logical verbal continuum, either out loud or in thought, and frequently inspires problem-solving; also referred to as Type I worry (Wells, 2005).

as all but unavoidable, though existentialists would place the onus on conditions for living, whereas Freud would point to unconscious dynamics as the source for anxiety (neurosis).

The contemplative view of anxiety, one based in Buddhist psychology, would also grant that anxiety is a nearly inevitable side effect of living. However, the contemplativist would argue that anxiety, as well as other forms of suffering, arises from wanting what one does not have, having what one does not want or being afraid of losing what one has now. Contemplativists argue that anxiety arises because we have difficulty accepting that all things and all feelings are impermanent and, consequently, we find it difficult to sit comfortably in the present moment (Wegela, 2014).

In contrast to Freudian, existential and contemplative theories, John Watson and his graduate student, Rosaline Rayner, were of a different mind about anxiety. Together in the laboratories of Johns Hopkins University, they conducted the now infamous Little Albert study in which they demonstrated that fear need not arise organically from unconscious drives or the stark but universal realities of choice or mortality, or even to clinging to some hoped for outcome, but could be learned and unlearned as well (Watson & Rayner, 1920). Later, cognitivist Aaron Beck also studied about anxiety. Like Watson and Raynor, he placed the source of anxiety within cognitive processes but argued that, " . . . the regulatory functions of the cognitive system leads one indiscriminately to interpret environmental events as dangers" (Beck & Emery, 1985, p. 86), forwarding the idea that anxiety is essentially the consequence of faulty thinking.

Much more recently John Bowlby, attachment theorist, attributed anxiety to early relational lapses (Fosha, 2000), a theory mirroring the self-psychology described by Kohut (Marmarosh & Mann, 2014). Finally, a recent biological theory has been advanced to explain differences in levels of anxiety experienced in response to stressful situations. Researchers believe that, for the rare person who experiences almost no anxiety, increased receptivity in the CB1 receptors in the brain may be responsible. This insight offers a new, and as yet unconfirmed, lead into the biological underpinnings of anxiety and points to its potential treatment (Murphy, 2019). While theories describing the origins of mental health disorders such as schizophrenia and autism have shifted significantly over time, these early and varied theories describing the sources of anxiety survive today in the contemporary theoretical models that describe anxiety and are evident in the wide variety of treatment approaches. Later in this chapter, we will explore cognitive theories that attempt to explain GAD, however, the reader should be aware of the rich history of theory related to anxiety and the wide variety of therapeutic approaches available to treat these disorders.

Disorders of the Anxiety Continuum

Separation Anxiety Disorder. With the printing of the fifth edition of the DSM, separation anxiety was included with the anxiety and related disorders. Setting this disorder apart from others in this grouping, the experience of separation anxiety is an expected milestone of early development, sometimes described as stranger anxiety. This phenomenon is usually observed in typically developing and securely attached children beginning around 6 months and lasting through the first year and may reappear at about age 2 (APA, 2013; Ehrenreich et al., 2008). Separation anxiety that arises as a course of normal development is distinguished from separation anxiety disorder when the anxiety persists beyond developmental norms, or arises later in life, and also interferes in the individual's ability to function. For example, though there are gaps in the research literature, many point to separation anxiety as one of the primary drivers behind a phenomenon known as school refusal, in which children and teens miss a great deal of school; thanks to intolerable anxiety (Elliott & Place, 2019). Though separation anxiety is most common in children, arising on average at age 7 (Bandelow & Michaelis, 2015), this diagnosis is not exclusive to children and adolescents. Research suggests that separation anxiety may be more common among older

BOX 8.02 CONSIDER THIS: REFLECTING ON YOUR OWN EXPERIENCE OF ANXIETY

Consider This

How does anxiety show up in your life? Read through the following. Do any of these resonate for you? Does your anxiety have other sources?

Existential

Do you find yourself reluctant to lean deeply into your own freedom to make choices or to take responsibility for getting what you want from life?

Cognitive

Does your anxiety arise out of things you tell yourself that are exaggerated, hurtful or perhaps not true?

Contemplative

Is your anxiety the result of grasping at one outcome over another, or avoiding less welcome outcomes, rather than holding situations with equanimity and accepting the impermanence of all things?

Behavioral

Can you trace your anxiety or fear to an event that has since stayed with you? Perhaps you are aware of an anxiety or phobia you may have learned from someone else, such as a caregiver?

adults than previously understood (Bögels et al., 2013; Shear et al., 2006; Wijeratne & Manicavasagar, 2003), and has been identified in those with substance use, anorexia, bulimia and dependent personality disorders (Loas et al., 2002). Still other research suggests a connection between posttraumatic stress disorder (PTSD) and separation anxiety in adults (Tay et al., 2015). Identifying separation anxiety in older adults will be discussed later in this chapter.

Selective Mutism. Selective mutism is an under-researched disorder, perhaps because it is relatively uncommon, seen in less than 1% of the population and becoming less and less common in later childhood and adolescence (Alyanak et al., 2013; APA, 2013; Bergman et al., 2002). Clients with selective mutism don't experience difficulties with speech fluency or language in general and typically speak as would be expected at home, but consistently decline opportunities to speak at school or other social settings. Conceptually, selective mutism is very similar to social anxiety disorder (SAD); both disorders arise out of a fear of being negatively evaluated, though selective mutism is more specific in its focus (speaking), whereas social anxiety encompasses a more general fear of negative evaluation. Research suggests that between 97% and 100% of those with selective mutism also endorse social anxiety

BOX 8.03 MEDICATIONS AND MEDICAL CONDITIONS THAT ARE CORRELATED WITH ANXIETY SYMPTOMS

Select Medications with Anxiety Side Effects

- Anesthetics
- Anticholinergics
- Anticonvulsants
- Antidepressants
- Antihistamines
- Antihypertensives
- Antiparkinsonian drugs
- Antipsychotics
- Amphetamines such as those used to treat ADHD
- Bronchodilators
- Caffeine found in medications that treat headache and migraine
- Corticosteroids
- Insulin
- Interferon
- Lithium
- Oral contraceptives
- Thyroid replacements

Select Medical Conditions with Anxiety Side Effects

- Adrenal insufficiency
- AIDS
- Brain tumor
- Cerebrovascular disease
- Cardiovascular conditions
- Chronic obstructive pulmonary disease (COPD)
- Diabetes
- Graves' disease
- Head trauma
- Hyperparathyroidism
- Hypothyroidism
- Thiamine deficiency

**Source:* Adapted from Culpepper (2009), Mayo Clinic (2019), and Morrison (2014).

(Bergman et al., 2002), though the reverse is not the case. Oppositional defiance seems to be comorbid in a significant subset of children with selective mutism (Chavira et al., 2007; Yeganeh et al., 2006). Selective mutism is considered a severe disorder because it creates significant social and educational impairments (APA, 2013). At least one study suggests a significantly elevated family history of selective mutism (37%) in those currently struggling with the disorder (Black & Uhde, 1995, in Alyanak et al., 2013). The typical onset of selective mutism is between age 2 and 5. While the symptoms of selective mutism do tend to dissipate over time and most often eventually disappear altogether, the mean duration of the disorder is 8 years (Muris & Ollendick, 2015), a period that would comprise a significant portion of a child's schooling and consequently entail a long period of suffering and struggle.

Specific Phobia. Though the object of a specific phobia varies a great deal, those with specific phobias share an exaggerated fear that is unresponsive to reason or reassurance. Specific phobias are best understood as a fear of an object, animal or situation that has become pronounced enough to interfere with a person's social or occupational functioning. In order for a phobia to be diagnosed, it should also be an enduring fear, lasting at least 6 months (APA, 2013).

A surprising amount of research has been dedicated to understanding children's fears: normative, subclinical and clinical. Early research suggests that children's fears have remained largely the same over decades of scientific documentation. For children aged 5-12, animals have ranked among the most prominent of fears, followed by monsters and ghosts, and potential dangers, such as robbers or kidnappers (Jersild & Holms, 1935 in Muris & Field, 2011). Muris and Merckelbach (2000) explored the seriousness of childhood phobias in interviews with parents of 160 children between the ages of 4 and 12. A full 17.6% of these parent interviews suggested that their children's fears interfered with their functioning. These researchers found that the five most common specific phobias included the dark, spiders, thunderstorms, blood and the doctor. For those with subclinical fears, the five most common fears were spiders, dogs, birds, snakes and wasps (Muris & Field, 2011). A review of the literature strongly suggests that children of Hispanic and those of African American descent tend to have much higher rates of fear and anxiety than among White children and adolescents of the same age (Chapman et al., 2008; Muris & Field, 2011).

Social Anxiety Disorder (SAD). In contrast to those struggling with a specific phobia, those experiencing an SAD also face a threat and a fear of pain, as Aristotle described, however, this threat is to the internalized self or ego structure rather than the physical body; the anticipated pain comes in the form of shame or embarrassment. Consequently, SAD describes troublesome worry and anxiety that arises in situations in which a person might be negatively evaluated (Bandelow & Michaelis, 2015). Common situations that trigger anxiety among those struggling with SAD generally feature some type of performance, such as offering a formal presentation at work or in the classroom, speaking in a meeting or attending an event in which attention might rest on the individual. As with all anxiety disorders, some kind of impairment is necessary before a diagnosis is given (APA, 2013). Research suggests that women are more likely to develop SAD than are men and seem to experience more severe psychological arousal than do men, however, men appear to be more likely to seek treatment for SAD than are women (Asher et al., 2017). Research also suggests that SAD is common among those 13-17 as well as among adults (Bandelow & Michaelis, 2015).

Culture and Prevalence of Social Anxiety. Hofmann et al. (2010) conducted a meta-analysis of available research on SAD that revealed dramatic differences in prevalence rates of social anxiety. For example, a study found that among women in a rural population of Russia, more than half met criteria for an SAD (using International Classification of Diagnoses [ICD-10] criteria), whereas a second study found a prevalence rate of less than half of 1% among a sample taken of participants in Taiwan. Hofmann, Asnaani and Hinton also found a number of differences within cultural groups within the United States. Their analysis suggests that factors that increased the likelihood of developing SAD included being young, Native American and experiencing low economic status. Factors that seemed to lower risk included Asian, Hispanic or African American heritage, male status or living in an urban area. For minority participants, these lowered rates of risk were more pronounced in those with lower education levels. Further, for Hispanic participants, the lowered risks were only felt for those under the age of 43. Among older participants, the rates of social anxiety were the same as the non-Hispanic White participants.

Taijin kyofusho: Taijin kyofusho (TKS) is organized within the culture-bound disorders of the DSM 5 and is seen most often in Japanese and Korean clients. TKS is very similar to SAD in that these clients fear social situations, however, not because they worry about embarrassing themselves but because they are concerned about embarrassing others. Most often these clients' concerns center on one of the five scenarios that make up the TKS subtypes: glancing at other's genitals, inappropriate blushing, inappropriate eye contact, offending others with their own imagined physical deformity or the fear that their own foul body odor would offend others. In their study, Hofmann et al. (2010) point out that though TKS is described as culturally bound, a 2005 study of 181 American students found that 75% of those diagnosed with SAD also endorsed at least one of the four subtypes of TKS, suggesting that TKS may be more common among the general population than previously understood. Consequently TKS has been included within this chapter.

Panic Disorder and the Panic Attack Specifier. Panic represents an experience of an abrupt and very intense onset of anxiety. Symptoms of a panic attack are largely, though not exclusively, physiological and as such are experienced as a physiological crisis. A person experiencing a panic attack may feel any combination of palpitations, sweating, difficulty catching one's breath, chest pain, nausea, dizziness, trembling, numbness, sensations of heat or cold or choking. These physical symptoms are often accompanied by a sense of derealization, a fear that one is dying or that one is losing one's mind. Panic attacks can accompany a number of disorders including any of the anxiety disorders, as well as in depression, PTSD, substance use disorders, and so on. However, panic attacks can also accompany medical disorders such as respiratory disorders, for example, asthma and chronic obstructive pulmonary disease (COPD), cardiac illnesses, digestive concerns such as irritable bowel syndrome, diabetes and vestibular ailments (APA, 2013; Chen & Tsai, 2016; Meuret et al., 2017). By themselves, panic attacks are considered a symptom rather than a disorder. Consequently, panic attack is included as a specifier when seen together with another disorder (APA, 2013).

However, panic disorder, first described by Robert Burton in 1621 (Bandelow & Michaelis, 2015) can be diagnosed independently. How are the panic specifier and panic disorder differentiated? Panic disorder is thought to be present when panic attacks recur and, as a result, the client has developed a troubling concern about the possibility of another attack and then adopts maladaptive behaviors to avoid another incidence of panic. For as many as a third of clients, panic disorder is resistant to treatment. Researchers attribute treatment-resistant panic to a number of intersecting factors including genetic predispositions coupled with altered brain function including "... brain-derived neurotrophic factor and long-term inflammation ..." (Chen & Tsai, 2016, p. 219). Between 30% and 60% of those with panic disorders also develop agoraphobia (Zalyte et al., 2017).

Agoraphobia. One of the more extreme manifestations of anxiety and fear comes in the form of agoraphobia, which features an inability to tolerate public spaces where the individual feels that easy escape or finding help would be difficult should strong anxiety symptoms arise. Agoraphobia is diagnosed when these fears lead an individual to avoid these spaces altogether or they are tolerated only with a great deal of discomfort. Agoraphobia can be diagnosed as a stand-alone disorder but is frequently comorbid with other disorders and, again, frequently goes hand-in-hand with panic disorder. As noted earlier, between 30% and 60% of those with panic disorders develop agoraphobia (APA, 2013; Sewart & Craske, 2018; Zalyte et al., 2017).

Generalized Anxiety Disorder (GAD)

GAD was included within the first edition of the DSM under the name *anxiety neurosis* (APA, 1952); the name was changed to *GAD* with the publication of the DSM III (APA, 1980), reflecting the philosophical shift in the manual as a whole toward the more theory-neutral tone taken in the third edition. The diagnostic criteria for GAD have gone largely unchanged since that time. Readers will note that the GAD construct includes both the phenomenological and physiological consequences of worry and anxiety. Indeed, when listening to the experiences of clients with GAD, clinicians can identify the threads of cognitive, dynamic, existential, behavioral and contemplative theories woven throughout their narratives. At its core, GAD describes a debilitating pattern of generalized and pervasive worry. Put another way, clients with GAD form a habit of worry that encompasses several areas of the individual's life, ranging from family, finances, health, work, and so on. The individual who struggles with GAD experiences persistent fears that are out of proportion to the actual likelihood or consequence of the scenarios that are generating concern. Further, these concerns are distracting or distressing enough to disrupt that person's ability to fulfill key social roles and additionally create obstacles to the person's ability to enjoy life fully. For example, people struggling with GAD tend to experience a significant number of

BOX 8.04 TRY THIS: WHEN TO USE PANIC SPECIFIER VERSUS PANIC DISORDER

In the following scenarios, Eddie and Jeanie have each experienced panic symptoms. As you read through each scenario, determine which requires a panic disorder diagnosis and which is a panic specifier more appropriate? What questions do you have that would lend more confidence to your decision?

Eddie: Eddie is collaborating with their counselor for issues related to family acceptance of their gender identity and has been working with their counselor on ongoing major depression. Recently, Eddie experienced a panic attack while shopping for groceries. Eddie is not worried about having another panic attack and has not altered their behavior in order to avoid a second occurrence.

Jeanie: Jeanie has had three panic attacks while in public spaces and finds herself avoiding the social situations that she once enjoyed. Initially her friends were willing to hang out with her at her apartment, but over time they began to gather without her when she declined their invitations to movies or dinners out. Now she finds herself alone most evenings and weekends feeling sad and angry.

what are called "disability days" or days when symptoms so overwhelm the person's ability to function that the individual misses work or school. Predictably, these clients also tend to access health care at a much higher rate than those without, presumably because they tend to carry more worries about their health than those without GAD (Wittchen et al., 2002). A more recent global epidemiology study of GAD, which included more than 147,000 participants, revealed an average of 41 days "out of role" in the past 12 months as a result of GAD symptoms; however, their findings showed that role impairment tended to be lower for those with no comorbid disorder (Ruscio et al., 2017). Taken together, the burden of suffering that accompanies GAD is quite high.

GAD is by its nature both pervasive and chronic. Client experiences of this disorder feature apprehensiveness, rumination and generally also come with experiences in the body, such as muscle tension. Although only one symptom is required in children, adults are diagnosed after evidencing at least three of the following six symptoms for a period of at least 6 months: restlessness, fatigue, difficulties with concentration, irritability, muscle tension and sleep disturbances (APA, 2013).

GAD and Its Relationship to Depression. Research available to data reveals a strong relationship between GAD and depressive disorders (Ballenger et al., 2001; Copeland et al., 2009; Moffitt et al., 2007; Wittchen et al., 2002). For years, the prevailing

BOX 8.05 TRY THIS: DIFFERENTIAL DIAGNOSIS OF PANIC

In the following examples, Jung-sook, Angelina and Noble, note that one of them might be diagnosed with panic disorder, one with agoraphobia and the other with panic disorder comorbid with agoraphobia. How would you diagnose each of these three? What questions would you have for each in order to confirm your diagnosis?

Jung-sook: Jung-sook has had nearly a dozen panic attacks, several in the subway on her way to work. She has decided to avoid the subway and drive to work or take cabs instead, which has increased her transportation costs and time considerably. Jung-sook sometimes worries she will have a panic attack while driving. At other times she has felt uncomfortable getting into a cab and on those days she has called in sick. She is considering looking for a new job closer to home, though she loves her work and the friends she has made there. She feels stuck.

Angelina. For the past 4 months, Angelina, aged 20, has gradually found herself more and more unwilling to leave her house. What began as a sinking feeling and an unanchored sense of impending danger when she was in the classroom or on campus, has spread to her travels from home to the city bus, and to her weekly errands. In the past month, Angelina decided to drop out of her fall courses and has used various delivery services to meet her basic needs rather than leaving her apartment.

Noble. Each morning before work, Noble steadies himself and, despite his worry, heads out the door and makes it to the office. A year ago, Noble had the first of a series of panic attacks, each before making a presentation for his supervisor and marketing team. Noble recently declined a promotion that would have meant more money and freedom for his family but would also have required more presentations. Noble and his wife have experienced tension over his decision since he declined the offer of promotion without talking with her, something that she took as a betrayal of trust.

understanding had been that GAD generally precedes and then converts to a depressive disorder; this idea was challenged by a longitudinal study, however, it revealed that in nearly half of their participants, depression had preceded GAD (Moffitt et al., 2007). A second longitudinal study designed to clarify relationships between early psychopathology and mental health patterns later in life followed a group of 1,420 children in cohorts aged 9, 11 and 13. This study affirmed the close relationship between depression and GAD. Indeed, GAD and depression have been found to be predictive of one another. However, whether clients experience GAD alone or GAD symptoms are complicated by depression, GAD has proven itself to be difficult to treat (Wittchen et al., 2002). Cognitive-behavioral therapy (CBT) in combination with medication have held their place as the gold standard for treating GAD for decades (Ballenger et al., 2001; Gautam et al., 2017; Stein, & Sareen, 2015). CBT will be discussed briefly later in the chapter.

Theories and Models Explaining GAD

A number of models have been formulated to describe the development of generalized anxiety, the bulk of which can be placed within cognitive or cognitive-behavioral theories. Consequently the interventions that have been developed for GAD are, by and large, also cognitive-behavioral in their orientation. Four of these theories are described briefly below: Attentional bias, Borkovec's avoidance model, Wells' meta-cognitive model (MCM) and acceptance-based model of GAD. Together, these models may create a comprehensive picture of the cognitive dynamics that converge and create the conditions for GAD patterns to take hold.

Attentional Bias in GAD. Cognitive bias is a broad term used to describe any number of mistakes in reasoning that can occur. A common attentional bias is the negative thought bias, in which negative thoughts are given more attention or weight than are positive or neutral ones. Using a version of the Stroop Visual Probe test modified for their research, Mogg and Bradley (2005) explored cognitive bias in those diagnosed with GAD and compared these results with the results of those diagnosed with either major depression or persistent depressive disorder (dysthymia). These researchers duplicated previous research that revealed those with GAD tend to hold a negative thought bias. Their research further revealed that those with GAD respond much more quickly to negative cues to threat stimuli in the environment than did those with depressive disorders. These researchers note that elevated external threat vigilance may draw attention to a wide array of "minor negative cues in the environment" (p. 42) that in turn may trigger anxious thoughts and feelings. These authors also theorize that a negative attentional bias may also create barriers to correcting thinking errors, such as catastrophizing.

The Role of Avoidance in GAD, Two Theories. The concept of avoidance has been present in one form or another in a variety of counseling theories attempting to explain anxiety. After all, what single word better captures Freud's theory of repression than avoidance, or the refusal to acknowledge the inevitability of isolation and death in existentialism, and so on? Hayes et al. (1996) have written extensively about the role of experiential avoidance, the practice and strategies for avoiding private experiences that might include unwelcome thoughts, memories and bodily sensation. They note that the practice of avoidance is pervasive, something most of us do to some degree or another, and also point out that these strategies take us out of contact with other key capacities that then limit our full pull potential, like dissociation, for example. Hayes et al. suggested that acceptance strategies, like those taught in dialectical behavioral therapy (DBT) or acceptance and commitment therapy (ACT), offer the best hope for managing unwanted experiences.

Other theorists have considered the experience of avoidance, this time focusing on the role of worry as an avoidance strategy. Borkovec argues that when a person imagines some threatening potential outcome, such as a feared poor performance on an exam, the imagery unfolds visually, emotionally and somatically, described as imaginal

BOX 8.06 TRY THIS: DIAGNOSING GAD

Read through the following two cases and then determine a diagnosis for each. Would you be hesitant to diagnose one or the other? If so, why? What questions might you ask to strengthen your diagnostic certainty?

Tadita. Tadita, a 53-year-old data-entry worker with late onset diabetes and heart disease, has been caring for her three grandchildren for a year. Tadita had been ill for some time with what she suspects is chronic bronchitis, but has been unable to see a doctor due to financial and transportation problems. Ultimately, Tadita lost her job due to missed work and has not found another position. Without health insurance, she has been forced to ration her insulin in recent weeks. She was also recently served an eviction notice citing the fact that she is delinquent in her rent. Tadita finds that she worries constantly. She worries the state will take her grandchildren if she can't find another job or loses her housing. She is concerned about being homeless and the impact homelessness will have on her health and her ability to find work again. She is concerned that without her insulin she may die. She also worries a great deal about the well-being of her grandchildren. She is kept up at night with concerns about the continued decline in her health and her loss of health insurance. Tadita is also concerned that her worry is making her more sick. She worries that the anxiety that keeps her awake at night and prevents her from eating is also making it more difficult to recover from her respiratory infection.

Mitch. Mitch is a 38-year-old pharmacist at a local hospital where he has worked for 9 years. He is married, has two children and another due in a few months. Mitch finds it very difficult to focus on his work, thanks to intrusive worry. Mitch worries that his younger son, Davis, aged 18 months, will not do well in school because he does not seem as "curious or quick" as his older sister was at the same age. He worries that if Davis fails at school, he will be bullied and have social problems. The family pediatrician has assured Mitch that Davis is meeting all his developmental milestones and seems to be thriving, but Mitch continues to worry. Mitch is also worried about finances. Though he and his wife are able to pay their bills and contribute to their savings each month, he worries that he and that his wife will lose their jobs and will not be able to support their kids. He finds himself lying awake at night concerned about news, such as changing EPA standards for water safety. Mitch also worries about his health. He recognizes that his worry is excessive and he worries that it is taking a toll on his health and his relationship with his wife and that if his coworkers were to find out that they would lose respect for him. Occasionally, Mitch has become so upset by his worries, he has had to call out sick at work and take a day to "get himself together."

activity. In Borkovec's model, this imagery is so uncomfortable that worry is triggered, a strategy that both examines the potentiality of the feared object and also begins the problem-solving process. By avoiding the imagery and the uncomfortable sensory experiences and shifting instead to the cognitive process of worry, the discomfort of the imagery is bypassed, but at a cost. In the long run, as worry becomes habitual, ultimately, the avoidance only serves to trade one discomfort for another (Sibrava & Borkovec, 2006).

Wells' Metacognitive Model (MCM) MCM. Wells' model is also one that features worry. Wells, however, describes a more complex cognitive dynamic that sets the GAD pattern of anxiety in motion. Wells' model begins with a trigger that initiates Type I worry, which describes those concerned thoughts about external conditions or internal sensations. In the Wells' model, however, metacognition, Type II worry, follows. Metacognition describes thoughts about thinking. Wells explains that clients with GAD generally hold both negative *and* positive thoughts about worry and that each type has a role in sustaining GAD (Wells, 2005; Wells & Carter, 2001).

The belief that worry is somehow helpful is fairly common. For instance, we might embrace the notion that worry helps a person to focus attention onto things that might otherwise be neglected, or that it spurs us to follow through on projects that we otherwise would not. At the same time, we may also endorse negative beliefs about worry. For example, some readers may carry concerns that worry can't be controlled or that it will eventually damage their health, a belief that can then lead to concerns about health generally. Wells asserts that in order to avoid potential negative consequences of worry, people often employ thought suppression, attempting to both block out the initial triggering thought and the worry that might follow, but these attempts frequently prove unsuccessful (Wells, 2005).

Although many people carry both positive and negative beliefs about worry, there is evidence that those with GAD endorse these negative beliefs at significantly higher rates than those without anxiety disorders but also at higher rates than those with panic or social phobia (Wells & Carter, 2001). Again, Wells has asserted that it is negative beliefs about worry that make the greater contribution to GAD-related struggles (Behar et al., 2009; Wells, 2005). More recently, researchers have examined the role of metacognition and anxiety in children as young as 7 years (Esbjørn et al., 2015). In a Danish study of children and their parents, children's negative beliefs about worry mediated the role of worry modeled by parents. More research is needed to understand the role of worry and metaworry in children and teens.

Roemer and Orsillo's Acceptance-Based Model of GAD. The acceptance-based model (Roemer & Orsillo, 2002, 2005) of GAD evolved from the theory that GAD results primarily from habitual avoidance of unwanted experiences. Roemer and Orsillo (2002) describe four key components to their understanding of the development of GAD. First, they argue that all people have internal experiences; these experiences, in and of themselves, are not seen as problematic. Instead, it is the problematic relationship to experiences that begins the process of GAD. A problematic relationship with worry might emerge from low tolerance for uncomfortable feelings, for example, or an inability to imagine alternative possibilities when troubling thoughts emerge. The third component of the acceptance-based model is avoidance. This model asserts that when the problematic relationship with the internal experience develops, clients with GAD then actively engage in avoidance of unwanted experiences. Finally, behavioral restriction results. Behavioral restriction includes all the ways that people alter their

BOX 8.07 WELLS' TYPE I AND TYPE II WORRY APPLIED TO MITCH AND TADITA

In looking back at Mitch and Tadita (Box 8.05), it is clear that both carry a number of concerns. Below, some of Wells' concerns have been organized using Wells' conceptualization model.

Type I Worry: Concerned thoughts about external events or internal sensation

Example: Mitch is concerned about finances, his son's developmental progress, news-related items, the economy and the stability of his marriage.

List Tadita's Type I Worries

Type II Worry: Also known as metaworry, this is worry about worry.

Example: Mitch is concerned that his worry will negatively impact his health or will interfere his relationship with his wife or potentially lessen his standing with coworkers.

List Tadita's Type II Worries

Consider this: What Type I worries are you aware of carrying? Do you also sometimes feel concerned about your worry; do you experience metaworry? How does metaworry look when it shows up for you?

Type I and Type II constructs are **drawn from** Wells (2005); Wells and Carter (2001).

Source: Adapted from Wells (2005); Wells and Carter (2001).

behavior in order to avoid unpleasant thoughts, feelings or experiences. The approach based on this model works to support clients in developing a more accepting stance in relationship to their internal experiences and to build capacities for holding negative experiences rather than responding with avoidance (Behar et al., 2009; Orsillo & Roemer, 2011).

The Skilled Diagnostician: Differential Diagnosis

Differentiation Between Specific and Social Phobia. Because fears tend to fall into predictable categories, such as animals, needles, closed-in spaces, presenting in front of large groups, and so on, differentiating between a specific and social phobia is almost always straightforward. Specific phobias feature a feared object or situation that is perceived to present a clear threat, such as a bite from a dog or spider. Social phobias, on the other hand, are based in fears of shame or embarrassment, for instance, terror at the thought of making a fool of oneself while offering an in-class presentation. Occasionally, however, a fear is presented that is less clear and will require exploration to understand more fully what exactly is feared in order to diagnose accurately.

Arguably, the distinction, in most cases, is a low-stakes diagnostic difference since the interventions for each are essentially the same.

Differentiating Separation Anxiety and SAD. Separation anxiety disorder is most common among younger children but may be seen in older children, sometimes manifesting in school refusal (Suveg et al., 2005) and has been documented in elderly adults, particularly those with a history of anxiety disorders (Wijeratne & Manicavasagar, 2003). Bögels et al. (2013) argue that separation anxiety in adults is likely underdiagnosed for two reasons: first, the DSM IV-TR organized the disorder under disorders identified in childhood, so the diagnosis may not have been considered for older clients. Second, the separation anxiety criteria listed in previous editions precluded diagnosis in those with an adult onset, though this is no longer the case. Bögels et al., note that adult separation anxiety frequently appears as a comorbid disorder with other anxiety disorders. Significantly, a 2006 study of over 9,000 participants revealed an adult lifetime prevalence rate of 6.6%. This study further revealed that of those who had a history of childhood separation anxiety, 36% continued to experience separation anxiety into adulthood. However, more than 77% of participants described having their first experience of separation anxiety in adulthood. Half of these respondents described significant impairment, thanks to separation anxiety (Shear et al., 2006). Studies like this one suggest that clinicians should screen for separation anxiety in adult clients presenting with symptoms of social anxiety or other anxiety disorders on the continuum.

BOX 8.08 TRY THIS: THE BEST-FIT DIAGNOSIS

A client's symptoms don't always fit comfortably into the criteria tables outlined in the DSM. Read the following case, Mariana, and identify a best-fit diagnosis:

Mariana. Mariana is a 17-year-old junior in high school who has noticed a growing fear of eating in front of others. She feels much more comfortable and relaxed if she can eat alone. Initially, Mariana was simply aware of this desire to eat alone and experienced it as a preference, and later as a wish. But more recently she has felt growing anxiety when she has to eat with others, particularly those who are not family. She describes feeling her palms become sweaty and her heart pounding at the thought of having dinner with others. Mariana shares that while she is not afraid of gaining weight and is not afraid of eating in general, only in front of others, she is seeking help from a counselor because food is central to so many social gatherings that she now believes her fear is "ruining her life."

What questions would you pose to Mariana in order to make a confident and accurate diagnosis? If Mariana can't clarify her fears further, what best-fit diagnosis would you select? Why?

Differentiation Between SAD and Selective Mutism. The DSM 5 criteria table for SAD notes that social anxiety can be expressed through a number of behaviors in children including but not exclusive to tantrums, clinging and "refusing to speak in social situations" (p. 202). There is some diagnostic ambiguity in whether or not a child who refuses to speak in social situations (as with selective mutism) would always be diagnosed with SAD or if the diagnosis of one obviates the need for the diagnosis of the other. The manual notes, however, that children who would be diagnosed with selective mutism alone (those without SAD) would not experience evaluation anxieties beyond those experienced when speaking (p. 207), making it possible, but also less common, to diagnose selective mutism without a comorbid SAD. Evaluation for social anxiety when selective mutism is present is best practice.

Differentiating "Normal" Worry, Worry Arising From GAD. It is important to be able to discern typical or appropriate worry from worry as it is seen in GAD. Few of us can claim that we have never been bothered by worry during difficult moments and fewer still can attest to having never experienced worry at all. Worries that are time limited and anchored in concerns that have some tangible basis, such as financial insecurities, the threats inherent in global pandemic, chronic or newly diagnosed health concerns, relationship problems, and so on, are all predictable sources of worry. However, when the worry and anxiety themselves take up a great deal of the individual's energy, when they are hard to quiet even for a little while or are longstanding and impair functioning, assessing for GAD is essential. To diagnose GAD, an impairment caused by the anxiety itself must be present.

Differentiating GAD From the Intrusive Thoughts Seen in obsessive compulsive disorder (OCD). Intrusive thoughts are generally understood to be unwelcome thoughts that arrive unbidden, seemingly out of the blue or as "spontaneous, quick and unwanted" thoughts (Rachman, 1981, in Turner et al., 1992, p. 868). These thoughts often inspire a feeling of dread that calls for some type of action, a compulsion, which serves to prevent the dreaded outcome from coming to fruition. Obsessive compulsive thoughts can vary widely but are often related to contamination, checking, parity, and so on, and may feature unwanted sexual or violent content. Common compulsions include tapping, touching, counting, praying, washing, and so on. A worry, on the other hand, can be thought of as more of a strategy. Worry is a line of thinking that the person actively engages in, though many describe worry as outside their control. The inspiration for the worry may arrive suddenly but the line of thinking takes on a purpose, either in fully mapping out the potential problem or searching for solutions. Compulsions differ from problem-solving in that compulsions are rarely linked logically to solving a potential problem.

Differentiation Between GAD, Illness Anxiety Disorder and Somatic Symptom Disorder. There is a great deal of symptomatic overlap between illness anxiety disorder (IAD), somatic symptom disorder (SSD) and GAD. IAD and SSD are new to the DSM 5 and replace the hypochondriasis diagnosis of previous editions. Because these two remodeled constructs are still relatively new, research on their individual comorbidity with disorders such as GAD is still being explored. However, because hypochondriasis had high comorbidity rates with GAD, the DSM 5 notes this may also be the case with IAD and SSD as well (APA, 2013). Consequently, assessment for IAD and SSD when GAD is suspected (and vice versa) is the best practice.

Further, GAD, like IAD and SSD, often includes physical symptoms and health concerns. Consequently, these disorders can be difficult to tease apart. However, when the client's concerns about health exist alongside a number of other worries, GAD is likely the more appropriate diagnosis and may adequately capture the client's diagnostic picture. In cases in which the individual's worry is almost entirely contained within the health domain, though no evidence of illness exists, the more appropriate diagnosis would be IAD (Stein & Sareen, 2015). When encountering a client who has developed a long-standing pattern of health-related worry with periods of generalized worry, addressing the two disorders separately may be necessary, in which case diagnosing both GAD and IAD together would be appropriate.

The Treatment of Anxiety

As mentioned earlier, theoretical and philosophical discussions of the origins of anxiety are many and reach deep into human intellectual history. Perhaps, as interesting is that a wide variety of these theories are still embraced by practitioners today and can be found woven into the fabric of best practice interventions. Though there are many very effective interventions for anxiety, we will briefly touch on only a few behavioral and cognitive-behavioral approaches here. A short list of additional approaches and their descriptions are also included.

Behavioral Interventions for Phobia. Many readers can identify one or more phobias that they have experienced themselves. Spiders, snakes, a visit to the dentist, and so on, frequently evoke strong feelings of distaste and fear. Common fears like these only rise to the level of diagnosis and require treatment when they interfere significantly with a person's day-to-day living. Behavioral interventions have a long history for treating those with specific phobias. These interventions gradually bring the client into contact with their feared trigger, either in actuality or virtually, often combining imagined, virtual and actual encounters. The aim of exposing clients to a feared object or situation is to dismantle irrational automatic responses to the object and to build insight in the actual degree of threat presented by the object while providing avenues for managing any residual distress caused by the trigger (Leahy, 2011). Current practices, however, generally combine behavioral approaches with cognitive therapies.

Behavioral interventions, such as in vivo or imaginal exposure, represent interventions of the first of the three waves of behavioral therapies. The second wave is composed of behavioral therapies that have been integrated together with cognitive interventions, creating the cognitive-behavioral approaches; the third wave includes,

BOX 8.09 TRY THIS: DIFFERENTIAL DIAGNOSIS OF NORMAL WORRY, GAD AND OCD

Read through the following three scenarios, Sy, Adrian and Apple. How might you identify the nature of each manifestation of thought: typical worry, generalized anxiety disorder (GAD) worry or obsessive compulsive disorder (OCD) intrusive thoughts?

Sy. While walking through the park with a friend, Sy spotted a police officer heading toward them. An image flashed through his mind in which he reached out and touched the officer's genitals as he passed. Sy immediately thrust his hands in his pockets and began counting silently in his head by multiples of seven as the officer walked by. Embarrassed by his thoughts, Sy hoped his friend wouldn't notice his strange behavior. He worried that he was losing his mind.

Adrian. Adrian has been very distracted at work all week after learning his wife will need a biopsy to determine whether she has breast cancer. He is worried about how he will be able to care for her and their young son. He is falling behind on an important project.

Apple. Apple, aged 24, has missed a lot of work and she is worried she may be in danger of losing her job. Sometimes her worries about finances, aging, friends, family and the climate keep her up late and she is too tired to go to work in the morning. She often worries about an odd body sensation or pain in her hip or her ears and finds herself at the doctor's office, though typically her doctor can find nothing physically wrong with her.

but is not exclusive to, the integration of Eastern mindfulness-based philosophies and approaches into the cognitive-behavioral models, as with ACT and DBT (Ost, 2008).

Cognitive-Behavioral Therapy for the Treatment of Anxiety. Therapists who use cognitive-behavioral therapy in the treatment of anxiety (CBT-A) work with their clients to identify thoughts that initiate and perpetuate anxious thoughts and the emotional and behavioral responses to those thoughts. After identifying anxiety-producing thoughts with their clients, the therapist supports clients in gaining the capacity to identify these thoughts as they arise and to replace them with more realistic supportive ways of thinking. CBT-A generally includes homework in which clients actively monitor thoughts, challenge and replace them. The results of a number of meta-analysis of CBT-A show moderate-to-high effect sizes and generally show promise for CBT-A for those with anxiety concerns ranging across the anxiety dimension (Carpenter et al., 2018; Hans & Hiller, 2013; Otte, 2011; Kaczkurkin & Foa, 2015).

Mindfulness-Based Stress Reduction. Mindfulness-based stress reduction (MBSR) is an 8-week group intervention that teaches participants mindfulness and meditation techniques for use in reducing anxiety and stress. A number of studies point to the

TABLE 8. 01 **Sample Cognitive Styles Common in Those with Anxiety**

Anxiety and Cognition Thinking Style	Defined	Example
Faulty cognitive map (Ingram, 2006)	Faulty beliefs, self-imposed rules, flawed schema (Gilbert, 1992: Ingram, 2006)	Yolanda believes she must both excel in all aspects of her career and function as a "perfect mother and partner." Yolanda feels anxious and worried that she is "falling short" and "dropping the ball."
Faulty information processing (Ingram, 2006)	All-or-nothing or black-and-white thinking, overgeneralization and "mind-reading" (Gilbert, 1992: Ingram, 2006)	John feels sure that his coworkers see him as incapable and foolish, though he has no tangible evidence to support his belief. He worries constantly that he will say something that will confirm their impression of him.
Unhelpful self-talk Cognitive styles identified in (Ingram (2006)	Internal dialogue that tends to discourage, dishearten or perpetuate misinformation (Gilbert, 1992: Ingram 2006)	Amy's inner voice features a running commentary, "You are so stupid," and "No one would hire you."

Source: Adapted from Gilbert (1992) and Ingram (2006)

efficacy of MBSR for those experiencing anxiety (Evans et al., 2008; Goldin & Gross, 2010; Hammond, 2015).

Response Prevention. Response prevention is an intervention that teaches clients to create spaces and times that are dedicated to worry and those that should be free from these kinds of thoughts (worry periods and worry-free zones). Response prevention aims to give clients control over where and when worrisome thoughts are entertained.

Worry Outcome Monitoring. This intervention attempts to address the tendency to overestimate the likelihood or severity of feared outcomes. The client is asked to keep a journal of worries and fears and then to document the actual result. For instance, a worry that a mysterious cough is a symptom of a threatening and as yet undetected illness would be recorded. When the cough resolves and no further illness manifests, this is noted by the client. The hope is that the client will gradually build evidence for more realistic expectations by drawing attention to actual outcomes rather than those that are feared (LaFreniere & Newman, 2016).

Imagery. In this intervention, clients are guided in imagining that they are encountering the feared event and that they are responding in very effective ways. Alternatively, clients are encouraged to imagine the more likely scenario rather than the feared outcome. Using the previous example, the client who is worried about a cough is encouraged to imagine that as spring passes and with the lowered pollen in the air, the cough naturally abates.

Mindfulness. Mindfulness practices are offered to clients in order to bring the fullness of their thoughts, feelings and sensations into awareness. Although this can be a frightening prospect for many who are beginning the process of addressing their anxiety, mindfulness practices also equip clients to hold these aspects of anxiety with less judgment and reactivity. A number of apps for tablets and smartphones support mindfulness interventions outside of the counseling setting, making them more accessible and affordable for clients (Hammond, 2015).

Biofeedback. Biofeedback is a process in which the client uses equipment that monitors breathing and heart rate variability in combination with relaxation techniques, frequently involving the breath, in order to regulate the physiological effects of anxiety and other mental health concerns. Although more research is needed, evidence for biofeedback as an augmentative approach to talk therapy is quite promising (Ratanasiripong et al., 2012; Reiner, 2008). More recently, inexpensive and compact equipment that can be used in conjunction with a smartphone has made this approach much simpler and cost effective to integrate into therapeutic approaches. Training and certification in biofeedback is also inexpensive and available both online and in person.

Definitional Cases

Levi

Levi, aged 6, will not speak to anyone at church or at school. He nods or uses gestures to indicate his needs, though his speech is normal at home. What diagnosis best fits Levi?

Jeb

Jeb becomes terrified and freezes at the sight of needles. He has been unable to follow through with the doctor's order for a blood panel to test his cholesterol. More recently, Jeb has resisted a blood test for a suspected cancer.

Daria

Daria was sent to the emergency room when she experienced difficulties in breathing, profuse sweating and a rapid heartbeat. The attending physician assured her that she was not experiencing a heart attack, as she had believed, but that her symptoms were emotionally based.

Ann

Though Ann is 12, she recently developed an intense fear of being apart from her mother. She has been unable and unwilling to go to school, swim lessons or her beloved ballet classes. What diagnosis best fits Ann's symptoms?

Jamal

Jamal, aged 7, has developed a fear of birds and cries in terror at the sight of these animals.

Rose

Rose has not been able to leave her home for 4 years because she is afraid of being in public, when she would have a panic attack. She is afraid that she would not be able to get help fast enough so she stays at home near the phone.

Jackie

Jackie has had multiple discrete episodes in which he experiences extreme anxiety coupled with physiological symptoms, such as palpitations and sweaty palms, trembling as well as subjective feelings of fear that she is having a heart attack and may die.

Fanta

Since moving out of her parent's home several years ago, Fanta has noticed that she worries "all through the day, nearly every day" and often feels restless, tensed and has difficulty concentrating. She describes worrying about many different things in her life, ranging from work, finances, parenting and relationships.

Serena

Serena would like very much to go out with friends on the weekend or see a movie but she worries that she will say or do the wrong thing. The fear is so strong that she stays home rather than putting herself in an awkward situation where she might say the wrong thing and be seen as "strange."

Narrative Cases in Anxiety

Philip

Philip has come to counseling hoping to get some help with anxiety. Philip shares that he remembers his mother describing him as "a nervous little goose from the get-go." Philip was the second child born to his parents and one of the five surviving siblings. His older brother, also named Philip, died unexpectedly at 22 months old. Philip was born a year later and was named for his older brother, something that sometimes led to confusion and angst. Philip shares, "It seemed like Baby Philip represented limitless possibility and I represented all the ways a boy could fall short of my parent's dreams.

TABLE 8.02 **Pivot Points: Anxiety Disorders**

	Consider
Pivot Point One: Are your client's struggles related to fear or worry about the physical integrity of the body or a threat to the body?	
• Does your client's struggle arise out of an exaggerated fear of injury to the physical body or concerns about personal safety? (fear of needles, elevators, dogs, etc.)	Specific phobia
• Does your client's struggle arise out of worries about the possibility of being or becoming ill?	Illness anxiety disorder
• Do your client's physical symptoms cause highly distressing worry and disruptions in your client's happiness?	Somatic symptom disorder
Pivot Point Two: Does your client's suffering arise from concerns of injury to the integrity of the self or to the ego, such as a fear of being judged or misunderstood?	
• Does this fear create discomfort in social settings where performance is expected?	Social anxiety disorder
• Does this fear create an inability or reluctance to leave a significant other that is unexpected to their developmental level?	Separation anxiety
• Does this fear lead your client to refrain from speaking in key environments, such as school or work?	Selective mutism
Pivot Point Three: Do your client's fears and anxieties restrict your client's movements and personal freedom?	Agoraphobia
Pivot Point Four: Do your client's anxieties and fears sometimes trigger physiological symptoms that remind your client of a heart attack or other acute health crisis?	Panic attack/disorder
Pivot Point Five: Do your client's worries and concerns encompass a broad range of your client's life ranging from health, relationships, work performance, money, and so on?	Generalized anxiety disorder
Pivot Point Six: Is your client's anxiety tied to a substance or medication that has been documented to have anxiety side effects?	Substance/medication-induced anxiety disorder
Pivot Point Seven: Have your client's anxiety symptoms coincided with a disorder known to lead to anxiety?	Anxiety disorder due to another medical condition
Pivot Point Eight: Does your Latino/a client's emotional anxiety follow on the heels of painful or shocking news and include a feeling of losing control of one's behavior and feelings?	Other specified anxiety disorder, Ataque de nervios

I could never quite live up to what Baby Philip might have been. I could see disappointment in their eyes, and sometimes I could hear their disappointment in what they said to me. They never got over Baby Philip's death and I don't think they ever stopped wishing I would be able to fill his shoes."

Four years after "Baby Philip" died, his parents would lose a second child, Erin, who was born with a heart defect and died despite a series of surgeries that doctors hoped would save her life. However, by the time Philip was 13, the family had grown to include five children; the loss of "Baby Philip" and Erin, however, hung like a dark cloud over Philip himself but also his mother, who struggled with severe bouts of depression and hospitalizations until she ultimately took her own life when Philip was 24.

Philip explains, "Ours was a busy house when I was growing up, as you can imagine. My dad worked a lot and my mom was distracted and often very depressed. I worried about her a lot and sometimes I didn't want to go to school because she wasn't getting out of bed and I wondered whether she would take care of the little ones without my help. We spent a lot of time together and I loved her a lot but, frankly, she wasn't really available for me when I needed her, she had too much on her mind. And I think my worrying about school and grades and various things got on her nerves. She didn't really have the capacity to deal with me and my issues. I had a lot of anxiety."

"I thought I'd kind of licked this anxiety when I was in college. I saw a counselor and had a chance to talk about my early life and eventually I stopped worrying so much about everything. Things were pretty good for a while, but lately I haven't been able to sleep and I've been distracted. The thing is that my wife and I are expecting a baby and I've been worrying about being able to be with her at the hospital when she goes into labor. I've been really nervous about hospitals and doctors since I was a kid and I get really sweaty and sick to my stomach just thinking of having to go to the hospital. To be honest, I haven't been to the doctor myself since I was about 15 because doctors make me so nervous. I haven't gone with my wife to her prenatal exams, which bothers me, but makes my wife really angry. We have argued about it so much that it is becoming a real sore spot in our relationship."

When asked about his fear of doctors and hospitals Philip shares, "I think it is two things, really. I get the creeps in the hospital and it reminds me of death—but to be honest, I get these thoughts that if I go there my baby or my wife will die. Ideally I could get over this fear of doctors and hospitals before the baby comes in a couple of months."

Damon

Damon, aged 30, met with his counselor for the first time looking a bit embarrassed. He shared that he had come to counseling to "get past my fear of elevators." When Damon was 3 years old, he and his mother were in an elevator when an electrical storm caused the lights to go out and the elevator stopped between floors. Damon shares, "My mother was terrified! She was screaming and banging on the walls and door calling out for help. She kept yelling that she couldn't breathe! I was so scared, I had never seen my mother come unglued like that. It was pitch black in the elevator and my mother's voice was amplified in that tiny closed-in space." Damon shares that since that incident he has been very uncomfortable in elevators. "When I can't avoid an elevator altogether I can make myself get on but if I can't stand right by the control panel and put my finger near the alarm button then I am just barely able to hold myself together. I sweat right through my shirt and I feel like there won't be enough air for everyone. Once the doors open I'm ok again." Damon continues, "Here's the kicker, I just got a job that I really like but it is on the 19th floor of a building downtown. I love the view from my office but it is a bit much for me to try to take the stairs every day," Damon says, "I really need some help with this fear or I will have to find another job." What diagnosis best fits Damon's situation?

Esther

Esther, aged 27, has come to counseling with concerns about anxiety. Esther shares, "I worked as a photographer for 3 years at an international magazine and did a lot of traveling. I've been in some places in the world that probably should have scared me to death. I've been in a rusted-out bus teetering dangerously close to the edge of a mountain road in Nepal, I've watched from a cage in shark-infested water, and I've ridden the rapids of Colorado. I generally think of myself as pretty independent and fearless. Now I work in New York about 10 blocks from where I live doing marketing for about 6 months, so I've left that travel behind me." Esther explains, "But that's not why I'm here. Seven months ago I was robbed in the subway, some guy came running by, grabbed my purse and I fell down. I wasn't hurt but I was shocked. Since returning home to New York I've been experiencing panic attacks. To be honest, I've been too afraid to go into the subway so I've been walking a lot and taking cabs when I'm running late or the weather is bad, which is very expensive. But I'm worried that I might be mugged in the subway!" She further shares, "Frankly, I'm more afraid that I will have another panic attack and will not be able to get off the train. I also feel really vulnerable when I'm standing in line on the subway platform. I can feel my anxiety start to build just thinking about waiting for the train. I have this same fear waiting in line at an outdoor market or those kiosks, so now I pack my lunch instead of getting a hot dog on the street." Esther's hesitancy to get on the train has led her to be late to work several times and her supervisor has confronted her about being on time for their morning team meetings. What diagnosis fits Esther best?

Leroy

Leroy, aged 53, worries about many things. He reports, "I guess my friends have always called me a bit of a 'Chicken Little,' way back to when I was still a kid." But he has noticed that his worries have amplified in the past 2 years. Leroy shares, "I go to bed distracted by a nagging feeling that I am in the early stages of Parkinson's. My dad's cousin has Parkinson's. I saw him at the family picnic last summer and I can't believe how much he's changed. All the life is gone out of his face and he moves in a very labored way. I know this disease can really sneak up on you and I'm worried that I may have it, too." Leroy has had a complete physical that showed him to be in good health, however, his fear persists.

Leroy further explains that he stays up nights worrying about money as well. "I do have a stable job, thank God, and right now we have no debt so we have been able to save some for retirement, but sometimes I can't sleep thinking that we might end up living in poverty when we are too old to work . . . or if I did get Parkinson's or cancer or something, I worry that we won't have enough money for good care and I'll end up in a dirty run-down nursing home with employees that hate their jobs. When I get started worrying about that, I feel sick inside." Leroy also confesses that he frequently worries that his wife is seeing someone else. "I have gone to her a couple of times and told her I was worried about this and I always feel so stupid. She tells me that she is committed to our marriage but I wonder how she could be when I must drive her crazy with all my fretting." Leroy told his intake worker, "I feel like all these worries have completely sapped any joy from my life." He describes feeling tired all the time, easily irritated and finds it difficult to concentrate thanks to his concerns. Which diagnosis fits his symptoms best?

Mim

Mim, aged 32, a mother of three young children, has come to counseling to address anxiety. She shares, "I have been working nights and spending my afternoons with my husband, Saul, who is homebound since returning from deployment 18 months ago. That's when the doctors had to amputate his left leg and he had a lot of other severe injuries that needed constant care." Mim reports she has noticed growing anxiety since her husband's return and reports she has experienced three separate situations in which she was sent to the emergency room. During these incidents, Mim reports, "I felt as if I was choking. I was really dizzy and had chills. Frankly, I was afraid I was losing my mind. On all three occasions, she was told she was having a panic attack. "For maybe about two months I've been avoiding going out too much because I'm afraid this is going to happen to me in the grocery store or out in public. I've had to ask my mom and my sister for help getting the kids where they need to be and help with picking up groceries. I have to spend a lot of time kind of building myself up so I can get out the door and go to work every night. I feel so ashamed. This is a time when I should be caring for my husband, and my children need to see my strength but, instead, Saul and the kids are trying to be my cheerleaders and help me through this. I'm desperate to get past this before it becomes impossible to go to work."

Dexter

Dexter, a 35-year-old father of two children, and his wife, Anna Jane, sit side by side on the couch across from their counselor. "I really can't figure out how to explain this fear I have of cereal boxes," Dexter begins, "but they just creep me out . . . a lot. Don't make me explain it, because I can't." Anna Jane adds, "Here's the problem. Since he's so afraid of these boxes of cereal he won't go to the grocery store, so I have to do it. When we were first married, I was willing to go along with this but now I work full time and the kids have their after-school things, so it is just too much. I need help with the shopping." Dexter adds, "Lately, this has been a real sore spot. We've gotten into some loud arguments over it and the kids have heard us . . . It's not good." Anna Jane, sitting forward a bit, explains pointedly: "It's not just that Dexter won't go into the grocery store, he doesn't want boxes of cereal in the house. So, in the garage I have to transfer the cereal to plastic bins or freezer bags. Now mind you, I don't need to do that with the boxes of crackers, or cookies, but the cereal I do or he will freak out. It is not nice to use this word but it is crazy. And besides, I don't know why his weird issue with cereal is my problem. I want him to deal with this, so that's why we are here." What diagnosis best fits Dexter's symptoms?

Dylan

Dylan, an avid outdoorsman, was excited to secure a job with a prominent law firm in Denver. Dylan had dreamed of moving out of New York City and into the Rocky Mountains where he could enjoy the outdoors year-round. He shares, "I found a large home outside of Denver with a beautiful southern view of the mountains and a river on the northern edge of the property. I love the house. I like that it is enough of a drive outside the city that I feel like I'm in the country. However, and this is what's bringing me in for some help, I notice myself getting increasingly more and more nervous when I encounter horses. I know it's strange. For about the past 8 months I've had several experiences where I've been driving behind a horse trailer or caught sight of a horse and rider and, how do I describe this? It's like a wave of anxiety." Dylan reports, "The last time I felt my whole body begin to tremble and I felt like I would vomit right there in the car! This last time it happened I thought I was losing my freaking mind! It's a problem because where I live there are a few people who have horses. I knew that when I bought the house but the problem wasn't too bad then. Now it is much worse." What diagnosis best fits Dylan's symptoms?

Bethany

Bethany, aged 14, is a new student at Harper High School and has been referred to outside counseling by her school counselor, Ms. May. With Bethany's permission and that of her parents, her counselor, Evan, has contacted Ms. May to get some additional information. Ms. May shares, "I'm relieved that Bethany has agreed to come to see you,

Evan. I don't know a lot about her, she only just came to Harper about 4 months ago, but since she got here she has not spoken in class or to her classmates at all. Several of her teachers have come to me with concerns about her, some of her teachers are worried and some are frustrated with her. I called her parents to talk with them about Bethany and they said that this problem was new to them. Apparently, she talks their ears off once she gets home. But they told me that she has always been shy and a little reluctant to speak up at school, though never to the degree that she wouldn't say anything at all." Ms. May paused and then continued, "I'm pulling up her report cards right now and it looks like she is doing pretty well in her classes. She's in advanced placement in English, history and math but she isn't doing too well in her Spanish class, probably because she isn't participating, but I can check that for you if you want. Her art teacher included some of her work at the gallery show at the hospital this semester, too. So she's got lots of different kinds of talent. Unfortunately, I haven't been able to figure out what is keeping her from speaking in class." What diagnosis should Evan consider given the information Ms. May has shared?

Tracy

Tracy, an 18-year-old college freshman, has scheduled an appointment with the campus career center and is meeting with the career counselor. When asked how the center might help her meet her goals, Tracy shares: "I need to find the best career for me." The career counselor, Annette, invited Tracy to take several career inventories and when she had completed those, the two sat down together. Annette described Tracy's results: "Tracy, it looks like you have lots of interests, talents and aptitudes that we can talk about. One of the main themes that I see, though, is an interest in medicine and the helping professions, like being a nurse or a medical doctor. Have you given this field any thought?" Tracy's eyes began to dampen as she replied, "All I've wanted since I was a kid was to be a nurse and follow in the footsteps of my mother, aunt and grandmother. So, when I got a chance to volunteer for about 3 months in a local hospital as part of a service learning project I was super excited about it. But any time I was in a situation where there was blood I experienced a wave of nausea and once I even passed out." Tracy continued, "It's beyond humiliating that my mom was able to be a surgical nurse and I get woozy at the sight of a blood draw! That service learning project was last year and I still feel sick just thinking about blood. I would really like to be a nurse but it looks like I wasn't cut out for it. That's why I'm here, to find something else to do with my life."

Elizabeth

Elizabeth, aged 44, shares: "I have been teaching in the chemistry department for 16 years. I've always liked my work, the students are great, I am fascinated by research and I have really enjoyed presenting at conferences both at the state and the national level. I've done a lot of speaking in front of others, so I just can't understand why I have been so anxious about teaching—it started at the opening of last semester and it is still a problem now that we are at final exam time. Right before class I start to feel really nervous and I have to go to bathroom. Usually I'm not sick, but sometimes I am." Elizabeth continues, "Before stepping into the classroom I feel the nervousness creeping in and then my palms begin to sweat. I've noticed, too, that my nerves are causing me to spend a lot of time preparing for lectures—probably over-preparing, because I can't really afford to put the hours in writing and re-writing lectures and handouts until they are 'perfect' but that is what is happening and it's frustrating and exhausting." Elizabeth further discloses, "I recently had a dream in which I went to class and found that I had to teach a course in Greek of all things! In my dream my dean was seated in the back of the room ready to evaluate me. I talked to a friend of mine about that dream, she is really interested in dreams, and she said that she thought it was a pretty straight-forward dream about evaluation and she suggested that I talk to someone about my reluctance to be evaluated and the anxiety I've been feeling about teaching. I thought about it and realized she was right, so here I am."

Mercedes

Mercedes, aged 15, is the eldest of three children. She and her mother have asked to meet with the school counselor, Theresa. Mercedes' mother shares, "I am really worried about Mercedes, she seems to be losing her spark for life. For the last three years she has volunteered at the SPCA. She has also helped out at the after-school program at the Stardust Elementary School in her freshman year of high school and they would like to have her back this year, too. Mercedes has lots of friends in her class and she has been pretty successful in school. But, as you know, lately Mercedes has missed a lot of school and it is starting to impact her grades."

Mercedes explains, "I genuinely do like school and getting out and doing things for people in the community but several months ago I started to have a nagging fear that something was going to happen to my mom. At first I just kind of tried to ignore it, but then I started to worry more and more that something terrible would happen. I didn't want to leave her alone in the house. When I would go to school or volunteer somewhere I was worrying the whole time about her. Then I started to check on her with texts, but that didn't really make me feel any better. After a while I just didn't feel like I could go to school and leave my mom alone anymore. I noticed that I started to feel sick in the morning just thinking about leaving her alone. I would get a headache or I would feel sick to my stomach or both and then I wouldn't feel good enough to go to school. That still happens when I try to leave my mom. So I've missed a lot of classes. I miss my friends and I want to do well in school, but I don't want my mom to get kidnapped by some pervert or something. I really hope I can get some help with this soon, I want to get my life back on track."

References

Alyanak, B., Kılınçaslan, A., Harmancı, H. S., Demirkaya, S. K., Yurtbay, T., & Vehid, H. E. (2013). Parental adjustment, parenting attitudes and emotional and behavioral problems in children with selective mutism. *Journal of Anxiety Disorders*, *27*(1), 9–15. https://doi.org/10.1016/j.janxdis.2012.10.001

American Psychiatric Association. (1952). *Diagnostic and statistical manual of mental disorders (DSM®)*. Author.

American Psychiatric Association. (1980). *Diagnostic and statistical manual of mental disorders (DSM-III®)*. Author.

American Psychiatric Association. (2013). *Diagnostic and statistical manual of mental disorders (DSM-5®)*. Author.

Asher, M., Asnaani, A., & Aderka, I. M. (2017). Gender differences in social anxiety disorder: A review. *Clinical Psychology Review*, *56*, 1–12. https://doi.org/10.1016/j.cpr.2017.05.004

Ballenger, J. C., Davidson, J. R., Lecrubier, Y., Nutt, D. J., Borkovec, T. D., Rickels, K., Stein, D. J., & Wittchen, H. U. (2001). Consensus statement on generalized anxiety disorder from the international consensus group on depression and anxiety. *The Journal of Clinical Psychiatry*, *62*, 53–58.

Bandelow, B., & Michaelis, S. (2015). Epidemiology of anxiety disorders in the 21st century. *Dialogues in Clinical Neuroscience*, *17*(3), 327.

Beck, A., & Emery, G. (1985). *Anxiety disorders and phobias: A cognitive perspective*. Basic Books.

Behar, E., DiMarco, I. D., Hekler, E. B., Mohlman, J., & Staples, A. M. (2009). Current theoretical models of Generalized Anxiety Disorder (GAD): Conceptual review and treatment implications. *Journal of Anxiety Disorders*, *23*(8), 1011–1023. https://doi.org/10.1016/j.janxdis.2009.07.006

Bergman, R. L., Piacentini, J., & McCracken, J. T. (2002). Prevalence and description of selective mutism in a school-based sample. *Journal of the American Academy of Child & Adolescent Psychiatry*, *41*(8), 938–946. https://doi.org/10.1097/00004583-200208000-00012

Bögels, S. M., Knappe, S., & Clark, L. A. (2013). Adult separation anxiety disorder in DSM-5. *Clinical Psychology Review*, *33*(5), 663–674. https://doi.org/10.1016/j.cpr.2013.03.006

Carpenter, J. K., Andrews, L. A., Witcraft, S. M., Powers, M. B., Smits, J. A., & Hofmann, S. G. (2018). Cognitive behavioral therapy for anxiety and related disorders: A meta-analysis of randomized placebo-controlled trials. *Depression and Anxiety*, *35*(6), 502–514. https://doi.org/10.1002/da.22728

Chapman, L. K., Kertz, S. J., Zurlage, M. M., & Woodruff-Borden, J. (2008). A confirmatory factor analysis of specific phobia domains in African American and Caucasian American young adults. *Journal of Anxiety Disorders*, *22*(5), 763–771. https://doi.org/10.1016/j.janxdis.2007.08.003

Chavira, D. A., Shipon-Blum, E., Hitchcock, C., Cohan, S., & Stein, M. B. (2007). Selective mutism and social anxiety disorder: All in the family? *Journal of the American Academy of Child & Adolescent Psychiatry*, *46*(11), 1464–1472. https://doi.org/10.1097/chi.0b013e318149366a

Chen, M. H., & Tsai, S. J. (2016). Treatment-resistant panic disorder: Clinical significance, concept and management. *Progress in Neuro-Psychopharmacology and Biological Psychiatry*, *70*, 219–226. https://doi.org/10.1016/j.pnpbp.2016.02.001

Copeland, W. E., Shanahan, L., Costello, E. J., & Angold, A. (2009). Childhood and adolescent psychiatric disorders as predictors of young adult disorders. *Archives of General Psychiatry*, *66*(7), 764–772. https://doi.org/10.1001/archgenpsychiatry.2009.85

Culpepper, L. (2009). Generalized anxiety disorder and medical illness. *The Journal of Clinical Psychiatry*, *70*(Suppl. 2), 20–24. https://doi.org/10.4088/JCP.s.7002.04

Ehrenreich, J. T., Santucci, L. C., & Weiner, C. L. (2008). Separation anxiety disorder in youth: Phenomenology, assessment, and treatment. *Psicologia Conductual*, *16*(3), 389.

Elliott, J. G., & Place, M. (2019). Practitioner review: School refusal: developments in conceptualisation and treatment since 2000. *Journal of Child Psychology and Psychiatry*, *60*(1), 4–15. https://doi.org/10.1111/jcpp.12848

Esbjørn, B. H., Lønfeldt, N. N., Nielsen, S. K., Reinholdt-Dunne, M. L., Sømhovd, M. J., & Cartwright-Hatton, S. (2015). Meta-worry, worry, and anxiety in children and adolescents: Relationships and interactions. *Journal of Clinical Child & Adolescent Psychology*, *44*(1), 145–156. https://doi.org/10.1080/15374416.2013.873980

Evans, S., Ferrando, S., Findler, M., Stowell, C., Smart, C., & Haglin, D. (2008). Mindfulness-based cognitive therapy for generalized anxiety disorder. *Journal of Anxiety Disorders*, *22*(4), 716–721. https://doi.org/10.1016/j.janxdis.2007.07.005

Fenichel, O. (1944). Remarks on common phobias. *The Psychoanalytic Quarterly*, *13*(3), 313–326. https://doi.org/10.1080/21674086.1944.11925574

Fosha, D. (2000). *The transforming power of affect: A model for accelerated change*. Basic Books.

Freud, S. (1936/2013). *The problem of anxiety*. W. W. Norton & Co.

Gautam, S., Jain, A., Gautam, M., Vahia, V. N., & Gautam, A. (2017). Clinical practice guidelines for the management of Generalised Anxiety Disorder (GAD) and Panic Disorder (PD). *Indian Journal of Psychiatry*, *59*(Suppl. 1), S67. https://doi.org/10.4103/0019-5545.196975

Goldin, P. R., & Gross, J. J. (2010). Effects of Mindfulness-Based Stress Reduction (MBSR) on emotion regulation in social anxiety disorder. *Emotion*, *10*(1), 83. https://doi.org/10.1037/a0018441

Grimaldi, W. M. (1980). *Aristotle, rhetoric I: A commentary* (Vol. 1). Fordham University Press.

Grimm, J., & Grimm, W. (2016). *The complete Grimm's fairy tales*. Chartwell Books.

Hammond, C. (2015). Mindfulness-based stress reduction. In E. Neukrug (Ed.), *Encyclopedia of counseling theories*. SAGE.

Hans, E., & Hiller, W. (2013). A meta-analysis of nonrandomized effectiveness studies on outpatient cognitive behavioral therapy for adult anxiety disorders. *Clinical Psychology Review*, *33*(8), 954–964. https://doi.org/10.1016/j.cpr.2013.07.003

Hayes, S. C., Wilson, K. G., Gifford, E. V., Follette, V. M., & Strosahl, K. (1996). Experiential avoidance and behavioral disorders: A functional dimensional approach to diagnosis and treatment. *Journal of Consulting and Clinical Psychology, 64*(6), 1152. https://doi.org/10.1037/0022-006X.64.6.1152

Hofmann, S. G., Asnaani, A., & Hinton, D. E. (2010). Cultural aspects in social anxiety and social anxiety disorder. *Depression and Anxiety, 27*(12), 1117–1127. https://doi.org/10.1002/da.20759

Huang, Y. Wang, Y., Li, X., Ren, L., & Zhao, J., Hu, Y., Zhang, L., Fan, G., Xu, J., Gu, X., Cheng, Z., Yu, T., Xia, J., Wei, Y., Wu, W., Xie, X., Yin, W., Li, H., Liu, M., ... Cheng, Z. (2020). Clinical features of patients infected with 2019 novel coronavirus in Wuhan, China. *The Lancet, 395*, (10223), 497–506 https://doi.org/10.1016/j.psychres.2020.112954

Ingram, B. L. (2006). *Clinical case formulations: Matching the integrative treatment plan to the client.* John Wiley & Sons.

Jungmann, S. M., & Witthöft, M. (2020). Health anxiety, cyberchondria, and coping in the current COVID-19 pandemic: Which factors are related to coronavirus anxiety? *Journal of Anxiety Disorders, 73*, 102239. https://doi.org/10.1016/j.janxdis.2020.102239

Kaczkurkin, A. N., & Foa, E. B. (2015). Cognitive-behavioral therapy for anxiety disorders: An update on the empirical evidence. *Dialogues in Clinical Neuroscience, 17*(3), 337.

LaFreniere, L. S., & Newman, M. G. (2016). A brief ecological momentary intervention for generalized anxiety disorder: A randomized controlled trial of the worry outcome journal. *Depression and Anxiety, 33*(9), 829–839. https://doi.org/10.1002/da.22507

Leahy, R. L. (2011). *Treatment plans and interventions for evidence-based psychotherapy* (2nd ed.). Guilford Press.

Loas, G., Atger, F., Perdereau, F., Verrier, A., Guelfi, J. D., Halfon, O., Lang, F., Bizouard, P., Venisse, J.-V., Perez-Diaz, Corcos, M., Flament, M., & Jeammet, P., M. (2002). Comorbidity of dependent personality disorder and separation anxiety disorder in addictive disorders and in healthy subjects. *Psychopathology, 35*(4), 249–253. https://doi.org/10.1159/000063830

Marmarosh, C. L., & Mann, S. (2014). Patients' selfobject needs in psychodynamic psychotherapy: How they relate to client attachment, symptoms, and the therapy alliance. *Psychoanalytic Psychology, 31*(3), 297. https://doi.org/10.1037/a0036866

Mayo Clinic (2019). *Anxiety disorders, symptoms and causes.* https://www.mayoclinic.org/diseases-conditions/anxiety/symptoms-causes/syc-20350961

Mertens, G., Gerritsen, L., Duijndam, S., Salemink, E., & Engelhard, I. M. (2020). Fear of the coronavirus (COVID-19): Predictors in an online study conducted in March 2020. *Journal of Anxiety Disorders, 74*, 102258. https://doi.org/10.1016/j.janxdis.2020.102258

Meuret, A. E., Kroll, J., & Ritz, T. (2017). Panic disorder comorbidity with medical conditions and treatment implications. *Annual Review of Clinical Psychology, 13*, 209–240. https://doi.org/10.1146/annurev-clinpsy-021815-093044

Moffitt, T. E., Harrington, H., Caspi, A., Kim-Cohen, J., Goldberg, D., Gregory, A. M., & Poulton, R. (2007). Depression and generalized anxiety disorder: Cumulative and sequential comorbidity in a birth cohort followed prospectively to age 32 years. *Archives of General Psychiatry*, *64*(6), 651–660. https://doi.org/10.1001/archpsyc.64.6.651

Mogg, K., & Bradley, B. P. (2005). Attentional bias in generalized anxiety disorder versus depressive disorder. *Cognitive Therapy and Research*, *29*(1), 29–45. https://doi.org/10.1007/s10608-005-1646-y

Morrison, J. (2014). *Diagnosis made easier: Principles and techniques for mental health clinicians*. Guilford Publications.

Muris, P., & Field, A. P. (2011). The "normal" development of fear. *Anxiety Disorders in Children and Adolescents*, *2*, 76–89. https://doi.org/10.1017/CBO9780511994920.005

Muris, P., & Merckelbach, H. (2000). How serious are common childhood fears? II. The parent's point of view. *Behaviour Research and Therapy*, *38*(8), 813–818.

Muris, P., & Ollendick, T. H. (2015). Children who are anxious in silence: A review on selective mutism, the new anxiety disorder in DSM-5. *Clinical Child and Family Psychology Review*, *18*(2), 151–169. https://doi.org/10.1007/s10567-015-0181-y

Murphy, H. (2019, March 30). *How pain tolerance and anxiety seem to be connected*. The New York Times. https://www.nytimes.com/2019/03/30/health/pain-anxiety-jo-cameron.html?action=click&module=RelatedCoverage&pgtype=Article®ion=Footer

Orsillo, S. M., & Roemer, L. (2011). *The mindful way through anxiety: Break free from chronic worry and reclaim your life*. Guilford Press.

Ost, L. (2008). Efficacy of the third wave of behavioral therapies: A systemic review and meta-analysis. *Behavioral Research and Therapy*, *46*(3), 296–321. https://doi.org/10.1016/j.brat.2007.12005

Otte, C. (2011). Cognitive behavioral therapy in anxiety disorders: Current state of the evidence. *Dialogues in Clinical Neuroscience*, *13*(4), 413–421.

Ratanasiripong, P., Sverduk, K., Prince, J., & Hayashino, D. (2012). Biofeedback and counseling for stress and anxiety among college students. *Journal of College Student Development*, *53*(5), 742–749. https://doi.org/10.1353/csd.2012.0070

Reiner, R. (2008). Integrating a portable biofeedback device into clinical practice for patients with anxiety disorders: Results of a pilot study. *Applied Psychophysiology and Biofeedback*, *33*(1), 55–61. https://doi.org/10.1007/s10484-007-9046-6

Roemer, L., & Orsillo, S. M. (2002). Expanding our conceptualization of and treatment for generalized anxiety disorder: Integrating mindfulness/acceptance-based approaches with existing cognitive-behavioral models. *Clinical Psychology: Science and Practice*, *9*(1), 54–68. https://doi.org/10.1093/clipsy.9.1.54

Roemer, L., & Orsillo, S. M. (2005). An acceptance-based behavior therapy for generalized anxiety disorder. In *Acceptance and mindfulness-based approaches to anxiety* (pp. 213–240). Springer.

Ruscio, A. M., Hallion, L. S., Lim, C. C., Aguilar-Gaxiola, S., Al-Hamzawi, A., Alonso, J., Helena Andrade, L., Borges, G., Bromet, E. J., Bunting, B., Caldas de Almeida, J. M., Demyttenaere, K., Florescu, S., de Girolamo, G., Gureje, O., Haro, J. M., He, J., Hinkov, H., Hu, C., . . . Scott, K. M. (2017). Cross-sectional comparison of the epidemiology of DSM-5 generalized anxiety disorder across the globe. *JAMA Psychiatry*, *74*(5), 465–475. https://doi.org/10.1001/jamapsychiatry.2017.0056

Sewart, A. R., & Craske, M. G. (2018). Panic disorder and agoraphobia. In J. Hunsley & E. Mash (Es.), *Assessments that work* (Vol. 6, p. 266). Oxford University Press.

Shear, K., Jin, R., Ruscio, A. M., Walters, E. E., & Kessler, R. C. (2006). Prevalence and correlates of estimated DSM-IV child and adult separation anxiety disorder in the National Comorbidity Survey Replication. *American Journal of Psychiatry*, *163*(6), 1074–1083. https://doi.org/10.1176/ajp.2006.163.6.1074

Sibrava, N. J., & Borkovec, T. D. (2006). *The cognitive avoidance theory of worry*. In G.C. Davey & A. Wells (Eds.), *Worry and its psychological disorders: Theory, assessment and treatment*. John Wiley & Sons.

Stein, M. B., & Sareen, J. (2015). Generalized anxiety disorder. *New England Journal of Medicine*, *373*(21), 2059–2068. https://doi.org/10.1056/NEJMcp1502514

Suveg, C., Aschenbrand, S. G., & Kendall, P. C. (2005). Separation anxiety disorder, panic disorder, and school refusal. *Child and Adolescent Psychiatric Clinics of North America*, *14*(4), 773–795. https://doi.org/10.1016/j.chc.2005.05.005

Tay, A. K., Rees, S., Chen, J., Kareth, M., & Silove, D. (2015). Pathways involving traumatic losses, worry about family, adult separation anxiety and posttraumatic stress symptoms amongst refugees from West Papua. *Journal of Anxiety Disorders*, *35*, 1–8. https://doi.org/10.1016/j.janxdis.2015.07.001

Tillich, P. (1952). *The courage to be*. Yale University Press.

Turner, S. M., Beidel, D. C., & Stanley, M. A. (1992). Are obsessional thoughts and worry different cognitive phenomena? *Clinical Psychology Review*, *12*(2), 257–270. https://doi.org/10.1016/0272-7358(92)90117-Q

Watson, J. B., & Rayner, R. (1920). Conditioned emotional reactions. *Journal of Experimental Psychology*, *3*(1), 1. https://doi.org/10.1037/h0069608

Wegela, K. K. (2014). *Contemplative psychotherapy essentials: Enriching your practice with Buddhist psychology*. W. W. Norton & Co.

Wells, A. (2005). The metacognitive model of GAD: Assessment of meta-worry and relationship with DSM-IV generalized anxiety disorder. *Cognitive Therapy and Research*, *29*(1), 107–121. https://doi.org/10.1007/s10608-005-1652-0

Wells, A., & Carter, K. (2001). Further tests of a cognitive model of generalized anxiety disorder: Metacognitions and worry in GAD, panic disorder, social phobia, depression, and nonpatients. *Behavior Therapy*, *32*(1), 85–102. https://doi.org/10.1016/S0005-7894(01)80045-9

Whitley, G. G. (1994). Expert validation and differentiation of the nursing diagnoses anxiety and *fear International Journal of Nursing Terminologies and Classifications*, *5*(4), 143–150. https://doi.org/10.1111/j.1744-618X.1994.tb00263.x

Wijeratne, C., & Manicavasagar, V. (2003). Separation anxiety in the elderly. *Journal of Anxiety Disorders, 17*(6), 695–702. https://doi.org/10.1016/S0887-6185(02)00239-6

Wittchen, H. U., Kessler, R. C., Beesdo, K., Krause, P., Höfler, M., & Hoyer, J. (2002). Generalized anxiety and depression in primary care: Prevalence, recognition, and management. *The Journal of Clinical Psychiatry, 63* (Suppl 8), 24–34.

Yeganeh, R., Beidel, D. C., & Turner, S. M. (2006). Selective mutism: More than social anxiety? *Depression and Anxiety, 23*(3), 117–123. https://doi.org/10.1002/da.20139

Zalyte, G., Neverauskas, J., & Goodall, W. (2017). Does the exposure method used in cognitive behavioural therapy for panic disorder with agoraphobia affect treatment outcome? *Biological Psychiatry and Psychopharmacology, 19*(1), 26–40.

9 Obsessive Compulsive and Related Disorders

I have a very distinct memory of a rather benign moment that unfolded while I was studying for my Ph.D. I had rented an apartment where I lived during the week and would go home to my family on the weekends. At home, my house, my work and my husband's work were all within a few blocks of one another. Forgetting something or getting locked out of the house would have been only a minor inconvenience when everything was so close and help was nearby. But because I lived alone in my apartment and I studied in the university library late into the night, getting locked out of my apartment would have been a real problem. So, I had developed a habit of double-checking that I had my keys and phone before shutting the front door behind me. But on this particular morning, I experienced a kind of mental glitch. I checked for my keys and confirmed they were in my bag. Then I checked again, and, again, confirmed they were there. Then as I reached for the doorknob, I checked a third time. Checking that third time I realized how tired I was, how I was looking at the keys but not registering or fully trusting what I was seeing. And I realized in that moment that I was also feeling anxiety about being completely on my own again and needing to take care of emergencies by myself. An experience like the one I had is uncomfortable but entirely normal, a product of circumstance and over-work.

For clients struggling with obsessive compulsive disorder (OCD) and its related disorders (OCRD), however, these same kinds of glitches of thought and behavior take on a regular pattern, they become taxing, extremely distracting and can escalate to an unrelenting stream of dread-filled forebodings and a constant demand for action, enslaving the client's mind and allowing little freedom of thought or action (American Psychiatric Association [APA], 2013; Fullana et al., 2009). This chapter will outline briefly four OCD-related disorders, body dysmorphic and hoarding disorders as well as trichotillomania (TTM) and excoriation disorder, and will then offer a deeper exploration of OCD. The OCD subtypes, and differential diagnosis, as well as current theories that work to explain the source of OCD will also be explored. A discussion of the implications of Covid-19 on the expression of OCD is included in this chapter as well as a brief description of treatments, followed by cases for diagnosis.

The Obsessive Compulsive Related Disorders

The OCRD spectrum of disorders contains five disorders: body dysmorphic disorder, hoarding disorder, TTM, excoriation disorder and OCD.

The obsessive compulsive dimension is set apart from other mental health concerns by the symptoms that give the dimension its name: obsessions and compulsions. While those with OCD generally present with both obsessions and compulsions, those with TTM and excoriation disorder are distinguished by their distinctive compulsions.

Obsessions. What exactly is an obsession? Obsessions are intrusive thoughts that are frequent, unwelcome, and patterned or themed. Though collectively obsessive thoughts vary quite a lot, obsessions tend to fall into one of several categories: checking, contamination, scrupulosity/religiosity, symmetry and sexual and aggressive themes. Less common obsessive thoughts are also seen, such as those pertaining to being in relationship with others, intense concerns about being understood perfectly or suicidal thoughts. Frequently, these intrusive thoughts are also abhorrent to the client and run counter to their deeply held values. Intrusive thoughts, such as images of committing violent acts, distasteful or illegal sexual acts, handling or eating filthy objects and so on are not uncommon. Because abhorrent-type obsessions are not only disruptive and distracting but represent violations to the client's own strongly held beliefs, they result in a great deal of persistent distress and shame and clients may be reluctant to disclose them (García-Soriano et al., 2011; Odriozola-Gonzalez et al., Perez-Alvarez et al., 2016; Weingarden & Renshaw, 2015). Obsessions and their subtypes will be discussed at greater length later in the chapter.

Compulsions. A compulsion is a behavior, which can be covert, such as praying or counting, or overt; for example, touching, blinking, hairpulling, skin picking and so on. When a behavior is a compulsion, the client feels an intense drive or urge to perform it (Abramowitz & Jacoby, 2015; APA, 2013).

These disorders evidence significant comorbidity with one another, consequently, when diagnosing one OCRD, it is good practice to assess for the presence of the others (APA, 2013).

Body Dysmorphic Disorder. Following considerable research, body dysmorphic disorder (BDD) was classified as an OCRD in the latest edition of the DSM (APA, 2013). This disorder features obsessive preoccupation with aspects of the body. The most common features of focus are facial features, such as the eyes, nose and teeth, though concerns about symmetry are common as is distress about the size of the pores of the skin or scarring. Less common but still noteworthy are fears related to the size of breasts or the size or shape of genitalia. Most people who suffer with BDD are distracted by more than one part of the body that they find to be terribly deficient, unappealing or even grotesque. Insight among this population tends to be much poorer generally than that of clients with OCD and these clients evidence a high rate of hospitalizations and suicidal ideation as well as attempted suicides (Mufaddel et al., 2013;

Toh et al., 2017). Phillips (2007), notes that 80% of those with BPD also experience suicidal thoughts and between 24% and 28% will make at least one attempted suicide.

These perceptions of the feature or features of their body have a costly impact on the individual's sense of self. These clients can become so ashamed of their perceived flaws that they find themselves canceling social engagements, avoiding intimacy and in some cases may avoid leaving their homes altogether. They may become convinced that others are as disgusted by their feature or features as they are and as a result may worry that they are the topic of criticism or disdain. Persons struggling with BDD will go to great lengths to disguise the offending feature, avoiding clothing that would reveal or emphasize the perceived flaw, avoiding mirrors, or seeking out surgery (Toh et al., 2017) or to improve it in some way (Mufaddel et al., 2013; Toh et al., 2017).

Hoarding Disorder. In the DSM 5, the APA removed hoarding as a subtype of OCD obsessions and established it as a stand-alone diagnosis, hoarding disorder. This happened primarily because conceptually, hoarding is not a ritual designed to stave off anxiety (compulsion) and because clients don't experience thoughts of acquiring objects as intrusive or as especially distressful (APA, 2013; Morein-Zamir et al., 2014). The compulsive amassing of items is a significant threat to the health and wellbeing of the people who struggle with it, however, justifying its addition to the nosology of disorder.

This isolating disorder can be easily overlooked in the therapy setting if it is not the client's primary concern since clients may be reluctant to broach this subject, or may not see the behavior as problematic (with poor insight). However, it is worth noting that clients struggling with hoarding have been reported to be as much as five times as likely to seek counseling as those who don't—but generally these clients are seeking counseling for another reason (Kress et al., 2016; Tolin et al., 2008). In its milder forms, hoarding creates piles of clutter that interfere with a person's ability to relax or entertain friends in the home. At its worst, hoarding leads to concerns that impact the individual's safety and health as well as those in the community. Severe hoarding can lead to extremely unsanitary and unsafe housing conditions and may lead to structural damage to the home or eviction from the property. Hoarding can also lead to public safety issues, such as fire hazards and pest infestations (Kress et al., 2016; Morein-Zamir et al., 2014; Tolin et al., 2008). Two types of hoarding have been observed: object and animal. Clients who hoard objects generally collect and keep items that others would find useless and have discarded, though sometimes hoarded items are purchased or even stolen. Other clients hoard animals. These clients tend to collect one type of animal, such as cats, and may be reluctant to give up animals even when they are not able to provide the food and medical care that the animals need. In some homes, animal feces and dead animals can be found, highlighting the poor insight of a subset of clients with hoarding disorders (Kress et al., 2016; Tolin et al., 2008). When children are living in these conditions, child protective services may become involved and families risk losing their children to foster care.

Trichotillomania. TTM is diagnosed in those who have developed a compulsive habit of pulling out hair from their scalp, eyebrows or pubic regions and despite wanting to end this habit have not been able to do so (APA, 2013; McGuire et al., 2019). TTM seems to express itself in one of two ways, focused pulling and automatic pulling styles. Focused pulling happens when a person experiences an overwhelming urge to pull hair and then deliberately, and sometimes ritualistically, gives into these urges and pulls out their hair. Automatic hairpulling, on the other hand, happens absentmindedly, as when watching movies or reading. Initial research suggests that those with focused hairpulling may respond better to standard treatment, habit reversal training (McGuire et al., 2019).

Excoriation/Skin Picking Disorder (ExD). Like TTM, ExD is a disorder of compulsion; however, this time the behavior is focused on picking at the skin to such a degree and frequency that lesions appear and the individual consequently experiences significant distress (APA, 2013). This disorder is sometimes described as neurotic excoriation or psychogenic excoriation. The standard treatment for ExD, as with TTM, is habit reversal training (Gupta & Gargi, 2012; Jones et al., 2018), though acceptance and commitment training, dialectical behavior therapy (Jones et al., 2018) as well as selective serotonin reuptake inhibitors (SSRIs) and lamotrigine, an anticonvulsant, have been used with varying degrees of success (Selles et al., 2016).

Obsessive Compulsive Disorder

Before 2013, both obsessions and compulsions had to be in evidence in order to diagnose OCD; however, the criteria have been changed; currently only obsessions or compulsions need to be observed in order to diagnose, though generally the two symptoms go hand and hand (APA, 2013). People burdened with symptoms of OCD report having a poor-quality life regardless of how severe their symptoms may be. Shame arising from OCD symptoms can lead clients to retreat from others, brings symptoms of depression and can be the source of difficulties in social relationships and even interfere with treatment (Remmerswaal et al., 2016; Weingarden & Renshaw, 2015). Shame, and a lack of education about the disorder, seems to contribute to the average 10-year gap between symptom onset and treatment (Glazier et al., 2015). It is not surprising, then, that as a group, clients with OCD are often diagnosed with comorbid disorders, such as anxiety and depression. A full 90% of those with OCD also have at least one other mental health disorder. Common among these are anxiety disorders (76%), major depressive disorders (40.7%) and substance use disorders (38.6%). This population also reports high rates of relational problems when compared to those without OCD (APA, 2013; Williams & Jahn, 2017). Currently somewhere in the neighborhood of one million children in the United States have OCD. Of these, about 62% also have a depressive disorder, and 32% carry an anxiety disorder. Tic disorders as well as disruptive behavioral disorders and separation anxiety disorders are

BOX 9.01 INVITING DISCLOSURES RELATED TO HOARDING

The following questions may help your client talk about difficulties of hoarding:

1. Tell me a little about your home.
2. When you are at home, are you able to relax and feel comfortable? Are you able to entertain friends in your home without too much trouble?
3. Is there a place in your home where you feel especially at peace?
4. Have you ever been in a situation in which you didn't want to let go of things that others saw as having little value; for instance, things that would need to be repaired in order to use them?
5. What pets do you have? Do you feel confident that all of your pets have enough food, veterinary care and space to roam?

Source: Kress et al. (2016) and Pertusa et al. (2011).

also very common among children with OCD (Fullana et al., 2009; Krebs & Heyman, 2015; Williams & Jahn, 2017).

Differentiating OCD Obsessions and Compulsions from Intrusive Thoughts and Compulsive Behaviors in Other Disorders. At first blush, the obsessive thoughts of OCD, and excessive, distracting and ruminative fears that are experienced by those with moderate to severe anxiety, or phobic-driven thoughts may be difficult to discern; however, on closer examination, differences can be seen. OCD-related obsessions frequently have a kind of "magical quality" to them or feature highly unlikely scenarios. For example, a client may report experiencing a strong sensation of heaviness on one side of the body that must be "evened out" by tapping the "heavy side" several times. In contrast, the worried thoughts seen in disorders such as generalized anxiety disorder (GAD) tend to include a wide array of worries typical of most age-related peers (work/school, finances, health etc.) but are amplified, out-of-proportion and prolonged. Phobias, on the other hand, tend to be specific to objects or experiences, such as snakes, flying, public speaking or the sight of blood. Clients struggling with phobias or anxiety disorders use avoidance as a primary line of defense, those with OCD use avoidance as well but tend to engage in counter-measures, known as compulsions, to ease anxiety.

Obsessional Themes in OCD. Researchers have long tried to operationalize obsessional themes and to clarify how, or if, various obsessive "types" respond differently to treatment or arise out of different processes, and have tried to organize these themes so that they can be measured reliably. Language describing these obsessional themes varies considerably within the research and between assessment tools. While the obsessive themes make a good deal of sense conceptually, for the most part the groupings don't seem to differentiate clients in etiology or treatment, except in two cases: hoarding obsessions, which have been reclassified as its own disorder, and OCD that manifests with tics. Despite extensive research using various metrics, diagnosticians and clinicians have not been able to agree definitively on reliable subtypes for OCD, with the exception of the "with tics" subtype. Consequently, the DSM 5 offers only the tic-related specifier for OCD and has provided specifiers indicating the client's degree of insight (APA, 2013; McKay et al., 2004; Moulding et al., 2013).

Though obsessive thoughts manifest in a dizzying variety and have been described using a wide range of descriptors, five primary categories emerge: checking, contamination, scrupulosity, symmetry and sexual and aggressive themes. While there is a wealth of literature describing OCD subtypes, their assessment and treatment, researchers have not been able to arrive at a shared language or parameters for these subtypes and, as a result, subtypes are not described in the DSM 5 (with the exception of the specifier applied when tics are part of the clinical picture). Consequently, the prevalence of these subtypes is very difficult to pin down. There does seem to be agreement across studies that checking and contamination are the most common manifestations of OCD, closely followed by symmetry, scrupulosity and aggressive and sexual obsessions, but not necessarily in that order. Again, the literature is mixed here. However, Ruscio et al. (2010), conducted an epidemiological study of more than two thousand respondents that showed that 28% of participants had experienced obsessions or compulsions at some point in their lives, the most common of which, by a large margin, was checking.

Checking. Clients for whom checking is their primary obsession and compulsion find themselves in a relentless loop triggered first by a question, "Did I remember to . . .", followed by a growing anxiety that an essential task was forgotten, and finally reassuring themselves by checking to see that the task was completed. Unfortunately, the checking does not satisfy the client's concern. Instead, a mental glitch prevents the client from registering fully their confirmation. Ultimately, clients find themselves checking over and over that they have locked doors, turned off appliances, shut off water taps and so on.

Recent studies have demonstrated that repeated checking can lead to loss of confidence in one's memory, even in people without OCD, and can also reduce how vividly something is remembered and how much detail remains in the memory. This erosion of memory seems to arise out of the checking itself rather than the other way around. It is important to clarify that the memory related to the event being "checked" is eroded, not memory generally (Radomsky et al., 2014). There is also growing evidence that repeated checking wears down a person's ability to later resist the urge to repeat the

BOX 9.02 KEY TERMS: OBSESSIVE COMPULSIVE RELATED DISORDERS

Obsession: Persistent and intrusive thoughts, images, impulses or doubts experienced as unwanted, unacceptable or senseless and are the cause of significant distress (Abramowitz & Jacoby, 2015; APA, 2013).

Compulsions: Overt or covert idiosyncratic rituals performed in order to manage distress that has been provoked by obsessive thoughts; these rituals are deliberate and goal-directed, often excessive and frequently have no direct connection to the desired outcome (Abramowitz & Jacoby, 2015; APA, 2013).

"Pure O": An abbreviation for "Pure Obsessional Obsessive Compulsive Disorders (OCD)," and refers to clients who evidence only obsessions and not compulsions (Moulding et al., 2014).

checking behavior, a capacity known as impetus control (Colas, 1999; Linkovski et al., 2016). These studies help to explain how OCD and checking in particular is sustained.

Contamination. Among the most common obsessions are those related to contamination. When contamination obsessions are present, clients describe being driven to distraction by the thought that some impurity, dirt, germ, poison and so on will cause them, or a loved one, to become ill or die. These fears lead people to avoid touching or getting near common objects such as door knobs, faucets, bathroom facilities, pencils and pens that belong to others and so on. People with contamination obsessions may describe a fear that a contaminant is spreading, or has spread, and may believe that there are only a few people or places that are free from taint. These types of thoughts can lead clients to limit the people that they will expose themselves to or the places that they will go, all of which impact their social relationships (Coughtrey et al., 2018; Tolin et al., 2004). For some, objects or places may become contaminated with "bad luck" rather than disease or filth. For instance, a man who was wearing his father's watch when his wife died believes strongly his beloved watch is contaminated by the horrible loss of his wife and now must be destroyed so that it doesn't cause further harm. In many cases, concerned clients insist that family members use the same caution (rituals) to keep themselves from being infected as the client themselves use. In this way, OCD often involves and impacts the whole family, causing tension and relationship problems (Amir et al., 2000). Ironically, some clients with contamination fears find themselves in very messy or unclean spaces because they are not able to touch the dirty items or surfaces and will not allow others to risk touching the items either (Schwartz & Beyette, 2016).

We see two types of contamination obsessions: contact and mental. The contact type involves fear of actually touching an impure or poisoned object. For some clients, it is not necessary to have touched an adulterated object; however, instead the mere thought of the item can cause the client to feel dirty or threatened. This is described as mental contamination because the contamination takes place in the person's mind. Clients with contamination obsessions nearly always make use of compulsive behaviors to either prevent contamination in the first place or to neutralize it, the most common approach being excessive washing and the use of hand sanitizers (Radomsky et al., 2018; Radomsky et al., 2014).

Aggressive and Sexual Obsessions. Much less well known or understood are obsessions with themes that are violent or sexually related. Often discussed together, clients may experience one or the other or both types. Though little is known about this presentation outside the medical community, these themes appear in as many as a quarter of those who suffer from OCD. It is not surprising, however, that researchers believe these symptoms are under-reported since they are the source of significant shame and guilt (Glazier, 2013, in Moulding et al., 2014; Vella-Zarb et al., 2017). These obsessions, sometimes referred to in the literature as "repugnant" or "taboo" obsessions or as Harm OCD, may include themes related to physical or emotional violence or sexual acts that the individual finds offensive. These clients are unable to dismiss these thoughts as random occurrences of mind, and instead attribute some deeper meaning related to their personal character. Stalked by these oppressive thoughts, clients fear or conclude that they are bad, evil or sick. This manifestation of OCD presents particular difficulties in differential diagnosis, which will be discussed in greater length later in the chapter (Moulding et al., 2014).

Symmetry. Symmetry obsessions are distinctive preoccupations with evenness. A client with this type of obsessive pattern would describe intense feelings of discomfort or foreboding when items on a shelf, books, for instance, are not even or symmetrical. The rule of symmetry is applied in a wide variety of ways; for example, a person may feel the need to pass through a hallway with their head and shoulders even and equidistant from each wall, or feel the need to hold a cup with both hands rather than just one, or to repeat actions so that they "come out even." The symmetrical obsession may be less evident to others than the contamination obsession. Clients with this type of presentation counter these uncomfortable feelings with excessive ordering (clothes by color, food labels, alphabetizing canned goods, throwing away or purchasing more items to make the number of items "just right," lining up items so that they are oriented in a particular direction and so on).

Scrupulosity or Religiosity. Somewhere between 10% and 33% of those with OCD also struggle with scrupulosity or religiosity. These clients feel they must do one or more activities perfectly and find that they either do tasks very slowly or complete the same task again and again until it is completed "perfectly." Alternatively, scrupulosity may manifest as distressing religious or moral fears. These clients experience intrusive concerns about having committed a sin or the fear that they might. Consequently, compulsive prayer is common among those with religious OCD (Siev et al., 2011).

Whatever the symptom subtype, OCD symptom types seem to remain relatively stable over time, meaning that those with contamination obsessions will likely continue to have contamination-themed obsessions, though the content of these thoughts may change (Fullana et al., 2009; Mataix-Cols et al., 2002). Each of the major obsessional themes have been associated with lowered scores in quality of life in health, social and leisure domains (Schwarzman et al., 2017). What's more, OCD is widely understood to be one of the more treatment resistant disorders; only about a quarter of clients are completely free of symptoms at the end of treatment (Marsden et al., 2017).

OCD Compulsions. Compulsions observed in OCD share three primary traits: drive, purpose and rigid rules (Abramowitz & Jacoby, 2015; APA, 2013). In contrast, people diagnosed with OCRD disorders, such as TTM, and those who experience tics sometimes describe a similar urge; however, an OCD compulsion has a distinct purpose: to address the anxiety produced by an obsessive thought and to neutralize the fear that results. OCD compulsions are rigid and must be performed according to a set of rules or the client will feel compelled to repeat them until completed "correctly" (Abramowitz & Jacoby, 2015; APA, 2013). The classic example of a compulsion is the client who has constant thoughts of becoming infected (obsession) and washes her hands many times a day in order to neutralize any germs or viruses and to eliminate her anxiety about becoming ill (compulsion). This person may have a very specific and complicated set of rules about how her hands are washed, with what kind of soap and for how long, before feeling she has done it well enough to prevent illness. Whatever the outward manifestation of the compulsion, the function remains the same: to neutralize the mounting anxiety caused by obsessional thoughts. Below you will find a list of 10 scenarios to practice your growing capacity for discerning obsessions and compulsions from anxieties, phobias and what are typical interests or distractions. Learning to distinguish frightening or disturbing obsessive thoughts from anxiety or phobias comes with practice and good supervision.

OCD and the Covid-19 Pandemic. While at the time of this writing few peer reviewed articles about OCD and Covid-19 are yet available, it does seem clear that the pandemic presents a uniquely challenging experience for people already struggling with OCD. Contamination fears may be fueled and amplified by the 24-hour news stream detailing the spread of the disease potentially exacerbating contamination-related compulsions and making them more difficult to cope with. Recommendations for frequent, extended and careful handwashing as well as recommendations for cleaning surfaces frequently touched by members of the household may feed into contamination rituals that were already present (Banerjee, 2020; International OCD Foundation, 2020). Banerjee (2020) notes, "Lack of inhibitory control in OCD can run into a vicious loop thus bringing in a chronic sense of vulnerability to the infection, hence increased thought of contamination and increased washing," (no p.). The

International OCD Foundation noted that people who struggle with other forms of OCD, such as perfectionism and fears of harming others may also find that the Covid-19 pandemic amplifies these concerns. News discussing asymptomatic spread may lead, for example, to intrusive worries about having infected others unintentionally. The need for the whole family to practice greater levels of hygiene and vigilance may also amplify OCD symptoms. Covid-19 will certainly complicate therapeutic approaches that challenge the rationality of contamination fears (Banerjee, 2020; International OCD Foundation, 2020).

Culture and OCD. Unfortunately, much of what we understand about OCD is based on White non-Hispanic children and adults. White participants are disproportionately represented in the pediatric OCD research (93%–95%) making it difficult to draw conclusions about how OCD presents in children across cultures. However, initial research suggests that African Americans tend to report more OCD symptoms than their White counterparts and have more fears about being perfectly understood (Williams & Jahn, 2017). A similar lack of representation of Latinx participants in adult OCD research is in evidence. For instance, Wetterneck et al. (2012) found that only 24% of the United States and Canadian studies they reviewed included Latino participants. Though epidemiological studies suggest similar prevalence rates among White and African American citizens, the latter are under-represented both in clinical settings and in research studies related to OCD (Williams et al., 2012). Much more research is needed to identify differences in presentation as well as treatment needs.

Etiological Theories of OCD and How OCD Is Sustained

OCD likely has at least four intersecting etiologies: biological, learning, cognitive and sociocultural. Below you will find a brief discussion of each.

Biological Contributions. There is growing evidence that OCD may have genetic origins (van Grootheest et al., 2005). For example, research seems to point to glutamate signaling dysfunctions within the brain as contributing to the development of OCD (Rajendram et al., 2017). In 2006, the National Institutes of Health sponsored a study in which a gene variant was found to double the risk of the development of OCD. This anomalous allele is found in the SERT gene responsible for the transportation of serotonin (Hasler et al., 2006). Further, evidence of neurological differences in those with OCD and those without has been identified, including, but not limited to, within the basal ganglia where cases of acquired OCD have been documented after injury to this area of the brain (Chacko et al., 2000; Harvey & McCabe, 2017). More recently a relationship has been found between OCD and dysfunction in the ventromedial cortex, an area of the brain responsible for signaling safety (Apergis-Schoute et al., 2017), further supporting a biological and brain-based theory of OCD. A complete

BOX 9.03 TRY THIS: DIFFERENTIAL DIAGNOSIS OF OBSESSIVE COMPULSIVE DISORDER (OCD) FROM OTHER ANXIETY SYMPTOMS

In order to diagnose OCD effectively, you will have to be able to accurately identify obsessions and compulsions and discern these from anxiety, phobia and more typical (not pathological) thoughts and behaviors. As you work through the following scenarios, be careful that you maintain a balanced perspective, neither pathologizing strong interests or distractions, nor ignoring the detrimental and unwelcome thoughts and behaviors of OCD. Indicate which of the following is likely an obsession, which more closely reflects a compulsion and which is neither a compulsion nor an obsession. If you find you are unsure about the nature of one or more of the following, jot down some questions that might clarify the example.

Cynthia, age 11, feels "funny inside" if things on her shelves are not arranged "just right." She gets out of bed several times a night to check on the arrangement of her things and has difficulty falling asleep again.

Arron, 23, is fascinated by roller-coasters and spends a lot of time daydreaming about how to build the perfect "coaster."

Lupita. Though she is too ashamed to tell anyone, Lupita is often jarred by the thought or image that she would reach into the toilet and pluck out feces and put it in her mouth.

Jimmy is worried that if he gives a presentation in front of the class that he will "make a fool of himself" and his classmates will laugh at him. He has three times skipped class to avoid presenting and has been kept awake distressed by thoughts of presenting.

Daisy, 15, worries a great deal that she will become sick from contaminated food and is very uncomfortable eating foods she has not prepared herself or watched being prepared.

Alissa, 29, has become concerned because her daughter's math homework is consistently taking much longer than she feels it needs to. Her daughter seems to have no trouble with the math itself, it's the copying and re-copying multiple times, until it's "just right" that is taking so long and causing her daughter to become upset, sometimes to the point of rage-filled tears.

Ellen, 54, a graduate student, has been worrying that she might lose control of herself, scream and run out of the classroom. The fear began several months ago after seeing a film in which a man suffering from schizophrenia attacked a nurse. Since that time, Ellen has been plagued with the idea that she would also lose control of her behavior.

Octavio's wife has been wanting to go camping with the children for over a year but Octavio is concerned that they will come across a rattlesnake or copperhead and that someone will be bitten. He worries he is running out of excuses for not going camping.

Wes has been bothered for more than a decade by the persistent feeling that his environment is not entirely clean. He frequently finds himself cleaning and re-cleaning the kitchen and bathroom, sometimes taking 3 or more hours of his day to complete these tasks to his satisfaction.

Bo, 45, spends a lot of time laying awake at night worrying about finances, about his daughters and whether or not they are getting the best education, and if he is a good father. He worries that the company he has contracted with will "go under," though they seem to be thriving. He worries his wife is not satisfied in their marriage. Though Bo admits "things seem good now," he always feels there is a "storm on the horizon."

discussion of neurological findings related to OCD is not possible given the confines of space, as the body of this literature is quite expansive.

PANDAS and the Onset of Pediatric OCD. Evidence seems to suggest that a rare complication of strep can lead to the sudden onset of OCD-like symptoms. Now described as PANDAS (pediatric autoimmune neuropsychiatric disorders associated with streptococcus). This autoimmune response appears to involve the basal ganglia, though researchers continue to try to support this theory more definitively (Harvey & McCabe, 2017; Swedo & Williams, 2017). PANDAS is distinct from typical OCD in that it involves a sudden and dramatic regression in the child's behavior, personality, movement and emotional wellness. Children who develop PANDAS evidence a combination of symptoms ranging from obsessions, compulsions, aggression, anxiety, depression, suicidality, vocal and motor tics, emotional lability and even visual or auditory hallucinations (Harvey & McCabe, 2017). Children have also acquired OCD after recovering from infections that were not strep-related, pediatric acute-onset neuropsychiatric syndrome (PANS), and suffer similar combinations of symptoms as a result. Currently it seems that about 5% of all pediatric OCD is related to PANS or PANDAS (Harvey & McCabe, 2017; Jaspers-Fayer et al., 2017). These children are treated with medications to address the initial infection, as well as SSRIs and Cognitive Behavioral Therapy (CBT) (Harvey & McCabe, 2017; Swedo & Williams, 2017).

Learning Theories. Learning theories have been forwarded that suggest that children acquire from their parents' patterns of responding to anxiety and of thinking about threats that then predispose them to OCD. For instance, parents who habitually avoid low-threat triggers, such as answering the phone, visits to the doctor or social gatherings, may instill both an exaggerated set of beliefs around threat and may model avoidance as a primary means of dealing with anxiety (Berman et al., 2018). Though current research shows that OCD does run in families, the specific obsessions don't seem to be transferred between family members but rather the tendency toward obsessions and compulsions (Berman et al., 2018). It is likely that there is an interaction between the genetic heritability of OCD and the learning environment.

Cognitive Models. Rachman (1997) published one of the earliest articles describing a cognitive model for OCD. Rachman argued that obsessive thoughts were born out of a tendency to catastrophize and misinterpret the significance and meaning of thoughts. More recent research has elaborated on Rachman's cognitive model elucidating obsessive thinking processes and the compulsive behaviors that result. Prominent among these is the thought-action fusion (TAF) model. In this model, an individual believes that the unwanted and intrusive thought is, in essence, equal to having acted out the thought in the real world. In other words, the thought and the action carry the same weight in the mind of the client. While most of us are able to disregard a thought that is not congruent with our values or seems to come "out of left field," clients with TAF don't.

This process has been further broken into two primary types of TAF: moral (TAF-M) and likelihood (TAF-L). A client who evidences TAF-M draws a moral equivalence between thoughts and behavior. For example, a child would view a wish that her brother would fall and actually shoving her brother with the intention that he will fall as morally the same. In contrast, the client who displays TAF-L believes that wishing that her brother will fall will make it *more likely* that her brother will later fall, and in effect she has endangered her brother with her thought. Of course, TAF-M and TAF-L beliefs can be held at the same time, but one belief generally predominates. Clients who come from homes that describe themselves as very religious are more likely to make these types of equivalencies than clients who don't and stronger TAF beliefs are associated with more debilitating OCD (Berman et al., 2018; Grøtte et al., 2015; Mauzay et al., 2016; Myers & Wells, 2013; Myers et al., 2009, in Odriozola-Gonzalez et al., 2016; Pichakolaei et al., 2014). Finally, parental accommodation of obsessive and compulsive symptoms contributes to the continuation of the disorder (Storch et al., 2007).

Family Accommodation. When a member of the family is very distressed by obsessions and compulsions, others in the family will often do what they can to help reduce the stress that this person feels, sometimes participating in rituals or making it easier for the family member to do so; these responses are described as family accommodation. Family members may try to avoid exposing the OCD sufferer to a particular trigger; for instance, by agreeing to change their shoes before coming into the house, or taking extra steps to assure that kitchen surfaces meet the client's cleanliness standards. Family members may constantly reassure the client, take them to unneeded medical appointments, adopt strict schedules for meals or alter routes of travel and so on. These accommodations come with a high cost to the family as a whole and are correlated with depression and anxiety in family members irrespective of the severity of the client's OCD symptoms (Amir et al., 2000). Family interventions are designed to educate families about OCD and provide effective strategies for supporting the family member struggling with OCD (Schwartz & Beyette, 2016; Storch et al., 2007).

The Skilled Diagnostician

Correctly diagnosing OCD can be more challenging than one might first imagine. While obsessions and compulsions have a distinctive quality to them, obsessions are neither uncommon nor do they arise exclusively in those with OCD, OCRD disorders or even exclusively within clinical populations generally. A comprehensive longitudinal study of 1,037 participants demonstrated just how common obsessions and compulsions are. Among study participants, made up of those with no clinical disorder, those with OCD and those with disorders other than OCD, more than a third reported experiencing either obsessions or compulsions. Notably, 13% of the study's non-clinical population endorsed these symptoms (Fullana et al., 2009).

Even among seasoned mental healthcare providers and primary care physicians, misdiagnosis of OCD is astonishingly high. In one study of 360 psychiatrists asked to rate one of five vignettes, an alarming 39% of the diagnoses were inaccurate. Vignettes depicting "taboo" obsessions were misdiagnosed at an even higher rate (homosexual obsessions, 77%; sexual obsession involving children, 43%) while contamination fears were misdiagnosed at a rate of about 16% (Glazier et al., 2013). In a similar study, primary care physicians, who are less well trained in psychiatric diagnosis but do most of the diagnosis and prescribing in the United States, also performed poorly, misdiagnosing half of the vignettes (Glazier et al., 2015). Differential diagnosis of obsessions and compulsions necessitates a careful look not only at the disorders within the OCRD dimension, but also a variety of disorders throughout the DSM. A discussion of the differential diagnosis of OCD is offered below and is organized by presenting symptoms.

Differential Diagnosis of Obsessions with Sexual and Aggressive Themes. Intrusive thoughts related to harming oneself or others are among the most distressing to clients and frequently present significant consequences if misdiagnosed. Reports from clients about intrusive thoughts of hurting or killing others, sexually or physically abusing children or injury to self all warrant careful consideration and assessment before a diagnosis is made. If you work in an environment that stresses a quick turn-around of diagnosis, these presentations may be worth lobbying for additional time in order to arrive at an accurate assessment of the client's difficulty.

Sexually-Themed Obsessive Thoughts. Perhaps one of the more difficult variants of OCD to diagnose is the pOCD subtype, or "pedophilia OCD." Those with the pOCD subtype find their lives disrupted by sexual thoughts and images of children or adolescents. These clients experience alarm, shame, guilt and deep self-doubt about their own moral fortitude. Over time, they begin to wonder if they are capable of the very acts they judge to be vile and may even become convinced that they are pedophiles (Moulding et al., 2014; Vella-Zarb et al., 2017). The OCD sufferer with pedophilic intrusive thoughts, however, differs from the client with true pedophilia in that the first is repulsed by the thoughts and imagery and is fighting their intrusion, while the client with true pedophilia is aroused by sexual thoughts and images of children and may or may not fight urges to act on this arousal (Moulding et al., 2014; Vella-Zarb et al., 2017).

A misdiagnosis of pedophilia for a client with pOCD would have dire implications for the client. A misapplied diagnosis would jeopardize treatment, and in this case would validate unnecessary fears about the client's personal character. Misdiagnosis of pOCD as pedophilia could damage the client's relationships, risk job and housing placements and even lead to the involvement of child protective services. Conversely, the misdiagnosis of OCD in a person with pedophilia could potentially create great risk to children and adolescents who would be the subject of the client's urges (Moulding et al., 2014; Vella-Zarb et al., 2017). Consequently, the stakes are particularly high in this symptom presentation.

Vella-Zarb et al. (2017) offer recommendations for assessing and diagnosing clients who experience sexualized obsessive content of harm to others (pedophilic, obsessions with sex with non-consenting adults, exposing themselves and so on). They suggest that first clinicians determine whether or not the client feels distress at the time of the intrusive thought and whether or not this distress continues after the thoughts have passed; for example, by ruminating about their meaning. They further recommend outlining the content of the cognitive, emotional and behavioral reactions to sexually-laden intrusive thoughts when discerning pOCD from pedophilia, and other paraphilic disorders (such as exhibitionism, frotteurism etc,).

Aggressive themes. As mentioned earlier, clients may present with intrusive thoughts of aggression toward others or toward themselves. Sometimes these fears are of intentional harm and sometimes they consist of fears of accidental injury; for instance, a fear of using a butcher knife and accidentally killing someone else in the kitchen. Suicide obsessions have also been documented. These types of obsessions, however, can be distinguished from true suicidality or homicidality by the fear the client expresses about these intrusive thoughts. However, some clients with suicidal obsessions may also be experiencing depression, clouding your ability to discern true suicidality and suicidal obsessions. Again, careful and ongoing assessment of your client's status accompanied by diligent consultation and documentation is essential.

Sexual and aggressive obsessions in post-natal men and women. Research has also shown evidence of post-natal obsessions in women and men with anxiety, depression and OCD. These obsessions may include thoughts and images of physical (such as shaking or suffocating) or sexual abuse of the newborn. As with pOCD, these clients experience a great deal of fear about what their obsessions might mean about their character and worry about the safety of their child, though if accompanied by severe depression the client may exhibit a flattened affect rather than fear. Research seems to suggest that most clients who experience post-partum OCD have experienced mental health concerns at some point prior to the birth of the child (Speisman et al., 2011; Zambaldi et al., 2009). Clients with aggressive obsessions that arise out of psychotic processes may be accompanied by flattened affect and delusional thoughts, but not in all cases. This differential diagnosis is also one with high stakes and requires careful assessment and diligent client monitoring. Precise clinical notes, meticulous documenting of the diagnostic process and frequent review of these notes, ideally augmented with skilled consultation or supervision, is advised when working with clients with aggressive and sexual obsessions, particularly when child safety is at risk.

Differential Diagnosis in Children. While special care must always be taken when diagnosing children, the diagnosis of OCD offers unique challenges that should be given attention. Developmentally, children are naturally given to magical thinking until about age 7 when they begin to replace these ideas with an understanding of physical realities. Consider the following scenarios of two children, each 6 years old:

Kelly. Now that the holiday decorations are up and her family is talking about Christmas each evening, Kelly has been nervous about her behavior. She hopes Santa will forget the times that she "got in trouble" over the last year. She is trying to be extra good so that Santa will bring her a kitten.

Daniel. Daniel has been worried for months that his "bad thoughts" will cause his mother to be ill again. She was sick last year with cancer but his parents have not been able to convince him that her illness wasn't due in part to his anger at her.

Kelly and Daniel each demonstrate a quality of magical thinking, Kelly in her belief in Santa's omniscience, and Daniel in his concern that thoughts can make others ill. It is important to remember that while magical thinking is developmentally appropriate, most typically developing children readily adopt information and adjust their beliefs when presented with information from trusted others, such as a sibling or adult. For the child with OCD, however, these beliefs are difficult to dislodge despite evidence or information to the contrary. Reassurances from adults rarely soothe these children's fears. Kelly's belief in Santa and her worries about her behavior would likely end if an older sibling revealed that Santa was actually her parents, while Daniel's fears have been much more steadfast despite the comfort and assurances of his parents. Accurate diagnosis of obsessional thoughts also has to take into consideration cultural normativity of the content of the belief.

While developmental issues may cloud OCD diagnosis in children, the converse is also true. The presence of OCD symptomatology may mimic developmental disorders such as learning disorders or autism. For example, children who struggle with scrupulosity may find that they work on homework and exams so slowly and meticulously that they can't complete their work and their grades suffer. Their slow work habits may also give the appearance that they are having difficulty comprehending or applying concepts (Krebs & Heyman, 2015).

Without careful consideration and evaluation, compulsive touching, counting or ordering can be confused with stereotyped movements or the rigid preferences seen in the autism spectrum and can closely resemble tics. However, OCD compulsions differ from both. The movements associated with tics are, by and large, involuntary and have no deliberate purpose, OCD compulsions, on the other hand, are aimed at reducing anxiety or neutralizing some feared event, such as a bad thought or feeling dirty. The compulsions of the child with OCD (counting, praying, repeating phrases) are more complex than stereotyped movements of the child with an autistic spectrum disorder (e.g., hand flapping or rocking) or the tics displayed by a child with a tic disorder (blinking or lip smacking) (Krebs & Heyman, 2015).

When assessing and diagnosing children presenting with these symptoms, clinicians should remember that comorbidity of these three disorders is very common. A full 59% of children with OCD also meet full criteria for tic disorders (Krebs & Heyman, 2015), those with autism are twice as likely to be diagnosed with OCD than their typically developing peers and a significant number of those on the autistic spectrum meet criteria for OCD (Meier et al., 2015).

The following pivot points may help to point you in the direction of one or more disorders that may be part of your differential diagnosis.

BOX 9.04 DIFFERENTIAL DIAGNOSIS OF PARAPHILIA AND OBSESSIVE COMPULSIVE DISORDER (OCD)

What level of distress is being described by your client?

- Suggests OCD: High level of distress is described (however, some clients with paraphilias have reported experiencing distress over their thoughts, particularly early in the development of the disorder)
- Suggests Paraphilia: Little/No distress

What is the nature of the distress experienced by the client?

- Suggests OCD: Client's concern is focused on what the thoughts and images might mean about their moral character
- Suggests Paraphilia: Client's concern is primarily focused on potential for negative consequences to the client (i.e., legal consequences if action would be discovered)

What are the physiological responses to the thoughts and images?

- Suggests OCD: Client reports or demonstrates fear and avoidance (note that clients may question whether or not their anxiety is a signal of underlying arousal or confuse anxiety for arousal, thus clouding the diagnosis and strengthening their obsessional fears)
- Suggests Paraphilia: Client becomes aroused when triggering thoughts and images arise

What gain or purpose does the obsessional content serve the client?

- Suggests OCD: Thoughts are unwanted and distressing: thoughts themselves offer no gain
- Suggests Paraphilia: Thoughts and images trigger sexual gratification and pleasure for the client or are used as an avenue for stress reduction

What are the subsequent behaviors engaged in by the client following an *obsessional*/triggering thought or image?

- Suggests OCD: Client attempts to neutralize the unwanted thoughts and reduce anxiety with compulsive actions (such as prayers, a safe word or phrase, reassurance seeking, "testing themselves," avoidance of children, etc.)
- Suggests Paraphilia: Client may masturbate, seek out pornography, or place themselves near children, for example

Source: Vella-Zarb, McCabe & Rowa, (2017).

A Brief Note on the Treatment of OCD and OCRD

As stated earlier, OCD is difficult to treat. Most studies suggest that only 25% of clients enjoy full remission of their symptoms by the end of treatment (Marsden et al., 2017; Wilhelm et al., 2015). Two therapies can be described as best-practices in treating OCD: CBT (Abramowitz & Arch, 2014) and exposure and ritual prevention (CBT/ERP) and selective serotonin reuptake inhibitors. Eye movement desensitization and reprocessing (EMDR) also offers promising results, particularly in conjunction with ERP and/or CBT. Finally, a brief group intervention, the Bergen 4-Day Treatment, has shown high recovery and remission rates in a 4-year follow-up study (Beck et al., 2006; Kvale et al., 2018; Foa et al., 2012; Williams et al., 2014). Specialized approaches to treating OCD require additional training; therapists interested in their use should study these approaches carefully, attend training and workshops and seek specialized supervision until sufficient mastery is achieved.

Pharmacological Approaches. The most commonly prescribed medications are selective serotonin reuptake inhibitors: fluoxetine, fluvoxamine and sertraline. Used together with therapy, these medications can be quite effective. These medications are frequently prescribed at higher doses than would be needed for depression or anxiety. Clinicians and clients should be aware that these medications often take 8-12 weeks before improvement in OCD symptoms is felt (Hirschtritt et al., 2017).

CBT and ERP. CBT/ERP works by identifying the client's specific fears and obsessions, evaluates the strength of those fears and triggers and then gradually exhausts or extinguishes the reactivity through exposure. During exposure, clients are supported in resisting compulsions that would otherwise reduce the anxiety produced by their fear and instead "ride out" the wave of anxiety until it is gone. Therapists using the CBT/ERP model work with clients to reduce underlying beliefs and schemas, such as the fusion between thoughts and actions, and as a result help clients to make gains in their OCD. A recent longitudinal study showed that at 3-year follow-up of clients who participated in CBT, a full 66% were in remission and nearly 20% of the remaining participants still showed a response to the treatment they received. These participants also showed improvements in their psychosocial functioning and a reduction in symptoms of depression. The participants in the study were also prescribed SSRIs and, where the SSRI was insufficient, were also prescribed a second-generation antipsychotic, pointing to the strength of the combination medication and therapy (Melin et al., 2018; Wilhelm et al., 2015).

Interestingly, in cases of OCD, neither client–therapist alliance nor the client or therapist's own belief that the client would improve, known as expectancy, has been shown to influence outcomes. Currently, the body of research demonstrating efficacy in OCD supports the use of CBT/ERP as the best practice approach (Wilhelm et al., 2015).

Eye Movement Desensitization and Reprocessing (EMDR). Marsden and colleagues (2017) note that of those that enter treatment for CBT/ERP, a quarter refuse to attempt exposure therapy, and of those who do try this kind of therapy, 20% experience no relief and another 20% eventually relapse. They argue that their research of the use of EMDR offers promise for these clients who are reluctant or unwilling to try therapies that involve exposure to their fears. EMDR was born out of Shapiro's

BOX 9.05 TRY THIS: RESPONDING TO UNCOMFORTABLE DISCLOSURES

Read the following scenario and note your immediate response. How might you experience a client who made the following report? What values, beliefs or personal experiences would support you or perhaps interfere with your ability to work effectively with this client from evaluation through treatment planning?

Scenario: You have been working with Edil, a 28-year-old father of two, for several months to help him deal with a tic disorder and OCD with contamination themes. In your seventh session together, Edil seems quite distressed as he discloses, "I think I could hurt a child in a sexual way, my head is filled with perverted thoughts and I can't make them stop no matter what I do. I need help before I damage a child, maybe even my own kids!"

(2001) *Adaptive Information Processing Model* and unfolds in eight phases that work to specifically identify threatening memories. Clients rate these memories and then therapists desensitize the client to those memories using targeted recall paired with eye movements, alternating bilateral auditory or tactile stimulations. In the Marsden et al. study, EMDR performed as well as CBT in therapy attendance; completion rates and the outcome measures between the two therapies were also similar at the completion of the study and at 6-month follow-up.

Definitional Cases in OCD and OCRD

Eastman

Eastman is a single 26-year-old living in New York. Eastman is a stage actor who has struggled to find the success that he would like to have. He is deeply troubled by what he believes is his "enormous and distorted nose" that he fears may be getting in the way of his success as an actor and in finding a relationship. Though many of his friends and family have tried to reassure Eastman that his nose is not out of the ordinary or in any way unappealing, he has undergone several plastic surgeries on his nose, none of which have eased Eastman's concerns.

TABLE 9.01 Pivot Points: Obsessive Compulsive and Related Disorders

	Consider
Pivot Point One: Does your client's suffering arise from intrusive, repetitive and distressing thoughts or from irresistible and unwelcome rituals?	
• Are your client's intrusive thoughts of a sexual nature that are repulsive or deeply disturbing to your client (e.g., forced/non-consensual sexual contact, pedophilic, incongruent homosexual, etc.)	Obsessive Compulsive Disorder
• Are your client's violent or non-consensual sexual fantasies arousing to your client or serve as a source of stress relief?	Explore various paraphilic disorders
Pivot Point Two: Does your client's suffering arise out of grossly distorted perceptions of the body?	
• Is your client's distorted body image related to an exaggerated or perceived physical flaw?	Body Dysmorphic Disorder
• Is your client's distorted body image related primarily to weight?	Anorexia Nervosa
• Is your client's distress about the body embedded in a feeling of incongruence between gender identity and the physical body?	Gender Dysphoria
Pivot Point Three: Do your client's distressing thoughts and compulsions manifest in an inability to let go of objects that have lost their functional value and create a cluttered and unsafe environment?	Hoarding Disorder
Pivot Point Four: Do your client's compulsions manifest in sounds or movements that your client can't control (tics)?	Consider Tic Disorders
Pivot Point Five: Does your client experience distress as a result of an irresistible urge to pull out their own hair?	Trichotillomania
Pivot Point Six: Does your client experience distress as a result of an irresistible urge to pick their own skin?	Excoriation Disorder

Dan

Dan, age 12, endures a lot of teasing from his friends about his habit of tapping any door frame before entering or exiting a room. Though he understands that the habit is strange, he feels he has no control over the tapping. Dan tries to hide this habit by being the last out of the room.

Emily

Emily, age 76, was recently moved from her rented duplex by adult protective services when it was found to be infested with rodents and roaches. The rooms were filled with discarded items, many of which were broken or dirty. When confronted by the social worker, Emily seemed confused about why the amassed clutter was problematic.

Todd

Todd has developed a habit of pulling out the hair above his temples when he is feeling stressed and has developed two distinctive bald spots.

Connor

Connor's arms are badly scarred thanks to his inability to refrain from picking at his skin. He sometimes spends hours squeezing pores and removing scabs.

Narrative Cases in OCD and OCRD

Devin

Devin, an 18-year-old White male student and recent transfer to his school, has asked to meet with the school counselor following an incident in his math class. Devin reports that his math teacher became irate and insisted he leave the class when Devin licked his finger and wiped it on a female student in the desk in front of him. His teacher had reported the incident to the vice-principal who told Devin that the other student had the right to press assault charges against him and that he would be suspended if it happened again.

Devin explains, "I don't expect anyone to understand or even believe me, but the edge of the chalkboard looked like it was touching her arm. I can't explain it but when straight lines intersect with somebody's skin I get a strong feeling that the person will be cut. The only way I can get the thought out of my head is to 'glue their skin' with saliva." Devin continues, "She was sitting in front of me for an hour with the line of the chalkboard intersecting her bare arm. I couldn't stand it! It was driving me crazy! Normally when I see a line run into a person I can take a deep breath and turn my head or walk away or move a little so the line doesn't intersect, but I was stuck in class. I asked to go to the restroom but my teacher wouldn't let me go. Nothing I tried helped. I finally gave up—I think I thought if I did it really quickly she wouldn't notice. But she did notice and now everyone thinks I'm a freak." Devin has no history of substance use and is not currently taking a medication that might account for his unusual thoughts or behavior.

Addie

Addie, age 6, has been experiencing a lot of teasing since she developed a bald spot on the crown of her head. Once barely perceptible, children frequently comment on the spot, which is now the size of a quarter. Several mornings a week, Addie resists going to school to avoid the teasing from classmates and questions from her teachers. Addie frequently worries about her parents, her sister and her friends and during these periods of worry, she finds herself pulling out the hair. Though her parents and teacher remind her often not to pull her hair, and despite the fact that she would like to stop this behavior, she has not been able to stop. Addie's parents were of the belief that the hairpulling was a "stage" and that if they didn't give it a lot of attention that she would eventually stop. However, when Addie began to miss school Addie's mother decided to take her to the doctor. Her physical showed that she is in good health and seems to be meeting all of her developmental milestones in a timely way. Her doctor referred Addie to counseling.

Marta

Marta, a 52-year-old White social worker, has come to counseling with concerns about intrusive thoughts that feel outside of her control. Marta explains, "This is not the first time I've been bothered by intrusive thoughts, but this time they are just really getting the better of me. A few months ago our department found a little girl beaten to death and stuffed in a dresser drawer. Her parents had done terrible things to her little body. Since then I have had these random thoughts that I was hurting a child or that I would. I open the file of a kid I have to go see and I get a flash of myself choking or beating that child or doing something to sexually violate that child. And I start to think, 'Am I really no different from the people who do this kind of thing? And I wonder if it's possible that I will do something really horrible.' So I've started carrying some charms with me that will help me to keep me and the kids safe. I touch each charm 13 times before I knock on the door. But I have to do it discreetly because I look a little crazy doing it."

Marta shares that she has a history of obsessive thoughts and compulsive behaviors reaching back into middle school. Most of these thoughts have revolved around themes of cleanliness or religiosity. Marta also has a history of motor tics when under stress, such as rolling her wrists.

Martin

Martin, 17, is seeking help. "I feel like I don't want to leave the house. I'm so ashamed of my face. I don't know what's wrong with me but every time I get a pimple or anything that looks or feels like an imperfection, I feel compelled to pick at it. And once I start it is like I can't stop. I keep picking and picking until sometimes it hurts, and of course they always bleed and look way, way worse than they would if I just left them alone. I can't stand to go into the bathroom because I know when I look in the mirror I am going to want to pick at my face. Sometimes I even get the urge when I am in class to just see if I can be excused so I can go pick at my face. I hate it and can't stop!"

Martin denies any negative thoughts about his appearance generally or his face or skin in particular. Martin also denies taking any medications or substances.

Cara

After returning from the Peace Corps after 2 years of service, Dee decided to spend a week with her sister, Cara, before beginning her new job. When she arrived at Cara's house, she was shocked to find that the whole of Cara's small space was filled, wall to wall and from the floor to the rafters, with second-hand items ranging from old discarded clothing to scratched or broken CD's and records. Key spaces such as the kitchen and bathroom were no longer usable, forcing Cara to use a local gym in order to shower. Exploring further, Dee found that the sinks were filled with dirty dishes, molding food, and other discarded detritus and filth. Cara explained that most of what was in the house were things that she would one day need. As Dee tried to help Cara sort through some of the items in order to throw things away, Cara became extremely anxious and angry. "Seriously, Dee, this is my house and I've been living here just fine without you sticking your nose in." Tension between the sisters escalated when Dee found that despite her efforts to help Cara to clean up the apartment, Cara continued to stop along her walk home from work picking items out of her neighbors' recycling bins and trash and bringing them into the house. Ultimately, Dee became so distressed by the filth and by her sister's state of mind and felt the best thing for her to do was to call a social worker.

Manny

Manny, a 16-year-old Laotian American high school student and dancer, has found himself to be more and more distracted by what he believes to be the "lopsided and pointed shape" of his ears. Manny frequently sits in front of the mirror trying to discern ways of holding his head that might de-emphasize his ears. He has grown his hair long and feels most comfortable when his hair rests over his ears but this isn't always possible when dancing. Manny has been told by friends and reassured by his agent that his ears are typical in both their shape and size. Manny, however, shares, "My ears are really uneven. They look like they are teeter-tottering in the sides of my head, so I try to tilt my head just a little to make them look straighter. And the left one is definitely bigger than the right, so I swivel my head just a very little so that one is less visible. I don't know what to do about how pointy they are except just have my hair lay over the tops. Sometimes my neck is so stiff and sore from trying to hold my head just right." Manny has started to save money toward plastic surgery and he hopes that a doctor can give him ears that aren't "horrible to look at." Manny shares, "I wish my friends could just be honest with me. I can take it. I see it every day when I look in the mirror. I don't know how they can deny something so obvious."

References

Abramowitz, J. S., & Arch, J. J. (2014). Strategies for improving long-term outcomes in cognitive behavioral therapy for obsessive-compulsive disorder: Insights from learning theory. *Cognitive and Behavioral Practice*, *21*(1), 20–31. https://doi.org/10.1016/j.cbpra.2013.06.004

Abramowitz, J. S., & Jacoby, R. J. (2015). Obsessive-compulsive and related disorders: A critical review of the new diagnostic class. *Annual Review of Clinical Psychology*, *11*, 165–186. https://doi.org/10.1146/annurev-clinpsy-032813-153713

American Psychiatric Association. (2013). *Diagnostic and statistical manual of mental disorders (DSM-5®)*. Author.

Amir, N., Freshman, M., & Foa, E. B. (2000). Family distress and involvement in relatives of obsessive-compulsive disorder patients. *Journal of Anxiety Disorders*, *14*(3), 209–217. https://doi.org/10.1016/S0887-6185(99)00032-8

Apergis-Schoute, A. M., Gillan, C. M., Fineberg, N. A., Fernandez-Egea, E., Sahakian, B. J., & Robbins, T. J. (2017). Neural basis of impaired safety signaling in obsessive compulsive disorder. *PNAS*, *114*(12), 3216–3221. https://doi.org/10.73/pnas.1609194114

Banerjee, D. (2020). The other side of COVID-19: Impact on Obsessive Compulsive Disorder (OCD) and hoarding. *Psychiatry Research*, *288*, 112966. https://doi.org/10.1016/j.psychres.2020.112966

Beck, A., Steketee, G., & Wilhelm, S. (2006). *Cognitive therapy for obsessive-compulsive disorder: A guide for professionals*. New Harbinger Publications, Inc.

Berman, N. C., Jacoby, R. J., Sullivan, A. D., Hoeppner, S., Micco, J. A., & Wilhelm. S. (2018). Parental-level risk factors for children's obsessive beliefs, interpretation biases, and compulsive symptoms: A cross-sectional examination. *Journal of Obsessive-Compulsive and Related Disorders*, *18*, 8–17. https://doi.org/10.1016/j.jocrd.2018.04.002

Chacko, R. C., Corbin, M. A., & Harper, R. G. (2000). Acquired obsessive-compulsive disorder associated with basal ganglia lesions. *Journal of Neuropsychiatry & Clinical Neuroscience*, *12*(2), 269–272. https://doi.org/0.1176/jnp.12.2.269

Colas, E. (1999). *Just checking: Scenes from the life of an obsessive-compulsive*. Washington Square Press.

Coughtrey, A., Shafran, R., Bennett, S., Kothari, R., & Wade, T. (2018). Mental contamination: Relationship with psychopathology and transdiagnostic processes. *Journal of Obsessive-Compulsive and Related Disorders*, *17*, 39–45. https://doi.org/10.1016/j.jocrd.2017.08.009

Foa, E., Yadin, E., & Lichner, T. (2012). *Exposure and response (ritual) prevention for obsessive-compulsive disorder: Therapist's guide* (2nd ed.). Oxford University Press.

Fullana, M., Mataix-Cols, D., Caspi, A., Harrington, H., Grisham, J., Moffitt, T., & Poulton, R. (2009). Obsessions and compulsions in the community: Prevalence, interference, help-seeking, developmental stability, and co-occurring psychiatric conditions. *American Journal of Psychiatry, 166*(3), 329–336. https://doi.org/10.1176/appi.ajp.2008.08071006

García-Soriano, G., Belloch, A., Morillo, C., & Clark, D. A. (2011). Symptom dimensions in obsessive–compulsive disorder: From normal cognitive intrusions to clinical obsessions. *Journal of Anxiety Disorders, 25*(4), 474–482. https://doi.org/10.1016/j.janxdis.2010.11.012

Glazier, K., Calixte, R. M., Rothschild, R., & Pinto, A. (2013). High rates of OCD symptom misidentification by mental health professionals. *Annals of Clinical Psychiatry, 25*(3), 201–209.

Glazier, K., Swing, M., & McGinn, L. K. (2015). Half of obsessive-compulsive disorder cases misdiagnosed: Vignette-based survey of primary care physicians. *Journal of Clinical Psychiatry, 76*(6), e761–e767. https://doi.org/10.4088/JCP.14m09110

Glazier, K., Wetternick, C., Singh, S., & Williams, M. (2015). Stigma and shame as barriers to treatment in obsessive-compulsive and related disorders. *Journal of Depression and Anxiety, 4*(3), 191. https://doi.org/10.4172/2167-1044.1000191

Grøtte, T., Solem, S., Vogel, P. A., Güzey, I. C., Hansen, B., & Myers, S. G. (2015). Metacognition, responsibility, and perfectionism in obsessive-compulsive disorder. *Cognitive Therapy and Research, 39*(1), 41–50.

Gupta, S., & Gargi, P. D. (2012). Habit reversal training for trichotillomania. *International Journal of Trichology, 4*(1), 39. https://doi.org/10.4103/0974-7753.96089

Harvey, J. E., & McCabe, H. P. (2017). A critical review of PANDAS research in the context of obsessive compulsive disorder. *Health Psychology Report, 6*(1), 1–9. https://doi.org/10.5114/hpr.2018.70356

Hasler, G., Kazuba, D., & Murphy, D. L. (2006). Factor analysis of obsessive–compulsive disorder YBOCS-SC symptoms and association with 5-HTTLPR SERT polymorphism. *American Journal of Medical Genetics Part B, 141B*, 403–408. https://doi.org/10.1002/ajmg.b.30309

Hirschtritt, M. E., Bloch, M. H., & Mathews, C. A. (2017). Obsessive-compulsive disorder advances in diagnosis and treatment. *Journal of the American Medical Association, 317*(13), 1358–1367. https://doi.org/10.1001/jama.2017.2200

International OCD Foundation. (2020). *COVID-19 vs. your OCD symptoms.* https://iocdf.org/covid19/covid-19-vs-your-ocd-symptoms/

Jaspers-Fayer, F., Han, S. H. J., Chan, E., McKenney, K., Simpson, A., Boyle, A., Ellwyn, R., & Stewart, S. E. (2017). Prevalence of acute-onset subtypes in pediatric obsessive-compulsive disorder. *Journal of Child and Adolescent Psychopharmacology, 27*(4), 332–341. https://doi.org/10.1089/cap.2016.0031

Jones, G., Keuthen, N., & Greenberg, E. (2018). Assessment and treatment of trichotillomania (hair pulling disorder) and excoriation (skin picking) disorder. *Clinics in Dermatology, 36*(6), 728–736. https://doi.org/10.1016/j.clindermatol.2018.08.008

Krebs, G., & Heyman, I. (2015). Obsessive-compulsive disorder in children and adolescents. *Archives of Disease in Childhood*, *100*(5), 495–499. https://doi.org/10.1136/archdischild-2014-306934

Kress, V. E., Stargell, N. A., Zoldan, C. A., & Maylo, M. J. (2016). Hoarding disorder: Diagnosis, assessment, and treatment. *Journal of Counseling & Development*, *94*, 83–94. https://doi.org/10.1002/jcad.12064

Kvale, G., Hansen, B., Björgvinsson, T., Børtveit, T., Hagen, K., Haseth, S., Kristensen, U. B., Launes, G., Ressler, K. J., Solem, S., Strand, A., van den Heuvel, O. A., & Öst, L-G. (2018). Successfully treating 90 patients with obsessive compulsive disorder in eight days: The Bergen 4-day treatment. *BMC Psychiatry*, *18*(1), 323. https://doi.org/10.1186/s12888-018-1887-4

Linkovski, O., Kalanthroff, E., Henik, A., & Anholt, G. E. (2016). Stop checking: Repeated checking and its effects on response inhibition and doubt. *Journal of Behavior Therapy and Experimental Psychiatry*, *53*, 84–91. https://doi.org/10.1016/j.jbtep.2014.12.007

Marsden, Z., Lovell, K., Blore, D., Ali, S., & Delgadillo, J. (2017). A randomized controlled trial comparing EMDR and CBT for obsessive-compulsive disorder. *Clinical Psychology & Psychotherapy*, *25*(1), e10–e18. https://doi.org/10.1002/cpp.2120

Mataix-Cols, D., Marks, I. M., Greist, J. H., Kobak, K. A., & Baer, L. (2002). Obsessive-compulsive symptom dimensions as predictors of compliance with and response to behaviour therapy: results from a controlled trial. *Psychotherapy and Psychosomatics*, *71*(5), 255–262. https://doi.org/10.1159/000064812

Mauzay, D., Spradlin, A., & Cuttler, C. (2016). Devils, witches, & psychics: The role of thought-action fusion in the relationships between obsessive-compulsive features, religiosity, and paranormal beliefs. *Journal of Obsessive Compulsive and Related Disorder*, *11*, 113–120. https://doi.org/10.1016/j.jocrd.2016.10.003

McGuire, J. F., Myers, N., Lewin, A. B., Storch, E. A., & Rahman, O. (2019). The influence of hair pulling styles in the treatment of trichotillomania. *Behavior Therapy*. https://doi.org/10.1016/j.beth.2019.12.003

McKay, D., Abramowitz, J. S., Calamari, J. E., Kyrios, M., Radomsky, A., Sookman, D., Taylor, S., & Wilhelm, S. (2004). A critical evaluation of obsessive-compulsive disorder subtypes: Symptoms versus mechanisms. *Clinical Psychology Review*, *24*, 283–313. https://doi.org/10.1016/j.cpr.2004.04.003

Meier, S. M., Petersen, L., Schendel, D. E., Mattheisen, M., Mortensen, P. B., & Mors, O. (2015). Obsessive-compulsive disorder and autism spectrum disorders: Longitudinal and offspring risk. *PloS ONE*, *10*(11), e0141703. https://doi.org/10.1371/journal.pone.0141703

Melin, K., Skarphedinsson, G., Skärsäter, I., Haugland, B. S. M., & Ivarsson, T. (2018). A solid majority remit following evidence-based OCD treatments: A 3-year naturalistic outcome study in pediatric OCD. *European Child & Adolescent Psychiatry*, *27*, 1373–1381. https://doi.org/10.1007/s00787-018-1137-9

Morein-Zamir, S., Papmeyer, M., Pertusa, A.., Chamberlin, R., Fineberg, N. A., Sahakian, B. J., Mataix-Cols, D., & Robbins, T. W. (2014). The profile of executive function in OCD hoarders and hoarding disorder. *Psychiatry Research*, *215*, 659–667. https://doi.org/10.1016/j.psychres.2013.12.026

Moulding, R., Aardema, F., & O'Connor, K. P. (2014). Repugnant obsessions: A review of the phenomenology, theoretical models and treatment of sexual and aggressive obsessional themes in OCD. *Journal of Obsessive-Compulsive and Related Disorders*, *3*(2), 161–168. https://doi.org/10.1016/j.jocrd.2013.11.006

Mufaddel, A., Osman, O., Almugaddam, F., & Jafferany, M. (2013). A review of body dysmorphic disorder and its presentation in different clinical settings. *Primary Care Companion of CNS Disorders*, *15*(4). https://doi.org/10.4088/PCC.12r01464

Myers, S. G., & Wells, A. (2013). An experimental manipulation of metacognition: A test of the metacognitive model of obsessive-compulsive symptoms. *Behaviour Research and Therapy*, *51*(4–5), 177–184. https://doi.org/10.1016/j.brat.2013.01.007

Odriozola-Gonzalez, P., Perez-Alvarez, M., Garcia-Montes, J., Perona-Garcelan, S., & Vallina-Fernandez, O. (2016). The mediating role of metacognitive variables in the relationship between thought-action fusion and obsessive compulsive symptomatology. *Suma Psicologica*, *23*, 80–89.

Pertusa, A., Nordsletten, A. E., de la Cruz, L. F., & Mataix-Cols, D. (2011). The Structured Interview for Hoarding Disorder (SIHD)©. *Journal of Obsessive Compulsive and Related Disorders*, *2*(3), 346–350. https://doi.org/10.1016/j.jocrd.2013.06.003

Phillips, K. A. (2007). Suicidality in body dysmorphic disorder. *Primary Psychiatry*, *14*(12), 58. https://doi.org/10.1037/e721432007-007

Pichakolaei, A., Fahimi, S., Roudsari, A ., Fakhari, A., Akbari, E., & Rahimkhsnli, M. (2014). A comparative study of thought fusion beliefs and thought control strategies in patient with obsessive-compulsive disorder, major depressive disorder and normal people. *Iran Journal of Psychiatry Behavioral Science*, *8*(3), 33–41.

Rachman, S. (1997). A cognitive theory of obsessions. *Behaviour Research and Therapy*, *35*(9), 793–802. https://doi.org/10.1016/S0005-7967(97)00040-5

Radomsky, A. S., Coughtrey, A., Shafran, R., & Rachman, S. (2018). Abnormal and normal mental contamination. *Journal of Obsessive-Compulsive and Related Disorders*, *17*, 46–51. https://doi.org/10.1016/j.jocrd.2017.08.011

Radomsky, A. S., Dugas, M. J., Alcolado, G. M., & Lavoie, S. L. (2014). When more is less: Doubt, repetition, memory, metamemory, and compulsive checking in OCD. *Behaviour Research and Therapy*, *59*, 30–39. https://doi.org/10.1016/j.brat.2014.05.008

Rajendram, R., Kronenberg, S., Burton, C. L., & Arnold, P. D. (2017). Glutamate genetics in obsessive-compulsive disorder: A review. *Journal of the Canadian Academy of Child and Adolescent Psychiatry*, *26*(3), 205.

Remmerswaal, K. C., Batelaan, N. M., Smit, J. H., van Oppen, P., & van Balkom, A. J. (2016). Quality of life and relationship satisfaction of patients with obsessive compulsive disorder. *Journal of Obsessive-Compulsive and Related Disorders*, *11*, 56–62. https://doi.org/10.1016/j.jocrd.2016.08.005

Ruscio, A. M., Stein, D. J., Chiu, W. T., & Kessler, R. C. (2010). The epidemiology of obsessive-compulsive disorder in the national comorbidity survey replication. *Molecular Psychiatry*, *15*(1), 53. https://doi.org/10.1038/mp.2008.94

Schwartz, J. M., & Beyette, B. (2016). *Brain lock: Free yourself from obsessive-compulsive behavior* (20th anniversary ed.). Harper Perennial.

Schwartzman, C. M., Boisseau, C. L., Sibrava, N. J., Mancebo, M. C., Eisen, J. L., & Rasmussen, S. A. (2017). Symptom subtype and quality of life in obsessive-compulsive disorder. *Psychiatry Research*, *249*, 307–310.

Selles, R. R., McGuire, J. F., Small, B. J., & Storch, E. A. (2016). A systematic review and meta-analysis of psychiatric treatments for excoriation (skin-picking) disorder. *General Hospital Psychiatry*, *41*, 29–37. https://doi.org/10.1016/j.genhosppsych.2016.04.001

Shapiro, F.. (2001). *Eye movement desensitization and reprocessing: Basic principles, protocols and procedures* (2nd ed.). Guilford Press.

Siev, J., Baer, L., & Minichiello, W. E. (2011). Obsessive-compulsive disorder with predominantly scrupulous symptoms: Clinical and religious characteristics. *Journal of Clinical Psychology*, *67*(12), 1188–1196. https://doi.org/10.1002/jclp.20843

Speisman, B. B., Storch, E. A., & Abramowitz, J. S. (2011). Postpartum obsessive-compulsive disorder. *Journal of Obstetric, Gynecologic, & Neonatal Nursing*, *40*(6), 680–690. https://doi.org/10.1111/j.1552-6909.2011.01294.x

Storch, E. A., Geffken, G. R., Merlo, L. J., Jacob, M. L., Murphy, T. K., Goodman, W. K., Larson, M. J., Fernandez, M., & Grabill, K. (2007). Family accommodation in pediatric obsessive–compulsive disorder. *Journal of Clinical Child and Adolescent Psychology*, *36*(2), 207–216. https://doi.org/10.1080/15374410701277929

Swedo, S., & Williams, K. (2017). PANDAS as a post-streptococcal autoimmune neuropsychiatric form of OCD. In C. Pinter (Ed.), *Obsessive-compulsive disorder: Phenomenology, pathophysiology, and treatment* (pp. 311–320). Oxford University Press.

Toh, W. L., Castle, D. J., & Rossell, S. L. (2017). Characterisation of Body Dysmorphic Disorder (BDD) versus Obsessive-Compulsive Disorder (OCD): In light of the current DSM-5 nosology. *Journal of Obsessive-Compulsive and Related Disorders*, *12*, 117–126. https://doi.org/10.1016/j.jocrd.2017.01.002

Tolin, D., Steketee, G., Gray, K., & Fitch, K. (2008). The economic and social burden of compulsive hoarding. *Psychiatry Research*, *160*, 200–211. https://doi.org/10.1016/j.psychres.2007.08.008

Tolin, D., Wohunsky, P., & Maltby, N. (2004). Sympathetic magic in contamination-related OCD. *Journal of Behavior Therapy and Experimental Psychiatry*, *35*(2), 193–205. https://doi.org/10.1016/j.jbtep.2004.04.009

van Grootheest, D. S., Cath, D. C., Beekman, A. T., & Boomsma, D. I. (2005). Twin studies on obsessive–compulsive disorder: A review. *Twin Research and Human Genetics*, *8*(5), 450–458. https://doi.org/10.1375/twin.8.5.450

Vella-Zarb, R. A., Cohen, J. N., McCabe, R. E., & Rowa, K. (2017). Differentiating sexual thoughts in obsessive-compulsive disorder from paraphilias and nonparaphilic sexual disorders. *Cognitive and Behavioral Practice*, *24*, 342–352. https://doi.org/10.1016/j.cbpra.2016.06.007

Weingarden, H., & Renshaw, K. D. (2015). Shame in the obsessive compulsive related disorders: A conceptual review. *Journal of Affective Disorders*, *171*, 74–84. https://doi.org/10.1016/j.jad.2014.09.010

Wetterneck, C. T., Little, T. E., Rinehart, K. L., Cervantes, M. E., Hyde, E., & Williams, M. (2012). Latinos with obsessive-compulsive disorder: Mental healthcare utilization and inclusion in clinical trials. *Journal of Obsessive-Compulsive and Related Disorders*, *1*(2), 85–97. https://doi.org/10.1016/j.jocrd.2011.12.001

Wilhelm, S., Berman, N. C., Keshaviah, A., Schwartz, R., & Steketee, G. (2015). Mechanisms of change in cognitive therapy for obsessive compulsive disorder: Role of maladaptive beliefs and schemas. *Behavioral Research & Therapy*, *65*, 5–10. https://doi.org/10.1016/j.brat.2014.12.006

Williams, M., Farris, S., Turkeimer, E., Franklin, M., Simpson, H. B., Liebowitz, M., & Foa, E. B. (2014). The impact of symptom dimensions on outcome for exposure and ritual prevention therapy in obsessive-compulsive disorder. *Journal of Anxiety Disorders*, *28*(6), 553–558. https://doi.org/10.1016/j.janxdis.2014.06.001

Williams, M., & Jahn, M. (2017). Obsessive–compulsive disorder in African American children and adolescents: Risks, resiliency, and barriers to treatment. *American Journal of Orthopsychiatry*, *87*(3), 291–303. https://doi.org/10.1037/ort0000188

Williams, M. T., Proetto, D., Casiano, D., & Franklin, M. E. (2012). Recruitment of a hidden population: African Americans with obsessive–compulsive disorder. *Contemporary Clinical Trials*, *33*(1), 67–75. https://doi.org/10.1016/j.cct.2011.09.001

Zambaldi, C. F., Cantilino, A., Montenegro, A. C., Paes, J. A., de Albuquerque, T. L. C., & Sougey, E. B. (2009). Postpartum obsessive-compulsive disorder: Prevalence and clinical characteristics. *Comprehensive Psychiatry*, *50*(6), 503–509. https://doi.org/10.1016/j.comppsych.2008.11.014

10 Sleep-Wake Disorders

Most of us are familiar with cycles in which we stay up late and rise early in order to meet some outside demand, if not in our lives now, then at some point in the past. The all-nighter, fueled by caffeine, anxiety and the blue light of computer screens are all but ubiquitous for high school, college and graduate students as well as for over-worked adults in the United States. However, these all-nighters are primarily driven by choice, fueled by some outside press or urgency. In these situations, a person chooses to stay up and study or work to meet tight deadlines, foregoing needed sleep in exchange for some other reward. For people experiencing insomnia and other sleep disorders, however, the night may stretch out in front of them like a desert, suspended in exhaustion and reaching for sleep that seems always just out of reach.

Often, the presence of disruptions to sleep can be readily identified when talking with clients. Still, students and seasoned clinicians alike find it difficult to parse out the unique etiology of an individual client's sleep disruption. It is often unclear when to make a sleep disorder diagnosis and when to refrain. Similarly, it can be challenging to decide where sleep should fall when prioritizing and treating presenting concerns. Diagnosis of sleep disorders is made more complex by the sheer number of mental health disorders that can include disruptions in healthy sleep patterns (APA, 2013; Dolsen et al., 2014). Likewise, a wide range of medical disorders have been documented to impede a person's ability to get good sleep, as do a number of common medications and substances (APA, 2013; Bos & Macedo, 2019; Spiegelhalder et al., 2019). Similarly, as most of us can attest, disrupted sleep amplifies other difficulties in our lives by sapping needed energy and concentration, taxing patience and relational capacities. This chapter will offer a brief overview of the sleep-wake disorders, focusing on those diagnosed in the therapy room (insomnia, nightmare disorder and circadian rhythm disorders [CRDs]). Also discussed in this chapter are the contributing factors to the sleep-wake disorders, focusing on insomnia; the chapter will also offer strategies for diagnosis. A differential diagnosis case is offered, as well as a sample treatment plan. At the end of this chapter, cases are offered for diagnosis.

Key Disorders of the Sleep-Wake Dimension

Circadian Rhythm Disorders. The CRDs are unique in that they feature a dysregulation of the biological sleep rhythm that leads a person to be out of sync with natural sleep patterns. Typically, sleep rhythms follow a predictable 24-hour cycle and as such are described as circadian rhythms. Circadian rhythms are encoded by clock genes and controlled by the hypothalamus and pituitary glands. The suprachiasmatic nucleus has come to be described as the brain's internal master clock. Ultimately, circadian rhythms dictate neurological, cellular and biochemical systems that mark the passing of time and signal the body to sleep (Faulkner et al., 2019).

The circadian rhythm family of sleep disorders arises when the client's natural sleep patterns run out of sync with the demands of work or social relationships. Typically, these disorders evidence themselves in clients who work at night, as with nurses or security guards (shift work type), but can also feature sleep patterns in which a person feels ready to sleep several hours before (advanced sleep phase type) or several hours after (delayed sleep phase type) conventional sleep expectations, leading to functional difficulties at work, school or in relationships (APA, 2013; Faulkner et al., 2019; Phelps, 2016).

The CRD Subtypes and Specifiers. The CRDs come with a complex array of specifiers. First, the DSM provides five primary subtypes, each carrying its own code, and are distinguished by the pattern of sleep: delay, irregular sleep, non-24-hour type and shift work type. Each of the subtypes can be specified with a familial pattern, when client history reveals this trait, and is then clarified with an episodic, persistent or recurrent pattern specifier (APA, 2013).

Nightmare Disorder. This sleep disorder features frequent disturbing dreams, generally with strong themes of threat to the person's life (APA, 2013; Germain & Nielsen, 2003; Gieselmann et al., 2019; Spiegelhalder et al., 2019; Swart et al., 2013). Somewhere in the neighborhood of 2%-5% of the general population experiences at least one nightmare a week, however, estimates place the prevalence of nightmare disorder at 1%-2% for the general population and as high as 39% among those being treated for serious mental health conditions (Swart et al., 2013). Research points to high rates of comorbid nightmare disorder among those with posttraumatic stress disorder (PTSD), depression and anxiety disorders (Swart et al., 2013), as well as among those with borderline personality disorder (Semiz et al., 2008; Swartet al., 2013). In those with dissociative disorders, concurrent nightmare disorder has been correlated with higher rates of self-harm and suicide attempts (Agargun et al., 2003). Both nightmare disorder and insomnia have been correlated with higher suicide risk generally (Nadorff et al., 2013) and specifically among military personnel with PTSD (Sullivan-Tibbs et al., 2019).

Insomnia. Sleeplessness or dissatisfaction with sleep is an experience that nearly every person will encounter at some point in their lives, but insomnia is only diagnosed when sleeplessness occurs at least three times a week for a period of no less than three months. Troublesome insomnia symptoms are estimated to affect 33% of the population (Dolsen et al., 2014), whereas diagnosable insomnia is thought to affect between 6% and 10% (APA, 2013). Comorbidity of insomnia and other mental health disorders hover between 41% and 53% (Dolsen et al., 2014). As many as 90% of older adults are thought to have insomnia that they describe as either moderate or severe (Brenes et al., 2009). Insomnia is comorbid with a wide range of mental disorders (see Table 10.01) and appears side by side with a long list of medical conditions (Table 10.02) (APA, 2013; Bos & Macedo, 2019; Spiegelhalder et al., 2019).

Bos and Macedo (2019) conducted an extensive review of the literature and found that the consequences of insomnia are significant and varied. They note that insomnia is associated with higher rates of tension headache (Ødegård et al., 2011 in Bos & Macedo, 2019), hypertension, heart attack (Fernandez-Mendoza et al., 2012 in Bos & Macedo, 2019) and increased mortality overall (Léger et al., 2012; Karlson et al., 2013 in Bos & Macedo, 2019). Insomnia has also been demonstrated to have consequences for cognition. Research reveals that insomnia is associated with impairments in working and episodic memory, as well as executive functioning (Fortier-Brochu et al., 2012, in Bos & Macedo, 2019).

Insomnia, Stress and Learning. Sleep has a two-fold role in learning. First, being rested facilitates focus, cognitive operations necessary for learning and organization. Second, sleep supports the consolidation of learning while we rest. Consequently, when we can't sleep we have both more difficulty understanding and more difficulty remembering what we learn. Problematic sleep has been documented to impair judgment and to cloud thinking (Fonseca & Genzel, 2020). A sizable range of learning impairments have been demonstrated; thank to sleep deprivation including verbal skills, abstract thinking and motor skills (Durmer & Dinges, 2005; Fonseca & Genzel, 2020). A "vicious cycle" (p. 54) of elevated stress hormones, glucocorticoids, causes sleeplessness and sleep deprivation, which then increases stress hormones (Sapolsky, 2017). When sleep does come, if stress levels remain high, the slow-wave restorative sleep cycles are reduced and the feeling of being rested will not be achieved. Because stress and sleep are so intricately tied, when sleep disturbance is present, it is essential to evaluate your client's stress levels and stress coping strategies, and to offer therapeutic support where needed.

Hypersomnia and Insomnia/Hyposomnia. Hypersomnia is not a codable disorder, but it is a term found in the DSM. It is listed among the criteria for major depressive episodes, within the persistent depressive disorder criteria table, and within the hypersomnolence disorder. Generally, hypersomnia is present when a client sleeps 10 or more hours per day yet still complains of not feeling rested. However, because the amount of sleep necessary varies from one person to the next, hypersomnia may be

TABLE 10.01 Health Concerns and Their Intersections with Sleep Disruption

Health Concern	Interference with Sleep
Asthma, chronic obstructive pulmonary disease (COPD), emphysema	Difficulty breathing; coughing; wheezing; medications that treat these illnesses can interfere with sleep
Cardiovascular disease	Irregular heart rhythms; fluid retention in the lungs; chest pain; fluctuations in circadian rhythms
Chronic pain (vast array of causes)	Interferes with ability to relax into sleep; night-time waking due to pain
Diabetes	Sugar fluctuations; night sweats; frequent urination
Enlarged prostate	Frequent need to urinate leads to sleep disruption
Gastroesophageal reflux disease (GERD)	Irritation of the esophagus when lying down
Hyperthyroidism	Over stimulation of the nervous system interferes with achieving sleep; night sweats
Hypothyroidism	Night sweats
Kidney disease	Unfiltered wastes induce insomnia; restless leg syndrome
Menopause	Night sweats; insomnia
Parkinson's disease	Nightmares: night-time jerking: restless leg syndrome
Sleep apnea	Difficulty breathing causes frequent waking

*Table compiled drawing from a wide range of sources including Sleep Foundation (2020b) https://www.sleepfoundation.org/insomnia/what-causes-insomnia

Source: https://www.sleepfoundation.org

considered when the client is sleeping 2 or more hours more than is typical each day without achieving a feeling of being rested (Phelps, 2016; Quitkin, 2002).

Sleep Disturbance as Symptom or Side Effect of a Medical Disorder or Its Treatment. The etiology of sleep disruptions and the patterns of interruption in sleep varies a great deal from one client to the next. Sleep disorders can arise either directly from the mechanism of a medical disorder, as with cardiovascular disease (which can interfere with circadian rhythms), or may be due to the symptoms of a medical disorder, as with coughing, wheezing and struggling to breathe in asthma, which in turn creates difficulties in either getting to sleep or maintaining sleep through the night (Sleep Foundation, 2020a). Additionally, sleep may be disrupted by the side effects of medications that treat a medical or mental health concern. For example, steroids used to treat asthma may cause wakefulness.

Again, a sizable number of the dimensions described in the DSM 5 feature disrupted sleep, most notably autism, depression, bipolarity, PTSD and anxiety, which will be discussed very briefly here. The overlapping symptoms and the frequent

BOX 10.01 KEY TERMS: SLEEP DISORDERS

Circadian Rhythm. In each 24-hour cycle, the body experiences natural changes in physical, mental and behavioral changes, known as circadian rhythms. Chief among these circadian cycles are sleep patterns. Two key influencers of circadian rhythms are the cycles of light and dark and the suprachiasmatic nucleus of the brain (Faulkner et al., 2019; Phelps, 2016).

Dream Anxiety. This term is sometimes used as a synonym for nightmare disorder, and features frequent, disturbing dreams with themes of threat to life or safety.

Drift. A phenomenon in which a person's sleep onset gradually "drifts" to a later and later point in the night.

Hypersomnia. This term refers to a pattern in which more sleep is required than is typical for the individual, and the extra sleep is not experienced as establishing a feeling of being rested.

Insomnia. This disorder describes difficulties falling asleep, staying asleep or waking early, that then cause disturbances in well-being.

Rapid Eye Movement (REM). These periods of sleep feature high brain activity and dreaming. During this time, the heart rate increases and movement, such as rapid eye movement, can be seen (Sun & Tan, 2019).

Shift Work. Shift work describes work that takes place at unconventional times of the day, as with hospital, security and cleaning staff who work during the night (Faulkner et al., 2019).

Sleep Hygiene. Sleep hygiene describes the basic practices necessary in order to get a good night's sleep (Sleep Foundation, 2020b).

Slow-Wave Sleep. This cycle of sleep is responsible for restoration and renewal. This cycle of sleep is dreamless and features a higher proportion of delta waves than other periods of the sleep cycle (Sun & Tan, 2019).

Zeitgebers (time giver): Social cues that support biological cycles, such as arriving at work at 8:30 each morning (Ehlers et al., 1993).

Zeitstorers (time disturber): Events that disrupt regular circadian cycles, such as irregular shift work (Ehlers et al., 1993). Sleep Disturbance and its Intimate Relationship with Mental Health Disorders

comorbidity of sleep disorders with other mental health concerns complicates the diagnostic process considerably (Dolsen et al., 2014).

Autism Spectrum Disorders and Sleep Disturbances. Parents of children with autism frequently express concerns about their children's sleep (Attwood, 2001; Katz, 2014). A comprehensive review of sleep in those with autism, conducted by Deliens et al. (2015), revealed that sleep difficulties tend to appear early in life, before age 2, and persist into adulthood. Sleep disturbance in autism, they found, is likely the result of the intersection of genetic predisposition, epigenetics and their interaction with the individual's social, psychological and environmental context, making sleep issues especially complex to address. Their review of the literature revealed that more significant sleep disturbances served to exacerbate symptoms, leading to greater difficulties with social communication, diminished emotion regulation capacities and poorer adaptive functioning. Identification and treatment of sleep disturbance should be prioritized when addressing the needs of persons with ASD.

Mood Disorders. Sleep disturbance is so deeply intertwined with the experiences of unipolar and bipolar mood disorders that it is listed among the criteria in both the manic and major depressive episodes (APA, 2013). Sleep disruption is particularly impactful for clients with bipolar disorder. Volumes of research link the disruption of circadian rhythms, particularly in sleep, to cycles of mood. Researchers have found a bidirectional relationship between circadian rhythms and the bipolar continuum that link presentations to different genetic markers. Stabilizing sleep is an essential step in the effective treatment of the bipolar disorders, and the prevention or reduction of manic mood episodes (Asarnow et al., 2014; Meloet al., 2017; Phelps, 2016).

Sleep is also a key factor in the development of depression and is a prominent symptom of the depressive episode. Baglioni et al. (2011) conducted an extensive meta-analysis of the available research and found that clients with insomnia but no depression were twice as likely to develop depression than those without insomnia. This relationship appears to be true across the life span. For example, sleep disturbance is widely documented among children and adolescents with depression (Tolêdo et al., 2020). Disruptions in sleep during and after pregnancy have long been understood to be a natural consequence of this stage of life, however, recent research suggests that the disruption in sleep may have a causal link to the onset of postpartum depression, highlighting the bidirectional relationship between sleep and this disorder (Okun, 2016). Similarly, far from being a trivial and inevitable aspect of aging, sleep disturbance among the elderly is the best predictor of future depression, higher than disability, living alone and being unmarried (Livingston et al., 1993).

Suicidality, Sleep and Mood. The link between suicidality and sleep disturbance is widely researched and documented, both for insomnia and nightmare disorder. Insomnia increases suicidal thoughts, attempts and the rate of death by suicide. Consequently, screening for insomnia and treatment must be prioritized (Bernert et al., 2015). Clients with a unipolar or bipolar mood disorder who also meet full criteria for a sleep disorder should receive an additional diagnosis for the sleep disorder if it appears that the difficulties with sleep are present even when the client is not experiencing a mood episode, or when it seems that the sleep-related symptoms will not resolve without independent treatment.

Insomnia that is a primary issue may differ from insomnia that is secondary to depression, according to Sun and Tan (2019). Their research revealed that rapid eye movement (REM) sleep is increased when insomnia and depression occur together, though the same did not appear to be true of insomnia and anxiety. Recommending a sleep study for depressed clients who suffer from insomnia may help to clarify the source of client sleep issues.

Anxiety, Generalized Anxiety Disorder and Insomnia. Insomnia is also a common complaint among those diagnosed with GAD across all age groups and seems most strongly correlated with the severity of generalized anxiety disorder (GAD) symptoms

(Ferre Navarrete et al., 2017). Children diagnosed with GAD display high rates of sleep disturbance, between 42% and 66% (Chorney et al., 2008). In fact, among children with anxiety disorders generally, 88% complain of sleep disturbances, disturbances that frequently do not resolve once the anxiety disorder is treated (Chorney et al., 2008). An extensive review of the literature, conducted by Tolêdo et al. (2020), found that the relationship between sleep disruption, and insomnia in particular, with adolescent anxiety was bidirectional, again highlighting the importance of giving priority to treating insomnia. In their study of elderly participants with GAD alone and GAD comorbid with depression, Brenes et al. (2009) found that both groups had much higher rates of insomnia than middle-aged counterparts.

Covid-19 and Insomnia, Initial Reports. Though limited research is available at this writing, the event of the Covid-19 pandemic appears to be having a significant impact on the mental health and well-being of Americans and people across the globe. For example, Pappa et al. (2020) have documented the impact of Covid-19 among healthcare workers and found that 40% described experiencing insomnia, while, only 20% reported depression or anxiety.

PTSD. Sleep disturbance is listed among the recurring symptoms in criteria for acute stress disorder and for PTSD (APA, 2013), and constitutes a burdensome symptom of the disorder. While for some, disruptions in sleep, both nightmares and insomnia, diminish over time, for many these become the source of ongoing suffering (APA, 2013; Harvey et al., 2003). Children suffering from PTSD following experiences of childhood sexual abuse report difficulties getting to sleep and struggling to stay asleep (Chorney et al., 2008). Similarly, among veterans with PTSD, as many as 44% have complaints about initiating sleep, contrasted with 91% of veterans with PTSD who described not being able to stay asleep once sleep was achieved (Harvey et al., 2003).

Frequent disturbing nightmares are also problematic for those with PTSD. A literature review of the content of PTSD dreams suggests that initially more than half of these dreams may be near exact replications of the traumatizing incident, which then change into dreams similar to the event, and then to dreams of threat with little resemblance to the triggering event. This is certainly not the case in all situations, however (Harvey et al., 2003). It bears repeating that, as with mood disorders, the influence of sleep disturbance on suicidality is considerable and should be a priority in the treatment of PTSD (Harvey et al., 2003; Sullivan-Tibbs et al., 2019).

Substance Use and Its Relationship to Sleep Disturbance. Whatever the cause of the initial sleep disruption or the way in which the fractured sleep presents, it is clear that adequate sleep is absolutely essential to our well-being. Without good sleep, our cognitive abilities quickly decline, memory and judgment are impacted. As we have seen, people who don't get enough sleep are given to depression and anxiety, all of which may lead to the misuse of substances in an effort to either achieve good sleep or to deal with the side effects of sleeplessness, again illustrating the bidirectional nature of sleep disorders and other mental health concerns (Manber & Carney, 2015). For example,

TABLE 10.02 Sleep-Wake Disorders and Their Intersection with Other Mental Health Disorders*

Diagnosis	Criteria, Associated Features and Comorbidity
	Neurodevelopmental Disorders
Autism spectrum disorder	*Comorbidity:* Medical conditions, including sleep problems, are commonly associated with ASD (p. 59)
	Schizophrenia Spectrum and Other Psychotic Disorders
Schizophrenia	*Associated Features:* Disrupted sleep pattern (p. 101)
	Bipolar and Related Disorders
Bipolar and related disorders: Manic and hypomanic episodes	*Criteria B2:* Decreased need for sleep (feels rested after only 3 hours of sleep) (p. 124)
Bipolar and related disorders: Major depressive episode	*Criteria A4:* Insomnia or hypersomnia nearly every day (p. 125)
	Depressive Disorders
Major depressive disorder	*Criteria A4:* Insomnia or hypersomnia nearly every day (p. 160)
Persistent depressive disorder (dysthymia)	*Criteria B2:* Insomnia or hypersomnia (p. 168)
Premenstrual dysphoric disorder	*Criteria C5:* Hypersomnia or insomnia (p.172)
Specifiers for depressive disorders: With melancholic features	*Criteria B3:* Early-morning awakening (i.e., at least 2 hours before usual awakening) (p. 185)
	Anxiety Disorders
Separation anxiety disorder	*Criteria A6:* Persistent reluctance or refusal to sleep away from home or to go to sleep without being near a major attachment figure (p. 191)
Panic disorder	*Associated features:* Waking from nocturnal panic attacks (p. 210)
Panic attack specifier	*Associated features:* Nocturnal panic attacks (p. 215)
Generalized anxiety disorder	*Criteria C6:* Sleep disturbance (difficulty falling or staying asleep, or restless, unsatisfying sleep) (p. 223)
Panic disorder	*Associated features:* Waking from nocturnal panic attacks (p. 210)
	Trauma- and Stressor-Related Disorders
Posttraumatic stress disorder	*Criteria E6:* Sleep disturbances (i.e., difficulty falling asleep or staying asleep or restless sleep) (p. 272)
Posttraumatic stress disorder for children 6 years and younger	*Criteria D5:* Sleep disturbances (i.e., difficulty falling asleep or staying asleep or restless sleep) (p. 272)

Diagnosis	Criteria, Associated Features and Comorbidity
Acute stress disorder	*Criteria:* Arousal symptoms: 10. Sleep disturbance (i.e., difficulty falling asleep or staying asleep or restless sleep) (p. 281)
	Dissociative Disorders
Dissociative identity disorder	*Comorbidity:* Highly comorbid with sleep disorders (p. 298)
	Feeding and Eating Disorders
Anorexia nervosa	*Associated features:* Seriously underweight individuals may show depressive symptoms, including insomnia (p. 341)
	Elimination Disorders
Enuresis	*Comorbidity:* Sleep-walking or sleep terror disorder may be present (p. 357)
	Substance Use Disorders
Alcohol use disorder	*Associated features:* Insomnia frequently accompanies and sometimes precedes heavy drinking (p. 492)
Caffeine intoxication	*Criteria B4:* Insomnia (p. 504) and *Comorbidity:* Is associated with sleep disorders (p. 506)
Cannabis use disorder	*Associated features:* Individuals often report it is used to help cope with sleep and other disorders (p. 512)
Cannabis withdrawal	*Criteria B3:* Sleep difficulty (e.g., insomnia, disturbing dreams) (p. 518)
Opioid use disorder	*Comorbidity:* Insomnia is common, especially during withdrawal (p. 546)
Opioid withdrawal	*Criteria B9:* Insomnia (p. 548)
Sedative, hypnotic or anxiolytic withdrawal	*Criteria B3:* Insomnia (p. 558)
Stimulant use disorder	May arise in those attempting to balance the sedative effects of medications used in treating sleep disruption and other concerns (p. 566)
Stimulant withdrawal	*Criteria B3:* Insomnia or hypersomnia (p. 569)
Tobacco use disorder	*Associated features:* Waking at night to smoke (p. 573)
Tobacco withdrawal (p.575)	*Criteria B7:* Insomnia (p. 575) and *Associated features:* Abstinence can increase dreaming and nightmares

Diagnosis	Criteria, Associated Features and Comorbidity
	Neurocognitive Disorders
Delirium	*Associated features:* Delirium is often associated with a disturbance in the sleep-wake cycle. Sleep-wake concerns are common with delirium and have been proposed as a core criteria for Dx (p. 600)
Major or mild neurocognitive disorder due to traumatic brain injury	*Associated features:* May be accompanied by physical disturbances, including sleep disorders (p. 625)
Substance/medication-induced major or mild neurocognitive disorder	*Associated feature:* Intermediate-duration neurocognitive disorders (NCD) induced by drugs can cause various kinds of sleep disturbance (p. 630)
Major or mild neurocognitive disorder due to Parkinson's disease	*Associated Features:* Frequently present features include rapid eye movement, sleep behavior disorder and excessive daytime sleepiness (p. 636)

Source: Adapted from American Psychiatric Association (2013).

substance use can trigger insomnia that may then lead to the use of substances to help bring on sleep (Manber & Carney, 2015; Provencher et al., 2020), feeding an endless cycle.

The following table illustrates the intersections between sleep-wake disorders and other mental health disorders described in the DSM 5.

Diagnostic Discernment: When to Diagnose a Sleep Disorder. A further complication in the decision to diagnose a sleep disorder, particularly insomnia, arises out of confusing instructions within the text of the DSM 5 itself. For example, when reviewing the F-H exclusion criteria for insomnia disorder (p. 362), you will note that the table excludes diagnosis when the sleep difficulty occurs as a direct result of another sleep-wake disorder, as a result of a substance, a mental disorder or medical condition. This seems clear enough until we read further. The note following the criteria table states, "The diagnosis of insomnia is given whether it occurs as an independent condition or is comorbid with another mental disorder . . . in the presence of insomnia and a comorbid disorder it is not necessary to make a causal attribution between the two conditions" (p. 363). This statement seems to contradict H criteria, which requires the clinician to consider the connection between the insomnia and a medical or mental disorder and to exclude diagnosis if there is a causal relationship. Further, the DSM notes that insomnia is comorbid with a number of medical, mental and substance use disorders (p. 368) implying that insomnia can be diagnosed when these other disorders are present. Ultimately, however, the APA advises, "A concurrent insomnia diagnosis should only be considered when the insomnia is sufficiently severe to warrant independent clinical attention, otherwise, no separate diagnosis is necessary" (p. 363 of the DSM 5).

BOX 10.02 GUIDING QUESTIONS FOR COMORBID OR CO-OCCURRING SLEEP DISORDERS:

The following questions may help to guide you when faced with a decision about diagnosing insomnia that is comorbid or co-occurring:

Do your client's sleep symptoms meet definitional, impairment and duration criteria for a sleep disorder? If so, also ask:

1. Are your client's symptoms unlikely to resolve without focused intervention?
2. Have your client's sleep difficulties continued despite treatment of the comorbid/primary mental health or medical diagnosis and seems to require separate intervention?
3. Did your client's sleep difficulty precede symptoms of your client's primary diagnosis?
4. Do the sleep disruptions continue between cycles of your client's primary diagnosis (for instance, between major depressive episodes)?
5. Are your client's sleep symptoms primary or a very high priority for your client? (Are your client's sleep symptoms the reason for your client's visit, for example?)

If the answer to any of these questions is affirmative, a diagnosis of insomnia is likely warranted.

Source: Adapted from American Psychiatric Association and Morrison, J. (2014).

Please note that the DSM 5 includes a number of sleep-wake disorders that are diagnosed following assessment by qualified physicians, such as restless leg syndrome and sleep apnea. Clients who have not spoken with a doctor recently about sleep disturbance, who do not respond to interventions after appropriate time and effort have been given, or for whom it is unclear what may be causing sleep difficulties, should be referred to their primary care physician to rule out medical causes or to a physician who specializes in sleep disorders. Breathing-related difficulties and most parasomnia sleep disorders have been excluded from the pivot points table below and from the cases in the sleep disorders since they are not diagnosed by mental health professionals.

Treating Sleep-Wake Disorders

Cognitive Behavioral Therapy for Insomnia. Cognitive behavioral therapy for insomnia (CBT-I) is a common and evidenced-based approach used with clients suffering with insomnia, which includes psychoeducation and tools designed to reshape behavior in

BOX 10.03 CONSIDER THIS: REFLECTING ON YOUR OWN SLEEP HYGIENE.

How are you caring for your sleep during your time as a student? What opportunities might there be for improving the quality of your sleep?

Creating a Regular Schedule

1. Can you create a regular sleep schedule for getting to bed and getting up in the morning?
2. Can you avoid using your bed for doing work, reading or spending time on the computer?

Incorporating Exercise or Meditation

1. Are you able to include 10 minutes of aerobic exercise before going to bed, such as walking or cycling (avoid heavy workouts)?
2. Are you able to include yoga or meditation as part of your evening routine?(Harvey & Buysse, 2017; Sleep Foundation, 2020b)

Setting Limits

1. Can you limit your screen time so that you are not working with screens for 2 hours before you go to sleep?
2. Can you limit daytime napping to no more than 20-30 minutes?
3. Can you limit caffeine, nicotine, alcohol and other substances in the late afternoon and evening?
4. Can you limit heavy and rich foods that can cause heartburn that might disrupt your sleep? (Harvey & Buysse, 2017; Sleep Foundation, 2020b)

Setting the Stage for Restful Sleep

1. Are your pillows and mattress comfortable?
2. Can you limit sources of light in your bedroom?
3. Can you leave your phone and other screens outside the bedroom while you sleep?
4. Are you able to control the temperature in your bedroom (between 60 and 67 degrees) (Harvey & Buysse, 2017; Sleep Foundation, 2020b)

Source: https://www.sleepfoundation.org

order to encourage sleep as well as approaches and strategies for maintaining sleep. A recent study of 301 participants with comorbid depression demonstrated reductions in insomnia severity after seven sessions as well as demonstrating reductions in symptoms of depression, both in the high- and low-depression groups (Manber et al., 2014). A number of techniques including sleep restriction therapy, a form of induced sleep deprivation, are used as a part of CBT-I (Perlis et al., 2008). Perhaps the gold-standard intervention in CBT-I is stimulus control, or the reduction of anxiety that arises around attempting to get to sleep. Stimulus control interventions include both relaxation techniques as well as teaching clients to associate the bed and bedroom

BOX 10.04 TRY THIS: CONSIDERATIONS FOR BIRGITTA'S DIAGNOSIS

1. As you read through Birgitta's story, what possible sources of sleeplessness do you note?
2. Given the information you have here, which diagnoses might you consider to describe her difficulties?
3. Which diagnosis would you prioritize and why?
4. What questions do you have for Birgitta that might clarify your diagnosis or diagnoses?
5. If you were to have a release of information, what clarifications might her doctor be able to bring to the diagnosis of her sleep difficulties?

with sleeping and to avoid using the bedroom for activities that discourage sleep, such as studying, reading or watching movies (Perlis et al., 2010).

Sleep Hygiene and Psychoeducation. The treatment of a client's sleep disturbance is generally crafted using the clinician's best understanding of the cause or causes of the disruption. Whatever the cause, however, most clients can benefit from education about sleep hygiene or sleep practices. Sleep hygiene are the essential practices necessary to getting a good night's sleep, which include, for example, limiting naps, reducing caffeine and nicotine before bedtime, using alcohol with moderation and limiting evening screen time (Sleep Foundation, 2020b). Together, the client and clinician can map the client's own patterns that contribute to disturbed sleep and determine which habits the client may be willing to shift. Changes in habits related to screen time, for example, may be difficult for some clients to embrace despite a real desire to get good sleep and to feel rested throughout the day.

Relaxation Techniques. Clinicians also make use of a variety of therapeutic interventions that are aimed at teaching relaxation before going to sleep, which can be especially effective with anxious clients. These techniques include, but are not exclusive to, diaphragmatic breathing, progressive muscle relaxation, meditation and yoga, each with different levels of efficacy (Emet, 2012; Gamaldo, 2017).

Pharmacological Approaches. CBT is considered the gold standard of sleep disorder treatment, however, when therapy is not available or is ineffective on its own, medications are frequently prescribed. Because of the high comorbidity rates, including substance abuse disorders, and the complicated interaction between pharmacological agents and the unique neurobiology of the individual, finding the right medication for each person can be challenging (Frase et al., 2018). While benzodiazepines are the most commonly prescribed medications for sleep disorders, they come with a large number of side effects. Further, the effects of these drugs seem to last only as long as the drug is taken. Some research seems to suggest that medications, such as trazodone, mirtazapine, and so on, may help to support better sleep while also treating comorbid mental health concerns (Atkin et al., 2018). The topic of pharmacology and the treatment of sleep disorders is vast, a detailed exploration of which is, unfortunately, outside the scope of this chapter.

Differential Diagnosis of Insomnia: Birgitta

Sleep disruptions that are uncomplicated by other mental or physical health concerns are the exception rather than the rule. The following case provides an opportunity to practice your developing skills in discerning more complex diagnoses that feature sleep disruption prominently. When reading Birgitta's case below, draw upon the diagnostic principles and recommendations from this chapter to arrive at your best clinical judgment in diagnosing this case. The questions below will help guide your diagnostic process. You may also want to make a list of additional questions you have and how your answers to those questions would influence a more confident diagnosis.

Birgitta

Birgitta, a 55-year-old night nurse in the ICU of a busy city hospital, is in counseling for the first time in 15 years. "I have to be honest," she shares, "I did not expect to ever need counseling again. I thought I had left the depression behind me a long, long time ago. But I find myself back in a place where I am sad and angry all the time." Birgitta explains, "I started to notice a slide back into depression about a year ago when I had to take the night shift because of a nursing shortage at the hospital. I started working four nights on and four nights off. It was supposed to be temporary but it wasn't. I felt betrayed by management because I had seniority and they gave me a promotion to a lead nurse position but when there was a need for a lead nurse at night, that was where I got put. So it feels like a demotion, which sucks because I've given the hospital so much." Birgitta further explains, "Now I'm always sleepy and just never feel rested. But as badly as I need sleep, I have the hardest time nodding off, between my hot flashes, feeling guilty for no discernable reason and my frustration with feeling stuck, I just can't get to sleep. I lay in bed for hours watching the clock and wishing I could get to sleep."

"I've also put on about 15 pounds this year and 10 the year before, so I don't even recognize myself when I look in the mirror—and I don't have time for exercise. My sister says that I should just expect weight gain, after all I'm in menopause now, and I know she's right, I'm a nurse after all. But knowing doesn't make it easier. I feel so guilty and gross when I look at how my body is changing and knowing I'm not taking care of my health. Everything seems off kilter now and has for a while. It's so hard to have a good balance in my life. I just can't stay in touch with friends and see my daughters, make it to Mass on Sunday, and keep up with the house when I'm working nights at the hospital. The confidence of my late 40s and early 50s is disappearing into a far-off memory."

Birgitta reports that she had her last physical 2 years ago. At that time, her doctor prescribed medication for hypothyroid, synthroid. She has remained on this dose for the last 2 years. Birgitta describes drinking "three or four 16 oz diet colas" while working, and at least three on her off-days. She frequently ends her day with "one or two glasses of red wine."

Birgitta's Treatment Plan

Below you will find a sample treatment plan for Birgitta, the case described in the differential diagnosis section of this chapter. As discussed earlier, quite a few factors in Birgitta's life are likely contributing to her sleeplessness. These contributing factors, such as her shift work and aggravation related to her transfer, a consumption of a great deal of caffeine and the onset of menopause all complicate the process of developing a clear diagnosis, however, each contributing factor helps to form the building blocks in the development of a comprehensive treatment plan.

In developing this treatment plan, Birgitta's counselor, Max, is working collaboratively with her to formulate goals for their work together. In his initial meeting with Birgitta, Max has developed a picture of the contributing factors that may be disrupting her sleep and together they have agreed that, though she is a nurse and holds a lot of knowledge about sleep and its contribution to health, they will make the fastest progress if they begin by reviewing basic information about sleep hygiene and identifying key changes that Birgitta would be willing to make. Together they have agreed that Birgitta would benefit from strategies that can be used before going to sleep, including meditation-based relaxation techniques. Finally, Birgitta and Max agreed that stressors that contribute to frustration and anxiety are likely contributing to her sleep disruption and that these frustrations should be explored in therapy. However, Max has not yet formed a hypothesis for how life stressors are connected to Birgitta's sleep (for instance, has she developed unreasonable expectations that cause excessive worry? Is she experiencing existential concerns related to menopause and aging? Something else entirely?) You will notice that he has kept his final goal broad with an intention to clarify it as therapy progresses. Finally, Birgitta and Max agree that given her shift work, there may be some limits to how much she will be able to improve her sleep, at least in the short term. Consequently, they have set "good enough for now" measures for sleep. What follows is the treatment plan Max has developed in collaboration with Birgitta.

TABLE 10.03 Sleep-Wake Disorders Pivot Points

Pivot Points: Sleep-Wake Disorders*	Consider
Pivot Point One: Does your client's suffering arise from difficulties falling asleep or staying asleep at night?	Insomnia disorder**
• Has your client's inability to sleep lasted less than 3 months?	Other specified insomnia disorder, brief insomnia disorder
• Are you unable to diagnose your client's impairing sleep deficits due to a lack of complete information?	Unspecified insomnia disorder
Pivot Point Two: Is your client's sleep disrupted by bad dreams or sleep walking?	
• Is your client experiencing very vivid and well-remembered nightmares?	Nightmare disorder
• Is your client frequently awoken, terrified, by dreams that are not well remembered?	Non-rapid eye movement sleep arousal disorder, sleep terrors
• Is your client's sleep marked with frequent episodes of sleep-walking?	Non-rapid eye movement sleep arousal disorder, sleep walking
Pivot Point Three: Does your client's suffering arise from excessive sleepiness even while getting 6-7 hours sleep at night?	Hypersomnolence disorder**
• Does your client's hypersomnolence fall short of the full criteria due to limited duration or another cause that you would like to document?	Specified hypersomnolence disorder (specify reason here)
• Are you unable to fully justify a diagnosis of hypersomnolence due to a lack of information?	Unspecified hypersomnolence disorder
Pivot Point Four: Is your client's primary sleep symptom limited to the inability to find restoration from sleep?	Other specified insomnia disorder, restricted to non-restorative sleep
Pivot Point Five: Has your client taken any substance or medication that could influence sleep quality? (Including alcohol, caffeine, amphetamines, etc.)	Substance/ medication-induced sleep disorder
Pivot Point Six: Is your client's sleep cycle out of sync with typical sleep schedule expectations and, as a result, causes functional difficulties?	
• Is your client falling asleep and rising several hours *later* than conventional expectations?	Circadian rhythm sleep-wake, delayed sleep phase type
• Is your client falling asleep and rising several hours *earlier* than conventional expectations?	Circadian rhythm sleep-wake, advanced sleep phase type

Pivot Points: Sleep-Wake Disorders*	Consider
• Are your client's sleep-wake cycles both out of sync with conventional cycles and gradually shifting so the sleep and wake times are later and later?	Circadian rhythm sleep-wake, non-24-hour sleep-wake type
Pivot Point Seven: If your client's symptoms are characteristic of a sleep disorder, but does not meet full criteria for any of them and you would like to specify the reason, then consider this diagnosis.	Other specified sleep-wake disorder (indicate sleep disturbance and reason it does not meet criteria)
Pivot Point Eight: Is your client's difficulty characteristic of a sleep disorder but you are unable to justify a diagnosis due to a lack of information?	Unspecified sleep-wake disorder

*This pivot table does not reflect all DSM 5 sleep-wake disorders. Those traditionally diagnosed by a sleep medicine specialists are not included.
***Note:* As of October 1, 2015, the codes for insomnia and hypersomnolence have changed, always check the most recent DSM 5 supplement for coding and content changes to diagnostic criteria.

Birgitta: Treatment Plan

OG1: Within 20 weeks of therapy, Birgitta will report restorative sleep in 7 of 10 days as measured by client report.

SG1: Within 2 weeks of therapy, Birgitta will have made an appointment with her primary care physician for a checkup and will consult with her doctor about age-related shifts, such as thyroid changes, that may disrupt sleep, as measured by client report.

SG2: Within 3 weeks of counseling, Birgitta will understand and implement key components of sleep hygiene, as measured by client report and counselor observation.

SG3: Within 6 weeks of therapy, Birgitta will be able to make use of relaxation techniques and meditation for the support of restful sleep, as measured by client report.

SG4: Within 20 weeks of counseling, Birgitta will explore and begin to find resolution for life stressors that contribute to disrupted sleep, as measured by client report.

OG2: Within 3 weeks of the onset of counseling, Birgitta will understand, articulate and implement key components of sleep hygiene, such as the importance of routine, limiting evening screen time, the influences of substances on sleep, and so on, as measured by counselor observation and client report.

SG1: Within the first week of counseling, Birgitta will be able to name three components of sleep hygiene that she is willing to integrate into her nightly routine, for example, avoiding screen time 2 hours before going to bed, as measured by counselor observation.

SG2: Within the second week of counseling, Birgitta will report the use of the identified and integrated sleep hygiene strategies and their impact on sleep and will work with the counselor to fine-tune strategies as needed, as measured by counselor observation.

SG3: Within the third week of counseling, Birgitta will regularly implement key strategies of sleep hygiene and make final adjustments to her sleep hygiene regimen, as measured by client report.

OG3: Within 6 weeks of therapy, Birgitta will be able to make use of evening relaxation techniques for the purpose of supporting sleep, as measured by counselor observation and client report.

SG1: Within 4 weeks of counseling, Birgitta will have an understanding of the use of meditation-based relaxation techniques in the support of sleep, as supported by counselor observation.

SG2: Within 5 weeks of counseling, Birgitta will be able to make use of key mindfulness-based relaxation techniques with counselor support.

SG3: Within 6 weeks of counseling, Birgitta will make use of meditation-based relaxation techniques independently, as measured by client report.

OG4: Within 20 weeks of therapy, Birgitta will be able to describe the connection between life stressors and her sleep disruption and will be able to articulate and enact strategies for addressing these challenges, as measured by counselor observation and client report.

What additions or changes would you make to this treatment plan?

Definitional Cases

What follows are a series of brief cases that capture the distinguishing feature of key sleep-wake disorders. These cases can function as an avenue to test your basic understanding of the range of sleep-wake disorders in DSM 5. Answers to select definitional cases are found at the end of this chapter. The above pivot table may help to point you in the direction of one or more sleep-wake disorders when diagnosing your client.

Abby

Abby can't seem to get enough sleep. Though she generally sleeps for 8-9 hours a night, she finds herself so drowsy while at work that she often falls asleep at her desk. The problem has persisted for nearly 3 months. Abby has no mental or physical complaints and has no other sleep-related disorders.

Daniel

Daniel complains of early evening sleepiness and reports that he is already sleepy by 6:30 p.m. and is unable to stay awake beyond 8:30 at night. Daniel also describes waking naturally, by 4:30 or 5:00 a.m. and is unable to fall asleep again. His sleep schedule has caused a great deal of family conflict.

Leigh

While Leigh falls asleep quickly when she goes to bed, she often will awaken after only an hour or two and struggle to go back to sleep. Sometimes she is awake for several hours before falling asleep again. She estimates that this has been happening for about 7 weeks.

Abe

Abe has been waking three or four nights a week screaming. Panicked, heart racing and sweating from head to toe, Abe believes these incidents follow bad dreams, though he is unable to remember his dreams.

Gurkiran

Gurkiran has been struggling with a major depression. He also complains of difficulty with excessive sleepiness. He reports sleeping as many as 12-14 hours in a 24-hour period. Gurkiran believes that the excessive sleepiness is the factor that is most responsible for his inability to work.

Jefferson

Jefferson recently began taking Imitrex for migraine headaches. While the headaches have improved, he has found that he is much more fatigued than before. He often gets 10 hours of sleep, but still feels sleepy during the day.

Vanessa

Vanessa is a writer who works from home. She often works late into the night and sleeps late into the morning. Over the last 3 months, however, she has noticed that she is gradually falling asleep and waking later and later. While she once fell asleep around 1 a.m. and slept until 9 a.m., more recently it is closer to 3 a.m. before she falls asleep; she struggles to get out of bed before 11 a.m.

Jalen

Jalen is 16 years old and has been waking only to find himself out of bed and in another part of the house. On occasion his parents have heard him wandering through the house in the middle of the night and have struggled to wake him up.

Mason

Mason has struggled nearly every night for the past 18 months with sleep initiation. He has no other physical or mental health complaints.

Ruby

For the last several weeks, Ruby has been feeling very tired during the day. She reports struggling to wake in the morning and feeling excessively tired for several hours after waking. Ruby reports feeling more awake midday and late in the evening and generally doesn't feel ready for sleep until 2 a.m., even on nights when she tries to go to bed earlier.

Ava

Ava has struggled with persistent depressive disorder for 3 years. During that time, she has found it very difficult to both get to sleep and remain sleeping through the night.

Emil

Several nights a week, Emil will wake in the middle of the night from a vivid and intense dream in which he is unable to get away from someone who is trying to kill him. He wakes feeling very anxious and is unable to fall back to sleep.

Hank

Hank works the night shift as a clerk in a local convenience store and sleeps during the day. Hank complains of "constant sleepiness" and is struggling to be fully available to his family and still get needed sleep.

Cases in Sleep-Wake Disorders: Narrative Cases

In the following pages, you will find a number of cases in sleep-wake disorders for you to diagnose. As in the sleep-wake pivot points table, diagnoses that are typically made by sleep specialists are not included. However, you should find that you have enough information within these cases to apply specifiers and to write complete justifications for your diagnoses. All narrative cases provide information through the voice of the individual struggling with symptoms, much as you might hear it in the therapy room, rather than the technical reporting offered in case studies in other texts. Remember that while these cases were written to satisfy criteria for specific diagnoses, your reading of the case may find ambiguities or differences in interpreting statements of experience. Should you find the individual's descriptions leave ambiguities that make it difficult for you to be certain of your diagnosis or its specifiers, make a list of the follow-up questions that you would like to ask and describe how the answers to those questions would guide your diagnosis. The diagnosis for alternating cases are offered in the appendix, as are select justifications.

It may be helpful to note that occasionally readers interpret statements within these cases differently from one another and differently than the author intended. These differences in interpretation point first to the ambiguity in language and also to our own individual differences in interpretation, assigning meaning to what we read, and sometimes even in the reader's own experiences of similar symptoms. It is often useful to make use of these differences in interpretation to note their implications for diagnosis in discussions with others.

Timeo

Timeo, age 36, and his wife, Heloise, moved to the United States 18 months ago from a small town, Eze, in the south of France, into the bustling Boston suburb of Brookline, Massachusetts. It is a move that has come with complications and unexpected consequences to their marriage and to Timeo's health. Timeo has come to speak to a doctor about his sleep difficulty. "I am not sure this is a problem that I should talk to a doctor about but my wife has insisted! About a year and a half ago we moved here from a small quiet town to an apartment right off a busy street. I had problems sleeping right away. I was very sleepy in the early evening and wide awake before dawn. I attributed the problem to jet lag and the noise of the street—since the evenings were quiet back home. Heloise and I thought that if I went to sleep early for a week or so that my sleep would normalize and wouldn't be a problem anymore. But that is not what happened."

He continues, "I started to go to bed around 9 p.m., which was very early for me. I tried this bedtime with a noise machine to block sounds from the street but I still felt tired. So I tried going to sleep at 8:00 or 8:30, which is really very early, but it helped a lot. I felt more rested in the day, but I was also still waking at about 4:30 or so every morning and couldn't get back to sleep, so I would just get up and get some work done. This pattern continues today." Timeo explains further, "Except for being a bit inconvenient, this sleeping pattern was working for me for about a year, but we now have a daughter, Ava, who is 6 weeks old. I am so tired in the evening I can't stay up and help with her—I'm in bed sleeping leaving my wife awake and alone. She is getting so angry and feels isolated. I feel terrible about it too. I work all day and when I get home I only see her and the baby for a few hours before I can't stay awake any longer and have to go to bed. I really need help synchronizing my sleep with Heloise. Can you help me?"

Jolanda

Jolanda, age 26, has made an appointment with her doctor to share concerns about her sleep. Her doctor notes that she has dark circles under her eyes and seems fatigued. Jolanda explains, "Most of the time I sleep just fine, but for the past 4 months I have really struggled to get to sleep. I can't put my finger on any particular thing stressing me out. My husband is on his second deployment which makes me a single mom for a while, but right now he is in Japan so I know he is safe. He has been away for about a year, and I do miss him, but I'm not sure that is the problem. The girls and I did get to go see him at Christmas and it was a great trip. Anyway, I lay in bed most of the night and then I eventually drop off to sleep for a couple of hours around 2 a.m." In meeting with her doctor, Jolanda denies any other mental or physical health concerns. Jolanda's religious beliefs preclude any use of substances such as caffeine or alcohol. Her physical exam revealed no medical cause for her sleeplessness. Jolanda shares, "Let me tell you, I don't know how much longer I can go on like this. I feel like I'm stumbling through the day, barely able to function. I'm just so, so tired."

Trenton

Three months ago, Trenton, aged 30, a doctoral student in electrical engineering came to speak with his primary care physician with worries about sleep. At that time Trenton explained, "I should probably not be surprised that I am tired and falling asleep all the time. I am pursuing my doctorate and I work for a small firm during the week. The truth is, though, that I finished my coursework and my comps and I have been working steadily and pretty effectively on my dissertation, so I don't really feel too stressed or especially taxed by it. I get to bed at a pretty reasonable time, too. I usually want to watch the local news at ten but I'm wiped out by 9 o'clock and never get to see it. I sleep pretty soundly through the night and I don't have to get up until about 7 a.m. or so. So I'm not sure what's going on. But I feel pretty tired most of the day, so tired that I feel like I could crawl under my desk like that character on Seinfeld, George!"

During his exam, Trenton's doctor had noted that Trenton had a large yellow bruise on his forehead. Trenton explained, "I've been biking to work every day because I'm trying to drop a little weight. I know that I'm about 60 or 70 pounds too heavy. Well, like a giant goofball, I decided to ride without a helmet and about a week and a half ago I hit a bump and flew off my bike and hit my head. I think it knocked me out for a second or two. I was sure seeing stars anyway! I scraped my pride off the pavement and went to work. I probably should have seen a doctor about it but I figured I was ok. Come to think of it, that's about the time I started to feel so sleepy all the time. It's pretty bad, though, I feel tired all the time." Trenton's doctor explained, "Trenton, it looks to me like you've had a concussion from this fall."

Trenton has now returned for a follow-up exam. Although his bruises have healed, Trenton continues to complain of excessive sleepiness throughout the day nearly every day. What diagnosis should be given for his sleep disturbance?

Jennica

Prior to her adoption from China, Jennica lived in an orphanage. Jennica seemed to respond fairly well to the caregivers in there, but there wasn't a lot of one-on-one attention offered to her. The care wasn't neglectful, but it also wasn't adequate. Within a week or so of arriving at her adoptive home, she began screaming out in the night. Her father offers, "Initially we thought she was having simple nightmares, but now we're not so sure. When this happens, there is no way to comfort her. She's clearly asleep, but nothing we do seems to reach her." Her mother adds, "Jennica looks just terrified and she is soaking wet from sweat. It's like she's possessed." These events happen several times a week, generally before midnight. Her parents are distressed, unsure why it is happening or how to help her in these moments. "We had thought that after she got used to sleeping here the nightmares would stop, but it has been going on for nearly two months now. After about twenty minutes or so she'll wake a little and then allow us to help her back to sleep. Then in the morning she wakes up with a smile as if nothing happened. Language is still an issue for us, though she is learning English, so we can't be sure she understands our questions about her dreams but it does seem that she remembers nothing about them. Maybe that is a blessing in this all," her father shares.

Rebecca

Rebecca has been a regular patient at the Anytown Sleep Hygiene Clinic, where she has been treated for several years for a moderate obstructive sleep apnea. Three years ago, Rebecca began using a Continuous positive airway pressure (CPAP) machine to assure that she continues breathing steadily throughout the night. Rebecca shares, "The trouble is that after several years of using the CPAP, I still haven't gotten used to the stupid thing. It really is not very comfortable, I always know that it is there. And even though this machine is more quiet than some of the older models, it still makes noise. I've tried using a sound machine, but that just isn't doing anything but adding noise to the noise of the CPAP. But none of that would be too awful except that now things have gotten more serious in my relationship with my boyfriend and he has moved in. At night as I'm getting into bed, I put on the CPAP and I feel like Darth Vader. Seriously! I feel ridiculous, it's embarrassing with my boyfriend laying next to me and me with this stupid mask. I feel like I'm starring in a ridiculous comedy instead of a romance. And, I'm still a little afraid that it won't work and I will be jolted awake. So, I don't sleep well at all. I just lay in bed feeling alternately really stupid or kind of tense. It's like that almost every night and I'm really, really tired, so tired it is hard to focus at work and I think it makes me cranky, too."

Cristabel

Cristabel, a 36-year-old newly immigrated Salvadoran woman living in southern Florida, is visiting a local clinic because for the last 2 months she hasn't been feeling like herself. Her children, 17-year-old twins, recently went to live with their father in Texas and she is living alone for the first time. She works as a housekeeper in a local motel, but the work has been sporadic lately and she sometimes won't have work more than 2 or 3 days a week. She has thought about getting a second job, but has been feeling so tired during the day that it has been hard to look for work, let alone go and fill out any applications. She reports that she has always struggled with sleep and often will be awake for a stretch of time in the middle of the night. Recently though, she's so sleepy during the day that she has begun to take 4- to 5-hour naps. She shared, "I just can't seem to get enough sleep. I go to bed around 10 or 11 each night and then wake up after two or three hours and often can't get back to sleep until 4 or 5 in the morning. Then, when I don't have work, I often won't wake until 9 or 10 a.m. and feel ready for a nap again after lunch. It feels like all I do is sleep, and yet, I'm so tired all of the time. I know I need to find another job, but on the days I do work, I feel like I'm moving through sludge, it's all I can do to keep going."

Gina

Gina is a 65-year-old retired attorney who is specialized in water law in the mid-Western states of the United States. She is meeting with a counselor for the first time at the recommendation of her primary care physician. She shares, "I had a pretty busy practice for almost 30 years and I have really been enjoying my retirement. I have been living retirement to the fullest, gardening, traveling and enjoying my grandchildren. But for years I have been bothered by nightmares. These are awful, awful dreams, and flashes of them come to me throughout the day. Sometimes the images are so upsetting I have to go to the bathroom and splash my face with water and take some deep breaths. And I really thought that when the stress of my work was over and I was retired, that I wouldn't have these dreams anymore, but they have continued. If anything, they are worse than they were when I was working. I'm having terrible dreams at least three times a week." Gina continues, "Just as an example, I had a dream a few nights ago that I was having a picnic in a beautiful apple orchard with my youngest grandson. The sun was shining and we were laughing. Suddenly, he noticed a spot of blood on my shirt near my belly button. I unbuttoned the button of my blouse near the red spot and I saw a wound opening from within. It was gradually opening wider and wider. I was terrified! Then, as I looked more closely, I could see maggots eating away at my stomach. My organs began to pour out of the wound. But my grandson was still playing, the sun was in his hair and he started to sing 'Ring Around the Rosie' and then he put his little hand in the grass where my insides were pouring out. His hands were covered in my blood and maggots. When I woke up I thought I was going to be sick, but after a few breaths I was ok again. I am here because I just can't take these terrible dreams any longer and I wonder if you can help."

Ken

Ken, aged 47, works in a high-pressure government position monitoring officers who work in undercover operations in Eastern Europe for the Central Intelligence Agency. Ken shares, "I love my job but it is pretty high pressure and there is a lot at stake. I don't have a lot of anxiety, but I do think it takes a toll on my body. I have had trouble with my stomach, for example, I have GERD. After I eat, my stomach juices come up into my esophagus. It really burns and I end up coughing. Sometimes I cough so hard and for so long that I throw up. It is a lot worse at night and it makes it really hard for me to get good sleep at night. When the GERD is better, then I get good sleep, but when the GERD flares up, well, then I can't sleep at all well. It's like a double whammy." Ken further explains, "Right now the GERD is pretty bad so for about 3 months I've been coughing and having a hard time sleeping almost every night. Since I can't sleep well I feel foggy and grumpy all the time. My irritation is causing problems between me and my wife. Plus, I feel really sleepy all day and I sometimes find myself nodding off while I'm driving, which really scares me. I feel like I have to do something about my sleep or I could fall behind at work or cause an accident!"

Dimitri

Dimitri is a 25-year-old man who moved in with his boyfriend three months ago. Dimitri works as an apprentice electrician, often putting in 11- or 12-hour days five days a week. At night he is exhausted and usually goes to bed around 10 p.m. His boyfriend, Jon, has insisted that Dimitri talk to his doctor citing the fact that several nights a week Dimitri wakes up and finds himself somewhere other than in his bed. Often he wakes up in the kitchen or living room, but on one or two occasions he has been on his way out of the apartment when Jon has heard him and has woken up. In one occurrence, Dimitri was opening the sliding glass door to their balcony and on another occasion he was walking down the hallway of their apartment building. Jon, who has come with Dimitri to the appointment, shares, "I am freaked out by the sleep-walking. I can't wake him up! Then, when he does wake up, Dimitri has no idea how he got there or what is going on." Jon continues, "It's creepy and now I'm not sleeping well because I'm worried about what might happen if I don't hear Dimitri get up." Turning to Dimitri he adds, "You have to figure this out. Your issues are not going to cut into my sleep." Dimitri admits that at different points in his life he has walked in his sleep, but this has been happening more lately. Dimitri sighs, sounding discouraged,

"I thought maybe it was just the stress of work, but even as things have gotten easier, this keeps happening. I'm so frustrated."

Darnell

Darnell, aged 11, a 5th grader, was held back in preschool when his parents and teachers felt his impulsiveness and immaturity made him a better fit for one more year to prepare for kindergarten. However, he continued to struggle with "wiggliness" and "inattention" through 1st, 2nd and 3rd grades. It wasn't until 5th grade that his academic work began to suffer, which led his parents to have Darnell assessed by the school psychologist and was diagnosed with ADHD 4 weeks ago. At that time Darnell was prescribed methylphenidate by his family physician based on the school's evaluation and also began therapeutic day treatment at school. Since that time, his mother reports improvement in his attention both at home and at school. While it is too soon to tell if his grades will be impacted, his homework does seem improved. Although he seems to like his counselor and overall school is improving, he has mentioned that he feels embarrassed about needing to be pulled out of class in front of his friends.

However, since beginning the medication Darnell has been awoken in the night by nightmares. At Darnell's one-month medication follow-up, his mother shares, "I'm concerned about Darnell. He's having terrible dreams about losing family members or getting lost in the woods and being torn apart by bears. I looked it up and I think that this might be a side effect of his medicine and I'm not sure that it is worth the trade-off. None of us are sleeping too well because he wakes the whole house with his crying. Is there something else that he could take that would help with the ADHD but wouldn't cause the nightmares?"

References

Agargun, M. Y., Kara, H., Özer, Ö. A., Selvi, Y., Kiran, Ü, & Özer, B. (2003). Clinical importance of nightmare disorder in patients with dissociative disorders. *Psychiatry and Clinical Neurosciences*, *57*(6), 575–579.

American Psychiatric Association. (2013). Sleep-Wake Disorders. In *Diagnostic and Statistical Manual of Mental Disorders: DSM 5* (pp. 361–422). Author.

Asarnow, L. D., Soehner, A. M., & Harvey, A. G. (2014). Basic sleep and circadian science as building blocks for behavioral interventions: A translational approach for mood disorders. *Behavioral Neuroscience*, *128*(3), 360.

Atkin, T., Comai, S., & Gobbi, G. (2018). Drugs for insomnia beyond benzodiazepines: Pharmacology, clinical applications, and discovery. *Pharmacological Reviews*, *70*(2), 197–245.

Attwood, T. (2001). *Asperger's syndrome: A guide for parents and professionals*. Jessica Kingsley Publishers.

Baglioni, C., Battagliese, G., Feige, B., Spiegelhalder, K., Nissen, C., Voderholzer, U., Lombardo, C., & Riemann, D. (2011). Insomnia as a predictor of depression: A meta-analytic evaluation of longitudinal epidemiological studies. *Journal of Affective Disorders*, *135*(1–3), 10–19.

Bernert, R. A., Kim, J. S., Iwata, N. G., & Perlis, M. L. (2015). Sleep disturbances as an evidence-based suicide risk factor. *Current Psychiatry Reports*, *17*(3), 15.

Bos, S. C., & Macedo, A. F. (2019). Literature review on Insomnia (2010–2016). *Biological Rhythm Research*, *50*(1), 94–163.

Brenes, G. A., Miller, M. E., Stanley, M. A., Williamson, J. D., Knudson, M., & McCall, W. V. (2009). Insomnia in older adults with generalized anxiety disorder. *The American Journal of Geriatric Psychiatry*, *17*(6), 465–472.

Chorney, D. B., Detweiler, M. F., Morris, T. L., & Kuhn, B. R. (2008). The interplay of sleep disturbance, anxiety, and depression in children. *Journal of Pediatric Psychology*, *33*(4), 339–348.

Deliens, G., Leproult, R., Schmitz, R., Destrebecqz, A., & Peigneux, P. (2015). Sleep disturbances in autism spectrum disorders. *Review Journal of Autism and Developmental Disorders*, *2*(4), 343–356.

Dolsen, M. R., Asarnow, L. D., & Harvey, A. G. (2014). Insomnia as a transdiagnostic process in psychiatric disorders. *Current Psychiatry Reports*, *16*(9), 471.

Durmer, J. S., & Dinges, D. F. (2005, March). Neurocognitive consequences of sleep deprivation. In *Seminars in neurology* (Vol. 25, No. 01, pp. 117–129). Thieme Medical Publishers, Inc.

Ehlers, C. L., Kupfer, D. J., Frank, E., & Monk, T. H. (1993). Biological rhythms and depression: The role of zeitgebers and zeitstorers. *Depression*, *1*(6), 285–293.

Emet, J. (2012) . *Buddha's book of sleep. Sleep better in seven weeks with mindfulness meditation.* Hay House, Inc.

Faulkner, S. M., Bee, P. E., Meyer, N., Dijk, D. J., & Drake, R. J. (2019). Light therapies to improve sleep in intrinsic circadian rhythm sleep disorders and neuro-psychiatric illness: A systematic review and meta-analysis. *Sleep Medicine Reviews*, *46*, 108–123.

Ferre Navarrete, F., Pérez Páramo, M., Fermin Ordoño, J., & López Gómez, V. (2017). Prevalence of insomnia and associated factors in outpatients with generalized anxiety disorder treated in psychiatric clinics. *Behavioral Sleep Medicine*, *15*(6), 491–501.

Fonseca, A. G., & Genzel, L. (2020). Sleep and academic performance: Considering amount, quality and timing. *Current Opinion in Behavioral Sciences*, *33*, 65–71.

Frase, L., Nissen, C., Riemann, D., & Spiegelhalder, K. (2018). Making sleep easier: Pharmacological interventions for insomnia. *Expert Opinion on Pharmacotherapy*, *19*(3), 1465–1473.

Gamaldo, C. (2017). *Your sleepless patient: Clinical considerations for non-sleep specialists treating patients with insomnia.* American Academy of Neurology Institute.

Germain, A., & Nielsen, T. (2003). Impact of imagery rehearsal treatment on distressing dreams, psychological distress, and sleep parameters in nightmare patients. *Behavioral Sleep Medicine*, *1*(3), 140–154. https://doi.org/10.1207/s15402010BSM0103_2

Gieselmann, A., Ait Aoudia, M., Carr, M., Germain, A., Gorzka, R., Holzinger, B., Kleim, B., Krakow, B., Kunze, A. E., Lancee, J., Nadorff, M. R., Nielsen, T., Riemann, D., Sandahl, H., Schlarb, A. A., Schmid, C., Schredl, M., Spoormaker, V. I., Steil, R., . . . Pietrowsky, R. (2019). Aetiology and treatment of nightmare disorder: State of the art and future perspectives. *Journal of Sleep Research, 28*(4), e12820.

Harvey, A., & Buysse, D. (2017). *Treating sleep problems: A transdiagnostic approach.* Guilford Press.

Harvey, A. G., Jones, C., & Schmidt, D. A. (2003). Sleep and posttraumatic stress disorder: A review. *Clinical Psychology Review, 23*(3), 377–407.

Jacobs, G. D. (2009). *Say good night to insomnia: the six-week, drug-free program developed at Harvard Medical School.* Macmillan.

Katz, T. (2014). *Solving sleep problems in children with autism spectrum disorders: A guide for frazzled families.* Woodbine House, Inc.

Léger, D., Morin, C. M., Uchiyama, M., Hakimi, Z., Cure, S., & Walsh, J. K. (2012). Chronic insomnia, quality-of-life, and utility scores: comparison with good sleepers in a cross-sectional international survey. *Sleep medicine, 13*(1), 43–51.

Livingston, G., Blizard, B., & Mann, A. (1993). Does sleep disturbance predict depression in elderly people? A study in inner London. *British Journal of General Practice, 43*(376), 445–448.

Manber, R., Berner, R., Suh, S., Siebern, A., & Ong, J. (2014). CBT for insomnia in patients with high and low depressive symptom severity: Adherence and clinical outcomes. *Focus, 12*(1), 90–98. https://doi.org/10.1176/appi.focus.12.1.90

Manber, R., & Carney, C. (2015). *Treatment plans and interventions for insomnia: A case formulation approach.* Guilford Press.

Melo, M. C., Abreu, R. L., Neto, V. B. L., de Bruin, P. F., & de Bruin, V. M. (2017). Chronotype and circadian rhythm in bipolar disorder: A systematic review. *Sleep Medicine Reviews, 34*, 46–58.

Nadorff, M., Nazem, S., & Fiske, A. (2013). Insomnia symptoms, nightmares, and suicide risk: Duration of sleep disturbance matters. *Suicide and Life-Threatening Behavior, 43*(2), 139–149.

Okun, M. L. (2016). Disturbed sleep and postpartum depression. *Current Psychiatry Reports, 18*(7), 66.

Pappa, S., Ntella, V., Giannakas, T., Giannakoulis, V. G., Papoutsi, E., & Katsaounou, P. (2020). Prevalence of depression, anxiety, and insomnia among healthcare workers during the COVID-19 pandemic: A systematic review and meta-analysis. *Brain, Behavior, and Immunity.*

Perlis, M., Junquist, C., Smith, M., & Posner, D. (2008). *Cognitive behavioral treatment of insomnia: A session-by-session guide.* Springer Publishing.

Perlis, M. L., Smith, M. T., Jungquist, C., Nowakowski, S., Orff, H., & Soeffing, J. (2010). Cognitive-behavioral therapy for insomnia. In H. Attarian & C. Schuman (Eds.), *Clinical handbook of insomnia. Current clinical neurology.* Humana Press.

Phelps, J. (2016). *A spectrum approach to mood disorders: Not fully bipolar but not unipolar—Practical management.* WW Norton & Company.

Provencher, T., Lemyre, A., Vallières, A., & Bastien, C. H. (2020). Insomnia in personality disorders and substance use disorders. *Current Opinion in Psychology, 34*, 72–76.

Quitkin, F. M. (2002). Depression with atypical features: Diagnostic validity, prevalence and treatment. *Primary Care Companion Journal of Clinical Psychiatry, 4*(3), 94–99.

Sapolski, R. (2017). *Stress, sleep, and lack of sleep. Stress & your body: Course guidebook. Great Courses.* Stanford University.

Semiz, U. B., Basoglu, C., Ebrinc, S., & Cetin, M. (2008). Nightmare disorder, dream anxiety, and subjective sleep quality in patients with borderline personality disorder. *Psychiatry and Clinical Neurosciences, 62*(1), 48–55.

Sleep Foundation. (2020a). *What causes insomnia?* https://www.sleepfoundation.org/insomnia/what-causes-insomnia

Sleep Foundation. (2020b). *What is sleep hygiene?* https://www.sleepfoundation.org/articles/sleep-hygiene

Spiegelhalder, K., Nissen, C., & Riemann, D. (2019). Clinical sleep–wake disorders II: Focus on insomnia and circadian rhythm sleep disorders. *Sleep-Wake Neurobiology and Pharmacology, 253*, 261–276.

Sullivan-Tibbs, M. A., Thompson, P., Nugent, W., & Baker, J. (2019). Sleep disturbances and suicide—New battles for veterans of US wars in Afghanistan and Iraq: A retrospective review. *Social Work in Mental Health, 17*(2), 222–236.

Sun, Q., & Tan, L. (2019). Comparing primary insomnia to the insomnia occurring in major depression and general anxiety disorder. *Psychiatry Research, 282*, 112514.

Swart, M. L., Van Schagen, A. M., Lancee, J., & Van Den Bout, J. (2013). Prevalence of nightmare disorder in psychiatric outpatients. *Psychotherapy and Psychosomatics, 82*(4), 267.

Tolêdo, J. M., Batista, J. F. D. O. L., Lyra, M. C. A., de VC Júnior, M. A., dos Santos, M. A. M., & Heimer, M. V. (2020). Sleep disturbance and depression in adolescence: An integrative review of literature. *International Journal of Adolescent Medicine and Health. (ahead-of-print).*

11 Trauma and Stressor-Related Disorders

The next three chapters, trauma and stress-related disorders, dissociative disorders and the somatic symptom and related disorders are organized next to one another in the DSM 5 thanks to their overlapping symptoms. Both the dissociative and the trauma and stress-related disorders are understood to be instigated by trauma experiences. In fact, as late as 2012, the DSM 5 working group was still considering including the dissociative disorders within the trauma and stressor-related continuum (Brand et al., 2012). Both the dissociative and trauma disorders share a great deal in common with the somatic symptom disorders. First, all three have a shared relationship within the history of hysteria, which will be discussed briefly in Chapter 12, Dissociative Disorders. Second, in those with dissociative and somatic symptom disorders, we see a psychological sidestepping of an underlying problem that is ultimately expressed indirectly. When a person divorces themselves from some or all of their immediate experience, or even the whole of their identity, this is dissociation; when the underlying issue undergoes a metamorphosis and manifests into another, more concrete and perhaps more socially consumable concern, such as a physical illness, this process is described as a somatoform disorder. As we will see later in this chapter, post-traumatic stress disorder (PTSD) features both somatic symptoms and, in some cases, dissociation.

There is a great deal to know about trauma in order to effectively treat those who have experienced it. Volumes of literature are devoted to detailing associations between trauma and chronic/complex trauma and any number of aspects of the human experience from learning, executive functioning, interpersonal and intrapersonal relationship, emotional regulation and well-being, life-long attachment capacities and so on (Ashton et al., 2016; McLean, 2016; Van der Kolk, 2017). However, for the purposes of this chapter, the discussion of trauma will focus primarily on its implications for diagnosis.

Stress, Trauma and The Trauma Continuum

Before exploring the continuum of trauma and stressor-related disorders, it is important to first understand what trauma and stress are and how to differentiate them. The concept of trauma is an evolving one. Once, the term "trauma" was reserved for horrifying events, such as kidnapping, rape or torture. Today there is a general consensus within the field that trauma exists on a continuum (Scaer, 2005; Shonkoff et al., 2005). Consequently, efforts to describe and quantify different types of trauma and their impact on development and well-being have given rise to a host of terms and categories; for instance, the differentiation of Type I and Type II traumas.

Stress, unlike trauma, can arise from positive or negative life events. For instance, the birth of a child, even when planned and welcomed with great anticipation and joy can be accompanied by significant stress. Similarly, learning new concepts generates stress as do other life events such as moving into a new home or taking a new position at work. Positive stress has been demonstrated to contribute to personal growth, meaning-making and learning while negative and chronic stress can impair cognitive function (McEwen & Sapolsky, 1995), diminish the capacity to sleep (Amaral et al., 2018) and impair overall health both immediately and in the long-term (Sapolsky, 2004).

Trauma, on the other hand, poses a threat to the physical, psychological or spiritual integrity of the person who experiences it. Type I traumas are the kind typically linked to PTSD. Type I trauma, sometimes described as acute trauma, might include a violent assault, a combat incident, an accident that results in severe injury or an unexpected life-threatening illness. Often these are single episode events. In contrast, Type II traumas tend to involve multiple incidents over a significant period of time, such as childhood physical, sexual or emotional abuse, or relational violence (Leahy & Clark, 1998) and have, consequently, been likened to the International Classification of Diagnoses (ICD)-11 construct, complex PTSD (Sage et al., 2018), which will be discussed in depth later in the chapter. When these incidents happen during childhood, their impact is described as developmental trauma. Race-related trauma results from systemic racism or direct experiences of racism, while historical trauma describes trauma experienced by a cultural or religious group as a result of historical events (Brave Heart, 2000; Evans-Campbell, 2008; Lazar et al., 2008; Nagata et al., 2019; Wilkins et al., 2013), something that will also be explored later in the chapter.

Disorders of the Trauma Continuum

Reactive Attachment Disorder (RAD). A major change to the RAD diagnosis was implemented in the 5th edition of the DSM when the diagnosis was split in two. In the DSM IV, RAD had two specifiers, emotionally withdrawn/inhibited and indiscriminately social/disinhibited, the latter of which has been separated and is now a stand-alone disorder, disinhibited social engagement disorder (DSED) (APA, 2013;

BOX 11.01 KEY TERMS: TRAUMA AND STRESSOR-RELATED DISORDERS

Acute Trauma/Type I Trauma: acute trauma is trauma resulting from a single incident

Complex post-traumatic stress disorder (PTSD)/ Developmental Trauma/Type II Trauma: this term describes those who have been exposed to multiple incidents of trauma, generally of a chronic nature and including a number of different types of trauma (Guina et al., 2017).

For example, Shannon has a complex history of a number of types of trauma: Shannon, a 26-year-old veteran, is seeking mental health services. Shannon has an early history of childhood physical abuse and was ultimately raised by her grandmother after her father was jailed for robbery. Shannon did poorly in school and was bullied often thanks to her tendency to be withdrawn and an occasional stutter. Shannon was raped while serving in Germany and became pregnant. She regrets her decision to abort the pregnancy and often feels "hopeless and disgusting."

Depersonalization: depersonalization is a phenomenon in which experiences are detached from the experience of self. For example, rather than feeling present in what is unfolding, one experiences events or sensations as an outside observer rather than a participant (APA, 2013).

Derealization: derealization is an experience of the outside world or surroundings as distorted, unreal or as having a dream-like quality (APA, 2013).

Dissociation: dissociation is a term describing the capacity for separating sensations, experiences or memories from one's awareness without intending or knowing that one has done so. Dissociation does not include instances in which a person isn't capable of understanding and integrating information, as when a child sees something that can't be understood developmentally or when a phenomenon, such as hypnosis or sedation, blocks the integration of information or stimuli (APA, 2013; Schore, 2012).

Moral Injury: describes the distress and profound existential crisis created when a person acts (or fails to act) in ways that then place them in violation of deeply held values or moral codes (Jinkerson, 2016).

Polytrauma Clinical Triad: this term refers to the comorbidity of chronic pain, traumatic brain injury (TBI) and PTSD (Held et al., 2018).

Positive Stress: these stressors tend to occur as part of everyday living, are brief and lend an opportunity for a person to develop stronger coping strategies. Examples of positive stress might include the demands on a child that come with moving from elementary to middle school, or in adulthood, the experience of being promoted to a more challenging position at work.

Post-Traumatic Growth: post-traumatic growth describes the growth that results thanks to having experienced, coped with and made meaning of traumatic situations.

Post-Traumatic Play: post-traumatic play is an organic play in which the trauma is re-enacted repetitively in a creative attempt to gain mastery over the event or events. For some children, post-traumatic play may serve to re-traumatize the child and often becomes the focus of attention in the clinical setting (Gil, 2016).

Race-Based Trauma: this term refers to reactions of distress following experiences of overt and covert racism experienced by People of Color and Indigenous persons (Comas-Díaz, 2019).

Situational Depression: this term is sometimes found in mainstream literature and describes an adjustment disorder with depressive features.

Small t Trauma: small t traumas describe disturbing and disruptive life events that lead to transient

(*Continued*)

(Continued)

and situational disturbances or distress. Small t traumas might include childhood bullying, losses such as parental separation, divorce or job loss, financial concerns, protracted illness and so on.

Trauma: trauma describes the negative physical, psychological and spiritual consequences that follow an event and threatens the physical or psychological safety of the experiencer (APA, 2013).

Trauma Continuum: the concept of a trauma continuum recognizes the mind–body impact of a host of traumas ranging from the painful experiences of daily life, such as childhood bullying, those more jolting life events such as parental divorce, one's own divorce or loss of job and those more horrific experiences, such as sexual assault, life-threatening injury or experiences of war as contributing to a person's physical and mental health and even shaping one's personal identity.

Trauma Resilience: trauma resilience describes traits that serve as protective factors in buffering the consequences of trauma (Lehavot et al., 2018).

Tolerable Stress: These stressors are ones that do hold the potential to negatively impact a child's development, such as when parents divorce, but thanks to the context, such as social support and infrequency, the child is able to integrate the experience without negative developmental consequences (Lehavot et al., 2018).

Toxic Stress: toxic stress describes stressful situations that tend to overwhelm a person's capacity to manage and recover from stressors (Lehavot et al., 2018).

Humphreys et al., 2017), which will be discussed next. RAD is defined by four key characteristics: inhibited and withdrawn behavior; for instance, failing to seek out comfort when comfort is needed; social and emotional disturbances, which might include persistent negative emotion and restricted emotional responses to others; inexplicable irritability or fearfulness in non-threatening situations and a documented history of extremely insufficient care, which may include frequent changes in primary caregivers, withholding of comfort or severely limited opportunities for building bonds of attachment (APA, 2013).

Disinhibited Social Engagement Disorder (DSED). Like RAD, clients diagnosed with DSED must have a documented history of extremely insufficient care in early childhood that results in disruptions in their ability to form bonds of attachment. However, these children, rather than withdrawing, as children and adolescents with RAD do, instead show indiscriminate and overly familiar social behavior with others; for instance, approaching, talking with or hugging strangers without demonstrating "checking" behaviors with caregivers that might offer reassurance of safety. Children with this disorder may walk away with strangers without ever looking back at their caregivers. The behaviors exhibited by a child with DSED should not be confused with the impulsive behaviors seen in children with attention deficit hyperactivity disorder (ADHD). Rather than arising from impulsivity, these behaviors are born out of a failure to attach properly with caregivers, combined with difficulties in recognizing social expectations around interactions with strangers (APA, 2013).

RAD made its entry into mainstream discussion following a wave of adoptions from Romania and other parts of Eastern Europe (Zeanah, 2000). By the year 2000, an estimated 40,000 children had been adopted from countries in that region, many from orphanages with few resources or caregivers; thousands more children were later adopted from Russia and China. These adoptions were also popular in Europe and Canada. During this time, both professional and mainstream literature were filled with stories of adopted children who displayed a range of significant health concerns, learning difficulties, disruptions in attachment, attention and behavioral problems, some so extreme many parents and therapists were unprepared to respond. Attempts to treat these children resulted in dangerous interventions, such as "holding therapy" that in some cases resulted in tragic deaths (Zeanah, 2000).

Though most of the extant research on RAD took place in the 1990s, interest seems to have been renewed in the last decade; several studies now examine RAD and its diagnostic sibling, DSED. A recent study, conducted by Humphreys et al. (2017) of more than 100 Romanian children who received different levels of skilled care, compared the number of institutionalizations and foster placements. Their research affirmed the importance of early quality care in the mental health outcomes of children living outside their birth homes. Research examining the care of children who are removed from abusive and neglectful caregiving situations and placed in different types of care demonstrate that while child-centered care and foster care placements do influence the course of RAD, the length of stay in institutional care also influences long-term outcomes (Guyon-Harris et al., 2019).

Acute Stress Disorder (ASD). ASD recognizes the immediate, psychological, cognitive and physiological consequences of a traumatic experience but differs from PTSD in its duration, lasting at least 3 days and no more than a month. By comparison, ASD offers more flexibility in the combination of symptoms that might be experienced than does PTSD. ASD draws from the following categories: intrusion symptoms, negative mood, dissociative, avoidance and arousal symptoms. To diagnose ASD a client must be experiencing at least nine of 14 listed symptoms; however, the DSM allows for any nine symptoms for the client to sufficiently meet criteria for diagnosis, rather than stipulating how many sub-criteria from each category as with PTSD (APA, 2013).

Adjustment Disorder. Prior to the addition of adjustment disorder to the second edition of the DSM in 1968, the term "transient situational disturbance" was frequently applied to shifts in well-being that followed what might now be described as small "t" traumas, such as divorce, loss of a job, serious financial stress, unexpected or protracted illness and so on (Carta et al., 2009). The person diagnosed with an adjustment disorder experiences a response to the triggering stressor significant enough to require support; however, the distress associated with the event generally resolves with time

BOX 11.02 CONSIDER THIS: ADJUSTMENT DISORDER

Read the following scenario. What thoughts or concerns might you have offering a diagnosis for Kriti given her circumstances? If Kriti could receive services without a diagnosis, how might you proceed? Would your decision to diagnose Kriti with an adjustment disorder change if diagnosis was required for treatment? What ethical considerations would you want to discuss with Kriti?

Kriti moved from Los Angeles to Atlanta about 2 months ago in hopes of securing a teaching position in her beloved hometown. Her partner planned to follow once he had sold their house. Kriti was adjusting to the city and had several job interviews but had not made many new friends when her partner called to say he would not join her in Atlanta and wanted to end their relationship. Jobless, recently separated and isolated, Kriti is finding that each day is harder to face than the last. For the past several weeks, she has been having a hard time finding the motivation to apply for teaching positions. She realizes that if she doesn't get some support soon, she may ultimately find herself in an emotional well that she can't climb out of.

either when the stressor or its consequences are no longer alive in the person's life. Adjustment disorder is not diagnosed when a client is experiencing normal bereavement, however (APA, 2013; Maercker & Lorenz, 2018). When a client experiences disruptions in well-being thanks to adjustment, specifiers lend clarity as to how those difficulties are manifesting: (1) depressed mood, (2) with anxiety, (3) mixed anxiety and depressed mood, (4) with a disturbance of conduct, (5) mixed disturbance of emotion and conduct and (6) an unspecified type.

This diagnosis is not without controversy. Some researchers and clinicians have voiced concerns that adjustment disorder as described in the DSM is over-broad and so inclusive that it is "virtually meaningless," and further argue that it represents a prime example of the medicalization of normal life, essentially conflating distress with disorder (Carta et al., 2009; Casey et al., 2001; Maercker & Lorenz, 2018). Other authors have argued that there is no biological evidence that adjustment disorder and major depression are different disorders and that they may in fact represent different manifestations of the same process (Kumano et al., 2007 in Carta et al., 2009). Notably, adjustment disorder is sometimes referred to as situational depression in mainstream literature (Psychology Today, 2019).

PTSD and Its Evolution

PTSD, A Brief History. The history of PTSD begins with the experiences of soldiers in war. Psychological crises experienced on the battlefield have been known by various names, including shell shock, war neurosis and battle fatigue, and has long been recognized as a problem. Public attitudes were once deeply divided about whether these problems developed due to the stress of the battlefield itself or were born out of individual weaknesses. At one point in World War II, the number of troops dismissed from the army on psychiatric grounds exceeded the number of new recruits being enlisted. During the Korean War, one in four evacuations from the battle field were psychiatric in nature adding to mounting evidence of the psychological impact of war on individual soldiers (Scott, 1990).

While the first edition of the DSM had contained a diagnosis of "gross stress reaction," which was frequently applied to soldiers, this diagnosis was not included within the DSM II. During this period, veterans suffering from mental health problems after war were often diagnosed with alcoholism, schizophrenia and depression. Sarah Haley, a social worker, Chaim Shatan and Robert Lifton, both psychiatrists and anti war activists, lobbied Robert Spitzer, chair of the DSM III, and ultimately developed the Vietnam Veterans Working Group. Together they gathered evidence and built an argument for the existence of PTSD and lobbied for its inclusion within the DSM III. Eventually, Shatan and Lifton were included in the DSM III working group, the Committee on Reactive Disorders, and in the end persuaded the other members that PTSD should be included (Scott, 1990).

PTSD's inclusion in the manual is due in part to the shifts in the DSM around the exclusion of homosexuality. In 1974, the field of psychiatry was split as to whether homosexuality was a natural variation of human sexuality or a psychiatric disorder. Spitzer decided to take the issue of the inclusion or exclusion of homosexuality to a vote by the membership of the American Psychiatric Association (APA) and the membership voted to remove homosexuality. Taking the issue to the APA membership introduced the idea of consensus into the decision-making process of diagnoses within the DSM. Thanks to this shift a host of suggested changes were then offered by researchers and practitioners; the status of "gross stress reaction," which would later become PTSD, represented but one of these (Scott, 1990).

PTSD in the DSM 5. PTSD is another of the few disorders of the DSM that stipulates a causal factor in its diagnostic criteria, "exposure to an event of actual or threatened death, serious injury or sexual violence" (APA, 2013, p. 271). The criteria for PTSD have undergone a number of key changes in the DSM 5, one of the most significant of which is the expansion of the criteria clusters from three to four. In order to be diagnosed with PTSD, a client must experience symptoms from each of the following categories: intrusion, avoidance, cognitive changes that negatively impact the client, negative shifts in mood and significant and unwelcome changes in arousal and reactivity (APA, 2013). Specifics outlining subjective experiencing of the traumatic event have been dropped in the DSM 5 while the "stressor" criterion has become more specific than previous editions. Additionally, an attempt has been made to make the diagnosis more developmentally sensitive by offering separate criteria for children and teens and those under the age of 6. Consult your DSM for details on the differences in diagnosing clients of different age groups.

Specifiers and Subtypes of PTSD. The diagnosis of PTSD comes with a pair of dissociative specifiers, depersonalization and derealization, as well as a delayed onset specifier, which can be applied where appropriate. Dissociation, as noted earlier, describes a phenomenon in which a person experiences discontinuity in their subjective experiences, sensations, feelings and so on. When this detachment involves the experience of self, it is described as depersonalization; detachment from the surrounding environment is known as derealization (APA, 2013). Dissociation, depersonalization and derealization will be explored at length in Chapter 12. These presentations when found together with PTSD are sometimes noted in the literature as PTSD + DS, PTSD dissociative subtype, or DPTSD. Between 15% and 30% of those with PTSD have been estimated to have the dissociative subtype of PTSD (Armour et al., 2014; Boyd et al., 2018; Hansen et al., 2017).

Do dissociative symptoms meaningfully influence presentation or prognosis of PTSD? Some research suggests it does. For example, Boyd et al. (2018) explored the role of dissociation in PTSD among veterans and first responders and found that the dissociative subtype of PTSD served a mediating role in PTSD severity, including increased functional impairment. This result was stronger among veterans than among first responders. It is important to note that PTSD symptoms don't always immediately follow the traumatic event. In those situations in which full diagnostic criteria are not met until 6 months after the incident, whether or not there are dissociative symptoms, clinicians should use the "delayed" specifier.

The Future of the PTSD Diagnosis

A Stand-Alone Disorder or a Specifier? The debate around whether or not PTSD should be a stand-alone disorder continues despite its current status in the DSM. Guina et al. (2017) argue, ". . . current nosology overemphasizes number of symptoms/clusters over level of dysfunction/distress, overemphasizes a traumatic event's details over its impact, and fails to capture the full spectrum of trauma-related psychopathology in a way that specifically identifies traumatic etiology. For these reasons . . . we argue that post traumatic stress (PTS) would be more accurate and useful if used as a specifier rather than a disorder" (p. 66). These authors argue that "trauma defies categories" (p. 67) and further point out that trauma is a risk factor "for virtually all mental disorders" (p. 66). Finally, Guina and colleagues note the inconsistency in the DSM 5 pointing out that some dimensions are organized primarily by a defining symptom, such as depression or anxiety, others are organized developmentally (neurodevelopmental and neurodegenerative), while the trauma continuum is held together by its cause. They argue that a post-traumatic stress (PTS) specifier would more accurately differentiate the manifestations of disorders across the DSM.

Complex PTSD and PTSD's Dissociative Subtypes. Before the publication of the DSM 5, there was a great deal of anticipation around the potential addition of a diagnosis described as complex PTSD, sometimes known as developmental trauma, which would describe those who had been exposed to more chronic forms of trauma, generally in childhood. Out of the explorations, a great deal of research concerning developmental trauma and its consequences has been published along with a simple and readily available measure, the Adverse Childhood Experiences (ACE) (Van der Kolk, 2017). In the past decade, complex trauma and the potential for another PTSD diagnosis has received a lot of attention outside the DSM; thousands of peer reviewed articles mention the construct and dozens of books have been dedicated to the topic. The World Health Organization has included complex PTSD in the ICD-11 (World Health Organization, 2018). Several diagnoses related to complex trauma diagnosis were proposed for the DSM 5 but none were included in the trauma continuum nor within the research section of the manual. The DSM 5 work group did not provide a reason for not including complex PTSD, however (Guina et al., 2017; van der Kolk & Najavits, 2013; van Huijstee & Vermetten, 2017). Some researchers argue that there is insufficient evidence to indicate that complex trauma is more than a severe form of PTSD and further argue that it responds to treatment for PTSD, increasing the likelihood that Complex PTSD and PTSD are the same construct. Finally, they point out that there is no evidence that PTSD and complex trauma have different origins, all of which, these authors argue, suggest that a separate diagnosis is not warranted (Resick et al., 2012).

Given the sheer volume of research and writing devoted to the concept of complex trauma, it is not surprising that there are many in the field who believe strongly that complex trauma should be understood as a separate construct. Bessel Van der Kolk (2017) describes complex trauma as unique in that it features multiple experiences of chronic and prolonged traumatic events, typically sexual or physical abuse, war or community violence or repeated invasive and painful medical procedures. He further notes, "Isolated traumatic incidents tend to produce discrete conditioned behavioral and biological responses to reminders of the trauma, such as those captured in the posttraumatic stress disorder (PTSD) diagnosis. In contrast, chronic maltreatment or inevitable repeated traumatization . . . have a pervasive effect on the development of mind and brain," (p. 401). Cook et al. (2017) outline distinct negative consequences of early prolonged trauma in seven developmental domains: attachment, biological, affect regulation, dissociation, behavioral control, cognition and self-concept. They argue that PTSD as described in the DSM 5 does not adequately reflect these symptoms.

Proposed Complex Trauma Diagnosis. Van der Kolk (2017) proposes the addition of a diagnosis, developmental trauma disorder (DTD) and offers recommended criteria. First, the proposed "A" criteria would be one of exposure to "one or more developmentally adverse interpersonal trauma" (p. 404), followed by a pattern of dysregulation responses arising from trauma cues ("B" criteria). Further, DTD would be defined by "persistent altered attributions and experiences," such as an expectation of future victimization and a distrust of protective caregivers ("C" criteria), and finally, functional impairment in family, peer, educational, vocational and perhaps legal arenas of life ("D" criteria). Van der Kolk (2017), along with other authors, further argue that PTSD as described in the DSM 5 does not adequately capture the disrupted affect regulation and attachment patterns or the emotional and behavioral regression, lack of striving and goal orientation, aggression and disturbances in sleeping, eating and so on. The APA (2013) counters that the revisions to the PTSD diagnosis have made the criteria more developmentally sensitive and encourages the use of specifiers to clarify the diagnostic picture.

Proposed diagnosis for subthreshold PTSD symptomatology. Guina et al., 2017, point out that because the DSM 5 criteria are organized in such a way that clients must meet criteria in each of the categories listed, clinicians are often faced with situations in which a client evidences many symptoms and is functionally impaired by these symptoms but may fail to demonstrate a symptom in one of the listed categories and, consequently, can't be diagnosed with PTSD. These researchers point out that rather than stipulating symptoms from each category, a total number of symptoms from any of the categories would better capture the true number of people in need of diagnosis and treatment.

Populations and PTSD

A number of special populations are especially vulnerable to developing PTSD after being exposed to trauma. Among these are veterans and those in active duty, and civilians who are living in war-torn conditions. First responders, such as EMTs, firemen, medical personnel and police and others who hold positions that place them in high-stress incidents also have elevated prevalence rates. Those exposed to sexual or physical violence in childhood, either personally or witnessing it in the home, have also been shown to be at elevated risk, both in childhood and later in life. Transgenerational trauma is also being investigated as a source of vulnerability for PTSD.

War-Related PTSD Among Active Duty, Veterans and Civilians. Elevated rates of PTSD are widely documented among deployed service men and women and military veterans (APA, 2013; Haugen et al., 2012), and even among those who operate remote drones (Chappelle et al., 2012). Female veterans appear to have higher rates of PTSD than their male counterparts (Lehavot et al., 2018). War presents a vast array of opportunities for exposure to traumatizing events that can lead to PTSD, including but not exclusive to sexual assaults that happen during the course of service, the threat to life experienced in battle, serious personal injury, witnessing serious injury and loss of life and experiencing violations of one's values. Among military personnel and veterans who develop PTSD, those with the dissociative subtype seem to experience greater PTSD severity, including increased functional impairment, something that also seems to be true among first responders, though to a lesser degree (Boyd et al., 2018).

As noted earlier, the very history of the PTSD diagnosis is directly tied to the experiences of war veterans (Scott, 1990); however, the larger proportion of people impacted by war are civilians, a group also subject to greatly elevated rates of PTSD. Those fleeing war, both adults and children, can experience trauma events in their home countries, as they leave their countries and while in the process of seeking asylum, placing them at considerable risk for significant mental health concerns (Alayarian, 2018). How much risk for PTSD is added when exposed to war? In attempting to answer this question Stevanović et al. (2016) compared women who had early experiences of trauma with those who had experienced traumas related to war and found that among their sample of 293 women who had survived war, nearly 21% could be diagnosed with PTSD while none of the 101 participants who had experienced other types of trauma met criteria for PTSD at the time of the study. In the United States, the 12-month prevalence rate for PTSD is 3.7%; however, for those exposed to war the estimated range between 30% and 50% (APA, 2013).

First Responders and High Stress Incidence Work. Service correlated with PTSD is not unique to active military and veterans, however. First responders, such as hospital personnel, emergency service workers, firefighters and police officers also experience greatly increased rates of PTSD, thanks to their frequent contact with potentially traumatic stressors (APA, 2013; Haugen et al., 2012).

Covid-19 and Trauma Experiences. In April of 2020, a Manhattan emergency room doctor's suicide made national headlines, an early warning of the potential toll the Covid-19 pandemic would have on those at the front lines (Romo, 2020). Healthcare professionals working with patients with Covid-19 are thought to be at elevated risk for mental health concerns and PTSD in particular (Greenberg et al., 2020). A *Washington Post* interview with healthcare workers revealed grief at the loss of colleagues who had succumbed to the disease, accompanied by feelings of helplessness at losing one patient after another despite their best efforts. Others described high levels of anxiety that they might themselves contract Covid-19 or spread it to their families; one interviewee with military experience likened the anxiety to what he felt on the battlefield (Leaming & Ribas, 2020). It is worth noting that the rates of mental health concerns and suicidality among medical professionals has long been a concern and focus of research (Petrie et al., 2019); however, the pressures of the pandemic has brought these concerns into the public spotlight.

Moral Injury. A phenomenon known as moral injury describes the distress and profound existential crisis created when a person acts (or fails to act) in ways that then place them in violation with deeply held values or moral codes. A moral crisis may be presented, for example, when a soldier kills another person despite religious beliefs against taking a human life, or when an ER physician must decide who will receive a scarce treatment intervention and who will be denied (Greenberg et al., 2020; Held et al., 2018; Jinkerson, 2016; Nash & Litz, 2013), or even when medical protocols force unnecessary and expensive testing (Bailey, 2020). Healthcare providers have described experiencing moral injury while treating Covid-19 patients after witnessing high death rates of patients in their care (Leaming & Ribas, 2020). These experiences can lead to shame, guilt, disgust and spiritual questioning and are thought to contribute to individual experiences of trauma (Greenberg et al., 2020; Held et al., 2018; Jinkerson, 2016; Nash & Litz, 2013).

At the time of this writing, literature is not yet available describing the experiences of mental health professionals during the early months of Covid-19 or their vulnerability to moral injury, trauma or other mental health concerns. In my own conversations with clinicians and clinicians in training, however, those who have made a quick pivot to telehealth have done so while trying to navigate their own anxiety and isolation. Many describe navigating child care and new homeschool demands, care of elderly family members, as well as personal financial stressors, experiences that parallel those of their clients. It seems clear that clinicians have suffered psychological stressors along with their clients. Anecdotally, clinicians have described feeling unsure about how to provide adequate support to clients when they don't feel confident about how to manage their own pandemic-related difficulties. Time is needed in order to fully understand the consequences of the pandemic on mental health providers and, indeed, the world as a whole.

High Stress Incidence Work. Clinicians should be aware that in addition to first responders and military personnel, other career choices can elevate exposure to trauma events. Those who conduct trains that are involved in "person under a train" incidents, journalists reporting in dangerous and war-torn areas, medical staff and those working during industrial disasters have all been documented to be vulnerable to PTSD (Skogstad et al., 2013). More recently, reports of PTSD among employees screening social media for content that violates community standards have also reported PTSD after long hours viewing and removing posts of murder, rape and child abuse (Solon, 2017).

Child Abuse Experiences and the Development of PTSD. It has long been understood that children who experience too much stress demonstrate observable disruptions in the architecture of the brain and its development (Ashton et al., 2016; Barlow, 2014; McLean, 2016; Schore, 2005; Schore, 2012; Shonkoff et al., 2005). The relationship between childhood sexual abuse and PTSD is widely documented (McTavish et al., 2019). Early childhood experiences of physical and sexual abuse predispose children to PTSD following a trauma, amplify the likelihood of developing PTSD later in life, and predispose children to developing a host of other mental health concerns. Research reveals that female veterans have a much higher incidence of past year PTSD than either the general public or their male veteran counterparts. In an effort to understand these contrasting prevalence rates, Lehavot et al. (2018) studied female veterans with PTSD. These researchers found that the number of types of trauma incidents mediated the difference in PTSD past year prevalence between female veterans and the general public while the presence of child abuse, interpersonal violence and stressful life events mediated the difference between female and male veterans (p. 943).

Traumatized children can display a wide range of symptoms including emotional dysregulation when exposed to trauma cues, expectations for future victimization, injury or abandonment, disruptions to sleeping and eating, difficulties with emotional regulations and so on (Van der Kolk, 2017). Children may also re-enact their trauma experiences repeatedly in an effort to gain understanding and mastery over the events. This type of play, known as post-traumatic play, can re-traumatize the child and should then become the focus of therapeutic intervention (Gil, 2016).

Historical Trauma. Typically, when we think of trauma, we are considering life events in either our recent past or within our childhood, that have served to overwhelm our resources and shape our thoughts, feelings and behaviors in ways that are ultimately unhelpful. Notably, however, research has demonstrated that the traumas experienced by our immediate ancestors and by those in our ethnic and religious communities also convey trauma and risk to the generations that follow (Lehrner & Yehuda, 2018). For example, genetic traces of trauma can be found in the grandchildren of Holocaust survivors (Kahane-Nissenbaum, 2011). Historical trauma is "a collective complex trauma inflicted on a group of people who share a specific group identity or affiliation—ethnicity, nationality, and religious affiliation," (Evans-Campbell, 2008, p. 320). Historical trauma works to shape the identity and culture of the impacted group. Research demonstrates, for instance, that the Holocaust is experienced as a cultural trauma in the same ways by Israeli Jewish youth who are the direct descendants of Holocaust victims as those Jewish youth who are not (Lazar et al., 2008). Historical traumas mar the timeline of American history with devastating impact on People of Color. Native Americans have endured a vast array of traumatic assaults including but not exclusive to genocide events such as those that unfolded at Wounded Knee, the deliberate introduction of disease, forced removal from ancestral land and removal of Native children and placement in mission schools and later, during the Indian Adoption Act era, through adoption (Brave Heart, 2000; Evans-Campbell, 2008; Fast & Collin-Vezina, 2019). The history of enslavement, lynchings, Jim Crow laws, mass incarceration, continued police brutality and systemic racism converge to create a complex historical trauma for African Americans (Wilkins et al., 2013). The internment of over 110,000 Japanese Americans during the 1940s serves as yet another example of historical trauma (Nagata et al., 2019).

Overt Racism, Microaggressions and Homophobia as Mediators of Trauma Symptoms. Trauma responses that arise out of experiences of overt and covert racism are described as race-based trauma or race-based stress (Comas-Dı́iaz et al., 2019). Helms et al. (2010) note that experiences of racism and ethnoviolence are often overlooked as sources of trauma and as the seeds for PTSD. Witnessing a steady stream of video-recorded incidents of police violence against African American and Latinx people for example, coupled with the nation's history of violence against People of Color leave many fearing for their safety and that of their family. Mounting evidence points to the impact of daily exposure to microaggressions, subtle and sometimes covert forms of racist or homophobic communication and its mediating effect on PTSD symptoms. Research suggests that both overt and covert forms of racial aggression have a similar impact on those who experience it (Jones et al., 2016; Schoulte et al., 2011; Torres & Taknint, 2015). Additionally, those exposed to microaggressive bias have been shown to have greater vulnerability to PTSD symptoms for example, in African American women (Moody & Lewis, 2019), in Latinx populations (Torres & Taknint, 2015) and in the lesbian, gay, bisexual and transgender questioning/queer (LGBTQ) community (Robinson & Rubin, 2016). Clinicians should be vigilant to the experiences of racist and homophobic aggressions of all types and consider their potential contribution to PTSD or its symptoms (Helms et al., 2010).

PTSD, Experiences of Potentially Traumatizing Events and Developmental Psychopathology. Clinicians have long observed that most people experience at least one potentially traumatic event over the course of their lifetimes but only a relatively small proportion of the general population develop PTSD; the research literature bears out these observations. For example, Kilpatrick et al. (2013) surveyed 2,953 participants and found that 89.7% endorsed at least one traumatic life event. Similarly, Ogle et al. (2013) conducted a study which included 3,575 older adults (age 55-69) and found that a full 90% reported at least one type of potentially traumatic life event, while 78.21% reported two or more types of traumatic events. Lifetime prevalence rates of PTSD, however, are placed at only about 8.3% (Kilpatrick et al., 2013; Lancaster et al., 2016).

Why, then, do some who experience trauma develop PTSD while the majority don't? Does the type of trauma, timing or frequency influence the development of PTSD either immediately or later in life? Research seems to suggest that frequent traumas that happen early in life, as with abuse or witnessing violence in the home during childhood, leads to more severe PTSD symptomatology (Lehavot et al., 2018; Ogle et al., 2013).

Trauma Resilience, Post-Traumatic Growth (PTG) and PTSD. While the number and type of early traumatic events contribute to the later development of PTSD (Lehavot et al., 2018; Ogle et al., 2013), some individual factors seem to serve as protective factors against serious mental health consequences. Among these, research suggests that the capacity to identify, understand, accept and regulate emotions may serve as a buffer between exposures to childhood sexual abuse and the development of PTSD (John et al., 2017). Another trait believed to protect against the development of PTSD is lower rates of neuroticism. Higher rates of neuroticism are thought to contribute to the process in which traumas are amplified, made central to one's personal identity narrative and the degree to which a person involuntarily rehearses the trauma or replays it in their minds (Ogle et al., 2017).

In contrast to the consequences of overidentification with a trauma, a study of 259 African American participants at high risk for PTSD and other mental health disorders revealed that purpose in life served as a key factor in both resilience and recovery from trauma (Alim et al., 2008). Attachment also seems to play an important role in whether or not PTSD develops later in life (Kanninen et al., 2003; O'Connor & Elklit, 2008; Twaite & Rodriguez-Srednicki, 2004). Secure attachment seems to serve to soften PTSD severity (O'Connor & Elklit, 2008). However, Kanninen et al. (2003) found securely attached political prisoners were more likely to develop PTSD from psychological torture than their insecurely attached counterparts. Though a complete model, Agaibi and Wilson (2005) conducted an early review of the literature and constructed a model documenting the interaction between personality traits, emotion regulation, coping style, ego defenses, community resources and the capacity to mobilize these resources when trauma is experienced. When trauma is the source of personal growth and meaning-making, this process is described as PTG.

Comorbidity in PTSD. Unfortunately, those with PTSD also have very high comorbidity rates with other mental health disorders including major depression, anxiety disorders, substance use and personality disorders (APA, 2013; van Minnen et al., 2015) as well as high rates of symptomatology such as dissociation and suicidality (van Minnen et al., 2015). This may be especially true for veterans. For example, Ginzburg et al. (2010) conducted a longitudinal study of 664 veterans spanning 20 years and found that a triple comorbidity of PTSD, depression and anxiety (26.7%-30.1%) was far more common than either PTSD alone, PTSD comorbid with depression (1.2%-4.5%) or PTSD with anxiety (2.9%-4.5%). Comorbid traumatic brain injury (TBI) is also very common among veterans (APA, 2013).

Suicidality, Veterans and PTSD. On any given day an average of 20 veterans take their own lives (Horwitz et al., 2018). Among veterans, a phenomenon known as the polytrauma clinical triad refers to the comorbidity of chronic pain, TBI and PTSD. Researchers exploring this triad have found a relationship to suicidality and violent thoughts; the functional interference caused by pain, rather than the intensity of the pain, was found to be more strongly related to suicidality and violent impulses (Blakey et al., 2018). Suicidality is also elevated among first responders. For example, a study examining completed suicides among police officers serving in the Bronx between 1955 and 2005 revealed a suicide rate eight times as high among those actively serving compared to those who were retired (Stanley et al., 2016). While the research is mixed, suicidality seems to be elevated among firefighters, some arguing that more firefighters die by suicide than fighting fires (Heyman et al., 2018). These staggering suicide statistics alert clinicians to the importance of screening for and immediately addressing suicidal thoughts in those with PTSD, especially veterans and first responders.

BOX 11.03 SUBTHRESHOLD SYMPTOMS AND DIAGNOSTIC CONUNDRUMS

Read the following case. What diagnostic options are available to you within and outside this continuum? How might you proceed?

Morgan, a 26-year-old contractor specializing in home remodeling, has been struggling with anxiousness and worry that has prevented him from getting good sleep for the past 10 months. Morgan shares, "Some days I don't want to leave my apartment, I feel so sad, and on those days I just sit in the dark and cry. Other days I'm ok, but the worry and the anger is pretty much always there. And some days I just call in sick to work because I just don't want to be around those guys at the site." Morgan further explains, "I work with a lot of ol' boys, red necks, you know. They like to crank the country music and the conservative talk radio and talk shit all day while we work on people's houses. I like to work the saw so I don't have to listen to most of it. But it is hard because they don't know that I'm gay and they don't know I am in a relationship with a man—if they did they would make life hell for me. So I've been choking back my anger for a long time. But almost a year ago, my partner and I were in the city at a gay bar with two of our friends and when we left to get in our car and drove away, we didn't see that just a half a block away some guys who were drunk out of their minds came up to our friends and started pushing them around and then started a fight. One guy smashed their car window and one of our friends was hurt pretty bad, broken nose, arm and had to have stitches. I felt so guilty that we weren't able to protect them but, honestly, I think we had pulled out of the driveway about the time they got jumped. When I heard the next morning what happened I was so angry and afraid for all of us. I can't believe this happened. I know it has been a while ago and we are ok but I keep thinking about it and I keep going in these loops between worry, grief and rage. I don't know how long I can go on like this."

Morgan needs help. His functioning is impaired (he sleeps poorly and has missed work) and he is experiencing significant distress (anger, anxiety and depression). Morgan's symptoms have been going on too long for an adjustment disorder. He doesn't have enough symptoms for a posttraumatic stress disorder (PTSD) diagnosis, though he certainly experienced trauma. He also doesn't fully meet criteria for depression or generalized anxiety. Assuming you must provide a diagnosis in order to provide treatment, how will you diagnose Morgan?

Here you have the option of an unspecified disorder—though you will have to decide if you will seat that diagnosis in the depression or anxiety continuum or within the trauma and related disorders dimension. What diagnostic option seems to fit best?

The Skilled Diagnostician

The diagnosis of trauma and dissociative disorders comes with some particular diagnostic challenges, some of which are described below.

Assessing for and Diagnosing Trauma Seeded in Overt and Microaggressive Racism and Homophobia. Clients of Color and sexual minorities require culturally competent assessment and intervention, including the use of assessment tools that are sensitive to racism, ethnoviolence, homophobia and its consequences. Helms et al. (2010) note that when People of Color present with trauma symptoms but the trauma trigger itself is ambiguous, clinicians should consider the possibility of overt and covert racism or homophobia as a potential source of distress and trauma.

Diagnosis of Subthreshold Symptoms When Trauma History Is Present. Some research suggests that 16% of the American population experience trauma-related distress but fail to meet full criteria for PTSD (Guina et al., 2017). Unspecified diagnoses are designed to capture these types of situations, but sometimes it can be difficult to identify the best fit for an unspecified diagnosis; the process can feel a bit like fitting a square peg in a series of round, oval or triangular holes. These situations may call upon your use of good clinical intuition to make the most of a difficult diagnostic situation.

Trauma, Substance Use Disorders, Sexual Disorders or other Mental Health Concerns. Early trauma increases the risk of nearly every other mental health issue and leaves those dealing with trauma, historical or recent, with additional challenges to contend with, such as depression and anxiety disorders (Hovens, 2015). The vast majority of those diagnosed with PTSD, 83%, are diagnosed with at least one other mental health disorder (Sharpless & Barber, 2011). For example, approximately half of those with PTSD are also experiencing a major depressive disorder (Flory & Yehuda, 2015) and among teens diagnosed with PTSD as many as 50% also have a substance use disorder (Mills et al., 2018). Substance use disorders in combination with PTSD seem to both worsen and perpetuate the other. Substance use also increases the risk for developing other mental health concerns such as depression and anxiety (Mills et al., 2018). Similarly, consequences to sexual functioning can follow traumatic or stressful life events which can, in turn, negatively impact relationships and well-being (Zoldbrod, 2015). In exploring the reasons behind the large comorbidity rates, research seems to point to genetic overlap in the vulnerability to depression, anxiety and PTSD (Smoller, 2016). Whether the cause is the nature of trauma itself or genetic predispositions, it is essential that we carefully screen for and treat other mental health concerns, including substance use disorders.

Diagnosis of Complex Trauma. Again, complex trauma describes trauma that is long-standing, generally interpersonal in nature, and frequently occurs early in development, as with early childhood sexual abuse. The literature describing long-term effects of early trauma includes an emotional pattern in which emotions are over-regulated and depersonalization or derealization can result, which contrasts with the more typical under-regulation pattern frequently seen in PTSD in which a client's inability to manage emotions triggered by PTSD cues reactivity, such as panic-like symptoms. As many as 15% to 25% of PTSD presentations are thought to include dissociative responses (APA, 2013; van Huijstee & Vermetten, 2017). Complex trauma presentations that feature dissociative symptoms should be diagnosed as PTSD using the appropriate specifiers (APA, 2013).

Treatments

Prevention Efforts. Anticipating the stress of battle and the elevated likelihood of encountering potential trauma-inducing events, pre-trauma prevention efforts have been made to stave off PTSD in military personnel (Galea et al., 2012). Prevention interventions have also been designed to immediately follow potentially traumatic events, such as post-trauma debriefing, though the utility of psychological debriefing has been challenged in a number of efficacy studies (Kearns et al., 2012). It is important to note that clinicians warn against single-session debriefing for medical personnel in distress that has been described as potentially harmful (Greenberg et al., 2020).

Early treatment at the first signs of ASD, before PTSD comes into full fruition, (Galea et al., 2012) has been implemented as part of efforts to protect service men and women from serious mental health consequences following a trauma. Most recently, researchers have begun to look into the potential of sleep deprivation immediately following a trauma in order to prevent the "over-consolidation of traumatic memories" (no p.); however, much more research is needed to determine the effectiveness of this intervention (Repantis et al., 2020).

Finally, pharmacological interventions for use in preventing PTSD have also been widely researched, including but not exclusive to corticosteroids, but with limited success (Galea et al., 2012; Searcy et al., 2012).

Psychotherapy. Therapies falling under the umbrella of cognitive-behavioral therapy (CBT) are the most broadly researched interventions for trauma and stress-related disorders, and show the greatest efficacy of treatment, particularly when combined with exposure interventions. CBT works to minimize guilt, shame and self-blame that can arise out of trauma experiences, as well as attending to key symptoms, such as flashbacks, avoidance and hypervigilance. Prolonged exposure interventions, a key element of some CBT approaches, have been shown to have faster results in reducing reexperiencing symptoms than have interventions like eye movement desensitization reprocessing (EMDR) and relaxation techniques using alternative exposure processes (Bradley et al., 2005; Sharpless & Barber, 2011; Taylor, 2017). The cognitive processing model (CPM), another CBT approach which has been found to be effective in both military and civilian populations, focuses on automatic thoughts using writing as its primary approach to exposure and also shows strong efficacy (Sharpless & Barber, 2011).

Promoting PTG. Trauma resilience describes a phenomenon in which a person who is exposed to a trauma is able to survive without symptoms or returns to pre-trauma functioning. PTG, on the other hand, describes the learning and positive meaning-making that can follow trauma. Researchers have documented PTG following a broad range of experiences, including childhood sexual abuse, combat experiences, serious illness, experiences of physical violence and so on (Ulloa et al., 2016). As many as 70% of those who experience trauma may also experience improvements in at least one domain of their lives (Linley & Joseph, 2004, in Jayawickreme & Blackie, 2014). Research suggests that intrinsic religiosity, purpose in life and social connectedness are all predictive of greater PTG (Tsai et al., 2015). Arguably, the ideal aim of trauma intervention is to facilitate PTG.

Body-Based and other Complementary Interventions. Perhaps because PTSD is notoriously difficult to treat and because its symptoms cut across a wide range of domains, a variety of complementary and alternative approaches have been applied and researched for the treatment of PTSD, among them yoga-based intervention, emotional freedom technique (EFT) and EMDR. Though sometimes difficult to define, complementary and alternative approaches are showing positive effects in the treatment of PTSD symptoms (Benedek & Wynn, 2016; Ritchie, 2013). Survey research reveals that yoga, meditation and mindfulness-based interventions have been used broadly in programs by the Veterans Administration (Libby et al., 2012) and are showing promising results. For example, a small study of the use of yoga with women diagnosed with PTSD or experiencing subthreshold symptomatology demonstrated decreases in hyperarousal symptoms (Mitchell et al., 2014).

EFT (Church, 2010; Church et al., 2013, 2018) and EMDR (Sharpless & Barber, 2011) also stand out in the research for their growing promise. EMDR techniques make use of approaches that are embedded in brain-based theories that describe the importance of physical movement in order to disrupt and rewire neural patterns thought to sustain PTSD symptoms and combine these with key elements of CBT and client-centered approaches. EMDR embraces the idea that trauma is not stored as memory but is, instead, treated by the brain as new stimuli. EMDR aims to rewire the traumatic experience so that it can be worked through (Sharpless & Barber, 2011). Both EMDR and EFT approaches incorporate imaginal exposure to traumatic events coordinated with body movement. Similarly, acceptance and commitment therapy (ACT), a mindfulness-based approach, is gaining attention in the literature as an approach to treating PTSD. ACT works to support clients in dealing with the gross and subtle layers of avoidance that come with PTSD (Orsillo & Batten, 2005). More recently, ACT has been manualized to treat co-occurring PTSD and substance use disorders (Hermann et al., 2016).

Play Therapy for Traumatized Children. Children who experience trauma can manifest a range of symptoms and problems that become the focus of attention in the counseling room. Play is a natural language for children and serves as an excellent platform for learning and mastery. Play therapy is a best practice intervention for very young children who have experienced trauma. Play therapy can be directive or non-directive and may include the use of art and sandtray as well as traditional playroom materials (Gil, 2006; Gil, 2016).

Pharmacological Interventions. Serotonin and norepinephrine reuptake inhibitors (SNRIs) and Selective serotonin reuptake inhibitors (SSRIs) are often used to treat symptoms of PTSD. Common among these are paroxetine and sertraline that have been approved for use in PTSD specifically (Koffel et al., 2016). Sleep disturbance among those with trauma symptoms and PTSD are both common and cause significant distress and functional disturbance; half of those with PTSD report significant sleep disturbance and as many as 70% report nightmares (Koffel et al., 2016). Detweiler et al., 2016, examined the literature for research on effective treatment of nightmares in veterans. They found that among the drug trials, prazosin has been shown to have some effectiveness in improving sleep and reducing nightmares while also having relatively fewer side effects.

Definitional Cases in Dissociative Disorders

Read through the following definitional cases and decide where your first diagnostic inquiries should be. What unanswered questions will you need to ask in order to confirm a diagnosis?

Theo

Three weeks ago, Theo, a state patrolman, was among the first responders in a highway accident in which a family was killed in a collision with a tractor trailer. For almost a month, Theo woke from nightmares of the accident, was distracted by intrusive images of the scene, and found himself worrying about his own wife and children. Gradually his distraction with the accident began to fade and he is no longer distressed by it.

Leon

Leon, age 3, was found 1 year ago by social workers, neglected, hungry and dirty and was ultimately removed from the home. Since that time, his foster parents have noticed that Leon does not seek out others when he is injured or upset and has a difficult time accepting care when it is offered. Leon seems isolated and often dissolves into tears or irritability for reasons that neither he nor his foster parents can identify.

Bellamy

Since moving into his 4th foster care placement in the past year and a half, Bellamy, age 7, has displayed increasing behavioral problems. There is no evidence of behavioral problems before placement in his most recent home, however.

Lea

One year ago, Lea, 27, was on her way home from a late shift at work when she was raped by a stranger who was never identified. Since that time Lea has struggled to feel

TABLE 11.01 **Pivot Points: Trauma, Stressor and Dissociative Disorders**

	Consider this Diagnosis
Pivot Point One: Does your client's (child) suffering result from insufficient or destructive relationships from caregivers?	
• Does your client's response to insufficient or destructive parenting manifest in marked difficulties seeking or receiving comfort, and emotional or social difficulties as a result?	Reactive Attachment Disorder
• Does your client's response to insufficient or destructive parenting manifest in a tendency to approach and interact with unfamiliar adults without hesitation?	Disinhibited Social Engagement Disorder
Pivot Point Two: Has your client directly experienced or witnessed an event so horrible as to leave your client fearing for their life or the life of a loved one? Does the horror from this event continue to interfere with functioning?	
• Has your client's reaction to this horrific event taken form immediately following a horrible event? (3 days to 1 month)	Acute Stress Disorder
• Has your client's reaction to this horrific event continued for more than a month?	Post-Traumatic Stress Disorder (PTSD)
Pivot Point Three: Is your client's suffering a direct response to an identifiable event or change in his or her recent life experience?	Adjustment Disorder
• Is your client's suffering a direct response to an identifiable event or change, a delayed reaction to something that occurred more than 3 months prior to symptom onset?	Other Specified Trauma- and Stressor-Related Disorder, Adjustment-like Disorders with Delayed Onset
• Has your response to a stressor continued for 6 months though the stressor itself has not continued?	Other Specified Trauma- and Stressor-Related Disorder, Adjustment-Like Disorders, Prolonged Duration without Prolonged Stressor
• Is your client's continued suffering the response to grief and loss?	Other Specified Trauma- and Stressor-Related Disorder, Persistent Complex Bereavement Disorder
• Have your Latino client's stress reactions manifested in anxiety, anger or grief, including attacks featuring crying, shouting or aggression that feel outside the client's control?	Other Specified Trauma- and Stressor-Related Disorder, Ataque de Nervios
• Does your Latino client attribute difficulties in fulfilling life roles and functioning to a frightening event?	Other Specified Trauma- and Stressor-Related Disorder, Susto

(Continued)

(Continued)

	Consider this Diagnosis
Pivot Point Four: Is your client unable to recall key autobiographical information?	
• Is your client's primary concern one of lost memories for traumatic events or even for their history and identity?	Dissociative Amnesia
Pivot Point Five: Do your client's thoughts or feelings seem unreal to them? Does your client feel as though her or his surroundings are not real?	
• Is your client's primary concern a feeling of distance from self-experiences or a dream-like quality of the external world?	Depersonalization/ Derealization Disorder
• Do your client's depersonalization or derealization accompany PTSD symptoms?	Use Appropriate Specifiers with PTSD Diagnosis

safe in her surroundings, is often haunted by memories and flashbacks of the rape, dreams of it frequently and feels anxious and depressed.

Galina

The Showalters adopted Galina, age 9, 2 years ago. They have become increasingly concerned with Galina's tendency to wander off and noted that she often approached and engaged with complete strangers without hesitation or fear. Despite explaining the dangers to Galina on a number of occasions, they have had to become very vigilant in crowded areas such as the farmer's market, grocery store or mall and worry constantly that she will be taken by a stranger.

Narrative Cases in Dissociative, Trauma and Stressor-Related Disorders

Ronin

Ronin, 35, has been separated from his wife, Tomone, for about 3 weeks. One year ago Ronin and Tomone moved to the United States with their son, Michio, when Ronin was given a promotion. By accepting the promotion, he had to agree to transfer to the American branch of his company. Tomone, who had worked as a consultant hiring models for an ad agency, immediately missed her work, family and friends. Ronin shares, "Tomone was very unhappy and decided to go back home and stay with her family. We were fighting a lot but I miss her and Michio a great deal. Now, when I get home from work the house is dark and quiet. I can't get anything I like to eat here and Tomone was such a good cook. And she is wise, so I could talk to her about what was going on at work. Now I am very lonely."

Ronin further shares, "Since Tomone went back to Tokyo I just hate coming home. I leave work and find myself driving around aimlessly until the early hours of the morning just to avoid coming home to an empty apartment. When we talk on the internet or after I talk to my son, I feel so hopeless and alone. My heart is not in my work. When I am at the office all I can do is think about how to get out of New York and back to my family. I can't get used to living in the U.S. and I can't get used to Tomone and Michio living in Tokyo. I want to tell her that she has to come back but I don't want her to be as miserable as I am."

Maggie

Maggie, age 10, has been living with her foster family for just over a year. During that time her foster parents have developed a habit of being very vigilant of Maggie when they are in public places or when they have guests over to the house. Maggie has little or no fear or hesitation about approaching complete strangers and asking them questions or asking to join them in their activities. For example, on one occasion, when the family had taken their dog to the park, Maggie noticed another family having a picnic birthday celebration and asked the family, whom she had never met, if she could join them for cake and ice cream. Maggie's foster father reports, "Maggie just seems really naïve about the world and just doesn't seem to understand the concept of a stranger."

Maggie came into foster care when she and her younger brother were found to be alone in their home after their mother had decided to go to Los Angeles for the weekend to sing with a local band. She had left no food in the refrigerator and had failed to tell the children when she would return. A neighbor found them alone when she had stopped by wondering why the sprinkler had been left running for 36 hours straight. Once in the custody of foster care workers, Maggie and her brother reported their mother was absent much of the time, and didn't pay much attention to them when she was home. They had grown used to asking neighbors for help and sometimes for food.

Marcel

Marcel is a 25-year-old client who has come in for counseling complaining that he experiences moments in which he feels as if the world around him is distorted and far away, almost as if he were in a dream. Marcel reports that he first began experiencing these symptoms after he returned to the United States from Peru, where he attends a graduate program in environmental sciences. Marcel returned early from his program following a mountain climbing accident in which he lost his left foot and three toes on his right foot. He explains that several months earlier, while on an ice climbing trip in Peru with a team of other French climbers, Marcel and his companions had been overcome by an unexpected and blinding snowstorm while crossing a ridge. Another climber, Jean, had lost his footing and fallen to his death while the rest of the team was stranded on the ridge. Marcel was sure he would lose his life as he realized he was developing frostbite in both his feet and that the frostbite would make it painful and dangerous to make it down the face of the mountain. Several days after they were expected, the team did make it back to their home base, badly dehydrated, suffering from hypothermia and grieving the loss of their team member. Marcel explains, "We didn't realize what we were getting ourselves into. I guess we thought we knew what we were doing but we hadn't planned well and didn't have the equipment we needed. In the end it cost Jean his life and it cost me a foot."

Since the accident on the ridge in Peru, Marcel has suffered from nightmares that wake him from his sleep. "All day these dreams stay with me. I see myself looking over the edge of the ridge and I see Jean lying there in the snow, holding my severed foot. If I'm not bothered by images of the dream I am haunted by actual memories of shivering in the cold and dark wondering if I would ever see my family again. I'm ashamed to admit it but I can't bring myself to talk with the other members of the team. The memories are just too painful. I'm so ashamed that I wasn't able to do something to save Jean and I guess I wonder if the team blames me. Besides that, I'm awful to be around. I am either feeling guilty or just really apathetic and don't want to do anything or talk. So why would they want to be near me anyway?"

Marcel reports that he decided not to return to classes this term. He reports that difficulties with sleep and concentration would make it impossible for him to study and to get ready for his comprehensive exams. Marcel reports, "All I want right now is to just be alone."

Eddie

Eddie, age 4, was recently placed in therapeutic foster care after his parents were found to have been negligent in Eddie's care, both physically and emotionally, and were unresponsive to attempts on the part of social services to support and educate the family in meeting Eddie's most fundamental needs.

Eddie's foster parents are seeking counseling for Eddie and education for themselves in understanding how to respond to Eddie's "sometimes perplexing needs." Eddie's foster father, Drake, shares, "We have three children of our own and they are each unique in their own ways, that is true, but Eddie's behavior is so different from the other kids we are completely at a loss about how to help. For instance, Eddie just won't come to us or the other kids when he needs help, like when he fell down and skinned his knee. There was blood all over the place and he was crying but he didn't come in the house to get help. When we do respond his body stiffens up like he expects us to hurt him or something." Eddie's foster-mother, Lena, adds, "Eddie seems really just so sad all the time, even at times when I would expect him to be happy. And he can be unpredictable, like the way he can be suddenly fearful and there doesn't seem to be a reason for it." Drake adds, "The social worker told us to expect some behavior problems and other stuff to come up since he didn't get good care when he was really little, so I guess we knew something was coming, but this is not something we really know how to respond to, so we just need some help."

Simon

The school counselor at Southern Plains Elementary has contacted Simon's parents with concerns about his behavior and adjustment at school. Simon, age 6, who is new to this public school, transferred 3 months ago after his parents decided to move him from a private Montessori school setting to the public school. However, since moving to his new school Simon has not fit in well with the other children and has resisted the more structured schedule his teacher provides. The classroom is much larger than Simon is used to—his other classroom had six children, this one has 25. His other classroom had "stations" for learning activities and he could move freely from one to the other. His current classroom has a clear schedule that all children must attend to. Simon regularly refuses to shift activities at transition times and yells or "throws tantrums" when redirected. Simon's parents report that his behavior at home is positive, that he responds well to direction and that he did not have behavior difficulties in his previous school setting.

Nadia

Nadia, a 22-year-old college student, was participating in a protest one evening about 3 weeks prior to her intake interview when police and protesters got involved in an altercation. Nadia reports, "Police were pushing and shouting at protesters and someone threw a rock. Suddenly things got really crazy, it was total chaos. A police officer grabbed the woman next to me by the hair and drug her to the ground. He kicked her and got his stick and hit her with it. I was screaming. Then another policeman grabbed my arm and pulled me to the ground and cuffed me. I felt so scared. I thought, '*This is it, I'm going to be killed and people are going to say it was my own fault.*' I have no idea what happened between when I was on the ground and when I got back home that night. It's just gone. I only remember the smell of the grass and the feeling of the weight of the officer pushing me into the ground."

Nadia shares that in the weeks following the incident, "I had such a hard time getting to sleep. I kept thinking about that woman and how she was screaming and crying and then how quickly that was me! And when I did fall asleep, I would dream about it. And those thoughts were bothering me a lot during the day and making it hard to concentrate." Nadia further explains "I wasn't even able to go downtown where the rally was held because being there would bring it all back for me in a flash. I just felt so, so upset all the time, I didn't think I was going to be able to shake it. Slowly but surely things started to get better. I started to be able to get to sleep without having bad dreams, and then I could get through the day without thinking about it. It still bothers me a lot, and I won't be going to any more marches, that's for sure, but at least I can get through the day without being so distracted and worried."

Tamika

Six months ago Tamika, age 9, was home with her sister and mother when an intruder broke into the house and assaulted and robbed her mother. Tamika hid in her bedroom with her younger sister while she listened to her mother's screams. She was able to contact 911 on a cell phone and told the operator, "I think someone is killing my mother." Since that time, Tamika has had difficulty concentrating in school. She frequently dreams of the incident and wakes up screaming. Consequently she often feels tired during the day. She is bothered by intrusive memories of her mother's screams and pleas for help and at those times her heart races and she feels "just like it is happening again." Tamika has refused to talk about the incident with a counselor or with her mother because "it bothers me too much to talk about it." Secretly Tamika believes that she did not do enough to help her mother, that it took too long for her to dial 911, and that she should not have hidden in her room. She feels she let her mother down.

Alice

Alice, a 55-year-old mother of two adult daughters, has come to see a counselor asking for help with symptoms of worry that began to emerge shortly after learning that her mother's recent biopsy was benign. Alice shares, "About four months ago my mother found a lump in her breast. My grandmother and my aunt both had breast cancer. It killed my grandmother and nearly killed my aunt. But when my mother found that lump I realized my mother and I, and maybe even my daughter, could all get cancer and die." Alice continues, "The problem is that even though my mom's results came out ok in the end, I still feel anxious a lot. Not so much about my mom having cancer but just about everyone's health and if everyone is going to be ok." When asked if she has acted on these worries Alice shares, "I worry more than I'd like to about whether or not one of us will get cancer, and I need some help with it, but I'm not going to the doctor all the time or checking for lumps or anything like that. My problem is more just worry that gets in the way of my sleep, which makes it hard to concentrate at work."

References

Agaibi, C. E., & Wilson, J. P. (2005). Trauma, PTSD, and resilience: A review of the literature. *Trauma, Violence, & Abuse*, *6*(3), 195–216.

Alayarian, A. (2018). *Handbook of working with children, trauma, and resilience: An intercultural psychoanalytic view*. Routledge.

Alim, T. N., Feder, A., Graves, R. E., Wang, Y., Weaver, J., Westphal, M., Alonso, A., Aigbogun, N. U., Smith, B. W., Doucette, J. T., Mellman, T. A., Lawson, W. B., & Charney, D. S., (2008). Trauma, resilience, and recovery in a high-risk African-American population. *American Journal of Psychiatry, 165*(12), 1566–1575.

Amaral, A. P., Soares, M. J., Pinto, A. M., Pereira, A. T., Madeira, N., Bos, S. C., Marques, M., Roque, C., & Macedo, A. (2018). Sleep difficulties in college students: The role of stress, affect and cognitive processes. *Psychiatry Research, 260*, 331–337.

American Psychiatric Association. (2013). *Diagnostic and statistical manual of mental disorders (DSM-5®)*. Author.

Armour, C., Karstoft, K. I., & Richardson, J. D. (2014). The co-occurrence of PTSD and dissociation: Differentiating severe PTSD from dissociative-PTSD. *Social Psychiatry and Psychiatric Epidemiology, 49*(8), 1297–1306.

Ashton, C. K., O'Brien-Langer, A., & Silverstone, P. H. (2016). The CASA Trauma and Attachment Group (TAG) program for children who have attachment issues following early developmental trauma. *Journal of the Canadian Academy of Child and Adolescent Psychiatry, 25*(1), 35.

Bailey, M. (2020, February). *Too many tests, too little time: Doctors say they face 'moral injury' because of a business model that interferes with patient care.* Washington Post, Health.

Barlow, J. (2014). Excessive stress disrupts the development of brain architecture. *Journal of Children's Services, 9*(2), 143–153.

Benedek, D. M., & Wynn, G. H. (Eds.). (2016). *Complementary and alternative medicine for PTSD.* Oxford University Press.

Blakey, S. M., Wagner, H. R., Naylor, J., Brancu, M., Lane, I., Sallee, M., Kimbrel, N. A., & Elbogen, E. B. (2018). Chronic pain, TBI, and PTSD in military veterans: A link to suicidal ideation and violent impulses? *The Journal of Pain, 19*(7), 797–806.

Boyd, J. E., Protopopescu, A., O'Connor, C., Neufeld, R. W., Jetly, R., Hood, H. K., Lanius, R. A., & McKinnon, M. C. (2018). Dissociative symptoms mediate the relation between PTSD symptoms and functional impairment in a sample of military members, veterans, and first responders with PTSD. *European Journal of Psychotraumatology, 9*(1), 1463794.

Bradley, R., Greene, J., Russ, E., Dutra, L., & Westen, D. (2005). A multidimensional meta-analysis of psychotherapy for PTSD. *American Journal of Psychiatry, 162*(2), 214–227.

Brand, B. L., Lanius, R., Vermetten, E., Loewenstein, R. J., & Spiegel, D. (2012). Where are we going? An update on assessment, treatment, and neurobiological research in dissociative disorders as we move toward the DSM-5. *Journal of Trauma & Dissociation, 13*(1), 9–31.

Brave Heart, M. Y. H. (2000). Wakiksuyapi: Carrying the historical trauma of the Lakota. *Tulane Studies in Social Welfare, 21*(22), 245–266.

Carta, M. G., Balestrieri, M., Murru, A., & Hardoy, M. C. (2009). Adjustment disorder: Epidemiology, Diagnosis and treatment. *Clinical Practice and Epidemiology in Mental Health, 5*(1), 15.

Casey, P., Dowrick, C., & Wilkinson, G. (2001). Adjustment disorders: Fault line in the psychiatric glossary. *The British Journal of Psychiatry, 179*(6), 479–481.

Chappelle, W., McDonald, K., Thompson, B., & Swearengen, J. (2012). *Prevalence of high emotional distress and symptoms of post-traumatic stress disorder in US Air Force active duty remotely piloted aircraft operators (2010 USAFSAM survey results)*. School of Aerospace Medicine Wright Patterson AFB OH Aerospace Medicine Dept.

Church, D. (2010). The treatment of combat trauma in veterans using EFT (Emotional Freedom Techniques): A pilot protocol. *Traumatology, 16*(1), 55–65.

Church, D., Hawk, C., Brooks, A. J., Toukolehto, O., Wren, M., Dinter, I., & Stein, P. (2013). Psychological trauma symptom improvement in veterans using emotional freedom techniques: A randomized controlled trial. *The Journal of Nervous and Mental Disease, 201*, 153–160.

Church, D., Stapleton, P., Mollon, P., Feinstein, D., Boath, E., Mackay, D., & Sims, R. (2018, December). Guidelines for the treatment of PTSD using clinical EFT (Emotional Freedom Techniques). In *Healthcare* (Vol. 6, No. 4, p. 146). Multidisciplinary Digital Publishing Institute.

Comas-Díaz, L., Hall, G. N., & Neville, H. A. (2019). Racial trauma: Theory, research, and healing: Introduction to the special issue. *American Psychologist, 74*(1), 1.

Cook, A., Spinazzola, J., Ford, J., Lanktree, C., Blaustein, M., Cloitre, M., & Mallah, K. (2017). Complex trauma in children and adolescents. *Psychiatric Annals, 35*(5), 390–398.

Detweiler, M., Pagadala, B., Candelario, J., Boyle, J., Detweiler, J., & Lutgens, B. (2016). Treatment of post-traumatic stress disorder nightmares at a veterans affairs medical center. *Journal of Clinical Medicine, 5*(12), 117.

Evans-Campbell, T. (2008). Historical trauma in American Indian/Native Alaska communities: A multilevel framework for exploring impacts on individuals, families, and communities. *Journal of Interpersonal Violence, 23*(3), 316–338.

Fast, E., & Collin-Vézina, D. (2019). Historical trauma, race-based trauma, and resilience of indigenous peoples: A literature review. *First Peoples Child & Family Review, 14*(1), 166–181.

Flory, J. D., & Yehuda, R. (2015). Comorbidity between post-traumatic stress disorder and major depressive disorder: Alternative explanations and treatment considerations. *Dialogues in Clinical Neuroscience, 17*(2), 141.

Galea, S., Basham, K., Culpepper, L., Davidson, J., Foa, E., Kizer, K., Koenen K., Leslie, D., McCormick, R., Milad, M., Ritchie, E. C., Rizzo, A. S., Rothbaum, B. O., & Zatzick, D. (2012). *Treatment for posttraumatic stress disorder in military and veteran populations: Initial assessment*. The National Academies.

Gil, E. (2006). *Helping abused and traumatized children: Integrating directive and nondirective approaches.* Guilford Press.

Gil, E. (2016). *Posttraumatic play in children: What clinicians need to know.* Guilford Publications.

Ginzburg, K., Ein-Dor, T., & Solomon, Z. (2010). Comorbidity of posttraumatic stress disorder, anxiety and depression: A 20-year longitudinal study of war veterans. *Journal of Affective Disorders, 123*(1–3), 249–257.

Greenberg, N., Docherty, M., Gnanapragasam, S., & Wessely, S. (2020). Managing mental health challenges faced by healthcare workers during covid-19 pandemic. *BMJ, 368*, 1–4.

Guina, J., Baker, M., Stinson, K., Maust, J., Coles, J., & Broderick, P. (2017). Should posttraumatic stress be a disorder or a specifier? Towards improved nosology within the DSM categorical classification system. *Current Psychiatry Reports, 19*(10), 66.

Guyon-Harris, K. L., Humphreys, K. L., Degnan, K., Fox, N. A., Nelson, C. A., & Zeanah, C. H. (2019). A prospective longitudinal study of reactive attachment disorder following early institutional care: Considering variable-and person-centered approaches. *Attachment & Human Development, 21*(2), 95–110.

Hansen, M., Ross, J., & Armour, C. (2017). Evidence of the dissociative PTSD subtype: A systematic literature review of latent class and profile analytic studies of PTSD. *Journal of Affective Disorders, 213*, 59–69.

Haugen, P. T., Evces, M., & Weiss, D. S. (2012). Treating posttraumatic stress disorder in first responders: A systematic review. *Clinical Psychology Review, 32*(5), 370–380.

Held, P., Klassen, B. J., Brennan, M. B., & Zalta, A. K. (2018). Using prolonged exposure and cognitive processing therapy to treat veterans with moral injury-based PTSD: Two case examples. *Cognitive and Behavioral Practice, 25*(3), 377–390.

Helms, J. E., Nicolas, G., & Green, C. E. (2010). Racism and ethnoviolence as trauma: Enhancing professional training. *Traumatology, 16*(4), 53–62.

Hermann, B. A., Meyer, E. C., Schnurr, P. P., Batten, S. V., & Walser, R. D. (2016). Acceptance and commitment therapy for co-occurring PTSD and substance use: A manual development study. *Journal of Contextual Behavioral Science, 5*(4), 225–234.

Heyman, M., Dill, J., & Douglas, R. (2018). *The Ruderman white paper on mental health and suicide of first responders.* Ruderman Family Foundation.

Horwitz, A. G., Held, P., Klassen, B. J., Karnik, N. S., Pollack, M. H., & Zalta, A. K. (2018). Posttraumatic cognitions and suicidal ideation among veterans receiving PTSD treatment. *Cognitive Therapy and Research, 42*(5), 711–719.

Hovens, J. G. F. M. (2015). *Emotional scars: Impact of childhood trauma on depressive and anxiety disorders.* Department of Psychiatry, Faculty of Medicine. Leiden University Medical Center (LUMC), Leiden University.

Humphreys, K. L., Nelson, C. A., Fox, N. A., & Zeanah, C. H. (2017). Signs of reactive attachment disorder and disinhibited social engagement disorder at age 12 years: Effects of institutional care history and high-quality foster care. *Development and Psychopathology*, *29*(2), 675–684.

Jayawickreme, E., & Blackie, L. E. (2014). Post-traumatic growth as positive personality change: Evidence, controversies and future directions. *European Journal of Personality*, *28*(4), 312–331.

Jinkerson, J. D. (2016). Defining and assessing moral injury: A syndrome perspective. *Traumatology*, *22*(2), 122.

John, S. G., Cisler, J. M., & Sigel, B. A. (2017). Emotion regulation mediates the relationship between a history of child abuse and current PTSD/depression severity in adolescent females. *Journal of Family Violence*, *32*(6), 565–575.

Jones, K. P., Peddie, C. I., Gilrane, V. L., King, E. B., & Gray, A. L. (2016). Not so subtle: A meta-analytic investigation of the correlates of subtle and overt discrimination. *Journal of Management*, *42*(6), 1588–1613.

Kahane-Nissenbaum, M. C. (2011). *Exploring intergenerational transmission of trauma in third generation Holocaust survivors.* Dissertation.

Kanninen, K., Punamaki, R. L., & Qouta, S. (2003). Personality and trauma: Adult attachment and posttraumatic distress among former political prisoners. *Peace and Conflict: Journal of Peace Psychology*, *9*(2), 97–126.

Kilpatrick, D. G., Resnick, H. S., Milanak, M. E., Miller, M. W., Keyes, K. M., & Friedman, M. J. (2013). National estimates of exposure to traumatic events and PTSD prevalence using DSM-IV and DSM-5 criteria. *Journal of Traumatic Stress*, *26*(5), 537–547.

Kearns, M. C., Ressler, K. J., Zatzick, D., & Rothbaum, B. O. (2012). Early interventions for PTSD: A review. *Depression and Anxiety*, *29*(10), 833–842.

Koffel, E., Khawaja, I. S., & Germain, A. (2016). Sleep disturbances in posttraumatic stress disorder: Updated review and implications for treatment. *Psychiatric Annals*, *46*(3), 173–176.

Lancaster, C. L., Teeters, J. B., Gros, D. F., & Back, S. E. (2016). Posttraumatic stress disorder: Overview of evidence-based assessment and treatment. *Journal of Clinical Medicine*, *5*(11), 105.

Lazar, A., Litvak-Hirsch, T., & Chaitin, J. (2008). Between culture and family: Jewish-Israeli young adults' relation to the Holocaust as a cultural trauma. *Traumatology*, *14*(4), 93–102.

Leaming, W., & Ribas, J. (2020). *Some fear covid-19's emotional trauma will have lasting effects for health-care workers.* Washington Post, National.

Lehavot, K., Goldberg, S. B., Chen, J. A., Katon, J. G., Glass, J. E., Fortney, J. C., & Schnurr, P. P. (2018). Do trauma type, stressful life events, and social support explain women veterans' high prevalence of PTSD? *Social Psychiatry and Psychiatric Epidemiology*, *53*(9), 943–953.

Lehrner, A., & Yehuda, R. (2018). Trauma across generations and paths to adaptation and resilience. *Psychological Trauma: Theory, Research, Practice, and Policy*, *10*(1), 22.

Libby, D., Reddy, F., Pilver, C., & Desai, R. (2012). The use of yoga in specialized VA PTSD treatment programs. *International Journal of Yoga Therapy*, *22*(1), 79–88.

Maercker, A., & Lorenz, L. (2018). Adjustment disorder diagnosis: Improving clinical utility. *The World Journal of Biological Psychiatry*, *19*(Supp. 1), S3–S13.

McEwen, B. S., & Sapolsky, R. M. (1995). Stress and cognitive function. *Current Opinion in Neurobiology*, *5*(2), 205–216.

McLean, S. (2016). The effect of trauma on the brain development of children. *Australian Institute of Family Studies CFCA Practice Resource*, 1–15.

McTavish, J. R., Sverdlichenko, I., MacMillan, H. L., & Wekerle, C. (2019). Child sexual abuse, disclosure and PTSD: A systematic and critical review. *Child Abuse & Neglect*, *92*, 196–208.

Mills, K., Barrett, E., Peach, N., Cobham, V., Ross, J., Perrin, S., Bendall, S., Back, S., Brady, K., & Teeson, M. (2018). Treating trauma and substance use in adolescents. In *Australasian Professional Society on Alcohol and other Drugs (APSAD)* (Vol. 37, pp. 14–14).

Mitchell, K. S., Dick, A. M., DiMartino, D. M., Smith, B. N., Niles, B., Koenen, K. C., & Street, A. (2014). A pilot study of a randomized controlled trial of yoga as an intervention for PTSD symptoms in women. *Journal of Traumatic Stress*, *27*(2), 121–128.

Moody, A. T., & Lewis, J. A. (2019). Gendered racial microaggressions and traumatic stress symptoms among Black women. *Psychology of Women Quarterly*, *43*(2), 201–214.

Nagata, D. K., Kim, J. H., & Wu, K. (2019). The Japanese American wartime incarceration: Examining the scope of racial trauma. *American Psychologist*, *74*(1), 36.

Nash, W. P., & Litz, B. T. (2013). Moral injury: A mechanism for war-related psychological trauma in military family members. *Clinical Child and Family Psychology Review*, *16*(4), 365–375.

O'Connor, M., & Elklit, A. (2008). Attachment styles, traumatic events, and PTSD: A cross-sectional investigation of adult attachment and trauma. *Attachment & Human Development*, *10*(1), 59–71.

Ogle, C. M., Rubin, D. C., Berntsen, D., & Siegler, I. C. (2013). The frequency and impact of exposure to potentially traumatic events over the life course. *Clinical Psychological Science*, *1*(4), 426–434.

Ogle, C. M., Siegler, I. C., Beckham, J. C., & Rubin, D. C. (2017). Neuroticism increases PTSD symptom severity by amplifying the emotionality, rehearsal, and centrality of trauma memories. *Journal of Personality*, *85*(5), 702–715.

Orsillo, S. M., & Batten, S. V. (2005). Acceptance and commitment therapy in the treatment of posttraumatic stress disorder. *Behavior Modification*, *29*(1), 95–129.

Petrie, K., Crawford, J., Baker, S. T., Dean, K., Robinson, J., Veness, B. G., Randall, J., McGorry, P., Christensen, H., & Harvey, S. B. (2019). Interventions to reduce symptoms of common mental disorders and suicidal ideation in physicians: A systematic review and meta-analysis. *The Lancet Psychiatry*, *6*(3), 225–234.

Psychology Today. (2019). *Adjustment disorder.* https://www.psychologytoday.com/us/conditions/adjustment-disorder

Repantis, D., Wermuth, K., Tsamitros, N., Danker-Hopfe, H., Bublitz, J. C., Kühn, S., & Dresler, M. (2020). REM sleep in acutely traumatized individuals and interventions for the secondary prevention of post-traumatic stress disorder. *European Journal of Psychotraumatology, 11*(1), 1740492.

Resick, P. A., Bovin, M. J., Calloway, A. L., Dick, A. M., King, M. W., Mitchell, K. S., Suvak, M. K., Wells, S. Y., Stirman, S. W., & Wolf, E. J. (2012). A critical evaluation of the complex PTSD literature: Implications for DSM-5. *Journal of Traumatic Stress, 25*(3), 241–251.

Ritchie, E. C. (2013). Complementary and alternative medicine for PTSD. *Psychiatric Annals, 43*(1), 36–37.

Robinson, J. L., & Rubin, L. J. (2016). Homonegative microaggressions and posttraumatic stress symptoms. *Journal of Gay & Lesbian Mental Health, 20*(1), 57–69.

Romo, V. (2020, April). *NYC emergency room physician who treated coronavirus patients dies by suicide.* NPR, Coronavirus Live Updates.

Sage, C. A., Brooks, S. K., & Greenberg, N. (2018). Factors associated with Type II trauma in occupational groups working with traumatised children: A systematic review. *Journal of Mental Health, 27*(5), 457–467.

Sapolsky, R. M. (2004). *Why zebras don't get ulcers: The acclaimed guide to stress, stress-related diseases, and coping-now revised and updated.* Holt paperbacks.

Scaer, R. C. (2005). *The trauma spectrum: Hidden wounds and human resiliency.* WW Norton & Company.

Schore, A. N. (2005). Attachment, affect regulation, and the developing right brain: Linking developmental neuroscience to pediatrics. *Pediatrics in Review, 26*(6), 204–217.

Schore, A. N. (2012). Relational trauma and the developing right brain: An interface of psychoanalytic self psychology and neuroscience. In A. Schore (Ed.), *The science of the art of psychotherapy* (Norton series on interpersonal neurobiology). WW Norton & Company.

Schoulte, J. C., Schultz, J. M., & Altmaier, E. M. (2011). Forgiveness in response to cultural microaggressions. *Counselling Psychology Quarterly, 24,* 291–300.

Scott, W. J. (1990). PTSD in DSM-III: A case in the politics of diagnosis and disease. *Social Problems, 37*(3), 294–310.

Searcy, C. P., Bobadilla, L., Gordon, W. A., Jacques, S., & Elliott, L. (2012). Pharmacological prevention of combat-related PTSD: A literature review. *Military Medicine, 177*(6), 649–654.

Sharpless, B. A., & Barber, J. P. (2011). A clinician's guide to PTSD treatments for returning veterans. *Professional Psychology: Research and Practice, 42*(1), 8.

Shonkoff, J. P., Boyce, W. T., Cameron, J., Duncan, G. J., Fox, N. A., Gunnar, M. R., Levitt, P., McEwen, B. S., Nelson, C. A., Phillips, D., & Thompson, R. A. (2005). *Excessive stress disrupts the architecture of the developing brain (Working paper no. 3).* National Scientific Council on the Developing Child.

Skogstad, M., Skorstad, M., Lie, A., Conradi, H. S., Heir, T., & Weisæth, L. (2013). Work-related post-traumatic stress disorder. *Occupational Medicine, 63*(3), 175–182.

Smoller, J. W. (2016). The genetics of stress-related disorders: PTSD, depression, and anxiety disorders. *Neuropsychopharmacology, 41*(1), 297.

Smucker, M. R. (1998). *Post-traumatic stress disorder.* In R. L. Leahy (Ed.), *Practicing cognitive therapy: A guide to interventions* (pp. 193–220). Jason Aronson, Incorporated.

Solon, O. (2017). Facebook is hiring moderators. But is the job too gruesome to handle? *The Guardian, 4.* https://www.theguardian.com/technology/2017/may/04/facebook-content-moderators-ptsd-psychological-dangers

Stanley, I. H., Hom, M. A., & Joiner, T. E. (2016). A systematic review of suicidal thoughts and behaviors among police officers, firefighters, EMTs, and paramedics. *Clinical Psychology Review, 44,* 25–44.

Stevanovic, A., Franciškovic, T., & Vermetten, E. (2016). Relationship of early-life trauma, war-related trauma, personality traits, and PTSD symptom severity: A retrospective study on female civilian victims of war. *European Journal of Psychotraumatology, 7*(1), 30964.

Taylor, S. (2017). *Clinician's guide to PTSD: A cognitive-behavioral approach.* Guilford Publications.

Torres, L., & Taknint, J. T. (2015). Ethnic microaggressions, traumatic stress symptoms, and Latino depression: A moderated mediational model. *Journal of Counseling Psychology, 62*(3), 393.

Tsai, J., El-Gabalawy, R., Sledge, W. H., Southwick, S. M., & Pietrzak, R. H. (2015). Post-traumatic growth among veterans in the USA: Results from the National Health and Resilience in Veterans Study. *Psychological Medicine, 45*(1), 165–179.

Twaite, J. A., & Rodriguez-Srednicki, O. (2004). Childhood sexual and physical abuse and adult vulnerability to PTSD: The mediating effects of attachment and dissociation. *Journal of Child Sexual Abuse, 13*(1), 17–38.

Ulloa, E., Guzman, M. L., Salazar, M., & Cala, C. (2016). Posttraumatic growth and sexual violence: A literature review. *Journal of Aggression, Maltreatment & Trauma, 25*(3), 286–304.

Van der Kolk, B. A. (2017). Developmental trauma disorder: Toward a rational diagnosis for children with complex trauma histories. *Psychiatric Annals, 35*(5), 401–408.

van der Kolk, B., & Najavits, L. M. (2013). Interview: What is PTSD really? Surprises, twists of history, and the politics of diagnosis and treatment. *Journal of Clinical Psychology, 69*(5), 516–522. https://is.muni.cz/el/1423/jaro2013/PSY403/um/Developmental_Trauma_Disorder_Kolk.pdf

van Huijstee, J., & Vermetten, E. (2017). The dissociative subtype of post-traumatic stress disorder: Research update on clinical and neurobiological features. In *Behavioral neurobiology of PTSD* (pp. 229–248). Springer Publishing.

van Minnen, A., Zoellner, L. A., Harned, M. S., & Mills, K. (2015). Changes in comorbid conditions after prolonged exposure for PTSD: A literature review. *Current Psychiatry Reports, 17*(3), *17*.

Wilkins, E. J., Whiting, J. B., Watson, M. F., Russon, J. M., & Moncrief, A. M. (2013). Residual effects of slavery: What clinicians need to know. *Contemporary Family Therapy, 35*(1), 14–28.

World Health Organization. (2018). *International classification of diseases for mortality and morbidity statistics* (11th Revision). https://icd.who.int/browse11/l-m/en

Zeanah, C. H. (2000). Disturbances of attachment in young children adopted from institutions. *Journal of Developmental and Behavioral Pediatrics, 21*(3), 230–236.

Zoldbrod, A. P. (2015). Sexual issues in treating trauma survivors. *Current Sexual Health Reports, 7*(1), 3–11.

12 Dissociative Disorders

Perhaps, you can remember a time when you realized you had dissociated? Likely, you have had an experience in which you have parked your car in front of your house after a long day at work only to realize that you have no memory of the drive home. This example is so broadly described as to be nearly universal in its quality. Similarly, you may have experienced moments while talking with someone when you have felt yourself drift away, not really hearing or absorbing what the other person was saying. Perhaps, you have experienced a time when things felt strange somehow, not quite real, as if you were walking in a dream. Though most of us will likely have experiences like these at some time in our lives, for people in the midst of a dissociative disorder or who experience dissociative symptoms as part of post-traumatic stress disorder (PTSD), these experiences are protracted, distressing and cause disruptions in their lives (APA, 2013).

Although there is considerable documentation of dissociative responses and their impact, this chapter will highlight another aspect of dissociation, one that serves as a cautionary tale for diagnosticians, reminding us of a painful chapter in the history of mental health treatment. This is a story that is at times both bizarre and heartbreaking and stands as a reminder to all of us who hold the power and responsibility inherent in diagnosis and therapeutic intervention to act with responsibility and care, and to approach theory with healthy skepticism and caution. The next few pages will describe the theory behind dissociation, touch briefly on the disorders of the continuum and will explore the history and evolution of the diagnosis once known as multiple personality disorder (MPD), now renamed dissociative identity disorder (DID).

What Is Dissociation? To understand the dissociative disorders, we first need a theoretical foundation for what dissociation is and for how it might manifest. Unfortunately, there is still no universal agreement among mental health practitioners about the "what" and "how" of dissociation. Serious discussion about the psychological barriers to the full awareness of one's experiencing began with Pierre Janet. Janet described a phenomenon instigated by trauma in which an individual failed to integrate these traumatic incidents into a coherent meaningful stream, which could be accessed later. Janet also asserted that this process seemed to stunt personality development. It is Freud, however, who deserves credit for the early and elaborate theories of dissociation, the bulk of which were set in the context of his discussions of hysteria. Much of the early literature on dissociation, however, was written by those who studied the field of hypnosis (Braude, 2009; Lynn, et al., 2014; Schore, 2012a; Scull, 2011).

When we talk about dissociation, we are likely using the term in one of two ways: as a capacity or as a state. When described as a capacity, dissociation is the ability to remove oneself from an uncomfortable or triggering moment by separating oneself from sensory information coming from either the environment or from within. Dissociation as a state of being is typically very brief, though not always, and can be likened to settling into an advanced "zoned out" status, removed from the psychological pressures and stimuli of the internal or external world or both. Braude (2009) argues that dissociation is a capacity shared by all people though the expression of which varies from modest to extreme.

Disorganized Attachment and the Development of Pathological Dissociation. Recall that the earliest developmental tasks are those that invite the infant into the symphony of human connection, cultivating a rhythm and harmony between parent and child in which the child's emotions are mirrored and co-regulated. These connections build capacities for self-regulation tools used throughout the life span. When this process runs smoothly, the child becomes securely attached; when disrupted, a host of difficulties unfold. Among these, researchers argue, is the development of disorganized attachment which, in turn, may then lay the neurological groundwork for dissociative processes (Schore, 1994; Schore, 2005; Schore, 2010; Schore, 2012a, 2012b).

Schore (2012a) argues that early affect regulating interactions between the parent and child "impact cortical and limbic-autonomic circuits of the developing right cerebral hemisphere" (p. 77), where emotion regulation patterns are stored. It is these patterns that shape our interactions through childhood and into adulthood. Schore (2012b) asserts that when an infant is traumatized, the child's initial reaction is one of hyperarousal and, later, a complimentary hypoarousal. Initially, the child responds with a startle response, elevated heart rate and crying, a kind of "frantic distress" (p. 260), which then triggers stress hormones that ultimately result in a hypermetabolic environment for the developing brain. When a child's caregiver supports the child in restoring equilibrium, the child's right brain capacities grow; without support the child's response is to withdraw from the psychic environment, resulting in a diminishing of "self-organizing capacities" (p. 270). The psychic withdrawal goes hand-in-hand with the parasympathetic nervous response, a response that aims to regulate and restore, but results in a much lowered metabolic responsiveness. This process becomes part of a pattern of responses to experiences that trigger memories of trauma, thus becoming a dissociative response pattern (Schore, 2012b). Schore's theory overlaps with theories that describe dissociation as primarily a function of emotion regulation.

The Polyvagal Model. The sympathetic and parasympathetic nervous systems work in harmony to activate and calm the system. Porges (2011) describes a third branch of this system, a social engagement system, that works to maintain connection with other people. When the "ventral vagal complex rapidly regulates cardiac output to foster fluid engagement and disengagement with the social environment, aspects of a secure attachment bond . . . on the other hand, activity of the dorsal vagal complex-associated with intense emotional states and immobilization-is responsible for severe metabolic depression, hypoarousal, and pain blunting of dissociation" (p. 61). Thus, the polyvagal system is responsible for creating a tripartite function: mobilization to action, immobilization or downregulation and social connection and communication. The sympathetic nervous system is responsible for the mobilization of the system in response to threat. The parasympathetic system restores the body to normalcy as it stabilizes the system. But the parasympathetic nervous system can over-function and bring the person into something that looks more like a shocked or frozen state with a concomitant downregulation of the metabolic system. The dorsal vagus nerve is responsible for this self-preserving shut-down process, though it may also provide a low metabolic state that enables a rest, digest and restore process. The vagus nerve is believed to be responsible for the connection between the right brain of one person and the next.

Dissociation as Emotion Modulation. Brand et al. (2012) place dissociation on a continuum of emotion modulation. In their model, flashbacks and intrusive re-experiencing of painful memories sit on the far end of the continuum of emotional under-modulation, and are considered dissociative because the flashback takes the individual out of contact with the environment and leaves the person entirely immersed in memories of the past. At the opposite end of this continuum, dissociation represents an emotional over-modulation. They describe three types of dissociation: (1) primary dissociation, re-experiencing/flashback; (2) secondary dissociation, depersonalization, derealization and analgesia (as in sedation) and (3) tertiary dissociation, the development of complex identity. Later in this chapter, the theory of tertiary dissociation and the diagnosis of DID, in particular, will be explored in greater depth.

Differentiating Dissociation from Altered States of Consciousness. How is dissociation different from other states of being that take us out of immediate and direct contact with the sensory environment? Van der Hart et al. (2004) note that a number of experiences of everyday living resemble dissociation but are distinct from it. For example, spaciness or daydreaming. Similarly, states such as creative flow in which a person is entirely absorbed in a creative effort, losing all sense of time, as described by Mihaly Czikszentmihalyi (1990) also fits these types of experiences. As I write this paragraph, sitting in my garden in the backyard, for instance, I lose awareness of the sound of the birds, the gentle breeze in the trees and even lose the sound of my neighbor's hammering on the other side of the fence. These types of temporary narrowing of the field of our consciousness are essential to completing complicated tasks and, again, should not be confused with pathological dissociation.

BOX 12.01 DISSOCIATIVE DISORDERS: KEY DEFINITIONS

Deaffectualization: This experience describes one in which emotions and emotional reactivity are diminished (Medford et al. 2005).

Example: Kai's friends and family have noticed that lately he has seemed somewhat emotionally remote. Kai has noted a sense of distance from his feelings as well, as if they were there, but somehow "over the horizon" or "not yet arriving." His girlfriend has shared her concern about how his lack of emotions has gotten in the way of their relationship in the last weeks.

Depersonalization: Depersonalization is a phenomenon in which experiences are detached from the experience of self, for example, rather than feeling present in what is unfolding, one experiences events or sensation as an outside observer rather than a participant.

Example: While shopping, Kerry's 2-year-old daughter threw herself onto the floor of the grocery aisle and screamed defiantly. Kerry was struck with a now-familiar sensation, as she picked up her daughter and tried to calm her. Kerry felt far away somehow, as if she was watching herself with her daughter through a window. This strange distanced feeling was happening more and more often and she wasn't sure what to make of it.

Derealization: Derealization is an experience of the outside world or surroundings as distorted, unreal or as having a dream-like quality.

Example: In the midst of teaching his advanced calculus course, Philippe suddenly felt as if the room was filled with an odd smoke or haze. He was certain that this was a feeling and not the true condition of the room because it had happened so suddenly and because there was no smell of smoke or shift in humidity. He wiped his eyes, but still the strange haze remained. He continued teaching, wondering what could be interfering with his senses.

Dissociation: Dissociation is a term describing the capacity for separating sensations, experiences or memories from one's awareness without intending or knowing that one has done so. Dissociation does not include instances in which a person isn't capable of understanding and integrating information, as when a child sees something that can't be understood developmentally or when a phenomenon, such as hypnosis or sedation, blocks the integration of information or stimuli (Schore, 2012b).

Example: Try as he might, 41-year-old Thad isn't able to remember any of a drowning accident in which his younger brother was killed. Though Thad knows the accident has happened and that he was a witness to it, he is unable to recover even a whisper of the memories of that day.

Desomatization: This phenomenon describes a change in one's relationship to bodily sensation, sometimes experienced as a disembodiment and occasionally accompanied by an increased threshold for pain (APA, 2013).

False Memory Syndrome: False memory syndrome describes false memories, usually of abuse or Satanic abuse in particular, which are embraced as factual but are false (Ost, 2017).

Recovered Memories: Now rejected as largely untrustworthy, recovered memories were "uncovered" through a number of suggestive processes, such as hypnosis, dream interpretation and the use of drugs, and often resulted in the production of false memories of experiencing or witnessing horrific abuse (Ost, 2017).

Repression: Repression is a psychoanalytic term for a theoretical phenomenon in which a person's unconscious psychological material is walled off from conscious awareness and can be accessed only indirectly, through means such as dreams and free association.

Example: Lying in the shadows of Isabella's unconscious, and completely outside her awareness, are lingering resentments toward her demanding parents and a wish that they would die and leave her free to live her life.

(Continued)

(*Continued*)

Structural *Dissociation: This term is one that describes dissociation within the structure of the personality and at its most extreme (tertiary) refers to dissociative identity disorder (Nijenhuis et al., 2010)*

Suppression: Suppression is a psychoanalytic term for the theoretical phenomenon in which a person shuts oneself off from information that was once in conscious awareness but is deliberately put out of the mind due to its potential to arouse anxiety or discomfort. Suppression does not include amnesia (Braude, 2009).

Example: Looking at the items displayed on the altar of her church, a thought crosses Mattie's mind that she could snap the head from the statue of the Virgin Mary and no one would suspect it was her. Mattie quickly put the sacrilegious thought out of her mind, and turned to her mother and said, "I love the Virgin Mary, she is so beautiful and reflects all that we should be in the world, nurturing, patient and loving. When I see her statue I think of sitting next to Nanna in church and it reminds me how much I miss her."

Iatrogenic: Illnesses or injuries that are the result of examination or treatment are described as iatrogenic, including but not exclusive to the side effects of medication.

Traumagenic: Illness that is the result of trauma, such as memory loss due to traumatic brain injury, or neurological deficits due to early abuse and neglect are described as traumagenic.

Differentiating Dissociation from Repression and Suppression. The term dissociation is sometimes used interchangeably with the Freudian defense mechanisms, repression and suppression. (Freud's theories and descriptions of the two changed over time, sometimes even using these terms interchangeably.) For our purposes, repression differs from both dissociation and suppression, however, in that what is repressed is alive only in the unconscious and was never consciously available to the individual. In contrast, anything dissociated or suppressed was first located in the individual's environment and would have been available under typical circumstances (Boag, 2010; Braude, 2009).

Suppression differs from both repression and dissociation because suppression is undertaken intentionally, for instance, putting out of one's mind the knowledge that this may be the last opportunity to see a loved one who is terminally ill, or suspecting a partner has been unfaithful and putting the thought to the back of one's mind. In other words, suppressed information is available but is deliberately sidestepped in order to avoid discomfort or pain. In dissociation, however, the mechanisms that take in information and store it don't do their job and the information is not recorded properly (Braude, 2009; Boag, 2010). The DSM defines dissociation as "a disruption of the normal integrative functions of consciousness, memory identity, and perception of the

BOX 12.02 TRY THIS

Read the following quote taken from Haruki Murakami's *The Wind-Up Bird Chronicle.* Is Creta Kano describing dissociation, repression or suppression? Support your argument.

"It may sound difficult when I describe it like this, but once you learn the method it is not difficult at all. When pain comes to me, I leave my physical self. It's just like quietly slipping into the next room when someone you don't want to meet comes along . . . I feel the existence of pain; but I am not there. I am in the next room. And so the yoke of pain is not able to capture me." —Creta Kano *in The Wind-Up Bird Chronicle (Murakami, 2010)*

environment" (p. 259), a bit like unintentionally forgetting to hit record on a recording device and being left with no audio or video record of an event. Using the definition offered by the DSM 5, neither repression nor suppression would be considered dissociative for two reasons: first, repressed materials are understood to arise from the unconscious and not the "environment," and second, suppression is a kind of practiced or skillful ignoring and not a disruption of the function of consciousness per se.

Disorders of the Dissociative Continuum

Depersonalization/Derealization Disorder. Depersonalization and derealization are perceptual anomalies in which a person feels disconnected from the body, thoughts, feelings or a sense of self (depersonalization) or experiences of detachment from or sensation of unreality about the surrounding environment (derealization) (APA, 2013; Madden & Einhorn, 2018; Spiegel et al., 2011). When a client feels disembodied or experiences diminished pain tolerance as a part of a dissociative process, this phenomenon has been described as desomatization, while the loss of emotion is described as deaffectualization (Medford et al., 2005). Ma Jian, in *Red Dust: A Path Through China*, evokes the experience of derealization when documenting his travels, "I feel I have walked onto a stage. The people around me are absorbed in their parts, putting on this great show, but nothing seems real. Every object looks like a prop."

Experiences of depersonalization and derealization are not, in and of themselves, disruptive or especially uncommon; some estimates suggest that as many as half of all Americans will have this kind of experience at least once in their lifetimes (APA, 2013). Arguably, experiences of depersonalization and derealization that result from sleep deprivation, mild or even moderate stress, illness, sensory deprivation or substance use may be closer to benign "alterations in consciousness" than true dissociative processes (Van der Hartm et al., 2004, p. 908). When depersonalization or derealization begin to impinge on a person's functioning, a diagnosis is considered. When this depersonalization or derealization reaches the level of disorder, it is set apart from a psychotic episode in that a person's reality testing remains intact throughout the experience; these clients never doubt their own substantiality or that of the world around them, except, perhaps, philosophically (APA, 2013; Madden & Einhorn, 2018).

Dissociative Amnesia. Dissociative amnesia has two forms, each with its own code. The more common form (without fugue) features scattered or localized amnesia in which traumatic or stressful memories are forgotten. Dissociative amnesia with dissociative fugue, also sometimes referred to as the Jason Bourne Syndrome, features amnesia for one's identity and personal history accompanied by a phenomenon in which the client wanders away from their home, sometimes for months or years; this form of amnesia is very rare. In each case, the amnesia far outpaces what might be expected in normal forgetting; the amnesia should not be better accounted for by brain injury, substance use, seizure, and so on. In previous editions of the DSM, dissociative fugue was coded separately; currently, a specifier is used to indicate fugue experiences (APA, 2013). Neurological explorations of retrograde (past) autobiographical memories have shown neuro-network changes that serve to undermine autobiographical information as a result of trauma, though more research is needed to fully understand this process, this research suggests biological underpinnings for the amnesia events (Staniloiu & Markowitsch, 2014).

Dissociative Identity Disorder (DID). This disorder describes a phenomenon in which a person experiences a profound disruption in the continuity of personal identity, and instead fosters the development of two or more personality states that can be distinguished from one another in thoughts, feelings, behaviors and preferences, as well as distinct memories. The recent edition of the DSM points out that these experiences may be described as possessions by some cultural groups but can be diagnosed despite this when the possession experienced is unwanted, unusual or is not sanctioned by the client's cultural group and, consequently, causes significant distress and dysfunction. Sanctioned practices that resemble DID should not be diagnosed, such as speaking in tongues. The diagnostic criteria for DID also stipulate gaps in memory that can't be attributed to normal forgetting as well as functional impairment in one or more areas of the client's life (APA, 2013; Spiegel et al., 2011).

In the next section, we will explore DID and its history in greater depth. Attention is being given to this disorder and its history because it highlights the importance of ethical practice in our roles as diagnosticians and mental health professionals as well as the importance of practice grounded in research, healthy skepticism and continual evaluation of the efficacy of our treatment plans.

DID/MPD and Its History: A Cautionary Tale

DID is new to the DSM 5 but not new to the field of psychiatry. Introduced in 1980 in the DSM III as multiple personality disorder (MPD), this diagnosis was once extraordinarily rare and fairly obscure, having been described in only 76 people prior to 1979. However, in 1973, Dr. Cornelia Wilbur's book, *Sybil* detailed her diagnosis and treatment of a client that she argued had 16 separate personalities. The book became a best seller and a popular movie of the same name soon followed. Directly after the publication of the DSM III, and the inclusion of MPD in that edition, the diagnosis proliferated dramatically. Between 1985 and 1995, an astonishing 40,000 cases were diagnosed in the United States. An academic journal devoted to the topic, "Dissociation," was founded, and the number of articles written on the topic of MPD lept 6,000% (Acocella, 1999; Piper & Mersky, 2004a). MPD had captured the imagination of the American public and the profession alike; the disorder and the people who were diagnosed with it were regularly featured on television programs popular at the time, such as Oprah and Donahue (Acocella, 1999; Spanos, 1996).

The earliest case studies of MPD, particularly those identified before the formal MPD diagnosis was introduced into the DSM, describe people who evidenced two personality presentations. A frequent example offered is that of Mary Reynolds who was treated in the 1860s. Ms. Reynolds presented with two primary states distinguishable from one another, one of a person with a thoughtless and rude temperament and one of "melancholic religiosity." At the time Ms. Reynolds was described as having a "double consciousness." Today proponents of the DID/MPD diagnosis point to her case as historical evidence for the disorder's existence. Others, however, believe Ms. Reynold's presentation is better described by the dramatic mood shifts of a bipolar disorder. By the mid-1980s, however, the average number of personalities identified in an individual diagnosed with MPD was 16, though some clients were thought to have "alters" numbering in the hundreds. Kluft (1984), a researcher and therapist, described having two patients each with a mind-boggling 4,000 alters. As the trend for patients to be "populated" by greater numbers of alter personalities, the nature of these personalities also became more and more unusual, and in some cases documentation of dogs, cats and even a lobster could be found in the literature (Acocella, 1999; Piper & Mersky, 2004a). MPD workshops, books and professional literature described a broad range of experiences that might trigger splintering of personalities, ranging from childhood abuse, war, severe illness, natural disasters and feeling rejected by one's parents, and with it a confusing list of symptoms that were purported to signal a potentially hidden dissociative identity, for example, depression, anxiety, eating disorders, believing one was sexually abused as a child . . . or believing one was NOT sexually abused as a child (Bass & Davis, 2002; Brand et al., 2016; Kluft, 1984).

The cases of MPD/DID were also unusual in that most patients eventually diagnosed showed no evidence of the disorder on initial interview with their therapist and had come seeking treatment for concerns related to depression, grief, psychosis, anxiety, and so on. The belief among researchers and clinicians of the time was that the multiples were hidden from view and had to be uncovered by a skilled professional and integrated before symptoms would resolve. Many therapists used hypnosis, with and without the use of drugs, dream interpretation, guided imagery and other suggestive methods to "uncover" memories and to reveal hidden alter personalities (Kluft, 1983). The recovery of these memories were often followed by family confrontations, severed relationships and, in some cases, lost jobs and criminal charges (Appelbaum, 2001; de Rivera, 1997).

By the late 1990s, however, hundreds of clients who had recovered memories of abuse during the course of therapy began to retract their claims, asserting their memories had been false and were cultivated within the therapeutic process itself. Family members and concerned therapists coined the term false memory syndrome to describe those who had, through the process of therapy, created false memories, which they believed were factual. The False Memory Syndrome Foundation ultimately created a hotline that logged nearly 6,000 reports of false memory syndrome between 1992 and 1994 (de Rivera, 1997). The methods used to recover memories would later be rejected in the courts; hundreds of therapists were sued for malpractice, some by their own clients and others by third-party complainants (Appelbaum, 2001; de Rivera, 1997; Loftus, 1997). These events helped to give rise to a field of study exploring how false memories are successfully implanted and sustained (Loftus, 1993, 1997).

At least one of the driving forces behind the dramatic rise in the diagnosis of DID was a cultural phenomenon, which coincided with the introduction of the disorder, the fear of underground cells of Satanic cults that were purported to abuse children sexually and physically, and were believed to engage in cannibalism and ritual sacrifice of infants, children, adults and animals. These cults were believed to have been centuries old and were thought to use brainwashing tactics to erase memories of abuse and murder and to encode instructions to abuse or kill children or to commit suicide (Acocella, 1999; Bikel & Dretzin, 1995). Reports of murders and sacrifices unearthed through recovered memories were so widespread as to trigger an extensive FBI investigation that resulted in a 1992 report. The report detailed its failure to find any evidence of Satanic cults or their reported murders (Acocella, 1999; National Center for the Analysis of Violent Crime, 1992).

Competing Theories of DID. Two competing theories have emerged to explain DID: the post-traumatic model (PTM) and the sociocognitive model (SCM). The PTM asserts that when a traumatic event is utterly horrific and inescapable, a person's capacity to integrate the experience is so overwhelmed that their personality is essentially shattered into parts that then take on a life and function of their own. In this model, a person loses awareness of activities and experiences when these other aspects of self-emerge. As a result, the person is said to lose chunks of memory and will experience unexpected consequences thanks to the behavior of the emergent personalities or "alters" (Acocella, 1999; Bass & Davis, 2002; Dorahy et al., 2014).

Structural Dissociation Theory. The structural dissociation theory is a more recent variant of the PTM of DID. This model describes two primary parts of the traumatized personality: the emotional part (EP) and the apparently normal part (ANP). The EP is thought to fixate on the traumatizing event, stuck in a defensive posture, ready to respond to threat, whereas the ANP is more attentive to the functions of daily life. This theory describes an alternation between the two aspects of self, in which the ANP is dissociated from the trauma, and consequently experiences different degrees of amnesia for it, and instead lends attention to matters of living, while the EP is vigilant and hyperaroused. This theory holds that those with PTSD have one ANP and one EP, those with complex trauma would have one ANP and two or more EPs, whereas the person with DID would have more than one ANP and more than one EP (Nijenhuis & den Boer, 2010).

Sociocognitive Model. The SCM, on the other hand, asserts that one's cultural environment and cognitive expectations shape the roles we take on, including how we act within our roles as client and therapist. In other words, these theorists argue that clients describe experiences in response to subtle and not-so-subtle expectations placed on them by social constructs and by the therapist themselves. In the case of DID, the SCM would point to the popular culture that framed the surge in these diagnoses, such as the popularity of movies like "The Three Faces of Eve" and "Sybil," in offering a template for client and therapist roles. Enhanced by the influence of drugs and hypnosis, these expectations worked together to shape the symptoms and roles that clients took on in therapy and ultimately resulted in their diagnosis (Boysen & VanBergen, 2013; Spanos 1996). The PTM theory would describe DID as "traumagenic," or arising out of trauma experiences, whereas the SCM would describe DID as essentially iatrogenic, or born out of the therapeutic process itself.

Researchers argue that if DID is a traumagenic disorder and not a socially constructed one, then experts trained to identify and diagnose should be able to differentiate those with true DID and those asked to simulate the disorder (to pretend they have DID). We would expect those pretending to have DID to respond to memory assessments and memory-based research tasks based on their assumptions about the disorder, whereas those diagnosed with DID would respond out of the cognitive capacities of their disorder (Boysen & VanBergen, 2013; Huntjens et al., 2006). What most studies have found, however, is that those diagnosed with DID and those simulating DID respond in the same ways, suggesting that those with DID manifest their disorder according to social expectations and not disorder (Boysen & VanBergen, 2013). In a 2006 study, for example, Huntjens et al. found that those simulating DID and those diagnosed with the disorder performed equally poorly on memory tests (answering less well than would be expected if they answered only by chance). These researchers concluded, "DID patients were found not to be characterized by an actual memory retrieval inability, in contrast to their subjective reports. Instead, the research results suggested that DID may more accurately be considered a disorder characterized by meta-memory problems, holding incorrect beliefs about their own memory functioning" (p. 857). These studies lend support to the sociocognitive model of DID. Brand et al. (2012) argue, however, that research on new assessment tools suggest some promise in differentiating "genuine from feigned DID" (p. 13), though they concede that additional research is needed to assist in this effort.

Given the historical timeline and the horrors of our world today and of our not so distant past, for example, colonization, wars, slavery, oppressive poverty, such experienced during the Great Depression, genocide, and so on, one might expect the psychiatric record to be choked with cases of splintered personality, and for these cases to be scattered evenly across the globe rather than concentrated among White middle class women. What the research shows, however, is that the vast majority of recorded cases have been diagnosed in the United States and Canada, followed by Europe and Turkey, and are diagnosed by a relatively small number of clinicians. What's more, a review of the literature "provided no direct evidence that DID exists outside of treatment" (Boysen & VanBergen, 2013, p. 8). In other words, we can easily meet people in everyday settings, those outside the therapy office, who describe symptoms that would meet criteria for major depression, PTSD, generalized anxiety, obsessive compulsive disorder (OCD), and so on, who are not receiving treatment; but this does not seem to be the case with people who are eventually diagnosed with DID.

Researchers also point out that the traumagenic theory of DID has not yet been supported by the research literature. A great deal of research literature points to an association between trauma and poor outcomes later in life, including dissociative patterns, but a causal process describing exactly how trauma would result in dissociation followed by multiplicity has not been born out in the scientific literature. Researchers and clinicians have also raised serious concerns about the therapeutic interventions designed for this population, noting that they tend to encourage clients to reinforce the substantiality of alters rather than working to integrate parts into the self, for example, inquiring about suicidal/homicidal intentions of individual alters, asking alters to interpret for one another or to care for/nurture one another, instructing alters to consult one another about how to solve problems, seeking consensus among alters for therapeutic treatment/goals, meeting separately with different alter identities, and creating developmentally sensitive interventions for "child alters." All of these interventions create a therapeutic environment that encourages clients to deepen and flesh out "alters" (Piper & Mersky, 2004b).

Ethical Considerations in the Diagnosis of DID. Clinicians should also be aware that validity problems have been identified in assessments used for evaluating dissociation (Brown, 2009; Gharaibeh, 2009). Gharaibeh (2009) uses the Adolescent Dissociative Experience Scale as an example of a questionable assessment tool. A sample question reads "I get so wrapped up in watching TV, reading, or playing a video game that I don't have any idea what's going on around me," something experienced by most teens and adults. Gharaibeh further points out that good diagnostic ethics involve a kind of "informed skepticism" in which the practitioner "challenges his or her assumptions about a possible diagnosis through a methodical process of inclusion, exclusion and hypothesis testing" (p. 31). He argues that without this kind of skepticism our care is substandard and perhaps neglectful. To this point, Gharaibeh notes that the diagnostic criteria themselves are tautological in nature, in that the A and B criteria are redundant to one another creating a circular reasoning increasing the likelihood of diagnosis. Again, extreme care should be used when exploring this diagnosis.

A 2001 survey of American and Canadian psychiatrists revealed that less than one in seven psychiatrists believed the MPD (DID) diagnosis was grounded in science (Lalonde et al., 2001). The chair of the DSM IV Task Force, Alan Frances, asserted his stance about the diagnosis saying, "I felt it was a hoax . . . certainly not a legitimate disorder. For better or worse, I chose not to impose my view on DSM-IV." Frances (2013) further warned, "Thankfully, the world has taken a break and for now has moved away from MPD, but I would expect other outbreaks in the future . . . We are always just a blockbuster movie and some weekend therapist's workshops away from a new fad . . ." (pp. 132-133). While the validity of the MPD/DID diagnosis has been and continues to be questioned, the impact of trauma is widely understood to have negative short- and long-term effects on well-being.

Cultural Considerations. A recent article bringing renewed interest to DID noted that cultural oppressions experienced by those living in inner-city areas made residents more vulnerable to trauma, dissociation and DID (Brand et al., 2016). Although it goes without saying that attending to the complex consequences of trauma within the context of multi-stressed families and communities is imperative, it is also essential that professionals avoid adding to the psychological consequences of these stressors and traumatic experiences by making use of harmful diagnostic practices or inaccurate diagnoses. Consequently, the utmost caution is advised when diagnosing clients already marginalized by social and economic oppression.

The Skilled Diagnostician: Differential Diagnosis

Differentiation of Depersonalization/Derealization and Psychotic Processes or Cannabis-Induced States. Depersonalization and derealization are generally seen in one of the five circumstances: (1) occurring on their own, idiopathically; (2) as part of a PTSD presentation; (3) triggered by the use of cannabis, ketamine, ecstasy and other drugs; (4) emerging as a feature of psychosis or (5) as part of religious or meditative practice. For the most part, depersonalization and derealization triggered by cannabis happens only during intoxication as a direct and immediate side effect of the substance, in which case, a substance intoxication diagnosis would be most appropriate. However, in some cases these experiences have persisted for days, weeks, months or even years after a person has stopped using the substance (APA, 2013; Madden & Einhorn, 2018), in which case depersonalization/derealization is diagnosed (APA, 2013).

When these experiences emerge as a part of a psychosis, they may be similar to a non-psychotic state but the relationship to, meaning-making of, and reality testing are different. In depersonalization/derealization disorder, the client's reality testing

BOX 12.03 TRY THIS: DIAGNOSE MANIFESTATIONS OF DEPERSONALIZATION/ DEREALIZATION

The following scenarios feature Javier, Elias, Mariana, Dennis and Fern, five people who share similar traits. Each is 21 years old, Presbyterian and a third-generation American, and each is experiencing similar symptoms. Read the following scenarios and notice how the differences in their descriptions pull you in different diagnostic directions. What first impressions do you have reading each that might point you in the direction of derealization/depersonalization disorder, substance-induced experiences, psychosis, post-traumatic stress disorder (PTSD) or a cultural experience that should not be diagnosed?

Javier: "Sometimes I get a really, really weird feeling and I never know when it will happen or how long it will last. What happens is that things just feel both far away and close at the same time. As if I am watching life on a movie screen or remembering a dream, but the whole time I know that it is just a jacked-up thing, it isn't real."

Elias: Elias shares, "Sometimes a sky spirit changes places with me and takes refuge behind my eyes. He watches my life while my consciousness rests in the sky. I see what he sees, and he sees what I see. When the spirit rests inside me the world looks far away; when the spirit sits in the sky I see up close again. He has chosen me because one day I will inherit this world and he will turn to silver-laced oxygen."

Mariana: Mariana has been plagued with flashbacks of a sexual assault that occurred four months ago while she was on an Army deployment. Since that time she has struggled to leave her home alone because, she has felt depressed and anxious. She also describes feeling like she is watching herself play out a scripted role in a novel rather than living in her 'real life.' "I know this is all real, but it doesn't really feel that way."

Dennis: Dennis started meditating and reading about Zen Buddhism at the suggestion of his counselor as part of an effort to reduce anxiety. He shares, "I really took to it. I didn't expect to, but I did. Early on in practicing open space meditations I had a few experiences where I could see the world a bit more clearly, with less intense emotional connection to everything and more like I was just observing. That gave me a lot of space and freedom from anxiety. I have had several experiences like that when I wasn't meditating, however, and at those times I don't really like that feeling. I would like to be able to control when I feel this distanced observing and when I don't."

Fern: "My sister and I got high a couple of weeks ago with some guys from the arcade that had some weed with them. I felt like everything around me was like a far off kind of whisper, but not exactly that, just more like maybe on a big movie screen but kind of far away, too. Like a drive-in theater where the sound comes in through a box. I don't know if that makes sense. But it is still kind of with me now even though I'm not high anymore. I'm not sure why it doesn't stop. It was cool when it started but it's getting on my nerves now."

remains intact throughout the experience, whereas the person experiencing a psychosis experiences a loosening of the relationship with reality (APA, 2013; Madden & Einhorn, 2018).

Recovered Memory and the Diagnosis of Trauma and Dissociative Disorders. A significant quantity of research documents the ease at which false memories of abuse can be formed (Garven et al., 1998; Ost, 2017; Pope, 1996). During the period of time when DID diagnoses were at their peak, practices aimed at uncovering lost memories of trauma became more popular. Highly suggestive and subjective methods were used, such as hypnosis (a state of suggestion itself), dream interpretation and the use of drugs (Appelbaum, 2001). However, by 1999, more than 200 lawsuits had been filed against therapists related to recovered memory practices (Acocella, 1999; Lief, 1999). The International Society for the Study of Trauma and Dissociation (2011) published guidelines for treating DID and noted that it is not the work of clinicians to investigate or uncover memories, nor is it the work of clinicians to evaluate the validity of memories that arise as either real or not real. Instead, they recommend "a respectful neutral stance" (p. 167) taking care to remember a client's "vulnerability to accommodate the therapist's authority" (p. 167). Ironically, Shirley Ardell Mason, the woman about whom the book and movie *Sybil* were written, would later admit that her alter personalities had been created to fulfill the expectations of her therapist (Borch-Jacobsen, 1997). In our work with clients who present with hazy, concerning, confusing or newly emerging memories of abuse, whether symptoms point to a trauma or dissociative disorder, extreme caution is recommended so that clients are not influenced, subtly coerced or shaped to meet the expectations, interests or curiosities of the clinician.

Differentiation of DID, Schizophrenia and Factitious Disorder. DID and schizophrenia can be confused and their differentiation can be complicated by the potential presence of a factitious disorder. A client with a presentation that resembles schizophrenia but also has features that mirror the DID criteria should be examined carefully. Consultation is a must and referral to a qualified practitioner licensed to conduct appropriate assessments is highly recommended. For initial support in deciding where best to refer this client, the use of the Structural Clinical Interview for DSM Disorders (SCID-D) will be helpful in suggesting the presence of one diagnosis over another (Welburn et al., 2003). Always take into consideration diagnostic principles when considering a diagnosis. Recall the principle *horses over zebras.* For example, a client in her early 20s with dramatic changes in personality, memory gaps, confusion and delusional beliefs is more likely to be experiencing the early symptoms of schizophrenia than a dissociative personality phenomenon.

Treatment Interventions for Dissociative Disorders

Pharmacological Interventions. A number of medications have been tested in the treatment of depersonalization, though the combination of the anticonvulsant lamotrigine

TABLE 12.01 **Pivot Points: Dissociative Disorders**

	Consider This Diagnosis
Pivot Point One: Has your client directly experienced or witnessed an event so horrible as to leave your client fearing for their life or the life of a loved one? Does the horror from this event continue to interfere with functioning?	
• Has your client's reaction to this horrific event taken form immediately following a horrible event? (3 days to 1 month)	Acute stress disorder
• Has your client's reaction to this horrific event continued for more than a month?	Post-traumatic stress disorder (PTSD)
Pivot Point Two: Is your client unable to recall key autobiographical information?	
• Is your client's primary concern one of the lost memories for traumatic events or even for their history and identity?	Dissociative amnesia
Pivot Point Three: Do your client's thoughts or feelings seem unreal to them? Does your client feel as though their surroundings are not real?	
• Is your client's primary concern a feeling of distance from self-experiences or a dream-like quality of the external world?	Depersonalization/ derealization disorder
• Do your client's depersonalization or derealization accompany PTSD symptoms?	Use appropriate specifiers with PTSD diagnosis
• Do your client's depersonalization or derealization follow substance use?	Substance-Induced depersonalization/ Derealization disorder
• Are your client's experiences of depersonalization or derealization a part of a culturally sanctioned or religious experience and cause no distress of functional difficulty?	No diagnosis
Pivot Point Four: If your client's suffering is characteristic of a dissociative disorder, but does not meet full criteria for any and you can specify the reason, then consider this diagnosis.	Other specified dissociative disorder (Specify the reason here)
Pivot Point Five: If your client's suffering is characteristic of a dissociative disorder but you do not have enough information to justify a diagnosis, then consider this.	Unspecified dissociative disorder

together with a selective serotonin reuptake inhibitor seems most broadly accepted (Medford et al., 2005).

Psychotherapy. Zerubavel and Messman-Moore (2015) argue that mindfulness-based approaches may be uniquely suited to support clients who struggle with dissociation. They assert that the key feature of dissociation is a retreat from present moment experiencing and argue that mindfulness offers clients an opportunity to cultivate awareness of their own dissociative processes and offers tools to stay within the present moment (p. 303). Acceptance and Ccommitment Therapy (ACT), a mindfulness-based approach, for instance, works with traumatized clients in targeting experiential avoidance, as with the avoidance of memories or emotion, while also supporting clients who tend to get caught in the past rather than occupying the present moment (Engle & Follette, 2015; Hayes et al., 2012).

Internal Family Systems. The internal family systems (IFS) model is an emergent model used in treating trauma and dissociation. IFS is one that integrates three streams of thought: normal multiplicity of mind, family systems theory and self-leadership. The concept of normal multiplicity draws from the Jungian idea that all of us contain parts of self, or subminds, that respond differently and with varied perceptions. For instance, we all have a child-like self that sees the world playfully and with wonder, as well as a skeptical and more practical self, though how often these parts of ourselves appear in relationship with others varies a great deal from one person to the next. Family systems theory considers the way that family members interact dynamically. IFS applies systems-style dynamics to the parts of self. Finally, "IFS posits the inherent existence of a spacious essence in each person that, when accessed spontaneously, manifests leadership qualities that include mindfulness, loving kindness, and compassion" (p. 130). This aspect is referred to as the Self. Together, these three streams assert that parts of self can be supported to work in harmony under the leadership of the wise compassionate Self, described as self-leading. This approach aims to support clients in embracing all parts of self rather than avoiding or ignoring unwanted parts and experiences (Schwartz & Sparks, 2015).

Definitional Cases in Dissociative Disorders

Read through the following definitional cases and decide where your first diagnostic inquiries should be. What unanswered questions will you need to ask in order to confirm a diagnosis?

Irene

Irene was found wandering around the subway of New York City. She doesn't know how she got into the subway or even who she is. Irene's driver's license indicates that she is 32 and that she lives in Boston.

Charlotte

Charlotte often feels detached from her feelings and thoughts as if they were happening to someone else.

Alisha

Alisha has virtually no memories before age 12 when she was placed in foster care and later adopted. Her memories seem largely intact from age 13 onward.

Takumi

Takumi has developed three distinct personalities. Takumi displays markedly different affect, ways of thinking and behavioral patterns from one personality style to the next.

Narrative Cases in Dissociative, Trauma and Stressor-Related Disorders

Serge

Serge, a 27-year-old welder, has been referred to a counselor where he reports, "I'm here because I keep having these weird experiences where things just feel really strange to me. It is very hard to explain. I tried to explain it to my doctor and he had me get some tests, one was a brain imaging test and then there was an eye exam and some blood tests, but they all came back fine so she told me to come to talk to a counselor. Here's what happens—and it really freaks me out—I'll be going along just fine and suddenly it is like the world around me is changing into some kind of other dimension. My wife calls it the Twilight Zone. Everything is there just like before but it is different somehow, just not as clear, not as real. It throws me off every time. And I really don't like for it to happen when I'm driving or when I'm welding. It doesn't feel safe. Nothing bad ever happens, it's just distracting and I can't focus on what I'm doing like I should." Serge further reports, "I just really want to figure out what is causing this and fix it because I'm not comfortable driving and I get nervous that it will happen at work. It's bothering me a lot."

Dickson

Dickson, age 16, was adopted at age 11 when courts removed him from his birth parents' home and jailed both parents on charges of child sexual abuse. Dickson shares, "I really don't have any memories of being abused in any way. I guess I believe it is true since my parents confessed that they did it. But I also don't remember anything from when I was a kid. I don't remember any birthdays or Christmas and I don't remember my grandparents or aunts or uncles. I don't even remember going to school or anything. It's like all of that is just a white board with nothing written on it. It makes me feel kind of empty inside. Like there is a big part of who I am just kind of wiped away. I feel embarrassed when my friends are talking about their memories and I am sometimes tense thinking they will expect me to say something about when I was a kid.

I wish I remembered something . . . anything. I know those memories could be hard but there could be good memories in there, too." Dickson's mother reports that she brought him to counseling because Dickson has told her that not having the memories is bothering him and that he worries that something is wrong with him that is causing him to be unable to recall his past. She believes that Dickson would benefit from being able to talk about the lost memories and if it is possible or even a good idea to try to get them back.

Bridget

Bridget, a 38-year-old mother of four, reports that she is unable to remember how she came to be in a downtown Denver spa when her home is located in a small town in Southern Utah. Police located Bridget by following her credit card usage after neighbors found the children alone in their home. Neighbors report that they had gone to check on the family and to bring food when they heard the news that Bridget's husband, Thom, had been killed on the job fighting a large office fire. Bridget explains, "The last thing I remember I was home, putting the laundry into the dryer. The phone rang, I remember that, and I remember reaching for it, but the rest is a blank. I don't remember anyone telling me about Thom and I don't remember getting in the car and driving to Denver, but I must have, because here I am." Bridget claims that neither she nor her husband drink or use substances and denies previous difficulties with memory or other mental health concerns.

References

Acocella, J. (1999). *Creating hysteria: Women and multiple personality disorder.* Jossey-Bass.

American Psychiatric Association. (2013). *Diagnostic and statistical manual of mental disorders (DSM-5®).* Author.

Appelbaum, P. S. (2001). Law & psychiatry: Third-party suits against therapists in recovered-memory cases. *Psychiatric Services, 52*(1), 27–28.

Bass, E., & Davis, L. (2002). *The courage to heal: A guide for women survivors of child sexual abuse.* Random House.

Bikel, O., & Dretzin, R. (1995). In search of satan. *Frontline, Episode 2.*

Boag, S. (2010). Repression, suppression, and conscious awareness. *Psychoanalytic Psychology, 27*(2), 164.

Borch-Jacobsen, M. (1997). Sybil: The making of a disease. *The New York Review of Books, XLIV,* 61–64.

Boysen, G. A., & VanBergen, A. (2013). A review of published research on adult dissociative identity disorder: 2000–2010. *The Journal of Nervous and Mental Disease*, *201*(1), 5–11.

Brand, B. L., Lanius, R., Vermetten, E., Loewenstein, R. J., & Spiegel, D. (2012). Where are we going? An update on assessment, treatment, and neurobiological research in dissociative disorders as we move toward the DSM-5. *Journal of Trauma & Dissociation*, *13*(1), 9–31.

Brand, B. L., Sar, V., Stavropoulos, P., Krüger, C., Korzekwa, M., Martínez-Taboas, A., & Middleton, W. (2016). Separating fact from fiction: An empirical examination of six myths about dissociative identity disorder. *Harvard Review of Psychiatry*, *24*(4), 257.

Braude, S. E. (2009). The conceptual unity of dissociation: A philosophical argument. In P. F. Dell & J. A. O'Neil (Eds.), *Dissociation and the dissociative disorders: DSM V and beyond*. Routledge.

Brown, L. S. (2009). True drama or true trauma? Forensic trauma assessment and the challenge of detecting malingering. In P. F. Dell & J. A. O'Neil (Eds.), *Dissociation and the dissociative disorders: DSM V and beyond*. Routledge.

Czikszentmihalyi, M. (1990). *Flow: The psychology of optimal experience*. Harper Perennial Modern Classics.

de Rivera, J. (1997). The construction of false memory syndrome: The experience of retractors. *Psychological Inquiry*, *8*(4), 271–292.

Dorahy, M. J., Brand, B. L., Şar, V., Krüger, C., Stavropoulos, P., Martínez-Taboas, A., Lewis-Fernández, R., & Middleton, W. (2014). Dissociative identity disorder: An empirical overview. *Australian & New Zealand Journal of Psychiatry*, *48*(5), 402–417.

Engle, J. L., & Follette, V. M. (2015). *Mindfulness and valued action: An acceptance and commitment therapy approach to working with trauma survivors*. In V. M. Follette, J. Briere, D. Rozelle, J. W. Hopper, & D. I. Rome (Eds.), *Mindfulness-oriented interventions for trauma: Integrating contemplative practices*. Guilford Press.

Frances, A. (2013). *Saving normal: An insider's revolt against out-of-control psychiatric diagnosis, DSM-5, big pharma, and the medicalization of ordinary life*. William Morrow.

Garven, S., Wood, J. M., Malpass, R. S., & Shaw, J. S. III. (1998). More than suggestion: The effect of interviewing techniques from the McMartin Preschool case. *Journal of Applied Psychology*, *83*(3), 347.

Gharaibeh, N. (2009). Dissociative identity disorder: Time to remove it from DSM-V? *Current Psychiatry*, *8*(9), 30–36.

Hayes, S. C., Strosahl, K. D., & Wilson, K. G. (2012). Psychological flexibility as a unified model of human functioning. In *Acceptance and commitment therapy: The process and practice of mindful change*. Guilford Press.

Huntjens, R. J., Peters, M. L., Woertman, L., Bovenschen, L. M., Martin, R. C., & Postma, A. (2006). Inter-identity amnesia in dissociative identity disorder: A simulated memory impairment? *Psychological Medicine*, *36*(6), 857–863.

International Society for the Study of Trauma and Dissociation. (2011). Guidelines for treating dissociative identity disorder in adults, Third revision. *Journal of Trauma & Dissociation*, *12*(2), 115–187.

Kluft, R. P. (1983). Hypnotherapeutic crisis intervention in multiple personality. *American Journal of Clinical Hypnosis*, *26*(2), 73–83.

Kluft, R. P. (1984). An introduction to multiple personality disorder. *Psychiatric Annals*, *14*(1), 19–24.

Lalonde, J. K., Hudson, J. I., Gigante, R. A., & Pope, H. G. Jr. (2001). Canadian and American psychiatrists' attitudes toward dissociative disorders diagnoses. *The Canadian Journal of Psychiatry*, *46*(5), 407–412.

Lief, H. I. (1999). Patients versus therapists: Legal actions over recovered memory therapy. *Psychiatric Times*, *16*.

Loftus, E. F. (1993). The reality of repressed memories. *American Psychologist*, *48*(5), 518.

Loftus, E. F. (1997). Creating false memories. *Scientific American*, *277*(3), 70–75.

Lynn, S. J., Lilienfeld, S. O., Merckelbach, H., Giesbrecht, T., McNally, R. J., Loftus, E. F. , Bruck, M., Garry, M., & Malaktaris, A. (2014). The trauma model of dissociation: Inconvenient truths and stubborn fictions. Comment on Dalenberg et al. (2012). *Psychological Bulletin*, *140*, 896–910.

Madden, S. P., & Einhorn, P. M. (2018). Cannabis-induced depersonalization-derealization disorder. *American Journal of Psychiatry Residents' Journal*, *13*(2), 3–6.

Medford, N., Sierra, M., Baker, D., & David, A. S. (2005). Understanding and treating depersonalisation disorder. *Advances in Psychiatric Treatment*, *11*(2), 92–100.

Murakami, H. (2010). *The wind-up bird chronicle: A novel.* Vintage.

National Center for the Analysis of Violent Crime. (1992). *Investigator's guide to allegations of "ritual" child abuse.* Federal Bureau of Investigations, Behavioral Science Unit.

Nijenhuis, E. R., & den Boer, J. A. (2010). Psychobiology of traumatization and trauma-related structural dissociation of the personality. In P. F. Dell & J. A. O'Neil (Eds.), *Dissociation and the dissociative disorders: DSM-V and beyond.* Routledge.

Nijenhuis, E., van der Hart, O., & Steele, K. (2010). Trauma-related structural dissociation of the personality. *Activitas Nervosa Superior*, *52*(1), 1–23.

Ost, J. (2017). Adults' retractions of childhood sexual abuse allegations: High-stakes and the (in) validation of recollection. *Memory*, *25*(7), 900–909.

Piper, A., & Merskey, H. (2004a). The persistence of folly: A critical examination of dissociative identity disorder. Part I. The excesses of an improbable concept. *The Canadian Journal of Psychiatry*, *49*(9), 592–600.

Piper, A., & Merskey, H. (2004b). The persistence of folly: Critical examination of dissociative identity disorder. Part II. The defence and decline of multiple personality or dissociative identity disorder. *The Canadian Journal of Psychiatry*, *49*(10), 678–683.

Pope, K. S. (1996). Memory, abuse, and science: Questioning claims about the false memory syndrome epidemic. *American Psychologist, 51*(9), 957.

Porges, S. W. (2011). *The polyvagal theory: Neurophysiological foundations of emotions, attachment, communication, and self-regulation* (Norton Series on Interpersonal Neurobiology). W. W. Norton & Co.

Schore, A. N. (1994). *Affect regulation and the origin of the self.* Erlbaum.

Schore, A. N. (2005). Attachment, affect regulation, and the developing right brain: Linking developmental neuroscience to pediatrics. *Pediatrics in Review, 26*(6), 204–217.

Schore, A. N. (2010). Relational trauma and the developing right brain: The neurobiology of broken attachment bonds. In T. Baradon (Ed.), *Relational trauma in infancy* (pp. 19–47). Routlege.

Schore, A. N. (2012a). Attachment, trauma and the developing right brain: Origins of pathological dissociation. In A. Schore (Ed.), *The science of the art of psychotherapy* (Norton Series on Interpersonal Neurobiology). W. W. Norton & Co.

Schore, A. N. (2012b). Right brain affect regulation: An essential mechanism of development, trauma, dissociation, and psychotherapy. In A. N. Schore (Ed.), *The science of the art of psychotherapy* (pp. 71–117). Norton.

Schwartz, R. C., & Sparks, F. (2015). The internal family systems model in trauma treatment: Parallels with Mahayana Buddhist theory and practice. In V. M. Follette, J. Briere, D. Rozelle, J. W. Hopper, & D. I. Rome (Eds.), *Mindfulness-oriented interventions for trauma: Integrating contemplative practices* (pp. 125–139). Guilford Press.

Scull, A. (2011). *Hysteria: The disturbing history*. Oxford University Press.

Spanos, N. P. (1996). *Multiple identities & false memories: A sociocognitive perspective*. American Psychological Association.

Spiegel, D., Loewenstein, R. J., Lewis-Fernández, R, Sar, V., Simeon, D., Vermetten, E., Cardeña, E., & Dell, P. F. (2011). Dissociative disorders in DSM-5. *Depression and Anxiety, 28*(9), 824–852.

Staniloiu, A., & Markowitsch, H. J. (2014). Dissociative amnesia. *The Lancet Psychiatry, 1*(3), 226–241.

Van der Hart, O., Nijenhuis, E., Steele, K., & Brown, D. (2004). Trauma-related dissociation: Conceptual clarity lost and found. *Australian and New Zealand Journal of Psychiatry, 38*(11–12), 906–914.

Welburn, K. R., Fraser, G. A., Jordan, S. A., Cameron, C., Webb, L. M., & Raine, D. (2003). Discriminating dissociative identity disorder from schizophrenia and feigned dissociation on psychological tests and structured interview. *Journal of Trauma & Dissociation, 4*(2), 109–130.

Zerubavel, N., & Messman-Moore, T. L. (2015). Staying present: Incorporating mindfulness into therapy for dissociation. *Mindfulness, 6*(2), 303–314.

13 Somatic Symptom and Related Disorders

The somatic symptom and related disorders' dimension of the DSM 5 is distinguished from the other dimensions of the DSM in that it is comprised of those disorders that are centered on the body and emerge either because a person is preoccupied with physical symptoms or illness or when a person is believed to have bypassed directly confronting emotional concerns by manifesting those issues as physical symptoms, as in a conversion disorder. Conversion disorders often carry with them a kind of metaphorical quality similar to a dream; for instance, the man who has not been able to "see" that his partner is having an affair, is suddenly blind, though nothing is physically wrong with his eyes, or the woman who is powerless to change her status at work and suddenly finds that she is too weak to lift her arms. In these examples, the psychological conflicts are believed to have manifested themselves in symbolic physical symptoms. In contrast to those clients who are believed to unconsciously manifest their distress through physical symptoms are clients who find the role of patient or caregiver so comforting or fulfilling that they deliberately produce symptoms, either in themselves or in others, in order to generate and sustain contact with medical professionals, as with factitious disorder (Hammond & Echterling, 2008). The long history of interest in somatic symptom disorders (SSD) and changing attitudes and understanding of them has, as a by-product, generated a long list of descriptors for these disorders, many now abandoned by the American Psychiatric Association (APA), or were never included within a DSM edition but have been used broadly in the literature. Box 13.01 includes some terms you are likely to encounter should you research these disorders further.

Somatic symptom and related disorders are somewhat complicated to identify and address because modern medical science is in a continual process of gaining a clearer picture of the process of disease within the body. Diseases once thought to be embedded largely in psychological processes have been found to have a physiological basis; for example, asthma (Aćimović, 2017), ulcerative colitis (Aronowitz & Spiro, 1988) and multiple sclerosis (VanderPlate, 1984) were all once thought to be manifestations of psychological processes but are now understood to be physiological illnesses exacerbated by stress. A dramatic example of

BOX 13.01 DESCRIPTORS USED TO DESCRIBE SOMATIC SYMPTOM DISORDERS FOUND OUTSIDE THE DSM 5

Briquet's Syndrome: a syndrome later named somatization disorder, Briquet's described those who generally thought of themselves as sickly and developed a number of unexplained symptoms judged to be hysterical in nature (Holder-Perkins & Wise, 2001).

Compensation Neurosis: a phenomenon in which an injured person with a current or pending litigation fails to recover from their injury as expected thanks to a combination of influences including somatization, suggestion and rationalization compounded by factors such as a need for justice, or an identification with the role of an injured or victimized person (Bellamy, 1997, p. 94; Charis, 2018).

Functional Somatic Syndromes (FSS): an umbrella term found in the medical literature describing a number of commonly recognized syndromes that cause distress, dysfunction or disability but to date have no identified medical explanation (Bourke et al., 2015).

Hypochondriasis: a disorder included within previous editions of the DSM describing a pattern in which a person tends to misinterpret bodily sensations as illness and carries a lot of worries about health-related issues (APA, 2013).

Hysteria: a psychoanalytic term that, in this context, describes symptoms manifested from the unconscious rather than from biological sources (Nicholson et al., 2016).

Medically Unexplained Symptoms (MUS): a term used in the medical literature to describe clusters of symptoms that have no known medical cause and are suspected to have psychological origins or contributions (Kirmayer et al., 2004).

Monosymptomatic Hypochondriacal Psychosis: describes hypochondriacal symptoms that feature delusions (Fallon & Feinstein, 2001).

Munchausen's Syndrome/Munchausen by Proxy: this term, frequently encountered in popular literature, refers to factitious disorder in which symptoms are deliberately feigned or produced, sometimes in oneself and sometimes perpetrated on some in one's care, in order to fill the role of patient or caregiver (Hammond & Echterling, 2009).

Psychogenic Illness/Disorder: illnesses with a psychological source.

Psychosomatic illness/Disorder: illnesses with a psychological source

Somatization: When first coined in 1943, this term was a synonym for Freud's term, conversion (Holder-Perkins & Wise, 2001). Currently the term refers to the presence of bodily symptoms without a known medical condition and does not immediately presume an underlying psychological cause, though it is not ruled out.

Somatization by Proxy: This phenomenon describes patterns of responding to physiological complaints, such as excessive worry of attention to benign sensations that are learned by observing caregiver responses to somatic experiences (Weisblatt et al., 2011).

the misdiagnosis of SSD is described in Cahalan's (2012) autobiographical telling of her month-long ordeal with psychosis, paranoid ideation and seizures that several doctors diagnosed as mental illness but was ultimately identified as an autoimmune disorder attacking her brain. Once identified, Cahalan's symptoms were treated successfully. Stories like Cahalan's remind us that accurately diagnosing SSDs is always subject to the limits of the current understanding of the physical body, of illness generally and by the physician's understanding of the individual client's body particularly, and, as such, must be undertaken with great care and humility.

Still, it is estimated that about once a month, the majority of the non-clinical population experiences symptoms pestersome enough that they seek help, for example through doctor's visits or by purchasing over-the-counter medications; as many as one-third of those symptoms are thought to be medically unexplained symptoms (MUS) (Cottingham, 2017). Fatigue and headache account for half of the complaints leading people to see their primary care physician, half of those have no medical explanation (Katon et al., 2001). An example of widespread MUS comes in the form of food allergies. Food allergies are serious and life threatening, causing vomiting, swollen tongue and throat or at its most extreme, anaphylaxis. In a study of more than 40,000 American adults, however, about 19% of those surveyed endorsed at least one food allergy; however, only about 10.8% of those allergies were judged to be "convincing" (Gupta et al., 2019). While MUS are very common and most of us experience some type of MUS that will come and go without remarkable interference in our lives, some functional somatic illnesses can lead to significant distress and even disability. A 2001 study conducted by the Division of Child and Adolescent Psychiatry revealed a startling picture of the degree to which clients can experience impairment. Those with chronic fatigue syndrome missed nearly seven times as many days of school than did those with depression and 10 times as many days as those with rheumatoid arthritis, for an average of 72 days, creating a significant barrier to their education (Manu, 2004). Similarly, psychogenic neurological disorders can be particularly debilitating; 50% of those affected are unemployed as a consequence, a quarter of whom turn to state funded disability (Cottingham, 2017). Further, it is important to keep in mind that among those diagnosed with a somatic symptom related disorder (SSRD), it is uncommon for a medical cause to be identified later, though this does sometimes happen (Crimlisk et al., 1998). It is clients for whom physical symptoms interfere significantly with functioning and well-being that the somatic symptom continuum is concerned.

Changes to the SSDs in the DSM 5

Criticisms of the category of SSDs as well as the individual disorders themselves have dogged the DSM's nosology. Attempts have been made to address some of these concerns while others remain, and unfortunately, new concerns have arisen; thanks to recent changes. Five key concerns have been voiced. First, the name of the category had been viewed as distasteful to clients, as it was associated with mental illness. Second, the early conceptualization of the SSDs embraced a mind–body dualism that is no longer reflective of the scientific literature and is out of step with the perspectives of most health professionals. A third concern swirled around the lack of clarity within the diagnostic criteria; for instance, poorly defined thresholds for impairment that contributes to low diagnostic reliability, and a failure to identify which medical diagnoses should be counted as a medical condition and which as a somatic symptom. Also, of concern to many diagnosticians is the lack of cohesion within the grouping, as the disorders are less a continuum than a collection of disorders that share a preoccupation with somatic symptoms. Finally, the SSDs have raised concerns because the group of disorders do not fit well within some cultural and religious frameworks where mind–body dualism is particularly incongruent, as with Asian medicine (American Psychiatric Association, 2018; Mayou et al., 2005).

In response to criticisms from the field and in order to address perennial difficulties with differential diagnosis, the SSDs grouping has undergone significant revision. The continuum has been renamed, Somatic Symptom and Related Disorders (previously the somatoform disorders). Several disorders were reconceptualized, collapsed and renamed in the latest edition (somatization disorder, hypochondriasis, pain disorder and undifferentiated somatoform disorder). Citing symptom overlap and a lack of clarity, somatization disorder and *undifferentiated somatoform disorder* are now merged into a single disorder, SSD (APA, 2013; Dimsdale et al., 2013). For all intents and purposes, hypochondriasis is essentially renamed illness anxiety disorder (IAD). Also new to the fifth edition is psychological factors affecting a medical disorder (PFMD) (APA, 2013). These disorders will be described briefly later in the chapter.

Some revisions to this continuum have raised concern among diagnosticians. The APA has attempted to shift the weight of diagnosis away from the necessity of exhaustive testing to determine the source of the symptoms and moves attention toward a consideration of a maladaptive relationship with the symptoms themselves (Dimsdale et al., 2013). In doing so, however, the revised criteria allow clinicians to diagnose an SSD in clients suffering from a credible or even serious health condition if the client also experiences considerable worry or anxiety about that illness. Critics feel this represents a potential for unnecessary and unhelpful overdiagnosis (Frances, 2013; Häuser & Wolfe, 2013).

The Somatic Symptom Continuum of Disorders

The SSDs are discussed in two ways within the literature: medically and psychologically. Though for two decades, medical researchers have been questioning whether or not MUS are all one or many different disorders (Wessely et al., 1999). In the medical literature, functional somatic syndromes are found within every discipline of the medical field from autoimmune, gastrointestinal, neurological and pediatric, and are described individually as syndromes, such as irritable bowel syndrome, persistent

BOX 13.02 KEY TERMS

Anosognosia: a failure to notice or to have any concern about physical symptoms, such as chest pain; this characteristic represents antithesis of health anxiety (Stone et al., 2006).

Central Sensitivity Syndrome: this syndrome describes a still-theoretical biological explanation for some functional pain syndromes that proposes a heightened sensitivity to sensation within the central nervous system that misinterprets benign sensations as pain (Yunus, 2008).

Cyberchondria: this safety-seeking behavior features repeated and excessive health-related internet research spurred by emotional stress, generally anxiety and tend to increase and reinforce worry rather than soothe it (Asmundson & Taylor, 2020).

Functional Somatic Syndromes (FSS): a term used to describe medically unexplained illness that avoids attributing the cause of the illness to psychological factors (Manu, 2004).

Health Anxiety: health anxiety refers to a protracted and distracting level of concern about one's physical health; the person struggling with illness anxiety is more concerned about becoming ill than with already being ill with something undetected, as in hypochondriasis/illness anxiety disorder (Asmundson & Taylor, 2020).

Illness Behavior: this term refers to the way people make sense of their symptoms, and take action to address them (Manu, 2004).

post-concussion syndrome or pervasive refusal syndrome, a syndrome in which children refuse to eat, drink or move at all and which threatens their health with infection from bed sores, pain and dehydration (Lask, 2004; Weisblatt et al., 2011; Wessely et al., 1999; Wessely & White, 2004; Youngjohn et al., 1995). The DSM 5, however, describes the somatic symptom continuum not according to the specific syndromes comprised of particular constellations of bodily complaints, but instead, identifies a few disorders that are discerned according to the client's relationship to their symptoms. This difference between how psychologically influenced physical symptoms are discussed within the medical and psychiatric fields adds a burden to mental health professionals to have a working knowledge of which diagnoses are medically unexplained and are believed to have their origins in psychological processes and which are biologically based. Adding to this challenge, some syndromes with medically based sounding names are diagnosed and treated by physicians without ever informing their patients that the syndrome is likely based in psychological sources, insomnia, fibromyalgia and irritable bowel syndrome representing three common examples. (It is worth noting, too, that while insomnia is described as medically unexplained in the medical literature, the DSM has placed it within the sleep disorders continuum.)

The SSDR continuum also includes a diagnostic category for clients who are suffering from psychological symptoms that are aggravating a diagnosed medical condition or interfering with its treatment, as is often seen with depression (DiMatteo et al., 2000).

Illness Anxiety Disorder (IAD). This diagnosis, previously named hypochondriasis and sometimes referred to as nosophobia, features a persistent and intensely distracting fear that one is ill with some undiagnosed condition. Clients plagued with this disorder spend an inordinate amount of time worried about health concerns, often researching them online and obsessively documenting symptoms. These clients may studiously avoid getting care for fear of having their fears confirmed, *care-avoidant type* or develop a relationship with healthcare professionals in which they frequently seek out help and consultation when it is not needed, specified as *care-seeking type*. Often care-seeking clients undergo many unnecessary and expensive medical procedures in order to rule out their fears, and are not easily reassured that they are well (APA, 2013; Axelsson et al., 2016). The most severely impacted may experience deep depression, hopelessness and intense fears of dying.

Lending evidence for how common IAD is, in 2017, Pandey et al. conducted a study of 400 consecutive medical outpatients at a large clinic in India. They found that 7% of patients met criteria for (IAD). Among these, two-thirds had a comorbid mental health condition, nearly one-third of which were anxiety disorders and more than a quarter were depression. There is some evidence for comorbidity with personality disorders as well. For example, Fallon et al. (2012), found that among those diagnosed with hypochondriasis/IAD, just over 40% also had a personality disorder, most frequently paranoid, avoidant and obsessive compulsive personality disorders. These studies and others like them strongly suggest that clients who present with IAD should be assessed for comorbid depression, anxiety and personality disorders.

Illness Anxiety and Covid-19. Health anxiety is a common experience and, up to a point, can serve an important function in maintaining both individual and community health. Measures needed to contain the spread of Covid-19, such as very frequent handwashing, frequent cleaning of "high-touch surfaces," wearing face coverings and social distancing, are served by those who have an appropriate level of concern for their own health and those around them. However, for those with IAD, these strategies may be accompanied by excesses. Too frequent handwashing, compulsive cleaning, fear-filled isolation, panic buying and overspending on unneeded products or purchasing excessive quantities of products such as disinfectants, hand sanitizers, masks and so on. Fear-driven purchases may contribute to supply shortages for service providers (Asmundson & Taylor, 2020). Mertens et al. (2020) conducted an online survey with 439 participants just 3 days after the World Health Organization declared Covid-19 to be a pandemic. They found four factors contributed to high levels of fear of Covid-19: health anxiety, high levels of media use, high levels of social media use and concerns about a loved one with high health risk. Affirming the Mertens et al. (2020) findings, Jungmann and Witthöft (2020) describe the role of safety-seeking behaviors in increasing pandemic fears, particularly a type of excessive exposure to media known as cyberchondria. Cyberchondria, describes a pattern of behavior in which a person returns to the internet again and again for health-related searches. Rather than finding solace, the searches amplify and fuel increasing anxiety.

However, low levels of illness anxiety can also jeopardize a person's health or that of others. Those who are not concerned about the spread of Covid-19, for example, and don't take recommended precautions, may expose themselves and others to disease (Asmundson & Taylor, 2020; Mertens et al., 2020).

Somatic Symptom Disorder. SSD is a diagnosis added to the latest edition of the DSM. This disorder is a re-imagining of the somatoform disorder, pain disorder and some key features of hypochondriasis. This diagnosis is given when a person is experiencing one or more physical symptoms that cause significant distress and distraction usually, but not always, lasting 6 months or more (APA, 2013; Axelsson et al., 2016; Dimsdale et al., 2013). Even before the publication of the DSM 5, clinicians were concerned about the diagnostic criteria for SSD. In contrast to IAD, SSD, they argued, is vague and has within it a heterogeneous quality that makes reliable diagnosis difficult and valid diagnosis questionable. Much of the discussion centers on the question whether or not SSD and IAD are two distinct disorders, as presented in the DSM 5 or are better framed as a single phenomenon, as was captured by hypochondriasis in past editions (Starcevic, 2013). However, evidence supporting the APA's position that IAD and SSD represent two different phenomena was offered in the form of a study of an assessment tool designed to identify and differentiate the two. The Health Preoccupation Diagnostic Interview (HPDI) has been found to discern the two disorders with some accuracy and consistency, though with less consistency in their specifiers (Axelsson et al., 2016).

Conversion Disorder (Functional Neurological Symptom Disorder). Conversion disorder, as described earlier, is understood to take place when a psychological stressor becomes too much to bear and a person unconsciously converts their pain into an illness as a means of escaping an intolerable emotional weight, in other words, "[an intrapsychic conflict is 'converted' into an external symptom]" (Burgeois et al., 2002, p. 488). These symptoms generally appear suddenly, can't be explained medically and usually manifest in ways that contradict human anatomy or the understanding of the function of the body; for instance, when pupils dilate in response to light in a person who is suddenly and inexplicably unable to see. Further, conversions generally follow a psychological trigger. Historically, it was asserted that clients who presented with conversion symptoms did not respond with the kind of distress in response to the converted symptom that one would expect, but instead seemed naive, indifferent or otherwise cheerful, a presentation described as *la belle indifference.* Research exploring la belle indifference has not borne out this sign as a reliable indicator of conversion; however, in part because this presentation has been documented in those with medically diagnosed disorders, indicating that it is not unique to the conversion phenomenon. What's more, conceptualization of *la belle indifference* has been criticized for failing to consider all plausible reasons for its presence. For instance, a client may try to "put on a brave face" in the midst of a perplexing physical condition, or may worry that they will be suspected of having a mental disorder and attempt to avoid a psychiatric diagnosis by presenting themselves as emotionally stable as possible (Stone et al., 2006).

Two types of gain are thought to result from conversion; escape from the painful feelings, described as the primary gain, any additional changes in circumstances brought about by the illness that might bring benefit (for instance, by drawing care or attention, by de-escalating conflict, avoiding a difficult work situation) would be described as secondary gain (Burgeois et al., 2002; Nicholson et al., 2016). Among the most common conversion symptoms: numbness, the inability to speak, disturbed balance, the lump-in-the-throat phenomenon, unexplained tingling, or other odd sensations or the inability to see or hear (Burgeois et al., 2002). However, some conditions can be easily confused with psychosomatic illness and should be ruled out before a diagnosis is made, including but not exclusive to the following: alcohol use or withdrawal, angina or arrhythmias, B6 and B12 deficiencies, brain abscesses or tumors, lupus, multiple sclerosis, thyroid abnormalities and so on (Pomeroy et al., 2008).

Freud postulated that conversion disorders featuring movement restriction were seated in an unconscious desire to escape a life event too terrible to face; he noted that these events were often repressed or minimized as the somatic symptom was generated. A comparison study of those with movement conversion disorders, those with depression and those with no diagnosis, attempted to test Freud's theory by assessing recent life events judged to be *severe, escape or severe escape*, such as rape or physical abuse. They found that among those with conversion disorder, 56% identified a recent severe "high escape" event, significantly more than in those with depression (21%) or in controls (0%). These researchers found a relationship between escape and severe escape events and conversion; however, they also found that 10% of those with a diagnosed conversion disorder reported no event at all, suggesting that while escape may serve as a key etiological factor, it did not seem to account for all conversions. Finally, this team did not find support for the repression of the events themselves nor did its finding support a minimization of their weight, as in la belle indifference (Nicholson et al., 2016).

Conversion disorders are frequently comorbid with other mental health concerns. A small study of participants diagnosed with conversion disorder revealed that nearly 90% had at least one other psychiatric diagnosis, half of the participants evidenced generalized anxiety disorder, the most severely impacted participants also manifested dissociative disorders (Şar et al., 2004).

Psychological Factors Affecting Other Medical Conditions (PFMC). First proposed by Mayou et al. (2005), this new addition to the DSM 5 has been included to describe situations in which a person's documented medical condition is being negatively affected by mental health concerns. The diagnostic criteria recognize three ways in which mental health may impair a client's progress in cultivating physical wellness. First, the mental health symptoms may seem to have instigated the health concern because the symptoms began at about the same time as the physical condition, suggesting a link between the two; for instance, when a person with newly emergent panic disorder also suddenly develops dangerous hypertension. Second, sometimes a client's mental health disorder or symptoms interfere with the treatment of a physical disorder, as when a depressed client lacks volition to take human immunodeficiency virus (HIV) medications as prescribed and does not follow through on appointments (DiMatteo et al., 2000). Third, a client can be diagnosed with PFMC when a client's mental health concern directly impacts the physical body and impedes treatment or hastens the health decline, as when a diabetic drinks heavily.

Factitious Disorder. The SSDs have been conceptualized as operating on a continuum, with deception of self at one end (SSD and conversion disorder) and deception of the other at the other extreme (factitious disorder) (Boone, 2017). Sometimes known as Munchausen's syndrome, factitious disorder describes a pattern of behavior in which a person so prizes the role of the patient that they deliberately exaggerate, induce or feign symptoms of a physical or mental illness. Though the behavior can be relatively benign and limited, as with single episode presentations, in extreme cases, affected persons can undergo unnecessary, intrusive, painful testing and even surgery. Some will suffer serious side effects or iatrogenic illness as a consequence of these unnecessary treatments and interventions. Some will take extreme measures to produce injury or illness; for example, introducing urine in the bloodstream to evoke infection. Presenting symptoms may be physiological or psychological in nature or a combination of the two (Hammond & Echterling, 2008). A 2006 study reviewing the records of 100 psychiatric hospital admissions determined that 6% of these admissions were factitious. These researchers found that depression, suicidal ideation and hallucinations were among the most commonly feigned symptoms (Gregory & Jindal, 2006).

A more dangerous variant of this behavior is factitious disorder imposed on another (FDIA). In this situation a person, most often a parent but sometimes another caregiver, deliberately creates the conditions for symptoms to arise in another targeted person, frequently a child. In these cases, the child (or other affected person) will manifest actual symptoms or illness (such as infection, dehydration, abnormal blood cell counts) that have been created by the perpetrator, or the child will be convinced of their illness; the target of this disorder is generally not feigning these symptoms, though this sometimes does occur. Presenting symptoms or illness can be physical, mental or cognitive in nature, as with factitious disorder imposed on the self. Those with this disorder tend to escalate their behavior, manipulating ever more dangerous symptoms and initiating increasingly more intrusive and risky interventions, including surgeries and sometimes resulting in death (Hammond & Echterling, 2009). Those with FDIA may shift their targets to younger children when a previous target becomes too old to manipulate easily. Some evidence exists that individuals may engage in both factitious symptom manifestation in themselves and in another at the same time (Feldman et al., 1997). When making a diagnosis, it is essential to note that when factitious disorder is imposed on another, for example on a child by a parent, the parent imposing the symptoms is given the diagnosis, the child can be given a Z code diagnosis of child abuse (APA, 2013).

Theories of Somatic Manifestation

It is likely that no single underlying cause can explain the development and continuation of an SSRD in an individual. Instead these disorders may arise out of a complex interplay of cognitive phenomena, such as somatic absorption and misinterpretation of sensation, anxiety and depression; and functional impairment that, in turn, increases illness anxiety and fixation on symptoms (Manu, 2004). Not surprisingly, a number of theories have been developed in an attempt to explain the phenomena. For centuries, Western thinkers held the concepts of mind and body as two separate phenomena, a philosophy known as Cartesian dualism (Demasio, 1994). Janet, and later Freud and Breuer, initiated a shift in thinking about physical symptoms when they asserted that medical symptoms could be manifested through dissociative psychological processes, described as hysteria or conversion (Nicholson et al., 2016; Şar et al., 2004). In their case studies and writings, patient's physical symptoms drew less concern and attention than did the psychological processes believed to instigate them and the unconscious dynamics they seemed to represent.

The most widely embraced theory is a cognitive theory that asserts that cognitive schemas or frameworks overinterpret benign sensation and result in unnecessary alarm and distress (Henningsen et al., 2011). Other researchers have argued for a tangible medical underlying cause for a number of functional somatic syndromes, such as fibromyalgia, irritable bowel syndrome (IBS), chronic fatigue and so on. This theory asserts that genetically based endophenotypes create a heightened central nervous system sensitivity that can express itself in a number of ways within the body. This theory, the central sensitization syndrome, was first introduced in 2008 and has gained continued attention since that time (Bourke et al., 2015; Yunus, 2008). In contrast, some theorists embrace a constructivist framework to understand somatic symptoms. Constructivists reject the notion that there is a single reality, for instance the presence or absence of illness, but argue instead that realities are many and all are constructed individually, the product of personal meaning-making. Rather than viewing MUS as distorted reality or misinterpretations, the task is to assist the client in developing an awareness of their contributions to their own reality, to acknowledge the consequences of those constructions and develop avenues for shifting toward health and vitality (Smith & Conway, 2009).

Mental health professionals and medical doctors alike have embraced a mind–body philosophy and frame for illness generally, asserting that psychological states and traumatic experiences can measurably and negatively impact the body, that injury

BOX 13. 03 CONSIDER THIS

As you consider these theories of medically unexplained symptoms and illness, what do you believe to be true about the body? Do you experience the mind and body processes as separate or as inextricably tied together? Both, perhaps? Do you embrace a concrete dualism of ill or not ill, or do you believe illness constructed? How might your beliefs influence how you listen to clients who describe medical concerns? How might your beliefs inform your diagnosis? What potential strengths and weaknesses do you see in bringing these beliefs into your diagnostic process?

and illness in the physical body can, in turn, lead to negative consequences for a person's mental health, and, indeed, mental health concerns can worsen biologically based conditions (Pomeroy et al., 2008; Van der Kolk, 2015). These shifting attitudes are evidenced by the popularity of books like, *The Body Keeps the Score,* by Bessel Van der Kolk. Both mind–body, cognitive and psychodynamic philosophies are reflected in the disorder constructs of this dimension.

SSD in Childhood and Adolescence

Anyone who has worked in schools or had other close contact with children can attest to the relationship between anxiety and stomach aches, evidenced, for example, by the steady stream of a subset of children asking to see the school nurse. For children with mental health concerns, such as depression and anxiety, somatic complaints are common. In their investigations, Ginsburg et al. (2006) found that among children diagnosed with an anxiety disorder, 70% complained of stomach aches, 45% described muscle tension, 45% sweating and 43% complained of trembling or shaking. An Italian study of children and adolescents, revealed that in those with depression alone, 11% complained of headache, 7% of stomach discomfort and 5% of abdominal pain, but among those diagnosed with both anxiety and depression, these numbers were doubled (Masi et al., 2000). Conversely, studies of children with functional abdominal pain (symptoms that could not be explained medically) being seen by gastroenterologists, have found between 42% and 85% also have an anxiety disorder, generalized anxiety disorder, social anxiety and separation anxiety being most commonly identified (Cunningham et al., 2015).

Though somatic symptoms frequently occur together with anxiety and depression, it is important to remember developmental norms, since children aren't always able to identify emotions or separate them from physical illness (Weisblatt et al., 2011). For example, I remember a moment when my son was very young, not quite 3 perhaps, after a fun-filled visit with my brother we had to say goodbye, we weren't sure when we would see him again. As we were waving goodbye and his uncle's car pulled out of the driveway, my son's face was visibly grief-stricken and he said, "Mommy, my throat hurts so much." He was interpreting the tightening in his throat that comes when we are "choked up" as a sore throat and not as grief or loss, perhaps because this was his first experience with this kind of feeling and he had not yet come to know its texture and qualities. Like my son in this example, young children who haven't yet linked typical physiological responses to emotion or don't have the vocabulary to describe emotional states, like grief, anxiousness or nervous anticipation, but will often be able to name the physiological discomfort that can come with those feelings. Consequently, somatic complaints seem to be more common among younger children than older children and adolescents (Masi et al., 2000). The skilled clinician will need to keep the individual developmental progress of each client in mind when diagnosing symptoms.

The Skilled Diagnostician: Differential Diagnosis

Complications in Diagnosing SSDs. Having read through the chapter, it is likely clear that diagnosing SSDs is complex. Among those that might be considered for diagnosis with an SSD, some will likely have an undiagnosed physical illness that is responsible for their psychological symptoms (Pomeroy et al., 2008), some diagnosed with physical illnesses have an undiagnosed somatic symptom illness that is responsible for or worsens the physical symptoms and some who are accurately diagnosed with a physical illness will also have an SSD that adds to symptoms or creates a great deal more distress than would otherwise be expected. Your role in diagnosing and treating these disorders will be focused less on the cause of the symptoms than on the client's relationship to them, the degree of disruption caused and the best way to support your client in managing symptom manifestation.

Differential Diagnosis of IAD, SSD and PFMC. The most immediate, but still not crystal clear, point of differentiation between the person who will be appropriately diagnosed with IAD, SSD or PFMC is the absence/near absence of symptoms or presence of physical symptoms that accompany the client's illness anxieties. Though the client's symptoms may be medically unexplained or have their origins in a documented biological cause, the distraction or distress caused by the symptoms is judged to be out of proportion with the symptoms themselves either in the emotional response or in the time and energy given to attending to them (APA, 2013; Axelsson et al., 2016; Dimsdale et al., 2013) a sometimes challenging clinical judgment. When considering whether or not a response is excessive, you may want to look for the following:

- Your client describes a mounting anxiety about a health concern and, as a result, spends a great deal of time searching the web for symptoms.

- Web searches for medical information increase anxiety and perpetuate anxiety.
- Time is lost while searching the web for medical information, or more time is taken than planned.
- Thoughts about symptoms are intrusive and attempts to ignore the thoughts are unsuccessful.
- Your client frequently seeks medical consultation but does not fully trust the reassurances that are offered and frequently seeks a second opinion.

Similarly, when a client presents with only one symptom, such as occasional headaches, the diagnostician will have to use clinical judgment to determine what presentations count for a "minimal" symptom, as with IAD, and which are not minimal but the reaction to them is still out of proportion (SSD) and which are not minimal but are made worse by mental health concerns. The client struggling with PFMC will have a documented medical condition that is being made worse by the psychological factors. The impact of the psychological factors in SSD and in PFMC differ, however, in two key ways: first, the psychological symptoms (worry, concern and distraction) are focused on the symptoms themselves, while the person struggling with PFMC is experiencing a psychological condition that is worsening their medical condition either directly or indirectly or causes the individual to neglect their treatment, for example. In contrast, the person with the SSD has physical symptoms that seem to function as the background for a psychological response.

Identifying Factitious Disorder. Bass and Halligan (2014) note that several patterns may serve as red flags for the possible presence of factitious disorder. Physicians and clinicians should be alert to the possibility of factitious disorder when an illness continues to worsen despite a history of a "remarkable number of tests, consultations, medical and surgical treatments" (p. 3) with no response. Most disease and injury have a natural course in which it begins to remediate or a typical pattern of decline. When this natural course is markedly different in a patient, consideration of faux symptoms or deliberately produced illness or injury should be considered. Additionally, when the patient (or parent of the patient) agrees to an invasive treatment without hesitation, this can signal feigned symptoms. Similarly, when psychiatric evaluation or recommendations for mental health counseling is resisted, this may also signal that symptoms are deliberately produced. Finally, clients with factitious disorders may not give consent to communicate with other healthcare providers and may fail to disclose concurrent medical treatments.

Though factitious disorder is likely more common in the medical profession, this disorder can also manifest in the form of psychological symptoms (APA, 2013). The literature contains numerous case studies documenting feigned psychological symptoms including but not limited to psychosis and schizophrenia (Pope et al., 1982; Welburn et al., 2003), dissociation (Brand et al., 2016; Welburn et al., 2003), suicidal and homicidal ideation (Thompson & Beckson, 2004), post-traumatic stress disorder

BOX 13.04 TRY THIS: DIFFERENTIATING ILLNESS ANXIETY DISORDER (IAD), SOMATIC SYMPTOM DISORDERS (SSD) AND PSYCHOLOGICAL FACTORS AFFECTING OTHER MEDICAL CONDITIONS (PFMC):

In the following four scenarios, Astrid, Kenji, Tess and Wilson, what is the most likely somatic symptom disorder for each? What questions do you have that would help lend support to a final diagnosis?

Astrid. Astrid, a 29-year-old art instructor at a local community college, has had asthma since childhood and takes a regular course of asthma medications. Though she has worked closely with a pulmonologist, they have not been able to remediate the daily use of her rescue inhaler or prevent the monthly visits to the emergency room. The key factor influencing the course of her asthma seems to be high levels of anxiety around her work and relationships that frequently trigger asthma attacks. Astrid has been reluctant to seek counseling despite her doctor's repeated recommendations.

Kenji. Kenji, 45, has noticed that when he wakes in the morning, until about midday, he experiences blurred vision in his right or left eye, but never both at the same time. He sometimes notes a vague dizzy feeling and some cognitive clouding that clears up by midafternoon. Kenji spends a lot of time distracted by his vision, covering one eye and then the other to check for blurriness. He often checks his heart-rate and jots notes in his diary about dizziness and other symptoms.

Tess. Tess, 24, has had difficulties with seizures for about 10 years. Though her seizures are "mostly controlled" (Tess experiences a seizure about once every 18 months), she worries constantly that she will have a seizure when she is in public. She has been reluctant to date or to socialize. She has noticed that she has become "obsessive" about things that might contribute to seizure; for instance, she is insistent on a rigid sleep schedule of 10 hours per night, to avoid sleep deprivation and will not work more than part time in order to control stress levels.

Wilson. While on the whole Wilson's health has been good and he is not experiencing a lot of consistent symptoms that he can put his finger on, he worries that he may be developing a brain tumor. Sometimes, Wilson worries that he may develop Parkinson's or Alzheimer's and worries there won't be anyone to take care of him when he is ill. These worries interfere with Wilson's ability to focus at work.

(PTSD) (Lynn & Belza, 1984) and so on, in order to gain psychiatric attention or hospitalization. Because psychiatric symptoms are mental events and client reports comprise the larger part of diagnosis, identifying factitious psychiatric disorders is

TABLE 13.01 **Differential Diagnosis of Illness Anxiety Disorder (IAD), Somatic Symptom Disorders (SSD) and Psychological Factors Affecting Other Medical Conditions (PFMC)**

Symptom	IAD	SSD	PFMC
Preoccupation with health	Yes	Yes	No
At least one somatic symptom is present that leads to significant concern or distress or functional disruption in day-to-day living	None (or minimal)	Yes	Yes
Fear of having or developing a severe physical illness	Yes	No	No
Duration of 6 months	Yes	No	No
Mental health factors exacerbate physical symptoms or interfere with treatment	No	No	Yes

Source: American Psychiatric Association (2013).

particularly challenging, especially in outpatients where it is not possible to document behavior outside of session; for example, relaxed socializing in a client presenting with factitious severe depression. Again, note the symptom's lack of response to numerous evidence-based interventions, illogical or inconsistent symptom presentations, inexplicable rapid decline and so on, when considering this diagnosis.

Differential Diagnosis of Factitious Disorder and Malingering. Factitious disorder and malingering share the same behavioral pattern, one of faking illness or injury, however the reasoning behind these behaviors differs. Malingering, once a codable disorder, is now noted using the Z code, Z76.5, and describes the misrepresentation of a person's physical or psychological health for the purposes of external gains. These might include pretended injury in order to avoid military service, avoid accountability for criminal behavior, seeking financial gain such as disability payments or workman's compensation and so on. The person with the factitious disorder finds reward in all that is derived from filling the role of the patient, or caregiver when symptoms are produced in another person (APA, 2013; Bass & Halligan, 2014; Hammond & Echterling, 2008). Neither the malingerer nor the person with a factitious disorder will have a strong motivation for disclosing their behavior, making the differentiation of these two behaviors difficult.

Morrison (2014) outlines a number of red flags for malingering, among them: (1) loss of memory with no other cognitive concerns; (2) personal amnesia for periods of time but intact memories for social events for that time; (3) very sudden onset of mental health symptoms that fully meet criteria for a disorder (as with a very sudden onset of schizophrenia); (4) an atypical or very rare presentation of a symptom or disorder, such as a hallucinated voice who has a name or elaborate identity/story; (5) the absence of expected or typical symptoms; (6) treatment does not work as expected; (7) surprising results on assessments, such as results below chance on a memory test, or a resistance to cooperating with assessment; (8) potential for secondary gain, such as a prescription and so on. Morrison notes that while any one of these flags may not be cause for suspicion, a collection of these indicators will warrant careful consideration.

The reader will note that the red flags for factitious disorder and malingering do overlap, such as with the atypical presentation of symptoms, the unusual or illogical progression of symptoms or their resistance to treatment. Ascertaining the primary reward for feigned symptoms, receiving attention and care in factitious disorder or secondary personal gain in malingering, will best serve you in determining how to code the behavior. The client's health history may also point in one direction over the other. The person with a factitious disorder is more likely to have a long history of medical difficulties and interventions since the aim of the disorder is contact with medical professionals. The person who is malingering is less likely to have a long perplexing health history.

Differential Diagnosis of SSRD's in Children. Children and adolescents can be influenced to develop patterns of somatization; thanks to the ways in which their parents or caregivers respond to their own complaints or to those of their children, a phenomenon described in the literature as *somatization by proxy* (Goldberg, 2017). Somatization by proxy is not a recognized disorder and should not be confused with FDIA. Somatization by proxy is a learned maladaptive behavioral and emotional response to benign symptoms, while FDIA is a phenomenon in which a child is injured or made ill deliberately by a parent or caregiver for the express purpose of securing attention and compassion for the perpetrator.

It is possible for children and adolescents who are victims of FDIA to develop an unhealthy relationship with physical symptoms and eventually meet criteria for a somatization disorder themselves, to develop their own factitious disorder or to later turn to malingering as an avenue of benefiting themselves, however. For example, a lonely or anxious child who experiences frequent MUS stomach pain (SSD) might one day feign a stomach ache in order to see the school nurse after having several experiences of the nurse's kindness (factitious disorder), or to be excused from an exam (malingering). Clinicians should keep in mind the ways in which the patterns of relationship with symptoms and illness can evolve. Finally, Weisblatt et al. (2011) remind us to keep in mind that children are in a process of developing skills for dealing with difficult emotional and social experiences and will seek out comfort for physical manifestations that are a consequence of these pressures. Clinicians will need to keep in mind that if these patterns aren't impairing functioning, they should not be diagnosed, but rather supported by building additional coping skills.

Aging and Somatic Symptom Manifestation. In aging populations, anxiety disorders are common, as high as 20%, but are less well-known concerns of later life than dementia, which impacts only 8%. Anxiety can be easily missed in older adults, who, like younger children, are more likely to somatize symptoms. Complicating differential diagnosis of anxiety and SSD in older adults, for example, is the fact that as people age and their bodies give in to chronic diseases, their symptoms can mimic anxiety and depression making an accurate diagnosis difficult. Regular screenings for depression and anxiety among aging clients is advised (Cassidy & Rector, 2008).

Culture and Somatic Symptoms. Those who embrace a belief in re-incarnation may also believe that past life experiences and karma carried from those past lives have a tangible impact on one's health in this and future lives (Hutchinson & Sharp, 2008). These beliefs can vary a bit; for example, some believe that injuries to the body or a violent death in a past life can show up as a bodily weakness, illness, malformation or a birthmark. Others, such as some Buddhist practitioners, hold that spiritual work and growth can be experienced as somatic symptoms, or can be accompanied by uncomfortable bodily experiences. For people with these beliefs, a great deal of focus and attention can be given to symptoms, interpreting their meaning and, frequently, individuals will use religiously grounded approaches to address symptoms. Similarly, significant amounts of energy may be given to building and sustaining prana (life energy) so that illness can be avoided or symptoms can be managed well if they arise. These practices may include adhering to dietary recommendations; adequate sleep; body movement, such as yoga, breathwork and mental relaxation and meditation (personal communication, Mary Pargas, M.A., C.Y.T., 12/22/18). Clinicians should be careful that they don't confuse cultural and religious beliefs that focus on sustaining good health with IAD or SSD.

Treatment

Cognitive-Behavioral Therapy (CBT). Holder-Perkins and Wise (2001) note that clients who are somatically preoccupied tend to have difficulties recognizing connections between their symptoms and psychological processes, complicating therapy. They add that short-term therapies, such as CBT seem to have more efficacy than do more open-ended therapies such as psychoanalysis or insight-oriented therapies. A review of the literature reveals that CBT has been used effectively with SSDR's like IAD. CBT works to identify and shift irrational thinking around illness and support clients in developing skills for disputing unproductive thoughts (cognitive errors and faulty schemas) in response to body sensations (Fallon & Feinstein, 2001; Smith & Conway, 2009). Exposure therapy has also been used to support clients in gradually reducing the anxiety felt when anxious thoughts arise (Fallon & Feinstein, 2001).

CBT and Exercise Therapy for Chronic Fatigue and Fibromyalgia. Clients with some functional somatic illnesses such as chronic fatigue syndrome and fibromyalgia may gradually develop sedentary habits that negatively impact tissue in the body that eventually increases pain, as in fibromyalgia, or perpetuates a cycle of physical exhaustion by impacting sleep. For these clients, regular aerobic exercise is recommended in addition to CBT (Creed et al., 2011).

Lifestyle Medicine. Lifestyle medicine is an evidenced-based approach that has been applied to chronic disease that arises out of lifestyle choices, such as nutritional choices, sleep and exercise habits, stress management and so on. This approach to medicine, largely implemented by physicians, is one that is patient-centered and places responsibility with the patient to create the conditions for sustained health and wellness. Chappell (2018) recommends a long-term collaborative relationship with patients with IAD that supports people in shifting their energies from worrying about their health to making and enacting lasting lifestyle choices that will both empower them and ensure greater long-term health outcomes. Mental health professionals may consider incorporating lifestyle medicine techniques into their current practices when supporting these clients; alternatively, identifying local physicians who take this approach and referring clients may be helpful.

Alternative Medicine and Somatic Disorders. Chun (2013) asserts that alternative medical approaches may be an excellent fit for clients with physical symptoms that can't readily be explained by Western science and further points out that there are more than 300 catalogued alternative, folk and non-Western medicines ranging from advanced energy healing to zone therapy. Clients presenting with functional somatic disorders describe a broad range of symptoms that don't fit neatly into Western understandings but are understood and described within other frameworks. Ni (1995) offers a number of examples in his translation of the Chinese classic penned by Huangdi Neijing in 2600 B.C.E., *The Yellow Emperor's Classic of Internal Medicine.* In one example, a patient, a pregnant woman, has suddenly and inexplicably lost her voice. Today in the United States, the problem would likely be diagnosed as a conversion disorder; however, this text asserts that the "collaterals of the uterus have been pinched . . . The collaterals of the uterus are connected to the kidneys and then travels upward, ending at the bottom of the tongue. Therefore, when the collaterals are obstructed, the connection up to the tongue is disrupted and speech is impaired" (Ni, 1995, p. 173). Both Chinese medicine and Kundalini Yoga Therapy, which works with movement, breath and mantras individualized to the client, which are meant to improve the function of the lymphatic and circulatory systems, expanding lung capacity and so on, are building recognition within the Western evidence-based practices and scientific communities as well as many other alternative systems (Chun, 2013; McCall, 2007).

Pharmacological Approaches. A number of medications have been prescribed for both primary and secondary hypochondriasis/IAD/SSD, often depending on what comorbid disorder exists. For example, fluvoxitine has been shown to be helpful for those with hypochondriasis secondary to obsessive compulsive disorder (OCD), amitriptyline for those with hypochondriasis secondary to depression and antipsychotics for those presenting with monosymptomatic hypochondriacal psychosis. In addition to medications, there is documentation of the use of electroconvulsive therapy in clients with hypochondria (Fallon & Feinstein, 2001). However, several studies have shown that the use of antidepressants in clients with IBS, for example, evidences no improvement beyond what might be expected for placebo (Creed et al., 2011).

Somatic Symptom and Related Disorders Cases for Diagnosis

The following pivot points may help to guide your diagnosis of clients manifesting unexplained symptoms, though, again, caution and careful and ongoing consultation with a medical professional is encouraged here.

BOX 13.05 DIMENSIONAL BRIDGE

Decades of research reveals considerable overlap and comorbidity with bipolar, depressive and anxiety disorders as well as with disorders of personality. Meta-analysis reveals that those with a bipolar or unipolar mood disorder are twice as likely as controls to have a functional somatic syndrome (Edgcomb et al., 2016; Manu, 2004). In their research, Katon et al. (2001) found a positive relationship exists between the number of functional somatic syndromes and the severity of anxiety and depression supporting the strong relationship between these dimensions.

Definitional Cases in Somatic Symptom and Related Disorders

Ellen

On Monday afternoon, Ellen watched in horror as her husband accidentally rolled over the beloved family pet with his sedan. Tuesday morning Ellen woke to find that she was unable to see anything. Her eyes were reactive to light when tested, however, and the examining physician could find no damage or illness in her eyes that would point to blindness.

Alex

Alex is troubled by frequent headaches that have been diagnosed as tension headaches. Though thorough medical exams have ruled out other more serious causes, Alex worries a great deal about these headaches and invests a great deal of money and time in herbal remedies, acupuncture and other measures he hopes will prevent "a stroke or something worse."

Chase

Chase is afraid to go to the doctor for his regular physical because he believes that he "probably has cancer." Though he has no symptoms that would point to cancer, Chase is very frightened and distracted by the cancer diagnosis he feels sure is coming if he were to visit the doctor.

Jessica

Jessica, 28, often pretends to be very ill in order to gain attention from the doctors and nurses in the emergency room or her physician's office.

TABLE 13.02 Somatic Symptom and Related Disorders Pivot Table

Pivot Points: Somatic Symptom and Related Disorders	Consider
Pivot Point One: Is your client's distress dramatically out of proportion to one or more symptoms your client has been experiencing?	Somatic Symptom Disorder
Pivot Point Two: Is your client's health-related distress born out of worry that he or she might have an illness or get sick? Is the distress clearly out of proportion with the risks of having that illness?	Illness Anxiety Disorder
Pivot Point Three: Is your client experiencing diminished motor or sensory function (blindness, deafness, paralysis, etc.) that can't be explained medically?	Conversion Disorder (Functional Neurological Symptom Disorder)
Pivot Point Four: Is your client's established medical condition made worse by psychological symptoms or behaviors?	Psychological Factors Affecting Other Medical Conditions
Pivot Point Five: Are your client's symptoms fabricated? • Has your client fabricated symptoms in order to avoid a consequence or for some gain?	Malingering
• Has your client fabricated symptoms (their own or in someone in their care) for the express purpose of receiving care and comfort from healthcare professionals?	Factitious Disorder
Pivot Point Six: Does your client suffer from subthreshold worries and behaviors related to health?	Other Specified Somatic Symptom and Related Disorders
Pivot Point Seven: Does your client falsely believe she is pregnant?	Other Specified Somatic Symptom and Related Disorders, pseudocyesis
Pivot Point Eight: Is your client worried or curious about confusing or problematic symptoms but not to the point of distress and distraction?	No diagnosis: distinguish from other specified somatic symptom and related disorders by lack of impairment

Doug

Doug drinks heavily and has been diagnosed with a substance use disorder. Doug also has epilepsy and has been treated for this condition since he was a child. Doug's drinking causes him to frequently forget his evening dose of anticonvulsants and as a consequence he has had a number of seizures in the last few months.

Chloe

Chloe has seen a number of specialists with concerns that she may soon lose her hearing. Though no disease or injury has been found, she continues to be distracted by what she believes to be the "very high likelihood" that she will lose her hearing.

Kiesha

Kiesha, a registered nurse, was recently found guilty of repeatedly introducing large amounts of salt into her daughter's feeding tube in order to induce prolonged illness.

Narrative Cases in Somatic Symptom and Related Disorders

Edmund

Edmund, a 54-year-old airline pilot has seen a number of doctors in the past year with complaints about a sharp pain that runs the length of his right leg. Though he has had several appointments with his doctor as well as magnetic resonance imaging (MRI) on his spine, no source for the pain could be identified. Ultimately, Edmund was then referred to counseling. Edmund reports, "I am pretty concerned about what could be causing all this pain. I have wondered if there could be a tumor in my spine or maybe some kind of degenerative nerve pain. I spend a lot of time researching pain but when I go to talk to these doctors they act like I don't know anything. I worry that it is going to get worse and worse. Maybe one day I will wake up and I won't be able to walk or move without pain."

Edmund further explains, "I have decided to cut way back on the number of flights that I make. The pain has just gotten to be too distracting."

Amal

Amal, a 43-year-old English teacher, has spent a significant amount of time over the past 5 years thinking about how to secure her health and prevent the multiple health concerns that she finds herself worrying about. "I spend a lot of time trying to stay fit and to eat right. I only eat an organic vegetarian diet and I juice at least one meal a day. I steer clear of dairy, gluten, sugar and salt—all that junky food can wreak havoc on the body! I get an hour of cardio every day and yoga every morning at home. I keep close tabs on my vitamin intake and all that. You see, I've been doing a lot of studying about heart disease, cancers, and neurodegenerative disorders that can come later in life and I try to do everything I can to make sure that this never happens to me. I'm not sick or anything but when I do get a symptom, it does freak me out a little bit, so I go to the doctor right away to get it checked out—better safe than sorry." Amal further shares, "I like to keep a health journal where I keep track of my diet, my exercise, any symptoms I've had and I store all my test results there so that my doctor has a really good record of what's going on if something strange happens, we can catch it right away."

Charlotte

Charlotte, 31, was recently released from the hospital after an incident in which her sister found her in a diabetic coma on the floor of their living room. Charlotte has been struggling with binge eating and though she attends a weekly therapy group to try to get the behavior under control, she sometimes lapses. Charlotte explains, "I feel a lot of stress. I feel like I should have made more of my life by this point. I'm married and divorced already and I live with my sister in a cramped apartment in the town I grew up in—the very place I wanted to get away from. Sometimes I feel so crushed and boxed in, and that is when I have these binging episodes. It always sends my sugar through the roof. Most times I can balance it with the right amount of insulin. But obviously, sometimes I lose track and end up in the hospital. It takes a long time to get back to normal and I miss work, which makes it hard to meet my rent, car payments and student loans. That also stresses me out and makes me feel like a loser, which can trigger a binge. This last time it almost cost me my life. It is a vicious and dangerous cycle." Charlotte denies any symptoms of depression and denies passive suicidal behavior by throwing off her glucose levels by overeating.

Vlad

Vlad and his wife have been arguing for years over his refusal to see a doctor. Vlad has just had his 60th birthday and his wife, Ruth, would like him to go to the doctor and get a regular checkup. "I just don't understand why he is so insistent that he not go to the doctor. He is scared to death that he will end up with prostate cancer like his brother did or colon cancer like his father. He talks about it all the time and once in a while I catch him on the internet looking up symptoms, but he refuses to just go get checked out." Vlad shares, "I remember the way my dad and my brother suffered at the end. I figure that is going to happen to me, too, after all, it's in my DNA. I just keep wondering who is going to take care of the family business if I get sick." Ruth interjects, "He's got to stop with all the obsession with checking his body for signs of cancer and just go to the doctor already! This has been going on for years and I am fed up!"

Didier

Didier, age 62, returned home from a business trip to find that his wife, Eva, was gone. "I went into the bedroom and called out to her but she wasn't there. She's always there when I come back from a trip. But after a few hours passed I got a funny feeling so I looked around and I realized that many of her things were gone, too. Her clothes were gone from the closet, her toothbrush and makeup. I wondered if I had forgotten something, maybe she was supposed to go to see her sister or something and I let it slip my mind, so I tried calling her. But Eva's phone was disconnected. And she took the car. The subway is in walking distance so we really only need one car, but she took it. I didn't know what to do so I just crawled into bed. The strange thing is that the next morning I woke up and I couldn't move my legs or feet. I couldn't get out of bed and I couldn't go to work. I was in the hospital for days before the feeling came back and I could walk again. The doctor never did figure out what was wrong with me."

Willow

Willow, age 13, has, for the past 3 days, been unable to speak. Willow has been to see her primary care physician and a neurologist, neither of whom could find anything that could explain Willow's inability to speak. For her part, Willow has been able to communicate by writing and reports that she would like to speak but that "the words won't come out." Willow denies any traumatic experiences, and reports that she has not been threatened, bullied or abused in any way. She writes, "When I open my mouth to speak, there just aren't any words to come out." Her parents report that Willow has been outgoing, has several good friends and does well in school. Her mother shares, "We are just completely flummoxed by this whole thing, we can't make heads or tails of it!"

Wilt

Wilt, a medical student has been studying to be a surgeon and has made an appointment with a counselor after meeting with several doctors with complaints about his right hand. "In the past month or so, since I got my match for a surgical residency, I have felt a kind of numbness or sometimes a painful tingling in the fingertips of my right hand. I went to a doctor—I was pretty worried this would mean that I couldn't be a surgeon if I didn't have the use of my hands—but there's nothing wrong with my hands or my fingers, and actually, there is no medically sound reason why I would have numbness in just the tips of my fingers, that isn't how the nerves in the hand work. My doctor thinks I'm stressed out about this match and should talk to a good counselor about it."

Brooklyn

Brooklyn, 35, is meeting with a forensic psychologist following charges that she deliberately poisoned her 7-year-old twins, Simon and Ian. Hospital social workers and physicians argue that Brooklyn has brought the boys to the hospital on a number of occasions. In the most recent incident, each of the boys was complaining of stomach pain and suffering from hemolytic anemia. In a turn for the worse, Ian fell into shock and required dialysis. Following testing it was discovered that the boys each had arsenic in their systems. Though the water at the family home and the boy's school showed no unusual levels of arsenic, the boys continued to show arsenic in their systems. The source of the arsenic was a mystery until Brooklyn was observed bringing the boys food from outside the hospital. When the food was tested, it was found to have arsenic in it. Brooklyn was charged with child endangerment and referred for psychological testing.

References

Aćimović, S. (2017). Bronchial asthma: From psychosomatic illness to proinflammatory cytokines and asthma phenotypes. *Vojnosanitetski Pregled, 74*(5), 399–401. https://doi.org/10.2298/VSP1705399A

American Psychiatric Association. (2013). *Diagnostic and statistical manual of mental disorders* (5th ed.). Author.

American Psychiatric Association. (2018). *Highlights of changes from DSM IV-TR to DSM-5.* http://www.dsm5.org/documents/changes%20from%20dsm-iv-tr%20to%20dsm-5.pdf

Aronowitz, R., & Spiro, H. (1988). The rise and fall of the psychosomatic hypothesis for ulcerative colitis. *Journal of Clinical Gastroenterology, 10*(3), 298–305. https://doi.org/10.1097/00004836-198806000-00013. http://journals.lww.com/jcge/abstract/1988/06000/the_rise_and_fall_of_the_psychosomatic_hypothesis.13.aspx

Asmundson, G. J., & Taylor, S. (2020). How health anxiety influences responses to viral outbreaks like COVID-19: What all decision-makers, health authorities, and health care professionals need to know. *Journal of Anxiety Disorders, 71*, 102211. https://doi.org/10.1016/j.janxdis.2020.102211

Axelsson, E., Andersson, E., Ljótsson, B., Wallhed Finn, D., & Hedman, E. (2016). The health preoccupation diagnostic interview: Inter-rater reliability of a structured interview for diagnostic assessment of DSM-5 somatic symptom disorder and illness anxiety disorder. *Cognitive Behaviour Therapy, 45*(4), 259–269. https://doi.org/10.1080/16506073.2016.1161663

Bass, C., & Halligan, P. (2014). Factitious disorders and malingering: Challenges for clinical assessment and management. *The Lancet, 383*(9926), 1422–1432. https://doi.org/10.1016/S0140-6736(13)62186-8

Bellamy, R. (1997). Compensation neurosis: Financial reward for illness as nocebo. *Clinical Orthopaedics and Related Research, 336*, 94–106. https://doi.org/10.1097/00003086-199703000-00013

Boone, B. (2017). *Neuropsychological evaluation of somatoform and other functional somatic conditions.* American Academy of Clinical Neuropsychology, Routledge.

Bourke, J. H., Langford, R. M., & White, P. D. (2015). The common link between functional somatic syndromes may be central sensitisation. *Journal of Psychosomatic Research, 78*(3), 228–236. https://doi.org/10.1016/j.jpsychores.2015.01.003

Brand, B. L., Webermann, A. R., & Frankel, A. S. (2016). Assessment of complex dissociative disorder patients and simulated dissociation in forensic contexts. *International Journal of Law and Psychiatry, 49*, 197–204. https://doi.org/10.1016/j.ijlp.2016.10.006

Burgeois, J., Chang, C., Hilty, D., & Servis, M. (2002). Clinical manifestations and management of conversion disorders. *Current Treatment Options in Neurology, 4*(6), 487–497. https://doi.org/10.1007/s11940-002-0016-2

Cahalan, S. (2012). *Brain on fire: My month of madness.* Simon & Schuster.

Cassidy, K. L., & Rector, N. A. (2008). The silent geriatric giant: Anxiety disorders in late life. *Geriatrics and Aging, 11*(3), 150–156.

Chappell, A. S. (2018). Toward a lifestyle medicine approach to illness anxiety disorder (Formerly Hypochondriasis). *American Journal of Lifestyle Medicine, 12*, 365–369. https://doi.org/10.1177/1559827618764649

Charis, C. (2018). Somatoform disorders from psychodynamic point of view. In Georgia Panayiotou (Ed.), *Somatoform and other psychosomatic disorders* (pp. 23–38). Springer.

Chun, S. (2013). The role of complementary and alternative medicine in somatic medicine. In K. B. Koh (Ed.), *Somatization and psychosomatic symptoms*. Springer.

Cottingham, M. E. (2017). Pseudotremor and other nonphysiologic movement disorders. In K. B. Boone (Ed.), *Neuropsychological evaluation of somatoform and other functional somatic conditions*. Routledge.

Creed, F., Kroenke, K., Henningsen, P., Gudi, A., & White, P. (2011). Evidence-based treatment. In F. Creed, P. Henningsen, & P. Fink (Eds.), *Medically unexplained symptoms, somatisation and bodily distress: developing better clinical services* (pp.69–96). Cambridge University Press.

Crimlisk, H. L., Bhatia, K., Cope, H., David, A., Marsden, C. D., & Ron, M. A. (1998). Slater revisited: 6 year follow up study of patients with medically unexplained motor symptoms. *BMJ, 316*(7131), 582–586. https://doi.org/10.1136/bmj.316.7131.582

Cunningham, N. R., Cohen, M. B., Farrell, M. K., Mezoff, A. G., Lynch-Jordan, A., & Kashikar-Zuck, S. (2015). Concordant parent-child reports of anxiety predict impairment in youth with functional abdominal pain. *Journal of Pediatric Gastroenterology and Nutrition, 60*(3), 312. https://doi.org/10.1097/MPG.0000000000000625

Demasio, A. (1994). *Descartes' error: Emotion, reason, and the human brain*. G. Putnam and Sons.

DiMatteo, M. R., Lepper, H. S., & Croghan, T. W. (2000). Depression is a risk factor for noncompliance with medical treatment: Meta-analysis of the effects of anxiety and depression on patient adherence. *Archives of Internal Medicine, 160*(14), 2101–2107. https://doi.org/10.1001/archinte.160.14.2101

Dimsdale, J. E., Creed, F., Escobar, J., Sharpe, M., Wulsin, L., Barsky, A., Lee, S., Irwin, M. R., & Levenson, J. (2013). Somatic symptom disorder: An important change in DSM. *Journal of Psychosomatic Research, 75*, 223–228. https://doi.org/10.1016/j.jpsychores.2013.06.033

Edgcomb, J. B., Tseng, C. H., & Kerner, B. (2016). Medically unexplained somatic symptoms and bipolar spectrum disorders: A systematic review and meta-analysis. *Journal of Affective Disorders, 204*, 205–213. https://doi.org/10.1016/j.jad.2016.06.029

Fallon, B. A., & Feinstein, S. (2001). Hypochondriasis. In K. A. Phillips (Ed.), *Somatoform and factitious disorders*. American Psychiatric Publishing.

Fallon, B. A., Harper, K. M., Landa, A., Pavlicova, M., Schneier, F. R., Carson, A., Harding, K., Keegan, K., Schwartz, T., & Liebowitz, M. R. (2012). Personality disorders in hypochondriasis: Prevalence and comparison with two anxiety disorders. *Psychosomatics, 53*(6), 566–574. https://doi.org/10.1016/j.psym.2012.02.002

Feldman, M. D., Rosenquist, P. B., & Bond, J. P. (1997). Concurrent factitious disorder and factitious disorder by proxy: Double jeopardy. *General Hospital Psychiatry*, *19*(1), 24–28. https://doi.org/10.1016/S0163-8343(96)00108-9

Frances, A. (2013). The new somatic symptom disorder in DSM-5 risks mislabeling many people as mentally ill. *BMJ*, *346*, f1580. https://doi.org/10.1136/bmj.f1580

Ginsburg, G. S., Riddle, M. A., & Davies, M. (2006). Somatic symptoms in children and adolescents with anxiety disorders. *Journal of the American Academy of Child & Adolescent Psychiatry*, *45*(10), 1179–1187. https://doi.org/10.1097/01.chi.0000231974.43966.6e

Goldberg, H. E. (2017). Somatization by proxy: Parental influences on the development of somatization in children and adolescents. In K. B. Boone (Ed.), *Neuropsychological evaluation of somatoform and other functional somatic conditions* (pp. 142–158). Routledge.

Gregory, R. J., & Jindal, S. (2006). Factitious disorder on an inpatient psychiatry ward. *American Journal of Orthopsychiatry*, *76*(1), 31–36. https://doi.org/10.1037/0002-9432.76.1.31

Gupta, R. S., Warren, C. M., Smith, B. M., Jiang, J., Blumenstock, J. A., Davis, M. M., Schleimer, R. P., & Nadeau, K. C. (2019). Prevalence and severity of food allergies among us adults. *JAMA Network Open*, *2*(1), e185630. https://doi.org/10.1001/jamanetworkopen.2018.5630

Hammond, C., & Echterling, L. (2008). Factitious disorders. In B. T. Erford (Ed.), *The ACA encyclopedia of counseling* (pp. 192–193). American Counseling Association.

Häuser, W., & Wolfe, F. (2013). The somatic symptom disorder in DSM 5 risks mislabelling people with major medical diseases as mentally ill. *Journal of Psychosomatic Research*, *75*(6), 586–587. https://doi.org/10.1016/j.jpsychores.2013.09.005

Henningsen, P., Fink, P., Hausteiner-Wiehle, C., & Rief, W. (2011). Terminology, classification and concepts. In F. Creed, P. Henningsen, & P. Fink (Eds.), *Medically unexplained symptoms, somatisation and bodily distress: Developing better clinical services* (pp. 43–68). Cambridge University Press.

Holder-Perkins, V., & Wise, T. N. (2001). *Somatization disorder*. In K. A. Phillips (Ed.), *Somatoform and factitious disorders*. American Psychiatric Publishing.

Hutchinson, J. F., & Sharp, R. (2008). Karma, reincarnation, and medicine: Hindu perspectives on biomedical research. *Genomic Medicine*, *2*(3–4), 107–111. https://doi.org/10.1007/s11568-009-9079-4

Jungmann, S. M., & Witthöft, M. (2020). Health anxiety, cyberchondria, and coping in the current COVID-19 pandemic: Which factors are related to coronavirus anxiety? *Journal of Anxiety Disorders*, *73*, 102239. https://doi.org/10.1016/j.janxdis.2020.102239

Katon, W., Sullivan, M., & Walker, E. (2001). Medical symptoms without identified pathology: Relationship to psychiatric disorders, childhood and adult trauma, and personality traits. *Annals of Internal Medicine*, *134*(9 Pt 2), 917–925. https://doi.org/10.7326/0003-4819-134-9_Part_2-200105011-00017

Kirmayer, L. J., Groleau, D., Looper, K. J., & Dao, M. D. (2004). Explaining medically unexplained symptoms. *The Canadian Journal of Psychiatry*, *49*(10), 663–672.

Lask, B. (2004). Pervasive refusal syndrome. *Advances in Psychiatric Treatment, 10*(2), 153–159. https://doi.org/10.1192/apt.10.2.153

Lynn, E. J., & Belza, M. (1984). Factitious posttraumatic stress disorder: The veteran who never got to Vietnam. *Psychiatric Services, 35*(7), 697–701. https://doi.org/10.1176/ps.35.7.697

Manu, P. (2004). *The psychopathology of functional somatic syndromes: Neurobiology and illness behavior in chronic fatigue syndrome, fibromyalgia, gulf war illness, irritable bowel, and premenstrual dysphoria.* The Haworth Medical Press.

Masi, G., Favilla, L., Millepiedi, S., & Mucci, M. (2000). Somatic symptoms in children and adolescents referred for emotional and behavioral disorders. *Psychiatry, 63*(2), 140–149. https://doi.org/10.1080/00332747.2000.11024905

Mayou, R., Kirmayer, L. J., Simon, G., Kroenke, K., & Sharpe, M. (2005). Somatoform disorders: Time for a new approach in DSM-V. *American Journal of Psychiatry, 162*(5), 847–855. https://doi.org/10.1176/appi.ajp.162.5.847

McCall, T. (2007). *Yoga as medicine: The yogic prescription for health and healing.* Bantam Books.

Mertens, G., Gerritsen, L., Duijndam, S., Salemink, E., & Engelhard, I. M. (2020). Fear of the coronavirus (COVID-19): Predictors in an online study conducted in March. *Journal of Anxiety Disorders, 74*, 102258. https://doi.org/10.1016/j.janxdis.2020.102258

Morrison, J. (2014). *Diagnosis made easier: Principles and techniques for mental health clinicians.* Guilford Publications.

Ni, M. (1995). *The yellow emperor's classic of medicine: A new translation of the Neijing Suwen with commentary.* Shambhala Press.

Nicholson, T. R., Aybek, S., Craig, T., Harris, T., Wojcik, W., David, A. S., & Kanaan, R. A. (2016). Life events and escape in conversion disorder. *Psychological Medicine, 46*(12), 2617–2626. https://doi.org/10.1017/S0033291716000714

Pandey, S., Parikh, M., Brahmbhatt, M., & Vankar, G. K. (2017). Clinical study of illness anxiety disorder in medical outpatients. *Archives of Psychiatry and Psychotherapy, 4*, 32–41. https://doi.org/10.12740/APP/76932

Pomeroy, C., Mitchell, J. E., Roerig, J. L., & Crow, S. J. (2008). *Medical complications of psychiatric illness.* American Psychiatric Publishing.

Pope, H. G., Jonas, J. M., & Jones, B. (1982). Factitious psychosis: Phenomenology, family history, and long-term outcome of nine patients. *The American Journal of Psychiatry, 139*(11), 1480–1483. https://doi.org/10.1176/ajp.139.11.1480

Rundell, J. R. (2000). Somatic symptoms in children and adolescents referred for emotional and behavioral disorders. *Psychiatry, 63*(2), 150. https://doi.org/10.1080/00332747.2000.11024906

Şar, V., Akyüz, G., Kundakçı, T., Kızıltan, E., & Doğan, O. (2004). Childhood trauma, dissociation, and psychiatric comorbidity in patients with conversion disorder. *American Journal of Psychiatry, 161*(12), 2271–2276. https://doi.org/10.1176/ajp.161.12.2271

Smith, L. W., & Conway, P. W. (2009). *The mind-body interface in somatization: When symptom becomes disease*. Jason Aronson, Incorporated.

Starcevic, V. (2013). Hypochondriasis and health anxiety: Conceptual challenges. *The British Journal of Psychiatry, 202*(1), 7–8. https://doi.org/10.1192/bjp.bp.112.115402

Stone, J., Smyth, R., Carson, A., & Warlow, C. (2006). La belle indifference in conversion symptoms and hysteria: Systematic review. *The British Journal of Psychiatry, 188*(3), 204–209. https://doi.org/10.1192/bjp.188.3.204

Thompson, C. R., & Beckson, M. (2004). A case of factitious homicidal ideation. *Journal of the American Academy of Psychiatry and the Law Online, 32*(3), 277–281.

Van der Kolk, B. (2015). *The body keeps the score: Brain, mind, and body in the healing of trauma*. Penguin.

VanderPlate, C. (1984). Psychological aspects of multiple sclerosis and its treatment: Toward a biopsychosocial perspective. *Health Psychology: Official Journal of the Division of Health Psychology, American Psychological Association, 3*(3), 253–272. https://doi.org/10.1037/0278-6133.3.3.253

Weisblatt, E., Hindley, P., & Rask, C. U. (2011). Medically unexplained symptoms in children and adolescents. In F. Creed, P. Hennignsen, & P. Fink (Eds.), *Medically unexplained symptoms, somatisation and bodily distress: Developing better clinical services*. Cambridge University Press.

Welburn, K. R., Fraser, G. A., Jordan, S. A., Cameron, C., Webb, L. M., & Raine, D. (2003). Discriminating dissociative identity disorder from schizophrenia and feigned dissociation on psychological tests and structured interview. *Journal of Trauma & Dissociation, 4*(2), 109–130. https://doi.org/10.1300/J229v04n02_07

Wessely, S., Nimnuan, C., & Sharpe, M. (1999). Functional somatic syndromes: one or many? *The Lancet, 354*(9182), 936–939. https://doi.org/10.1016/S0140-6736(98)08320-2

Wessely, S., & White, P. D. (2004). There is only one functional somatic syndrome. *The British Journal of Psychiatry, 185*(2), 95–96. https://doi.org/10.1192/bjp.185.2.95

Youngjohn, J. R., Burrows, L., & Erdal, K. (1995). Brain damage or compensation neurosis? The controversial post-concussion syndrome. *The Clinical Neuropsychologist, 9*(2), 112–123. https://doi.org/10.1080/13854049508401593

Yunus, M. B. (2008, June). Central sensitivity syndromes: A new paradigm and group nosology for fibromyalgia and overlapping conditions, and the related issue of disease versus illness. *Seminars in Arthritis and Rheumatism*, 37(6), 339–352. https://doi.org/10.1016/j.semarthrit.2007.09.003

14 Feeding and Eating Disorders

By now it is becoming clear that all of the dimensions of mental health concerns within the DSM come with their own complexity, complexity in both the converging contributors to the development of each disorder as well as its interactions with nearly every aspect of an individual's life. Eating itself is unique in that it occupies a space that is both vital to health and well-being, immediately and in the long term, but also holds a distinctly social and cultural meaning. Consequently, eating disorders have the capacity to quickly and negatively impact one's physical health and are felt deeply in the psychological and social aspects of the individual's life. Eating disorders (EDs) tend to be chronic, have high relapse rates and impact a range of physiological systems. Anorexia nervosa (AN) is believed to have the highest mortality rate of any of the psychiatric disorders, though mortality rates for other EDs are also very high. Deaths result from a range of physical complications, including but not limited to heart failure and suicide (Arcelus et al., 2011; Harrop & Marlatt, 2010). The peak period for the onset of EDs is during adolescence (Rosenvinge & Pettersen, 2015b). EDs are the source of tremendous suffering for the person who carries the diagnosis but also for their family members and friends.

Rosenvinge and Pettersen (2015a) point out that at one-time EDs were something of a curiosity, poorly understood and ill defined. Today, although the ED dimension continues to be refined, serious questions have been raised about the utility of the current configuration to adequately capture ED complexity or to meet the needs of clinicians in identifying best-fit interventions (Dazzi & Di Leone, 2014). Because the disorders of the ED dimension share a great deal of overlap in symptoms, behaviors and comorbidities, this chapter will talk about the disorders collectively rather than focusing primarily on one, as has been done in the rest of this text. As you read through this chapter, you will find descriptions of each disorder, theories that describe the etiology of the ED spectrum, discussions of comorbidity and points of differential diagnosis. The end of this chapter will feature cases for you to diagnose.

BOX 14.01 KEY DEFINITIONS: EATING DISORDERS

Acrocyanosis. Acrocyanosis describes a blue or purple discoloration of hands and feet that results from poor circulation and is sometimes observed in persons with anorexia who are experiencing cardiovascular problems (Mitchell & Crow, 2010).

Amenorrhea/Oligomenorrhea. Amenorrhea describes a phenomenon in which a person's menstrual cycle is interrupted. Oligomenorrhea describes a menstrual cycle that is less frequent than is typical, a span of more than 35 days between cycles. Both amenorrhea oligomenorrhea can be indicators of metabolic disturbances (Attia & Roberto, 2009).

Bigorexia/Muscle Dysmorphia. A subtype of body dysmorphic disorder, this experience features a perception of the body as smaller and weaker than it is. Clients experiencing muscle dysmorphia may adopt extreme measures in eating and exercise to build the desired body mass (Pope et al., 2005).

Bradycardia. Bradycardia describes a heart rate that is too slow to deliver enough oxygen to the body and may result in dizziness or fainting, a lack of energy for everyday activities or shortness of breath (Mitchell & Crow, 2010).

Compensatory Behavior. A compensatory behavior, for the purposes of this chapter, is one of any number of strategic actions designed to limit weight gain, lose weight or shift body shape. Compensatory behaviors might include, but are not limited to, the misuse of alcohol, drugs and medications, excessive exercise, purging, and so on (Fitzpatrick et al., 2019).

Diabulimia. Describes persons with Type I diabetes who deliberately skip insulin in order to induce weight loss. This risky practice can result in diabetic ketoacidosis, which may lead to hospitalization or death (Ruth-Sahd et al., 2009).

Edema. A medical condition in which water collects in the tissues of the body, such as in the legs or lungs (Mitchell & Crow, 2010).

Fatosphere. The fatosphere refers to an online community of those promoting fat acceptance. It is a forum for working with weight-based stigma rather than a promotion of weight gain (Dickins et al., 2011).

Female Athlete Triad. The female athlete triad refers to three co-occurring phenomena: amenorrhea, osteoporosis and disordered eating among female athletes (Stand, 2007).

Food Neophobia. Seen largely in very young children, food neophobia refers to the fear of and the significant reluctance to try new foods (Dovey et al., 2008).

Hyperphasia. Often associated with damage to the hypothalamus, hyperphasia describes an abnormally elevated appetite for food (Mitchell & Crow, 2010).

Lanugo. Lanugo describes the fine hair that covers the body of newborns and serves as a natural insulator. Lanugo may regrow in those who are malnourished when temperature regulation has been disrupted and is often seen in those with anorexia or bulimia (Mitchell & Crow, 2010).

Marasmus. Marasmus is the wasting of muscle tissue to fuel the body when a person has not consumed enough protein and other vital nutrients. Marasmus is a marker of severe malnourishment (Mitchell & Crow, 2010).

Obesity. Obesity is a medical term that describes body weight that is 20% above the ideal weight for that individual, or a body mass index of 30 or greater. Obesity is a condition that is distinct from the eating disorders listed in the DSM (APA, 2013).

Orthorexia Nervosa. Orthorexia describes an unhealthy fixation on healthy eating that generally

(*Continued*)

(*Continued*)

includes obsessive and anxious thoughts about food purity and the health benefits of food. While the fears concerning food purity and nutritional value lead to significant food restriction and weight loss, the individual's concerns do not generally include concerns about weight or weight gain. Orthorexia is not currently included in the DSM nomenclature but is discussed in the literature (Dunn & Bratman, 2016).

Pro-ana/Pro-mia. These terms refer to communities and their media products that promote anorexia or bulimia as a lifestyle rather than a disorder. Pro-ana and pro-mia resources often provide encouragement and ideas for how to sustain these practices and how to avoid detection (Borzekowski et al., 2010).

Refeeding Syndrome. This describes a situation in which a person is so malnourished, the introduction of foods begins a metabolic process that results in death. People who have been starving, have severe anorexia, cancer and other medical conditions are at risk for this phenomenon (Hearing, 2004).

Russell's Sign. A term describing calluses that develop on knuckles and the backs of hands that result from frequent self-induced vomiting over an extended period of time (Mitchell & Crow, 2010).

Selective Eating. Typically seen in childhood, selective eating describes a strong preference for a very narrow range of foods, often carbohydrates, and is not accompanied by concerns about weight.

Thinspiration. Thinspiration describes any media, be it video, blogs, pictures, poetry, music, and so on, designed to inspire very low and unhealthy body weight.

The ED Continuum

Six disorders of eating occupy this continuum: pica, rumination disorder, avoidant/restrictive food intake disorder (ARFID), AN, bulimia nervosa (BN) and binge-ED. Two of these disorders, pica and rumination disorder, were previously organized under the disorders of infancy and childhood, but are now included here to create a more cohesive dimension.

Pica. Pica describes a persistent habit of eating items with no nutritional value. In order to diagnose pica, this habit should not be reflective of the individual's developmental age and should have continued for more than one month. For example, an 18-month-old child who eats things found on the floor would not be diagnosed with pica, but an 18-year-old with a cognitive age of 10 who does the same thing would be. Before diagnosing this disorder, one should rule out items eaten as part of a ritual, as with the cultural practice of eating ashes in funeral ceremonies. The incidence of pica is correlated with the increased severity of intellectual disabilities (American Psychiatric Association [APA], 2013; Delaney et al., 2015).

Pica has gained some recent attention in the media; thanks to television programs, like *My Strange Addiction*, in which episodes feature adults who describe their irresistible urges to eat non-nutritive items like laundry detergent, bricks or cremated ashes. Although the actual prevalence of pica among typical adults has been difficult to ascertain, in part because of differences in how pica is measured (e.g., should ice or uncooked rice be included in non-nutritive items) and because it seems that clients are very reluctant to disclose pica until some medical consequence results. Common complications that come with pica include broken or chipped teeth, gastrointestinal obstructions and heavy metal intoxications. Higher rates of pica have been noted among pregnant women, children with intellectual disabilities and persons with iron deficiencies. Pica is also more common among children in sub-Saharan Africa (Delaney et al., 2015).

Rumination Disorder. This disorder is more commonly seen in infants and very young children and features a pattern of regurgitating food, which is then rechewed and then either swallowed again or spit out. Those with rumination disorder are able to bring up their food without deliberately inducing vomiting and without retching. Rumination disorder is not diagnosed when associated with a medical condition, as with gastroesophageal reflux disorder (GERD). However, rumination disorder is not without its consequences. Rumination can result in electrolyte imbalances, weight loss, malnutrition, tooth decay, and so on (APA, 2013; Delaney et al., 2015).

Avoidant/Restrictive Food Intake Disorder. ARFID has undergone a name change since the publication of the new edition of the DSM, once named feeding disorder of infancy or early childhood, and its criteria have been expanded. This disorder, is one sometimes seen in infants or very young children newly introduced to solids as well as older children, teens and sometimes lasting into adulthood. Typically, ARFID does not develop later in life, however. ARFID describes a phenomenon in which the food itself, it's texture, scent, taste or the sensation of eating is experienced as highly aversive and is consequently avoided. Persons struggling with ARFID, like those with AN, show concerning weight loss, or a failure to meet expected growth milestones; thanks to their avoidance of food and eating. Of course, this diagnosis is not applied in situations in which food restrictions are cultural or religious in nature, as with those who avoid pork or shellfish, and is not diagnosed in those who avoid one or a few foods that are perceived to be aversive if weight loss or other impairments are not experienced (APA, 2013; Fisher et al., 2014; Norris & Katzman, 2015; Norris et al., 2014).

An ED Spectrum: Anorexia, Bulimia, Binge Eating and Purging Disorder

The next four disorders listed in the EDs continuum, anorexia, bulimia, binge eating and purging disorder, share a great deal of symptom overlap as well as high rates of diagnostic migration, sometimes described as crossover or conversion, in which a person switches between diagnoses. It may be helpful to remember while reading this chapter that these diagnostic migrations are so common that they are frequently observed within research studies that are attempting to describe features of specific disorders, significantly clouding any differences that may be present between groups and suggesting to some that differences observed in these studies may be unreliable. Symptom overlap and diagnostic conversion are two of the primary drivers behind challenges to the current DSM ED structure (Agras, 2010; Dazzi & Di Leone, 2014; Gleaves et al., 2000). Let's first explore the DSM diagnostic structure and then touch briefly on proposed changes.

Anorexia Nervosa (AN). Anorexia nervosa, meaning a nervous loss of appetite (Meyer & Deitsch, 1996), may be the most broadly recognized ED on this dimension. Anorexia is an ED that carries profound medical consequences, a high mortality rate and significant comorbidity with disorders that also have significant mental and physical consequences, such as substance use disorders (SUDs). The defining feature of AN is an intense fear of weight gain and deluded perceptions of their own body. Those with anorexia have a low body mass index (BMI), 17 or less, but perceive themselves to be overweight. In response to fears and misperceptions of their own body size, clients with anorexia put significant energy, effort and focus into restricting their caloric intake (APA, 2013).

Anorexia has two sub-types, those that limit their efforts to restricting how many calories they consume and to exercise, described as the restricting type (AN-R) and those who also binge or purge in order to eliminate calories, binge eating/purging type (AN-BP) (APA, 2013; Zipfel et al., 2015). Researchers note crossover rates from anorexia to BN is as high as 1 in 3 (Eddy et al., 2008).

Changes to the criteria for the DSM 5 included the removal of the requirement that women experience a disruption in their menstrual cycle, in order to be diagnosed with AN (APA, 2013). Diagnosticians had long argued that while the cessation of the menstrual cycle offered a concrete diagnostic marker, its value in differentiating the psychological or physiological statuses of clients was marginal and did not serve as a meaningful marker distinguishing treatment outcomes. What's more, clients who met all but the amenorrhea criteria were virtual diagnostic orphans. Further, this criterion did not address the needs of post-menopausal women, young women who have not yet begun menstruating regularly, or men (Attia & Roberto, 2009; Zipfel et al., 2015), nor does it address the needs of transgendered or intersex persons who do not menstruate.

Although anorexia is seen in people across ages, genders, sexual orientations, races and socioeconomic classes, women in their teens and early 20s are most at risk. Most often this disorder is protracted and marked by relapses. Recovery rates are higher for those in their teens; older clients with AN evidence higher mortality (Button et al., 2010; Zipfel et al., 2015).

Bulimia Nervosa (BN). Bulimia, meaning "the hunger of an ox" (Meyer & Deitsch, 1996) describes a pattern of disordered eating in which cycles of binging and purging or other compensatory behaviors are in evidence at least once a week for three consecutive months. Binging episodes are often triggered by acute stress and increases in negative emotion (Fitzpatrick et al., 2019). The severity of this disorder is judged by examining the frequency of compensatory behaviors, 1–3 being mild, 4–7 moderate, 8–13 severe and 14 or more described as extreme (APA, 2013). Though binging and purging are central to the bulimia diagnosis, a network analysis of core symptoms of bulimia, depression and anxiety conducted by Levinson et al. (2017) identified fear of weight gain as the core bulimia symptom; fear of weight gain correlated most strongly with anxiety and depression symptoms, although binging and purging were strongly correlated with one another.

The criteria for bulimia have also undergone some revision with the fifth edition. First the criteria threshold has been lowered by reducing the required number of binging and compensatory behaviors from at least twice a week to once (APA, 2013), a move that has been welcomed by some and criticized by others (Frances, 2013). By reducing the threshold for BN, the total number of persons diagnosed with an unspecified ED was reduced. The subtypes of BN, purging and non-purging, have also been removed (APA, 2013).

Compensatory Behaviors. Compensatory behaviors among those with EDs describes strategies for either balancing calories with exercise or eliminating them through the use of laxatives and purging, or by using alcohol, drugs or medication to influence body weight or shape. Compensatory behaviors are a defining feature of bulimia but are also evidenced in those with AN-BP. Both food restriction, binging and compensatory practices have significant physiological and psychological consequences (APA, 2013; Mitchell, 2016; Mitchell & Crow, 2010), which will be described later in this chapter.

A particularly dangerous compensatory behavior has been documented among clients with Type I diabetes and has been unofficially dubbed "diabulimia." These clients skip insulin for the purpose of weight loss. This tactic can lead to headache, lethargy and poor concentration, and in severe instances, result in diabetic ketoacidosis, which may lead to coma or death. The incidence of those who endorse having engaged in this practice in order to manage weight is high among those with diabetes, ranging between 5% and 14%. When seen together with binge eating, this practice is diagnosed as BN, however, when occurring together with severe food restriction should be diagnosed as AN, binging/purging type (AN-BP) (Ruth-Sahd et al., 2009).

Binge Eating Disorder (BED). Binge eating disorder (BED) appears to be a familial disorder and is likely influenced by the interplay of "genetic and environmental variables" (Agras, 2010, p. 3). BED and BN share symptom overlap, recurring binging episodes. As with those with BN or AN-BP, episodes are accompanied by a feeling of having lost control over how much was eaten and is generally followed by feelings of disgust, distress and shame. Unlike those diagnosed with BN, those with BED do not engage in compensatory behaviors such as vomiting, using laxatives, excessive exercise, and so on. In contrast to those with AN, those with BED do not habitually restrict their food intake (APA, 2013). Those with BED are more likely to be of average weight or to be overweight than are others on the EDs continuum (APA, 2013;

Mitchell, 2016; Mitchell & Crow, 2010). BED makes its first official appearance in the EDs dimension after having been placed in the research section of the previous edition (APA, 2013). In those with BED, the likelihood of crossover to BN is more likely than is retaining the BED diagnosis (Bohon, 2017).

Newly Identified Disorders: The ED Horizon

Until recently, anorexia and bulimia comprised the core EDs and all other disordered eating, save those first arising in childhood or infancy, fell into an unspecified ED category. The unspecified group of EDs, which described the larger proportion of people presenting with EDs, captured a widely varied group of symptoms. Revisions in criteria and the addition of binge ED were aimed at creating greater diagnostic specificity and better treatment outcomes (APA, 2013), an aim that continues today. Three disordered eating phenomena have been identified and are explored within the research literature, two of which are included within the presentations of other specified feeding or ED: night eating syndrome and purging disorder. A third, orthorexia nervosa, is not discussed in the DSM 5. Each is described briefly below.

Night Eating Syndrome (NES). NES was first described in 1955 and has been slow to make an appearance in the DSM. Currently, it is included with the five variations of the other specified feeding and EDs. NES describes recurrent episodes of eating large quantities of food after the evening meal (APA, 2013). Researchers have noted that those with this syndrome may eat 25% or more of their total food intake for the day during these night eating episodes, though this feature is not a part of the diagnostic criteria. NES shares some features with sleep disorders and may be the consequence of

FIGURE 14.01 **Re-envisioning the Eating Disorder Dimension**

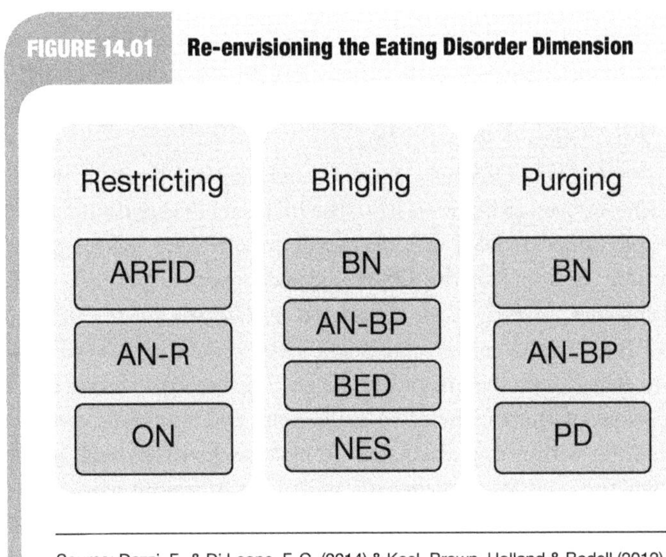

Source: Dazzi, F., & Di Leone, F. G. (2014) & Keel, Brown, Holland & Bodell (2012).

disrupted circadian rhythms. Often, these clients find it difficult to fall asleep without eating and may either eat before going to bed or wake during the night, eat and only then return to sleep. Research suggests that symptoms seem to worsen with increasing body mass (Allison et al., 2010; Costa et al., 2015).

Purging Disorder (PD). Purging disorder describes behavior in which a person attempts to control their weight by purging but does not restrict, as with anorexia, and does not binge, as with bulimia and AN-BP type (APA, 2013). There is some evidence that the clinical severity of PD roughly matches that of BN, and that the incidence rate of PD among teens and young women are similar. Currently, however, not enough is known about the diagnostic reliability in the field or about the clinical utility of differentiating PD for treatment outcomes, consequently, it has not been included as an independent diagnostic disorder. It is, however, included within the other specified feeding and EDs category (Keel, 2007; Keel & Striegel-Moore, 2009).

Orthorexia Nervosa (ON). Though not included in the feeding and EDs dimension nor mentioned in the research section of the DSM 5, orthorexia is drawing considerable attention from clinicians and researchers. Diagnostic criteria have been proposed (Dunn & Bratman, 2016) and a diagnostic questionnaire has been developed (Donini et al., 2005), however, sufficient consensus has not been reached for its inclusion (Costa et al., 2017). Orthorexia describes a phenomenon in which a person develops "a fixation on the virtue of food or unhealthy obsession with healthy eating" (Bratman, 1997, p. 980, in Costa et al., 2017). This problematic presentation often begins as an interest in healthy eating as a part of preventing chronic disease but evolves into a fixation that often leads to food restriction and ultimately to malnutrition (Dunn & Bratman, 2016). Common focuses of concern among this group are foods that have been treated with chemicals, contain artificial ingredients or have a high fat, salt or sugar content. As a result, a great deal of time and effort are given to selecting ingredients, planning and preparing meals. Food and its preparation begins to overshadow other aspects of life and concerns about food then lead to distress. Orthorexia is not a weight loss strategy, though weight loss may result, and body weight is not a central concern for those with this presentation (Costa et al., 2017; Dunn & Bratman, 2016).

Challenges to the DSM Diagnostic Structure and Proposals for New Models. The high degree of symptom overlap between EDs, the high rate of diagnostic conversions and the questionable utility of BMI as a diagnostic marker have led researchers to challenge the current structure of the DSM and led others to propose new diagnostic models. For instance, investigations conducted by Gleaves et al. (2000) suggest that AN-BP and BN are closely related constructs. They found that AN-BP type was more different from AN-R type than from BN, suggesting a reorganization may be needed.

The full scope of the variety of investigations and proposals are too broad for careful exploration within this discussion. In essence, however, each of the proposed changes recognize a core set of diagnostic traits: fear of weight gain, food restriction, binge eating and purging and other compensatory actions, though each varies slightly in how these are described (Keel et al., 2012). Dazzi and Di Leone (2014) recommend a new organization made up of three categories: those with binging and purging, those with binging alone and those with food restriction without either binging or purging. They note that such a structure would include those with NES, purging disorder and those with anorexia but who are not fat-phobic, obviating the need for another specified category.

Medical Complications Associated with EDs. EDs have a direct impact on a number of systems of the body. Particularly among those diagnosed with anorexia or bulimia, systems that can be impacted include cardiovascular, dermatologic, skeletal, gastrointestinal, metabolic and endocrine, renal and neurological. Among those with AN and BN, cardiac problems can manifest as a very low heart rate, bradycardia, which can lead to dizziness, fainting, shortness of breath and other heart-related concerns, the most significant of which is heart failure. These clients may experience yellowing of the skin thanks to high consumption of green leafy vegetables, and a blue or purple hue to the hands and feet due to poor circulation. Decreases in bone density can lead to osteopenia or osteoporosis in more extreme cases.

Medical Problems Tied to the Binging and Purging Process. Dental problems are very common among those who use vomiting as an avenue to purge calories. A wide variety of gastrointestinal difficulties have been linked to AN and BN including swelling in the salivary glands, slowed digestive processes that result in constipation and other difficulties, including in more severe instances, gastric dilation and gastric rupture, which can lead to death. Metabolic and endocrine systems are also impacted and are evidenced in a number of symptoms, such as electrolyte imbalances, disrupted (amenorrhea) or irregular menstrual cycles (oligomenorrhea), reproductive difficulties, thyroid dysfunction, and so on. Neurological shifts associated with AN include enlarged ventricles and pseudoatrophy as well as Wernicke's encephalopathy, which may result in weakness, involuntary movement or confusion (APA, 2013; Mitchell, 2016). Among those with binge-ED, many but not all of the medical consequences are tied to obesity that often accompanies the disorder. Among this group, higher rates of diabetes are widely documented (APA, 2013; Mitchell, 2016; Mitchell & Crow, 2010). A study of 1,892 patients found that those with AN were 10 times more likely to experience an early death than were matched controls. Of those diagnosed with AN who had passed away, 70% were in their 20s (Button et al., 2010).

Medical Problems Tied to the Binging and Purging Process. Though many of the medical concerns are seen across the ED spectrum, those with binging and purging behaviors can trigger specific physiological changes. Some of these changes might include cavities and enamel loss, esophageal tears, swelling of the parotid glands, creating a chipmunk like effect, scarring on the backs of the hand and fingers, known as Russell's sign, dry mouth and chronic hoarseness. Physiological consequences to binging and purging that are shared with AN and BED include electrolyte imbalances, disruptions in menstrual cycles and reproductive problems, heart dysrhythmia, diabetes, cholesterol problems, electrolyte imbalances and so on (APA, 2013; Mitchell, 2016; Mitchell & Crow, 2010).

Mental Health Comorbidities. In addition to the associated physical health disorders associated with EDs, EDs also have very high rates of comorbidity with other mental health concerns including suicide. EDs and their severity have been correlated with the childhood trauma (Groth et al., 2019). EDs are frequently seen together with depression, bipolar disorder, anxiety disorders, PTSD as well as substance abuse disorders (Halmi, 2010; Herpertz-Dahlmann, 2009; Levinson et al., 2019; Pisetsky et al., 2015; Woodside & Staab, 2006; Zipfel et al., 2015). Across all racial groups, unipolar and bipolar disorders are the most common comorbid psychological disorders in those diagnosed with EDs (Halmi, 2010; Levinson et al., 2019). Nearly 75% of those with AN experience a mood disorder sometime over the course of their lifetimes, whereas somewhere between 25% and 75% experience an anxiety disorder. Research suggests that more often than not these anxiety disorders precede the anorexia. Nearly 80% will experience some kind of obsession or compulsion and between 15% and 29% will eventually meet criteria for OCD (Halmi, 2010; Zipfel et al., 2015).

Cognition. Cognitive shifts have been observed and documented in those with anorexia. These changes include difficulties in shifting tasks and difficulties with global or big-picture thinking. These shifts are often not recovered when anorexia resolves. Cognitive difficulties resulting from anorexia also reach into the social domain. People diagnosed with anorexia have shown impaired emotional recognition, diminished emotional expression and attentional bias. Like the neurocognitive symptoms, these sociocognitive skill deficits may not fully resolve with recovery from anorexia (Zipfel et al., 2015).

Substance Use Disorders: A Special Consideration. SUDs and EDs make dangerous bedfellows. When clients present with both an ED and one or more SUDs, their symptoms tend to be worsened, they show longer recovery times, their outcomes are poorer and their relapse rates are higher (Dansky et al., 2000; Gregorowski et al., 2013; Harrop & Marlatt, 2010). Clients with EDs seem to misuse substances for different purposes, sometimes to aid in weight-loss attempts, as with stimulants, laxatives, thyroid medications, insulin and so on. Alcohol is sometimes used to suppress appetite, induce vomiting or dehydration (Franko et al., 2005). Other clients use substances for emotion regulation, and at other times to supply energy that has not been gained by eating regular meals (Franko et al., 2005; Gregorowski et al., 2013). While precise comorbidity rates are difficult to pin down, thanks to differences across studies in inclusion categories, including changes in the SUD nosology, high crossover rates between EDs and other complicating factors, it does seem to be clear that those with EDs have a higher incidence of substance use than do those without (Harrop & Marlatt, 2010; Zipfel et al., 2015). An early study suggests that for those with comorbid SUDs and EDs, well over half had the ED first (57%), whereas only 27% reported the SUDs preceded the ED (Halmi, 2010). SUDs have been shown to contribute to the high mortality rate of those with EDs (Button et al., 2010).

Suicide and Deliberate Self Harm and EDs. Suicide rates among those with EDs are alarmingly high. A systematic analysis of studies describing mortality rates among those with EDs revealed both high rates of suicide and death from associated medical causes (Arcelus et al., 2011). Research conducted on the rates of suicide among large samples of those diagnosed with AN, BN and BED revealed that overall rates of suicide death were much higher among those with AN than BN (this study did not find an incidence of suicide among their BED sample). They also found that over time the incidence of suicide decreased for those with AN, whereas for those with BN longer illness duration was correlated with higher suicide rates (Preti et al., 2011). Studies examining suicidal behavior in those diagnosed with BN found that between 20% and 27% had attempted suicide (Pisetsky et al., 2015). Pisetsky et al. (2015) explored mental health correlations between BN and suicide attempts and found that depression, identity problems and attachment style were most highly correlated with suicide attempts while a range of tested personality traits showed no correlation. Across diagnoses, comorbid depression and SUDs appear to increase suicide rates among those with EDs (Button et al., 2010; Eddy et al., 2008). These studies point to the urgency in offering quick, comprehensive assessment and skilled intervention to these vulnerable clients.

Race, Ethnicity and Gender. For some time, EDs were perceived to be a problem primarily of White women, however, decades of research demonstrates that EDs are evident across racial groups. For instance, Neumark-Sztainer et al. (2002) explored body satisfaction among 4,746 adolescents attending urban public schools. They found that weight-related concerns and behaviors aimed at controlling weight were prevalent across racial groups. Similarly, Marques et al. (2011) report study results that suggest anorexia and binge-EDs have prevalence rates that were roughly the same across groups, but found that BN was more common among those of African American and Latino respondents. Shuttlesworth and Zotter's (2011) research suggested that African American women may identify with beauty ideals that shield them from eating-disordered behavior aimed at weight loss but does not protect them from those that cause weight gain, as with binging. As is so often the case, lifetime service utilization for the treatment of EDs was lower among all ethnic groups than among non-Latino White participants. A meta-analysis conducted in 2006 found that African American women have better body image esteem and report fewer concerns with weight and shape, though this difference was small and differences on other measures were close to zero (Grabe & Hyde, 2006). Inconsistencies across studies and the utilization of very broad racial and ethnic groups make a clear and definitive understanding of ED prevalence among racial and ethnic minorities difficult to ascertain. However, it does seem clear that EDs are in evidence across racial groups.

Race, Ethnicity, Gender and the Identification of EDs. Sala et al. (2013) conducted a study of 663 participants examining their ability to recognize EDs portrayed in vignettes and measured the participant's judgement about whether or not the person depicted in the vignette should receive medical help. Of particular interest to these researchers was whether or not race or gender interaction effects between the reviewer and the vignette would influence whether or not an ED was recognized. Overall, these researchers found that the rates of recognition of problematic eating were low, especially for bulimia and binge eating. Their results demonstrated that men were less likely to recognize an ED and less likely to indicate the need for medical help than were women. Across all groups, AN was most easily recognized and accurately named, however, among those that saw problematic behaviors within the vignettes, the bulimia vignette was more likely to be identified as needing intervention. Researchers found there were no differences in race and ethnicity interactions in either the rater or in the vignette with the exception that White participants were slightly more likely to identify BED, independent of the race or ethnicity depicted in the vignette.

Eating and Gender Transition. Early research seems to show that transgender youth experience EDs at higher rates than their cisgendered counterparts and that female to male (FTM) transgendered persons are more apt to experience an ED than are male to female (MTF) transitioning persons. Clinicians should be aware that disordered eating, either restriction or overeating, can be used as an avenue to achieve a body type that more closely fits a person's own gender identity without making use of hormones. For instance, a person considering an MTF transition may intentionally overeat in order to attain a "curvier" and more "feminine" figure, while a person considering an FTM transition may restrict their calorie intake in order to reflect a more androgenous or "typically masculine" look. These differences in motivation may influence a client's experience of and response to treatment. Conveying understanding about these dynamics are potentially important to the client–therapist relationship (Diemer et al., 2018; Duffy et al., 2016).

Theories of Etiology and Factors that Sustain EDs

Family Systems. Salvador Minuchin can be credited with bringing family members back into the therapy room when treating EDs after a long period of exile. Historically, parents had alternatively been criticized in their unhelpful role in the ED and sometimes outright blamed. Minuchin believed that an ED could arise out of a family dynamic that featured a "rigid, enmeshed, over-involved and conflict avoidant" (p. 373) family system (Le Grange & Hoste, 2010). Rosman, Minuchin and Liebman (1975) describe their work with families framing the problem eating as "one of parental management of a balky rather than sick child" (p. 847). They note that the parents often undermine one another's efforts to get their child to eat, use emotional blackmail to implore the child to eat, make demands or physically attempt to force the child to eat. Minuchin et al. theorized that the problematic eating was a response to difficulties within the family system's interpersonal relationships themselves, rather than one located solely in the child, the "identified client." They asserted that the child's eating behaviors provided a conflict detour for the parents, accommodating the family's conflict avoidance.

Primarily focused on girls and women, family systems theorists of the time, such as Masterson and Bruch, incorporated attachment theory in order to better describe the role of family dynamics in the development of EDs. Chief among these is the assertion that autonomy failure resulting from intrusive and overly controlling caregivers leads the client to develop a "false self" one of the "good girl," which serves as a defense against intrusion. The consequence is an inability to express emotions, such as anger, that don't match the good girl persona. Finally, it is theorized the parents' wishes become confused with her need for food, creating an ambivalent or hostile relationship with food (Dallos, 2004).

Self-psychology and the Vertical Split. Another view of the etiology of EDs, also involving family dynamics, is one of the disorganized self-experience. Readers will recall Kohut's discussion of the importance of mirroring in early childhood to healthy adult outcomes. Mirroring is the experience of having one's feelings identified and accepted rather than being missed altogether or chastised and rejected. When aspects of a child's self-experiencing are rejected, the theory asserts, the child is left with a choice between expressing those feelings and risk rejection from parents or to disavow themselves of those feelings, disguising them even from themselves, a process described as the vertical split. Cowan and Heselmeyer have described this process in bulimia. They describe the dys-integrated part of self that steps behind the wall of the vertical split as the dissociated bulimia identity, the DBI (Cowan & Heselmeyer, 2011; Cowan, 2017).

Researchers note the presence of dissociative symptoms within the binging and purging cycles. (Dallos, 2004; La Mela et al., 2010). These dissociations happen, Cowan and Heselmeyer assert, when food is used as a substitute for the disavowed need for affirmation and relational nurturance. Rather than risk rejection by acknowledging these needs, the client is said to dissociate, escaping their stress and receiving the needed support through food and the comfort of the dissociated bulimia identity. Once the dissociation has ended and the individual recognizes what they have done, shame about the eating as well as about their own needs leads to renewed rejection in the form of purging and turning away from their needs. Healing of the dissociative binging and the resultant purging cycles comes, thanks to the therapeutic relationship and the embracing of the rejected identity and the needs the identity represents (Cowan, 2017; Heselmeyer & Cowan, 2012).

Cultural Influences and EDs. Feminist scholars place responsibility for EDs at the feet of sociocultural norms that idealize unnaturally thin bodies and create standards for beauty that are nearly impossible to realize (Gurrieri & Cherrier, 2013; Malson & Burns, 2009). These theorists point to examples such as "heroin chic," a trend toward very thin and pale bodies, the widespread use of prepubescent models used as stand-ins for full grown women and photoshopping of models as examples of unhealthy culturally inspired beauty standards. The pervasiveness of the Internet has deepened concerns about the ubiquity of these influences (Eckermann, 2009).

Media: Pro-Ana and Pro-Mia and Their Effect on Eating and Body Image. One of the most influential avenues through which culture and cultural expectations is communicated is through the media. Traditionally, media has included television, movies and print, such as magazines and newspapers, but for over a decade media has included the sizable presence of the Internet, which besides serving as a conduit for all other forms of media, also now includes blog forums and websites that focus on a seemingly limitless range of topics, including pro-ED content. Websites and content dedicated to the promotion of EDs and very thin body types generally are referred to as "thinspiration," pro-ana (pro-anorexia) or pro-mia (pro-bulimia) (Borzekowski et al., 2010;

BOX 14.02 TRY THIS: DISCERNING THE BINGE EPISODE

In the following scenarios, consider Elise and Joy. Do either of these scenarios resemble a binging episode? What questions would you have for each to confirm your initial thoughts?

Elise. Elise and her husband are celebrating their fifth wedding anniversary in Florence with her parents. They have decided to have an authentic Italian seven-course meal. Over the course of 2 hours, the waiter has brought an apertivo that included a selection of olives and bread, followed by the antipasti, a platter of thinly sliced meats and one each of a small broccoli and carrot souffle. The primi platter consisted of a large bowl of risotto drizzled with truffle oil, which was followed by the secondi, the house specialty lamb chops. With the secondi came the contorni, in this case a plate of white beans with black pepper, and then a plate of roasted brussel sprouts. Though Elise felt she could not eat another bite, the family was then served a selection of cheese and fruit drizzled with seasoned honey. They finished the meal with a traditional slice of grandmother's cake and espresso. Before ending the meal, each had a shot of limoncello. Everyone left stuffed to the gills and feeling a walk around the Duomo was in order. Though she enjoyed her meal thoroughly, she wondered how she had managed to consume so much food in so little time.

Joy. Joy arrived home exhausted from yet another trying day at the office. In her long commute home, she could think of little else than slipping into her sweatpants and eating dinner to the flickering light of a movie. But Joy knew she would need to do the week's shopping first. So she stopped by the grocery store on her way home and purchased a family-sized frozen mac and cheese, a hot rotisserie chicken from the deli and a pint of mashed potatoes. She grabbed a variety of fresh and frozen vegetables, some fruit, chips, soda, some yogurt, goat cheese and crackers and a box of breakfast cereal. Once home, she changed her clothes and popped the frozen pasta and the pie into the oven, planning to have the mac and cheese Monday, Wednesday and Friday and the chicken Tuesday and Thursday. She turned on a movie and began eating the chicken and potatoes, planning just a quick taste to hold her over until dinner was ready. Once the timer for the mac and cheese went off, the chicken and potatoes were eaten and she began eating the pasta, followed by the pie. Her stomach ached, and she felt both nauseous, ashamed and deeply regretful. The whole of the week's groceries consumed in just over 2 hours. She hardly remembered any of it, almost as if it had been another person eating. She tearfully began cleaning up the dishes piled on her coffee table.

Eckermann, 2009; Harper et al., 2008). Content analysis of 220 of these sites revealed that nearly all were open to the public, and consequently easily accessible by children and adolescents, nearly 80% of which had interactive features. Further, the majority 84% offered pro-ana material, whereas 64% provided pro-mia content. Eighty-five percent of the sites reviewed offered "thinspiration" in the form of images, music or poetry, and 83% offered ideas for food restriction, eliminating or burning calories and disguising disordered eating behaviors. Just under 40% provided information and links to recovery information (Borzekowski et al., 2010).

The Body-Positive Moment. A contrasting, but still controversial presence on the web are those that work to push back against cultural beauty norms and work instead to celebrate fat bodies (Gurrieri & Cherrier, 2013). Some research suggests that the stigma associated with obesity has grown with the increase in focus on the medical consequences of very high BMI. In response to cultural weight stigma and biases, empowerment groups have formed; this online community has become known as the "fatosphere," and promotes ideas such as health at every size (HAES) and the body-positive movement (Dickins et al., 2011). Although many therapists work to promote healthy eating and weight loss, other therapists and writers, such as Matacin and Simone (2019) assert the importance of challenging systemic weight bias and encouraging clients to explore body-positive activism in order to promote mental health and well-being. These contrasting viewpoints challenge clinicians to consider the most appropriate and ethical approach to working with clients for whom eating patterns have resulted in obesity.

Appetitive Function and Anorexia and Bulimia. It may be worth noting that some researchers are exploring potential psychophysiological etiologies for anorexia and bulimia, looking at the brain and appetitive functions of the body. Appetitive functions are complex and involve hormones, neuropeptides and the limbic and cortical regions of the brain, making it difficult to nail down the potential source or sources of appetite difficulties in these disorders. Complicating these efforts further is the fact that malnourished and emaciated clients with anorexia do exhibit changes in organ function that may impact appetitive functions, however, it is difficult to know whether these differences preceded or followed illness. There is some evidence that the anterior insula of the brain, for example, plays a role in disrupting an otherwise appropriate hunger response, which then leads to emaciation (Kaye & Oberndorfer, 2010).

Neurological and Genetic Factors. EDs appear to have high rates of heritability. AN, for instance, has heritability rates ranging from 28% to 74%. Most of the research examining the neurobiological traits of those with AN have been conducted on those who were very ill making it difficult to discern which observed structural differences preceded and are causal or are a result of the ED. Reductions in global gray matter and white matter have been observed as have increased cerebrospinal fluid. Decreases in the gray matter of the hypothalamus have also been observed (Zipfel et al., 2015).

PANDAS and Anorexia. Researchers are investigating a possible link between pediatric autoimmune neuropsychiatric disorders associated with streptococcal infection

(PANDAS) and its role in pediatric anorexia. Non-specific bio-markers for PANDAS complicate the validation of this theoretical association leaving the medical community divided on its relationship to anorexia and other theorized disorders such as OCD and movement disorders. Currently, PANDAS-AN is considered when the onset of anorexia is sudden, meets full DSM 5 criteria for anorexia and follows a confirmed strep infection (Puxley et al., 2008; Vincenzi et al., 2010).

Skilled Diagnostician

Scope of Practice. Lazzer and Muhlheim (2016) point out that because anorexia and bulimia have both a significant impact on the physical health of the client, and have high mortality rates and because the psychological comorbidities are also high, the skills needed for treating these patients usually outpaces the skills of outpatient therapists who do not specialize in ED treatment. They further note that while mandates for operating within the scope of training are included in the ethical standards for counselors, social workers, nurses, psychologists and psychiatrists, many of those who indicate their ability to treat EDs on therapist finder websites or insurance listings have minimal formal exposure to specialized training. Lazzer and Muhlheim advocate for a standardization of knowledge and skill for those diagnosing and treating EDs. They point to the recommendations of the American Psychiatric Association (Yager et al., 2006), which outline the following for the adequate assessment of those who are suspected of having an ED. These recommendations include the following:

1. Height and weight history
2. Patterns and changes in restrictive and binge eating
3. Patterns and changes in exercise
4. Patterns and changes in purging and other compensatory behaviors
5. A thorough evaluation and history of core attitudes and beliefs about weight, shape, eating and exercise
6. A thorough evaluation of mental health concerns

As with any assessment, clients who have not recently had a physical exam should be referred for medical examination to identify or rule out medical problems that may be the source of the ED or a consequence of it.

Diagnosis of Atypical Presentations. In a few cases, clients with anorexia symptoms lose a great deal of weight but do not fall at or below the 17 BMI threshold and may even be overweight. These clients are described as having atypical AN and are diagnosed with other specified feeding and ED (APA, 2013).

Rigid Eating Patterns in Persons with Autism Spectrum Disorders. In situations in which a client diagnosed with autism spectrum disorder (ASD) also evidences

TABLE 14.01 Differentiating Eating Disorders (EDs)

	Restricts	Binges	Purges	Distorted Body Image	Weight Change	Dissociative
Avoidant/ restrictive food intake disorder (ARFID)	Yes: Aversions to taste, texture, smell, etc.	No	No	Not characteristic	Significant loss or failure to meet expected gains	No
Anorexia nervosa as the restricting type (AN-R)	Yes: Weight control	No	No	Yes	Yes: Loss	No
Anorexia nervosa as the binge eating/ purging type (AN-BP)	Yes: Weight control	Yes	Yes	Yes	Yes: Loss	No
Bulimia nervosa (BN)	No	Recurrent episodes	Recurrent episodes	Not a defining characteristic	May gain or maintain stable weight	Yes
Binge eating disorder (BED)	No	Recurrent episodes	No	Not a defining characteristic	May gain or maintain stable weight	Yes
PD	No	No	Yes	Not a defining characteristic	May lose or maintain stable weight	No
Night eating syndrome (NES)	No	Yes	No	Not a defining characteristic	Yes: Gain	No
Orthorexia Nervosa (ON)	Yes: Avoids "unhealthy" or "impure" foods	No	No	Not a defining characteristic	Yes: Loss	No

Source: American Psychiatric Association (2013).

restricted eating patterns, it may be necessary to determine whether or not a diagnosis of ARFID would be appropriate. Children on the autism spectrum have high rates of food selectivity and a limited food repertoire (Bandini et al., 2010). When an individual's diet is made so narrow by the selection of tolerated foods that their health is impacted or, as in the case of children, they fail to make expected gains, an additional diagnosis of ARFID should be considered.

Discerning Anorexia from Avoidant/Restrictive Food Intake Disorder. Anorexia and ARFID share similar qualities and may, at initial presentation, be difficult to discern. Norris et al. (2014) conducted a study to explore similarities and differences between these two disorders and began with ED assessments of 699 patients, of which 205 met initial inclusion criteria. However, only 5% of these participants met full criteria for ARFID. These 34 participants were matched with 36 participants diagnosed with anorexia and then compared. They found that those diagnosed with ARFID were younger and more likely to be male (20.6% vs. 8.3%). This group also held more fears of vomiting and reported more abdominal pain. Those diagnosed with ARFID were hospitalized at lower rates than were those with anorexia. However, in this study, three-fourths of the ARFID group eventually met criteria for anorexia. In a similar study, Fisher et al., (2014) examined the traits and experiences of just over 700 participants with EDs and concluded that ARFID was distinct from anorexia and other disorders in that the ARFID participants had longer illness duration, were significantly underweight and had higher rates of comorbid medical illness and higher rates of comorbid anxiety, though lower rates of depression. When discerning anorexia and ARFID, these studies may be helpful in that they point out that those with ARFID report much earlier difficulties with resistance to food and eating, and that these early experiences were often accompanied by experiences of vomiting or choking and then fears of vomiting or choking developed. Many of these clients experience abdominal discomfort. In discerning these two diagnoses note the reasoning behind the avoidance; disgust with some aspect of the food or fear of choking, throwing up or experiencing a stomach ache without fears of gaining weight, point to ARFID.

Discerning AN, Binge-Eating/Purging Type from BN. Bulimia and anorexia with binging and/or purging are very closely related disorders with significant conversion from one to the other. The diagnostic differentiation comes in the assessment of body weight. Those with a BMI of 17 or less are diagnosed with anorexia, whereas those with a BMI greater than 17 are diagnosed with bulimia. The severity of anorexia is determined by the BMI range. Both disorders are dangerous and both can be deadly. It is important for clinicians to understand that there is something of a challenge presented by the weight criteria as a point of differentiation between these two presentations (APA, 2013).

As noted earlier, many clients will shift back and forth between these diagnoses over the course of their illness and treatment. Clinicians may wonder whether there is utility in changing the client's diagnosis with these shifts, a question that Agras (2010) points out has been the source of considerable controversy. Agras argues that the change of diagnosis suggests that one disorder has resolved and another has arisen, something that often does not seem to fit the client's presentation. Instead, the manifestation of the disordered eating has shifted but the underlying disorder remains the same. Agras recommends against changing the diagnosis frequently.

Another diagnostic principle forwarded by some authors is to adopt the stance, *anorexia trumps bulimia* because the consequences of malnourishment are thought to be objectively more severe than are those of purging (Birmingham & Beumont, 2005). Once a client has been diagnosed with either type of anorexia, this diagnosis is retained and differences in the specification of type would then be applied. Careful documentation of shifts in weight and eating patterns will clarify the diagnostic picture and direct treatment intervention. However, clinicians are advised to use clinical supervision and consultation in cases where differential diagnosis seems foggy and a clearer picture is needed in order to map a treatment plan.

Treatments For EDs

Refeeding and Refeeding Syndrome. Refeeding is a medical term for the reintroduction of nutrition in patients who are starving for the purpose of weight restoration. Refeeding syndrome is a metabolic phenomenon triggered by insulin and serum phosphate often in response to carbohydrates that results in sudden death, within 2 weeks, of the reintroduction of food. Refeeding syndrome can unfold even with the introduction of small amounts of carbohydrates (Kohn et al., 2011). Clinicians should be aware that the dietary needs of clients with EDs should be addressed by those fully qualified and with specialized understanding of the physiological needs of these clients. Dietary and medical consultation is absolutely essential when working with clients with EDs particularly when working toward weight restoration.

Cognitive-Behavioral Therapy for EDs (CBT-E). Across ED diagnoses CBT-E has demonstrated among the highest efficacy rates for clients. Fairburn is credited with developing the manualized adaptation of CBT for EDs and it is this first adaptation that has since spawned a number of adapted approaches for this dimension. CBT-E tends to span 4–5 months with between 12 and 20 sessions. These sessions are strategic and aim to motivate change while supporting clients in developing healthy eating, eliminating extreme strategies, such as purging, helping the client to build a realistic and supportive body image and to shift an inappropriate focus on weight, and, finally, to guard against relapse (Linardon et al., 2017; Linardon et al., 2017; Wilson, 2017; Wilson et al., 2002). A systematic review of the literature that included a meta-analysis found that results were not enhanced when coupled with medications. Further CBT, when compared to interpersonal therapy, demonstrated better outcomes on cognitive and behavioral measures, but only on cognitive measures at follow-up (Linardon et al., 2017).

CBT-E in its various forms has been used across EDs and in different settings. CBT has been adapted for those receiving intensive inpatient therapy with some success (MacDonald et al., 2017) as well as in groups. Brief group approaches, as little as four sessions, have shown initial support in treating BED (Ashton et al., 2009). A meta-analysis of group CBT for EDs did not show superior efficacy over other forms of group therapy, though it did show a significant advantage over wait-list controls (Grenon et al., 2017). Brief Adaptations of CBT with features of integrative dynamic therapy for BN have also shown efficacy (Richards et al., 2016). However, the efficacy of CBT-E does seem to be correlated with the therapist's adherence to the treatment protocol (Folke et al., 2017; Linardon et al., 2017).

Family Therapy and EDs. Family issues have long been thought to instigate and sustain disordered eating, making family therapy a logical treatment modality for this dimension. For adolescents, family therapy is the most often used approach (Le Grange & Hoste, 2010). A seminal randomized control study of 80 participants diagnosed with an ED and ranging in age compared family and individual therapy. Their research did not find definitive differences for those with BN or those with suffering from AN for more than 3 years, but for adolescents with an early onset and short illness duration (<3 years), outcomes were positive and were sustained at 5-year follow-up (Russel et al., 1987, in Le Grange & Host, 2010). A number of family approaches have followed, including, for example, emotion-focused family therapy that has four primary aims: recovery coaching, emotion coaching, relational repair and working through relational blocks (Dolhanty & Lafrance, 2019). Another approach, ED-focused family therapy, has been shown to have efficacy in children and adolescents in randomized control studies (Jewell et al., 2016). Family approaches embrace a wide range of theoretical underpinnings, though each shares the family systems relationship. These approaches have been used for inpatient and outpatient clients. For adolescents, however, family-based therapies are the intervention of choice (Gorrell & Le Grange, 2019).

Dialectical Behavioral Therapy (DBT). Frequently binging episodes are triggered by stressors or difficulty with emotion regulation. DBT was first designed to treat the suicidal and parasuicidal behaviors of those diagnosed with borderline personality disorder but has been adapted to treat a number of other disorders including EDs. This adaptation, the Stanford DBT Model, is frequently used as an adjunctive therapy in order to offer support to clients in developing emotion regulation skills. DBT therapists frame the purging behaviors as having the same function as self-injury. DBT aims to support these clients in identifying and coping with negative emotions effectively. The Stanford DBT Model differs from the standard DBT in that standard DBT includes both group and individual sessions, whereas the Stanford model uses either group or individual sessions alone (Chen & Safer, 2010; Linehan & Chen, 2005).

Definitional Cases

Sadie

When stressed, Sadie sometimes "zones out" and eats large quantities of food. After these episodes, she often forces herself to vomit so that she does not gain weight.

Keith

Keith, age 35, has experienced some stressors in the past 7 months. As many as 5 times a week since the stressors began, Keith has found himself in his apartment alone, eating large amounts of food in a single sitting, often enough for three or four people. He describes having no control over these episodes.

Bethany

Bethany is haunted by the fear that she will "become fat like my mother." Though her current BMI is 16.5, she consistently restricts her food intake.

Bobby

Bobby, age 5, has been diagnosed with an autism spectrum disorder and is currently attending a special education program for help with behavioral issues. One of the issues his teachers are working with is his tendency to eat glue and paper, though he has sampled crayons and once swallowed a very small plastic toy construction hat.

Trish

Trish, age 9, refuses any food that she finds to be too "spicy" or "feel funny" in her mouth. As a result, she will not eat any foods that are tangy, sour, savory, and avoids dairy and most cooked vegetables. She will eat bread, pasta and roasted chicken, if unseasoned as well as some cereal and toaster pastry. She is significantly underweight and has failed to meet growth milestones for her age group.

Narrative Cases

Katrina

Katrina, 38, is currently admitted to a local hospice center where she is receiving end of life care. For 26 years, Katrina has received treatment for eating and substance use disorders. Katrina, who stands 5' 9" and now weighs 102 pounds, has imagined her skeletal frame to be "doughy and disgusting." Katrina's problems began after she started dancing and cheering in middle school and felt she could never be thin enough to be truly graceful. Her mother remembers her saying, "I want to float across the stage like a ribbon drifting on a barely perceptible breeze." No matter how thin Katrina became, her perception of herself as "too fat" did not waver. She did not begin her menstrual cycles and does not recall if she has ever had a period. Over the past 15 years, Katrina has tried several residential treatment centers in an attempt to overcome her painful relationship with eating. As a result of her restricted diet, she has also struggled with heart problems, as well as osteoporosis. Family members have noticed significant cognitive dulling over the past 10 years.

Gina

Gina, age 27, shares, "I come from a family of big girls. My mom, aunts, sisters and grandma are all big. I was a little on the rounder side in school and I wasn't too worried about it until I started to feel some changes in my health, especially in the last two years when I put on a lot of weight, almost 120 pounds, pretty fast. That's why I decided to go ahead and make an appointment with the bariatric center at the hospital, just to see." Already she has been diagnosed with Type II diabetes and more recently she has been prescribed a Continuous positive airway pressure (CPAP) machine to help assure that she is breathing steadily through the night, a problem her doctors attribute to her weight. As she describes her eating habits with the nutritionist she notes, "Most of the time I eat a reasonable meal and the food choices I make are healthy ones . . . usually. I don't really eat a lot of fast food or food loaded with fat or sugar. But about 6 or 7 times a week I find myself sitting down for what was supposed to be a normal meal and suddenly I realize that I have eaten much, much more than I meant to. Sometimes I make a dish that is supposed to last several days and I eat it all in one sitting while streaming some show. I don't know how I manage to eat so much in so little time." When these episodes are over she describes having a terribly uncomfortable stomach ache. She shares, "I feel so ashamed and guilty, I can't tell you what an awful feeling this is. When that happens I usually just go to bed and watch a movie there until I fall asleep." Gina reports that she does not purge, use laxatives or exercise to excess. She is hoping that bariatric surgery will help her to stop the binging cycles and lose the weight that she believes has held her back for so long.

Behir

Mr. and Mrs. R are very concerned about their son, Behir, aged 7. He is quite thin and small for his age and has large dark rings under his eyes and sits listlessly on the exam table as they talk with his pediatrician. Mrs. R explains, "Behir is just getting more and more sickly and weak looking. He has no energy for going out with his friends. He refuses to eat most things I make for him, but thankfully he will take the vitamins I give him and will drink protein shakes. This has been a problem since he was a baby, he was difficult to encourage to nurse and would often fall asleep before he had enough to eat. We got some help from a lactation aide that seemed to work for a while but as soon as we introduced solids, our problems with food started again. It only got worse as he got older." Responding to the doctor's inquiry, Behir shares, "A lot of food smells gross or it makes my tounge prickly and the sides of my mouth water. I am afraid I will throw up and then choke. I do eat some things, though." His pediatrician can find no medical reason for his lack of appetite or failure to meet expected gains in weight and height.

Mindy

Mindy, a 46 year-old real estate agent, has come for counseling following the recent dissolution of her 20-year marriage. Mindy reports, "I just need to talk about the end of my marriage and about some old problems that seem to be coming back since he moved out 6 months ago." When asked to elaborate on the old problems, Mindy explains, "When I was in college I had this, well I guess you would call it a problem, a problem with the way I ate. Sometimes I would eat A LOT and I was afraid of gaining a ton of weight so when I over-ate or drank too much I would just throw it up. But I stopped that when I got married. It has started up again since my husband moved out, though. One day I was in the kitchen cooking and I just kind of started eating and eating and eating. I was really kind of zoned out. It felt like I wasn't really in control, like someone else was doing the eating. And when I realized what I had done and noticed how much my stomach hurt, well I felt like I *had* to throw up. So I did." Mindy further explains, "So then I started to throw up a lot, sometimes twice or three times in a week, and all I could think about was that I COULD NOT GET FAT or I would be alone forever. But in the past three weeks it is a little better. I throw up maybe once a week and I know that all this obsession with my weight has been a little crazy. I think with some help I can get this under control again."

Darian

Darian, age 13, and his parents are sitting in the emergency room waiting to be seen, his parents are sitting cross-armed and angry while Darian complains about the pain in his stomach. This scenario has, by now, become something of a familiar one to the family since Darian has had several hospitalizations resulting from his habit of eating things that aren't food and can't be digested safely. Darian's first incident happened shortly after he began to walk and he had found a paper clip in the carpet. Since that time his parents had been very careful about keeping the floor and counter surfaces free of items that could be swallowed, but after a decade, both had become somewhat tired of this vigilance. Despite their care, Darian had managed to swallow a number of odd items that resulted in injury to his esophagus and stomach or have made him sick. Darian has swallowed thumb-tacks, plastic candy bar wrappers, laundry detergent, pencil lead, paper, and so on. Despite efforts to curb Darian's behavior, including the use of behavioral interventions, Darian's habit of eating items that threaten his health continues.

Anna-Jane

Anna-Jane, age 12, has been brought to counseling by her concerned parents, Mike and Shannon. Shannon reports that Anna-Jane frequently complains that she is "too fat" though at her last physical she fell 5% below the normal weight expectancy for a child her height and age. Mike shares, "Anna-Jane pouts through dinner and picks at her food, making a spectacle of herself and ruining dinner for everyone else." In private conversation the intake worker asked Anna-Jane why she felt her parents had brought her to counseling, to which Anna-Jane replied, "Well, my friend's mom called my mom and told her that I had been throwing up and my mom really flipped her shit. I was surprised! She came into my room and started to cry and then later my dad yelled at me. But really that has only happened twice after a party at school when I had pizza or ice cream or something like that. It isn't a regular thing and it is nothing to worry about. Anyway, all my friends do it sometimes. You know that mom that called my mom? Her daughter does it too, I just didn't tell my parents about it or she would probably be here, too. It's not really fair if you think about it."

Kelly

Kelly, age 29, lost her father a year ago. Kelly's father was cremated and Kelly has kept his ashes on her mantle. However, her sisters have been distressed to learn that Kelly has been eating her father's ashes. Kelly shares, "A month or two after my dad passed away, I was still pretty paralyzed by my father's death. I would go to the mantle and hold his ashes and cry. Sometimes I would open the lid and look down at my father's ashes. I could see my tears mixing with the ashes and there was something so comforting about that. And then one day I put my finger in the ashes and tasted them. After that I started to taste the ashes once a week or so. Then I started to eat a little bit at a time. I do understand that this is strange, and I know why it upsets my sisters, but I haven't been able to stop."

Felicity

Felicity, age 16, has been experimenting with a male to female transition. For years she has known that she is a female, though she occupies a male body. Though she does not yet feel fully ready to share this with her parents or to talk to a doctor about hormones, she has gradually shifted to more gender neutral clothing and has grown her hair out. For the last 6 months, she has been strategically eating extra helpings of dinner nightly and about twice a week, when alone, large amounts of carb, fats and sugar heavy foods in order to gain weight. She shares that during this time she feels "completely out of control." "The extra helpings at dinner I do on purpose, but the binging in my room, not so much." Felicity describes feeling "pretty gross and ashamed" after these binging episodes but hopes the weight she is gaining will add some additional curviness to her once very slim figure.

References

Agras, W. S. (Ed.). (2010). *The Oxford handbook of eating disorders.* Oxford University Press.

Allison, K. C., Lundgren, J. D., O'Reardon, J. P., Geliebter, A., Gluck, M. E., Vinai, P., Mitchell, J. E., Schenck, C. H., Howell, M. J., Crow, S. J., Engel, S., Latzer, Y., Tzischinsky, O., Mahowald, M. W., & Stunkard, A. J. (2010). Proposed diagnostic criteria for night eating syndrome. *International Journal of Eating Disorders, 43*(3), 241–247. https://doi.org/10.1002/eat.20693

American Psychiatric Association. (2013). Diagnostic and statistical manual of mental disorders. *BMC Medicine, 17,* 133–137. https://doi.org/10.1176/appi.books.9780890425596

Arcelus, J., Mitchell, A. J., Wales, J., & Nielsen, S. (2011). Mortality rates in patients with anorexia nervosa and other eating disorders: A meta-analysis of 36 studies. *Archives of General Psychiatry, 68*(7), 724–731. https://doi.org/10.1001/archgenpsychiatry.2011.74

Ashton, K., Drerup, M., Windover, A., & Heinberg, L. (2009). Brief, four-session group CBT reduces binge eating behaviors among bariatric surgery candidates. *Surgery for Obesity and Related Diseases, 5*(2), 257–262. https://doi.org/10.1016/j.soard.2009.01.005

Attia, E., & Roberto, C. A. (2009). Should amenorrhea be a diagnostic criterion for anorexia nervosa? *International Journal of Eating Disorders, 42*(7), 581–589. https://doi.org/10.1002/eat.20720

Bandini, L. G., Anderson, S. E., Curtin, C., Cermak, S., Evans, E. W., Scampini, R., Maslin, M., & Must, A. (2010). Food selectivity in children with autism spectrum disorders and typically developing children. *The Journal of Pediatrics, 157*(2), 259–264. https://doi.org/10.1016/j.jpeds.2010.02.013

Birmingham, C. L., & Beumont, P. (2005). *Medical management of eating disorders: A practical handbook for health care professionals.* Cambridge University Press.

Bohon, C. (2017). Research domain criteria: The impact of RDoC on the conceptualization of eating disorders. In W. S. Agras (Ed.), *The Oxford handbook of eating disorders* (pp. 24–32). Oxford University Press.

Borzekowski, D. L., Schenk, S., Wilson, J. L., & Peebles, R. (2010). e-Ana and e-Mia: A content analysis of pro–eating disorder web sites. *American Journal of Public Health, 100*(8), 1526–1534. https://doi.org/10.2105/AJPH.2009.172700

Button, E. J., Chadalavada, B., & Palmer, R. L. (2010). Mortality and predictors of death in a cohort of patients presenting to an eating disorders service. *International Journal of Eating Disorders, 43*(5), 387–392.

Chen, E. Y., & Safer, D. L. (2010). *Dialectical behavior therapy for bulimia nervosa and binge-eating disorder.* In C. Grilo & J. Mitchell (Eds.), *Treatment of eating disorders: A clinical handbook* (pp. 294–316). Guilford Press.

Costa, C. B., Hardan-Khalil, K., & Gibbs, K. (2017). Orthorexia nervosa: A review of the literature. *Issues in Mental Health Nursing, 38*(12), 980–988. https://doi.org/10.1080/01612840.2017.1371816

Costa, M. B., Stein, A. T., Trevisani, V. F. M., Valente, O., Harb, A., & Melnik, T. (2015). Pharmacological and psychosocial interventions for night eating syndrome in adults. *Cochrane Database of Systematic Reviews, 4.*

Cowan, E., & Heselmeyer, R. (2011). Bulimia and dissociation: A developmental perspective. *Journal of Mental Health Counseling, 33*(2), 128–143. https://doi.org/10.17744/mehc.33.2.08m34u3h2575t588

Cowan, E. W. (2017). Oh mother where art thou: Interpersonal origins of self experience. In *Ariadne's thread: Case studies in the therapeutic relationship.* James Madison University.

Dallos, R. (2004). Attachment narrative therapy: Integrating ideas from narrative and attachment theory in systemic family therapy with eating disorders. *Journal of Family Therapy, 26*(1), 40–65. https://doi.org/10.1111/j.1467-6427.2004.00266.x

Dansky, B. S., Brewerton, T. D., & Kilpatrick, D. G. (2000). Comorbidity of bulimia nervosa and alcohol use disorders: Results from the National Women's Study. *International Journal of Eating Disorders, 27*(2), 180–190.

Dazzi, F., & Di Leone, F. G. (2014). The diagnostic classification of eating disorders: Current situation, possible alternatives and future perspectives. *Eating and Weight Disorders-Studies on Anorexia, Bulimia and Obesity, 19*(1), 11–19. https://doi.org/10.1007/s40519-013-0076-1

Delaney, C. B., Eddy, K. T., Hartmann, A. S., Becker, A. E., Murray, H. B., & Thomas, J. J. (2015). Pica and rumination behavior among individuals seeking treatment for eating disorders or obesity. *International Journal of Eating Disorders, 48*(2), 238–248. https://doi.org/10.1002/eat.22279

Dickins, M., Thomas, S. L., King, B., Lewis, S., & Holland, K. (2011). The role of the Fatosphere in fat adults' responses to obesity stigma: A model of empowerment without a focus on weight loss. *Qualitative Health Research, 21*(12), 1679–1691. https://doi.org/10.1177/1049732311417728

Diemer, E. W., White Hughto, J. M., Gordon, A. R., Guss, C., Austin, S. B., & Reisner, S. L. (2018). Beyond the binary: Differences in eating disorder prevalence by gender identity in a transgender sample. *Transgender Health, 3*(1), 17–23. https://doi.org/10.1089/trgh.2017.0043

Dolhanty, J., & Lafrance, A. (2019). Emotion-focused family therapy for eating disorders. In L. S. Greenberg & R. N. Goldman (Eds.), *Clinical handbook of emotion-focused therapy* (pp. 403–423). American Psychological Association.

Donini, L. M., Marsili, D., Graziani, M. P., Imbriale, M., & Cannella, C. (2005). Orthorexia nervosa: Validation of a diagnosis questionnaire. *Eating and Weight Disorders-Studies on Anorexia, Bulimia and Obesity, 10*(2), e28–e32. https://doi.org/10.1007/BF03327537

Dovey, T. M., Staples, P. A., Gibson, E. L. , & Halford, J. C. (2008). Food neophobia and 'picky/fussy'eating in children: a review. *Appetite, 50*(2-3), 181–193.

Duffy, M. E., Henkel, K. E., & Earnshaw, V. A. (2016). Transgender clients' experiences of eating disorder treatment. *Journal of LGBT Issues in Counseling, 10*(3), 136–149. https://doi.org/10.1080/15538605.2016.1177806

Dunn, T. M., & Bratman, S. (2016). On orthorexia nervosa: A review of the literature and proposed diagnostic criteria. *Eating Behaviors*, *21*, 11–17. https://doi.org/10.1016/j.eatbeh.2015.12.006

Eckermann, L. (2009). Theorising self-starvation: Beyond risk, governmentality and the normalizing gaze. In H. Malson & M. Burns (Eds.), *Critical feminist approaches to eating dis/orders* (pp. 31–43). Routledge.

Eddy, K. T., Dorer, D. J., Franko, D. L., Tahilani, K., Thompson-Brenner, H., & Herzog, D. B. (2008). Diagnostic crossover in anorexia nervosa and bulimia nervosa: Implications for DSM-V. *American Journal of Psychiatry*, *165*(2), 245–250. https://doi.org/10.1176/appi.ajp.2007.07060951

Fairburn, C. G., Bailey-Straebler, S., Basden, S., Doll, H. A., Jones, R., Murphy, R., O'Connor, M. E., & Cooper, Z. (2015). A transdiagnostic comparison of Enhanced Cognitive Behaviour Therapy (CBT-E) and interpersonal psychotherapy in the treatment of eating disorders. *Behaviour Research and Therapy*, *70*, 64–71. https://doi.org/10.1016/j.brat.2015.04.010

Fisher, M. M., Rosen, D. S., Ornstein, R. M., Mammel, K. A., Katzman, D. K., Rome, E. S., Callahan, S. T., Malizio, J., Kearney, S., & Walsh, B. T. (2014). Characteristics of avoidant/restrictive food intake disorder in children and adolescents: A "new disorder" in DSM-5. *Journal of Adolescent Health*, *55*(1), 49–52. https://doi.org/10.1016/j.jadohealth.2013.11.013

Fitzpatrick, S., MacDonald, D. E., McFarlane, T., & Trottier, K. (2019). An experimental comparison of emotion regulation strategies for reducing acute distress in individuals with eating disorders. *Canadian Journal of Behavioural Science/Revue Canadienne des Sciences du Comportement*, *51*(2), 90. https://doi.org/10.1037/cbs0000119

Folke, S., Daniel, S. I., Gondan, M., Lunn, S., Tækker, L., & Poulsen, S. (2017). Therapist adherence is associated with outcome in cognitive–behavioral therapy for bulimia nervosa. *Psychotherapy*, *54*(2), 195. https://doi.org/10.1037/pst0000107

Frances, A. (2013). Saving normal: An insider's revolt against out-of-control psychiatric diagnosis, DSM-5, big pharma and the medicalization of ordinary life. *Psychotherapy in Australia*, *19*(3), 14.

Franko, D. L., Dorer, D. J., Keel, P. K., Jackson, S., Manzo, M. P., & Herzog, D. B. (2005). How do eating disorders and alcohol use disorder influence each other? *International Journal of Eating Disorders*, *38*(3), 200–207. https://doi.org/10.1002/eat.20178

Gleaves, D. H., Lowe, M. R., Green, B. A., Cororve, M. B., & Williams, T. L. (2000). Do anorexia and bulimia nervosa occur on a continuum? A taxometric analysis. *Behavior Therapy*, *31*(2), 195–219. https://doi.org/10.1016/S0005-7894(00)80012-X

Gorrell, S., & Le Grange, D. (2019). Update on treatments for adolescent bulimia nervosa. *Child and Adolescent Psychiatric Clinics*, *28*(4), 537–547. https://doi.org/10.1016/j.chc.2019.05.002

Grabe, S., & Hyde, J. S. (2006). Ethnicity and body dissatisfaction among women in the United States: A meta-analysis. *Psychological Bulletin*, *132*(4), 622. https://doi.org/10.1037/0033-2909.132.4.622

Gregorowski, C., Seedat, S., & Jordaan, G. P. (2013). A clinical approach to the assessment and management of co-morbid eating disorders and substance use disorders. *BMC Psychiatry*, *13*(1), 289. https://doi.org/10.1186/1471-244X-13-289

Grenon, R., Schwartze, D., Hammond, N., Ivanova, I., Mcquaid, N., Proulx, G., & Tasca, G. A. (2017). Group psychotherapy for eating disorders: A meta-analysis. *International Journal of Eating Disorders*, *50*(9), 997–1013. https://doi.org/10.1002/eat.22744

Groth, T., Hilsenroth, M., Boccio, D., & Gold, J. (2019). Relationship between trauma history and eating disorders in adolescents. *Journal of Child & Adolescent Trauma, 13,* 443–453. https://doi.org/10.1007/s40653-019-00275-z

Gurrieri, L., & Cherrier, H. (2013). Queering beauty: Fatshionistas in the fatosphere. *Qualitative Market Research: An International Journal*, *16*(3), 276–295. https://doi.org/10.1108/13522751311326107

Halmi, K. A. (2010). *Psychological comorbidity of eating disorders.* In W. S. Argas (Ed.), *The Oxford handbook of eating disorders* (pp. 292–203). Oxford University Press.

Harper, K., Sperry, S., & Thompson, J. K. (2008). Viewership of pro-eating disorder websites: Association with body image and eating disturbances. *International Journal of Eating Disorders*, *41*(1), 92–95. https://doi.org/10.1002/eat.20408

Harrop, E. N., & Marlatt, G. A. (2010). The comorbidity of substance use disorders and eating disorders in women: Prevalence, etiology, and treatment. *Addictive Behaviors*, *35*(5), 392–398. https://doi.org/10.1016/j.addbeh.2009.12.016

Hearing, S. D. (2004). Refeeding syndrome. *British Medical Journal*, *328*(7445), 908–909. https://doi.org/10.1136/bmj.328.7445.908

Herpertz-Dahlmann, B. (2009). Adolescent eating disorders: Definitions, symptomatology, epidemiology and comorbidity. *Child and Adolescent Psychiatric Clinics of North America*, *18*(1), 31–47. https://doi.org/10.1016/j.chc.2008.07.005

Heselmeyer, R., & Cowan, E. W. (2012). Understanding bulimic dissociation: Creating new pathways to change for clients with bulimia, *Counseling Today*, December 2012. https://doi.org/https://ct.counseling.org/2012/12/understanding-bulimic-dissociation-to-create-new-pathways-for-change/

Jewell, T., Blessitt, E., Stewart, C., Simic, M., & Eisler, I. (2016). Family therapy for child and adolescent eating disorders: A critical review. *Family Process*, *55*(3), 577–594. https://doi.org/10.1111/famp.12242

Kaye, W. H., & Oberndorfer, T. (2010). Appetitive regulation in anorexia nervosa and bulimia nervosa. In W. S. Agras (Ed.), *The Oxford handbook of eating disorders.* (pp. 75–102). Oxford University Press.

Keel, P. K. (2007). Purging disorder: Subthreshold variant or full-threshold eating disorder? *International Journal of Eating Disorders*, *40*(Suppl. 3), S89–S94. https://doi.org/10.1002/eat.20453

Keel, P. K., Brown, T. A., Holland, L. A., & Bodell, L. P. (2012). Empirical classification of eating disorders. *Annual Review of Clinical Psychology*, *8*, 381–404. https://doi.org/10.1146/annurev-clinpsy-032511-143111

Keel, P. K., & Striegel-Moore, R. H. (2009). The validity and clinical utility of purging disorder. *International Journal of Eating Disorders*, *42*(8), 706–719. https://doi.org/10.1002/eat.20718

Kohn, M. R., Madden, S., & Clarke, S. D. (2011). Refeeding in anorexia nervosa: Increased safety and efficiency through understanding the pathophysiology of protein calorie malnutrition. *Current Opinion in Pediatrics*, *23*(4), 390–394. https://doi.org/10.1097/MOP.0b013e3283487591

La Mela, C., Maglietta, M., Castellini, G., Amoroso, G., & Lucarelli, S. (2010). Dissociation in eating disorders: Relationship between dissociative experiences and binge-eating episodes. *Comprehensive Psychiatry*, *51*(4), 393–400. https://doi.org/10.1016/j.comppsych.2009.09.008

Lazzer, S. D., & Muhlheim, L. (2016). Eating disorders and scope of competence for outpatient psychotherapists. *Practice Innovations*, *1*(2), 89. https://doi.org/10.1037/pri0000021

Le Grange, D., & Hoste, R. R. (2010). Family therapy. In W. S. Agras (Ed.), *The Oxford handbook of eating disorders*. (pp. 259-266). Oxford University Press.

Levinson, C. A., Sala, M., Murray, S., Ma, J., Rodebaugh, T. L., & Lenze, E. J. (2019). Diagnostic, clinical, and personality correlates of food anxiety during a food exposure in patients diagnosed with an eating disorder. *Eating and Weight Disorders-Studies on Anorexia, Bulimia and Obesity*, *24*(6), 1079–1088.

Levinson, C. A., Zerwas, S., Calebs, B., Forbush, K., Kordy, H., Watson, H., Hofmeier, S., Levine, M., Crosby, R. D., Peat, C., Runfola, C. D., Zimmer, B., Moesner, M., Marcus, M. D., & Bulik, C. M. (2017). The core symptoms of bulimia nervosa, anxiety, and depression: A network analysis. *Journal of Abnormal Psychology*, *126*(3), 340.

Linardon, J., Fairburn, C. G., Fitzsimmons-Craft, E. E., Wilfley, D. E., & Brennan, L. (2017). The empirical status of the third-wave behaviour therapies for the treatment of eating disorders: A systematic review. *Clinical Psychology Review*, *58*, 125–140.

Linardon, J., Wade, T. D., de la Piedad Garcia, X., & Brennan, L. (2017). The efficacy of cognitive-behavioral therapy for eating disorders: A systematic review and meta-analysis. *Journal of Consulting and Clinical Psychology*, *85*(11), 1080. https://doi.org/10.1037/ccp0000245

Linehan, M. M., & Chen, E. Y. (2005). Dialectical behavior therapy for eating disorders. *Encyclopedia of Cognitive Behavior Therapy* (pp. 168–171). Springer.

MacDonald, D. E., McFarlane, T. L., Dionne, M. M., David, L., & Olmsted, M. P. (2017). Rapid response to intensive treatment for bulimia nervosa and purging disorder: A randomized controlled trial of a CBT intervention to facilitate early behavior change. *Journal of Consulting and Clinical Psychology*, *85*(9), 896. https://doi.org/10.1037/ccp0000221

Malson, H., & Burns, M. (Eds.). (2009). *Critical feminist approaches to eating dis/orders*. Routledge.

Marques, L., Alegria, M., Becker, A. E., Chen, C. N., Fang, A., Chosak, A., & Diniz, J. B. (2011). Comparative prevalence, correlates of impairment, and service utilization for eating disorders across US ethnic groups: Implications for reducing ethnic disparities in health care access for eating disorders. *International Journal of Eating Disorders*, *44*(5), 412–420. https://doi.org/10.1002/eat.20787

Matacin, M. L., & Simone, M. (2019). Advocating for fat activism in a therapeutic context. *Women & Therapy*, *42*(1–2), 200–215.

Meyer, R. G., & Deitsch, S. E. (1996). *The clinician's handbook: Integrated diagnostics, assessment, and intervention in adult and adolescent psychopathology*. Waveland Press.

Milos, G., Spindler, A., Schnyder, U., & Fairburn, C. G. (2005). Instability of eating disorder diagnoses: Prospective study. *The British Journal of Psychiatry*, *187*, 573–578. https://doi.org/10.1192/bjp.187.6.573

Mitchell, J. E. (2016). Medical comorbidity and medical complications associated with binge-eating disorder. *International Journal of Eating Disorders*, *49*(3), 319–323. https://doi.org/10.1002/eat.22452

Mitchell, J. E., & Crow, S. J. (2010). Medical comorbidities of eating disorders. In S. Argas (Ed) *The The Oxford handbook of eating disorders* (pp. 259–266). Oxford University Press.

Mortimer, R. (2019). Pride before a fall: Shame, diagnostic crossover, and eating disorders. *Journal of Bioethical Inquiry*, *16*(3), 365–374. https://doi.org/10.1007/s11673-019-09923-3

Neumark-Sztainer, D., Croll, J., Story, M., Hannan, P. J., French, S. A., & Perry, C. (2002). Ethnic/racial differences in weight-related concerns and behaviors among adolescent girls and boys: Findings from Project EAT. *Journal of Psychosomatic Research*, *53*(5), 963–974. https://doi.org/10.1016/S0022-3999(02)00486-5

Norris, M. L., & Katzman, D. K. (2015). Change is never easy, but it is possible: Reflections on avoidant/restrictive food intake disorder two years after its introduction in the DSM-5. *Journal of Adolescent Health*, *57*(1), 8–9. https://doi.org/10.1016/j.jadohealth.2015.04.021

Norris, M. L., Robinson, A., Obeid, N., Harrison, M., Spettigue, W., & Henderson, K. (2014). Exploring avoidant/restrictive food intake disorder in eating disordered patients: A descriptive study. *International Journal of Eating Disorders*, *47*(5), 495–499. https://doi.org/10.1002/eat.22217

Pisetsky, E. M., Wonderlich, S. A., Crosby, R. D., Peterson, C. B., Mitchell, J. E., Engel, S. G., Joiner, T. E., Bardone-Cone, A., Le Grange, D., Klein, M. H., & Crow, S. J. (2015). Depression and personality traits associated with emotion dysregulation: Correlates of suicide attempts in women with bulimia nervosa. *European Eating Disorders Review*, *23*(6), 537–544. https://doi.org/10.1002/erv.2401

Pope, C. G., Pope, H. G., Menard, W., Fay, C., Olivardia, R., & Phillips, K. A. (2005). Clinical features of muscle dysmorphia among males with body dysmorphic disorder. *Body Image*, *2*(4), 395–400. https://doi.org/10.1016/j.bodyim.2005.09.001

Preti, A., Rocchi, M. B. L., Sisti, D., Camboni, M. V., & Miotto, P. (2011). A comprehensive meta-analysis of the risk of suicide in eating disorders. *Acta Psychiatrica Scandinavica*, *124*(1), 6–17. https://doi.org/10.1111/j.1600-0447.2010.01641.x

Puxley, F., Midtsund, M., Iosif, A., & Lask, B. (2008). PANDAS anorexia nervosa—Endangered, extinct or nonexistent? *International Journal of Eating Disorders*, *41*(1), 15–21. https://doi.org/10.1002/eat.20462

Richards, L. K., Shingleton, R. M., Goldman, R., Siegel, D., & Thompson-Brenner, H. (2016). Integrative dynamic therapy for bulimia nervosa: An evidence-based case study. *Psychotherapy*, *53*(2), 195. https://doi.org/10.1037/pst0000054

Rosenvinge, J. H., & Pettersen, G. (2015a). Epidemiology of eating disorders part II: An update with a special reference to the DSM-5. *Advances in Eating Disorders: Theory, Research and Practice*, *3*(2), 198–220. https://doi.org/10.1080/21662630.2014.940549

Rosenvinge, J. H., & Pettersen, G. (2015b). Epidemiology of eating disorders part III: Social epidemiology and case definitions revisited. *Advances in Eating Disorders*, *3*(3), 320–336. https://doi.org/10.1080/21662630.2015.1022197

Rosman, B. L., Minuchin, S., & Liebman, R. (1975). Family lunch session: An introduction to family therapy in anorexia nervosa. *American Journal of Orthopsychiatry*, *45*(5), 846. https://doi.org/10.1111/j.1939-0025.1975.tb01212.x

Ruth-Sahd, L. A., Schneider, M., & Haagen, B. (2009). Diabulimia: What it is and how to recognize it in critical care. *Dimensions of Critical Care Nursing*, *28*(4), 147–153. https://doi.org/10.1097/DCC.0b013e3181a473fe

Sala, M., Reyes-Rodríguez, M. L., Bulik, C. M., & Bardone-Cone, A. (2013). Race, ethnicity, and eating disorder recognition by peers. *Eating Disorders*, *21*(5), 423–436. https://doi.org/10.1080/10640266.2013.827540

Shuttlesworth, M. E., & Zotter, D. (2011). Disordered eating in African American and Caucasian women: The role of ethnic identity. *Journal of Black Studies*, *42*(6), 906–922. https://doi.org/10.1177/0021934710396368

Stand, P. (2007). The female athlete triad. *Medicine & Science in Sports & Exercise*, *39*(10), 1867–1882. https://doi.org/10.1249/mss.0b013e318149f111

Vincenzi, B., O'Toole, J., & Lask, B. (2010). PANDAS and anorexia nervosa—A spotters' guide: Suggestions for medical assessment. *European Eating Disorders Review: The Professional Journal of the Eating Disorders Association*, *18*(2), 116–123. https://doi.org/10.1002/erv.977

Wilson, G. T. (2017). Cognitive behavioral therapy for eating disorders. In W. S. Agras, (Ed.), *The Oxford handbook of eating disorders* (pp. 331–347). Oxford University Press.

Wilson, G. T., Fairburn, C. C., Agras, W. S., Walsh, B. T., & Kraemer, H. (2002). Cognitive-behavioral therapy for bulimia nervosa: Time course and mechanisms of change. *Journal of Consulting and Clinical Psychology*, *70*(2), 267. https://doi.org/10.1037/0022-006X.70.2.267

Woodside, B. D., & Staab, R. (2006). Management of psychiatric comorbidity in anorexia nervosa and bulimia nervosa. *CNS Drugs*, *20*(8), 655–663. https://doi.org/10.2165/00023210-200620080-00004

Yager, J., Devlin, M., Halmi, K., Herzog, D. B., Mitchell, J. E., & Powers, P. (2006). American Psychiatric Association practice guideline for the treatment of patients with eating disorders. *American Journal of Psychiatry*, *163*(7 Suppl.), 4–54.

Zipfel, S., Giel, K. E., Bulik, C. M., Hay, P., & Schmidt, U. (2015). Anorexia nervosa: Aetiology, assessment, and treatment. *The Lancet Psychiatry*, *2*(12), 1099–1111. https://doi.org/10.1016/S2215-0366(15)00356-9

15 Sexual Dysfunctions

Sex is broadly understood to be an important part of the human experience. A person's sexuality is a key avenue for connection and bonding with one's partner, a source of pleasure and even an avenue for deeper self-understanding. Our sexuality and sexual experiences are also often bound up in our personal identity and are shaped and defined by our sociocultural contexts. Human sexuality is a broad concept that begins with a sense of oneself as a sexual being and includes one's gender identity, sexual orientation, sexual desire, as well as the experiences of arousal and orgasm (Laurent & Simons, 2009; Ramlachan & Campbell, 2014). At its best, human sexuality can be the source of deep meaning and connectedness to oneself and others; however, when difficulties develop in either desire or the ability to engage sex in a way that is satisfying, a variety of problems can follow, including anxiety, shame, guilt, a feeling of isolation and so on.

Though data differs from study to study, it is clear that sexual dysfunction is common among the general population and very common among those who suffer from mental health concerns, particularly those with anxiety, depression and obsessive compulsive disorder (OCD). Among the general population, the estimates of sexual dysfunction among women is about 32% and among men is about 23% (Apantaku-Olajide et al., 2011). Among those with mental health concerns such as depression and anxiety, rates have been reported to be as high as 40%-60% (Preeti et al., 2018). It is important to note here that most of the research studies conducted in sexual health and dysfunction are composed disproportionately of White participants leaving the experiences of People of Color much less clear. In one of the few studies available to explore prevalence across race, however, Laumann et al. (2007), found that while overall 22% of men report erectile dysfunction; 19.9% of Hispanic men, 21.9% of White men and 24.4% of Black men reported erectile dysfunction. Similarly, the bulk of the research and discussion of sexual health and satisfaction of sexual dysfunction and, in fact, mental disorders generally, describes individuals that identify as male or female leaving scant research to describe sexual health or dysfunction of those that describe themselves as sitting somewhere on the non-binary gender continuum;

for example, those who identify as gender-neutral or bigender. This research is badly needed and would be a welcome addition to the DSM discussions, where it is currently absent.

The Disorders of the Sexual Dysfunction Continuum

Sexual functioning can be thought of as unfolding in stages beginning with desire, arousal, orgasm and ending with the closure of the intimacy (Ramlachan & Campbell, 2014). The DSM 5 addresses dysfunction in the first three of these stages. Two disorders of this continuum address difficulties experienced with desire: female sexual interest/arousal disorder and male hypoactive sexual desire disorder. These two disorders describe difficulties related to diminished interest in sexual fantasies, sex itself, a lack of response to sexual cues and little to no interest in initiating sex. Erectile disorder addresses difficulty with arousal. This disorder describes problems in either attaining or sustaining an erection during sexual activity. Three disorders are included that describe difficulties related to orgasm: delayed ejaculation, premature ejaculation and female orgasmic disorder. In these cases, clients either find it very difficult to arrive at orgasm, arrive at orgasm too soon to fully enjoy the sexual encounter or, in the case of female orgasmic disorder, may not experience the intensity of orgasm that is desired. Finally, a sexual dysfunction related to pain is included as well, genito-pelvic pain/penetration disorder (American Psychiatric Association [APA], 2013). These disorders of the different phases of sexual intercourse are treated differently and may often have different origins.

Changes in The DSM 5 and Their Implications

Three changes were made to the diagnostic criteria within this dimension. First, all of the disorders now share a duration criterion of 6 months. It is widely understood that transient difficulties with sexual drive and performance are normal and should not be pathologized. Second, in order to give a diagnosis, your client must describe having these difficulties nearly all the time, meaning somewhere between 75% and 100% of the time, rather than occasionally. The third change requires that the individual also experiences distress as a consequence of the sexual difficulties. It is hoped that these changes in criteria will reduce "false positives" in diagnosis (APA, 2013; Mitchell et al., 2016). Not all clinicians within the field of sexual medicine are happy with these changes and raise concerns about false negatives; consequently, the changes are the subject of continued discussion and debate. Indeed, initial research suggests that the addition of these criteria does appear to lessen significantly the number of persons who would meet criteria for diagnosis. In their study of 15,162 British men and women, a full 38.2% of men and 22.8% of women described experiencing one or more sexual difficulties outlined in the DSM; however, only 4.2% of men and 3.6% of women would meet the full criteria of the DSM 5 (Mitchell et al., 2016).

TABLE 15.01 **Sexual Dysfunctions**

Categories of Sexual Dysfunction	Related Disorder
Desire	• Female Sexual Interest/Arousal Disorder • Male Hypoactive Sexual Desire Disorder
Arousal	• Erectile Disorder • Female Sexual Interest/Arousal Disorder
Orgasm	• Female Orgasmic Disorder • Premature (Early) Ejaculation
Pain	• Genito-Pelvic Pain/Penetration Disorder

Source: American Psychiatric Association (2013).

Applying Specifiers. A complete diagnosis of a sexual dysfunction includes specifiers that describe the consistency and pervasiveness of the difficulties. In making this diagnosis, you are asked first to consider whether the problem has always been present, in which case it is specified as lifelong, or is acquired and follows a period of relatively satisfying sexual functioning. Next you are asked to specify whether the difficulty arises with all partners or types of stimulation, referred to as generalized, or happens only with a particular partner or during a specific type of sexual activity, situational. These specifiers greatly clarify the clinical picture.

The Biopsychosocial Model for Understanding Sexual Disorders

Again, lifetime prevalence rates for sexual problems are quite high (Mitchell et al., 2016; Vegunta et al., 2016). These difficulties arise out of biological, psychological and sociocultural factors that work together to create obstacles to satisfying sexual lives. These three factors can impact sexual functioning at all four stages of the encounter, beginning with desire and ending with resolution. Because the factors contributing to sexual dysfunction are complex, the need for comprehensive intake evaluations that draw information from each domain, including medically based conditions that may be at the root of your client's difficulty, are essential. In the next few pages, we will consider very briefly some of the biological, psychological and psychosocial contributors to sexual dysfunction, particularly those that will influence your diagnosis of these disorders.

Biological: Medical Conditions and Their Relationship to Sexual Dysfunction. An examination of the literature highlights the close relationship between physical and mental health and sexual functioning and well-being. Decades old research reveals that chronic health problems, particularly high blood pressure, hypertension and other forms of heart disease, negatively impact desire, arousal and orgasm. Diabetes, thyroid disease (both hyper and hypo), epilepsy, multiple sclerosis and so on have also been linked to sexual dysfunction as has arthritis (Gandaglia et al., 2014; McCabe et al., 2016; Simon & Lukas, 2017). Congenital disorders, such as spina bifida, or those that directly impact the development of sex organs can also affect sexual function (Brotto et al., 2016). Gathering health information, including a timeline of symptoms, and consultation with your client's physician will help to clarify whether or not a medical condition is the cause of your client's difficulty or is simply happenstantial to it.

Infertility. For some couples, intimacy becomes complicated when they are faced with difficulties conceiving. This often unexpected interruption in plans for growing their families comes with tremendous pressure and strain. Couples often find that their intimacy shifts from whatever it was before they began planning for children and becomes more utilitarian and much less spontaneous. With time, sexual dissatisfaction and even sexual dysfunction can develop. Both men and women can experience depression related to difficulties with conception, and as will be discussed at greater length later, depression is closely tied to sexual dysfunction. What's more, the treatments used to address infertility can directly impact sexual functioning (Brotto et al., 2016; Pasha et al., 2018), self-esteem concerns, social and relational expectations and the financial cost of those treatments can take a toll on both individuals and the couple system that, in turn, impacts sexual functioning (Brotto et al., 2016; Monga et al., 2004).

Menopause and Andropause. Aging and age-related changes frequently bring with them changes in sexual satisfaction and functional declines in both men and women; however, as you work with aging clients, it is important to keep in mind that pleasure in sexual activity is possible at any age and for many it continues to be valued as important to a healthy relationship (Vegunta et al., 2016). In half of all women, however, menopause brings with it discomfort related to vaginal dryness, burning and irritation, known as genitourinary syndrome of menopause (GSM) which, in turn, makes sexual intercourse unappealing and uncomfortable. GSM can also lead to urinary incontinence and frequent urinary infection, which also lowers sex drive, interferes with pleasure and makes orgasm difficult (Jannini & Nappi, 2018; Simon & Lukas, 2017; Vegunta et al., 2016).

As men age, they also experience changes in sexual function that come with the decline in testosterone levels, known as andropause. These changes can mark impaired sex drive, difficulties achieving an erection as well as declines in the capacity to achieve orgasm (Simon & Lukas, 2017; Vegunta et al., 2016). Vegunta et al. (2016) point out that as couples age together these problems often coincide, compounding one another, a phenomenon they describe as *couplepause.* These researchers recommend that clients in menopause or andropause who are experiencing sexual difficulties be treated together with their partners using approaches that take into account the needs of both partners rather than each individual separately.

Biological: Medications and Side Effects. Historically, sexual dysfunction was attributed to psychosomatic origins. However, in the 1960s, physicians began to take note of the relationship between medications and sexual side effects that lead to sexual dysfunction, a phenomenon that has come to be referred to as treatment emergent sexual dysfunction (Story, 1974). Psychotropic medications have long been known to have this effect and include, but are not limited to antidepressants, antipsychotics and anxiolytics (Apantaku-Olajide et al., 2011; Clayton et al., 2016; McCabe et al., 2016; Montejo et al., 2001; Serretti & Chiesa, 2009; Stimmel & Gutierrez, 2006; Story, 1974).

Montejo et al. (2001) surveyed 1,022 participants with no history of sexual dysfunction and found that just over 62% of men and 57% of women reported sexual dysfunction while on antidepressants. In another survey of clients being treated for mental health concerns, researchers revealed that about 41% reported sexual dysfunction, which they had attributed to medications. Not surprisingly, these clients reported much more negative attitudes toward their medications than those who did not experience sexual side effects (Apantaku-Olajide et al., 2011; Stimmel & Gutierrez, 2006).

Cancer Treatments. Rates of sexual dysfunction among those being treated for cancer are also quite high despite improvements in treatment technologies. Cancer treatments such as chemotherapy and radiation can impair the production of sex hormones and damage nerves and blood vessels that support healthy sexual function (Schover et al., 2014). Among those being treated for breast or pelvic cancers, 50% report severe sexual dysfunction that is lasting. Similarly, colon and rectal cancers are also associated with elevated rates of sexual dysfunction (Den Oudsten et al., 2012). Rates of sexual dysfunction are also higher than the general population among those being treated for lung cancer (Reese et al., 2011, in Schover et al., 2014), hematological cancers (Thygessen et al., 2012, in Schover et al., 2014) and even among those who were treated for cancer in childhood (Bober et al., 2013, in Schover et al., 2014). This suggests that clients with a medical history featuring cancer should be screened for sexual dysfunction even if neither cancer nor sexual dysfunction is the presenting problem.

Biological: Substances. The use and abuse of non-prescription legal substances, such as alcohol and tobacco, and illicit substances such as amphetamines, marijuana, opioids and barbiturates have all been tied to sexual dysfunction and can be seen to impact all stages of the sexual encounter. Alcohol is thought to inhibit genital responses, for example, increasing the likelihood of erectile dysfunction, though use of alcohol at "non-abusive levels" does not appear to have this same effect. Similarly, tobacco seems to also reduce genital responses but not subjective interest in sex (Brotto et al., 2016; McCabe et al., 2016; Rao et al., 2018). Research suggests that those who smoke are 1.5 times more likely to experience erectile dysfunction than those who don't (Rao et al., 2018). Consequently, a frank discussion with clients about their use of substances is necessary to gaining a clear picture of biological factors that may be contributing to sexual complaints. Rao et al. (2018) also note that for clients with substance addictions, sexual dysfunction is a frequent issue that can complicate therapy and sometimes persists after the substance abuse issue has been addressed.

Psychological Sources of Sexual Dysfunction. Psychological difficulties such as anxiety and depression are frequently comorbid with sexual dysfunction and also are strong predictors for sexual dysfunction later in life (Brotto et al., 2016; McCabe et al., 2016; Preeti et al., 2018; Vegunta et al., 2016). Laurent and Simons (2009) point

BOX 15.01 CONSIDER THIS: DISCERNING PRIMARY FROM SECONDARY SEXUAL DYSFUNCTION

What questions might you ask Amelie in order to discern whether her complaints should be diagnosed as a primary sexual dysfunction or are a side effect or symptom of another disorder or medication used to treat it or some intersection of causes? What consultation might you elicit in order to hone your diagnosis?

Amelie. Amelie is a 53-year-old married woman who was referred to mental health counseling by her pastor who has been meeting with Amelie and her husband for spiritual guidance and marital counseling for about 6 months. Amelie explains, "I think I first noticed a change in my life after the last of our children went to college about 4 years ago. Ours was the house where all the kids in the neighborhood basically grew up and our family really helped shepherd dozens of children out into the world. Now Louis and I are left in our giant house all alone and it feels like a ghost town. I started to feel sad all the time, I stopped doing much cooking or baking and the house got pretty run down inside. I don't work and so I spent a lot of time at home alone just staring at the walls or streaming movies."

"Louis did some internet research and he thought I might be just having a little bit of empty nest syndrome on top of menopause, so I saw my doctor and he prescribed something for depression and something to help me sleep at night, so I have been taking that for a couple of months. It did help with the sadness, but our relationship was still suffering. I didn't really want to be intimate with Louis, which hurt his feelings. It's complicated because sometimes when I do feel interested, which isn't that often, Louis will have trouble getting aroused and then the evening becomes another disappointment for both of us. But to be honest, sex isn't very fun for me since I started menopause, it's uncomfortable. We didn't get into all that with our pastor, of course, but Louis is losing his patience with this long period of grieving that I've been going through since the kids flew the nest and we need help to regroup and get our lives together back on track."

out that although the relationship between mood and anxiety disorders and sexual dysfunction is bidirectional, sexual dysfunctions have long been conceptualized as an aspect of sexuality. These authors draw attention to the fact that early conceptualizations of sexual disorders were framed as a function of anxiety. Substantial support exists for the link between anxiety disorders such as panic disorder, social phobia and generalized anxiety disorder and sexual dysfunction. Researchers have measured significant delays in arousal to stimulating materials in depressed men, for example, and cognitions associated with depressive thinking have been shown to depress sexual response in both men and women. Anxiety and stress particularly have long been associated with problems with arousal as well as known contributors to painful sexual intercourse in women. Perhaps not surprisingly, both chronic stress and daily hassles seem to contribute (Brotto et al., 2016; Dunn et al., 1999; Laurent & Simons, 2009; McCabe et al., 2016).

TABLE 15.02 Medical Conditions, Their Treatments and Sexual Side Effects in Men and Women

Medical Condition	Men	Women	Medications Known to Lead to Sexual Dysfunction
Anxiety Disorders	x	x	Anxiolytics, such as benzodiazepines, clomipramine (Anafranil) lorazepam (Ativan) buspirone (Buspar, etc.)
Cancer	x	x	Chemotherapies; Radiation
Chronic Pain		x	Muscle relaxants
Depression	x	x	Antidepressants: e.g., Tricyclics (e.g., clomipramine, amitriptyline and imipramine), Selective Serotonin Reuptake Inhibitors, fluoxetine (Prozac), sertraline (Zoloft) etc. monoamine oxidase inhibitors (MAOIs)
Diabetes	x		
Endometriosis		x	
Epilepsy	x	x	Anticonvulsants, such as carbamazepine and phenytoin
Fibromyalgia		x	
Heart Disease	x	x	
Hysterectomy		x	
Hypertension	x		Diuretics, such as hydrochlorothiazide Beta-blockers like Atenolol (cause ED)
Menopause/ Andropause	x	x	
Multiple Sclerosis	x	x	
Parkinson's	x		Anti-Parkinsonians, such as levodopa (Sinemet)
Spinal Cord Injury	x	x	
Sleep Apnea	x	x	
Schizophrenia	x	x	Antipsychotics, such as haloperidol, risperidone, quetiapine
Substance Abuse	x	x	Methadone
Thyroid Disease (Hypo/Hyper)		x	

Source: APA (2013).

The relationship between depression and anxiety to sexual dysfunction is so strong that it has led some clinicians and researchers to question whether or not sexual dysfunction should be conceptualized as an internalizing disorder (Forbes et al., 2017; Laurent & Simons, 2009). By way of example, a study of men with erectile dysfunction found that this group was about twice as likely as men without ED to experience depression (Dunn et al., 1999, in Laurent & Simons, 2009). Similarly, a second study found that men who reported stress or other emotional problems were more than twice as likely to experience premature ejaculation (Johnson et al., 2004, in Laurent & Simons, 2009). Further supporting this argument, their survey of the literature found a similarly strong relationship between mood disorders and sexual dysfunction in women; for example, 38% of depressed women reported being "not at all satisfied with their ability to reach orgasm" (Frank et al., 2004, in Laurent & Simons, 2009, p. 578). In another more recent study, an association was identified between sexual dysfunction and suicidality among female military persons struggling with post-traumatic stress disorder (PTSD), depression or both disorders together (Blais et al., 2018).

While depressive and anxiety disorders can impact sexual functioning as a kind of external influencing factor, anxiety can also impact sexual function when it manifests out of concerns about performance within the sexual encounter itself, commonly referred to as performance anxiety. Performance anxiety can be felt in the arousal or orgasm phases (Barlow, 1986; Brotto et al., 2016).

Chronic and Acute Trauma. Mounting evidence ties chronic and traumatic stress to sexual dysfunction. Multiple research studies spanning decades have shown a connection between war veterans with PTSD and low sexual desire, difficulties with arousal and orgasm as well as sex avoidance. Similarly, research indicates that traumatic incidents unrelated to combat, such as being the victim of violent crime or involvement in a life-threatening accident has also been associated with sexual dysfunction (Brotto et al., 2016; Yehuda et al., 2015). Though it is not yet entirely clear how trauma impacts sexual function, one theory asserts that because the biological responses in arousal are similar to those in fear responses that individuals with PTSD are unable to differentiate or uncouple the physiological responses from the trauma become overwhelmed, leading to avoidance (Yehuda et al., 2015).

Sociocultural Factors Associated with Sexual Dysfunction. The incidence of sexual dysfunction appears to be much lower among women who live in societies where genders are more equal than among women who live within male-dominated cultures, particularly those in which the priority of sex is reproduction and the satisfaction, pleasure and meaning-making of women's sexual experiences is minimized. These societies tend to be more socially and religiously conservative and embrace attitudes that inhibit sexual education. Additionally, some cultural practices deliberately aim to impair sexual pleasure among women, such as female genital mutilation; among women subject to these practices sexual dysfunction is very high (McCabe et al., 2016; McCool-Myers et al., 2018).

A history of childhood sexual abuse or one or more experiences of unwanted sexual experiences in adulthood comprise another of the sociological/environmental factors that have been demonstrated to have a negative impact on sexual desire and functioning in both men and women (Brotto et al., 2016; Dunlop et al., 2015; Maseroli et al., 2018; McCabe et al., 2016). Whatever the cause of the sexual dysfunction, whether arising out of biological, psychological, sociological or some combination of the three, when one member of a couple experiences sexual dysfunction, the partner's satisfaction and functioning can be affected. Studies seem to indicate that when a male partner experiences ED or premature ejaculation, for example, his partner is more likely to report sexual difficulties (Brotto et al., 2016; Çayan et al., 2004; Maseroli et al., 2016) and the same appears to be true when women experience sexual dysfunction such as pain with sex or difficulty reaching orgasm (Brotto et al., 2016; Davies et al., 1999). For both men and women who experience sexual dysfunction, the burden to the relationship can be quite high. Research by Rowland and Kolba (2018) suggests that for women, distress about her own sexual dysfunction predicts her perception of distress in her partner, while for men, personal distress as well as the quality of relationship influenced the level of distress sensed in his partner. These authors strongly recommend that when one partner is experiencing a sexual dysfunction that both partners be interviewed, as both are impacted and the partner's distress increases the overall burden of the difficulty.

The Skilled Diagnostician

Diagnosis when mental health concerns are the suspected source of the dysfunction. Much of the complexity in diagnosing sexual dysfunction comes from determining the source of the difficulty (biological, psychological or social) and deciding if the dysfunction is primary or secondary to another cause. If after gathering information and considering your client's symptoms, your clinical judgment leads you to believe that the sexual dysfunction arises out of another mental health concern, such as depression or anxiety, a sexual disorder is **not** diagnosed in addition to the primary diagnosis. Creating a timeline in which clients identify as best they can when the first instance of sexual dysfunction arose and if these difficulties preceded difficulties with anxiety or depression, for example, and whether or not these symptoms continue between mood episodes, will help you to determine whether or not the sexual dysfunction is independent of or a function of another mental health concern.

Diagnosis when substance use is the suspected cause of sexual dysfunction. Similarly, in clients whose use or abuse of a substance seems to have triggered the dysfunction, as with the use of alcohol, tobacco, marijuana, your diagnosis would then be substance/medication-induced dysfunction. This is also true when, in your judgment, the symptoms are a direct response to prescribed medications, such as a Selective Serotonin Reuptake Inhibitor (SSRI) (APA, 2013).

When after thoughtful consideration it seems very likely that a medical condition is the source of the dysfunction, do not diagnose your client's concern as a sexual dysfunction (APA, 2013). If diagnosis is necessary and no mental health concern is present, consider an adjustment disorder to describe the distress that comes with dealing with the symptoms of a medical condition.

In situations in which your client is describing very high relationship stress, such as domestic violence, or significant life stressors and it is your judgment that these stressors are the cause of the sexual dysfunction, use appropriate Z codes located in the back of your DSM rather than diagnosing sexual dysfunction (APA, 2013).

Screening and outside referrals. Throughout this book and within this brief chapter, the importance of including a medical history at intake and keeping these records up to date has been emphasized for accurate diagnosis of any disorder and for sexual disorders in particular. Spending time talking about your client's health is helpful in conveying that physical, emotional, cognitive and sexual health are all tied together. Including questions about sexual satisfaction within your intake will create a space in which issues like these can be discussed more comfortably and addressed when they are problematic. Ramlachan and Campbell (2014) recommend that a sexual history include the client's sexual orientation, history of sexual activity, key sexual experiences, including trauma, body image, sexual cycle, fertility needs and a comprehensive understanding of symptoms or complaints.

When clients are able to trust clinicians with the sensitive disclosure of sexual dissatisfaction or dysfunction, it is important to take this opportunity to consider the client's health fully. For instance, studies suggest that the presence of erectile dysfunction often predates and predicts the later development of cardiovascular problems or diabetes, something like a canary in the coal mine. These clients should be strongly encouraged to have a complete medical checkup if they have not had one recently (Gazzaruso et al., 2008; McCabe et al., 2016).

As mentioned earlier, there is also considerable support for a bidirectional relationship between depression and sexual dysfunction. Consequently, clinicians are advised to screen for depression in clients who report sexual dysfunction and to screen for sexual dysfunction in those who report depression and, from there, make a determination of which is primary (Atlantis & Sullivan, 2012).

Asexual Identities. As society becomes more aware of variations within the continuum of human sexuality, both in levels of desire and in the orientation of those feelings, the mental health field and individual clinician's knowledge, skill and awareness will likely become more refined. An important piece of cultural competence in the diagnosis of sexual dysfunction includes an awareness of asexuality. Asexuality is an identity in which a person experiences no desire for sexual contact with others of any gender and also does not feel distress over the absence of these feelings. Some skill may be needed in parsing out the difference between the client with little to no sexual desire and the client who is asexual. This is true in part because not all clients who might eventually identify as asexual are aware that such an identity exists. Further muddying the waters

TABLE 15.03 **Pivot Points: Sexual Dysfunctions**

	Consider this Diagnosis
Pivot Point One: Are your client's sexual difficulties tied to the process of arousal?	
• Is your client's struggle related to a dramatically reduced interest in sex or sexual arousal?	Female Sexual Interest/ Arousal Disorder *Or* Male Hypoactive Sexual Desire Disorder
• Is your client's struggle related to not being able to obtain or sustain an erection?	Erectile Disorder
Pivot Point Two: Does your client struggle to experience a satisfying orgasm?	
• Does your client's struggle arise from having difficulty with or not being able to ejaculate?	Delayed Ejaculation
• Is your client's suffering related to experiences of ejaculating before he would like to?	Premature (Early) Ejaculation
• Does your client experience an unsatisfying delay, infrequency, absence of orgasms or perceive a lack of intensity?	Female Orgasmic Disorder
Pivot Point Three: Does your client's struggle arise from an experience or fear of vaginal pain during intercourse?	Genito-Pelvic Pain/ Penetration Disorder
Pivot Point Four: Is your client's sexual concern related to a substance or medication?	Substance/Medication-Induced Sexual Dysfunction
Pivot Point Five: If your client's suffering is characteristic of the diagnoses above, but does not meet full criteria for any of them and you would like to specify the reason, consider this diagnosis (as with a medical disorder).	Other Specified Sexual Dysfunction
Pivot Point Six: If your client's suffering is characteristic of a sexual dysfunction, but you do not yet have enough information to justify a diagnosis, consider this diagnosis.	Other Unspecified Sexual Dysfunction

is that some asexual persons do experience and embrace romantic feelings for others, and some also engage in and enjoy activities that are preliminary to sexual intercourse but are not interested in intercourse itself, challenging what are described as essentialist views of sex (Scherrer, 2008). Clinicians should be aware that this identity lies on a continuum of human sexuality that is both diverse and complex. Variations in human sexual preference or experience are not pathological unless they cause that individual distress (sexual dysfunction) or threaten the rights or safety of another person (some paraphilias) (APA, 2013).

Differential Diagnosis: Beatriz

Beatriz is a 52-year-old Brazilian philosophy doctoral candidate in New York City where she has lived with her husband and two children for 7 years. Beatriz explains, "I have a group of friends who are all in their dissertation stage of their studies and we all made a pact to help to make offerings to the research gods by participating in at least one study. We were hoping it would help all of us have good research karma, and that is how I landed here," she noted with a touch of irony in her voice. "My research participation was basically just an interview about my health perceptions and about relationships, but a lot of the interview was about marriage and intimacy. As I was talking to the researcher I realized I should really talk to someone about my sex life, I hadn't realized just how unsatisfied I am in that department. It's not something I would have normally sought out counseling for but it could be good to just figure out what is happening to my body and what it means."

In her counseling intake, Beatriz explains that she and her husband married when she was 25 and he was 35; they had no children for 10 years, during that time, Beatriz describes traveling often and enjoying each other's company; she remembers their sex life was "really good" but "it suffered a lot after their children were born." She further explains that their sex life had rebounded when both of their children were sleeping through the night and slept in their own rooms. "My husband, Arsenio, and I are very close and we have been through a lot together. I've learned I can depend on him. Right after we moved from Lisbon to New York I was diagnosed with uterine cancer. We were lucky because it was pretty bad and the doctor wasn't too sure about how it was going to go. I went through several rounds of chemo and I got really sick. It was terrible to be sick in a city where I didn't know anyone, I was scared and Arsenio was at work a lot of the time, so I was lonely, too. As I began to recover from the cancer my doctor noticed that I had become depressed and so she convinced me that I should take an SSRI to see if it was helpful. After about 3 months on that medication I did start to feel a little better. I was still depressed but I wasn't immobilized by it. Since then I have had depression on and off . . . Wow! I'm realizing this has been 7 years of these cycles of depression."

Beatriz also shares that sex is physically uncomfortable for her. "I don't remember the last time that Arsenio and I were intimate. It's been a while, that much I know. I think he avoids asking because he knows it hurts. Part of me is ok with that—that's the part that remembers that I am getting older, I'm past the age of having children and I don't feel especially sexy anymore. But I think it is the other part of me, the part of me that misses that part of my life with my husband, that part of me with good memories of our early years is dragging the other part in here hoping there is something that I can do to turn this around. I don't know, what do you think? Is this something that I can change how my body responds to intimacy or is my body just different than it once was and I just have to accept that?"

Treatment for Sexual Dysfunction

Psychological Interventions. Treatments for this dimension are similar across dysfunctions and draw from psychotherapy, psychoeducation and the use of medications. The four most common (and most effective) psychological approaches for addressing sexual dysfunctions include cognitive-behavioral therapy (CBT), systematic desensitization, marital therapy and sex therapy. CBT focuses on thoughts and expectations that undermine enjoyment of sex at any of the four stages (Brotto et al., 2016; McCabe, 2001). In the 1970s, systematic desensitization was adapted for sexual dysfunction. Systematic desensitization worked, in part, by focusing on gradually reducing performance anxiety responses that were believed to inhibit sexual function and pleasure. In an early study, systematic desensitization demonstrated much stronger outcomes with clients with "severe sexual disorders" when compared with the psychoanalytically oriented approach to which it was compared (Obler, 1973), and has since been shown to have about the same efficacy as sex therapy (Everaerd & Dekker, 1985; Rao et al., 2018).

Sex therapy is a specialization area that recognizes the sexuality and needs of men and women as different and needing specialized attention and response. This approach tends to focus less on anxieties and more on the desired outcomes of their clients and how to help their clients achieve those desires (Leiblum, 2006). All four of these therapies seem to be equally efficacious with some advantages given to one or the other depending upon the specific dysfunction (Rao et al., 2018).

Educational Interventions. This category of intervention includes sexual skills training as well as essential education about the fundamentals of sexual functioning and healthy living strategies that contribute to positive sexual experiences, such as exercise, diet and avoiding the abuse of substances. Education that includes both partners is also common and tends to be helpful, particularly in those with age-related sexual dysfunction. By themselves, educational interventions are less likely to fully remediate sexual dysfunction than when used in combination with other approaches (Frühauf et al., 2013; Rao et al., 2018).

Pharmacological Interventions. The most commonly used medication for sexual dysfunction in both men and women is sildenafil (Brotto et al., 2016; Nurnberg et al., 2008). Sildenafil has been used with efficacy with a number of disorders including erectile dysfunction and premature ejaculation (Brotto et al., 2016) as well as a range of sexual side effects in women suffering from depression (Nurnberg et al., 2008). Another common approach, used in both men and women with anxiety and depression who are experiencing sexual dysfunction is to switch medications from those with higher rates of sexual side effects to those with fewer reported effects, such as bupropion. Psychotherapy paired with bupropion has also been found to improve sexual dysfunction in women with depression (Pasha et al., 2018). Further, a number of SSRIs have been shown to be helpful to those who experience premature ejaculation (Althof et al., 2010).

BOX 15.02 DIAGNOSTIC BRIDGE

Again, because the comorbidity rates of sexual dysfunction is so high with depression and anxiety and medical disorders such as heart disease and diabetes, clients presenting with sexual dysfunction should be screened for these disorders and referred for medical exams if they have not had a recent physical (Preeti et al., 2018).

Definitional Cases in Sexual Dysfunctions

Christian

Christian has become frustrated by his inability to remain engaged in sexual activity since he regularly ejaculates before he is ready and before his partner has experienced pleasure from their time together.

Zoe

Zoe, age 22, experiences intense pelvic pain when she anticipates her husband will want to have sex with her. The pain is intense enough to prevent sexual activity.

Tunde

Tunde and his wife have been trying to have a baby for a year. Since they decided to have a child, Tunde has been unable to ejaculate during intercourse.

Martina

Martina has all but given up the idea that she would ever be interested in sex. She does not have fantasies or experience arousal and resists her partner's advances.

Timothy

Timothy, age 30, reports that for the last 8 months, he has lost all interest in sexual activity. Timothy is distressed because his partner is ready to leave him if things don't improve.

Victoria

Victoria and her partner have been quite distressed at Victoria's inability to reach orgasm during intercourse. The problem is one that Victoria has struggled with since she began having sex as a teen.

Dale

Dale has become distracted and worried because in the past year, he has found it difficult to obtain and keep an erection during sexual activities.

Narrative Cases in Sexual Dysfunctions

Brent

Brent and his wife celebrated the birth of their first child a year ago. Brent shares, "I was present for Noah's birth and, on one hand, it was a really incredible experience. Sarah was such a trooper. I couldn't believe how she stuck through the process with so much grace and grit. She was beautiful. The actual birth was pretty amazing, too. When Noah emerged it was as if a part of me was being born at the same time. However, and this is a big however, ever since I saw the baby come out of Sarah's vagina, bloody and everything stretched and slimy, well, my sex drive vanished. I don't have any desire at all to have sex and I don't even have fantasies. At first Sarah didn't notice, she was focused on Noah and healing her own body. But now it's been a year and I just can't get there, if you know what I mean. So I'd like to get my sex drive back before it drives a wedge between me and Sarah."

Jennifer

Jennifer, 36, has never been free of pelvic pain when she attempts to engage in sexual intercourse. "I can't really describe this pain, but what happens is the muscles in my pelvic floor start to tense up as soon as my partner and I start to get close, even just touching or kissing. I can sense myself getting more and more tense even when there is a really big part of me that wants to be with this guy. But when it comes to the act itself, that is really painful, usually unbearable. Most of the time I can't go through with sex at all. Over the years I have lost several relationships because of this problem. My partners just get fed up, some thought I was a 'tease,' some thought I was a head-case, and twice I was raped. I asked them to stop but they didn't. One guy told me he thought that once I let him in I would like it and then I wouldn't have this problem anymore. It took a long time to get over that. So now I have all but given up on the idea that I will ever have a sex life or a partner. Who would be willing to put up with this?"

Logan

Logan has asked to meet with a counselor about difficulties securing and maintaining a romantic relationship. Logan explains, "I've never really been that confident with women. I always feel so awkward. I have had a lot of girlfriends online, we meet in chat rooms and get to know each other. I can usually feel pretty relaxed when I'm behind a screen. But when we meet I start to feel insecure. I notice things about her that I guess I don't like and things about myself that I don't like either and I start to lose interest. What usually kills the whole process is when she finally starts hinting at sex, which I try to avoid as long as possible. It is always so embarrassing and disappointing. It would be great if I could have a normal sex life but every time I get with a girl I, well you know, I have an orgasm, or whatever before I really get started. It's always been like this and it's humiliating."

Petra

Petra, 43, and her partner Amanda have made an appointment with a counselor to explore ongoing difficulties with their sexual relationship. Petra explains, "For about the past 8 months I have found it very difficult to have an orgasm. Amanda is afraid it is a case of LDB, you know lesbian death bed, move in together and kill the sex life. But I don't think that is it. I can't put my finger on it exactly but maybe it has something to do with work. Things changed for me in the bedroom around the time of my promotion. There is a lot of stress at work and it has been really hard for me to relax—I find my mind drifting to work projects when I should be focused on our time together. Maybe that has something to do with it. But whatever it is, it is getting in the way. Sex feels more like work than it should. We'd like some help before it starts to create a rift between us."

Keith

During a physical, Keith, age 52, responded to his doctor's inquiry about his sexual health. "I don't have any problem getting excited. What is a problem is reaching a climax. Most of the time I don't climax at all, it just doesn't happen. When it does happen, it takes a long time, I mean a very long time. It's a problem. My wife thinks it's her, but it has always been that way for me. If I approach her for sex she's hesitant because she knows it's going to be a while, there's no such thing as a quickie for us. So she has to be in the mood. So it puts a bit of a damper on our sex life. You wouldn't think it would cause so much problem, but it does."

Matteo

Sitting on the subway on the way into work, Matteo thought again about the conversation he and his partner, Ira, had at the breakfast table earlier in the week when Ira had asked, "So when are you going to talk to someone about your ascension deficit disorder?" "You mean attention deficit?" Matt asked? "No, I mean that your Johnson has lost his magic and it is time to get that looked into," Ira retorted wryly. Matteo tried to think back to when he first started to experience some inconsistency with his erections. "I guess I've always had a little problem during really stressful times at work but never for more than a week at a time, but this has been going on longer, maybe 6 or 8 months. Has it really been that often that this has been going on, though . . . I guess it has been most of the time, my God, I just lost track." Matteo thought to himself. "I hope something isn't really wrong . . ." As the train raced forward, Matteo's thoughts circled back to thoughts of sex and his difficulties. "It has been going on a while and does happen a lot but it's almost guaranteed to be a no-go when Ira wants some kind of role play . . . I think I'm all played out."

References

Althof, S. E., Abdo, C. H., Dean, J., Hackett, G., McCabe, M., McMahon, C. G., Rosen, R. C., Sadovsky, R., Waldinger, M., Becher, E., Broderick, G. A., Buvat, J., Goldstein, I., El-Meliegy, A. I., Giuliano, F., Hellstrom, W. J. G., Incrocci, L., Jannini, E. A., Park, K., . . . International Society for Sexual Medicine. (2010). International society for sexual medicine's guidelines for the diagnosis and treatment of premature ejaculation. *The Journal of Sexual Medicine*, *7*(9), 2947–2969. https://doi.org/10.1111/j.1743-6109.2010.01975.x

American Psychiatric Association. (2013). Sexual dysfunctions. In *Diagnostic and statistical manual of mental disorders (DSM-5®)*. Author.

Apantaku-Olajide, T., Gibbons, P., & Higgins, A. (2011). Drug-induced sexual dysfunction and mental health patients' attitude to psychotropic medications. *Sexual and Relationship Therapy*, *26*(2), 145–155. https://doi.org/10.1080/14681994.2011.567259

Atlantis, E., & Sullivan, T. (2012). Bidirectional association between depression and sexual dysfunction: A systematic review and meta-analysis. *The Journal of Sexual Medicine*, *9*(6), 1497–1507. https://doi.org/10.1111/j.1743-6109.2012.02709.x

Barlow, D. H. (1986). Causes of sexual dysfunction: The role of anxiety and cognitive interference. *Journal of Consulting and Clinical Psychology*, *54*(2), 140. https://doi.org/10.1037/0022-006X.54.2.140

Blais, R. K., Monteith, L. L., & Kugler, J. (2018). Sexual dysfunction is associated with suicidal ideation in female service members and veterans. *Journal of Affective Disorders*, *226*, 52–57. https://doi.org/10.1016/j.jad.2017.08.079

Brotto, L., Atallah, S., Johnson-Agbakwu, C., Rosenbaum, T., Abdo, C., Byers, E. S., Graham, C., Nobre, P., & Wylie, K. (2016). Psychological and interpersonal dimensions of sexual function and dysfunction. *The Journal of Sexual Medicine*, *13*(4), 538–571. https://doi.org/10.1016/j.jsxm.2016.01.019

Çayan, S., Bozlu, M., Canpolat, B., & Akbay, E. (2004). The assessment of sexual functions in women with male partners complaining of erectile dysfunction: Does treatment of male sexual dysfunction improve female partner's sexual functions? *Journal of Sex & Marital Therapy*, *30*(5), 333–341. https://doi.org/10.1080/00926230490465091

Clayton, A. H., Alkis, A. R., Parikh, N. B., & Votta, J. G. (2016). Sexual dysfunction due to psychotropic medications. *Psychiatric Clinics*, *39*(3), 427–463. https://doi.org/10.1016/j.psc.2016.04.006

Davies, S., Katz, J., & Jackson, J. L. (1999). Sexual desire discrepancies: Effects on sexual and relationship satisfaction in heterosexual dating couples. *Archives of Sexual Behavior*, *28*(6), 553–567. https://doi.org/10.1023/A:1018721417683

Den Oudsten, B. L., Traa, M. J., Thong, M. S. Y., Martijn, H., De Hingh, I. H. J. T., Bosscha, K., & Van De Poll-Franse, L. V. (2012). Higher prevalence of sexual dysfunction in colon and rectal cancer survivors compared with the normative population: A population-based study. *European Journal of Cancer*, *48*(17), 3161–3170. https://doi.org/10.1016/j.ejca.2012.04.004

Dunlop, B. W., Hill, E., Johnson, B. N., Klein, D. N., Gelenberg, A. J., Rothbaum, B. O., Thase, M. E., & Kocsis, J. H. (2015). Mediators of sexual functioning and marital quality in chronically depressed adults with and without a history of childhood sexual abuse. *The Journal of Sexual Medicine*, *12*(3), 813–823. https://doi.org/10.1111/jsm.12727

Dunn, K. M., Croft, P. R., & Hackett, G. I. (1999). Association of sexual problems with social, psychological, and physical problems in men and women: A cross sectional population survey. *Journal of Epidemiology & Community Health*, *53*(3), 144–148.

Everaerd, W., & Dekker, J. (1985). Treatment of male sexual dysfunction: Sex therapy compared with systematic desensitization and rational emotive therapy. *Behaviour Research and Therapy*, *23*(1), 13–25.

Forbes, M. K., Baillie, A. J., Eaton, N. R., & Krueger, R. F. (2017). A place for sexual dysfunction in an empirical taxonomy of psychopathology. *The Journal of Sex Research*, *54*(4–5), 465–485. https://doi.org/10.1080/00224499.2016.1269306

Frühauf, S., Gerger, H., Schmidt, H. M., Munder, T., & Barth, J. (2013). Efficacy of psychological interventions for sexual dysfunction: A systematic review and meta-analysis. *Archives of Sexual Behavior*, *42*(6), 915–933. https://doi.org/10.1007/s10508-012-0062-0

Gandaglia, G., Briganti, A., Jackson, G., Kloner, R. A., Montorsi, F., Montorsi, P., & Vlachopoulos, C. (2014). A systematic review of the association between erectile dysfunction and cardiovascular disease. *European Urology*, *65*(5), 968–978. https://doi.org/10.1016/j.eururo.2013.08.023

Gazzaruso, C., Solerte, S. B., Pujia, A., Coppola, A., Vezzoli, M., Salvucci, F., & Garzaniti, A. (2008). Erectile dysfunction as a predictor of cardiovascular events and death in diabetic patients with angiographically proven asymptomatic coronary artery disease: A potential protective role for statins and 5-phosphodiesterase inhibitors. *Journal of the American College of Cardiology*, *51*, 2040–2044. https://doi.org/10.1016/j.jacc.2007.10.069. https://www.sciencedirect.com/science/article/pii/S0735109708009480

Jannini, E. A., & Nappi, R. E. (2018). Couplepause: A new paradigm in treating sexual dysfunction during menopause and andropause. *Sexual Medicine Reviews*, *6*, 384–395. https://doi.org/10.1016/j.sxmr.2017.11.002

Laumann, E. O., West, S., Glasser, D., Carson, C., Rosen, R., & Kang, J. H. (2007). Prevalence and correlates of erectile dysfunction by race and ethnicity among men aged 40 or older in the United

States: From the male attitudes regarding sexual health survey. *Journal of Sex Medicine*, *4*(1), 57–65. https://doi.org/10.1111/j.1743-6109.2006.00340.x

Laurent, S. M., & Simons, A. D. (2009). Sexual dysfunction in depression and anxiety: Conceptualizing sexual dysfunction as part of an internalizing dimension. *Clinical Psychology Review*, *29*, 573–585. https://doi.org/10.1016/j.cpr.2009.06.007

Leiblum, S. R. (Ed.). (2006). *Principles and practice of sex therapy*. Guilford Press.

Maseroli, E., Fanni, E., Mannucci, E., Fambrini, M., Jannini, E. A., Maggi, M., & Vignozzi, L. (2016). Which are the male factors associated with female sexual dysfunction (FSD)? *Andrology*, *4*(5), 911–920. https://doi.org/10.1111/andr.12224

Maseroli, E., Scavello, I., Campone, B., Di Stasi, V., Cipriani, S., Felciai, F., Camartini, V., Magini, A., Castellini, G., Ricca, V., Maggi, M., & Vignozzi, L. (2018). Psychosexual correlates of unwanted sexual experiences in women consulting for female sexual dysfunction according to their timing across the life span. *The Journal of Sexual Medicine*, *15*(12), 1739–1751. https://doi.org/10.1016/j.jsxm.2018.10.004

McCabe, M. P. (2001). Evaluation of a cognitive behavior therapy program for people with sexual dysfunction. *Journal of Sex & Marital Therapy*, *27*(3), 259–271. https://doi.org/10.1080/009262301750257119

McCabe, M. P., Sharlip, I. D., Lewis, R., Atalla, E., Balon, R., Fisher, A., Laumann, E., Lee, S. W., & Segraves, R. T. (2016). Risk factors for sexual dysfunction among women and men: A consensus statement from the fourth international consultation on sexual medicine 2015. *Sexual Medicine*, *13*, 153–167.

McCool-Myers, M., Theurich, M., Zuelke, A., Knuettel, H., & Apfelbacher, C. (2018). Predictors of female sexual dysfunction: A systematic review and qualitative analysis through gender inequity paradigms. *BMC Women's Health*, *18*, 108. https://doi.org/10.1186/s12905-018-0602-4

Mitchell, K. R., Jones, K. G., Wellings, K., Johnson, A., Graham, C., Datta, J., Copas, A. J., Bancroft, J., Sonnenberg, P., Macdowal, W., Field, N., & Mercer, C. H. (2016). Estimating the prevalence of sexual function problems: The impact of morbidity criteria. *The Journal of Sex Research*, *53*(8), 955–967. https://doi.org/10.1080/00224499.2015.1089214

Monga, M., Alexandrescu, B., Katz, S. E., Stein, M., & Ganiats, T. (2004). Impact of infertility on quality of life, marital adjustment, and sexual function. *Urology*, *63*(1), 126–130. https://doi.org/10.1016/j.urology.2003.09.015

Montejo, A. L., Llorca, G., Izquierdo, J. A., & Rico-Villademoros, F. (2001). Incidence or sexual dysfunction associated with antidepressant agents: A prospective multicenter study of 1022 outpatients. *The Journal of Clinical Psychiatry*, *62*(Suppl. 3), 10–21.

Morrison, J. (2014). *Diagnosis made easier: Principles and techniques for mental health clinicians*. Guilford Publications.

Nurnberg, H. G., Hensley, P. L., Heiman, J. R., Croft, H. A., Debattista, C., & Paine, S. (2008). Sildenafil treatment of women with antidepressant-associated sexual dysfunction: A randomized controlled trial. *JAMA*, *300*(4), 395–404. https://doi.org/10.1001/jama.300.4.395

Obler, M. (1973). Systematic desensitization in sexual disorders. *Journal of Behavior Therapy and Experimental Psychiatry*, *4*(2), 93–101. https://doi.org/10.1016/0005-7916(73)90051-7

Pasha, H., Basirat, Z., Faramarzi, M., & Kheirkhah, F. (2018). Comparative effectiveness of antidepressant medication versus psychological intervention on depression symptoms in women with infertility and sexual dysfunction. *International Journal of Fertility & Sterility*, *12*(1), 6.

Preeti, S., Jayaram, S. D., & Chittaranjan, A. (2018). Sexual dysfunction in patients with antidepressant-treated anxiety or depressive disorders: A pragmatic multivariable longitudinal study. *East Asian Archives of Psychiatry*, *28*(1), 9. https://doi.org/10.12809/eaap181664

Ramlachan, P., & Campbell, M. M. (2014). An integrative treatment model for patients with sexual dysfunctions. *SAMJ*, *104*(6), 440–445. https://doi.org/10.7196/SAMJ.8374

Rao, T. S., Maheshwari, S., George, M., Chandran, S., Manohar, S., & Rao, S. S. (2018). Psychosocial interventions for sexual dysfunction in addictive disorders. *Indian Journal of Psychiatry*, *60*(Suppl. 4), S506.

Rowland, D. L., & Kolba, T. N. (2018). The burden of sexual problems: Perceived effects on men's and women's sexual partners. *The Journal of Sex Research*, *55*(2), 226–235. https://doi.org/10.1080/00224499.2017.1332153

Scherrer, K. S. (2008). Coming to an asexual identity: Negotiating identity, negotiating desire. *Sexualities*, *11*(5), 621–641. https://doi.org/10.1177/1363460708094269

Schover, L. R., van der Kaaij, M., van Dorst, E., Creutzberg, C., Huyghe, E., & Kiserud, C. E. (2014). Sexual dysfunction and infertility as late effects of cancer treatment. *European Journal of Cancer Supplements*, *12*(1), 41–53. https://doi.org/10.1016/j.ejcsup.2014.03.004

Serretti, A., & Chiesa, A. (2009). Treatment-emergent sexual dysfunction related to antidepressants: A meta-analysis. *Journal of Clinical Psychopharmacology*, *29*(3), 259–266. https://doi.org/10.1097/JCP.0b013e3181a5233f

Simon, J. A., & Lukas, V. A. (2017). Distressing sexual function at midlife: Unmet needs, practical diagnoses, and available treatments. *Obstetrics & Gynecology*, *4*, 889–905. https://doi.org/10.1097/AOG.0000000000002268

Stimmel, G. L., & Gutierrez, M. A. (2006). Sexual dysfunction and psychotropic medications. *CNS Spectrum*, *9*, 24–30. https://doi.org/10.1017/S1092852900026730

Story, N. (1974). Sexual dysfunction resulting from drug side effects. *The Journal of Sex Research*, *10*(2), 132–149. https://doi.org/10.1080/00224497409550840

Thygesen, K. H., Schjødt, I., & Jarden, M. (2012). The impact of hematopoietic stem cell transplantation on sexuality: A systematic review of the literature. *Bone marrow transplantation, 47*(5), 716–724.

Vegunta, S. Kling, M. J., & Faubion, S. S. (2016). Sexual health matters: Management of female sexual dysfunction. *Journal of Women's Health*, *25*(9), 952–954. https://doi.org/10.1089/jwh.2016.5991

Yehuda, R., Lehrner, A., & Rosenbaum, T. Y. (2015). PTSD and sexual dysfunction in men and women. *The Journal of Sexual Medicine*, *12*(5), 1107–1119. https://doi.org/10.1111/jsm.12856

16 Disruptive, Impulse and Control Disorders

The ability to enact self-control, the counterpart to impulsivity, is a central feature of a child's development and thriving, and pays dividends later in life. In the late 1960s and early 1970s, Walter Mischel, a psychologist at Stanford, conducted a now-famous experiment in delayed gratification. Mischel offered children a small reward, a marshmallow, cookie or pretzel. The children participating in the study were told they could eat the snack immediately or wait 15 minutes when they would be given a larger reward. The researcher would then leave the room and the child would be left with a tasty treat and a dilemma: eat the treat now or wait for the promised reward. Mischel and his team later gathered evidence demonstrating that children who were able to postpone gratification had higher Scholastic Assessment Test (SAT) scores, educational attainment and lower body mass index in adolescence (Mischel, 2015). With this study and others that would follow, Mischel began to build an argument for the relationship between self-control and life satisfaction.

Another essential element of the natural human growth and development process is learning to comfort ourselves when we are upset, to identify our feelings as they emerge and to respond to those feelings in ways that support our relationships with our families, friends and communities. Sometimes, however, children, teens and adults experience difficulties that impair their ability to manage negative emotions, to think through their actions or the potential consequences of those actions to themselves or to others, in developmentally appropriate ways. For those who aren't able to master the ability to identify and meet their own emotional needs or to ask for comfort and support from others, hostility, emotional intensity and impulsivity can result. As Barkley (2013) notes, "The children who need love the most will always ask for it in the most unloving ways." Perhaps all of us have, at one time or another, acted spitefully toward a loved one when, in fact, we craved closeness, or fantasized some retaliation, fulfilling a vengeful wish without carrying it out. When this behavior is played out in real time, and becomes a relational pattern rather than a momentary lapse or fantasy, the consequences to the client's relationships can be profound. It is at these times when challenging behavior and deficits in emotion impair relationships or alienate clients from their community, that diagnosis on the disruptive, impulse control and conduct continuum.

The Disorders of the Continuum

The disorders that comprise this dimension include two that feature behavioral difficulties, oppositional defiant disorder (ODD) and conduct disorder (CD). A third disorder, intermittent explosive disorder (IED), is diagnosed when a person experiences frequent, destructive tantrums. Included within this continuum are two impulse control disorders, kleptomania and pyromania. Also discussed, but not formally included within the continuum, is antisocial personality disorder (ASPD). Each of these will be described briefly in the next few pages and will be followed by a discussion of the current understanding of the developmental course and nuanced relationship between ODD, CD and ASPD.

Oppositional Defiant Disorder (ODD). Children and adolescents diagnosed with ODD present with an angry and irritable mood much of the time. Because ODD is an externalizing disorder, parents and teachers see the client's anger expressed outwardly in the form of vindictiveness, intentional acts designed to rile others and, most notably, in their defiance of adults. These children can find it difficult to take responsibility for their behaviors and may develop a pattern of blaming others for their actions. Since all children (and perhaps people generally) have the potential to sustain anger or resentment, or to act vindictively, this diagnosis is given only when these patterns are present most of the time for a period of 6 months or more. This diagnosis is nearly always given to children or adolescents, though adults are not excluded (American Psychiatric Association [APA], 2013; Cavanagh, et al., 2017).

The lifetime prevalence rates of ODD seem to hover at around 10% and, as will be discussed later, ODD is frequently comorbid with other disorders (Nock et al., 2007). In a longitudinal study designed to identify early predictors of adult psychopathology, Copeland et al. (2009) found that while adolescent depression was significantly predictive of a range of disorders in young adulthood, the effect of depression later in life was accounted for by comorbidities of ODD, substance abuse and anxiety. This study and others like it point to the importance of preventing the development of ODD in order to prevent mental health concerns later in life.

The DSM 5 points out that many children with ODD eventually develop conduct disorder, and further notes that neurobiological markers have not distinguished the two disorders, suggesting that they may, in fact, represent two subtypes of the same disorder. However, in a study of 4,380 children, researchers Cavanagh et al. (2017) explored whether or not ODD and CD were expressions of the same underlying deficit or represented independent constructs. In their factor analysis, emotional lability and irritability grouped with ODD but not with CD, pointing to two separate constructs

BOX 16.01 DISRUPTIVE, IMPULSE CONTROL AND CONDUCT KEY TERMS

Acquired Sociopathy: this umbrella term describes situations in which injury to the brain resulting from head trauma or illness, such as dementia, results in antisocial behavior where no problematic antisocial behaviors existed before (DeLisi et al., 2018).

Equifinality: a principle recognizing that a diverse range of risk factors and pathways can lead to the same outcome (Cummings et al., 2002).

E.g., Two children, one from a middle-income single-parent family and the other from a low-income two-parent family, experience depression in adulthood.

Externalizing Behaviors: when people respond to difficult feelings and situations by striking out, such as through bullying or antagonizing others, destroying property or defying authority, these behaviors are described as externalizing. Consequently, conduct disorders are often referred to as externalizing disorders.

Developmental Psychopathology: this branch of scholarship explores the developmental course of the evolution of mental disorders, specifically exploring the multiple origins and pathways of particular disorders and the multiple outcomes of similar early experiences (Cummings et al., 2002).

Internalizing Behaviors: a response to painful or distressing feelings or circumstances by turning inward; for example, by withdrawal, self-injury, depression, anxiety and so on.

Multifinality: a principle that acknowledges that similar beginnings may result in dissimilar outcomes across different persons (Cummings et al., 2002).

E.g., Two children, both with similar documented childhood sexual trauma, later in life one child experiences depression and anxiety in adulthood while the other experiences no mental health concerns.

Psychopath/sociopath. for the purposes of diagnosis and within the DSM 5 nomenclature, the terms, psychopath, sociopath and dyssocial personality, all serve as synonyms for antisocial personality disorder (ASPD), the current diagnostic name for the cluster of defining traits that feature a lack of concern for and frequent violation of the rights of others, and a concomitant lack of remorse for harmful or amoral behaviors (American Psychiatric Association [APA], 2013).

However, the study of criminology has taken a keen interest in differentiating the terms psychopath, sociopath and ASPD. These researchers have begun efforts to describe each as different constructs (Pemment, 2013; Tracy (2015). Some differentiate these terms this way: ASPD is the diagnostic and legal term for patterns of amoral and antisocial behaviors; sociopathy describe the behaviors resulting from the neurological consequences of adverse environmental experiences; psychopathy, on the other hand, is thought to be a naturally occurring personality trait that makes it possible for some people to meet their goals and needs free of guilt and without considering the needs of others (Walsh & Wu, 2008).

in which ODD is more likely manifested from a deficit in emotion regulation while CD is capturing disruptive behavior. These researchers also report that while they did not find support for ODD subtypes, they assert that subtyping may still be useful

BOX 16.02 A LETTER TO THE READER

Working with children, adolescents and adults with disruptive disorders requires a diagnostician to don a particular clinical hat. In my experience, it has been the rare clinician in training who sets out to work with this population. As they say, however, the squeaky wheel gets the grease, so clinicians often see this constellation of disorders in their work. In supervising counselors in training, I've noticed that clinicians who see these kinds of symptoms are often challenged to monitor their own counter-transference while remaining mindful of the power they hold in their role as counselor and diagnostician. Frequently, this challenge shows up as a response that is evoked by a client's presentation in session that mirrors behaviors in the home or in the community that consistently elicit negativity from others. In other words, these clients, particularly those with conduct disorder, don't make it easy to work collaboratively with them. Fantasies about warm connections, gratitude and ready change in clients who present with these patterns can quickly give way to impatience, irritation and dreading sessions, or worse, power struggles, passive aggressive and counterproductive responses to client behaviors.

If you are a highly empathic person, the frustration, anger and, frankly, a dislike for the client that is often held by those who have referred them, coupled with the client's own difficulties connecting positively with others, may be absorbed by the clinician early in the process and interfere with the ability to see the client clearly. Should this happen, you may fail to see signs of distress or maltreatment that would otherwise be evident in a child whose distress response was more anxious or depressed.

After working for several years with children and adolescents with these diagnoses, and experiencing failures in my own approaches, I realized that I held a bias for internalizing behaviors, those that were more comfortable for me and for society as a whole. At some point, it became evident that this bias was getting in the way of seeing the suffering that was driving negative behaviors and prevented me from cultivating a genuine compassion for the pain these clients experienced. Seeing this bias, I was better able to respond in a balanced way and, as a result, I witnessed a change in the therapeutic relationships I was able to develop.

This diagnostic continuum requires counselors to find compassion and understanding for difficult behaviors but also requires frank, direct and immediate communication along with clear boundary-setting. Compassion and genuine appreciation alone will likely not be enough to shift very difficult patterns, however. Students who find it difficult to say what is on their minds if there is a danger that it may not be received warmly or with appreciation may find this work especially challenging. Building confidence in your work through practice and good supervision will benefit your therapeutic relationships with these clients.

Reflections for those working closely with clients who display difficult behaviors:

1. What would it be like for you to work with a teen who did not seem to like you, who assumed immediately that you had nothing of value to offer or that you didn't have a clue how to survive in their world? How would it be to work with someone who did not want to work with you or participate in counseling at all?
2. What personal biases and stereotypes related to race, ethnicity, faith, gender, sexual orientation, language, dialect and so on do you hold? What potential do these biases hold for polluting your ability to diagnose your client appropriately?
3. What "tender spots" do you carry? For instance, do you have sensitivities about your weight, height or appearance? Your race, gender, sexual orientation or faith? Do

you hold fears about your abilities, your age or your belongingness? How would it be for you if a client were to disparage you around one or more of these areas?

4. What are the sources of reward for you in your work as a counselor? Do you hold a private hope for appreciation, gratitude or recognition for yourself within the relationship? How about a wish for rapid or steady client change? How can you respond if these restorative pieces of the counseling encounter are not present in your work?

5. How will you know if your negative experience of a client is coloring your diagnostic lens or impairing your ability to provide an appropriate standard of care? Where could you turn to for support?

for predicting later outcomes, something that will be discussed later in this chapter. However, while not all children with ODD will later develop CD, research reveals that as many as 42% of clients with ODD also meet criteria for CD, alerting diagnosticians to the close relationship and the need to screen for both when conduct or disruptive symptoms are present (Nock et al., 2007; Riley et al., 2016).

Intermittent Explosive Disorder (IED). IED is diagnosed when a person experiences frequent, highly disruptive tantrums but does not experience difficulties in temperament or a tendency to deliberately defy or annoy others. These frequent outbursts are marked by aggression, verbal and sometimes physical, destructive behavior or both. These incidents are believed to be born out of impulse control problems and not deliberate attempts to harm, manipulate or control others or as demonstrations of social protest, instead, they are spontaneous and judged to be grossly out of proportion to the triggering event. Children under the age of 6 should not receive this diagnosis since very young children are not prepared to manage their feelings and impulses fully before this time (APA, 2013).

Though considered to be less severe than either ODD or CD, international studies of the prevalence and impact of IED indicate that IED may be both more common than one might expect and quite burdensome to the person who experiences it and to those in relationship with them. The typical age of onset seems to be somewhere in the 13-23 years of age range and is more typically seen in males. Other demographic predictors, however, have been less consistent (Kessler et al., 2006; Scott et al., 2016). Like other impulse control disorders, IED is frequently comorbid with disorders such as mood, anxiety and substance use disorders (Kessler et al., 2006). Research suggests that IED may also contribute to poor health later in life. Using logistic regression analysis

BOX 16.03 TRY THIS: THE CALLOUS-UNEMOTIONAL SPECIFIER

In the following example, note Grant's responses. Identify the feathers that support a callous-unemotional specifier.

Grant. Grant and his childhood friend, Andy, both 15, skipped school and got high and then drank what alcohol they could find in his parent's house. That afternoon, they decided to take a commercial scooter and ride it around the wharf. In a moment of impulsivity, Grant aimed the scooter for the pier and ran it off into the water. Grant swam to the dock but Andy hit his head on a rock and was in an ICU unit for several days before he finally recovered. During that time, Grant was very worried that Andy's parents would blame him if Andy died and he would be charged criminally or sued. Grant's parents noticed that Grant seemed to show no concern for Andy nor did he seem to feel any remorse or guilt for his role in the accident.

Source: American Psychiatric Association (2013).

of over 10,000 participants, McCloskey et al., (2010) found that IED was a risk factor for nine of 12 health outcomes assessed, including heart disease, hypertension, stroke, diabetes and arthritis.

Conduct Disorder (CD). In theory, ODD, IED and CD can be easily discerned from one another in that the child or adolescent struggling with symptoms of a CD demonstrates behaviors that tend to violate the rights of others. In contrast, the child struggling with oppositional defiance is more likely to aggravate, annoy or to refuse to comply with requests, while the child with IED is unskilled at managing outbursts but is otherwise constructive and, for the most part, cooperative with others. In the field, the line between these three may be much more blurred. However, CD itself describes a significantly impairing presentation and can lead to weighty legal, social and relational consequences (APA, 2013; Frick, 2016). Children and adolescents with CDs display behaviors that fall into four categories: serious violation of rules, such as running away and truancy, deceitfulness and theft, destruction of property and aggression that is directed at people or animals. To diagnose this disorder at least three of the 15 behaviors described in the criteria table must be present for a minimum of 12 months, and one consistently for the past 6 months. Because a broad range of behaviors is described and because only a fraction of these must be in evidence, these clients can differ from one another a great deal (APA, 2013; Berkout et al., Frick, 2016).

The fifth edition of the DSM marked the addition of a specifier to CD, the callous and unemotional trait, the implications of which will be discussed later in this chapter. This specifier is applied when a person demonstrates a marked disregard for the feelings or needs of others and is instead focused primarily on the impact of behaviors on themselves.

Pyromania. Pyromania is an impulse disorder and features a fascination with fire and fire setting that is accompanied by either a build-up of tension or emotional arousal that is then satisfied by setting destructive fires. Pyromania is not diagnosed when fires are set in order to exact revenge, hurt another person or to profit in some way. Nor is pyromania diagnosed when fires are set in protest or political demonstration (APA, 2013). Very little research has been done on pyromania, so little is known about its development, how to treat it effectively or its comorbidities. However, a small study of 21 subjects, half of whom were women, found that 62% of the participants also had a comorbid mood disorder and 48% had an additional impulse control disorder at the time of the study, suggesting that the comorbidity rates among those with pyromania may be quite high, though more research is needed to confirm these results (Grant & Won, 2007).

Kleptomania. Kleptomania is also conceptualized as an impulse control disorder and is diagnosed when a person experiences an irresistible urge to take items that ultimately have little or no use to them and have no significant monetary value; in other words, the urge is unrelated to personal gain. As with pyromania, kleptomania is not diagnosed when a client steals out of vengeance, protest or profit (APA, 2013). Grant and Chamberlain (2018) conducted research with a sample of 112 adult participants in an effort to explore contributors to more significant severity of illness in kleptomania. Their research revealed stronger symptom severity in those that also had a comorbid anorexia or OCD diagnosis. Grant and Chamberlain assert that this research suggests that kleptomania may be more closely related to OCD than to the impulse control disorders with which it is currently organized. Much more research will be needed to support this idea and to explore its implications.

Antisocial Personality Disorder (ASPD). ASPD is organized within the cluster "B"personality disorders of the DSM but is also discussed with the impulse and disruptive behavior disorders, largely due to its close relationship to CD. ASPD and CD have very similar diagnostic criteria and are differentiated, in large part, by the age of the client displaying the symptoms. While not all of those diagnosed with CD will eventually develop ASPD, the criteria as written in the current edition of the DSM require a previous diagnosis of CD (criteria "C," p. 659). Some adults who did not have a documented history of conduct symptoms in childhood or adolescence do later meet all but the C criteria, and have been diagnosed with ASPD despite not meeting fully the diagnostic criteria outlined in the DSM. These adult diagnoses without history of CD are not currently sanctioned by the APA but are described in the research literature as "late onset" autism spectrum disorder (ASD) or as acquired sociopathy (DeLisi et al., 2018; Pemment, 2013).

Do persons with late onset ASPD differ from those with a history of CD? The answer to this question may offer direction in the future of the ASPD construct. A survey of the literature conducted by DeLisi et al. (2018) revealed mixed results and

BOX 16.04 EVERYDAY PSYCHOPATHS

Antisocial traits don't always emerge as aggressive or otherwise criminal behavior. Dr. J. Fallon, a professor of human behavior at the University of California, Irvine School of Medicine and author of *The Psychopath Inside* was interviewed by National Public Radio (NPR) in the summer of 2015. In that interview, he describes his research on psychopaths and some of his findings. In this interview, he also explores his personal journey after realizing that he was himself a psychopath and describes his efforts to change. You can find that interview by using the search term "The Scientist and the Psychopath" or by following this address: https://www.npr.org/2015/07/10/421625310/the-scientist-and-the-psychopath

little consensus. A quantity of studies suggest equifinality among these two groups. Equifinality describes a phenomenon in which people with different early experiences, diagnostic profiles or risk factors converge later in life in their expression of a similar diagnostic outcome (Cummings et al., 2002). Surveyed literature suggests that typical and late onset ASPD clients score similarly on measures of impulsivity, irritability, unlawful behavior, non-conformity to social norms, recklessness with self and others, irresponsibility and aggressiveness. However, equally compelling research suggests that those who were first diagnosed with CD before meeting criteria for ASPD demonstrate both more proactive and reactive criminality, may be more sadistic, demonstrate higher levels of egocentricity and so on (DeLisi et al., 2018).

Developmental Psychopathology and the Disruptive, Impulse Control and CDs

Developmental Psychopathology and the Disruptive Disorders. Berkout et al. (2011) frame the developmental context of CD succinctly when they note, "From a contextual developmental perspective, CD can be conceptualized as an antisocial behavioral repertoire shaped by parental use of harsh and inconsistent discipline, with behavioral difficulties leading to failure at school and rejection by normative peers, followed by subsequent association with a deviant peer group and engagement in antisocial actions," (p. 504). Other contextualizing factors also contribute, such as low household income, exposure to violence and the prolonged effects of marginalization, such as racism (Mizock & Harkins, 2011). Together these factors create the fertile ground for difficulties in school, within personal relationships and with those in the greater community. The development of CD also places a client at an elevated risk for the development of other mental health concerns, including ASPD.

Though it is generally assumed that there is a developmental process leading from ODD to CD and later to ASPD, the research supporting this process has been mixed. For example, a longitudinal study of 1,420 participants conducted by Roweet et al., (2010) found that the conversion of ODD to CD was not as common as they had anticipated. Instead, they found that those with pure ODD (no CD symptoms) were more apt to develop emotional disorders while pure CD (those that did not also meet criteria for ODD) was predictive of behavioral disorders later in life. These researchers identified a subtype of ODD featuring "headstrong" and "irritable" traits with a much stronger developmental progression to CD. Similarly, when Burke (2009) conducted a longitudinal study breaking out ODD symptoms into two groups, negative affect (angry, touchy or spiteful) and oppositional symptoms (such as defiance, arguing with adults and losing one's temper) differences in developmental progress emerged. Those with oppositional traits were more apt to develop CD while those with negative affect were more apt to develop depressive symptoms.

The Callous-Unemotional Trait and Its Role in the Progress of CDs. Some researchers suspect that a much stronger predictor of the progression from ODD to CD and to ASPD is the callous-unemotional (CU) trait sometimes present in those with disruptive behavior disorders. This trait has garnered a great deal of attention in the research and several assessment tools contain scales that measure it, such as the Inventory of CU Traits (Paiva-Salisbury et al., 2017). The CU trait features a disposition that is striking in its lack of empathy for others and an absence of remorse for wrongdoing (Frick et al., 2016; Masi et al., 2018). In fact, researchers have found this trait to be predictive, irrespective of whether or not a CD is present (Frick et al., 2003; Frick & White, 2008). Clinicians will want to note that research also suggests that CU traits are not as stable over time as once thought; more often than not, these traits decrease over time. CU traits also seem to be responsive to treatment intervention in many, though in those in which these traits persist, outcomes are poorer (Masi et al., 2018). Recent research mapping the neurobiology of the CU trait suggests a unique neural pathway from deficits in empathy to CD, research that links behavioral observational research with neuroscience (Moulet et al., 2018).

Narcissism. Another trait seen in a subset of clients with disruptive behavior disorders is narcissism. These clients present with grandiosity, manipulation, deceit and egocentricity. This trait seems to have the strongest correlation with unprovoked aggression and aggression used to maintain dominance over others. People who score high on measures of narcissism also seem to be more hypervigilant to cues indicative of social distress. A third trait, impulsivity/irresponsibility, which describes a pattern of disinhibition and a tendency to seek out novel and often risky behaviors, has been closely correlated with reactive aggression (Masi et al., 2018).

As noted earlier, increasingly people are diagnosed with ASPD though they do not meet the "C" criterion for the disorder stipulating a history of CD before the age of 15. DeLisi et al. (2018) examined archival data including early mental health records of 865 persons currently in the correctional system, adults diagnosed with ASPD without a history of CD. They found that a number of disorders increased the likelihood of an ASPD diagnosis without a history of CD: ADHD by 75%, frotteurism by 311%, bipolar I by 328% and sexual sadism by an alarming 1,033%. While the DSM seems to conceptualize these ODD, CD and ASPD almost as if they were the same disorder expressed differently at different stages across the lifespan, research like that conducted by DeLisi et al. (2018), Rowe et al. (2010) and by Burke (2009) points to a more subtle or nuanced relationship.

Diathesis Stress Models of Development. As noted above, research strongly suggests that early experiences of maltreatment have negative consequences for brain development which, in turn, negatively impacts a host of developmental processes, including the ability to regulate emotion and control impulses. A diathesis-stress model, one in which a latent genetic predisposition holds the potential for a particular trait or set of traits is then triggered by environmental factors, is frequently used to explain conduct and impulse disorders. In this case, early maltreatment contributes one of the stressors that activate the biological contributors to conduct and/or impulse difficulties (McCrory et al., 2010). Some of these biological contributors may include structural neural deficits that may impede empathy (Sterzer et al., 2007), Alternatively or in addition, hypoactive amygdala function may contribute (Jones et al., 2009).

Three primary systems, the hypothalamus–pituitary–adrenal system (HPA axis), the autonomic nervous system (ANS), of which the polyvegal nerve system is a part and the serotonergic system (SS) control three key domains thought to be central in the development of CD, punishment and reward processing and cognitive control over impulses. Matthys et al., (2013) argue that for a person to operate in a way that is socially congruent, all three domains must be functioning well; a deficit in any of these areas may increase the potential for the development of a disruptive behavior disorder.

The Skilled Diagnostician

Differential Diagnosis of ODD, IED and Normative Behavior. A host of mental health professionals have expressed concerns that the APA and the DSM have lost sight of the difference between pathology and normal responses to life's challenging moments (Frances, 2013; Keenan & Wakschlag, 2004). Exploring this question, Keenan and Wakschlag (2004) acknowledge that very young children are prone to tantrums when tired, hungry or stressed and pose the question, can an ODD diagnosis be appropriately applied to very young children? In order to answer this question, these researchers explored differences between children aged 2.5-5.5 who had been referred for mental health services and those who were not. They found that very young referred children did, in fact, differ from non-referred children in the rates of CD symptoms present. While non-referred children had a base rate of symptoms ranging from 0% to 8%, the referred children's base rates ranged from 31.6% to 72.2%. Keenan and Wakschlag argue that while behavior problems such as defiance, dishonesty and tantrums are evident in non-referred children, the difference in the degree to which these symptoms are manifested are large enough to lend ODD discriminative validity. Still, caution should be used in diagnosing very young children with behavioral disorders. An unwarranted diagnosis can create for a child a self-fulling prophecy or an identity as unruly or bad, while failure to acknowledge and address difficulties in managing behaviors and emotion can lead to a significant and life-long burden to that child's physical and mental health.

Concerns Regarding the Broadening of the IED Diagnostic Criteria. In contrast to findings affirming the validity of ODD, concerns have been voiced regarding the diagnosis of IED. IED underwent changes in the DSM 5 that significantly broadened the scope of behaviors that could be included within this diagnosis. The DSM IV criteria required that loss of control be evidenced by instances of physical aggression or the destruction of property. The DSM 5, however, did away with this criteria specificity. The current criteria require verbal or physical aggression a minimum of twice a week for 3 months. Doing the math, 24 verbally aggressive outbursts in the span of 3 months without any evidence of physical aggression or of damage to property would satisfy criteria, provided they were not pre-meditated and were out of proportion with a given situation. Some authors assert that this broadened criteria will result in an overdiagnosis of the disorder (Wakefield, 2016).

Cultural Considerations in Diagnosing CDs. Mizock and Harkins (2011) note that youth of color, especially African American and Latinx, particularly those from urban areas and low-income families, are diagnosed disproportionately with CDs. They further note that once diagnosed these youths have poorer outcomes than White counterparts. Studies spanning decades indicate that given the same behavioral symptoms, White clients are more apt to be diagnosed with adjustment disorders, mood, anxiety or developmental disorders than their Latinx or African American counterparts (Mizock & Harkins, 2011; Schwartz & Feisthamel, 2009).

The reader will note in the following pages that the appropriate differential diagnosis of the conduct and impulse spectrum of disorders and those of mood, anxiety, adjustment and developmental disorders can be complex and have the potential to be clouded by bias. Being aware of one's own stereotypes of racial groups different from your own when diagnosing is an essential first step in removing bias from your diagnostic process. A second step is to cultivate a strong working understanding of the different ways that cultural groups may frame and describe behaviors and subjective symptoms and to note how you may be interpreting or misinterpreting these descriptions.

Nearly all of the diagnoses of the DSM 5 contain an exclusion criterion within the criteria table itself designed to remind the reader to avoid cultural bias in diagnosis or to consider other diagnostic possibilities before making a final clinical decision, the "not better accounted for" criteria. The CD criteria table, however, is comprised exclusively of symptoms and specifiers and it is not until three pages later in the manual, in only two sentences, that the reader is cautioned to take context into consideration as a primary causal factor for the client's behavior (APA, 2013, see p. 474). As mentioned earlier, several contextualizing factors that raise the risk for developing behavioral symptoms should be taken into consideration before considering a CD: socioeconomic status, exposure to violence and a history of victimization and racial discrimination (Mizock & Harkins, 2011).

Gender Differences in CD. Research reveals that statistically male clients are much more likely to develop antisocial behaviors (such as physical and relational aggression, oppositional behavior and criminal acts): 10:1 in early onset CD and 5:1 in late onset (Fontain et al., in Berkout et al., 2011) and consequently are much more likely to go on to be diagnosed with a CD. Differences in male and female early childhood aggression ratings have been documented indicating that the propensity to develop CDs begins early in life. Perhaps two key differences emerge in comparing the manifestation of CD among boys and girls: first, research suggests that boys score higher on physically aggressive manifestations of CD than do girls, but some research suggests that they score similarly on relational aggression, lying, stealing and so on (Berkout et al., 2011; Tiet et al., 2001). Another important difference that is being explored is the assertion that while girls are less likely to develop CD overall, those that do seem to develop more problems related to the disorder. In their study of over 300 boys and girls, ages 4-18, Tiet et al. (2001), explored gender and age effects on the expression of conduct problems. These researchers found that girls tended to have fewer conduct problems overall; however, when comparing high-risk boys and girls, girls seemed to have more pervasive problems, something the researchers described as a "gender paradox."

Differential Diagnosis of ODD and Depression. Children who experience depression may also evidence negative affect, irritability and may resist adult authority. Frances (2013) notes that developmentally, children have few outlets for expressing pain and anger than to tantrum and act out. When symptoms consistent with ODD appear exclusively in the context of depression, the additional diagnosis of ODD should **not** be given.

Differential Diagnosis of ODD and Adjustment Disorder with Disturbance of Conduct, and Complex Trauma. Adjustment disorder with a disturbance of conduct can resemble ODD. For example, when a child or adolescent is placed in foster care and foster parents and teachers notice irritable mood, persistent angry outbursts, defiance and reluctance to take responsibility for behavior, there may be a temptation to apply an ODD diagnosis. In cases of significant transition or trauma, even if this behavior continues for 6 months, diagnosis of an adjustment disorder is often the more appropriate. However, ongoing trauma can result in ODD that is sustained long after the trauma has ended, in which case post-traumatic stress disorder (PTSD) and ODD should be considered.

Again, in the best of circumstances, children have few avenues of emotional outlet besides protest and defiance and are still learning healthy and effective methods of managing painful emotions and overwhelming situations (Frances, 2013). However, when early childhood is marked by substandard care and trauma, impairments are thought to follow. The survival model describes a domino effect that is believed to unfold when children experience repeated early trauma that then leads to ODD behavior. This process is thought to unfold in three steps: (1) childhood victimization; (2) a deterioration of emotion regulation capacities coupled with diminished ability to process social cues (described as "survival coping") and (3) two-fold symptom development of oppositional and defiant behaviors paired with symptoms of trauma (described in this model as "victim coping") (Ford, 2002). Currently, the DSM has not adopted a complex trauma diagnosis that would include behavioral symptoms. Consequently, children and adolescents with complex trauma who display these symptoms are diagnosed with PTSD and a comorbid ODD. The differential diagnosis of adjustment with conduct, ODD or PTSD with ODD is complicated to parse out and should be made balancing best fit and least stigmatizing diagnosis considerations in mind. Consultation is recommended.

Differential Diagnosis of ADHD and ODD. Children with ADHD can develop a pattern of failing to follow directions given by parents and teachers particularly in settings where there is a demand for sustained attention. These children may fail to follow directions because their attention is somewhere else and they may not register the instructions, or they may lose track of what they are doing and fail to follow through. This failure to remain on task and attentive to instructions can be mistaken for a pattern of refusal to cooperate and then misdiagnosed as ODD. Frequently, however, ADHD and ODD are comorbid; ADHD is estimated to occur in 14%-40% of those diagnosed with ODD (Nock et al., 2007; Riley et al., 2016). In these children and teens, threads of both patterns are in evidence. In other words, the client at times legitimately fails to attend to instructions and at other times refuses to cooperate with directions. Discerning which diagnosis is the best fit, or if both diagnoses are appropriate can be a challenging task. You will want to give some thought to a few of the following before deciding the best diagnosis for your client:

1. After listing your client's symptoms, signs and behaviors, consider whether your client would most appropriately be diagnosed with both ADHD and ODD together. Ask yourself, "How would this client's behavior and temperament be different if ADHD were not in evidence? How about CD? Would your client's diagnostic picture change significantly?" These questions

may help to decide if one or the other diagnosis is sufficient rather than assigning both.

2. American Counseling Association (ACA) ethics establish an expectation that clients will not be harmed by the diagnosis or the diagnostic process (E.5.d, ACA, 2014, p. 11), suggesting that when a less stigmatizing diagnosis (or no diagnosis at all) would be appropriate, then clinicians should select that option. ADHD is probably the less stigmatized diagnostic label of either ADHD or ODD. If ADHD would fully account for your client's symptoms, ADHD is the better diagnostic option.

3. It is important to remember that medications used to treat ADHD, methylphenidate or Amphetamine, hold a small but not insignificant risk for the development of symptoms of psychosis, increasing the risk that would come with a misdiagnosis of ADHD (Moran et al., 2019).

4. Remember that you don't need to make difficult diagnostic decisions alone. Careful consultation with a well-informed supervisor or colleague with expertise, the use of assessments, including assessments for teachers and parents, will all support stronger diagnostic decision-making. Transparency with parents and education about the use and risks of medications will also strengthen your confidence in diagnostic decisions.

Differential Diagnosis of Pyromania, Kleptomania and CD. In CD, children and adolescents frequently commit acts of property destruction, which may include setting fire to something in order to destroy it. Theft and deceitfulness are also common in clients with CD. Though it is possible for a client to have a comorbid diagnosis of pyromania or kleptomania, these later diagnoses can be distinguished from the behaviors arising from CDs in the feeling tone behind the actions. People who struggle with pyromania or kleptomania have a difficulty that seems to be seated in impulsivity. For these clients, an urge arises, tension builds and is relieved by either setting fires (pyromania) or taking an item (kleptomania). For the person with a CD, the fire setting is generally driven by anger, while the theft is driven by impulsive self-satisfaction or negative emotion. When vengeance or anger are behind these actions, they are attributed to CD and pyromania and kleptomania are ruled out (APA, 2013).

IED in Adulthood. Though IED is most often diagnosed in childhood or adolescence, diagnosis of adults is also appropriate. Adult clients who evidence frequent outbursts can suffer significant consequences to their relationships both personally, professionally and within the community. Note the following case example, Dierdre.

Deirdre, 52, has had trouble keeping a job for more than a year at a time, due to frequent conflicts in the workplace, and describes being very irritated with other people's 'mamby-pamby-beating-around-the-bush.' Deirdre prefers a more direct way of communicating with others that many find abrasive. However, what gets Deirdre into trouble in most of her relationships is her tendency to 'fly off the handle' at the least

BOX 16.05 DIFFERENTIAL DIAGNOSIS: DISRUPTIVE, CONDUCT AND IMPULSE

Reading through the following examples, decide whether the best fit diagnosis is more likely pyromania, kleptomania, conduct disorder or if no diagnosis should be given. What questions would you ask in order to confirm your hunch?

Cooper: Gazing into the top drawer of his desk, Cooper looks with puzzlement at the pile of useless objects assembled there: a lipstick, a pair of nail scissors, a duck call, a paperweight from a state he has never visited, a key fob representing a university he did not attend. "All this useless junk . . . why do I take this shit?" Cooper can't remember when he first began taking things, it had been a long time, that much he knew. But there was something about acting on the impulse to steal little things that was a source of instant relief. Still, he wished he could stop.

Mike: Mike, 18, and his friends have been working on an effort to stop a pipeline from being constructed near their town's main water source. Mike's involvement in the efforts to stop the pipeline began as a school project but grew to be a passion and singular focus of his growing concerns about the environment. However, Mike and his community members were not able to stop the construction and a month earlier, workers began clearing space to lay the pipe. One evening, Mike and his friends drove to the site and set fire to the trucks and destroyed the fencing around the project. Mike is facing charges for destruction of property.

Pim: Pim likes to slip out to his father's shed and spend time alone. His father has cleared a space on the workbench for Pim to try his hand at woodworking. Over the past few years, however, Pim has been burning bits of wood and other materials when he is alone. He finds that when he has been feeling tense, burning things seems to help, though he can't explain why. Pim's father was furious and concerned when recently one of Pim's fires got out of control and badly damaged the shed and caused minor smoke damage to the house.

Sheela: Sheela, 16, had been eyeing her sister's state swim trophy for weeks. Martha had only just begun competing in swim this year but already she was ranked in the top five in the state. Her parents were very proud of Martha and everyone had made a big deal of her trophy. Sheela, who had a difficult year, had been suspended from school twice and in and out of other kinds of trouble much of the year. Thinking of all the praise her sister got while she was constantly criticized made her so angry she was beside herself. Sheila took Martha's trophy, burned it in the fire pit on the patio, and then returned the charred trophy to the mantle where she found it. She felt a rush of pleasure when she heard her sister's dismay at finding the trophy.

Source: American Psychiatric Association (2013).

provocation; it is these incidents that generally lead to her being fired. She has also had run-ins with people in the community while doing weekly errands. Deirdre shares, 'Just last Tuesday I was at the superstore downtown and some idiot forgot to take down the sale sign on their steaks before they changed the price in the computer. When I was in the aisle they looked like they were on sale and so I filled up my cart. Well when I got to the check-out and they rang it up it was something like $50 more than it should have been. I hit the roof! The lady said she was sorry and all that, but I told her,

You're god-damned right you should be sorry! What the hell kind of business are you running here anyway?! I told her I wanted the price I saw in the aisle. But she wouldn't give it to me so I yelled at her to shove that meat where the sun don't shine, and then I turned the cart over and just left. When I went back in on Thursday they told me I wasn't welcome. So yeh. I've got a short fuse for sure and could use some help with it.'

The Likelihood of a Dual Diagnosis. When assessing clients with symptoms of ODD, clinicians should be aware that the comorbidity rates for these clients is quite high. In their study of the prevalence and correlates of ODD, Nock et al. (2007) found that of participants with lifetime ODD, a full 92% also met criteria for another lifetime disorder (p. 706). Chief among these disorders were ADHD, CD or other impulse control disorder, substance use disorders, bipolar disorder and OCD (Nock et al., 2007; Riley et al., 2016).

Treatment for CDs

Intervention Approaches: Parent-Focused versus Client Interventions. For children and adolescents with CD particularly, interventions that include parents and offer parenting skills (sometimes referred to as parent management training or PMT) may be especially important given the role that parenting styles seem to play in the development of ODD, CD and ASPD (Berkout et al., 2011; Sukhodolsky et al., 2016). PMT interventions are aimed at softening harsh parenting styles, and to ameliorate parenting approaches that will lead to tantruming and other negative behaviors in the first place, while increasing consistency (Sukhodolsky et al., 2016). The efficacy of interventions that include parents is supported by decades of research literature. For example, an often cited study, Webster-Stratton and Hammond (1997) compared interventions with 97 families aimed at improving behavior in children with early onset conduct problems. This research compared outcomes between those clients offered parent training, those offered client training and those that offered both parent and client training. Though parent training offered benefits over client training and vice versa, it comes as little surprise that those who were offered both interventions had the better outcomes of either group. Ultimately, intervention programs for CDs that include or are exclusive to parents have proliferated. By way of example, home-based family counseling models, such as multisystemic therapy, are supported by research that suggests efficacy with adolescents with a history of juvenile offenses (Curtis et al., 2004; Hammond & Czyszczon, 2014; Schaeffer & Borduin, 2005).

Key Features for Successful Intervention. With so many different parent training models and home-based approaches available, it can be difficult to find the right approach for your client. Kaminski et al., (2008) conducted an extensive survey of the literature exploring programs that include parents and found that parent training programs with the best outcomes shared key features. First, the most effective programs supported parents in cultivating consistency in parenting and developing more positive parent–child relationships by requiring parents to practice skills with their children. It should be noted that programs that taught parents to support their child's social skills had smaller effect sizes. These authors concluded that parent training programs do seem to be effective in reducing early childhood behavior problems but can also be beneficial to the parents. Programs that included emotional communication skills and practicing with their children, those that included supporting children with academic skills, problem-solving or attaining ancillary services have also shown efficacy.

Cognitive Behavioral Therapies (CBT) for Disruptive, Impulse and CDs. CBT has been utilized extensively in the treatment of both conduct and impulse control disorders. Ample research supports the efficacy of CBT in a variety of formats and modes of delivery. Findings from meta-analysis of these studies conclude that CBT is an effective treatment for ADHD, ODD and the reduction of externalizing symptoms generally, particularly when included with multimodal approaches. CBT for externalizing disorders includes interventions that address emotional awareness, perspective taking, problem-solving, anger management and goal development (Battagliese et al., 2015; Lochman et al., Sukhodolsky et al., 2016).

Sukhodolsky et al. (2016) point out that combining post-traumatic model (PTM) and CBT models may be especially efficacious because each works on different contributors to the problem. While PTMs shape parenting skills and likely work to strengthen the parent–child relationship, CBT works to address deficits in emotion regulation and problem-solving skills that are characteristically problematic for these clients. Consequently, using both approaches together is a best practice recommendation. However, in a study of clients with comorbid conduct and depressive disorders, researchers found that CBT was more effective in addressing depression than it was in treating the conduct symptoms, leading researchers to caution that when treating children and adolescents with comorbid disorders it is important to be certain that the interventions specifically address both disorders (Rohde et al., 2004).

Cavanagh et al. (2017) argue that ODD specifically may be better understood as a deficit in the capacity for emotion regulation and assert that interventions designed at shoring up executive functioning skills may best serve these children and adolescents. Recall that executive functioning skills include the capacity to gather and sustain needed focus and attention, plan, stay on task and manage steps of a process, and monitor and manage one's emotions, skills that have the potential to support children through difficult emotional upheavals and in completing the tasks asked of them.

Definitional Cases in Disruptive, Impulse Control and CDs

Jackson

Jackson, age 4, struggles to maintain his temper and often seems angry and resentful. Jackson has a tendency to argue with parents and his daycare workers, and offers resistance to most directions or requests from adults.

TABLE 16.01 Pivot Points: Disruptive, Impulse Control and Conduct Disorders

	Consider this Diagnosis
Pivot Point One: Are your client's concerns rooted in difficulties controlling impulses?	
• Are your client's difficulties primarily related to controlling outbursts of verbal or behavioral aggression?	Intermittent Explosive Disorder
• Is your client having difficulty resulting from an inability to resist the impulse to set fires?	Pyromania
• Do your client's difficulties arise out of an inability to resist the impulse to take unneeded items or items of little worth?	Kleptomania
• Do your client's impulse control difficulties seem to be related to hyperactivity?	Attention Deficit/Hyperactivity Disorder
• Do your client's difficulties controlling impulses co-occur with symptoms suggestive of the autism spectrum, such as repetitive behavior or narrow interests?	Autism Spectrum Disorder
Pivot Point Two: Do your client's struggles include difficulty extending respect to others or intruding on the rights of others?	
• Has your client developed a habit of acting in opposition to parents and other adults?	Oppositional Defiant Disorder
• Do your client's behavioral problems follow an identifiable stressor, such as placement in foster care, significant loss, illness etc.	Adjustment Disorder, with Disturbance of Conduct
• Does your client's behavior regularly violate the rights of others?	Conduct Disorder
• Has your adult client developed a life-long pattern of taking advantage of and harming others, while violating social norms and laws without remorse?	Antisocial Personality Disorder
Pivot Point Three: Do your client's defiant behaviors and tantrums occur exclusively in the context of anxiety?	Social Anxiety Disorder
Pivot Point Four: Does your client's defiant behavior and tantrums occur exclusively during episodes of mood?	Depressive Disorders or Bipolar Disorders
Pivot Point Five: Is your client struggling with symptoms characteristic of a conduct or impulse disorder but does not meet full criteria for any of these? Would you like to specify the reason criteria are not fully met?	Other Specified Disruptive, Impulse Control and Conduct Disorder
Pivot Point Six: Is your client's struggle characteristic of an impulse or conduct disorder, but you don't have enough information to justify a diagnosis?	Unspecified Disruptive, Impulse Control and Conduct Disorder

Lena

Lena, age 30, regularly sets fires in order to relieve tensions that build over the week. She would like to stop but finds she can't.

Ethan

When Ethan, age 12, becomes frustrated, he often has difficulty containing an outburst. Ethan is not, however, deliberately non-compliant and his overall demeanor is usually content and cooperative.

Anika

For several years, Anika has struggled against the urge to take trivial items of almost no value. She reports feeling a building tension until she finally takes an item.

Eric

Eric, 14, has for several years engaged in behaviors that consistently violate the rights of others, and has encountered legal problems and alienated classmates and family as a consequence.

Narrative Cases in Disruptive, Impulse Control and CDs

Jude (age 6)

Jude's parents, Ed and Sarah, have brought him to counseling following 2 years of trying a number of different parenting interventions and seeking several consultations for Jude's behavior. Ed and Sarah report that "Jude is a delight most of the time, but several times a week he loses it completely." Sara adds, "I know that children have tantrums and two or three tantrums a week may not sound like a lot but it is the quality of the meltdowns that worry us. A lot of the time it is in response to the smallest thing, but it is followed by a violent outburst, sometimes screaming and biting. And it is always just out of the blue, there doesn't seem to be a way to predict when it will happen. The tantrums seem to surprise him as much as us." Ed offers, "If we are really honest, these meltdowns and explosions are putting us on edge. We would like to have another child but right now we just don't have the energy to give to another child, so we are thinking about how this is impacting the family but we are also worried about the way that Jude is starting to think about himself. He doesn't have any other bad behaviors, nothing else is worrying us about his mood, but he is starting to think of himself as a bad kid and that can't be good for him. Can you help us help Jude?"

Kris

An unusual string of small fires on municipal properties broke out in a coastal village in Maine. After a town hall meeting and increased vigilance on the part of the citizens, the community was shocked to learn that Kris,16, the junior class president and SPCA volunteer had been setting the fires. The sheriff and key city administrators decided to initiate a restorative justice process with Kris. As step one of the process, he was asked to speak at the next town hall to describe what had prompted his behavior and to listen to the impact it had on the community. During the town hall, Kris explained that he had been fascinated with fire for as long as he could remember. He further explained, "I used to fish birthday candles out of the trash and burn them in my room, or go out into my fort in the wooded area behind my house and burn little things. I love the smell, the heat and the sound, everything about it. I noticed later that when I was stressed that I could just feel the pressure building inside my body, setting fires seemed to make the feeling go away almost immediately and replaced it with a surge of adrenaline. But it got out of hand, and I'm sorry. I know I could have hurt someone and I know I let all of you down." Kris has no history of other impulsive behaviors and has never had conduct problems at home or at school.

Crystal

Crystal, 9, is in the school counselor's office at the request of her classroom teacher who reports that she has witnessed Crystal "deliberately annoy" other students by pinching them when Crystal believes the teacher is not watching, though she often blames other children for this behavior and for other behaviors that she is herself responsible for. Consequently, she draws a good deal of negative attention from teachers and peers. Crystal has a reputation for being a bit "touchy" and can quickly become cross with her peers and others. In her most difficult moments, she flatly refuses to cooperate with classroom rules or to participate in classroom activities. Though her experiences at school are marked with conflict, she appears to do well in her after-school gymnastics class and gets along well with her coach. However, Crystal has a great deal of difficulty making friends and other children tend to give her a wide berth. Crystal does not seem to meet criteria for a mood disorder and takes no medication. Crystal's teacher shares, "I just don't know what to do with this kid. I checked her file and she was doing this stuff last year, too. I don't know what else to try, maybe you can come up with something?"

Bruce

Bruce, age 15, was recently accused of forcing his way into his neighbor's home and robbing them while threatening them with a baseball bat and is facing charges for this incident. Bruce's school record is marked by a long history of disciplinary action and suspensions for bullying and often finds himself in fights with his classmates. A year ago, Bruce was in a fight with a younger boy, breaking the boy's rib and in a second incident, Bruce assaulted another boy with a skateboard, which left the other teen with a concussion. After the second incident, Bruce was placed in an alternative educational setting where, his parents note, he "learned several new tricks for misusing other's trust and injuring people he views as vulnerable."

The beginning of Bruce's life was filled with emotional and physical violence. When he was 5 years old, he was removed from his biological mother's home by social services following founded allegations of abuse and neglect. Bruce was adopted by his foster parents when he was 7 years old after several unsuccessful foster placements. He has not learned to trust others and, his parents share, "He seems to hold most of the world with contempt."

"From the beginning Bruce had a lot of trouble controlling his temper, we expected that, but we also really hoped it would get better with lots of love. But he seemed to delight in being cruel to other children and sometimes to animals as well. At first, we made excuses for it and sometimes looked the other way hoping that he would slowly recover from his time with his biological parents. But he didn't seem to," his mother shares. In the past few years, Bruce has become increasingly dishonest with his mother and has taken money from her purse without permission. Also worrisome to his parents is the fact that Bruce's school performance has been in steady decline. Bruce's mother reports that she can't remember Bruce ever showing regret for having hurt someone, though he does sometimes seem concerned that he will get into trouble.

Felicia

Felicia, 21, has lived a privileged life filled with travel and opportunity. The daughter of diplomats, Felicia has seen much of the world and admits that she has never really wanted for anything. One morning while in an open market in Istanbul with her mother, she took a small trinket from a display table and slipped it into her pocket and walked on. When she and her mother sat down at a local cafe, her mother confronted Felicia, telling her that she had seen her take the item and had stayed back and paid for the item. "Why? Why Felicia, do you do this? Help me understand." Staring into her coffee and blushing, Felicia shares, "I am utterly perplexed and completely ashamed of the stealing. But I can't explain it . . . I wish I could. I can tell you what happens though. Sometimes when I'm out somewhere, especially if it is noisy and very stimulating, I can feel a tension building and my body starts to kind of tingle, though that doesn't really capture it. Then the body feeling just kind of builds until I release it and the only way I know how to do that is to take something. So I swipe some odd thing, often it doesn't matter what it is, but it never amounts to anything pretty, useful or even remotely valuable. I feel guilty afterward and want to hide. I'm confused and disappointed in myself but no matter what I try I can't seem to prevent myself from taking little nothings. I'm sorry, it's been going on for years and I really want to stop."

References

American Counseling Association. (2014). *ACA code of ethics*. Author.

American Psychiatric Association. (2013). Disruptive, impulse & conduct disorders. In *Diagnostic and statistical manual of mental disorders: Diagnostic and statistical manual of mental disorders* (5th ed.). Author.

Barkley, R. (2013). *Taking charge of ADHD, 3rd edition: The complete authoritative guide for parents*. Guilford Press.

Battagliese, G., Caccetta, M., Luppino, O. I., Baglioni, C., Cardi, V., Mancini, F., Buonanno,C., 2015. Cognitive-behavioral therapy for externalizing disorders: A meta-analysis of treatment effectiveness. *Behaviour Research and Therapy*, *75*, 60–71. https://doi.org/10.1016/j.brat.2015.10.008

Berkout, O. V., Young, J. N., & Gross, A. M. (2011). Mean girls and bad boys: Recent research on gender differences in conduct disorder. *Aggression and Violent Behavior*, *16*(6), 503–511. https://doi.org/10.1016/j.avb.2011.06.001

Burke, J. D. (2009). The relationship between conduct disorder and oppositional defiant disorder and their continuity with antisocial behaviors: Evidence from longitudinal clinical studies. In *Externalizing disorders of childhood: Refining the research agenda for DSM-V*. American Psychiatric Association.

Cavanagh, M., Quinn, D., Duncan, D., Graham, T., & Balbuena, L. (2017). Oppositional defiant disorder is better conceptualized as a disorder of emotional regulation. *Journal of Attention Disorders*, *21*(5), 381–389. https://doi.org/10.1177/1087054713520221

Copeland, W. E., Shanahan, L., Costello, E. J., & Angold, A. (2009). Childhood and adolescent psychiatric disorders as predictors of young adult disorders. *Archives of General Psychiatry*, *66*(7), 764–772. https://doi.org/10.1001/archgenpsychiatry.2009.85

Cummings, E. M., Davies, P. T., & Campbell, S. B. (2002). *Developmental psychopathology and family process: Theory, research & clinical implications*. Guilford Press.

Curtis, N. M., Ronan, K. R., & Borduin, C. M. (2004). Multisystemic treatment: A meta-analysis of outcome studies. *Journal of Family Psychology*, *18*(3), 411. https://doi.org/10.1037/0893-3200.18.3.411

DeLisi, M., Drury, A. J., Caropreso, D., Heinrichs, T., Tahja, K. N., & Elbert, M. J. (2018). Antisocial personality disorder with or without antecedent conduct disorder: The differences are psychiatric and paraphilic. *Criminal Justice and Behavior*, *45*(6), 902–917. https://doi.org/10.1177/0093854818765593

Ford, J. D. (2002). Traumatic victimization in childhood and persistent problems with oppositional-defiance. *Journal of Aggression, Maltreatment and Trauma*, *11*, 25–58.

Frances, A. (2013). *Saving normal: An insider's revolt against out-of-control psychiatric diagnosis, DSM-5, big pharma, and the medicalization of ordinary life*. William Morrow.

Frick, P. J. (2016). Current research on conduct disorder in children and adolescents. *South African Journal of Psychology*, *46*(2), 160–174. https://doi.org/10.1177/0081246316628455

Frick, P. J., Cornell, A. H., Bodin, S. D., Dane, H. E., Barry, C. T., & Loney, B. R. (2003). Callous-unemotional traits and developmental pathways to severe conduct problems. *Developmental Psychology*, *39*(2), 246. https://doi.org/10.1037/0012-1649.39.2.246

Frick, P. J., & White, S. F., (2008). Research review: The importance of callous-unemotional traits for developmental models of aggressive and antisocial behavior. *Journal of Child Psychology and Psychiatry*, *49*(4), 359–375. https://doi.org/10.1111/j.1469-7610.2007.01862.x

Grant, J. E., & Chamberlain, S. R. (2018). Symptom severity and its clinical correlates in kleptomania. *Annals of Clinical Psychiatry: Official Journal of the American Academy of Clinical Psychiatrists*, *30*(2), 97.

Grant, J. E., & Won, S. K. (2007). Clinical characteristics and psychiatric comorbidity of pyromania. *The Journal of Clinical Psychiatry*, *68*(11), 1717–1722. https://doi.org/10.4088/JCP.v68n1111

Hammond, C., & Czyszczon, G. (2014). Home-based family counseling: An emerging field in need of professionalization. *The Family Journal*, *22*(1), 56–61. https://doi.org/10.1177/1066480713505055

Jones, A. P., Laurens, K. R., Herba, C. M., Barker, G. J., & Viding, E. (2009). Amygdala hypoactivity to fearful faces in boys with conduct problems and callous-unemotional traits. *American Journal of Psychiatry*, *166*(1), 95–102. https://doi.org/10.1176/appi.ajp.2008.07071050

Kaminski, J. W., Valle, L. A., Filene, J. H., & Boyle, C. L. (2008). A meta-analytic review of components associated with parent training program effectiveness. *Journal of Abnormal Child Psychology*, *36*(4), 567–589. https://doi.org/10.1007/s10802-007-9201-9

Keenan, K., & Wakschlag, L. S. (2004). Are oppositional defiant and conduct disorder symptoms normative behaviors in preschoolers? A comparison of referred and nonreferred children. *American Journal of Psychiatry*, *161*(2), 356–358. https://doi.org/10.1176/appi.ajp.161.2.356

Kessler, R. C., Coccaro, E. F., Fava, M., Jaeger, S., Jin, R., & Walters, E. (2006). The prevalence and correlates of DSM-IV intermittent explosive disorder in the national comorbidity survey replication. *Archives of General Psychiatry*, *63*(6), 669–678. https://doi.org/10.1001/archpsyc.63.6.669

Lochman, J. E., Powell, N. P., Boxmeyer, C. L., & Jimenez-Camargo, L. (2011). Cognitive-behavioral therapy for externalizing disorders in children and adolescents. *Child and Adolescent Psychiatric Clinics*, *20*(2), 305–318. https://doi.org/10.1016/j.chc.2011.01.005

Masi, G., Milone, A., Brovedani, P., Pisano, S., & Muratori, P. (2018). Psychiatric evaluation of youths with disruptive behavior disorders and psychopathic traits: A critical review of assessment measures. *Neuroscience & Biobehavioral Reviews*, *91*, 21–33. https://doi.org/10.1016/j.neubiorev.2016.09.023

Matthys, W., Vanderschuren, L. J., & Schutter, D. J. (2013). The neurobiology of oppositional defiant disorder and conduct disorder: Altered functioning in three mental domains. *Development and Psychopathology*, *25*(1), 193–207. https://doi.org/10.1017/S0954579412000272

McCloskey, M. S., Kleabir, K., Berman, M. E., Chen, E. Y., & Coccaro, E. F. (2010). Unhealthy aggression: Intermittent explosive disorder and adverse physical health outcomes. *Health Psychology*, *29*(3), 324. https://doi.org/10.1037/a0019072

McCrory, E., De Brito, S. A., & Viding, E. (2010). Research review: The neurobiology and genetics of maltreatment and adversity. *Journal of Child Psychology and Psychiatry*, *51*(10), 1079–1095. https://doi.org/10.1111/j.1469-7610.2010.02271.x

Mischel, W. (2015). *The marshmallow test: Why self-control is the engine of success*. Little Brown & Company.

Mizock, L., & Harkins, D. (2011). Diagnostic bias and conduct disorder: Improving culturally sensitive diagnosis. *Child & Youth Services*, *32*(3), 243–253. https://doi.org/10.1080/0145935X.2011.605315

Moran, L. V., Ongur, D., Hsu, J., Castro, V. M., Perlis, R. H., & Schneeweiss, S. (2019). Psychosis with methylphenidate or amphetamine in patients with ADHD. *New England Journal of Medicine*, *380*(12), 1128–1138. https://doi.org/10.1056/NEJMoa1813751

Moul, C., Hawes, D. J., & Dadds, M. R. (2018). Mapping the developmental pathways of child conduct problems through the neurobiology of empathy. *Neuroscience & Biobehavioral Reviews*, *91*, 34–50. https://doi.org/10.1016/j.neubiorev.2017.03.016

National Public Radio. (2015, July 10). *The scientist and the psychopath*. Snap Judgement. https://www.npr.org/2015/07/10/421625310/the-scientist-and-the-psychopath

Nock, M. K., Kazdin, A. E., Hiripi, E., & Kessler, R. C. (2007). Lifetime prevalence, correlates, and persistence of oppositional defiant disorder: Results from the national comorbidity survey replication. *Journal of Child Psychology and Psychiatry*, *48*(7), 703–713. https://doi.org/10.1111/j.1469-7610.2007.01733.x

Paiva-Salisbury, M. L., Gill, A. D., & Stickle, T. R. (2017). Isolating trait and method variance in the measurement of callous and unemotional traits. *Assessment*, *24*(6), 763–771. https://doi.org/10.1177/1073191115624546

Pemment, J. (2013). Psychopathy versus sociopathy: Why the distinction has become crucial. *Aggression and Violent Behavior*, *18*(5), 458–461. https://doi.org/10.1016/j.avb.2013.07.001

Riley, M., Ahmed, S., & Locke, A. (2016). Common questions about oppositional defiant disorder. *American Family Physician*, *93*(7), 586–591.

Rohde, P., Clarke, G. N., Mace, D. E., Jorgensen, J. S., & Seeley, J. R. (2004). An efficacy/effectiveness study of cognitive-behavioral treatment for adolescents with comorbid major depression and conduct disorder. *Journal of the American Academy of Child & Adolescent Psychiatry*, *43*(6), 660–668. https://doi.org/10.1097/01.chi.0000121067.29744.41

Rowe, R., Costello, E. J., Angold, A., Copeland, W. E., & Maughan, B. (2010). Developmental pathways in oppositional defiant disorder and conduct disorder. *Journal of Abnormal Psychology*, *119*(4), 726. https://doi.org/10.1037/a0020798

Schaeffer, C. M., & Borduin, C. M. (2005). Long-term follow-up to a randomized clinical trial of multisystemic therapy with serious and violent juvenile offenders. *Journal of Consulting and Clinical Psychology*, *73*(3), 445. https://doi.org/10.1037/0022-006X.73.3.445

Schwartz, R. C., & Feisthamel, K. P. (2009). Disproportionate diagnosis of mental disorders among African American versus European American clients: Implications for counseling theory, research, and practice. *Journal of Counseling & Development*, *87*(3), 295–301. https://doi.org/10.1002/j.1556-6678.2009.tb00110.x

Scott, K. M., Lim, C. C. W., Hwang, I., Adamowski, T., Al-Hamzawi, A., Bromet, E., Bunting, B., Ferrand, M. P., Florescu, S., Gureje, O., Hinkov, H., Hu, C., Karam, E., Lee, S., Posada-Villa, J., Stein, D., Tachimori, H., Viana, M. C., Xavier, M., & Kessler, R. C. (2016). The cross-national epidemiology of DSM-IV intermittent explosive disorder. *Psychological Medicine*, *46*(15), 3161–3172. https://doi.org/10.1017/S0033291716001859

Sterzer, P., Stadler, C., Poustka, F., & Kleinschmidt, A. (2007). A structural neural deficit in adolescents with conduct disorder and its association with lack of empathy. *Neuroimage*, *37*(1), 335–342. https://doi.org/10.1016/j.neuroimage.2007.04.043

Sukhodolsky, D. G., Smith, S. D., McCauley, S. A., Ibrahim, K., & Piasecka, J. B. (2016). Behavioral interventions for anger, irritability, and aggression in children and adolescents. *Journal of Child and Adolescent Psychopharmacology*, *26*(1), 58–64. https://doi.org/10.1089/cap.2015.0120

Tiet, Q. Q., Wasserman, G. A., Loeber, R., McReynolds, L. S., & Miller, L. S. (2001). Developmental and sex differences in types of conduct problems. *Journal of Child and Family Studies*, *10*(2), 181–197. https://doi.org/10.1023/A:1016637702525

Tracy, N. (2015, August 5). *Psychopath vs. Sociopath: What's the difference? HealthyPlace.* https://www.healthyplace.com/personality-disorders/psychopath/psychopath-vs-sociopath-what-s-the-difference

Wakefield, J. C. (2016). Diagnostic issues and controversies in DSM-5: Return of the false positives problem. *Annual Review of Clinical Psychology*, *12*, 105–132. https://doi.org/10.1146/annurev-clinpsy-032814-112800

Walsh, A., & Wu, H. H. (2008). Differentiating antisocial personality disorder, psychopathy, and sociopathy: Evolutionary, genetic, neurological, and sociological considerations. *Criminal Justice Studies*, *21*(2), 135–152. https://doi.org/10.1080/14786010802159814

Webster-Stratton, C., & Hammond, M. (1997). Treating children with early-onset conduct problems: A comparison of child and parent training interventions. *Journal of Consulting and Clinical Psychology*, *65*(1), 93. https://doi.org/10.1037/0022-006X.65.1.93

17 Substance-Related and Addictive Disorders

Most of us have experienced a moment of deep craving, an irresistible urge for just one more cigarette, for example, or found ourselves mindlessly eating one after another salty delight just after whispering a pledge to ourselves to taste just one. Or perhaps, as part of your training and coursework, you have been asked to give up a pleasure that has become something of a habit, like coffee, smoking, sweets, streaming movies or using social media in order to simulate the experience of trying to give up an addictive substance. When I engaged this experiment in my own training, and have witnessed others go through it in the years since, I have noticed two things. First there is a similar pattern of suffering that arises in each person as they experience the loss, sometimes physiological and nearly always including a great deal of grumbling as well as irritation, either with themselves or with the process generally. And each year I've heard participants in this experience acknowledge that the whole exploration reflects a mere shadow of the discomfort, pain, effort and struggle experienced by those trying to disentangle themselves from substances like heroine, methamphetamines or other drugs.

While students explore the ways in which substances and, even some behaviors, can wrestle a powerful hold over a person's body, mind and spirit, the nation as a whole is coming to terms with the devastating impact of the now epidemic proportions of opioid addiction and the jarring spike in overdose deaths that has resulted. In 2015, 35,000 overdose deaths were attributed to opioids alone (Weiner et al., 2017), a number roughly matching the size of the entire 2010 population of Tupelo, Mississippi, Beverly Hills or West Hollywood (Democrat & Chronicle, 2019). Additionally, the estimated overdose death rate in the United States in 2016 for all drugs was 63,600 people; leaders in these deaths included West Virginia, Ohio, New Hampshire, Washington D.C. and Pennsylvania. In 2015, we witnessed for the first time in U.S. history that heroin overdose deaths surpassed American gun homicides (Ingraham, 2016). Reflecting another shift in trends, in 2015, those between 45 and 54 had the highest rate of drug overdose deaths of any other group (Hedegaard et al., 2017). A Kaiser Family Foundation study illustrated the reach of the epidemic, finding that of those surveyed, 16% indicated personal knowledge of someone who had died as a result of opioid overdose (Weiner et al., 2017). Overall, overdose deaths among women have risen 260% in the past 20 years; however, among women 30-64, the increase was 492%, the bulk of which can be attributed to fentanyl, followed by heroin and prescription opioids (Miller, 2019; Substance Abuse and Mental Health Services Administration, 2018). While the number of opioid deaths provides a hint of the much larger population of people struggling with opioid use disorders, opioids themselves reflect only one of nearly a dozen classes of drugs that are taking a toll on public health and well-being. Though you may not choose to specialize in the treatment of substance use disorders (SUDs), you will certainly encounter clients who either experience this difficulty themselves or are living with the consequences of loving someone who does.

This chapter will focus on the diagnostic paradigm introduced in the DSM 5, one that reflects a significant shift in thinking about these disorders (Robinson & Adinoff, 2016); we will explore briefly the reasoning that led to some of these changes. However, readers should be aware that substance abuse treatment is an area of specialization and constitutes a body of knowledge that is far too broad and deep to cover adequately here. Instead, this chapter will focus on how these disorders are diagnosed and how to address complications in diagnosis. One such common complication that will be discussed here is the dual diagnosis phenomenon, in which a client experiences both an SUD as well as another mental health concern.

Substance Use and Cultural and Theoretical Shifts: Implications for the New Diagnostic Paradigm

The most recent edition of the DSM was published in 2013, making it a bit of a stretch to describe any of the introduced changes as "new." However, in the context of the long history of the Western world's relationship with substances, this most recent diagnostic paradigm is still quite young. Robinson and Adinoff (2016), point out that the historical record is rich with descriptions of the use and misuse of substances and note that even ancient literary classics, such as Homer's *The Odyssey*, include references to the use of substances to dull emotional experiencing. Substance use, such as alcohol and opiates have been a part of social and religious practices not only in the West but across the globe (Robinson & Adinoff, 2016; Straussner, 2013). Consequently, attitudes toward the use of substances run the gamut between total abstention to embracing their use as part of personal growth and development of spiritual domains of the self.

The earliest understanding of why people might misuse a substance was lodged in assessments of the individual's moral character or strength of will. In the 1960s, Jellinek began to change this narrative, helping to shift conventional thinking to a medical model for making sense of alcohol addiction, an idea that was then applied to other substances (Jellinek, 1960). The medical model attends to the biochemical

BOX 17.01 CONSIDER THIS: REFLECTING ON YOUR ATTITUDES ABOUT AND EXPERIENCE OF SUBSTANCE USE

Substance use disorders (SUDs) and their consequences have long been a part of the American story, a story that has become a part of the lives of an ever-increasing number of families. Perhaps your own life narrative has been touched by substance use. Has someone you love experienced the pain of addiction? Maybe members of your family or friends have lived with the heartache of watching a person caught in the cycle of use and misuse of substances. Perhaps you have experienced this struggle yourself? Though public attitudes are shifting around the causes of SUDs, arguably, each of us carry beliefs that have the potential to impair our ability to work effectively with this population. Reflect on the following questions:

1) What personal experience do you have with SUDs? How have these experiences influenced your ability to work with these clients? For example, have these experiences sensitized you to daily challenges faced by this population, or, conversely, left you feeling angry and resentful or finding it difficult to muster compassion for those who misuse substances at the expense of others?
2) What stereotypes do you hold about those who use substances? For instance, when you think of someone who is a heavy user of heroine, what comes to mind? How about crack cocaine? Do you romanticize or minimize the use of some drugs over others?
3) If you or someone close to you has experienced or is now experiencing an SUD, what work have you done to understand its place in your life and personal development? What work is still left to be done?
4) If you have no personal experience with substance use or misuse, how might this lack of experience show up in your work with clients? What potential obstacles might this pose?
5) What fears do you have about working with clients struggling with SUDs?
6) What skills or abilities do you have that you feel would be helpful in this work?
7) What traits or tendencies do you carry that might get in your way of working effectively with addiction?
8) What cultural and religious beliefs do you have about alcohol and other drugs? What role might these beliefs serve in your work with these clients?
9) What do you believe is the source of and solution to addiction? How might your theory of addiction support you or get in your way when working with clients?

consequences of long-term substance use; for instance, various metabolic changes. For other thinkers, the process of addiction is one primarily of psychic dynamics, sociological or even political causalities (Granfield & Reinarman, 2015).

BOX 17.02 KEY DEFINITIONS: SUBSTANCE-RELATED AND ADDICTIVE DISORDERS

Detoxification: detoxification, or detox, describes the physiological process undertaken primarily by the liver, in releasing the substance from tissues of the body (Straussner, 2013).

Diversion: refers to the practice of taking prescribed medication and diverting it to persons for whom the medication was not prescribed for purposes other than its medical use. Medications that have been prescribed for pain and for attention deficit hyperactivity disorder (ADHD) are frequently diverted and misused (Faraone et al., 2019).

Early Stage Addiction: this term, used more often among substance treatment specialists, is roughly equivalent to a "mild" substance use disorder (SUD) described in the DSM 5 in which a client experiences one or two symptoms associated with use.

End/Late Stage Addiction: described in the recovery literature and used primarily among substance use treatment specialists, in this stage of the use cycle, the entirety of the client's life focuses on the use of the substance in an effort to avoid experiencing symptoms of withdrawal. The medical consequences of late stage use can include concerns such as cirrhosis of the liver, hepatitis and even brain damage and differs from substance to substance.

Intoxication: describes a "reversible substance-specific syndrome," or collection of symptoms, directly resulting from ingesting a substance. Intoxication is common among those with SUDs but is also prevalent among those without an SUD. Though symptoms of intoxication vary from one substance to another, common symptoms include shifts in perception, impairments in attention, focus, judgment, decreased emotion control and so on (APA, 2013).

Process Addiction. Also sometimes referred to as a behavioral addiction, this term denotes an addiction to a behavior, action or process, such as gambling, sex or social media (APA, 2013).

Substance Induced Mood Disorder an acronym reflecting substance-induced mood disorder; this term refers to symptoms of mood disorders, unipolar or bipolar, that result as a direct consequence of the use of, intoxication with or withdrawal from a substance.

SIP: this acronym denotes a substance-induced psychosis and is differentiated from psychosis that arises out of a primary mental health disorder.

Substance-Induced Persisting Disorder. This term applies to those situations in which a client's use of a substance precipitated structural changes within the central nervous system that have resulted in symptoms that persist after use has ended and the substance's toxins have left the body.

Tolerance: tolerance describes changes in the effect of a particular substance when either the same dose leads to less than the desired effect or when a higher dose of a substance is needed to gain a particular effect. Tolerance is evident, for example, when high levels of the substance are present in the bloodstream but there is little outward evidence of intoxication (Kuerbis et al., 2013).

Withdrawal: withdrawal describes a collection of symptoms that emerge as the concentration of a substance, once used for a prolonged period of time, drops within the system. These symptoms vary in type and duration from one substance to another and may include but are not exclusive to physical pain, nausea, sweating, hot and cold flashes, sleep, agitation and so on. Avoidance of withdrawal symptoms contributes to the perpetuation of the substance use cycle (APA, 2013).

Withdrawal Management: withdrawal management describes the medical supervision of the detoxification process as well as the clinical assessment of the physical and mental health difficulties experienced by the client, and includes initial diagnosis (American Addiction Centers, 2019).

The Moral Model. Models developed for understanding and treating SUDs have been heavily influenced by cultural beliefs; new models tend to emerge with shifts in cultural attitudes. Again, the earliest understanding of the misuse of substances, described today as the moral model, placed the onus for problematic use on the individual and attributed these behaviors to weak moral character and, sometimes, on the basic sinful nature of human beings. The idea that whether or not one decided to use substances with moderation was widely believed to be a choice and entirely within the individual's power to manage if the courage of one's convictions was applied with diligence. Capuzzi and Stauffer (2016) point out that while the moral model has been largely discredited by modern science, traces of these beliefs are still with us in the law, policies and in the social stigma that continues to surround SUDs.

Cognitive-Behavioral Model. Applying the principles of learning theory and behaviorism, theorists have developed an understanding of the cycle of use and misuse of substances based in concepts of positive and negative reinforcement. At its essence, the cognitive model asserts that the experience that comes with the use of a substance is pleasurable (positively reinforcing/rewarding) and, as a result, the person is likely to repeat this behavior and use the substance again. Because ending substance use after heavy use can come with very unpleasant consequences, such as the illness that comes with withdrawal from heroin, people are thought to avoid these consequences and continue use (negative reinforcement). Using this model, cognitive-behavioral theorists understand the development of dependent behavior to be a function of the power of subtle and gross manifestations of the positive and negative reinforcement (Baker et al., 2004).

Biological Models. Biological models, sometimes referred to as the medical model, assert that the propensity to develop an SUD is dependent in large part in the physical makeup of the body, determined by genetics and their influences in the metabolic and neurological interplay between the brain, the environmental context in which the individual develops and the substances themselves. A great deal of research has been devoted to identifying genetic markers shared by those with SUDs (Agrawal & Lynskey, 2008; Baker et al., 2016; Kreek et al., 2005; Uhl et al., 2008), examining potential DNA links to contributing factors such as impulse control (Kreek et al., 2005) and dynamics of reward sensitivity (Agrawal & Lynskey, 2008) and so on. For example, researchers believe that they have gathered enough genetic data to confidently assert that at least one-fifth of the variance in vulnerability to SUDs can be attributed to a set of common genetic variations known as single nucleotide polymorphisms (SNPs). SNPs are sections of our genetic code, each with a slight variation, that occur normally within each person's individual DNA. All of us carry SNPs within our DNA, almost always with no medical impact; however, as in the case of the set of SNPs identified by researchers, these particular variations are thought to create a vulnerability to substance addiction (Palmer et al., 2015). Other researchers have focused their attention on neurocognitive structures. But perhaps the most compelling body of research is that which combines biological findings with other contemporary theories of addiction, such as personality theory (Conrod & Nikolaou, 2016), or, for example, exploring the neurological basis of reward and motivation, a cognitive-behavioral concept (Baskin-Sommers & Foti, 2015; Koob, 2008; Koob & Volkow, 2016).

Sociocultural Models, Rat Park and Addiction as a Function of Attachment. At the epicenter of the debate around the causes of SUDs and the concept of addiction is the idea that substance addiction is not a biological process but a sociological one arising out of a lack of connection to others. For example, the now famous work of Bruce Alexander et al. (1981) commonly known as the "rat park study" challenged prevailing views about the inherent addictive qualities of substances such as opioids and alcohol. Alexander and colleagues noticed that much of the research on addiction that used rats had what he asserted was a key flaw, the rats were isolated in cages with nothing to distract them, their only task was to choose between one of two water bottles, the first spiked with the drug being studied and the other with untainted water. Predictably, in study after study rats would return to the tainted water again and again until they overdosed and died. Alexander conducted studies in which rats were provided with environments that would satisfy their needs for connection, curiosity and play. They found that very few rats resorted to drug-spiked water under these conditions. Research replicating these early findings suggest that social disconnection may play a key role in whether or not a person develops an SUD (Schenk et al., 1987; Solinas et al., 2009).

In this vein, the central role of healthy attachment as a protective factor against addiction has been explored. Writers such as Philip Flores, 2004/2011, assert that when a person has not developed a healthy attachment style, and does not enjoy the neurological benefits that result, their ability to manage their own emotions is compromised, self-care is hampered, self-esteem is diminished and the capacity to navigate the complexities of relationship is impaired. As a result, Flores argues, drugs and alcohol are used as substitutes for the internal systems that would normally regulate emotion and maintain human connection. Likely the truth of the development of SUDs lies in the points of intersection between these models. Early childhood experiences, cultural beliefs and attitudes, early learning, cognitive reward processes, neurological processes, genetics, sociological factors such as socioeconomics, structural oppressions such as racism and homophobia and so on all seem to play their own part in the development of SUDs.

Shifts in the Diagnostic Language and Criteria Structure. The diagnostic paradigm for the addictions continuum shifted dramatically with the publication of the DSM 5. Marking a significant change in the diagnostic nosology of addictions, the concepts of abuse and dependence are no longer differentiating points, instead one diagnosis, SUD, is used to include both types of problematic use. The concepts of dependence and abuse arose from a construct developed by Edwards and Gross in 1976 in making sense of alcohol addiction. This construct became the predominant understanding of addiction and was later applied to other substance disorders. This system became known as the biaxial system, dependence comprising one axis and consequences of use comprising the other (Jones et al., 2012). Both the dependence criteria and the consequences criteria have come under considerable criticism leading many to call for changes in the diagnostic criteria (Hasin et al., 2013; Jones et al., 2012; Martin et al., 2014; Peer et al., 2013).

Dependence and abuse were originally conceived as two different levels of substance misuse severity, abuse being less severe than dependence and were embraced along with the popular understanding that abuse eventually led to dependence. However, while the dependence construct was supported in the literature, abuse was harder to define and much less reliable than its counterpart. Further, the research supporting the conversion from abuse to dependence was not as strong as researchers had anticipated. Ultimately, however, the primary reason given for the construct shift was to bring the DSM into alignment with findings which revealed that the two concepts were, in fact, more accurately captured by the single construct, SUD (Denis et al., 2015; Jones et al., 2012; Martin et al., 2014; Robinson & Adinoff, 2016). The consequences construct of the nosology was retained despite considerable criticism.

Later in the chapter, you will notice that nearly half of the 11 symptoms of the SUDs relate directly to the consequences of use. Martin et al. (2014) note a number of key concerns with criteria related to consequences. They first point out that negative consequences experienced by those with SUDs can arise out of the individual's context and may be difficult to pull apart from the direct contributions of the substance use; for example, developmental differences, age, race and socioeconomics, to name a few. They further note that for some, high socioeconomic status protects them from consequences that would otherwise be felt, making the validity of the criteria questionable. Other contributing factors to observed consequences might include situational factors, individual impulsivity, personality traits and so on. They further point out that while an individual may experience consequences, those consequences may only be exacerbated by the substance use or may be entirely independent of it. They offer the example in which a student drinks heavily before a test and fails their exam. While alcohol may have played a role in the student's failure, a lack of knowledge, skill or strong study habits may be primarily responsible. Martin et al. (2014), offer instead the concept of a core illness dimension: "heavy use, compulsive use, the incentive salience of substance use and physiological features" (p.1776). They recommend that consequences be used only to assist in determining the severity of the disorder.

Second, researchers challenged the validity of the symptom constuct of past editions of the DSM arguing that it was so lenient as to be overinclusive, and asserted that it created such heterogenous diagnostic populations that it had lost its utility diagnostically or as a research measure (Martin et al., 2011). Too frequently, this single criteria was met by a drunk driving incident, highlighting validity problems and pointing to bias in the diagnostic process. For example, early criticism of the risk criteria can be seen in works like those published by Hasin et al. (1999) who pointed out that about 50% of a sample of community members diagnosed with an alcohol abuse disorder had received this diagnosis based on drunk driving alone. Curious about the validity of this diagnosis, these authors were prompted to conduct a large scale study of over 22,000 participants; they found significant differences between those diagnosed with an alcohol abuse disorder based on drunk driving criteria alone, those with no diagnosis and those who were diagnosed based on additional criteria (with or without drunk driving). While some authors certainly argued that diagnosis based upon the risky behaviors criteria alone was likely overinclusive, others argued that so many alcohol abuse disorders were diagnosed based upon drunk driving that likely groups of people who did not own cars, such as persons with fewer socioeconomic resources, may not have been appropriately included (Keyes & Hasin, 2008). (Borges et al., 2010 in Robinson & Adinoff, 2016; Jones et al., 2012; Martin et al., 2014; Robinson & Adinoff, 2016).

The current edition requires two or more criteria to be met before diagnosis. Finally, the criterion describing recurrent legal difficulties has been dropped in favor of a criterion for cravings, which will be described at greater length later in this chapter (American Psychiatric Association [APA], 2013; Denis et al., 2015; Robinson & Adinoff, 2016). While there were concerns that the diagnostic construct was overinclusive, there were also concerns that the criteria excluded too many at the mild end of the spectrum who were in need of treatment, those described as diagnostic orphans. Diagnostic orphans were substance users who under the DSM IV criteria met one or two criteria; for example, tolerance and abuse but none for consequences and consequently could not be diagnosed (Martin & Winters, 1998; Peer et al., 2013).

Have Changes to the DSM Criteria Improved Reliability? Denis et al. (2015) set out to explore the inter-rater reliability of four DSM 5 SUDs (alcohol, cannabis, cocaine and opioids) and compare those results with a study they conducted exploring the inter-rater reliability of the DSM IV-TR. Using the same methodology used in their first study, they found the reliability of the DSM 5 to be "at least as reliable" (p. 235) as the DSM IV-TR construct. Inter-rater reliability was good to excellent for moderate to severe levels of all four diagnoses, and slightly less strong for the mild range. Reliability rates were also lower when anxiety or mood disorders were present, presumably because this presentation clouds the diagnostic process. In addition to the modest improvements in reliability, the changes to the diagnostic construct seem to do a better job of including affected clients, particularly those at the mild end of the spectrum and those that would otherwise have been diagnostic orphans (Bartoli et al., 2015; Peer et al., 2013).

The Inclusion of Process Addictions in the Addiction Conversation. Early discussions and outright debates supporting the description of gambling as an addiction (Blanco et al., 2001; Robinson & Adinoff, 2016) and contesting this conceptualization (Walker, 1989) mirror the larger discussion of the validity of process addictions. A process addiction, also described as a behavioral addiction, is one that is not tied to a substance but to an activity, behavior or process (APA, 2013; Kardefelt-Winther et al., 2017).

The idea of a process addiction represents a shift in thinking about what constitutes an addiction and what is a compulsion, as is seen in obsessive compulsive processes, and how the two can be differentiated. As attitudes have shifted from the belief that addiction must include a chemical that stimulates the neuropsychological processes that are characteristic of addiction, conventional thinking began to include activities believed to be capable of triggering the addictive cycle. Investigations into neurochemical processes have given strength to the concept of process addiction, which includes investigations into sex addiction (Zapf et al., 2008), binge eating (Cassin & von Ranson, 2007), compulsive purchasing (Christenson et. al., 1994), internet addiction (Widyanto & Griffiths, 2006) and technology addiction (Pearson & Hussain, 2017). A scale has been developed to measure workaholism (Andreassen et al., 2012) and there has even been research into dance addiction (Maraz et al., 2015).

Expressing concern for the growing array of experiences that have been explored for inclusion within the process addictions and noting their fear that common behaviors will be pathologized, Kardefelt-Winther et al. (2017) suggest the addition of four exclusion criteria. First, behaviors better explained by another underlying mental health concern, such as anxiety or depression, should not be diagnosed as a process addiction. Second, they argue that it is problematic to include consequences of high-risk hobbies or sports, as impairment; for example, sports such as boxing, climbing, base jumping and so on, should not include anticipated injuries among consequence criteria. Third, these authors argue that if the involvement is prolonged and intensive but does not include a functional impairment, it should not be diagnosed. Finally, they recommend that exclusion criteria be added for behaviors that are coping mechanisms.

Despite the wide range of behaviors that have been explored in the context of addiction, only gambling addiction has been included in the DSM 5, a disorder that was moved from the impulse control disorders to the addictions continuum, and only internet gambling addiction has been included in the section reserved for disorders for research (APA, 2013; Kardefelt-Winther et al., 2017).

The Diagnostic Process

Each dimension of the DSM presents its own diagnostic challenges; the substance and addictive behaviors are no different. What's more, the changes that have come with the publication of the DSM 5 came with some controversy and differs significantly from the rest of the disorders organized in the manual. To understand this dimension, it is important to know first that two primary types of disorders are included, substance and process; the bulk of these disorders involve consequences related to substance use and the other is behavioral, gambling disorder specifically. Nine classes of substances are described within the DSM 5: alcohol, caffeine, tobacco, cannabis, hallucinogens, inhalants, opioids, and sedative, hypnotic or anxiolytic-related substances. The substance-related disorders are then broken down into one of three categories: intoxication, use and withdrawal, since each of these circumstances brings with it its own symptoms and each requires different treatment responses. Finally, all of the substance-related and addictive behavior disorders are then given appropriate specifiers to clarify the diagnostic picture (APA, 2013).

Diagnosis of Substance-Related Disorders: A Three-Step Process. The symptoms within the substance-related and addiction continuum overlap significantly with disorders throughout the DSM, making their diagnosis particularly complicated. The first step in mastering the diagnosis of substance-related disorders is grasping the general concept of SUDs, followed by a narrowing to a specific class or classes of drugs. The third step in diagnosis is identifying the unique symptom sets that most frequently accompany each substance as well as the mental health disorders that can result as a consequence of the misuse of each. Finally, clinicians must then do the critical and often very difficult work of pulling apart the original source of the client's symptoms, either as originating with a primary mental health disorder (PMHD), an SUD or as arising from both simultaneously.

Substance Use Disorders. SUDs are diagnosed when the use of a substance or substances results in a cluster of symptoms and behaviors that impair functioning. These symptoms are organized into four categories: (1) impaired control, (2) social impairment, (3) risky use and (4) pharmacological criteria.

Impaired Control. When substance use grows more and more problematic and rises to the level of diagnosis, one of the first developments we observe is a shift in the client's ability to control use. This may evidence itself when a client gradually increases the amount and frequency in which the substance is used, often using more than was intended. The second criteria in the control category is met when clients attempt to reduce or stop use of a substance and are unable to do so, finding themselves using despite a deep wish to stop. Criterion 3 describes the increasing amounts of time that is dedicated to obtaining, using or recovering from the use of the substance. For those with an SUD, the amount of time devoted to using carves out a greater and greater portion of the client's life, leaving other areas neglected (APA, 2013; Morrison & Flegel, 2016; Robinson & Adinoff, 2016). Finally, criterion 4 is craving (APA, 2013; Morrison & Flegel, 2016; Robinson & Adinoff, 2016), a symptom frequently associated with relapse (Robinson & Adinoff, 2016). These four experiences are obviously deeply intertwined and are frequently met together.

Social Impairment. As a client's involvement with a substance grows and demands more and more of the client's time and attention, substance use slowly but surely wedges out other important areas of the client's life. Client's may neglect family members and sacrifice key relationships, they may neglect their work, or do poorly in school, in any of these situations, criterion 5 is met. Criterion 6 is met when despite these consequences, the client continues to use the substance. Finally, criterion 7 describes behavior in which the client gives up what was once important to them in favor of substance use (APA, 2013; Morrison & Flegel, 2016; Stevens et al., 2019). Criteria

BOX 17.03 SHIFTING DEFINITIONS

In April of 2011 the American Society of Addiction Medicine (ASAM) adopted a new definition that was inclusive of process addictions.

Addiction is a primary, chronic disease of brain reward, motivation, memory and related circuitry. Dysfunction in these circuits leads to characteristic biological, psychological, social and spiritual manifestations. This is reflected in an individual pathologically pursuing reward and/or relief by substance use and other behaviors

(ASAM, 2011; Smith, 2012).

Kardefelt-Winther et al. (2017), Proposed Definition of Process Addiction

A repeated behavior leading to significant harm or distress. The behavioral addiction is not reduced by the person and persists for a significant period of time. The harm or distress is of a functionally impairing nature (p. 1710).

5-7 represent a gradual worsening of symptoms in that the client is progressing from neglect of some role responsibilities to largely giving these up altogether.

Risky Use. Here the clinician is evaluating the client's relative ability to control use when using presents some kind of significant risk to the client, either physically, emotionally or socially (APA, 2013; Morrison & Flegel, 2016), such as when use of a substance would constitute a parole violation and legal consequences.

Pharmacological Criteria. The final criteria, 10 and 11, relate specifically to tolerance and withdrawal. Tolerance refers to the process by which a person gradually needs ever-increasing doses in order to achieve the desired result, or conversely, notices the same dose results in less than hoped for results (APA, 2013). Withdrawal describes the symptoms that accompany the cessation of substance use and their exit from the body. Withdrawal symptoms vary a great deal from one substance to the next and are outlined in detail within the DSM 5 (APA, 2013).

Intoxication. Intoxication is a diagnosis given when the client is evidencing the immediate physiological and psychological consequences of ingesting drugs and/or alcohol. The nature of intoxication is that its effects are temporary, though duration and the symptoms themselves vary from substance to substance. To diagnose a client with intoxication, clinicians must be able to attribute the observed symptoms directly to the substance that has been used. It is important to remember that intoxication can be diagnosed in absence of a use disorder, in other words, a client can be under the influence without having an alcohol use disorder (APA, 2013).

BOX 17.04 CODING NOTE

Please note, the coding for substance disorders have been updated in recent supplements, the most extensive were to be implemented in October of 2017 and a few additional changes to text within the dimension that went into effect as of October 2018. Similarly, revisions to text and coding have been made across dimensions; however, the revisions to coding of the substance use disorders is significant. Check the American Psychiatric Association (APA) website for the most recent coding for each of these disorders (APA, 2018).

Withdrawal. The consequences of the misuse of substances extend beyond the period of use or intoxication. For many, symptoms experienced in withdrawal are very uncomfortable or even life threatening. Withdrawal symptoms can be so uncomfortable that they create a strong drive to avoid pain and, consequently, perpetuates the substance use cycle. Not all classes of drugs result in withdrawal, however; for example, neither inhalants nor hallucinogens are associated with withdrawal symptoms. On the other hand, abrupt withdrawal from alcohol for a person in the late stage of alcoholism or a person suffering from a heroin addiction are notoriously uncomfortable. Withdrawal from heroin generally includes severe flu-like symptoms including chills, body aches, diarrhea and vomiting that can last as many as 5 days. When withdrawal from alcohol includes seizures, delirium or hallucinations, medical supervision of the detoxification process may be necessary (APA, 2013; Straussner, 2013). Similarly, frequent users of cannabis have been shown to exhibit clusters of withdrawal symptoms, such as irritability, restlessness, aggression and so on; more than half of these experience six or more symptoms (Budney et al., 1999).

Substance Use and Special Populations

Phase of life, gender, racial and cultural differences present clients and clinicians with contextual and personal differences in the development of SUDs as well as their treatment. Here we will take a brief look at some of the considerations to keep in mind as you approach potential diagnosis of an SUD.

Adolescents. The cultural context for many teens in the United States is one that includes expectations for experimentation with alcohol and drugs, though these expectations vary from one group to another, both within groups and between groups, in the degree to which this expectation is present and also for what kinds of experimentation is encouraged. How would you describe the social pressures and expectations in your own school experience as a teen? What, if any, substances were your peers experimenting with when you were in high school? Middle school? How did you respond to those pressures?

For many, substance use as a right of passage is a contextual consideration in both the onset and sustaining of an SUD. Though parental, sibling and peer substance use have all been shown to influence adolescent substance and alcohol use, it has long been understood that peer substance use exerts the greatest effect (Windle, 2000). Research shows that these types of experimentation are not without risk, however. For example, a study of e-cigarette use among teens found that for those that used both e-cigarettes and regular tobacco products, there was an elevated incidence of binge drinking and marijuana use, as well as increases in the use of other types of drugs (McCabe et al., 2017). Some clinicians and researchers have explored the efficacy of working with teens and their families together to shift cultural beliefs around substance use in order to reduce substance disorders among teens (Marsiglia et al., 2016).

While cultural expectations and peer pressure can be significant contributors to substance use and abuse, marginalization can have the same effect. Benner and Wang (2015) conducted a path analysis study of nearly 8,000 participants, which included both boys and girls with White, African American, Latinx and Asian American identities. They found that marginalizing experiences, for instance, those in which less than 15% of their school peers were of matched race, experienced lower rates of school attachment, which, in turn resulted in higher levels of depression that were then associated with higher levels of alcohol and marijuana use. Similar studies have found that the marginalizing impact of bullying perpetrated against lesbian, gay, bisexual, transgender, transsexual and queer (LGBTQ) teens is also connected to substance use (Huebner et al., 2015). Studies like these point to the importance of considering contextual and cultural considerations in the lives of teens that may contribute to the development of a substance use or PMHDs.

As with adults, adolescents with mental health concerns are at an elevated risk for SUDs (Conway et al., 2016; Merikangas et al., 2010). Conway et al. (2016) conducted a comorbidity study of more than 10,000 American teens and found that SUDs were highest among those with anxiety disorders, closely followed by conduct disorders. They also found that when an adolescent had any primary mental health disorder , the likelihood of progressing from first time use to problematic use increased compared to those who did not. This study and others like it (Welsh et al., 2017; Yoshimasu et al., 2016) suggest that initial assessment for SUDs should be followed by periodic follow-up assessment for drug and alcohol use and misuse.

Women. A report published by the Centers for Disease Control reports that over the past two decades we have seen a dramatic increase of substance use and abuse and consequently overdose deaths (VanHouten et al., 2019). As with the population at large, genetic factors, poverty and early exposure to substances are all correlated with SUDs in women. In 2017, more than 5% of women over the age of 12 had a substance abuse

BOX 17.05 TRY THIS: IDENTIFYING CRITERIA

It is not always easy to pull apart one criterion from another when symptoms are interconnected as they are in substance use. Practice can support you in avoiding double-counting a presentation; for example, or missing a symptom embedded in the client's presentation. In the following scenarios, identify one or more of the matching criteria for substance use disorders (SUDs) in each: control of amounts used, inability to stop using, time devoted to the substance, role neglect and risk.

Jamie woke feeling hungover but determined to make it to her 10 a.m. scheduled supervised visitation with her son. Looking in the mirror she thought, "I look like yesterday's warmed over pizza. I can't go in looking like this. I'll just have a shot to get my head on straight, I'll wash my face and brush my teeth and it will be ok." Three hours later, Jaimie realized she had drained what was left of her bottle of vodka and she had missed her appointment. "I'm losing everything in my life, one shot at a time," she whispered to herself.

Alex shares with his Narcotics Anonymous (NA) group, "When I first started using H, I used it at parties with friends on the weekend but it didn't take long before I was using after work, too, and then before work, after work and always at parties . . . and I started to party every weekend, all weekend long. Then I lost my job. Before I went into treatment I used all the time, trying to get high but also trying to avoid the crash. When I wasn't using or hustling to get some heroin, I was high or sick. Drugs was just everything."

Sheldon, 15, has asthma and juvenile diabetes. Despite these conditions, Sheldon drinks heavily and smokes pot with his friends. Sheldon has twice been hospitalized following diabetic emergencies that resulted from drinking. He sometimes uses a nebulizer to treat smoking-induced asthma.

Holly, 24, has been using meth for 3 years. She has been in treatment three times in the last 2 years but despite her desire to quit using meth once and for all and to go back to school and become a vet, she is unable to stop using.

Dan, 43, has a big project that has to be completed by the end of the week. A lot is on the line in this project. If he does well his supervisor has promised a promotion and his family could use the money. Dan's son's Little League team is playing in the city championships today as well. Dan feels he "can't really get motivated" for this project or the game without first doing a line—or two—of coke and "giving himself a minute for himself."

disorder (Center for Behavioral Health Statistics & Quality, 2017). The contributing factors to addiction in women are complex and begin early in life.

Research has demonstrated that adverse childhood experiences (ACE) scores, a measure of adverse experiences in childhood including sexual abuse, are positively correlated with both primary mental health concerns and SUDs (Anda et al., 2006). While ACE are not unique to women, gender does establish a unique context that can create vulnerabilities to SUDs. For example, Carr and Szymanski (2011) conducted a study of women's experiences of sexual objectification and its connection to substance use. They found that while sexual victimization, such as childhood sexual assault, were correlated with substance abuse, everyday objectification experiences, such as body evaluation, were also correlated with the abuse of alcohol, nicotine and other drugs. Similarly, experiences of intimate partner violence, particularly when paired with post-traumatic stress disorder (PTSD) are also correlated with SUDs (Sullivan et al., 2016).

Pape and Elias (2013) note that substance abuse assessments have been largely normed using male research participants, making them less valid for women, frequently under-including women. They also note that for women, eating disorders as well as mood disorders are frequently comorbid with SUDs and recommend including eating disorders in a thorough assessment. Finally, they advise that women who have substance use concerns and are of childbearing age should have a thorough medical exam to rule out pregnancy.

Substance assessment and treatment for women must take into consideration issues related to pregnancy (McLafferty et al., 2016; Pape & Elias, 2013) and breastfeeding (Reece-Stremtan et al., 2015). Estimates place the rate of illicit substance use during pregnancy at about 11% and 75% of that use is thought to be of cocaine (Schueller, 2015). Perhaps it is not surprising then, that the rate of neonatal abstinence syndrome, NAS, a condition in which infants exposed to substances in utero experience withdrawal symptoms after birth, increased 380% between 1999 and 2013. Infants with NAS can experience a host of dangerous symptoms including tremor, seizure, temperature regulation difficulties and so on (Ko, 2016).

Women may be very reluctant to discuss substance use problems due to social stigmas that associate substance use problems in women with immorality and promiscuity and thanks to fears about the legal ramifications should their abuse be found out and their children be taken from them (Brogly et al., 2018; Pape & Elias, 2013). What's more, women describe childcare as an obstacle to getting the treatment they need particularly when treatment would be residential (Brogly et al., 2018). However, women have been found to be more likely to remain in treatment than men once they have access (Choi et al., 2015).

Elderly Populations. Alcohol is the substance of choice among older adults (Blazer & Wu, 2009; Kuerbis et al., 2013). While substance use seems to decline as people age, the estimated prevalence of SUDs among the elderly ranges, some placing this number as high as 17%. Aging brings with it biological changes that alter the way that we metabolize alcohol, which can decrease tolerance levels. Other biological changes that can impact tolerance include the softening of the blood brain barrier, higher neurological receptivity to alcohol and lower effectiveness of liver function. Since rising tolerance is a key diagnostic criterion, accurate diagnosis is made more complicated in this population (Kuerbis et al., 2013).

Racial and Ethnic Minority Groups and Substance Use. Between group and within group, differences in attitudes about substance use and SUDs are documented across the literature. Understanding why these differences exist and what sustains them requires that we not only understand the unique cultural norms and stressors of each specific group but also how those dynamics intersect with the social and political dynamics of society at large, including trends and influences of the social, educational, legal, and media processes and so on. Systemic oppression of racial and ethnic minorities, for example, plays out in each of these domains, each having a potential impact that touches mental health and substance use.

One of the places where these dynamics can play out is in the therapy office during assessment and diagnosis, highlighting the importance of cultural competence in mental health clinicians. Research reveals that ethnic minority clients identify a number of obstacles to treatment, including discrimination. Mays et al. (2017) surveyed California residents during healthcare visits including for mental health and SUD care. They found high rates of reported healthcare discrimination among Latinos, African Americans and the uninsured. Race and ethnicity were the most common reasons given for discrimination followed by lack of adequate insurance. These experiences of discrimination resulted in lowered helpfulness ratings among Latino and White uninsured clients and early termination among African American clients (Mays et al., 2017).

SUDs are not distributed proportionately to population sizes. The highest prevalence rates of SUDs are among Native Americans and Native Alaskans (12.8%) followed by White, African American and Latinx populations (7.7%, 6.8% and 6.5%, respectively) and then Native Hawaiian and Pacific Islanders (4.6%) and Asian Americans (3.8%) (Center for Behavioral Health Statistics & Quality, 2017). However, prevalence for PMHDs, which contribute to the development of SUDs, is not distributed proportionately either. In 2017, the group with the highest rates of any mental illness were multiracial persons (28.6%) followed by Caucasians (20.4%), Native Hawaiians (19.4%), Native Americans (18.9%), African Americans (16.2), Latinx (15.2%) and Asians (14.5%) (National Institute of Mental Health [NIH], 2019). While the between group differences are evident, within group differences have also been identified. For example, research suggests that Latinos born in the United States are much more likely than their foreign-born counterparts to experience an SUD, and consequently more likely to have co-occurring disorders. In contrast, Latino immigrants have lower rates of mental health difficulties generally, have later age of onset for those illnesses and a slower rate of progression of SUDs (Vega et al., 2009).

Another aspect of cultural identity, religiosity, has also been researched and may play a role in whether or not a person develops an SUD. Religiosity seems to provide a protective factor for African Americans, Latinx Americans as well as for Whites, however, not in the same ways. Meyers et al. (2017) found that for African American participants public religiosity was an effective buffer for alcohol use disorder while for Latinx, intrinsic religiosity was a more powerful buffer. Religiosity served as a stronger buffer for both groups than for Whites. Studies like these point to the complex interplay between identities, such as race, gender, religious affiliation and so on, of which all contribute to a mosaic of factors that explain the development of an SUD.

Covid-19 and Its Implications. Overdose events and deaths have risen dramatically with the Covid-19 pandemic. According to reporting from Wang and Long (2020) of the *Washington Post*, suspected overdoses rose by 18% nationally (as of July 1), though in some jurisdictions the toll increased more than 50%. The rise is attributed to the reduction in services available; in some cases, clinics have been forced to close. Compounding factors include high unemployment rates, isolation from family and friends thanks to social distancing measures, and mounting anxiety and depression.

Diagnostic Complexity: Dual Diagnosis

Decades of research demonstrate the high prevalence of SUDs and their comorbidity with other mental health disorders. Complexity in the diagnostic process arises when a clinician must determine what symptoms are a direct consequence of the substance or substances being used, and what symptoms may arise from another independent mental health concern. Once a clinician has determined that a second (or perhaps multiple) mental health disorder coexists with an SUD, the next task is to determine which is primary. A disorder is determined to be primary when it seems to cause the greatest risk to the client or contributes the greatest burden of suffering. Sometimes, risk and suffering are balanced, however, as when a person uses a highly toxic substance, like fentanyl, but also experiences very severe depression with active suicidal ideation. PMHDs have an exceedingly complicated relationship with SUDs; PMHDs can precede SUDs, worsen their effects, co-occur with them or significantly elevate the risk for developing them later in life (Bennett et al., 2018; Freshman, 2013; Quello et al., 2005). Among the most common co-occurring disorders are the mood disorders, both unipolar and bipolar, for which some studies indicate co-occurrence at more than 40% (Freshman, 2013; Quello et al., 2005). Also common are personality disorders, such as borderline personality and antisocial personality, estimated at nearly 20% (Bennett et al., 2018; Tolliver & Anton, 2015; Torrens et al., 2011). Comorbidity between anxiety disorders and alcohol use are particularly high (Bartoli et al., 2015). A 2008 study of over 43,000 participants revealed that 17% of those with an SUD also met criteria for one or more anxiety disorders (Back & Brady, 2008).

One might reasonably ask why the co-occurrence rates are so dramatic. The answer is, of course, complex, but begins with the fact that the regular use of substances seems to elevate the risk of developing a mental health disorder where none had been present before. Further, while substances can provoke serious mental health symptoms, including psychosis, substances are often used to self-medicate bothersome mental health symptoms, creating a painful cycle that further burdens a person already experiencing significant suffering (Atkins, 2014; Bennett et al., 2018; Caton et al., 2000; Freshman, 2013; Quello et al., 2005). Bennett et al. (2018) point out that the issue of co-occurring disorders is further complicated by the high rate of multiple co-occurring disorders, particularly among those with severe SUDs, making both diagnosis and treatment much more complex. Adherence to best practices necessitate that when assessing clients with SUDs, clinicians also provide a thorough evaluation for the presence of other mental health disorders and to make every effort to determine which diagnosis is the primary cause of the client's symptoms (Atkins, 2014; Bennett et al., 2018; Caton et al., 2000; Freshman, 2013; Quello et al., 2005).

The Skilled Diagnostician

Comorbid Mood Disorders and SUDs. A number of national epidemiological surveys reveal that roughly 40% of those who have experienced major depressive disorder in their lifetimes also have an alcohol use disorder; however, few, less than 1% of those currently meeting criteria for a mood disorder, were thought to have a substance-induced mood disorder (SIMD), in other words, the vast majority of these are primary mood disorders rather than instigated by substance use. However, when SUDs and disorders of mood co-occur, researchers have noted a significant worsening of the mood disorder symptoms (Tolliver & Anton, 2015). These studies suggest that when differentiating primary and SIMD, in absence of evidence to the contrary, a primary diagnosis of mood disorder, either unipolar or bipolar, is appropriate. Three key diagnostic pieces of information will be vital in differentiating cloudy clinical pictures: the timing of the onset of mood symptoms, the symptom picture following a reasonable period of abstinence and to a lesser degree, a family history of mood disorder. Substance-induced mood symptoms that result from lingering effects of a substance typically begin within 4 weeks of the last use. Later onset suggests a primary mental health concern. Mood symptoms that seem much more intense than those typically seen as a consequence of intoxication or withdrawal, particularly when a history of mood symptoms is documented or a family history is present, suggest a primary mood disorder (Quello et al., 2005). However, others assert that consideration of risk should be prioritized in determining which disorder is primary. For example, they argue that while the burden of suffering with severe anxiety may be quite high and may have preceded the use, it is more likely that their addiction to alcohol will result in their death, and consequently the SUD should be described as primary.

Psychosis and Substance Use, Intoxication and Withdrawal. A number of substances are known to provoke substance-induced psychosis (SIP) including alcohol, amphetamines, cannabis and cocaine (Caton et al., 2000; Fiorentini et al., 2011). Though the extant data is not definitive, some researchers believe that cannabis can cause psychosis to develop in those who would not otherwise manifest it. We do know that as many as half of all cannabis users have experienced a psychotic symptom and there is evidence that the risk for developing schizophrenia among cannabis users is dramatically elevated (Caton et al., 2000; DeLisi, 2008; Ferdinand et al., 2005; Fiorentini et al., 2011; Green et al., 2004; Hall et al., 2004; Nielsen et al., 2017). These studies and others like them suggest that for clients who use cannabis regularly, particularly those who report psychotic symptoms, it is important to be alert to the possibility of conversion to a schizophrenia spectrum disorder.

Substance and Addiction Treatment: A Brief Overview

Withdrawal Management/Detoxification (Detox). The first step toward healing and change for a significant number of people who are in substance use recovery is detoxification, often referred to as *detox,* within the greater process of withdrawal management. Detoxification is a process in which the liver does the work of cleaning the body of a substance. Withdrawal management, on the other hand, a term introduced by the World Health Organization (WHO), describes the work of the clinician or medical professional who supports clients through the symptoms of withdrawal (American Addiction Centers, 2019; WHO, 2009). In any given year, over 300,000 people go through detoxification/withdrawal management programs (Center for Substance Abuse Treatment, 2006), a staggering number roughly equivalent to a city the size of Lexington, Kentucky. Withdrawal management has three primary aims: (1) evaluation, which includes lab work for the presence of an array of substances and evaluating for the presence of co-occurring mental health disorders; (2) stabilization, which includes a process of safely shepherding an individual, physically and psychologically, from intoxication, through withdrawal and into a state free of substances and (3) fostering the entry into an appropriate treatment setting. This process is understood to be a type of palliative care rather than a formal part of the substance abuse treatment; however, the comprehensive evaluation that is part of the withdrawal management process provides the foundation for the client's intervention plan (Center for Substance Abuse Treatment, 2014; Center for Substance Abuse Treatment, 2006; Friedman, 2013; WHO, 2009).

Pharmaceutical Interventions. Pharmaceutical interventions are used when withdrawal from one or more substances may be painful or even dangerous. For example, some clients may be prone to suffer seizures when withdrawing from alcohol use. While pharmaceutical interventions can be used to soften symptoms that come with withdrawal, they may also be used to replace one very dangerous substance, such as heroin, with a less dangerous substitute, such as methadone or LAAM, both of which are synthetic painkillers with fewer side effects than heroin. Methadone and LAAM are long-acting, however, LAAM is attractive to some clients because it effectively blocks heroin's effects for as long as 3 days and has few side effects, allowing clients to take this medication three times a week rather than daily, as is necessary with methadone and thus requiring fewer clinic visits (Friedman, 2013). Thus, pharmaceutical interventions can be both a temporary part of the detoxification process or part of a bridge to maintaining client recovery.

Withdrawal management is a medical specialization made more imperative due to the complexities presented by special populations. For example, alcohol-dependent pregnant women must be given careful consideration in the process of detoxification since anticonvulsants, frequently used in alcohol withdrawal support, are dangerous to the unborn baby; instead, when necessary, short-acting benzodiazepines are recommended. Similarly, care and attention must be given to monitoring the withdrawal process of elderly clients since they are more likely to have one or more co-occurring medical conditions or physical disabilities that complicate or might be complicated by withdrawal or its medical treatment (Center for Substance Abuse Treatment, 2006). Clearly, supporting clients through withdrawal from substance use should only be undertaken in collaboration with trained and qualified health professionals. Once a client is stabilized and their needs are understood, the next step is formal treatment that may come in the form of a residential treatment placement or take place within an outpatient treatment setting.

Residential Care. Residential treatment care for substance use is recommended for those clients who are seen to be a danger to themselves or others, are in need of stabilization, or who have not responded to outpatient treatment (Liddle et al., 2018). Residential treatment can vary from one setting to the next but most residential settings share common features. First and most obviously, clients live in the treatment center for a specified amount of time, ranging from a week to many months. For adolescent clients, a significant amount of literature supports the efficacy of residential treatment in treating the teen substance use. Some research suggests that the ideal window for treatment efficacy for teens in residential treatment is somewhere between 1 and 6 months but not longer than 10 (Strickler et al., 2016, is subsumed in Liddle et al., 2018). For adults, too, length of stay in treatment is correlated with better outcomes, such as lower post-treatment substance use rates and lower readmission rates (Choi et al., 2015). Residential treatment facilities provide clients with structure and as a result, these facilities generally embrace regimented schedules and strict rules that clients must abide by, the most important of which is that clients abstain from using substances and participate in therapeutic interventions. These settings typically provide a number of different types of intervention including psychiatric care, individual therapy, group therapy and sometimes family intervention. Some form of therapy is generally experienced every day, and usually more than one. Taking responsibility for one's own self-care is also generally an important part of residential treatment, and consequently clients are required to contribute to chores and general upkeep (Center for Substance Abuse Treatment, 2006; Straussner, 2013).

An important guiding principle for residential treatment is the concept of *least restrictive care* (LRC), the medical equivalent to the *least restrictive environment* concept embraced within the education system. LRC serves to protect client civil rights and in so doing embraces four primary stipulations: (1) each patient's civil rights should be preserved to the greatest extent possible, including safeguarding their rights to participate in society, (2) clients should have the right to disagree with the level and type of care that they are receiving, (3) care should be developed and delivered in full collaboration with clients and their healthcare providers and (4) providers must carefully abide by the law in attending to the needs of those who are at risk of harming

BOX 17.06 EIGHT KEY STEPS FOR DIFFERENTIAL DIAGNOSIS OF CO-OCCURRING DISORDERS

1. *Identify your client's primary presenting problem.*
   Question: Are your client's concerns potentially the consequence of use or withdrawal from substances?
2. *Identify and list your client's symptoms.*
3. *Identify and list the substance or substances that your client describes using.*
4. *Examine your client's symptoms.*
   Question: Are these symptoms potentially produced by heavy use of this substance or withdrawal from its use?
5. *Examine your client's timeline and reasoning for substance use. Might your client's use of substances be a response to mental health symptoms?*
   Questions: What is your client's hope for use? (E.g., will help me sleep) What triggers use, internal or external? (E.g., Emotional experiencing or social situations)
6. *Examine your client's timeline and reasoning for substance use.*
   Question: Might your client's use of substances be a response to a medical condition?

Determining the Primary Disorder

7. *Establish a timeline. Which disorder seems to have arisen first?*
8. *Determine Primacy. Which do you believe presents the most significant risk to your client?*
   Question: Is your client at greater risk of deliberate suicidal behavior; for example, with severe depression, or of accidental overdose?

Source: American Psychiatric Association (2013).

themselves or others or are unable to make their own decisions. Attending to state case law regarding commitment is essential since states differ in the degree to which they lean toward protecting clients with commitment or protecting clients by preserving their right to choose to decline treatment (Center for Substance Abuse Treatment, 2006; WHO, 2009).

Obstacles to receiving treatment differ from one population to the next. For example, some research suggests that for women, the percentage who enter treatment compared to men is vastly disproportionate to their relative substance use (Greenfield et al., 2007; Pape & Elias, 2013). What creates obstacles to women who need treatment for their substance use? Among pregnant and parenting women, obstacles to seeking help generally included fear of negative repercussions, such as with Child Protective Services, if substance abuse were discovered, the status of their pregnancy,

TABLE 17.01 Substances and Their Shared Symptoms with Mood Disorder Symptoms

Substance	Mania	Depression	Psychosis
Alcohol	Yes Intoxication and Withdrawal	Yes Intoxication and Withdrawal	Yes Intoxication and Withdrawal
Cannabis	-	Yes, in Withdrawal	Yes Intoxication
Hallucinogens	Yes Intoxication	Yes Intoxication	Yes Intoxication
Opiates	-	Yes Intoxication and Withdrawal	Yes Intoxication
Sedatives	Yes Intoxication and Withdrawal	Yes Intoxication and Withdrawal	Yes Intoxication and Withdrawal
Stimulants	Yes Intoxication	Yes Intoxication and Withdrawal	Yes Intoxication and Withdrawal

Source: American Psychiatric Association (2013).

TABLE 17.02 Substances and Their Shared Symptoms with Anxiety and Sleep Disorder Symptoms

Substance	Anxiety	Sleep
Alcohol	Yes Intoxication and Withdrawal	Yes Intoxication and Withdrawal
Cannabis	Yes Intoxication	Yes Intoxication and Withdrawal
Hallucinogens	Yes Intoxication	-
Opiates	-	Yes Withdrawal
Sedatives	Yes Withdrawal	Yes Intoxication and Withdrawal
Stimulants	Yes Intoxication and Withdrawal	Yes Intoxication and Withdrawal

Source: American Psychiatric Association (2013).

BOX 17.07 TRY THIS: DIAGNOSING MADISON

Read the following brief scenario. What questions do you have for Madison and her family that might clarify the source of her psychotic symptoms? After considering carefully what each family member describes, what is your initial diagnostic hunch?

Madison. Madison, 32, sat across from her mother, father, younger brother and Jerome, the intervention specialist facilitating their intervention. After being prompted by Jerome, Madison's father began, hands shaking as he glanced at the hand-written note he used as a guide, "It is hard for me to put into words the utter dismay, complete anguish and barely contained rage as I watch you drink yourself into a stupor day-in and day-out, throwing away every talent you once had, leaving us to care for your kids when we should be retired, and worrying constantly about what you are doing to get all this booze. I can't stand to watch you stumble around our house incoherent and I can't concentrate when you are gone because I'm so worried about what might happen to you while you are out on the streets. Your mom, your brother and I, we are terrified and we want our lives back." Madison's mother adds, "We love you, Maddie, but here you are, showing up drunk to your intervention, we haven't seen you in three days and didn't even know if you would show up until you finally walked through the door . . ." Her brother interrupts, "And you haven't even asked about your kids! Maddie, you've always been like this, such a drama queen, stomping around the house or hijacking every family meal with your issues, then the cutting and suicide attempts, creating chaos wherever you go. And now that you've added alcohol to that mess the rest of the family is left to clean-up from Hurricane Maddie, except this storm never ends! It's time for you to get some real help this time, Maddie. You've got to commit yourself to being healthy, if not for us or yourself, for your kids."

Sobbing, Madison shares, "I never meant for things to get so bad, Dad . . . Mom? You know that. I'm scared, too. I'm scared of what will happen to me but I'm afraid of what is happening to my mind. Sometimes when I haven't had a drink for a while I see things that I know are not there. If I don't get help I won't be able to take care of my kids, drunk or sober."

"What are you experiencing, Maddie, that is scaring you so much?" Jerome asks.

"When I haven't had a drink in a while, I see a black dog, or maybe it is a shadow dog, I'm not sure. It usually just stares at me in a very creepy way. When I'm drinking it disappears again."

1. What do you think is the source of Madison's repeated visual hallucination? Do you believe it is substance-induced or represents a primary psychosis?
2. Does Madison's brother's description of her behavior before her drinking began offer any clues? Does his description describe good, fair or poor prior functioning?
3. How about her relationship to the shadow dog? What sense do you get about her insight about the shadow dog?
4. What more would you like to know before giving Madison a diagnosis?

issues with their partners and so on (Jessup et al., 2003). Among African American women, barriers may include childcare responsibilities, lack of money or insurance and community-based obstacles (Allen, 1995). Residential treatment programs are expensive and are also in high demand. Not all private insurance providers adequately cover

BOX 17.08 DIAGNOSTIC BRIDGE: SUBSTANCE-INDUCED PSYCHOSIS (SIP) AND THE SCHIZOPHRENIA SPECTRUM

Differentiating between SIP and florid or prodromal psychosis is one of the more difficult diagnostic challenges. Key to this challenge is constructing an accurate and detailed timeline of symptoms. However, when it is not possible to create an adequate timeline or the accuracy of the timeline is in question, turning to research that describes differences in the psychotic symptoms themselves may help differentiate these two continuums and support you in arriving at an accurate diagnosis. For a detailed discussion of the differentiation of schizophrenia spectrum disorders and SIPs, turn to the Schizophrenia and Related Disorders chapter in this book.

residential treatment costs, and a significant portion of those who need medical coverage don't have it, leaving too many clients without this option and others without enough coverage to complete programs. Consequently, outpatient programs are used to fill gaps left by availability and access problems with residential treatment. Outpatient treatment also provides relapse prevention following completion of residential programs.

Outpatient Treatment. When discussing outpatient treatment, it is helpful to know that there are two primary levels of intervention. The most comprehensive of the outpatient treatment programs are referred to as "intensive outpatient" treatment. These programs can run 4-6 hours a day and include a variety of interventions and approaches. Other outpatient treatment programs may meet as little as once a week, and, of course, there are programs that run the continuum of intensity between these two extremes (O'Dwayer, 2013).

Half-Way Houses and Sober Living/Therapeutic Communities. For most clients, the environment and the people within it are as important a factor in their substance use or sobriety as their personal commitment to their recovery. Consequently, communities where residents share the intention to remain drug and alcohol free is a draw. The first treatment communities were established in the late 1950s for those with opiate addiction. A movement followed and treatment communities began to appear all over the country in the 1960s and 1970s. Where once these communities were primarily for those addicted to opiates, it is now much more common for residents to be experiencing addiction to multiple substances (Polcin et al., 2010). Sober living communities are non-licensed homes where clients agree to abstain from substance use, to attend 12-step programs (see peer-based programs below), pay rent and contribute to chores, similar to residential treatment but do not provide formal treatment on site or require that residents participate in outside therapy. Half-way houses, on the other hand, generally are funded entirely or in part by government sponsored grants, are licensed and include some form of integrated treatment that is a mandated part of living in the house. Both half-way houses and sober living environments have demonstrated efficacy in supporting clients in maintaining sobriety and improving various measures of wellness (Polcin et al., 2010).

Family Treatment. Family-based interventions are broadly researched and enjoy very strong efficacy rates. Though there are a number of these programs, the most widely available include brief strategic family therapy (BSFT), multidimensional family therapy (MDFT) and functional family therapy (FFT). These interventions share key elements in addition to treatment of the substance addiction including teaching parenting strategies that are developmentally appropriate, supporting family members in repairing and rebuilding damaged relationships and guiding families in dealing with systems outside the family such as legal and educational systems (Hogue et al., 2017).

Though the bulk of available research suggests that residential and family treatment of substance abuse in teens are roughly equivalent in their efficacy, Liddle et al. (2018), conducted a randomized clinical trial of 113 adolescents assigned to either residential treatment or to MDFT and followed these participants through treatment, assessing progress at 2, 4, 12 and 18 months after baseline scores were taken. Their research found that early in treatment, the first 2 months, clients receiving either treatment showed significant improvements in substance use reduction, frequency of use, externalizing and delinquency. However, those who were assigned to MDFT faired better in their ability to sustain those gains in substance use and frequency of use than did those who received residential treatment, though both groups were roughly similar in maintaining decreases in delinquent behavior and externalization. Similarly, Hartnett et al. (2017) conducted a meta-analysis of randomized and non-randomized comparative studies of functional family therapy, control groups, alternative treatments and treatment as usual groups. These authors found support for the effectiveness of FFT compared to each of these groups, including cognitive-behavioral therapy as well as other models of family therapy.

Peer-Based Recovery. Peer-based recovery programs are often used to support clients in maintaining a sober status. These programs, also known as 12-step programs, are widely available, hold regularly scheduled meetings, are generally free of charge, and are frequently, but not always, open to all. Probably the most famous of the peer-based groups is Alcoholics Anonymous (AA), closely followed by Narcotics Anonymous.

These groups provide peer support by allowing people with addictions a space to listen to others share about their journey through substance abuse, talk about their own struggles and provide one-to-one support and guidance in the form of a peer sponsor, who is typically available by telephone when urgent support is needed. These groups embrace the medical model of addiction, provide a culture of honesty and confrontation and the expectation of confidentiality (Spiegel & Fewell, 2013; White, 2009). Twelve-step groups have been shown to have very high attrition rates, attendance generally declining between 3 and 6 months after beginning (Laudet, 2003). The 12-step process itself, sometimes described as "working the steps," includes a series of beliefs and related actions that have drawn concern and criticism. Among the concerns expressed by mental health professionals and clients alike are issues that range from the untrained leadership of the programs, risk of bad advice from leaders or other members, risk of dependence on the group and the emphasis of religion and personal powerlessness that many find aversive or counter to their personal beliefs (Laudet, 2003; Laudet & White, 2005). Some have raised concerns that AA in particular has taken on a cult-like quality, thanks in part to its focus on religion, and the concept that only with the help of God can those addicted to substances maintain sobriety. Critics assert that the dependence on substances is simply replaced with a dependence on the group, though supporters of the program argue that AA is effective, democratic, constitutes a healthy dependency and provides inclusion, community and support (Vaillant, 2005).

Definitional Cases in Substance-Related and Addictive Disorders

As you read through the following cases, you will want to use both your printed DSM 5 and the most recent available DSM 5 Supplement. Again, significant revisions to the codes and some criteria and text revisions were made in the 2017, and to a lesser extent, the 2018 supplements (APA, 2018). As is always the case, definitional cases do not always lend themselves to full coding. An answer key providing answers to alternating cases can be found in the appendix of this text. Again, when considering diagnosis around the misuse of substances, it is essential to remember that a given substance can have one effect that results from ongoing use, another during the moment of intoxication and still another when the substance is removed, that of withdrawal. Consequently, the DSM 5 organizes the SUDs first by type of substance and then by whether the ill effects are the consequence of use, intoxication or of withdrawal. The pivot table is organized with this in mind.

David

A police officer brought David to the hospital after he was found unconscious, dirty and disheveled, in an alley next to a large trash can outside a restaurant. Blood tests revealed the presence of heroin in his system. What diagnosis is appropriate for David?

Dana

Though she has tried many times to stop, Dana feels a continuous pull to place bets on racehorses. Over the past few years, she finds that she must bet more and more money in order to feel the same excitement she felt when she first began gambling.

Mike

Mike, 65, has been in an alcohol recovery program for 48 hours following years of heavy alcohol use. Since entering the program, Mike has experienced anxiety, insomnia, tremor, nausea and vomiting.

Holly

Holly, 42, is the mother of three young daughters. Though she always has the intention to restrict her drinking to "just a glass or two of wine" by the time her daughters get home from school they generally find Holly passed out on the couch and unable to help them with their homework or make their dinner.

Simone

Simone, who is on a week-long vacation from medical school, is complaining of a debilitating headache, fatigue and general crankiness. Simone has only had one cup of coffee in the past 24 hours compared to her usual 8-10 when she is doing her rotations.

Desmond

Desmond, 19, would like to cut back on his use of cannabis but every time he has gotten together with friends over the past year, he has found himself using more than he intended. Desmond is worried that his use of the drug is interfering with his willingness to go to class or study and he has noticed his grades dropping.

Libby

Libby, 27, was brought into the hospital by police officers after answering a call and finding Libby attacking her roommate and screaming obscenities. Upon examination, she was found to have delusions, visual disturbances (nystagmus) and a large quantity of PCP in her system.

Anar

Anar, 13, has been spending a great deal of time in his basement alone or with his cousin "huffing." Anar has lost interest in spending time with friends and has dropped out of ice hockey because he would rather spend time getting high.

Narrative Cases in Substance-Related and Addictive Disorders

Because of the high rate of co-occurring disorders, some of the following cases will require a dual diagnosis.

Ann

Ann, a 35-year-old nurse who works for a pain management clinic has come to mandated counseling following a DUI. Ann shares, "This is how the DUI happened, I'm not sure it is really that big a deal. The ladies from the pain clinic like to go out for a drink on Fridays and so I like to go along. I am really kind of an introvert and I always have been. It's not easy for me to just let loose and have a good time like it is for everyone else. I worry a lot about how the others will perceive me, and I feel embarrassed to say anything or to dance or whatever, so for a long time I wouldn't go out with them because I just felt too stupid. But finally I did go and I discovered if I have a few drinks then I can have a lot of fun and people really think I'm funny. I do have a good sense of humor when I'm not monitoring myself so much. But then I started to come home really wasted and it pissed my husband off a lot. So I promised him that I would tone it down a bit. He knows that when I start to party, it is hard for me to slow down. The problem for me is that I always mean to have just one or two drinks but once I get started, I just kind of lose track and end up drinking more than I planned. The night of the DUI, I just had a little too much to drink before I got in the car." Ann further shares, "Sometimes my husband and I fight about my weekend drinking. It's just the weekend but he says that I get carried away and I am too drunk or hungover to be a good mom to the kids."

Dale

Dale, a 24-year-old dental student, was meeting with his advisor when she expressed concern about his flushed face, nervous energy and restlessness. Dale shared with his advisor that he was, in fact, not feeling well and that he was experiencing a racing heart, and insomnia. Dale admits that he has been drinking a lot of coffee and energy drinks to try to stay awake while he studies for his exams. "Sometimes I can drink two or three of those energy drinks in a day and coffee in between. It makes me pretty jittery,

TABLE 17.03 Pivot Points: Substance-Related and Addictive Disorders

	Consider this Diagnosis
Pivot Point One: Is your client's suffering related to consuming alcohol?	Alcohol-Related Disorder
• Does your client consume too much alcohol and struggle to cut down on the amount of alcohol they consume?	Alcohol Use Disorder
• Do your client's symptoms follow the recent consumption of alcohol?	Alcohol Intoxication
• Is your client's suffering a result of attempting to stop drinking alcohol?	Alcohol Withdrawal
Pivot Point Two: Is your client's suffering related to consuming a high dose of caffeine (> 250 mg)?	Caffeine Intoxication
• Does your client's suffering arise from abruptly stopping or drastically reducing caffeine intake?	Caffeine Withdrawal
Pivot Point Three: Does your client's suffering arise from problematic use of cannabis?	Cannabis Use Disorder
• Has your client recently used cannabis?	Cannabis Intoxication
• Does your client's suffering arise from abruptly stopping their use of cannabis?	Cannabis Withdrawal
Pivot Point Four: Is your client's suffering related to the use of PCP or another substance that produced dissociation or hallucinations?	
• Does your client have a pattern of using phencyclidine or similar substance?	Phencyclidine Use Disorder
• Is your client suffering from using a hallucinogenic substance other than phencyclidine?	Other Hallucinogen Use Disorder
• Is your client currently experiencing the effect of PCP or other hallucinogenic substance?	Phencylidine Intoxication Other Hallucinogen Intoxication
• Is your client still experiencing changes in their perception after they've stopped using a hallucinogenic substance?	Hallucinogen Persisting Perception Disorder
• Is your client's experience related to the diagnoses above, but does not meet full criteria for any?	Other Phencyclidine-Induced Disorders Other Hallucinogen-Induced Disorders Unspecified Phencyclidine-Related Disorder Unspecified Hallucinogen-Related Disorder
Pivot Point Five: Is your client's suffering related to a pattern of inhaling a hydrocarbon-based inhalant?	Inhalant Use Disorders

(Continued)

	Consider this Diagnosis
• Did they recently use an inhalant?	Inhalant Intoxication
• Is your client's experience related to the diagnoses above, but does not meet full criteria for any?	Other Inhalant-Induced Disorders Unspecified Inhalant-Related Disorder
Pivot Point Six: Does your client's suffering result from opioid use?	Opioid Use Disorder
• Recent use of an opioid?	Opioid Intoxication
• Does your client's suffering arise from the cessation of opioid use?	Opioid Withdrawal
• Is your client's experience related to the diagnoses above, but does not meet full criteria for any?	Unspecified Opioid-Related Disorder
Pivot Point Seven: Does your client's suffering arise from a pattern of sedative, hypnotic or anxiolytic use?	Sedative, Hypnotic or Anxiolytic Use Disorder
• Are they currently under the influence of such substances?	Sedative, Hypnotic or Anxiolytic Intoxication
• Is their suffering a result of withdrawal from such substances?	Sedative, Hypnotic or Anxiolytic Withdrawal
• Is your client's experience related to the diagnoses above, but does not meet full criteria for any?	Unspecified Sedative-, Hypnotic- or Anxiolytic-Related Disorder
Pivot Point Eight: Does your client struggle with a pattern of amphetamine-type substance, cocaine or other stimulant use?	Stimulant Use Disorder
• Are they currently under the influence of such substances?	Stimulant Intoxication
• Is their suffering related to the cessation of using such substances?	Stimulant Withdrawal
• Is your client's experience related to the diagnoses above, but does not meet full criteria for any?	Other or Unspecified Stimulant-Induced Disorder
Pivot Point Nine: Is your client's suffering related to the use of tobacco?	Tobacco Use Disorder
• Is their suffering related to the cessation of tobacco use?	Tobacco Withdrawal
• Is your client's experience related to the diagnoses above, but does not meet full criteria for any?	Unspecified Tobacco-Related Disorder
Pivot Point Ten: Does your client's suffering arise from a problematic pattern of substance use that does not fit the criteria for the diagnoses above?	Other (or Unknown) Substance Use Disorder Other (or Unknown) Substance Intoxication Other (or Unknown) Substance Withdrawal
Pivot Point Eleven: Is your client's suffering a result of problematic gambling behavior?	Gambling Disorder

it's the trade-off, I guess. I must have had two of those energy drinks on the train to school this morning."

Sachiko

Sachiko, a 23-year-old art student, has come to the campus health clinic with a number of complaints "I can't sleep at all, I've lost my appetite and I just don't feel like myself. My roommate is asking me why I'm so irritated and angry all the time." Sachiko shares, "These problems all started about a week after I stopped smoking pot. I got a job and they do drug testing there so I had to stop if I wanted to keep my job. I used to smoke a little every day after classes, and with my friends at parties and stuff. But I haven't smoked at all in the last week and now I feel terrible." Sachiko denies using any other substances.

Sachiko asks, "Is there any way I can get something for sleep? I think the sleep issue is my real problem, that's why I'm so cranky. I've been having trouble getting any sleep since I was a kid, way before I started smoking pot. I've always had a hard time getting good rest, even if I sleep a lot. As long as I can remember I lay in bed thinking and having a hard time getting to sleep or sometimes waking up so early it is still dark out and not being able to get back to sleep. And then I would start thinking about how I am such a loser and not as smart as my sister or not good at things and on and on. Then I would think about how guilty I feel for taking up space in the family. At least when I was smoking I wouldn't have such dark thoughts about being worthless. I didn't feel so hopeless about my future. I can feel the edge of those feelings creeping back in. Maybe if I got better sleep things would get better?"

Shelby

Shelby, 20, was dropped by the emergency room, unconscious and covered in vomit. Once conscious Shelby met with a social worker and reported, "I was at a party with some guys I met at a club. We had laced some weed and then me and Simon were sitting on his bed, lost in the K-hole. So we were smoking and I guess I just got really sick." Shelby also shares that while she had been a good student in her freshman and sophomore years of high school, she had been less successful academically and less involved socially after she and her friends began drinking and smoking marijuana. While her friends seemed to be able to balance their use of drugs and alcohol, Shelby found this to be much more difficult. "My grades dropped a lot, I lost a lot of friends that were doing things like journalism club and track and found friends who liked to smoke with me. So I didn't get into college, but I did take a few classes at the community college. While I was there I met a guy who was selling Special K. I never tried that before, and when I mixed it with pot it was great. I tried K by itself but it was too much, it scared me, but with pot it was just right. After that, I stopped going to class and just worked enough hours at a coffee shop to pay for the pot and the K. In the morning when I wake up I miss that old me, the person I was in high school before I got in trouble but by afternoon, well, I just want to get high. My family won't have anything to do with me so why bother, right?"

Sawyer

Sawyer, 26, has been brought to a free clinic in the middle of a busy Wednesday morning. Sawyer's head is bleeding and he has a gash across the back of his skull where his friend reported that Sawyer fell and hit his head. While meeting with a nurse Sawyer explains, "I was huffing glue and I tried to walk across the street. Everything was blurry and I felt dizzy and lost my balance. I hit my head on the curb or something, I'm not sure, and it won't stop bleeding so Jake brought me in." Jake confirms that he and Sawyer use glue or other inhalants to get high four or five times a week. Sawyer notes, "Jake and I get ahold of this stuff and I end up doing a lot more than I thought I would. I'd like to stop, and I've tried, but you know how it is, it's there and I can't stop in the moment. It's a problem because I get high instead of looking for a job or going to see my kids. I've missed a bunch of appointments with the social services to see my kids because I was high. I know using is ruining my life and I still can't stop."

Jerry

Jerry, now 27, was in a motorcycle accident 2 years ago in which he was badly injured and spent nearly 3 weeks in the hospital. He shares, "After I got out of the hospital the doctor gave a scrip' for oxycodone for the pain in my back and legs. It was like knives running up and down my legs and made it impossible to concentrate or sleep." Jerry's pain, however, did not seem to ease as the year unfolded so his doctor gradually increased his dose. Jerry reports, "It got so that I had to have that oxy just to get through the day but if I wanted to get to sleep I had to add sleeping pills and beer. I had to stop doing that after it caused a seizure and I spent another night in the hospital. Since then I've decided I'm going off oxy once and for all." Jerry stopped taking all medication 24 hours ago and decided to do a juice cleanse. Since stopping the medication, Jerry has experienced stomach cramping, nausea, vomiting, body pain and a feeling of intense anxiety. He reports he is unable to sleep.

Ingrid

Ingrid, 26, has been struggling with her use of Valium. Nine months ago, Ingrid was in a car accident. Since that time, she has struggled with symptoms of anxiety, including panic when faced with the prospect of driving, nightmares about her accident, sleeplessness, distraction and "brain fog," and idiopathic muscle spasm. Ingrid's primary care physician prescribed Valium for the anxiety and muscle pain; however, after a few weeks, Ingrid found that she needed more and more medication to feel relaxed and get to sleep. Her doctor increased her dosage but when Ingrid returned to her physician complaining that the medication needed increased again because it was not having the effect it once had, her physician declined and suggested counseling. Ingrid shares, "I can get it on campus from a guy I know but that feels shady and I'm not sure I want to go down that road. I'm embarrassed to admit it but I think I need some help with this."

References

Agrawal, A., & Lynskey, M. T. (2008). Are there genetic influences on addiction: Evidence from family, adoption and twin studies. *Addiction*, *103*(7), 1069–1081.

Alexander, B. K., Beyerstein, B. L., Hadaway, P. F., & Coambs, R. B. (1981). Effect of early and later colony housing on oral ingestion of morphine in rats. *Pharmacology Biochemistry and Behavior*, *15*(4), 571–576.

Allen, K. (1995). Barriers to treatment for addicted African-American women. *Journal of the National Medical Association*, *87*(10), 751.

American Addiction Centers. (2019). *Is detox always necessary?* https://americanaddictioncenters.org/drug-detox/is-it-necessary

American Psychiatric Association. (2013). *Diagnostic and statistical manual of mental disorders (DSM-5®)*. Author.

American Psychological Association. (2018). *Supplement to diagnostic and statistical manual of mental disorders (DSM-5-UPDATE)*. Author.

American Society of Addiction Medicine. (2011). *Definition of addiction*. https://www.asam.org/resources/definition-of-addiction

Anda, R. F., Felitti, V. J., Bremner, J. D., Walker, J. D., Whitfield, C. H., Perry, B. D., Dube, S. R., & Giles, W. H. (2006). The enduring effects of abuse and related adverse experiences in childhood. *European Archives of Psychiatry and Clinical Neuroscience*, *256*(3), 174–186.

Andreassen, C. S., Griffiths, M. D., Hetland, J., & Pallesen, S. (2012). Development of a work addiction scale. *Scandinavian Journal of Psychology*, *53*(3), 265–272.

Atkins, C. (2014). *Co-occurring disorders: Integrated assessment and treatment of substance use and mental disorders*. PESI Publishing & Media.

Back, S. E., & Brady, K. T. (2008). Anxiety disorders with comorbid substance use disorders: Diagnostic and treatment considerations. *Psychiatric Annals*, *38*(11).

Baker, T. B., Piper, M. E., McCarthy, D. E., Majeskie, M. R., & Fiore, M. C. (2004). Addiction motivation reformulated: An affective processing model of negative reinforcement. *Psychological Review*, *111*(1), 33.

Baker, T. E., Stockwell, T., Barnes, G., Haesevoets, R., & Holroyd, C. B. (2016). Reward sensitivity of ACC as an intermediate phenotype between DRD4-521T and substance misuse. *Journal of Cognitive Neuroscience*, *28*(3), 460–471.

Bartoli, F., Carrà, G., Crocamo, C., & Clerici, M. (2015). From DSM-IV to DSM-5 alcohol use disorder: An overview of epidemiological data. *Addictive Behaviors*, *41*, 46–50.

Bartoli, F., Carretta, D., Clerici, M., & Carrà, G. (2015). Comorbid anxiety and alcohol or substance use disorders: An overview. In el-Guebaly, G. Carrà, M. Galanter, & A. M. Baldacchino, *Textbook of addiction treatment: International perspectives* (pp. 1971–1983). Springer Milan.

Baskin-Sommers, A. R., & Foti, D. (2015). Abnormal reward functioning across substance use disorders and major depressive disorder: Considering reward as a transdiagnostic mechanism. *International Journal of Psychophysiology*, *98*(2), 227–239.

Benner, A. D., & Wang, Y. (2015). Adolescent substance use: The role of demographic marginalization and socioemotional distress. *Developmental Psychology*, *51*(8), 1086.

Bennett, M. E., Peer, J., & Muralidharan, A. (2018). The problem of dual diagnosis. In D. C. Beidel & B. C. Frueh (Eds.), *Adult psychopathology and diagnosis* (Vol. 5, pp. 45–103).

Blanco, C., Moreyra, P., Nunes, E. V., Saiz-Ruiz, J., & Ibanez, A. (2001, July). Pathological gambling: Addiction or compulsion? *Seminars in Clinical Neuropsychiatry*, *6*(3) 167–176.

Blazer, D. G., & Wu, L. T. (2009). The epidemiology of substance use and disorders among middle aged and elderly community adults: National survey on drug use and health. *The American Journal of Geriatric Psychiatry*, *17*(3), 237–245.

Borges, G., Ye, Y., Bond, J., Cherpitel, C. J., Cremonte, M., Moskalewicz, J., Swiatkiewicz, G., & Rubio-Stipec, M. (2010). The dimensionality of alcohol use disorders and alcohol consumption in a cross-national perspective. *Addiction*, *105*(2), 240–254.

Brogly, S. B., Link, K., & Newman, A. (2018). Barriers to treatment for substance use disorders among women with children. *Canadian Journal of Addiction*, *9*(3), 18–22.

Budney, A. J., Novy, P. L., & Hughes, J. R. (1999). Marijuana withdrawal among adults seeking treatment for marijuana dependence. *Addiction*, *94*(9), 1311–1322.

Capuzzi, D., & Stauffer, M. D. (2016). *Foundations of addictions counseling* (p. 528). Pearson.

Carr, E. R., & Szymanski, D. M. (2011). Sexual objectification and substance abuse in young adult women. *The Counseling Psychologist*, *39*(1), 39–66.

Cassin, S. E., & von Ranson, K. M. (2007). Is binge eating experienced as an addiction? *Appetite*, *49*(3), 687–690.

Caton, C. L., Samet, S., & Hasin, D. S. (2000). When acute-stage psychosis and substance use co-occur: Differentiating substance-induced and primary psychotic disorders. *Journal of Psychiatric Practice*, *6*(5), 256–266.

Center for Behavioral Health Statistics & Quality. (2017). *Mental health services administration. 2017. Results from the 2016 national survey on drug use and health: Detailed tables.* Author.

Center for Substance Abuse Treatment. (2006). *Detoxification and substance abuse treatment* (Treatment Improvement Protocol (TIP) Series 45, DHHS Publication No. (SMA) 06-4131). Substance Abuse Mental Health Services Administration.

Center for Substance Abuse Treatment. (2014). *Treatment Improvement Protocol (TIP) Series.* Substance Abuse and Mental Health Services Administration. https://store.samhsa.gov/system/files/sma14-4849.pdf

Choi, S., Adams, S. M., Morse, S. A., & MacMaster, S. (2015). Gender differences in treatment retention among individuals with co-occurring substance abuse and mental health disorders. *Substance Use & Misuse, 50*(5), 653–663.

Christenson, G. A., Faber, R. J., De Zwaan, M., Raymond, N. C., Specker, S. M., Ekern, M. D., Mackenzie, T. B.., & Eckert, E. D. (1994). Compulsive buying: Descriptive characteristics and psychiatric comorbidity. *The Journal of Clinical Psychiatry, 55*, 5–11.

Conrod, J. P., & Nikolaou, K. (2016). Annual research review: On the developmental neuropsychology of substance use disorders. *Journal of Child Psychology and Psychiatry, 57*(3), 371–394.

Conway, K. P., Swendsen, J., Husky, M. M., He, J. P., & Merikangas, K. R. (2016). Association of lifetime mental disorders and subsequent alcohol and illicit drug use: Results from the national comorbidity survey–adolescent supplement. *Journal of the American Academy of Child & Adolescent Psychiatry, 55*(4), 280–288.

DeLisi, L. E. (2008). The effect of cannabis on the brain: Can it cause brain anomalies that lead to increased risk for schizophrenia? *Current Opinion in Psychiatry, 21*(2), 140.

Democrat & Chronicle. (2019). *Population of U.S. cities.* http://rochester.nydatabases.com/database/population-us-cities

Denis, C. M., Gelernter, J., Hart, A. B., & Kranzler, H. R. (2015). Inter-observer reliability of DSM-5 substance use disorders. *Drug and Alcohol Dependence, 153*, 229–235.

Faraone, S. V., Rostain, A. L., Montano, C. B., Mason, O., Antshel, K. M., & Newcorn, J. H. (2019). Systematic review: Nonmedical use of prescription stimulants: Risk factors, outcomes, and risk reduction strategies. *Journal of the American Academy of Child & Adolescent Psychiatry, 59*(1), 100–112.

Ferdinand, R. F., Sondeijker, F., Van Der Ende, J., Selten, J. P., Huizink, A., & Verhulst, F. C. (2005). Cannabis use predicts future psychotic symptoms, and vice versa. *Addiction, 100*(5), 612–618.

Fiorentini, A., Sara Volonteri, L., Dragogna, F., Rovera, C., Maffini, M., Carlo Mauri, M., & Altamura, A. C. (2011). Substance-induced psychoses: A critical review of the literature. *Current Drug Abuse Reviews, 4*(4), 228–240.

First, M. B. (2013). Differential diagnosis step by step. In *DSM-5 handbook of differential diagnosis.* American Psychiatric Pub.

Flores, P. J. (2004). *Addiction as an attachment disorder.* Jason Aronson.

Freshman, A. (2013). Assessment and treatment of adolescents with substance use disorders. In S. L. A. Straussner (Ed.), *Clinical work with substance abusing clients*. Guilford Press.

Friedman, E. G. (2013). Assessment and treatment of individuals dependent on opioids. In S. L. A. Straussner (Ed.), *Clinical work with substance abusing clients*. Guilford Press.

Granfield, R., & Reinarman, C. (2015). *Expanding addiction: Critical essays*. Routledge.

Green, A. I., Tohen, M. F., Hamer, R. M., Strakowski, S. M., Lieberman, J. A., Glick, I., Clark, W. S., & HGDH Research Group. (2004). First episode schizophrenia-related psychosis and substance use disorders: Acute response to olanzapine and haloperidol. *Schizophrenia Research*, *66*(2–3), 125–135.

Greenfield, S. F., Brooks, A. J., Gordon, S. M., Green, C. A., Kropp, F., McHugh, R. K., Lincoln, M., Hien, D., & Miele, G. M. (2007). Substance abuse treatment entry, retention, and outcome in women: A review of the literature. *Drug and Alcohol Dependence*, *86*(1), 1–21.

Hall, W., Degenhardt, L., & Teesson, M. (2004). Cannabis use and psychotic disorders: An update. *Drug and Alcohol Review*, *23*(4), 433–443.

Hartnett, D., Carr, A., Hamilton, E., & O'Reilly, G. (2017). The effectiveness of functional family therapy for adolescent behavioral and substance misuse problems: A meta-analysis. *Family Process*, *56*(3), 607–619.

Hasin, D., Paykin, A., Endicott, J., & Grant, B. (1999). The validity of DSM-IV alcohol abuse: Drunk drivers versus all others. *Journal of Studies on Alcohol*, *60*(6), 746–755.

Hasin, D. S., O'Brien, C. P., Auriacombe, M., Borges, G., Bucholz, K., Budney, A., Compton, W. M., Crowley, T., Ling, W., Petry, N. M., Schuckit, M., & Grant, B. (2013). DSM-5 criteria for substance use disorders: Recommendations and rationale. *American Journal of Psychiatry*, *170*(8), 834–851.

Hedegaard, H., Warner, M., & Miniño, A. M. (2017). *Drug overdose deaths in the United States, 1999–2015*. Department of Health and Human Services. https://www.semanticscholar.org/paper/Drug-Overdose-Deaths-in-the-United-States%2C-Hedegaard-Warner/d9fb9f85f17b86409fb1980955ff4e9a51eb086e

Hogue, A., Bobek, M., Dauber, S., Henderson, C. E., McLeod, B. D., & Southam-Gerow, M. A. (2017). Distilling the core elements of family therapy for adolescent substance use: Conceptual and empirical solutions. *Journal of Child & Adolescent Substance Abuse*, *26*(6), 437–453.

Huebner, D. M., Thoma, B. C., & Neilands, T. B. (2015). School victimization and substance use among lesbian, gay, bisexual, and transgender adolescents. *Prevention Science*, *16*(5), 734–743.

Ingraham, C. (2016, August 12). *Heroin deaths surpass gun homicides for the first time, CDC data shows*. The Washington Post. https://www.washingtonpost.com/news/wonk/wp/2016/12/08/heroin-deaths-surpass-gun-homicides-for-the-first-time-cdc-data-show/?utm_term=.b3ad39c2e7d6

Jellinek, E. M. (1960). *The disease concept of alcoholism*. Hillhouse Press.

Jessup, M. A., Humphreys, J. C., Brindis, C. D., & Lee, K. A. (2003). Extrinsic barriers to substance abuse treatment among pregnant drug dependent women. *Journal of Drug Issues*, *33*(2), 285–304.

Jones, K. D., Gill, C., & Ray, S. (2012). Review of the proposed DSM-5 substance use disorder. *Journal of Addictions & Offender Counseling, 33*(2), 115–123.

Kardefelt-Winther, D., Heeren, A., Schimmenti, A., van Rooij, A., Maurage, P., Carras, M., Edman, J., Blaszczynski, A., Khazaal, Y., & Billieux, J. (2017). How can we conceptualize behavioural addiction without pathologizing common behaviours? *Addiction, 112*(10), 1709–1715.

Keyes, K. M., & Hasin, D. S. (2008). Socio-economic status and problem alcohol use: The positive relationship between income and the DSM-IV alcohol abuse diagnosis. *Addiction, 103*(7), 1120–1130.

Ko, J. Y, Patrick, S. W., Tong, V. T., Patel, R., Lind, J.N., & Barfield, W.D. (2016). Incidence of neonatal abstinence syndrome—28 states, 1999–2013 *Morbidity and Mortality Weekly Report,* 65(*31*), 799-802.

Koob, G. F. (2008). Hedonic homeostatic dysregulation as a driver of drug-seeking behavior. *Drug Discovery Today: Disease Models, 5*(4), 207–215.

Koob, G. F., & Volkow, N. D. (2016). Neurobiology of addiction: A neurocircuitry analysis. *The Lancet Psychiatry, 3*(8), 760–773.

Kreek, M. J., Nielsen, D. A., Butelman, E. R., & LaForge, K. S. (2005). Genetic influences on impulsivity, risk taking, stress responsivity and vulnerability to drug abuse and addiction. *Nature Neuroscience, 8*(11), 1450.

Kuerbis, A. N., Hagman, B. T., & Sacco, P. (2013). Functioning of alcohol use disorders criteria among middle-aged and older adults: Implications for DSM-5. *Substance Use & Misuse, 48*(4), 309–322.

Laudet, A. B. (2003). Attitudes and beliefs about 12-step groups among addiction treatment clients and clinicians: Toward identifying obstacles to participation. *Substance Use & Misuse, 38*(14), 2017–2047.

Laudet, A. B., & White, W. L. (2005). An exploratory investigation of the association between clinicians' attitudes toward twelve-step groups and referral rates. *Alcoholism Treatment Quarterly, 23*(1), 31–45.

Liddle, H. A., Dakof, G. A., Rowe, C. L., Henderson, C., Greenbaum, P., Wang, W., & Alberga, L. (2018). Multidimensional family therapy as a community-based alternative to residential treatment for adolescents with substance use and co-occurring mental health disorders. *Journal of Substance Abuse Treatment, 90*, 47–56.

Maraz, A., Urbán, R., Griffiths, M. D., & Demetrovics, Z. (2015). An empirical investigation of dance addiction. *PLoS One, 10*(5), e0125988.

Marsiglia, F. F., Ayers, S. L., Baldwin-White, A., & Booth, J. (2016). Changing Latino adolescents' substance use norms and behaviors: The effects of synchronized youth and parent drug use prevention interventions. *Prevention Science, 17*(1), 1–12.

Martin, C. S., Langenbucher, J. W., Chung, T., & Sher, K. J. (2014). Truth or consequences in the diagnosis of substance use disorders. *Addiction, 109*(11), 1773–1778.

Martin, C. S., Steinley, D. L., Vergés, A., & Sher, K. J. (2011). Letter to the editor: The proposed 2/11 symptom algorithm for DSM-5 substance-use disorders is too lenient. *Psychological Medicine, 41* (9), 2008–2010.

Martin, C. S., & Winters, K. C. (1998). Diagnosis and assessment of alcohol use disorders among adolescents. *Alcohol Health and Research World, 22*(2), 95.

Mate, G. (2010). *The realm of the hungry ghosts: Close encounters with addiction.* North Atlantic Books.

Mays, V. M., Jones, A., Delany-Brumsey, A., Coles, C., & Cochran, S. D. (2017). Perceived discrimination in healthcare and mental health/substance abuse treatment among blacks, latinos, and whites. *Medical Care, 55*(2), 173.

McCabe, S. E., West, B. T., Veliz, P., & Boyd, C. J. (2017). E-cigarette use, cigarette smoking, dual use, and problem behaviors among US adolescents: Results from a national survey. *Journal of Adolescent Health, 61*(2), 155–162.

McLafferty, L. P., Becker, M., Dresner, N., Meltzer-Brody, S., Gopalan, P., Glance, J., Victor, G. S., Mittal, L., Marshalek, P., Lander, L., & Worley, L. L. (2016). Guidelines for the management of pregnant women with substance use disorders. *Psychosomatics, 57*(2), 115–130.

Merikangas, K. R., He, J. P., Burstein, M., Swanson, S. A., Avenevoli, S., Cui, L., Benjet, C., Georgiades, K., & Swendsen, J. (2010). Lifetime prevalence of mental disorders in US adolescents: Results from the National Comorbidity Survey Replication–Adolescent Supplement (NCS-A. *Journal of the American Academy of Child & Adolescent Psychiatry, 49*(10), 980–989.

Meyers, J. L., Brown, Q., Grant, B. F., & Hasin, D. (2017). Religiosity, race/ethnicity, and alcohol use behaviors in the United States. *Psychological Medicine, 47*(1), 103–114.

Miller, S. (2019). *Drug overdose death rates in US women rise 260% in 2 decades.* LiveScience. https://www.livescience.com/64466-drug-overdose-deaths-women.html

Morrison, J., & Flegel, K. (2016). *Interviewing Children and adolescents: Skills and strategies for effective DSM-5? Diagnosis.* Guilford Publications.

National Institute of Mental Health. (2019). *Mental health.* https://www.nimh.nih.gov/health/statistics/mental-illness.shtml

Nielsen, S. M., Toftdahl, N. G., Nordentoft, M., & Hjorthøj, C. (2017). Association between alcohol, cannabis, and other illicit substance abuse and risk of developing schizophrenia: A nationwide population based register study. *Psychological Medicine, 47*(9), 1668–1677.

O'Dwayer, P. (2013). Assessment and treatment of individuals dependent on alcohol and other central nervous system suppressants. In S. L. A. Straussner (Ed.), *Clinical work with substance abusing clients.* Guilford Press.

Palmer, R. H., Brick, L., Nugent, N. R., Bidwell, L. C., McGeary, J. E., Knopik, V. S., & Keller, M. C. (2015). Examining the role of common genetic variants on alcohol, tobacco, cannabis and illicit drug dependence: Genetics of vulnerability to drug dependence. *Addiction, 110*(3), 530–537.

Pape, P. A., & Elias, S. (2013). Assessment and treatment of women with substance use disorders. In S. L. A. Straussner (Ed.), *Clinical work with substance abusing clients.* Guilford Press.

Pearson, C., & Hussain, Z. (2017). Smartphone use, addiction, narcissism, and personality: A mixed methods investigation. In *Gaming and technology addiction: Breakthroughs in research and practice* (pp. 212–229). IGI Global.

Peer, K., Rennert, L., Lynch, K. G., Farrer, L., Gelernter, J., & Kranzler, H. R. (2013). Prevalence of DSM-IV and DSM-5 alcohol, cocaine, opioid, and cannabis use disorders in a largely substance dependent sample. *Drug and Alcohol Dependence, 127*(1–3), 215–219.

Polcin, D. L., Korcha, R. A., Bond, J., & Galloway, G. (2010). Sober living houses for alcohol and drug dependence: 18-month outcomes. *Journal of Substance Abuse Treatment, 38*(4), 356–365.

Quello, S. B., Brady, K. T., & Sonne, S. C. (2005). Mood disorders and substance use disorder: A complex comorbidity. *Science & Practice Perspectives, 3*(1), 13.

Reece-Stremtan, S., Marinelli, K. A., & Academy of Breastfeeding Medicine. (2015). ABM clinical protocol# 21: Guidelines for breastfeeding and substance use or substance use disorder, revised 2015. *Breastfeeding Medicine, 10*(3), 135–141.

Robinson, S., & Adinoff, B. (2016). The classification of substance use disorders: Historical, contextual, and conceptual considerations. *Behavioral Sciences, 6*(3), 18.

Schenk, S., Lacelle, G., Gorman, K., & Amit, Z. (1987). Cocaine self-administration in rats influenced by environmental conditions: Implications for the etiology of drug abuse. *Neuroscience Letters, 81*(1–2), 227–231.

Schueller, J. R. (2015). Use of cocaine by pregnant women: Child abuse or choice? The;note. *Journal of Legislation, 25*(2), 163.

Smith, D. E. (2012). Editor's note: The process addictions and the new ASAM definition of addiction. *Journal of Psychoactive Drugs, 44*(1), 1–4.

Solinas, M., Thiriet, N., El Rawas, R., Lardeux, V., & Jaber, M. (2009). Environmental enrichment during early stages of life reduces the behavioral, neurochemical, and molecular effects of cocaine. *Neuropsychopharmacology, 34,* 1102–1111.

Spiegel, B. R., & Fewell, C. H. (2013). 12-Step programs as a treatment modality. In S. L. A. Straussner (Ed.), *Clinical work with substance abusing clients.* Guilford Press.

Stevens, J. E., Steinley, D., McDowell, Y. E., Boness, C. L., Trull, T. J., Martin, C. S., & Sher, K. J. (2019). Toward more efficient diagnostic criteria sets and rules: The use of optimization approaches in addiction science. *Addictive Behaviors, 94,* 57–64.

Straussner, S. L. A. (Ed.). (2013). *Clinical work with substance-abusing clients.* Guilford Publications.

Substance Abuse and Mental Health Services Administration. (2018). *Key substance use and mental health indicators in the United States: Results from the 2017 National Survey on Drug Use and Health* (HHS Publication No. SMA 18-5068, NSDUH Series H-53). Center for Behavioral Health Statistics and Quality, Substance Abuse and Mental Health Services Administration. https://www.samhsa.gov/data/

Sullivan, T. P., Weiss, N. H., Flanagan, J. C., Willie, T. C., Armeli, S., & Tennen, H. (2016). PTSD and daily co-occurrence of drug and alcohol use among women experiencing intimate partner violence. *Journal of Dual Diagnosis*, *12*(1), 36–42.

Tolliver, B. K., & Anton, R. F. (2015). Assessment and treatment of mood disorders in the context of substance abuse. *Dialogues in Clinical Neuroscience*, *17*(2), 181.

Torrens, M., Gilchrist, G., & Domingo-Salvany, A. (2011). Psychiatric comorbidity in illicit drug users: Substance-induced versus independent disorders. *Drug and Alcohol Dependence*, *113*(2–3), 147–156.

Uhl, G. R., Drgon, T., Johnson, C., Li, C. Y., Contoreggi, C., Hess, J., Naiman, D., & Liu, Q. R. (2008). Molecular genetics of addiction and related heritable phenotypes. *Annals of the New York Academy of Sciences*, *1141*(1), 318–381.

Vaillant, G. E. (2005). Alcoholics anonymous: Cult or cure? *Australian and New Zealand Journal of Psychiatry*, *39*(6), 431–436.

VanHouten, J. P., Rudd, R. A., Ballesteros, M. F., & Mack, K. A. (2019). Drug overdose deaths among women aged 30–64 years—United States, 1999–2017. *Morbidity and Mortality Weekly Report*, *68*(1), 1.

Vega, W. A., Canino, G., Cao, Z., & Alegria, M. (2009). Prevalence and correlates of dual diagnoses in US Latinos. *Drug and Alcohol Dependence*, *100*(1–2), 32–38.

Walker, M. B. (1989). Some problems with the concept of "gambling addiction": Should theories of addiction be generalized to include excessive gambling? *Journal of Gambling Behavior*, *5*(3), 179–200.

Wang, W., & Long, H. (2020, July 1). 'Cries for help': Drug overdoses are soaring during coronavirus pandemic. *Washington Post.*

Weiner, S. G., Malek, S. K., & Price, C. N. (2017). The opioid crisis and its consequences. *Transplantation*, *101*(4), 678–681.

Welsh, J. W., Knight, J. R., Hou, S. S. Y., Malowney, M., Schram, P., Sherritt, L., & Boyd, J. W. (2017). Association between substance use diagnoses and psychiatric disorders in an adolescent and young adult clinic-based population. *Journal of Adolescent Health*, *60*(6), 648–652.

White, W. L. (2009). Peer-based addiction recovery support: History, theory, practice, and scientific evaluation executive summary. *Counselor*, *10*(5), 54–59.

Widyanto, L., & Griffiths, M. (2006). 'Internet addiction': A critical review. *International Journal of Mental Health and Addiction*, *4*(1), 31–51.

Windle, M. (2000). Parental, sibling, and peer influences on adolescent substance use and alcohol problems. *Applied Developmental Science*, *4*(2), 98–110.

World Health Organization. Department of Mental Health, Substance Abuse, World Health Organization, International Narcotics Control Board, United Nations Office on Drugs & Crime. (2009). *Guidelines for the psychosocially assisted pharmacological treatment of opioid dependence.* Author.

Yoshimasu, K., Barbaresi, W. J., Colligan, R. C., Voigt, R. G., Weaver, A. L., & Katusic, S. K. (2016). Mediating and moderating role of depression, conduct disorder or attention-deficit/hyperactivity disorder in developing adolescent substance use disorders: A population-based study. *PLoS One*, *11*(6), e0157488.

Zapf, J. L., Greiner, J., & Carroll, J. (2008). Attachment styles and male sex addiction. *Sexual Addiction & Compulsivity*, *15*(2), 158–175.

18 Personality and Related Disorders

In the 1990s, a shift in thinking about personality disorders began to take shape. A classification of disorders that clinicians had long felt largely helpless to change seemed to reveal glimmers of hope and even documentation of recovery. Sperry (2016) notes that prior to this time, clients with a personality disorder diagnosis sometimes found it difficult to secure insurance coverage for mental health services because the view that personality disorders were untreatable was so widely held, which, in turn, left clinicians hesitant to diagnose personality disorders if doing so might create an obstacle to treatment. Also of concern was the significant stigma attached to a personality disorder diagnosis, particularly borderline personality or antisocial personality disorders.

Thirty years later, the conceptualization of the personality disorders is again, or perhaps still, in transition and is receiving a great deal of attention and discussion from clinicians and researchers in the field. The personality continuum is the only continuum in the DSM 5 in which two different frameworks for diagnosis are described, reflecting the degree to which the discussion is still ongoing. As is often the case with the DSM, efforts to strengthen validity and reliability are at the bottom of the proposed changes to the traditional framework. Looking more deeply, however, there is another discussion, one about the construct of personality itself, its origins and when (and if) personality crystallizes. Swept up in this debate is the long-held tradition of refraining from diagnosing children and adolescents with a personality disorder when presumably children and teens are still in a state of significant developmental change. Also swirling within these discussions are conversations about the origins of traits attributed to personality and whether or not, as in the case of borderline personality disorder (BPD), the origin and manifestation of these traits bear closer kinship with another continuum, namely the bipolar and related disorders or trauma and related disorders dimension.

In this chapter, we will touch upon the questions and the arguments offered within the field that have specific bearing on the diagnostic process. This chapter will explore aspects of the constructs of borderline personality disorder (BPD) and bipolar II (BPII), which complicate differential diagnosis and will draw from the wisdom of the field to offer recommendations for how to diagnose and, to a lesser degree, how to proceed safely with treatment when diagnosis is less than certain. Though the chapter will include an overview of the continuum, touching on the traditional framework and the proposed changes, the focus of this chapter will be on BPD. Let's begin with a description of the continuum of personality disorders as it is described in the main body of DSM 5 and its alternate framework located in the back of the manual.

The Personality Disorders Continuum

Though the DSM 5 as a whole makes an effort to move away from categorical diagnosis and into a more dimensional framework, the personality disorder nosology remains firmly in the categorical camp, while the alternative framework, which will be described briefly, comprises an effort to understand personality dimensionally. Like previous editions, the DSM 5 recognizes 10 distinct personality disorders and also describes a general personality disorder (GPD) configuration that is non-specific. The GPD criteria outline the defining qualities of the personality disorders continuum while the 10 distinct personality disorders serve to specify the unique configurations of personality and how they contribute to distress or impairment. GPD describes an enduring pattern of thoughts and behavior that includes the way the client thinks about the world, themselves and others (cognition) and includes a pattern of intensity and lability of emotion (affect) that is strikingly different than the client's cultural expectations. GPD is evidenced in both the interpersonal functioning and in the client's impulse control. Importantly, personality disorders are described as enduring, inflexible and pervasive, meaning they are stable overtime and don't change from one environment to the next. These patterns result in significant distress in relationships, at work and school and other areas of functioning (American Psychiatric Association [APA], 2013; Sperry, 2016).

Ten distinct manifestations of personality are described, each of which is placed into one of three clusters: A, B and C. Cluster A contains the personality disorders that share an "odd" or "eccentric" quality; cluster B includes the personality disorders that feature dramatic, erratic and highly emotional traits and cluster C includes those that are better described as anxious or fearful (APA, 2013). It is important to remember that the following personality disorders exist on the extreme end of a continuum of behaviors, with normal or typical presentations at one end, disorders seated at the other and various degrees of manifestation in between. Consequently, readers may see aspects of themselves within one or more of these disorders.

Cluster A. Three personality disorders form a family of similar presentations: paranoid, schizoid and schizotypal. These disorders share features with schizophrenia and related disorders. A discussion of differential diagnosis between features of disorders in cluster A and the schizophrenia spectrum is included within the schizophrenia and related disorders chapter. Paranoid personality disorder features a strong and predictable tendency to distrust others' motivations and to assume ill-will. People with this personality are filled with doubt about trustworthiness and are highly reluctant to disclose to others for fear of being manipulated later. Those with this personality configuration tend to misperceive intent and meaning and then hold grudges about these perceived slights for a long time. The DSM notes that this pattern of thought should be distinguished from paranoia that arises during the course of schizophrenia, bipolar disorder with psychotic features or another psychotic disorder or medical condition that instigates a paranoid episode (APA, 2013).

Schizoid Personality. In contrast, schizoid personality disorder features a discomfort with social interaction and results in social withdrawal. Unlike persons on the autism spectrum who generally want friendships and enjoy others, but may have difficulties with social skills, persons with schizoid personality configurations don't seem to experience pleasure in connecting with others, often lacking, for example, connections with family or a desire for sexual closeness with another. Those with a schizoid personality are not usually distressed by these symptoms and are instead indifferent to them. People with this disorder are often experienced as detached, cold or emotionally flat. As with all cluster "A" personality disorders, schizoid personality should be discerned from experiences that arise within the context of psychosis, as with schizophrenia or bipolar disorder with psychotic features, in depression or within the autistic spectrum (APA, 2013). Schizoid personality should also be differentiated from those who would identify themselves as asexual, those who enjoy emotional intimacy with others but do not seek or enjoy sexual contact, an experience that is a preference and not a disorder (Scherrer, 2008).

Schizotypal Personality. Schizotypal personality shares features with both paranoid and schizoid personalities. Like the schizoid personality, schizotypal personality includes patterns of detachment and of restricted emotional expression. However, the schizotypal personality configuration often carries features of paranoid personality in the form of suspiciousness or even paranoid ideation. People who carry this diagnosis tend to avoid others but are motivated by their fear and distrust rather than a lack of interest as with the schizoid personality type. Again, this personality structure may be difficult to differentiate from a disorder that lies on the schizophrenia spectrum, from bipolar disorder when psychotic features are present or from the autistic spectrum (APA, 2013).

Cluster B. Cluster B may be the group of personality disorders that garners the most attention from the general public and within the mainstream media. Four disorders are included within this grouping: antisocial, borderline, histrionic and narcissistic personalities. Antisocial personality is a personality disorder that must evidence itself by age 15 and includes a callous disregard for and evidence of the violation of the rights of others (APA, 2013). Antisocial personality is explored in the chapter describing disruptive, conduct and impulse disorders.

Borderline Personality. BPD, which will be explored at much greater length later in the chapter, is characterized by high emotional lability, intense fears of abandonment and, as a consequence, extreme measures to prevent separation. Persons with BPD, experience instability in a number of key domains, including within their sense of self, within their relationships and, again, in their emotions. These clients also demonstrate patterns of impulsivity that can expose them to risk, including suicidal behavior and non-suicidal self-injury (APA, 2013).

Histrionic Personality. Histrionic personality is described as a pattern of high emotional intensity and a need to draw attention to the self. Clients with this disorder may rely on inappropriate sexual behavior to secure this attention. The emotions of those diagnosed with histrionic personality can seem mercurial and shallow, and these clients frequently communicate with what is described as "impressionistic speech," a communication style that reveals little detail and emphasizes emotional content. These clients are described as being very uncomfortable when they are not the focus of attention. Finally, many of these clients are thought to be highly suggestible and frequently infer a closer relationship to others than is actually the case (APA, 2013).

Narcissistic Personality. The last disorder of cluster B is narcissistic personality disorder (NPD). NPD is one in which an individual craves admiration and, as a result, habitually engages in grandiose behavior or fantasies that they might garner widespread respect. Another key feature of this disorder is a notable deficit in empathic skills. These traits may manifest in a number of ways, including but not exclusive to an inflated sense of self-importance. These clients often believe they are so special that they can only be understood by other equally elite and special people, exude a sense of entitlement and are exploitative of others (APA, 2013; Vater et al., 2014). While there are within group differences among those diagnosed with NPD, a recent study of 96 German clients with the disorder found that the most common of these traits included need for admiration, followed closely by fantasies of unlimited success, and envy, exploitativeness and grandiosity. Envy, need for admiration and grandiosity seemed to have had the greatest stability over the 2-year period of this longitudinal study (Vater et al., 2014). Narcissistic personality should not be confused with the grandiose delusions that can arise during manic episodes of bipolar disorder or schizoaffective disorder, nor with grandiosity that is sometimes evidenced in those with substance use concerns (APA, 2013; Vater et al., 2014).

Cluster C. The third and final cluster includes personality disorders that share anxiety and fear as their defining feature: avoidant, dependent and obsessive compulsive personality disorders. Avoidant personality disorder, like schizoid and schizotypal personality, features an avoidance of others; however, the client with avoidant personality has another reason for isolating themselves from others, fear of criticism. The fear of negative evaluation is so strong that these clients will avoid work situations where they might be evaluated by others. Their relationships are restricted in number, depth and level of intimacy since these clients will seek to limit exposure to shame, embarrassment and the forms of criticism that exposure might make them vulnerable to. Clients with this diagnosis are highly risk aversive. In direct contrast to the narcissistic client, the avoidant client believes themselves to be particularly inept, inferior and unappealing to others. Avoidant personality can be confused with other personality disorders, or with symptoms of social withdrawal seen in substance use disorders (SUDs) (APA, 2013) and resembles the isolation and self-deprecation often manifested in depression.

Dependent Personality. Dependent personality disorder, on the other hand, features a strong desire to be taken care of which manifests in fears of separation and "clinginess." These clients frequently adopt a submissive role strategy in an attempt to secure their relationships with others. These clients strongly prefer others to take responsibility for major areas of their lives and often have difficulty making everyday decisions independently. Frequently, these clients fear that if they assert themselves or contradict others they will be abandoned. Ultimately, these clients are very uncomfortable when they are alone because they don't feel adequately skilled to care for their own needs. Consequently, their relational dynamics center around subservience and securing other's care. Dependent personality should not be confused with other personality disorders, particularly those in which fears of being alone or unattended to are central, as with borderline personality or histrionic personality, with a manifestation of depression, panic or agoraphobia (APA, 2013; Bornstein, 2011).

Obsessive Compulsive Personality. The final disorder of cluster C is obsessive compulsive personality disorder. People who manifest this personality structure are most comfortable when their environment is very orderly and predictable. They tend to become captivated by their own vision of perfection and can be very rigid in their thoughts, ideas and behaviors. This may manifest in a strong preoccupation with details, lists, rules, schedules and so on. Frequently, their perfectionism becomes an obstacle to their completing projects, though they may give preference to work over relaxation, fun or hobbies. People who meet criteria for obsessive compulsive personality disorder seem to have difficulty letting go of items that have little value or are worn-out, even when there is no sentimental value to the object, and can have difficulty spending money. This diagnosis should not be confused with obsessive compulsive disorder, which features true obsessive thoughts and compulsions designed to stave off the fears that emerge; thanks to those unwanted thoughts; however, when criteria are met for both, both disorders should be diagnosed. Hoarding disorder can be confused with obsessive compulsive personality. However, in the case of hoarding disorder, the inability to let go of worthless or broken items becomes so extreme that health, safety or well-being are impacted by the collected clutter. These disorders can also be diagnosed together when appropriate (APA, 2013).

Winds of Change: The Alternative Framework

An Alternative Framework. For nearly a decade before the publication of the DSM 5 work was being done to construct a new framework for diagnosing personality disorders. This new framework would bring these disorders into alignment with the rest of the DSM by attempting to distance itself from a categorical approach to personality disorder diagnosis and moving toward a dimensional understanding. What does this

BOX 18.01 PERSONALITY DISORDERS AND THEIR CLUSTERS

Cluster A: Odd or Eccentric

Paranoid: Features a pervasive distrust and suspicion that others will hurt or take advantage of them if given the opportunity

E.g., David is unable to build satisfying relationships with others thanks to his constant doubt in others' intentions and hypervigilance about breaks in trust.

Schizoid: Feature a preference for solitary life and avoids social and emotional contact with others

E.g., Sherman has no one that he would call a friend and prefers to spend time alone.

Schizotypal: Sharing features with both paranoid and schizoid personalities, these clients experience social impairments paired with odd beliefs and paranoid features that work together to create thoughts, feelings and behaviors that alienate and isolate the client from those in the social environment

E.g., Lenard's fears of being controlled by unnamed government agencies and uncomfortable interactions with others have contributed to his homelessness.

Cluster B: Dramatic, Erratic and Highly Emotional

Antisocial: Features a pattern of disregarding and violating the rights of others

E.g., Laurie, a landlord and small business owner, makes her living by making high-interest pay-day loans to low-income community members. Some of these loans are made to people who also rent apartments from her.

Borderline: A collection of patterns that include instability of emotion, relationship and of understanding the self. This disorder also includes intensely uncomfortable fears of abandonment and feelings of emptiness.

E.g., Barb has had a series of failed relationships, each ending dramatically following fears that she would be left alone.

Histrionic: A pattern of behaviors featuring rapidly shifting and shallow emotion, impressionistic speech and a desire for attention from others that manifests in inappropriate behaviors that may include sexualized or seductive behavior.

E.g., Dannie feels very uncomfortable if she is left out of the spotlight. She has used her sexuality to gain the attention she craves.

Narcissistic: Persons displaying a grandiose demeanor, a high need for admiration and affirmation while displaying difficulties with empathy.

E.g., Gavin often exaggerates his accomplishments and feels entitled to only the best in life. He often belittles others and has alienated his coworkers thanks to his inability to accept constructive feedback.

Cluster C: Anxious and Fearful

Avoidant: This personality disorder features a strong preference to avoid situations in which these clients may expose themselves to criticism, shame or embarrassment. These clients perceive themselves to be inept and inferior so, consequently, they are risk avoidant and prefer solitary work and restricted social circles.

E.g., Nevin likes to stay under the radar at work and in social situations. He is so concerned about embarrassing himself that he has isolated himself from others.

Dependent: This personality structure features a core belief that the client is not themselves able to care for their own needs and as a result believes themselves to require others to make important decisions and attend to their needs. In order to secure the care they desire, and because they are convinced of their own incompetence, they adopt a subservient role to the person upon whom they depend.

E.g., Max is very dependent on his wife. His family describe their 25-year marriage as more akin to director and assistant than a partnership. Internally, Max feels inadequate and believes he is incapable of most any task without his wife's direction and supervision.

Obsessive Compulsive: This personality configuration features a strong preference for orderliness, control and perfectionism and as a result finds flexibility and openness to be challenging and will often favor ways of approaching tasks and problems that fit their preferences at the expense of efficiency.

E.g., Esther has been denied a promotion. She has been told that, while she is very capable, her inflexibility and demandingness have brought complaints from coworkers, making her a poor candidate for the leadership position. Esther has heard complaints like this from her family, as well.

Source: APA (2013) and Sperry (2016).

mean? When thinking about a personality disorder using a categorical approach, a client is determined to have a particular disorder based upon whether or not they meet a threshold of listed symptoms. Clinicians and researchers alike point out that these thresholds are, in the end, somewhat arbitrary, and frequently, those who don't fully meet criteria for a disorder are still functionally impaired, leaving some clients diagnostic orphans. A dimensional approach, researchers argue, grants clinicians freedom to focus primarily on personality factors and their impact on the client's functioning (Oldham, 2015; Skodol et al., 2011; Sperry, 2016).

Other problems, too, spurred the development of a new framework. Researchers and clinicians alike have long been concerned about the excessive comorbidity among the personality disorders. Sperry (2016) notes that the point of describing 10 distinct personality disorders was to provide the diagnostician with an opportunity to convey a clear idea of the dynamics that were interfering with the client's well-being, in other words to lend specificity. Clients, however, rarely fit neatly into these personality patterns and are often diagnosed with multiple personality disorders in order to fully capture the array of symptoms. Another problem with the categorical approach is that the traits that makeup each of the diagnoses lie on a continuum, with a healthy range at one end and a decidedly unhealthy manifestation at the other, determining where these traits cross over into disorder has proven to be more challenging for diagnosticians than is presented in the DSM. The alternative framework aims to address these concerns.

Elimination of the Multiaxial System. In an earlier chapter, we discussed the multiaxial system of diagnosis, introduced with the publication of the DSM III and used until the DSM 5 was published in 2013. You'll remember that in this system, Axis I disorders were those that required immediate clinical attention, and were referred to as "principal" or "primary" diagnoses. Axis II was reserved for pervasive disorders, those that had broad implications for the individual, such as cognitive impairment or personality disorders. Axis III held relevant medical conditions that impacted well-being, such as chronic pain or heart disease. Axis IV described the sociocultural environment and its influence on the client and Axis V captured the client's overall functioning. The demise of the multiaxial system came with the convergence of three primary issues: (1) changing attitudes about the distinction between physical and mental disorders, (2) arguments that the DSMs placement of disorders within Axis I and Axis II were arbitrary; for example placing autism on Axis I despite the fact that it is a pervasive developmental disorder and (3) growing evidence that personality disorders may share stability rates with other Axis I disorders, obviating the need to segregate them into separate categories (Kress et al., 2014; Røysamb et al., 2011). So, in this way, the conceptualization of personality disorders has experienced two major shifts: first the door has been opened to think about personality disorders along a continuum and, second, the prevailing attitude about the relative fluidity of personality disorders is also changing, a topic we will revisit later in the chapter. Let's first take a brief look at the alternative framework for diagnosing personality disorders.

The alternative framework is located in the back of the DSM 5, pages 761-781. The APA asserts that by including two frameworks, the original and the alternative, within the same manual, they can retain "continuity with current clinical practice" (APA, 2013, p. 761) while also providing a format that addresses the shortcomings

BOX 18.02 KEY DEFINITIONS: PERSONALITY DISORDERS

Identity Diffusion: identity diffusion refers to the condition of having failed to cultivate a coherent understanding of one's self, one's own thoughts, motivations and wishes, often attributed to a lack of adequate mirroring in early childhood (Bateman & Fonagy, 2016).

Impressionistic Speech: A style of communication that features emotional impressions but lacks details that might support or explain the impressions that were experienced (APA, 2013).

E.g., A client notes, "My last therapist was simply wonderful, just fantastic!" When asked to describe a few things that were most appreciated about the therapist, the client replies, "Oh, I don't know, he was just awesome, just so, so good. I LOVED him!"

Neurosis. The quality of being troubled by some state of mind, such as anxiety, depression or obsession, while also maintaining a firm grasp on reality. A person suffering from a neurosis understands at some level that the trouble is born out of their own thought processes (McWilliams, 1994).

Personality: A construct describing the dynamic and individual coalescing of patterns of thought, feelings, behavior and motivations that together create the foundation for one's being in the world and one's relationship to self and others (APA, 2013).

Personality Disorder: "An enduring pattern of inner experience & behavior that deviates markedly from the expectations of the individual's culture, is pervasive and inflexible, has an onset in adolescence or early adulthood, is stable overtime, and leads to distress or impairment," (APA, 2013, p. 645).

Projective Identification: A defense mechanism in which a person externalizes a part of self that is unrecognized and often unwelcome, as when one's own unintegrated hostility is seen in another (Bateman & Fonagy, 2016).

Psychosis. Psychosis is an experience of having lost touch with external reality and, as a result, being both deeply troubled by one's distorted perceptions as well as experiencing functional consequences such as communication impairments and difficulties with self-care (McWilliams, 1994).

Splitting: Splitting describes both a cognitive style and a defense mechanism. At its essence, splitting is the inability to see events and people in a full, balanced and realistic way and instead events and people are seen in sharp dichotomies of good and bad. People who habitually engage in splitting have a difficult time integrating evidence that contradicts their Black and White perceptions, leaving them with a skewed vision of the world (Sperry, 2016).

of the original model. The alternative model has five key features: (1) describes core impairments of personality function, (2) describes pathological traits, (3) provides an outline for the GPD criteria, (4) provides narrative descriptions of each of the major personality criterion, A-G and (5) reduces the specific personality disorders from 10 to 6: antisocial, avoidant, borderline, narcissistic, obsessive compulsive and schizotypal (APA, 2013; Skodol et al., 2011; Sperry, 2016).

Shared Structure of the A Criteria. The alternative model conceptualizes personality as impacting aspects of relationship to self and others through four key components: identity, self-direction, empathy and intimacy. Each of the six specific disorders are described by their particular manifestations in each of these four domains. Box 18.03 provides an example of how each of the six disorders manifests on the empathy domain in the alternative model.

The Personality Functioning Scales. Pages 775-777 of the DSM 5 include a table that is designed to assist diagnosticians in assessing the client's functioning on each of these domains on a scale from 0 (indicating little or no impairment) to 3 (an indication of severe impairment). Together the assessment of these factors are thought to create a high degree of specificity and descriptive quality (APA, 2013; Skodol et al., 2011; Sperry, 2016).

Three Points of Controversy Regarding the Personality Disorder Construct

Three seismic points of discussion stand out when exploring the literature concerning personality disorder constructs. First, there are those that passionately argue against the idea of the stability of personality disorders, a belief long-held by the clinical and research community. Second, a question has been raised about whether children would benefit from the diagnosis and treatment of personality disorders. Finally, the criteria of the personality disorders have been challenged by those who raise concerns about culture and gender bias. Each of these challenges is explored briefly in the following pages.

The Question of Personality and Stability Overtime. A key discussion within the literature around personality disorders generally centers around the notion of the stability of personality overtime. For much of the history of modern mental health, these disorders have been thought to be largely resistant to intervention (Hopwood & Bleidorn, 2018; Sperry, 2016). Perhaps one of the key turning points in this changing perception unfolded when Marsha Linehan took her place among the major theorists of the counseling and psychotherapy field, after sharing her own struggles with BPD, and then outlined dialectical behavioral therapy (DBT) describing how it had transformed her life and those of her clients. Since that time DBT has taken its place as one of the evidence-based practices that demonstrate efficacy for BPD. Overtime, attitudes about the stability of personality disorders have gradually changed, and as a result, some research has been done to explore this question (Hopwood & Bleidorn, 2018; Zanarini et al., 2012; Zanarini et al., 2005). For example, researchers exploring the temporal stability of narcissistic personality found recovery rates of about 53% on

BOX 18.03 "A" CRITERIA FOR EMPATHY FOR EACH OF THE SIX PROPOSED PERSONALITY DISORDERS (PDS) OF THE ALTERNATIVE MODEL

Antisocial PD: In clients with this disorder, there is generally a lack of concern for others' feelings, needs, rights or suffering (APA, 2013, p. 764).

Avoidant PD: These clients are preoccupied by the possibility of negative evaluation from others and frequently carry a perception of others' feelings as more negative than they are in reality (APA, 2013, p. 765).

Borderline PD: These clients are often blind to the feelings and needs of others while also being hypersensitive to what they perceive as intentional slights from others (APA, 2013, p. 766).

Narcissistic PD: Clients with this personality configuration may have difficulty identifying with others' feelings or needs, while at the same time are especially attuned to reactions to themselves by others and frequently fail to accurately evaluate how they affect others (APA, 2013, p. 767).

Obsessive Compulsive PD: These clients may have difficulty understanding the feelings or actions of others or may fail to appreciate ideas different from their own (APA, 2013, p. 768).

Schizotypal PD: Clients with this personality structure often misperceive others' intentions and may fail to fully apprehend their impact on others (APA, 2013, p. 769).

Source: American Psychiatric Association (2013).

categorical measures, meaning the participants no longer met criteria thresholds for NPD. However, their results also revealed dimensional stability, meaning the study participants retained subclinical narcissistic traits over time (Vater et al., 2014). A 10-year longitudinal study of 290 persons with BPD found that half achieved recovery from BPD, while 86% experienced a remission of symptoms lasting 4 years (Zanarini et al., 2010). These studies suggest that while personality disorders may be treatable, subclinical traits tend to be stable over time. Much more research is needed to understand this dynamic across personality disorders.

Do Children and Teens Sometimes Have Personality Disorders? A second discussion influencing our diagnostic process swirls around a debate concerning three questions.

BOX 18.04 TRY THIS: SCALING PERSONALITY FUNCTIONING

Turn to Table 2 in your DSM 5, located on page 775. Read through the following examples and assign a level of impairment score for Diane and Eric for the empathy domain. How confident are you in this score? What questions might you have for Diane or Eric that could help you to feel more certain of your score?

Diane. Diane works in a large office building in the center of a sprawling metropolitan area. She enjoys her management position and has a comfortable apartment that she shares with her husband and their two children. Each morning for nearly a year, she has passed the same homeless woman, Sandy, who sits outside the front entrance of the office building where she works. No matter the weather, Sandy is always there, collecting coins. One morning just before Thanksgiving a coworker, Linda, started a collection for Sandy to get her a coat. When asked if she would like to contribute, Diane replied, "I think that we are going to have to do something about that woman, she is a blight on the city and tarnishes the prestige of the businesses in this building. Plus she creeps me out with her dirty mismatched clothes. I honestly think she chooses to haunt our doorstep because she knows it bothers me. She can go somewhere else for her handout as far as I'm concerned."

Eric. Eric has an office just three doors down from where Diane works. Like Diane, he would describe himself as "comfortably middle-class." Talking to his wife Eric shares, "Today there was a collection for Sandy, the homeless lady who is always outside our office building. I contributed some money so that Linda could get her a coat and a few things for the winter months. I was thinking about it on the way home and feeling a little embarrassed. I wondered why I didn't think about taking up a collection for her myself and why I'm not nicer to her when I pass by her in the morning. I barely look at her. I think if I'm honest, seeing her there makes me feel guilty and then I feel a little angry, too, because I shouldn't feel guilty that I work and have a nice house. Should I? I do want to help, but I realized this morning that there was a part of me that would be happy if she moved on."

First, when in the life span should we begin to consider diagnosing a personality disorder? Second, where should we look for early signs of pathology? And third, when should we begin treating these manifestations? The diagnostic criteria as currently described presume that these traits don't emerge suddenly in adulthood, but that their origins must have evidenced themselves in adolescence. The second ongoing debate asks if children and adolescents should be assessed for early signs of traits associated with personality disorder, diagnosed and then treated (Swit et al., 2018). The benefit in early assessment comes with the possibility of preventing full-blown personality disorder later in life, while the caution comes from those in the profession who are concerned about overdiagnosis and its consequences to individuals and to society at large.

Culture, Gender and Personality Construct and Disorder. Some researchers and clinicians have asked whether or not the construct of personality disorder is one built almost entirely around stereotyped notions of gender, class and ethnicity (Becker, 1997; Henry & Cohen, 1983; Kaplan, 1983; Landrine, 1989; Morey et al., 2002). Numerous studies demonstrate that a subset of these disorders are much more common in men (antisocial, schizoid, schizotypal and narcissistic personality) and another subset are much more common among women (borderline, dependent and histrionic) (APA, 2013; Trull et al., 2010). In their quest to explain this dynamic, a number of researchers have looked to gender bias and stereotypes for answers; for example, Kaplan (1983), argued that the histrionic and dependent personality disorder criteria were virtual caricatures of the traditional female role (p. 787) and further argued that women were in danger of diagnosis if they overperformed or underperformed gender roles prescribed for them. Landrine's (1989) study found that persons depicted in vignettes portraying prototypical personality disorders but without a gender indicated were assigned a gender along gender stereotypes associated with those disorders. Landrine notes:

> "The question that arises at this point is why the gender-roles and stereotypes of both sexes might be reflected in the personality disorder categories. The purposes of masquerading gender roles as madness may be (a) to locate falsely within persons all of the ludicrous cognitive and behavioral limitations that actually reside in gender roles and stratification, so that (b) to direct our attention-not to changing gender roles or to eradicating gender stratification—but to changing individuals through therapy and to eradicating their ostensible personal problems" (p. 332).

Ultimately, Landrine (1989) argues that the personality disorders are so reliably distributed within gender groups not solely as a result of the bias on the part of the clinician but due to the mirror-like quality of the diagnostic criteria that reflect gender stereotyped role expectations.

Morey et al. (2002) examined four key indicators that might serve to point to gender bias in diagnosis: (1) differences in prevalence rates of specific personality disorders within a non-clinical sample, (2) implications of gender differences among non-professionals, (3) an evaluation of the internal consistency of the criteria for these disorders as a function of gender and (4) the gender-normative quality of the criteria. Among other findings, these researchers found that criteria that were found to be more prevalent in one gender were also perceived to be a greater problem for that gender than for the other.

Trull et al. (2010) conducted a study that included over 43,000 participants. They compared diagnoses of personality disorders using an assessment, National Epidemiologic Survey on Alcohol and Related Conditions, or the National Epidemiologic Survey on Alcohol and Related Conditions (NESARC), that requires the endorsement of at least five criteria, at least one of which must be reported to cause some kind of impairment, and then examined the prevalence of these diagnoses along racial and gender lines. The team then used NESARC-REVISED. In this assessment, all endorsed symptoms must also be reported to cause impairment before inclusion for diagnosis. As anticipated, these researchers found that by raising the demand for meeting full criteria for each diagnosis, that overall prevalence rates fell. They also found that while many of the diagnoses did not change in terms of the predominance of diagnosis within one gender or another, some differences were observed. For example, mirroring past research, they found that men were significantly more likely to be diagnosed with antisocial, schizoid and NPDs, but this was not true for schizotypal personality. Using the NESARC-REVISED assessment, these researchers also found that women were significantly more likely to be diagnosed with histrionic personality or obsessive compulsive personality than were men, but not borderline personality. Research like this raises questions about the validity of personality disorder constructs and their intersection with gender.

Initial investigations into the Prevalence of Personality Disorder Among Transgendered Persons. Most of the extant research related to gender and personality focuses on cisgendered persons; however, Lingiardi et al. (2017) conducted a study of 44 transgendered persons diagnosed with gender dysphoria and examined the presence of traits indicative of personality disorder, the presence of personality disorder and attachment styles. These researchers found that among the transgendered persons in their small study, 16% presented with a personality disorder. Much more research is needed to fully understand the prevalence of personality disorders among those who identify as transgendered or non-binary.

Borderline Personality Disorder

Brief History of BPD. Historically, the earliest discussions of personality disorders would have unfolded within a time when psychodynamic theories were the dominant framework. The psychodynamic nosology organized the severity of psychological disorders into two major tiers: neurotic and psychotic. The neurotic disorders were those of everyday life, anxieties, depressions and obsessions, for example, in which a client was observed to have a strong relationship with reality but was thought to be rigid in their use of defense mechanisms, which resulted in unhelpful ways of thinking, feeling and behaving. Conversely, psychotic disorders were those in which the individual had lost contact with reality creating a distortion that was the source of a great deal of suffering, such as paranoid delusions of persecution. Freudians believed that psychosis sprung from defense mechanisms that were too weak to manage the dynamics of the unconscious and the drives and impulses unfolding there. (Recall that defense mechanisms are unconscious strategies that protect the conscious mind from the anxiety producing urges, drives and desires of the unconscious.) Resting within the borderlands between these two experiences were those clients who existed primarily within neurotic states of mind but when very stressed crossed over into brief psychotic periods and then back again (Becker, 1997; McWilliams, 1994). A further division within this framework made a distinction between neurotic symptoms and neurotic character; for example, giving rise to a spectrum of personality function, the neurotic-borderline-psychotic personality spectrum, which would later be known as the BPD (McWilliams, 1994).

A contemporary understanding of BPD. BPD was first formally described in 1938 and included those who demonstrated a marked difficulty in maintaining emotional stability, exhibited impulsivity and also seemed to share a fear of rejection within their relationships as well as a tendency to experience transient periods of psychosis. Early descriptions of BPD placed transient psychotic episodes at the core of this diagnosis, (Becker, 1997) though it is somewhat more peripheral to the contemporary criteria. Today BPD carries roughly the same incidence rate as schizophrenia, impacting about between 1% and 2% of the population (APA, 2013; Paris, 2018; Zanarini, 2000). On the whole, many assert that BPD affects males and females equally, but because women are more likely to seek help, more women are seen for the disorder than are men (Paris, 2018). While a great deal of the diagnostic features described by early psychodynamic thinkers remain within the DSM 5 criteria, the criteria now reflect greater specificity than they once did.

A hallmark of BPD is the felt experience of instability in self-image that often includes a great deal of self-criticism and feelings of emptiness. People with BPD may find it difficult to settle on goals or career plans. Those with BPD are often challenged to recognize others' feelings and needs; thanks to their own tendency to be hypersensitive in interpersonal relationships. When in relationship with others, they often find it difficult to fully trust and are given to either idealize or devalue others and may swing suddenly from periods of overinvolvement to times of withdrawal. Triggering these rapid shifts in relational style are deeply held fears of being abandoned (APA, 2013; Sperry, 2016; Zanarini, 2000). Consequently, these clients often report having very tumultuous or chaotic relationships. These clients also tend to find it difficult to manage their emotions and frequently find themselves overcome by anger and feel extremely stressed, to the point of occasional dissociation. Finally, clients with BPD can be impulsive in ways that jeopardize their well-being; for example, by spending a great deal of money, entering into sexual relationships with those they don't know well, misusing substances or risking injury or death as with suicidal behavior or deliberate self-harm (APA, 2013; Latalova et al., 2011; Paris, 2018; Sperry, 2016).

Suicidality and Deliberate Self-Harm (DSH) in BPD. A defining feature and one that likely challenges clinicians most while working with clients with BPD is that of suicidal behavior and self-harm. These concerning behaviors not only threaten the lives of clients but are also one of the primary drivers behind hospitalizations. Generally, personality disorders increase the likelihood of suicidality by six times in women and by seven times in men (Soloff & Chiappetta, 2017). Some estimates place the rate of suicide attempts among those with BPD as high as 75% (Black et al., 2004).

Between 3% and 10% of clients with BPD complete suicide (Paris, 2018; Soloff & Chiappetta, 2017; Zanarini et al., 2008), a sobering statistic. As one might anticipate, comorbid depression or substance abuse seems to increase the likelihood of completed suicides (Black et al., 2004). Importantly, the incidence of DSH is also quite high. Well over half of those who have attempted suicide have also engaged in DSH; similarly, a history of DSH doubles the likelihood of suicide (Black et al., 2004). Among the most common DSH activities include cutting, overdose, burning, walking into traffic, hanging and suffocation (Black et al., 2004; Soloff & Chiappetta, 2017).

Soloff and Chiappetta (2017) conducted an 8-year longitudinal study of 123 participants diagnosed with BPD without comorbid bipolar disorder and found that just over 20% made medically significant suicide attempts during the course of the study. Variables that correlated with these attempts included minority status, and having been recruited while inpatients as well as those in job transitions. Age, socioeconomic status, marital status or whether or not there were children in the home did not differ significantly between groups; however, formal education surfaced as a protective factor. If there is good news in the relationship between suicidality, DSH and BPD, it is that the tendency for suicidal behavior appears to decrease overtime (Soloff & Chiappetta, 2017; Zanarini et al., 2010; Zanarini et al., 2008; Zanarini et al., 2007). For example, in their longitudinal study, Zanarini et al. (2008) found that while just over 90% of their sample of 290 participants had engaged in some type of self-mutilation, at the 10-year follow-up only 13% reported doing so.

Early Trauma and BPD. A key risk factor that emerges in correlation with the development of BPD is childhood abuse and neglect (Chanen & Kaess, 2012; Zanarini, 2000; Zanarini et al., 2019). A full one-third of persons with BPD report early childhood trauma and sexual trauma in particular (de Aquino Ferreira et al., 2018; Frost et al., 2018; Menon et al., 2016; Paris, 2018). At least one study places this estimate at 60%-80% (Fosatti et al., 1999, in Sperry, 2016). A study conducted by Shevlin et al. (2007) using 8,580 participants in Great Britain suggests that there is a strong relationship between the severity of the early trauma and the severity of BPD symptoms. These events are thought to interact in a diathesis-stress model between genetic predisposition and temperament creating the fertile ground for the seeds of BPD. Notably, initial thesis research seems to suggest that emotional awareness may mediate the effects of childhood abuse on measures of disturbed relatedness and emotional dysregulation in those with BPD (Westbrook & Berenbaum, 2017).

Prevalence of Substance Use Disorders (SUDs). To date, Trull et al. (2018) have conducted the most recent and thorough review of the frequently co-occurring BPD and SUDs. A precise and detailed discussion of co-occurrence rates is complicated by changes in the diagnostic structure for SUDs that has been implemented since many of these studies were published, a discussion of which is, unfortunately, prohibitive for inclusion in this space. Broadly, however, across the 70 reviewed studies, which in total included more than 10,000 individuals diagnosed with at least one SUD, just over

22% were also determined to meet criteria for BPD while half of those with BPD had at least one SUD. Alcohol, cocaine and opioids are among the most frequently abused. Needless to say, in the co-occurrence of BPD and SUDs, each greatly complicates the treatment of the other. Theorists point to shared traits that are risk factors for both disorders, such as impulsivity and emotional dysregulation, when explaining the high rates of co-occurrence. These figures point to the importance of screening for SUDs when BPD is suspected.

The Skilled Diagnostician

Is BPD Better Understood as a Variant of Bipolar Disorder? For some time, there has been a conversation within the field about the appropriate placement of BPD. The question on the lips of a number of practitioners is whether or not the overlapping symptoms between the two disorders is pointing to a diagnostic kinship (Becker 1997; Paris, 2018; Philips, 2016). In our discussion of mood disorders, Chapter 7, we touched briefly on the similarities between BPD and BPII, which will be reviewed very briefly below.

Differential Diagnosis of BPD and BPI/II. People diagnosed with BPD and those with bipolar disorders share experiences of unstable mood, including intense feelings of anger, as well as suicidal, self-harm and risk-taking behaviors. Both groups can experience transient psychosis. Difficulties in relationships are a feature of both those with BPD and BPI/II (Ha, 2018; Perugi et al., 2015; Phelps, 2016). While BPD and BPI/II share a great deal of symptom overlap, researchers offer insights into how to effectively differentiate the two disorders by examining the ways that manic and depressive symptoms present differently in BPD and BPI/II. Those with BPD and bipolar disorder differ in the types of depression symptoms that evidence themselves, the duration of those symptoms and in their triggers (Kernberg & Yeomans, 2013; Paris, 2018; Perugi et al., 2015; Phelps, 2016; Zimmerman & Morgan, 2019).

Bipolar depressions differ from depressive symptoms in BPD in that the bipolar depressions are more apt to feature episodic and classic symptoms including slowing of cognition, lack of self-care, guilt, self-blame, apathy, changes in sleeping and eating and lack of emotion and so on (Kernberg & Yeomans, 2013; Perugi et al., 2015; Phelps, 2016; Zimmerman & Morgan, 2019). The person with a borderline personality structure, on the other hand, tends to experience chronic, very short-lived depressive feelings that are highly situational (Kernberg & Yeomans, 2013; Paris, 2018). Feelings of depression by those with BPD are more likely to be expressed through descriptions of sadness marked by anger or rage (Kernberg & Yeomans, 2013). Kernberg and Yeomans (2013) further argue that the "neurovegetative symptoms" are more indicative of bipolar disorder than of personality disorders; these include severe insomnia, particularly when featuring early waking, loss of appetite along with severe weight loss, loss of interest in sex or impotence, heightened sensitivity to cold, severe constipation, loss of menstrual cycles and a mask-like quality to the person's facial expression (p. 7).

Clients with BPD may have experienced and described recurrent periods of subclinical depressive symptoms over the span of many years. For the client with BPD, depressive traits frequently are observed to be woven into the fabric of their thoughts, feelings and behaviors, described as trait depression, and represents a contrast to the state depression seen in bipolar disorder. The client with BPD may endorse hopeless feelings but often struggles to meaningfully describe what the hopeless feelings are about (Kernberg & Yeomans, 2013). In their study of affective instability and impulsivity in borderline and bipolar disorders, Henry et al. (2001) examined 148 participants and found that while both groups experienced significant emotional fluctuations, differences emerged in how these fluctuations manifested. Participants with BPII fluctuated between euthymia, depression and elation while fluctuations of mood between euthymia, anger and anxiety were more typical of those with BPD.

The triggers for depressive episodes in bipolar disorder and BPD also differ. For those with BPD, relatively minor events seem to carry a significant symbolic value and result in very strong emotional reactions, while those with bipolar depressions are less sensitive to environmental triggers (Ha, 2018; Kernberg & Yeomans, 2013; Perugi et al., 2015; Phelps, 2016; Zimmerman & Morgan, 2019).

Further differentiating the two, the literature seems to show that clients with pure bipolar disorder "do not show severe pathology of object relations during periods of normal functioning, and even chronic bipolar patients . . . maintain the capacity for relationships in depth, stability in their relations with others, and the capacity for assessing themselves and the most significant persons in their [lives] appropriately" (Kernberg & Yeomans, 2013, pp. 3-4). This means that while clients with bipolar disorder may diminish themselves during depressive periods and experience paranoia about others during manic episodes, when experiencing emotional stability their assessment of others and of themselves remains relatively stable. Clients with BPD, however, find it difficult to evaluate others, themselves or their relationships accurately or with any real depth.

The Danger of Misdiagnosis. Both bipolar disorder and BPD are subject to false positive and false negative misdiagnosis. A misdiagnosis of either BPI/II or BPD come with their own set of problems. When a bipolar disorder is misdiagnosed, especially when depressive symptoms are then treated with antidepressant medications, conditions can be set in motion for triggering rapid cycling mood episodes and the erratic and sometimes dangerous behaviors that can accompany them. On the other hand, a missed BPD diagnosed as BPII exposes a client unnecessarily to medications and their side effects (Phelps, 2016; Zimmerman & Morgan, 2019), medications that tend not to be effective in clients with BPD (Paris, 2018). A missed BPD diagnosis will likely cheat the client of appropriate interventions, since these disorders are treated very differently.

Recommendations. Zimmerman and Morgan (2019) recommend the Structural Clinical Interview for DSM Disorders (SCID), describing it as the gold standard for differentiating BPI/II and BPD, in addition to the Hypomania Checklist-32. Additionally, Kernberg and Yeomans (2013) recommend that intake questions about depressive symptoms be asked in an open-ended way and probed in order to gain an accurate picture of the presentation. Hurrying through intake questions may lead to building a flawed picture of your client's experiences. For example:

> **AVOID:** Have you noticed any of the following feelings in the past 2 weeks: sadness, guilt, shame, hopelessness . . .
>
> **TRY INSTEAD:** Can you describe some of the feelings you have been experiencing that have most bothered you in the past few weeks?
>
> **Follow with a probe:** You've described feeling hopeless. Can you say a bit more about what has left you feeling this way?
>
> **Follow with probes that might reveal hypomania:** You mentioned earlier that you had feelings of regret about some spending. Can you say more about what that looked like and the circumstances that led up to it?

Managing the False-Positives in Personality Disorder Diagnoses. Two approaches may help to stem the overdiagnosis of personality disorders, time and caution, and careful consideration of each criterion met. First, remember the diagnostic principle, using caution in crisis. During crisis, transition or when intoxicated or dependent on substances, clients may regress to less skilled relational and behavioral patterns. Relationships may be strained, and stress and exhaustion may amplify normal but less adaptive personality traits. When first encountering a client, it is best practice to wait before giving an initial diagnosis of personality disorder until it is clear that the traits that are in evidence are long standing, evident in early adulthood or late adolescence and not simply transient maladaptive responses to stress. A very thorough history is always needed before applying any diagnosis and never less so in the diagnosis of a personality disorder. Rapid shifts in personality are red flags for both substance use as well as for possible medical conditions, such as head injury or brain tumor (APA, 2013; Frances, 2013).

Returning to the work of Trull and colleagues (2010) described earlier, they outline an approach that may bring greater accuracy to diagnosis. Again, they recommend applying the criteria more stringently. In this case, rather than referring to the criteria table to determine if each criterion is met, a second step is taken, the determination of whether or not each criterion met is also leading to impairment. Trull and colleagues have found that applying this method brings the prevalence rates into expected ranges.

Differential Diagnosis of BPD and PTSD and Complex PTSD. For some time, researchers have asked whether BPD might represent a particular manifestation of post-traumatic stress disorder (PTSD), and complex PTSD (CPTSD) in particular.

BOX 18.05 DIAGNOSTIC BRIDGE TO THE BIPOLAR DISORDERS

This chapter discusses the intersection of symptom sets between bipolar disorder and borderline personality disorder. The differential diagnosis is complex and the stakes are high for appropriate diagnosis in these clients. One complicating factor is the underdiagnosis of bipolar II (BPII); thanks to poor recognition and reporting of hypomanic states (Zimmerman & Morgan, 2019). Turn to Chapter 7, Disorders of Mood, for a full discussion of hypomanic episodes, and appropriate diagnosis of BPI/II as well as a more complete discussion of depressive symptoms.

CPTSD is recognized in the ICD-11 but is not currently included within the DSM nosology (a more complete discussion of PTSD and CPTSD can be found in the trauma and stress-related disorders chapter of this book). CPTSD and BPD share key symptoms including affective dysregulation, negative self-concept and difficulties within interpersonal relationships, creating the potential for diagnostic confusion. Both disorders also share a risk factor, namely childhood physical and sexual abuse (Becker, 1997; Frost et al., 2018; Knefel et al., 2016). Recent research exploring these diagnostic constructs have not found BPD and CPTSD to be describing the same disorder however (Cloitre et al., 2014; Frost et al., 2018). Though symptom overlap does exist and some comorbidity between PTSD and BPD is in evidence, the two disorders may best be distinguished by four key features that point to BPD: (1) frantic efforts to avoid abandonment, (2) unstable sense of self, (3) highly unstable and emotionally intense interpersonal relationships and (4) the endorsement of impulsiveness (Cloitre et al., 2014). Frost et al., note that the treatment goals for CPTSD and BPD differ. Consequently, comorbid diagnosis of PTSD, when evidence supports this diagnosis, would be important in assuring the client receives optimal care.

Etiology Theories of Borderline Personality

Kernberg. In the mid-1970s, Kernberg attempted to both explain borderline personality and to describe the disorder with greater specificity. Kernberg turned to object relations and self-psychology to make sense of BPD. Recall that object relations describe the internalized representations of early figures, primarily our parents. This theory purports that when we develop healthy, realistic and inclusive representations of our caregivers (integrated objects), the internal representation is supportive of our growth and serves as a resource in difficult times. Conversely, Kernberg argued, when we develop problematic, rigid and unidimensional internal representations (unintegrated), we are unable to access reliable internal resources and find, instead, internalized representations are a source of pain, suffering and confusion. Kernberg argued that the person with a borderline personality construction is unable to accept the presence of both positive and negative traits in their understanding of self and other and instead engages in *splitting*, a pattern in which a two-dimensional understanding of self and other is created and traits and behaviors that contradict these constructions are denied, leaving a distorted perception of both others and of the self. Kernberg further argued that this inability to integrate both positive and negative traits was exacerbated by stunted growth resulting from oral fixations. Kernberg argued that oral fixations cultivated excessive anger, which was then projected onto the mother and to a lesser degree on the father (Becker, 1997; Reich & Frances, 1984; Zanarini, 2000).

Parental Styles and Early Attachment. A second theory, forwarded by Adler and Buie, also of the psychodynamic school, placed responsibility for the development of BPD at the hands of inconsistent, unemphatic and insensitive mothering. This theory asserted that, thanks to insensitive parenting, children were not able to cultivate a vision of others or themselves that was stable or consistent and consequently have no solid ground from which to respond when under stress (Zanarini, 2000). Mahler and Masterson also placed the origins of personality disorders in early development and misguided parenting. These theorists argued that failure to allow their children sufficient autonomy strivings, specifically by withdrawing when their children evidenced independence, leaving children with an awful choice between their own autonomy and their parent's love. This dynamic served, they argued, as the fertile ground for the intense abandonment fears among those with BPD (Becker, 1997; Zanarini, 2000).

Similar to Adler and Buie and Masterson and Mahler, constructs of attachment examine the relative strength of the parent–child relationship. Attachment styles describe the qualities and patterns of bonding between parent and child and are thought to fall into four broad but distinct categories: secure, preoccupied, fearful and disorganized (Choi-Kain et al., 2009; Fonagy, 2000). Exploring this theory Choi-Kain et al. (2009) studied over 200 participants and found that those diagnosed with BPD were most likely to fit a preoccupied and fearful attachment style and were much less likely to endorse a secure attachment style than those without BPD, confirming previous research. They further found that the preoccupied and fearful style differentiated those with BPD from participants with major depression and from the non-borderline controls except when comorbid PTSD or when other personality disorders were present. These researchers also suggest that those with BPD are more likely to exhibit a hybrid attachment style that combines features of the preoccupied and fearful types. They found that endorsing elements of both attachment styles conveyed greater risk for BPD than did either style alone. Finally, they found that the endorsed features of these attachment styles were correlated strongly with defining features of BPD such as fear of abandonment. It is worth noting, however, that other studies have found high

BOX 18.06 SYMPTOM OVERLAP AND CONTRASTING MANIFESTATIONS OF BORDERLINE PERSONALITY DISORDER (BPD) AND BIPOLAR I/II (BPI/II)

Symptom	BPD	BPI/II
Impulsivity	Coping mechanism	Arises out of Manic/Hypomanic episodes
Relational Instability	Client fears abandonment and these fears create problematic relational patterns	Emotional volatility leads to distress in the relationship
Risk-Taking	Reactive to environmental triggers	Transient with mania
Evaluation of Self and Other	Unrealistic evaluation of self and others; splitting into good and bad	May devalue self while in depressed episode: typically able to accurately evaluate others and status of relationships
Suicidality and Self-Harm	Coping mechanism used during periods of intense emotional experiences and frustration; communicative, conveying distress	Accompanies severe depression
Depressive Symptoms	Rapid and intense mood shifts (chronic minor depressive episodes) lasting a few hours or days	Major Depressive episodes may be present, including slowed thinking, reduced self-care and hopelessness, changes in sleeping and eating etc. May include vegetative symptoms
Hypomanic/ Manic Symptoms	Rapid but brief shifts in mood, often featuring irritability	Manic/hypomanic episode is a defining feature of this dimension
Paranoia	Transient	Transient with mania
Psychosis	Transient: generally auditory	Transient with mood episodes
Dissociation	Transient and Stress-Related	Transient

Source: Ha, 2018; Kernberg & Yeomans, 2013; Perugi, Hantouche, Vannucchi, & Pinto, 2015; Phelps, 2016 (see page 40) Zimmerman & Morgan, 2019.

BOX 18.07 CONSIDER THIS: DISCERNING DEPENDENT PERSONALITY DISORDER

Consider the following two examples, Jenna and Devin. In your clinical opinion do both Jenna and Devin meet criterion A1 of dependent personality disorder (p. 675 of the DSM 5), difficulty making decisions without an excessive amount of advice or reassurance? What questions might you have to help you feel more confident in your decision? In your initial clinical opinion, do either Jenna or Devin experience difficulty making decisions without excessive reassurance that also causes impairment? How might cultural differences influence how you would assess their functioning? Do gender expectations play a role here?

Jenna and Devin are 32-year-old fraternal twins who grew up in a home in which they were not encouraged to trust their own experience or intuition. Each leaned heavily on their parents to make decisions well into their senior year of college. The outside observer would likely describe their parents as both domineering and intrusive. Both Devin and Jenna confess feeling uncomfortable taking initiative without consulting someone and often feel they are not capable of making fully informed decisions entirely on their own. Devin regularly consults his parents about any important matter before making a decision. He is relieved to be living with his parents and working in the family business where he knows he can count on his parents to guide him when important work or financial issues arise. Jenna, however, despite her secret concern that she may not be fully competent, resists consulting others and is determined to live and work independently, despite considerable fears that sometimes arise. Jenna does, however, check her decisions with trusted friends if she feels the decision will have lasting consequences, such as selecting a graduate school or making a major purchase.

rates of disorganized attachment among those with BPD (Bateman & Fonagy, 2010; Levy, 2005).

Mentalization. Mentalization is a theory of mind skill through which people are able to create a meaningful understanding of our own thoughts, feelings, wishes and motivations and those of others. Through successful mentalization, we are able to interpret and navigate social interactions, both implicit and explicit. When successful, mentalization assures that we are in harmony with others, responding to implicit communications and lending a coherent quality to our understanding of others. However, when the mentalization processes are impaired, social interactions become difficult to navigate leaving a person frustrated, anxious and volatile. While theory of mind and mentalization capacities are developmental milestones, the strength of these skills seems to be influenced by early care, attachment and emotional mirroring (Bateman et al., 2007; Bateman & Fonagy, 2010, 2016; Fonagy, 2000).

Treatment Approaches for Personality Disorders

Earlier we explored theories that attempt to describe the origins of BPD. Below you'll find a very brief description of three prominent therapeutic approaches used in the intervention for BPD: DBT, Transference Focused Therapy (TFT) and Mentalization Focused Therapy, each of which finds its origins in one of the theories described above. A lesser known but promising group approach is also included.

Dialectical Behavioral Therapy. In recent decades, DBT has emerged as the therapeutic mainstay of those treating personality disorders, particularly BPD. DBT is comprised of three components: personal therapy, group psychoeducational therapy and telephone coaching in which clients are able to reach out for immediate help in moments when they might otherwise respond impulsively and in ways that would be harmful to themselves. Ideally, this approach is delivered by two or more therapists, each taking responsibility for one of the three modes of therapy. This approach was specifically developed with suicidal and parasuicidal clients in mind and aims to provide them with support and skills that reduce self-injurious behavior, cultivate a stable sense of self, build skills for emotion regulation, stress tolerance and a repertoire of skillful responses to conflict. Other aims include building a capacity to observe the present moment without judgment and to reduce dependency on others. Weekly therapy sessions focus on problem-solving, giving priority to suicidal and DSH behavior and then addressing behaviors that might pose an obstacle to therapy working with PTSD-like responses and finally, supporting the development of a strong self-image. Group therapy is focused on psychoeducation, combining CBT and mindfulness techniques to deliver four modules: mindfulness, interpersonal effectiveness, distress tolerance and emotion regulation (Frost et al., 2018; Kliem et al., 2010; Koerner & Linehan, 2002; Linehan, 1993/2018; Linehan et al., 1993; Lynch et al., 2007; Perseius et al., 2003; Zanarini et al., 2010).

Multiple Family Group Treatment. The Multiple Family Group Treatment (MFT) approach recognizes the empirical efficacy of key elements of DBT and the central importance of family intervention in shifting relational patterns. Consequently, this approach incorporates psychoeducational models with family in group contexts in order to provide information, skills and group support. MFT pre-supposes that the family member with BPD has difficulty clearly expressing emotional needs and that family members often miss or fail to hear the subtext of these communications. Finally, MFT acknowledges that many of these families have developed patterns of operating within a high degree of emotional intensity that is overwhelming and difficult for members to navigate. MFT works to support families in reducing emotional intensity while strengthening communication and educating the family about BPD generally (Koerner & Linehan, 2002; Whitehurst et al., 2004). This approach is thought to be both cost effective and efficacious with families of teens (Uliaszek et al., 2014) as well as with adults (Linehan et al., 1993; Lynch et al., 2007; Zanarini et al., 2010).

Kernberg's Object Relations and TFT. TFT is sourced from object relations theory originated by Kernberg. This approach has three primary aims, the first of which is to reduce suicidality; second, to address tendencies among BPD diagnosed clients to engage in behaviors that undermine therapy and, finally, to repair object relations patterns through the use of the therapeutic relationship (Linehan et al., 2001). A fairly recent randomized study of TFT that included just over 100 participants who received either a year of TFT or community counseling from an experienced therapist found superior outcomes for the TFT group in personality organization, borderline symptomatology and psychosocial functioning. In this study, suicide rates dropped but self-harm did not; however, neither of these domains changed in the comparison groups (Doering et al., 2010).

Attachment and Mentalization-Based Therapy. The aim of mentalization-based therapy (MBT) is to restore mentalization capacities to functional levels. Aware that those with BPD are highly sensitive to interpersonal interactions, a great deal of attention is given to the therapeutic relationship. The first order of business in MBT is to stabilize emotional responding, since this functioning is important in preventing suicidal and self-harming behaviors and because it is believed that emotional stability is necessary in order for the client to begin to work on internal representations of self or in undertaking therapy generally (Bateman & Fonagy, 2010; Bateman & Fonagy, 2016; Paris, 2010; Linehan et al., 2001). Research suggests that DBT and MBT each demonstrate strong efficacy in the treatment of BPD (Paris, 2010). MBT has shown efficacy in reducing BPD symptoms, including demonstrating ever-important reductions in suicidal and self-harm behaviors (Bales et al., 2012; Bateman & Fonagy, 2016).

Definitional Cases

Junji

Junji, 36, is a very driven accountant who lives with his wife and three children. Junji's wife has asked him if he will go with her to marriage counseling. She is feeling at the breaking point in trying to tolerate Junji's rigid behavior and his tendency to put his family second to his work. Because of his perfectionistic tendencies, his work takes hours longer than the other accountants and consequently he works late into the night, often getting home long after the children are in bed. Junji is confused and irritated by his wife's request.

Cyndi

Cyndi, is a 29-year-old writer for an online magazine who is living with her parents and younger sister. While she longs to move to Paris and attend a culinary school, she is convinced that ultimately she is "too socially awkward and functionally inept" to make the move. Cyndi avoids any situations in which she might expose herself to evaluation, since any perceived criticism is deeply painful for her, often deciding to stay home rather than go out with friends fearing she might make a mistake and her friends would laugh. When she does spend time with friends, she avoids asserting herself and lets others take the lead.

Maureen

Maureen is a 56-year-old hospice nurse and part time minister in the small town where she has lived her whole life. Maureen showed no remorse when she was recently arrested for scamming elderly patients out of their social security checks through her "ministry" and for shorting her patients' medication doses, in order to use or resell the drugs.

Art

Art is a 35-year-old dentist who is hoping to become a partner in the large dental clinic where he currently works. Art is having a great deal of difficulty accepting constructive feedback from the partners who have received a number of complaints about his tendency to describe at length to the dental clients what he sees as his many talents and his superior intellect. When his coworkers have come to him with these concerns, Art has flown into a rage, and accused others of trying to undermine him or of being jealous.

Ernesto

Ernesto, 22, is not able to hold down a job or go to school, though he would like to. Ernesto, often fails to notice important details about his dress, his clothes are often dirty, mismatched or his pants left unzipped. He doesn't filter his thoughts, and sometimes is unsure if he's said something aloud or simply thought it in his head, and as a result often offends or makes others uncomfortable. His life goals shift rapidly and are often fairly unrealistic or strange. He finds it difficult to read others' feelings and intentions and as a result often feels anxious and lacks trust. He has no friends but prefers being alone when given the chance.

Lee Anna

Lee Anna has a long history of volatile relationships. She holds deep fears that she is not lovable; that she will not be able to keep a partner or friend close to her. She finds herself vacillating between being too clingy or shutting others out, but always wishing for closeness. At her lowest points she has hurt herself, and once was hospitalized when she threatened suicide.

Narrative Cases

Anushka

Anushka, 34, shares that she and her mother are best friends. "She's also kind of been like my life coach and agent my whole life." Anushka went to college for 3 years before returning home and studied architecture but found the competitive and masculine environment left her with intense anxiety and occasional panic attacks. She now works at a small grocery store where she sells specialty meats and cheeses. She further shares, "My mom is my greatest ally. She takes care of me at home and coaches me on important decisions. Sometimes I call her from work when I feel stressed or I'm having a hard time making a decision on an order or dealing with my boss or coworkers. My mom arranges my doctor's appointments for me and that kind of thing, which I appreciate, because I guess I'm not sure I've got my stuff together enough to do that kind of thing myself without screwing it up. I worry a lot about how I will get along without my parents. I seriously feel I would be completely lost without them." At work Anushka admits that she will often volunteer to do the least preferred tasks in order to ingratiate herself to her coworkers. "I know they take advantage sometimes, but I'm just really lucky to have their friendship and I want to keep it that way."

Rodrick

For his whole life, Rodrick has done things in his own time, in his own way and often on his own, out of the view of others. He first concerned his parents when he seemed to be catching on slowly to reading and then one day reading as if out of the blue. Roderick has long been sensitive to other's evaluation and has cultivated a pattern of avoiding the possibility of criticism by keeping a very low profile. Now 27, he kept his head down all through school, generally earning very good grades along the way but never entering into a spotlight where he might shine . . . or fail, which was and is his primary fear.

Rodrick has been carrying feelings of inadequacy for as long as he can remember. Even small corrections and criticisms, such as teasing about spelling errors, stung terribly. Mounting sensitivity over the years has led Rodrick to "tuck in," as he describes it, by avoiding work or social situations where he might draw attention. He's now settled on remote consultation with a computing firm where he rarely meets with coworkers. He rarely goes. More recently, however, Roderick has begun a relationship with a woman he met in college, Eva. He is seeking counseling because Eva has noticed that he is remote and reluctant to share his feelings with her. She has shared that she would like to introduce him to her friends, but Rodrick has resisted and Eva's feelings have been hurt. Rodrick knows that underlying both of Eva's concerns is his fear. This fear has stalked him his whole life, "If people really knew me they would laugh at me and see me as an ass that I am." Rodrick is afraid that if he were to meet Eva's friends they wouldn't like him and, in turn, she would reject him. He has lost sleep imagining having a beer with Eva's friends and envisioning a nice evening crumbing into a scenario in which he is the butt of jokes. But a deeper concern, Rodrick feels, is that if he were to share his fears with her, she would certainly find him to be ridiculous or even pathetic. Rodrick feels he can "see the writing on the wall." He believes Eva will leave, either because he shows himself and all his inadequacies or because he is not able to be open with her. He misses her already.

Eric

Eric, 64, is so angry, he is beside himself. Looking out the window of his small duplex he can see his neighbors walking their dog, who invariably makes its way onto his grass. "They could walk on the other side of the street but they do this because they know I don't want that damn dog in my yard!" Eric thinks to himself. Grabbing his bb gun Eric opens his door and shouts, "Get that dog off my yard or I'll shoot him! I know my rights!"

Eric holds a long list of grudges against community members and family and has, as a result, only one person he can call a friend, Dexter, whom he has known since he was a child. Eric regularly gets into yelling matches with city officials at town hall meetings, for example, with police officers, store managers and the like, all of whom he believes are trying to take advantage of him or refuse him his rights. Eric has filled dozens of ledgers documenting slights and noting opportunities that others have failed to take to make things right again. Eric is very reluctant to share his feelings with anyone, including Dexter, because he is sure that if he were to "show the soft parts of myself, they'd go in for the kill." But when he is honest with himself, he knows that he is very lonely and would like nothing better to than to have a friend or partner he could spend time with. However, he has extended enough trust to show Dexter some of his ledgers over the years in an attempt to support his claims that people are deliberately treating him unfairly. Eric has felt angry and betrayed when Dexter has failed to see how some of the listed incidents have caused so much upset in the first place or why he hasn't been able to let them go. Though Dexter is diplomatic, it is clear that he doesn't understand the incidents in the same way Eric himself does. "Eric, some of the things you have written in here, Dude, they happen to everyone, like this paperboy grudge, or the thing complaint you've got going with the UPS guy. I've had some of these same experiences, and they are annoying for sure, but they don't deserve so much of your attention. Maybe if you could relax a little you'd be happier."

Irenka

Irenka, 19, is in trouble again. While walking through a gallery with a friend, she spotted a small Versace clutch resting on a couch beneath a painting. Irenka walked casually over to the painting, discretely slipped the small purse into her own bag and slowly moved on to the next painting. Irenka and her friend left the museum and then went to dinner. She'd nearly forgotten she'd taken the clutch until she reached in her bag to pay the bill. Inside she found several credit cards as well as cash, which she used to pay for her dinner. Irenka's troubles came when she attempted to use one of the credit cards to purchase tickets to Vail. Though this is not Irenka's first arrest, her parents have been able to get her out of these scrapes without a criminal record or consequence.

Though still a young woman, Irenka already has a history of running roughshod over those around her. Irenka's parents acknowledge that they have raised her to be the "Princess of New York City" and have made every effort to give her the life that royalty might expect. They are perplexed, however, at why Irenka would feel the need to steal anything, since she has always had a sizable allowance and has not been denied any request. Irenka has cultivated a belief that rules don't apply to her and are put in place for "common people who don't know how to work around them." Irenka can be mean-spirited, often mocking those less fortunate than herself. She has difficulty forming and keeping friendships because her cruel comments and tendency to steal from others are sometimes aimed at friends. Because she feels little remorse or guilt, she is not one to apologize, but instead, blames others or rationalizes her actions. She is bright but has not been able to finish college or even give much thought to what she might do with her life. She finds such lines of thinking to be "far too tedious" and "beneath her."

Wainwright

Wainwright and his soon to be ex-wife, Kim, are meeting with a psychologist who will help them determine custody of their two children. Kim shares, "I knew I had to get out of that relationship and get the kids away from him but I was scared, scared for us and for him."

"When I met Wain he was very attentive and kind," Kim continues. "Wain had a pretty traumatic childhood, his dad was abusive and his mom had a drinking problem that eventually killed her. Still, despite all that hardship he was kind. He put me and our first child on a pedestal, but by the time the second baby, Tim, came along, Wain, seemed to have switched and he had me characterized as some villainous woman like Maleficent in the fairy tales. Everyone in his world is like that, I wish I'd seen that sooner. There's just no grey in Wain's world, a person is either really, really bad or a saint-like-hero-genius figure. That got really old. But when he said that if I left him he would kill himself, and said it in front of the kids, I knew I had to get them out of that environment, and that's why I'm trying to get full custody. He scares the crap out of them with talk like that."

In Wain's discussion with the psychologist, he shares his anger at discovering that Kim was "a terrible person" and nothing like the sweet woman she had seemed to be when they met. "It's been my lot in life to have relationships with women who pretend to be good as long as it suits them and then to show their true colors later." Wain shares that he has struggled with bouts of dejection and rage and has even tried to kill himself once, resulting in a hospitalization. Wain asserts that he is not sure that he really meant to kill himself in those events but admits he was "pretty drunk the first time that happened." When asked, Wain shares that he had two other attempts, one when he was fired and a second following a fight with his wife Kim early in their relationship. Wain offers, "I do have an anger problem but I've been working on it. I've been in therapy for a while working on anger and trying to figure out why I feel so empty all the time. I probably drink too much, not like my mom did, but too much, so I'm working on that, too. But none of this should keep me from my kids. They are the glue that is keeping me pasted together.

References

American Psychiatric Association. (2013a). Personality disorders. In *Diagnostic and statistical manual of mental disorders* (Vol. 17, pp. 133–137). BMC Med.

American Psychiatric Association. (2013b). Alternative diagnostic model for personality disorders. In *Diagnostic and statistical manual of mental disorders* (Vol. 17, pp. 133–137). BMC Med.

Bales, D., van Beek, N., Smits, M., Willemsen, S., Busschbach, J. J., Verheul, R., & Andrea, H. (2012). Treatment outcome of 18-month, day hospital Mentalization-Based Treatment (MBT) in patients with severe borderline personality disorder in the Netherlands. *Journal of Personality Disorders*, *26*(4), 568–582.

Bateman, A., & Fonagy, P. (2010). Mentalization based treatment for borderline personality disorder. *World Psychiatry*, *9*(1), 11.

Bateman, A., & Fonagy, P. (2016). *Mentalization-based treatment for personality disorders: A practical guide*. Oxford University Press.

Bateman, A. W., Ryle, A., Fonagy, P., & Kerr, I. B. (2007). Psychotherapy for borderline personality disorder: Mentalization based therapy and cognitive analytic therapy compared. *International Review of Psychiatry*, *19*(1), 51–62.

Becker, D. (1997). *Through the looking glass: Women and borderline personality disorder*. Routledge.

Black, D. W., Blum, N., Pfohl, B., & Hale, N. (2004). Suicidal behavior in borderline personality disorder: Prevalence, risk factors, prediction, and prevention. *Journal of Personality Disorders*, *18*(3: Special issue), 226–239.

Bornstein, R. F. (2011). Reconceptualizing personality pathology in DSM-5: Limitations in evidence for eliminating dependent personality disorder and other DSM-IV syndromes. *Journal of Personality Disorders*, *25*(2), 235–247.

Chanen, A. M., & Kaess, M. (2012). Developmental pathways to borderline personality disorder. *Current Psychiatry Reports*, *14*(1), 45–53.

Choi-Kain, L. W., Fitzmaurice, G. M., Zanarini, M. C., Laverdière, O., & Gunderson, J. G. (2009). The relationship between self-reported attachment styles, interpersonal dysfunction, and borderline personality disorder. *The Journal of Nervous and Mental Disease*, *197*(11), 816–821.

Cloitre, M., Garvert, D. W., Weiss, B., Carlson, E. B., & Bryant, R. A. (2014). Distinguishing PTSD, complex PTSD, and borderline personality disorder: A latent class analysis. *European Journal of Psychotraumatology*, *5*(1), 25097.

de Aquino Ferreira, L. F., Pereira, F. H. Q., Benevides, A. M. L. N., & Melo, M. C. A. (2018). Borderline personality disorder and sexual abuse: A systematic review. *Psychiatry Research*, *262*, 70–77.

Doering, S., Hörz, S., Rentrop, M., Fischer-Kern, M., Schuster, P., Benecke, C., & Buchheim, P. (2010). Transference-focused psychotherapy v. treatment by community psychotherapists for borderline personality disorder: Randomised controlled trial. *The British Journal of Psychiatry*, *196*(5), 389–395.

Fonagy, P. (2000). Attachment and borderline personality disorder. *Journal of the American Psychoanalytic Association*, *48*(4), 1129–1146.

Frances, A. (2013). *Saving normal: An insider's revolt against out-of-control psychiatric diagnosis, DSM-5, big pharma and the medicalization of ordinary life.* William Morrow.

Frost, R., Hyland, P., Shevlin, M., & Murphy, J. (2018). Distinguishing complex PTSD from borderline personality disorder among individuals with a history of sexual trauma: A latent class analysis. *European Journal of Trauma & Dissociation*, *4*, 2–29.

Ha, T. H. (2018). The border between Bipolar disorder and personality disorders. *Journal of Korean Neuropsychiatric Association*, *57*(4), 308–316.

Henry, C., Mitropoulou, V., New, A. S., Koenigsberg, H. W., Silverman, J., & Siever, L. J. (2001). Affective instability and impulsivity in borderline personality and bipolar II disorders: Similarities and differences. *Journal of Psychiatric Research*, *35*(6), 307–312.

Henry, K. A., & Cohen, C. I. (1983). The role of labeling processes in diagnosing borderline personality disorder. *The American Journal of Psychiatry*, *140*(11), 1527–1529.

Hopwood, C. J., & Bleidorn, W. (2018). Stability and change in personality and personality disorders. *Current Opinion in Psychology*, *21*, 6–10.

Kaplan, M. (1983). A woman's view of DSM-III. *American Psychologist*, *38*(7), 786.

Kernberg, O. F., & Yeomans, F. E. (2013). Borderline personality disorder, bipolar disorder, depression, attention deficit/hyperactivity disorder, and narcissistic personality disorder: Practical differential diagnosis. *Bulletin of the Menninger Clinic*, *77*(1), 1–22.

Kliem, S., Kröger, C., & Kosfelder, J. (2010). Dialectical behavior therapy for borderline personality disorder: A meta-analysis using mixed-effects modeling. *Journal of Consulting and Clinical Psychology*, *78*(6), 936.

Knefel, M., Tran, U. S., & Lueger-Schuster, B. (2016). The association of posttraumatic stress disorder, complex posttraumatic stress disorder, and borderline personality disorder from a network analytical perspective. *Journal of Anxiety Disorders*, *43*, 70–78.

Koerner, K., & Linehan, M. M. (2002). Dialectical behavior therapy for borderline personality disorder. In Stefan G. Hofmann and Martha C. Tompson (Eds) *Treating Chronic and Severe Mental Disorders: A Handbook of Empirically Supported Interventions* (pp. 317–342). Guilford Press.

Kress, V. E., Minton, C. A. B., Adamson, N. A., Paylo, M. J., & Pope, V. (2014). The Removal of the Multiaxial System in the DSM-5: Implications and Practice Suggestions for Counselors. *Professional Counselor*, *4*(3), 191–201.

Landrine, H. (1989). The politics of personality disorder. *Psychology of Women Quarterly*, *13*(3), 325–339.

Latalova, K., Prasko, J., Pastucha, P., Grambal, A., Kamaradova, D., Diveky, T., & Vrbova, K. (2011). Bipolar affective disorder and dissociation-comparison with healthy controls. *Biomedical Papers of the Medical Faculty of Palacky University in Olomouc*, *155*(2), 181–186.

Levy, K. N. (2005). The implications of attachment theory and research for understanding borderline personality disorder. *Development and Psychopathology*, *17*(4), 959–986.

Linehan, M. M. (1993/2018). *Cognitive-behavioral treatment of borderline personality disorder*. Guilford Publications.

Linehan, M. M., Cochran, B. N., & Kehrer, C. A. (2001). Dialectical behavior therapy for borderline personality disorder. In D. H. Barlow (Ed.), *Clinical Handbook of Psychological Disorders: A Step-By-Step Treatment Manual*, (pp 470–522). The Guilford Press.

Linehan, M. M., Heard, H. L., & Armstrong, H. E. (1993). Naturalistic follow-up of a behavioral treatment for chronically parasuicidal borderline patients. *Archives of General Psychiatry*, *50*(12), 971–974.

Lingiardi, V., Giovanardi, G., Fortunato, A., Nassisi, V., & Speranza, A. M. (2017). Personality and attachment in transsexual adults. *Archives of Sexual Behavior*, *46*(5), 1313–1323.

Lynch, T. R., Trost, W. T., Salsman, N., & Linehan, M. M. (2007). Dialectical behavior therapy for borderline personality disorder. *Annual Review of Clinical Psychology*, *3*, 181–205.

McWilliams, N. (1994). *Psychoanalytic diagnosis: Understanding personality structure in the clinical process*. Guilford Press.

Menon, P., Chaudhari, B., Saldanha, D., Devabhaktuni, S., & Bhattacharya, L. (2016). Childhood sexual abuse in adult patients with borderline personality disorder. *Industrial Psychiatry Journal*, *25*(1), 101.

Morey, L. C., Warner, M. B., & Boggs, C. D. (2002). Gender bias in the personality disorders criteria: An investigation of five bias indicators. *Journal of Psychopathology and Behavioral Assessment*, *24*(1), 55–65.

Oldham, J. M. (2015). The alternative DSM-5 model for personality disorders. *World Psychiatry*, *14*(2), 234.

Paris, J. (2010). Effectiveness of different psychotherapy approaches in the treatment of borderline personality disorder. *Current Psychiatry Reports*, *12*(1), 56–60.

Paris, J. (2018). Clinical features of borderline personality disorder. In W. J. Livesley, & R. Larstone (Eds.). *Handbook of personality disorders: Theory, research, and treatment*, (2nd ed., p. 419). Guilford Publications.

Perseius, K. I., Öjehagen, A., Ekdahl, S., Åsberg, M., & Samuelsson, M. (2003). Treatment of suicidal and deliberate self-harming patients with borderline personality disorder using dialectical behavioral therapy: The patients' and the therapists' perceptions. *Archives of Psychiatric Nursing, 17*(5), 218–227.

Perugi, G., Hantouche, E., Vannucchi, G., & Pinto, O. (2015). Cyclothymia reloaded: A reappraisal of the most misconceived affective disorder. *Journal of Affective Disorders, 183*, 119–133.

Phelps, J. (2016). Bipolar or Borderline (or PTSD or ADHD)? In *A spectrum approach to mood disorders: Not fully bipolar but not unipolar--Practical management*. Norton Press.

Reich, J., & Frances, A. (1984). The structural interview method for diagnosing borderline disorders: A critique. *Psychiatric Quarterly, 56*(3), 229–235.

Røysamb, E., Kendler, K. S., Tambs, K., Ørstavik, R. E., Neale, M. C., Aggen, S. H., & Reichborn-Kjennerud, T. (2011). The joint structure of DSM-IV Axis I and Axis II disorders. *Journal of Abnormal Psychology, 120*(1), 198.

Scherrer, K. S. (2008). Coming to an asexual identity: Negotiating identity, negotiating desire. *Sexualities, 11*(5), 621–641.

Shevlin, M., Dorahy, M., Adamson, G., & Murphy, J. (2007). Subtypes of borderline personality disorder, associated clinical disorders and stressful life-events: A latent class analysis based on the British Psychiatric Morbidity Survey. *British Journal of Clinical Psychology, 46*(3), 273–281.

Skodol, A. E., Clark, L. A., Bender, D. S., Krueger, R. F., Morey, L. C., Verheul, R., & Oldham, J. M. (2011). Proposed changes in personality and personality disorder assessment and diagnosis for DSM-5 Part I: Description and rationale. *Personality Disorders: Theory, Research, and Treatment, 2*(1), 4.

Soloff, P. H., & Chiappetta, L. (2017). Suicidal behavior and psychosocial outcome in borderline personality disorder at 8-year follow-up. *Journal of Personality Disorders, 31*(6), 774–789.

Sperry, L. (2016). *Handbook of diagnosis and treatment of DSM-5 personality disorders: Assessment, case conceptualization, and treatment*. Routledge.

Swit, C. S., McMaugh, A. L., & W. L. (2018). Teacher and parent perceptions of relational and physical aggression during early childhood. *Journal of Child and Family Studies, 27*(1), 118–130.

Trull, T. J., Freeman, L. K., Vebares, T. J., Choate, A. M., Helle, A. C., & Wycoff, A. M. (2018). Borderline personality disorder and substance use disorders: An updated review. *Borderline Personality Disorder and Emotion Dysregulation, 5*(1), 15.

Trull, T. J., Jahng, S., Tomko, R. L., Wood, P. K., & Sher, K. J. (2010). Revised NESARC personality disorder diagnoses: Gender, prevalence, and comorbidity with substance dependence disorders. *Journal of Personality Disorders, 24*(4), 412–426.

Uliaszek, A. A., Wilson, S., Mayberry, M., Cox, K., & Maslar, M. (2014). A pilot intervention of multifamily dialectical behavior group therapy in a treatment-seeking adolescent population: Effects on teens and their family members. *The Family Journal*, *22*(2), 206–215.

Vater, A., Ritter, K., Strunz, S., Ronningstam, E. F., Renneberg, B., & Roepke, S. (2014). Stability of narcissistic personality disorder: Tracking categorical and dimensional rating systems over a two-year period. *Personality Disorders: Theory, Research, and Treatment*, *5*(3), 305.

Westbrook, J., & Berenbaum, H. (2017). Emotional awareness moderates the relationship between childhood abuse and borderline personality disorder symptom factors. *Journal of Clinical Psychology*, *73*(7), 910–921.

Whitehurst, T., Ridolfi, M. E., & Gunderson, J. (2004). Multiple family group treatment for borderline personality disorder. In S. G. Hofman & M. C. Tompson (Eds.), *Treating chronic and severe mental disorders: A handbook of empirically supported interventions*, (pp *343*, 343–364). Guliford Press.

Zanarini, M. C. (2000). Childhood experiences associated with the development of borderline personality disorder. *Psychiatric Clinics of North America*, *23*(1), 89–101.

Zanarini, M. C., Frankenburg, F. R., Hennen, J., Reich, D. B., & Silk, K. R. (2005). The McLean Study of Adult Development (MSAD): Overview and implications of the first six years of prospective follow-up. *Journal of Personality Disorders*, *19*(5), 505–523.

Zanarini, M. C., Frankenburg, F. R., Reich, D. B., & Fitzmaurice, G. (2010). Time to attainment of recovery from borderline personality disorder and stability of recovery: A 10-year prospective follow-up study. *American Journal of Psychiatry*, *167*(6), 663–667.

Zanarini, M. C., Frankenburg, F. R., Reich, D. B., & Fitzmaurice, G. (2012). Attainment and stability of sustained symptomatic remission and recovery among patients with borderline personality disorder and axis II comparison subjects: A 16-year prospective follow-up study. *The American Journal of Psychiatry*, *169*(5), 476–483.

Zanarini, M. C., Frankenburg, F. R., Reich, D. B., Fitzmaurice, G., Weinberg, I., & Gunderson, J. G. (2008). The 10-year course of physically self-destructive acts reported by borderline patients and axis II comparison subjects. *Acta Psychiatrica Scandinavica*, *117*(3), 177–184.

Zanarini, M. C., Frankenburg, F. R., Reich, D. B., Silk, K. R., Hudson, J. I., & McSweeney, L. B. (2007). The subsyndromal phenomenology of borderline personality disorder: A 10-year follow-up study. *American Journal of Psychiatry*, *164*(6), 929–935.

Zanarini, M. C., Temes, C. M., Magni, L. R., Aguirre, B. A., Hein, K. E., & Goodman, M. (2019). Risk factors for borderline personality disorder in adolescents. *Journal of Personality Disorders*. *33*, 1–8.

Zimmerman, M., & Morgan, T. A. (2019). Interface between borderline personality disorder and bipolar II disorder. In H. A. Swartz & T. Suppes (Eds.), *Bipolar II disorder: Recognition, understanding, and treatment*. American Psychiatric Publishing.

19 Paraphilia

Sexual desire is a powerful driving force in the human experience and sexual contact can be counted among the most profound bonding experiences, representing a key opportunity to strengthen and deepen intimacy in a relationship. However, when clients' own sexual impulses and desires are troubling to them, or they infringe on the rights or safety of others, those desires and impulses become the focus of clinical and very often legal attention. For some clients, urges, such as surreptitiously observing others in their most private moments, or exposing themselves to unwilling persons, represent experiences that place clients in conflict with society and threaten belongingness. In addition to the legal problems these impulses and the behaviors carry, feelings of shame and isolation are common. In some cases, such as with pedophilia, the urges and behaviors also represent a profound danger to the emotional and physical well-being of children, making identification and treatment important for the client as well as for potential victims.

Most often clients who are being evaluated for paraphilic disorders are involuntary clients, encountered either through the court system or custody hearings. This dimension is the only dimension in the DSM 5 in which legal considerations played an important role in the development and refinement and, in some cases, the exclusion, of disorders and their criteria over time (First, 2010, 2014). Consequently, many of the diagnostic challenges that come with this dimension of disorders hover around issues of the law and their implications for clients, their treatment as well as for actual and potential victims. This chapter will provide an overview of the disorders of the paraphilic dimension, the changes represented in the DSM 5 and their implications, as well as the diagnostic challenges presented. Also included in this chapter is a brief discussion of our current understanding of norms among the general/nonclinical population related to sexual fantasies, an understanding that is essential to diagnosticians. The chapter concludes with definitional and narrative cases for diagnosis.

Donning Your Clinical Hat. Ample evidence suggests that mental health professionals are more likely to have experienced childhood sexual assault (CSA) than the population as a whole (Bach & Demuth, 2018; Pope & Feldman-Summers, 1992); research suggests that this is true even among those who treat sex offenders. For example, a 2004 study found that 75% of their sample of therapists who treat sex offenders had been victims themselves (Way et al., 2004, in Bach & Demuth, 2018). Readers who have experienced unwanted sexual experiences (USE) or CSA should be aware that this content may be personally triggering, bringing back memories and still-tender feelings of sadness, anger, betrayal and so on. It may be helpful before progressing through the chapter, to pause and take a moment to dawn your clinical hat, reminding yourself of the wisdom, strength and courage that has brought you to a space where you are now doing the work of a graduate student and preparing to serve as a resource, a source of strength, light and healing. Through that lens, you can begin to understand the impulses and behaviors of this continuum and resultant suffering while focused on the people who experience them. My recommendation is that if you find that the chapter is very triggering and difficult to read thanks to your own experiences, seek counseling if you are not receiving counseling already. Unfortunately, the sexual assault of children and adults is terribly, terribly common and no counselor, psychologist, psychiatrist or social worker will be able to do work that does not include the capacity to facilitate discussions around these events.

The Disorders of the Paraphilic Dimension

Before exploring the specific disorders and criteria of the paraphilias, it is important to note that this chapter of the DSM 5 has been marked by considerable controversy; some researchers and diagnosticians have called for its removal from the diagnostic nosology altogether (Joyal, 2018; Moser & Kleinplatz, 2006), while some have argued for its expansion (Stern, 2010). Central, to the debate and core to the contention are three challenges. The first challenge comes in maintaining the central ethic of the DSM, which is to describe mental illness and provide a valid and reliable nosology for its identification and organization. In service of this aim, the first task is determining what kinds of fantasies, sexual behaviors and preferences are to be considered pathological in nature and which are simply atypical, taboo or socially distasteful. The American Psychiatric Association (APA) (2013) is explicit in stating that disorder is not a function of acting in conflict with societal preferences (social deviance) but that the distress experienced must arise independently out of a dysfunction within the individuals themselves (APA, 2013; Wakefield, 2012). Second, the criteria of "intense sexual arousal" that distinguishes these disorders must have some kind of reliable benchmark, which discerns experiences that would be considered pathological from experiences that are not. Some authors point out that the DSM seems to frame behaviors and interests that are prevalent among the non-clinical population as pathological (Joyal, 2018). In other words, the concerns surrounding the diagnoses in this dimension are tied to reliability, validity, and the potential for conflating socially accepted morals and values with mental health. Notably, voices from the field are questioning whether pedophelia, for example, should be thought of as a moral and social wrong, a mental illness or both, a topic that will be discussed later in this chapter.

Notable Changes in Response to Long-Standing Criticism

In 2006, Moser and Kleinplatz conducted an extensive review of the paraphilias and the available research, which led them to voice a number of concerns about the structure and content of the paraphilias. These concerns, which have been partially remediated with the publication of the DSM 5, centered on five main points: (1) the DSM's failure to keep pace with current research, including the unsubstantiated statements peppered throughout the section; (2) vague language that complicated diagnosis; (3) inconsistencies in the decision-making process for the inclusion or exclusion of disorders from the text; (4) a tendency to equate social deviance and criminality with disorder and (5) equating of consensual role-play or fantasy with criminal/disordered behavior. They pointed out that much of the content of the DSM had gone unrevised since the third edition, further suggesting that the text of the DSM had not kept pace with available research nor was it in line with current social understandings and norms.

Moser and Kleinplatz (2006) also pointed to the difficulty in the language of the A criteria of each of the paraphilic disorders, such as "intense sexually arousing fantasies," and the difficulty in discerning the difference between the intensity of healthy sexual arousal and the intensity of unhealthy arousal. They noted that, in this dimension the DSM has not employed descriptors found elsewhere in the manual, such as obsessive, compulsive or impulsive, suggesting that the A criteria "intense sexual interest/arousal" must mean something other than these three indicators (p. 96).

In response to some of these questions, the DSM 5 now discerns paraphilic interests from paraphilic disorders, taking a step toward untangling questions of mental illness from departures from social norms and values, and bringing the DSM more in line with current research. The DSM 5 has not, however, resolved its problem with inconsistency in deciding which socially destructive and odious behaviors are included as disorders and which are not. For example, compulsive rape disorder was considered for the fifth edition but ultimately was not included due in part to fears that the diagnosis would be used inappropriately as a defense in legal cases and because many in the field pointed out that there was no evidence that compulsive rape was born out of disorder per se, and argued that it was instead simply a criminal behavior (Wollert, 2011). However, similar disorders such as pedophilia and frotteuristic disorder, disorders that also feature unwanted and illegal sexual contact, remain in the manual. A discussion about the role of the law and its intersection with the diagnostic process as well as a brief discussion of current understandings of normative sexual fantasies will be explored later in this chapter.

Shared Criteria

All paraphilic disorders share three criteria: duration, intense sexual arousal associated with the arousal target and distress. Each of these disorders require a duration of 6 months before a diagnosis can be made. Second, the intense arousal derived from each of these domains are understood to outpace or replace other more typical fantasies or behaviors. Third, the client diagnosed with a paraphilic disorder should either be experiencing distress or impairment as a result of these preferences or impulses or the gratification of these interests must be causing harm to the client or potential or actual harm to others. It is important to note that a diagnosis of a paraphilic disorder is not made on the basis of the behavior or interest alone; in order to meet diagnostic criteria for a paraphilic disorder, the behavior must result in distress for the client or actual or potential risk of harm to others (APA, 2013).

This adjustment in the framing of paraphilic disorders marks a significant shift in the understanding of this dimension and is responsive to research. For example, Dunsieth et al. (2004) demonstrated that not all persons who engage in criminal acts of voyeurism, exhibitionism, pedophilia or the sexual assault of other adults also meet criteria for paraphilic disorders. Instead, many of these crimes are committed for reasons unrelated to sexual arousal. In their study of male sex offenders, 25.7% did not meet the criteria for a paraphilia. The shift in framing also better fits with research about normative sexual fantasies and practices, which will be discussed later in this chapter.

Shared Traits across Paraphilic Disorders

Recent research describing comorbidity among clients with paraphilic disorders is scarce. Most of the available research centers around violent sex offenders (rape) and those who commit sexual assault of children; much of this research is decades old and is in need of renewed exploration and additional depth and sophistication in analysis (Moulden et al., 2014). Dunsieth et al. (2004) conducted a study of 113 men in a treatment facility for those who had served time for sex offenses. Among the paraphilic offenders, 85% had substance use disorders, more than half had a mood disorder, usually bipolar disorder, nearly a quarter had an anxiety disorder and just under 10% had an eating disorder. These findings mirrored the findings of Kafka and Hennen (2002) who studied 120 men being treated on an outpatient basis for paraphilias. Like Dunsieth et al. (2004), they also found that offenders with paraphilic disorders struggled with high rates of substance abuse (40.8%). Also common were mood disorders, a 71.6% lifetime prevalence. Notably, their participants showed high rates of dysthymia and attention deficit hyperactivity disorder (ADHD). A 2012 meta-analysis revealed predictably varied results but affirmed high rates of substance abuse, fetal alcohol spectrum disorders, depressive and bipolar disorders, social phobia and panic disorder (Kafka, 2012).

It is difficult to discern comorbidity for each of the individual paraphilic disorders. However, first, as mentioned earlier, because much of the research organizes participants by offenses and not specifically by paraphilia, and second because there is so much overlap within the population with paraphilias. In their study of men convicted of sex offenses, three-fourths had at least one paraphilia and just over a quarter of those met criteria for three or more (Dunsieth et al., 2004). Finally, the bulk of the available research on paraphilias focuses on pedophilia, leaving the remaining disorders largely unexplored.

Almost without exception, men are much more likely than women to report paraphilic interests, therefore, men are much more likely to be diagnosed, with the exception of masochism, which appears to be more common among women. A 2011 community sample found that 64% of male respondents endorsed at least one paraphilic interest and 44% affirmed paraphilic activity (Ahlers et al., 2011, in Dawson et al., 2016). Dawson et al. (2016) found men to be more likely to endorse arousal in any of the paraphilias except exhibitionism, scatologia, transvestic fetishism, masochism, scatophilia and zoophilia, which were endorsed about equally by both men and women.

As you consider the disorders of this dimension, you might break them into three basic categories: those involving an unsuspecting or an unwilling person or persons; those involving giving or receiving some form of verbal, psychological or physical harm, real or imagined and those that involve fixation on a particular target of sexual desire. Included in the group of interests involving unsuspecting or unwilling persons, are voyeuristic disorder, exhibitionistic disorder and frotteuristic disorder. The second group includes sadistic and masochistic disorders both of which require some degree of physical or verbal abuse. Finally, those that involve a particular consuming target of sexual desire include pedophilia, transvestic disorder and fetishistic disorder. The distinguishing features of each are noted below along with any changes in the DSM 5 discussion or criteria.

Voyeuristic Disorder

The person evidencing a voyeuristic disorder experiences a great deal of sexual arousal from watching others undress or having sex without their consent or knowledge. Sometimes this pattern may come in the form of the stereotypical "peeping Tom" while others have made use of more modern technologies such as using smart phones to capture images beneath women's skirts, "upskirting," or using hidden cameras in public restrooms. Voyeurism is the one disorder in which the client who is being assessed must be at least 18 years old, the justification offered by APA being that voyeuristic interests might be a natural developmental part of developing sexuality (APA, 2013; First, 2014).

Exhibitionistic Disorder

Those diagnosed with exhibitionistic disorder experience intense arousal by surprising unsuspecting and unwilling persons by exposing their genitals. Not nearly enough research is available to describe with confidence comorbidities; however, the few studies available note that individuals who engage in this behavior are more likely to have other mental health problems, they report lower satisfaction with life and higher rates of drug and alcohol use (Långström & Seto, 2006).

Frotteuristic Disorder

The person diagnosed with frotteuristic disorder derives sexual pleasure from rubbing against or otherwise touching unwilling and unsuspecting persons. Frequently, these behaviors will happen in very crowded areas, such as subways during rush hours, where touching might be mistaken as accidental.

Sexual Masochism Disorder and Sexual Sadism Disorder

Sexual masochism is a practice of role-playing or actually experiencing, for the purpose of sexual pleasure, some harm inflicted by another person. These forms of harm can come in the form of physical abuse, such as spanking, binding, cutting or beating, or may come in the form of verbal humiliation. Some masochists also participate in sexual activity while reducing the flow of oxygen to the brain, a practice known as erotic asphyxiation or hypoxyphilia, a practice coded with the specifier *asphyxophelia*. An online study of men and women who engage in this practice affirmed previous research that noted a high overlap with other masochistic behaviors, such as the use of bondage, as well as transvestic fetishism (37%) (Hucker, 2011). Conversely, sexual sadism is the pleasure derived from inflicting pain or humiliation on a partner.

Transvestic Disorder

This relatively rare disorder is diagnosed when significant distress or impairment arises from sexual pleasure derived from cross-dressing. Two specifiers are given, one for arousal from certain materials or garments, coded as "with fetishism," the second specifier, autogynephilia, is given when arousal arises when a male imagines himself as a female.

Pedophilic Disorder

Significant research points to the harm done to children as a result of CSA. Globally, the incidence of CSA is estimated to hover around 7.9% for men and 19.7% for women. More than a quarter of American women are estimated to have been victims

BOX 19.01 KEY DEFINITIONS

Paraphilic Interests/Paraphilia: "Any intense and persistent sexual interest other than sexual interest in genital stimulation or preparatory fondling with phenotypically normal, physically mature, consenting human partners," (APA, 2013, p. 685).

Paraphilic Disorder: Paraphilic interests (see above) of a duration of 6 months or more, causing distress or dysfunction (anxiety, obsessions, guilt, shame or social or relational difficulties stemming from these interest, etc.) or causes actual or potential risk of harm to another person (APA, 2013).*

Dunkelfeld: A German word meaning "dark field," this term refers to the number of undetected sexual offenses against children. Dunkelfeld is also the name applied to programs designed to prevent child sexual abuse or the use of child pornography.

Phallometry: Also known as penile plethysmography (PPG), this method of assessment measures blood flow to the penis, as an avenue for determining sexual arousal. The phallometry measures responses to images of children, adults and nonhuman objects (Seto et al., 2006).

*Note: Paraphilic *interests* can be thought of as an arousal pattern that does not harm or infringe on the rights or safety of the individual or of others, while a paraphilic *disorder* is a phenomenon in which paraphilic interests have impinged on the functionality or well-being of the individual or of other people.

of CSA, among the highest in the world after Australia, Costa Rica, Tanzania, Israel and Sweden. Documented difficulties correlated with CSA include but are not exclusive to post-traumatic stress disorder (PTSD), depression and suicidality and substance use (Bach & Demuth, 2018; Singh et al., 2014) to name a few. Only a small percentage of CSA incidents are believed to come to the attention of authorities, some estimates put this number at 30%, the remainder fall into what is known as the *Dunkelfeld,* a German word, literally translated "dark field," and refers to incidents that have gone unreported (Kuhle & Beier, 2014).

Extant research points to a high incidence of personality disorders among those who molest children. A recent study comparing those convicted of child molestation, who also met criteria for paraphilias, and those who did not revealed differences in incidences of certain types of personality disorders. Those who molest children have been shown to have much higher rates of borderline, histrionic, obsessive compulsive and depressive personality disorders. Obsessive compulsive personality disorder (OCPD), however, stood out among the four as being much more prevalent than the other three among paraphilic offenders, suggesting to researchers important connections between tendencies toward obsession and paraphilia (Bogaerts et al., 2008).

Conceptualizing "Normal" Sexual Fantasies

Before donning the hat of a diagnostician, it is always important to have a good sense of the boundary between what is "normal" or "typical" and what kinds of thoughts, feelings and behaviors are both anomalous and the source of distress, otherwise we run the risk of pathologizing ways of being based on our own values, experience and comfort. Perhaps there is no topic so prone to this kind of clinical error as sexual behavior and sexuality.

Cultural values and thinking can change a great deal in a relatively short period of time. For instance, a review of surveys archived at Cornell University over the past 80 years revealed that American attitudes have changed significantly along a range of issues. For instance, in 1968, 50% of respondents reported that they would not allow their son to grow long hair; in contrast, 15% of those surveyed in 2018 responded in the same way. Of those surveyed in 1938, 22% approved of women working outside the home if her husband had the means to support her, while 92% of respondents in 2018 endorsed women's freedom to work irrespective of her husband's income (Edwards-Levy, 2019). How much have attitudes about sexuality changed in the past several decades? Researchers have argued that the DSM 5's framing of paraphilias is out of step with changing sexual values and practices.

In order to shed light on what types of sexual fantasies are common among the general population, Joyal et al. (2014) conducted an internet survey of more than 1,500 adults from which they analyzed the sexual fantasies of men and women. Beginning with a list of 55 sexual fantasies, they identified those that were rare (occurring in 2.3% or less of the sample), those that were uncommon (15.9% or less), common (50% or more) and typical (endorsed by 84.1% of respondents). They found that a broad range of submission and dominance fantasy themes, for example, were common among both men and women. They also found that only two sexual fantasies were rare, fantasies involving children and those involving animals. Nine fantasies were found to be uncommon, among them forcing someone to have sex, sexually abusing someone drunk or unconscious, wearing clothing associated with the opposite sex and urination fantasies. Voyeuristic fantasies were common among men and women (63.4% and 31.8%, respectively) as was exhibitionism, though less so (23.3% of men and 16.6% of women). A similar study conducted in Italy of more than 700 college-aged participants found similar results. Among these participants, 532 of which were women and 243 were men, just over 41% of women endorsed at least one paraphilic behavior while slightly more than 50% of men did (Castellini et al., 2018). These studies demonstrate that fantasies once thought to be "odd" or unusual appear to be much more common than once understood, though fantasies of sexual contact with children, animals and vulnerable adults remain uncommon or rare (Joyal & Carpentier, 2017).

BOX 19.02 SHARED SPECIFIERS OF THE PARAPHILIC DISORDERS

In a Controlled Environment: This specifier is reserved for those living in environments where freedom of movement and behavior is restricted, as in prisons, hospitals, rehabilitation facilities, nursing homes and so on.

In Full Remission: This specifier is applied when a person has refrained from acting on their paraphilic urges with a non-consenting person, and has not experienced distress or occupational impairment while in an *uncontrolled environment* for at least 5 years. Consequently, this specifier can't be applied to a person currently in restricted settings such as the hospital or prison.

Source: American Psychiatric Association (2013).

The Skilled Diagnostician

Clinician Self-Awareness

The vague language of the DSM 5 and its predecessors leaves a great deal of space for clinical judgment. Where guidelines are absent, clinicians may fall back on their own cultural norms, religious beliefs, morals or personal practices and preferences for reference points of what is and is not pathological behavior. However, evaluating clients based on our own beliefs and values jeopardizes culturally sensitive diagnostic practice. Clinicians are encouraged to cultivate a strong awareness of their own cultural and religious beliefs and to be aware of the boundaries between their beliefs and preferences and the beliefs, practices and needs of their clients.

Accurate Diagnosis of Pedophilia

When diagnosing any paraphilic disorder, remember that behavior alone does not qualify an individual for a paraphilic disorder. The DSM 5 has included language across the A criteria that inadvertently allows for a diagnosis of pedophilia in those who have committed the crime of child sexual abuse but have committed the crime for reasons other than an intense sexual attraction to children, such as intoxicated opportunistic sex with a teen under the age of consent. First (2014) notes, the language of the A criteria reads "... recurrent, intense sexually arousing fantasies, sexual urges or behaviors involving sexual activity with a prepubescent child or children...." He notes that the "or behaviors" was added with intention to highlight the fact that it is behaviors that bring these clients to the attention of clinicians; he argues that the use of the word "or" was not intended to create room to diagnose pedophilia in those without sexual attraction to children.

Typically, diagnosis of pedophelia is made by drawing from three sources of information: (1) client self-report of attraction and preferences, (2) client's history of sexual contact with children and (3) the use of assessment tools including phallometry (Seto et al., 2006). The diagnosis of those who have molested children but deny attraction to children is one that requires specialized assessment. Those that molest children are not reliable in disclosing their fantasies and desires, making it difficult to determine whether or not the client's behavior is sourced from pedophilic preferences and urges or from psychotic, sociopathic, opportunistic or substance-driven behaviors.

While child sexual offense in and of itself may not serve as a reliable and definitive marker of pedophilia, Seto et al. (2006) argue that the use of child pornography can be used as a valid indicator of pedophilia, though it is not explicitly listed within the A criteria of the disorder. Using phallometic assessments, these researchers found that among their sample of 685 males, child pornography offenders were three times as likely to be identified as pedophilic than those who were convicted of CSA but denied the use of child pornography and nearly six times as frequently as general sexology clients. They theorize that the use of child pornography is a stronger indicator of pedophilic disorder than child sexual offenses alone because, while in general, child sex offenders may target children for a number of reasons (ranging from pedophilia, sociopathy, substance use etc.), people will choose pornography that best fits their preferences and are unlikely to go out of their way to secure illegal child pornography when legal adult pornography is widely available unless their interests are pedophilic (Seto et al., 2006). The use of child pornography has been included within the DSM 5 under associated features supporting diagnosis (APA, 2013).

Sexually Violent Predator Civil Commitment Laws

As of this writing, 20 states have established what are known as sexually violent predator (SVP) commitment laws. These laws are aimed at preventing future violent sexual assaults by those identified as having a mental disorder, which would predispose them to such behavior. Those evaluated as being at high risk first serve their prison terms and then are committed indefinitely to mental hospitals. Currently, as many as 4,000 persons are being held in hospitals as SVPs in what some have described as "de facto life sentences" (Douard, 2007; First, 2010, 2014; Hafemeister, 2001; Smith, 2015).

These SVP laws have been opposed by the APA and other mental health organizations, arguing that psychiatric science does not have the ability to predict future sexually violent behavior and because sexual violence has not been established to be caused by any mental illness. These organizations argue that, to date, science cannot

BOX 19.03 CONSIDER THIS: A YOUNG MAN'S STORY OF HIS PEDOPHILIA

When calling to mind the idea of a pedophile, what images arise? Who is this person? What qualities or traits come to mind? Male? Female? Young? Old? Successful? Living on the edges of society? What feelings are you aware of? How might these images and feelings influence how you respond to a client who discloses pedophilic interests?

For any person, including healthcare professionals, generating compassion for and desire to help people with pedophilic interests may present a significant challenge. One may even wonder if such compassion is necessary, particularly since the harm done by child sexual assault is so grave. Also challenging is the fact that many mental health clinicians have their own histories of childhood sexual abuse creating additional barriers to understanding this perplexing and odious behavior.

However, for an unknown number of persons with a pedophilic predilection, the preference is experienced as a curse that they would like to get help with but have nowhere to turn. Journalist Luke Malone has researched pedophiles who would like help and are committed to preventing child sexual abuse and the use of child pornography. Adam, a teen seeking such help and who hosts an online support group, highlights the lives of young men fighting this disorder alone.

Listen to Adam's story on NPR's *This American Life*: *"Help Wanted"* by Luke Malone, or read it on medium.com: *"You're 16. You're a Pedophile. You Don't Want to Hurt Anyone. What Do You Do Now?"*

back up claims that would attempt to predict sexually violent behavior in an individual. They further assert that psychologists, psychiatrists and other mental healthcare professionals can't reasonably claim "expertise" in making such predictions. When these kinds of predictions are made in these cases, they have sometimes resulted in hospitalizations lasting decades. Recently, these laws have been met with legal challenges. For example, a Minnesota program for SVPs, which detained 700 men, was determined to be unconstitutional for three key reasons: (1) the men detained had already served their sentences, (2) the SVP program was punitive and not therapeutic and (3) because the participants were not re-evaluated and thus had no opportunity to be released (Smith, 2015).

The status of these laws pertains to diagnosticians because a diagnosis of a paraphilia or paraphilic disorder can be used in court to argue that a client should be committed, in the case of SVP laws, or used in family court to argue that a parent should not be awarded custody of a child, or used to withhold security clearances, making this issue one of human rights (Merrick, 2016; Moser & Kleinplatz, 2006; Wright, 2014). Wright (2014) notes, however, that the recent changes to the DSM, which discern paraphilic interests from paraphilic disorders, has made a measurable difference in the number of child custody cases ruling against parents with Bondage and Discipline, Dominance and Submission, Sadochism and Masochism (BDSM), swing or polyamory preferences—preferences she argues should not, by themselves, prohibit parental custody.

Differentiating Transvestic Disorder from Gender Dysphoria

Transvestic disorder has had an interesting history in its journey to becoming a stand-alone diagnosis. The changes in the conceptualization and placement of this disorder reflects shifting social views around gender, sex and sexuality. The DSM 5 itself has left room for how and when to diagnose the disorder if gender dysphoria is also present, noting that those with transvestic disorder don't experience gender confusion or dysphoria; however, you'll note that the criteria table offers a specifier, autogynephilia. This specifier is applied to those who are aroused by imagining themselves as a woman (APA, 2013). This specifier is not indicating a desire to be a woman, only the experience of being aroused by imagining themselves as a woman, a subtle but important difference.

Thoughtful discussion with clients will help to clarify whether the distress felt by the client arises from being aroused by dressing in clothing traditionally reserved for women (transvestic disorder), from arousal at imagining himself as a woman (transvestic disorder, with autogynephilia) or if instead the distress comes from feeling as if their assigned gender is not a true reflection of themselves (gender dysphoria). It is possible for clients to experience both phenomena together however, in which case the DSM 5 advises that both diagnoses be given (APA, 2013).

Treating Paraphilias

Pharmacological Interventions

Androgen deprivation therapy (ADT) employs a class of steroid drugs used to inhibit sexual drive and is frequently prescribed for sex offenders. Though there are a number of such drugs available, which work in different ways, each reduce production or block the uptake of sex hormones. These drugs are prescribed in just under 20% of clients in residential and community treatment programs. However, while research results are mixed, the empirical evidence for their efficacy is quite low, sometimes as low as placebo. Meta-analysis of ADT efficacy shows that initial reductions in recidivism are modest and diminish over time. Research does seem to suggest that a client's willingness to use these drugs may indicate an authentic wish to eliminate pedophilic urges and prevent abuse of children (Amelung et al., 2012; Thibaut, 2012).

In addition to ADT, a number of selective serotonin reuptake inhibitors (SSRIs) have been prescribed for clients with paraphilic disorders generally with varied results. SSRIs are hypothesized to have the potential to reduce paraphilic interests by those

BOX 19.04 TRY THIS: DIFFERENTIATING PEDOPHELIA

Three scenarios are offered below: Brett, Davis and Sedrick. In each case, an adult male has had sexual contact with a minor who can't legally give consent. What similarities do you note? What differences? What diagnosis would you consider for Brett? And for Davis? What about Sedrick? What questions do you have for each that would help you to clarify and justify your diagnoses?

Brett. Brett, a 22-year-old college student, spent his Friday and Saturday partying to the point of blackout, much as he did every weekend of the spring and fall semesters. Brett admits that he "drank heavily and smoked a lot of pot" over the weekend. At the party, Brett met Alison, a 13-year-old student at a local middle school, who was attending the party with a college-aged cousin. Alison also drank and smoked with Brett and the two had sex Friday night. For Brett, drinking, smoking and "hooking up" with virtual strangers at these parties was a familiar pattern. However, Brett's contact with Alison has led to criminal charges, filed by Alison's parents. Brett's parents have convinced him to go into rehab and to try to get a handle on his drinking and drug use. During his intake and evaluation, the diagnosing psychologist has decided to assess Brett for a pedophilic disorder since Alison was under the age of consent and because he has been charged with criminal sexual contact with a minor.

Davis. Davis, a 22-year-old college senior majoring in kinesiology, has been volunteering with the girls gymnastics team at a local middle school. He has been sexually attracted to girls between the ages of 12-14 for as long as he can remember and does not feel any attraction to women his own age. Davis has used his role on the team to gain access and trust. He regularly offers to massage the cramped feet and legs of team members, buys them food and gifts and invites them to his apartment for movies where he has provided the teens with beer and pizza during their "movie nights." Davis feels he has fallen in love with 13-year-old Macie and he has had sex with her on two occasions.

Sedrick. Sedrick, 22, has lived in a group home for 3 years after being hospitalized for an attempted suicide and where he was treated for paranoid delusions and command hallucinations. For several weeks, Sedrick had been hearing a voice telling him that he should "unite with Annalise," a 13 year old with developmental disabilities who attends the same state-sponsored mental health "clubhouse" that he attends on weekends. Sedrick had come to believe that Annalise has special spiritual powers that she could transfer to him through sexual intercourse. Sedrick and Annalise were discovered having sex at the clubhouse and Sedrick has since been readmitted to the hospital while charges are being considered.

who see paraphilia as similar to the obsessive and compulsive process in obsessive compulsive disorder (OCD) (Abouesh & Clayton, 1999). Though research in the use of these drugs for paraphilia are few and have significant limitations (such as being small or single case studies, or retrospective studies) some support for drugs such as fluoxetine and sertraline have been described as useful for paraphilic disorders such as sadism, exhibitionism, voyeurism and pedophilia (Abouesh & Clayton, 1999; Saleh & Guidry, 2003; Thibaut, 2012).

Psychotherapy

Cognitive-behavioral therapy (CBT) has been used to help clients with pedophilic disorder to challenge and restructure beliefs that support or justify offenses against children. These cognitions might include beliefs like, "children can be quite seductive" or "sexual contact with an adult can be helpful to a child's development." CBT for this population also aims to improve social skills training and to cultivate empathy for victims (Beier et al., 2015; Grossman et al., 1999). Also common in CBT is the use of aversion therapy and covert sensitization. These therapies pair target paraphilic stimuli with punishments, such as electric shock (Grossman et al., 1999). Relapse prevention is an intervention that teaches clients to recognize high-risk situations or experiences that may make it more likely that they would reoffend. Clients are taught to avoid or cope with these situations so that they do not relapse. The efficacy of cognitive-behavioral interventions vary widely from one study to the next ranging from post-treatment recidivism rates of 6%-36% (Beier et al., 2015; Grossman et al., 1999).

Definitional Cases in Paraphilic Disorders

The following definitional cases will provide you some practice in narrowing diagnoses quickly. The narrative cases will provide you enough information to both provide a full diagnosis, offer a justification for that diagnosis and to develop a treatment plan. You may want to use the pivot table to help you to narrow your diagnosis.

Kenneth

Kenneth can't get aroused unless he begins foreplay dressed in women's underwear and a wig. His wife feels the cross-dressing interferes with her arousal and would like to have sex without the "dressing up" at least some of the time, so consequently the couple argues about sex frequently.

Andrew

Andrew is ashamed and distressed by his need to be physically and verbally abused in order to become sexually aroused.

Donna

Donna, a 32-year-old middle school teacher, was recently found guilty of multiple charges of possessing child pornography and of sexual abuse of a minor.

BOX 19.05 TRY THIS: DIFFERENTIATING TRANSVESTIC DISORDER FROM OTHER PARAPHILIAS

In the following three scenarios, match the best fit diagnosis: A. Gender dysphoria; B. Transvestic disorder, with autogynephilia; C. Transvestic disorder, with fetishism or D. No Diagnosis. Note any questions you would ask in order to confirm your tentative diagnosis.

Eliot. When Eliot, 24, was born his doctor passed him to his mother and declared, "Congratulations, you have a fine baby boy!" But Eliot has never felt like a boy, and has identified strongly with all things feminine since early childhood. Eliot often dresses as a woman when alone and imagines how life would be better in the body of a woman. Gender identity is the source of considerable guilt and shame for Eliot and has led to a recent suicide attempt.

Martin. Martin, 46, is satisfied and comfortable with his male identity, so he and his girlfriend are a little perplexed by the fact that he is not able to become fully aroused without first dressing in silk panties. About a year ago, Martin began "borrowing" his girlfriend's panties but when this caused conflict between them, he started buying women's underwear for himself, often wearing them once, promising himself it was the last time, and then throwing them away, only to purchase more undergarments later. Martin would like to be rid of the habit but he is not sure what to do.

Russell. Russell, 32, a sheriff's deputy has been asked by his supervisor to meet with a staff psychologist for his "problem." Russell, who was in a brief sexual relationship with another officer, disclosed that he was very comfortable with being a man and happy in his body but that he was only very aroused when imagining himself "as a high class lady," and consequently he preferred to begin sex dressed as a woman wearing lipstick. His partner immediately broke off their relationship and raised concerns to their supervisor that Russell was "perverted and maybe a child molester."

Suresh

Suresh has always had a "thing" for women's gloves. Recently, however, he finds that discarded surgical gloves are his primary object of arousal. Suresh describes being disgusted by his interest.

Clarke

After months of complaints in a small neighborhood near the local university, Clarke, 26, was arrested and identified as the man who, on a number of occasions, was seen masturbating while watching unsuspecting women disrobe.

Phillipa

Phillipa and her partner have had a number of angry conversations about the way that their sexual intercourse seems to escalate until Phillipa becomes violent. Phillipa is afraid to tell her partner that without the aggression she can't become aroused.

Brian

Brian was recently beaten badly on a subway train after rubbing against a man on the train and fondling him. Brian admits that for several years he has been surreptitiously touching strangers on the train for his own sexual gratification.

Melinda

Melinda is unable to explain why she can't gain sexual gratification unless her stuffed toy kitten is in the bed with her. She is ashamed and wonders how she will be able to have an adult sexual relationship.

Todd

Todd regularly drives to a town 30 minutes from where he lives, finds a crowded space where he can escape easily and exposes his genitals. Todd gains a great deal of sexual excitement from the planning and execution of this behavior.

Narrative Cases in Paraphilic Disorders

Ion

Ion and Celeste, both 36 and parents of two daughters, have come for marriage counseling. Celeste shares that their sex life has suffered in the past few years and that Ion has not seemed interested in having sex with her; her feelings have been hurt when she has come into the bedroom and found him masterbating. After some discussion, Ion discloses, "I know that this is going to be very hard to hear, and it is really, really hard to say, but for almost a year I have had these urges that I can't really explain and they have completely taken the place of anything that used to excite me." Ion explains, "I have this repeat fantasy that I am in the grocery store standing in line and I move closer and closer to the person in front of me and find a way to rub up against that person. In my fantasy I say I'm sorry but that person, usually a woman but sometimes a man, can see I'm aroused. Sometimes I fantasize about it and just masterbate, but a couple of times, when I was out of town, I actually did it." Ion further explains, "I'm really concerned that this is getting out of control. I don't know if I can stop this without help."

BOX 19.06 DIMENSIONAL BRIDGES

A number of researchers have suggested that the paraphilias have a close relationship to the obsessive compulsive disorders (OCD), some arguing that these disorders should be organized within the OCD and related disorders dimension (Krueger & Kaplan, 2001). A significant number of persons with OCD have obsessions with sexual themes, including themes featuring children (García-Soriano et al., 2011). Numerous studies have found comorbid personality disorders in paraphilic sexual offenders. At least one study found obsessive compulsive personality to be more common among this group, leading them to hypothesize that the obsessive traits of obsessive compulsive personality disorder (OCPD) may contribute to the offending patterns of this population (Bogaerts et al., 2008).

Wyatt

Wyatt, a 27-year-old, part-time landscaper, has been referred to counseling as part of his sentencing following a guilty plea for several "peeping" incidents spanning a year. Wyatt shares, "I can't explain why I do it, but I like watching people get undressed. It gets me excited. I usually key in on someone when I am out on a landscaping job. The excitement builds as I check out the house and the landscape for ideal places to hide and that gives me a good view. It can take several visits to get this planning all lined up. When it's all worked out, I come back later and just get a little peek. I don't mean to make light. I get that it upsets people, and even though I know it is hypocritical, I'd rain holy hell on anyone who did this to my mom or my wife. But I'm not out to hurt anybody and I really can't stop myself."

Blaine

Blaine, a 46-year-old corporate accountant, is facing criminal charges after an IT worker found child pornography featuring both boys and girls around the ages of 4-6 on his computer when making a regularly scheduled upgrade to Blaine's computer and reported him to police. When speaking with his lawyer Blaine shares, "It was really so stupid of me to have that stuff on my office computer, I guess to have it all was just was just really, really stupid." Blaine admits, "I know it is against the law so I assume it is against corporate policy, too. But I think society has this whole thing wrong, and I want you to help me fight this thing in court. I think children are perfectly capable of loving, and, of course, humans are sexual beings, so children are naturally sexual, too. They just have to learn about their sexuality, the same way that they have to learn about

TABLE 19.01 Pivot Table

Pivot Points: Paraphilic Disorders	Disorder to Consider
Pivot Point One: Do your client's impulses infringe on the rights, safety or privacy of others?	
• Do your client's impulses or behaviors infringe on the rights, safety, and privacy of children? Are children the object of the client's sexual desire, impulses and behavior?	Pedophilic Disorder
• Does your client expose their genitals to non-consenting adults or children?	Exhibitionistic Disorder
• Does your client rub his or her genitals against non-consenting persons?	Frotteuristic Disorder
• Does your client gain sexual gratification from observing a non-consenting person while dressing, bathing or having sex?	Voyeuristic Disorder
• Does your client need or prefer to inflict pain or humiliation in order to gain sexual gratification?	Sexual Sadism Disorder
• Does your client need or prefer to receive pain or humiliation in order to gain sexual gratification?	Sexual Masochism Disorder
• Does your client's sole or preferred means of sexual gratification come from forced sexual contact with a non-consenting person (rape)?* *This category does **not** apply to all persons who commit rape, only to those who can only gain sexual gratification through this means or who very strongly prefer gratification through this means, and should be applied only with extreme caution.	Unspecified Paraphilic Disorder, Non-consent
• Have your client's violations of others' rights come as a result of diminished inhibitions, dementia, psychosis, mania or substance abuse?	Diagnose underlying cause; do not diagnose paraphilia
Pivot Point Two: Are your client's fantasies or impulses troubling to your client or the source of relational difficulties?	
• Does your client require an object not normally associated with sexual activity in order to stimulate sexual arousal?	Fetishistic Disorder
• Is your client unable to gain sexual arousal without cross-dressing? Does your client find this necessity to be troublesome?	Transvestic Disorder
Pivot Point Three: Does your client have intrusive thoughts of violent sexual acts or acts against children that are experienced as unwanted, vile, objectionable, stress-inducing or otherwise impairing? (Thoughts have not been acted upon.)	Obsessive Compulsive Disorder

everything an adult teaches them. I admit that I've always been attracted to children. I've never been attracted to teens or adults, too much hair. But I reject the idea that there is something inherently wrong with that, especially if your intentions are for a loving sexual relationship. Anyway, I would never touch a child without their consent. As for these pictures, I don't see the problem. The children seem well taken care of, they aren't being hurt. I think this is a law that needs to be challenged."

Tina

Tina, 27, and her husband, Paul, have made an appointment with a couple's counselor in hopes of staving off divorce. Paul shares, "Tina is my best friend and I don't want to end this marriage but the way things are going I just don't know how we can continue. I can't in good conscience keep doing this, it is giving me nightmares." Tina explains, "About two years ago I encouraged Paul to get a little bit more adventurous in bed. I was tired of the same old thing. We tried a few things but I found that I just couldn't get excited until we started to get rough." Paul shares, "We hadn't been married that long and I thought it was just something fun to try but this has been going on for over a year and it is escalating, she needs more and more abuse to get aroused. It isn't doing anything for me. She wants me to hit her, force myself on her, and now it's this fascination with being strangled. I do it but it is taking a toll on me. I feel like a monster."

"Paul has said he's done with it and if I keep pressing he gets angry. So our sex is a train wreck. I don't know if you can help us get our sex life back on track so that we are both happy, because right now it is a disaster and its wrecking our relationship!"

Dane

Dane, a 45-year-old factory worker, has come to counseling seeking help. Dane initially sought help for symptoms of depression related to guilt and shame. He described feeling "worthless and of no use to anyone." After 4 weeks of therapy, Dane disclosed to his therapist, "I feel sick to my stomach admitting this but I keep having these weird fantasies that I flash my privates on the playground down the street from my house. The first time it happened in a dream, about a year and a half ago, and I didn't think much of it. I remember that I woke up excited, but since it was just a dream I didn't think too much about it. But now I have random thoughts of doing it and other times I have fantasies . . . on purpose. The fantasies get me excited but they also make me kind of sick. The guilt isn't really about the other stuff we've been talking about since I came, it's about this. I don't want to turn into some kind of pervert . . . So I need help!" Dane denies experiencing any other intrusive thoughts, urges or behaviors, either sexual or nonsexual in content.

Amiko

Amiko, 32, has come for counseling following a falling out with a friend. "What happened was that my friend, Marion, was having a party, there were lots of people there, drinking cocktails and the whole thing. Well, I slipped upstairs and into her bedroom and I was going through her closet. She has a lot of really beautiful shoes, a gorgeous pair of Jimmy Choos and a pair of spikey-healed Pradas. I was sitting on the floor of her closet turning the shoes over in my hands and getting really turned on. I could imagine her slender foot resting there and I thought of gently caressing her foot. I was just going to borrow the shoe and I was slipping it into my bag when she walked in. I was mortified! She thought I was going to steal the pair but really I just wanted one, just for the evening and then I would bring it back, but I couldn't tell her that I have this thing with feet and shoes, I just couldn't. So she kicked me out and she's not speaking to me. I feel really ashamed and I don't really know what to do about it. But I'd like to get control of this shoe issue and I'd like to clear things up with my friend. I guess it's better that she know that I'm a freak instead of thinking I'm a thief."

Adam

Adam, age 35, has recently been charged with sexually abusing several young boys in his neighborhood. In his meeting with a forensic psychologist, Adam reports, "I started having thoughts of touching boys, usually between the ages of 6-9, when I was in middle school. My brother did it to me when I was a kid and so did my uncle so maybe that is how the idea got imprinted on my brain. I mostly resisted the urge until I was in high school. I got a job as a camp counselor and sometimes the temptation was too much for me to resist. I was sure someone would catch me, but it never happened. I stopped for a while after I married my wife, and we even had a pretty good sex life, but then we moved to this neighborhood where there are a lot of children and a lot of social get-togethers, potlucks and block parties, that kind of thing. It got to the place where I was thinking about the boys in the neighborhood a lot. And then I started to touch them. Then it just escalated from there. It got out of hand fast. Then one of the boys told his father. Part of me was relieved, so I agreed to cooperate and here I am."

Lenora

Lenora is a 56-year-old artist living on the beaches of Hawaii selling her hand-painted sea shells to tourists. She has been arrested on a number of occasions after flashing glimpses of her genitals to unsuspecting beach-goers and tourists in local shops. Lenora does not expose herself to children, however. Lenora explains her situation this way: "I don't remember when I started doing it exactly, it's been a couple of years, though. It started out that I felt excited walking around with a towel wrapped around my middle with nothing underneath, just my little secret. But one day the towel slipped off when I was walking down the beach. The guy that saw it looked so shocked and he covered his eyes and ran off. It was really exciting! So then I started to do it on purpose, just once in a while and then more often. But I guess my guilty habit has gotten me in trouble so I suppose I have to find a new hobby, but this is my only sexual outlet and it will be hard to give up."

Leland

Leland, age 82, is faced with an eviction from his retirement community following a string of complaints over 7 months asserting that he has slipped into other residents' rooms and attempted to watch them shower, and on at least two occasions was found masturbating while surreptitiously observing others while bathing. Leland has refused to talk with staff counselors about his behavior. However, his adult son, Howard, shares that Leland was once charged for similar behavior about 20 years ago when he was finally identified as the man who had been eluding police in a number of peeping incidents in his neighborhood. Leland had once shared with Howard that he felt deeply ashamed of the seeming irresistible urge to watch others and the inexplicable intensity of the sexual satisfaction he derived from it, but had promised to never again act on the urge to "spy on others."

Palmer

Palmer, 20, has recently been charged with three separate rapes in as many months. In a plea agreement, Palmer agreed to talk with a forensic psychologist and disclose his crimes fully. During his interview, Palmer disclosed that his father had abused him sexually beginning at the age of 8 and, in his early adolescence, his father exposed him to pornography. Palmer reported, "So I think it started a long time ago, a kind of fascination with pain. I was in college when I got turned on to torture porn. It turned everything up to full volume for me. I couldn't get enough of it, but eventually, even that didn't always get me worked up. That's when I first started to get violent with the girls I was with. I couldn't get off unless I got really rough. After a while I wondered what it would be like if the girl wasn't into it, if it wasn't just a sex game. I was really bored with pretending and not all these girls were great actresses. So that's when I raped the first girl. She didn't call it that because we started out with rough sex but she was on board with it, but I pushed it until I thought it was more than what she wanted and then raped her. After that I raped a couple of other girls, one I followed from the library at the university and another after a football game and then one at a friend's party. Planning rape or remembering it is about the only way I can get excited."

Victor

A little less than a year ago Victor's wife, Alyssa, was in a scary car accident. While she suffered very few lasting injuries, it really shook Victor. When faced with the possibility of losing her, he experienced a fear and sadness he hadn't known before. In the weeks after the accident, on the evenings that she worked late, he was particularly emotional and after their kids were in bed he would sit on the closet floor smelling her clothing and crying, imagining what it would be like if she had died. He found himself really drawn to the silk nightgowns that she would wear. At first he enjoyed the way they felt in his hands and the fact that he felt aroused and not just overwhelmed by sadness and fear. But over time as his sadness subsided, he enjoyed the arousal he felt as he held the nightgown and developed a curiosity about what it would feel like covering his body. Wearing her nightgown increased his arousal and he began to have intense sexual fantasies both when thinking about wearing and actually wearing the nightgowns. While he had been engaging with this activity privately for nearly 8 months, he only recently shared his ritual and fantasies with Alyssa. She is very disturbed that dressing in a woman's nightgown arouses her husband so much and she has a lot of questions about what this means about his sexuality. She has more recently become overwhelmed thinking that her children could have found him wearing the nightgown and she has started to talk about the possibility of separation. Victor, sharing with his therapist, says, "I don't know what to do. I am afraid I'm going to lose my family over this, but I'm not sure that I can change this either. Even though I've stopped wearing the nightgowns, how do I stop the fantasies and urges?"

References

Abouesh, A., & Clayton, A. (1999). Compulsive voyeurism and exhibitionism: A clinical response to paroxetine. *Archives of Sexual Behavior*, *28*(1), 23-30.

Amelung, T., Kuhle, L. F., Konrad, A., Pauls, A., & Beier, K. M. (2012). Androgen deprivation therapy of self-identifying, help-seeking pedophiles in the Dunkelfeld. *International Journal of Law and Psychiatry*, *35*(3), 176-184.

American Psychiatric Association. (2013). *Diagnostic and statistical manual of mental disorders (DSM-5®)*. American Psychiatric Pub Author.

Bach, M. H., & Demuth, C. (2018). Therapists' experiences in their work with sex offenders and people with pedophilia: A literature review. *Europe's Journal of Psychology*, *14*(2), 498-514.

Beier, K. M., Grundmann, D., Kuhle, L. F., Scherner, G., Konrad, A., & Amelung, T. (2015). The German Dunkelfeld project: A pilot study to prevent child sexual abuse and the use of child abusive images. *The Journal of Sexual Medicine*, *12*(2), 529-542.

Bogaerts, S., Daalder, A., Vanheule, S., Desmet, M., & Leeuw, F. (2008). Personality disorders in a sample of paraphilic and nonparaphilic child molesters: A comparative study. *International Journal of Offender Therapy and Comparative Criminology*, *52*(1), 21-30.

Castellini, G., Rellini, A. H., Appignanesi, C., Pinucci, I., Fattorini, M., Grano, E., Fisher, A. D., Cassioli, E., Lelli, L., Maggi, M., & Ricca, V. (2018). Deviance or normalcy? The relationship among paraphilic thoughts and behaviors, hypersexuality, and psychopathology in a sample of university students. *The Journal of Sexual Medicine*, *15*(9), 1322–1335.

Dawson, S. J., Bannerman, B. A., & Lalumière, M. L. (2016). Paraphilic interests: An examination of sex differences in a nonclinical sample. *Sexual Abuse*, *28*(1), 20–45.

Douard, J. (2007). Loathing the sinner, medicalizing the sin: Why sexually violent predator statutes are unjust. *International Journal of Law and Psychiatry*, *30*(1), 36–48.

Dunsieth, N. W., Jr., Nelson, E. B., Brusman-Lovins, L. A., Holcomb, J. L., Beckman, D., Welge, J. A., Taylor, P., Jr., Soutullo, C. A., McElroy, S. L., & McElroy, S. L. (2004). Psychiatric and legal features of 113 men convicted of sexual offenses. *The Journal of Clinical Psychiatry*, *65*, 293–300.

Edwards-Levy, A. (2019). *These polls show how American thinking has (and hasn't) changed in 80 years*. Huffington Post. https://www.huffingtonpost.com/entry/historical-polls-2018-20th-century-america_us_5c2a47aae4b05c88b7029f37

First, M.B. (2010). DSM-5 Proposals for paraphilias: Suggestions for reducing false positives related to use of behavioral manifestations. *Archives of Sexual Behavior*, *39*, 1239-1244.

First, M. B. (2014). DSM-5 and paraphilic disorders. *Journal of the American Academy of Psychiatry and the Law Online*, *42*(2), 191-201.

García-Soriano, G., Belloch, A., Morillo, C.,& Clark, D. A. (2011). Symptom dimensions in obsessive–compulsive disorder: From normal cognitive intrusions to clinical obsessions. *Journal of Anxiety Disorders*, *25*(4), 474-482.

Grossman, L. S., Martis, B., & Fichtner, C. G. (1999). Are sex offenders treatable? A research overview. *Psychiatric Services*, *50*(3), 349-361.

Hafemeister, T. L. (2001). Sexual predator laws: Is an irresistable impulse required to involuntarily commit offenders? *Judicial Notebook*, *32*(8).

Hucker, S. J. (2011). Hypoxyphilia. *Archives of Sexual Behavior*, *40*(6), 1323-1326.

Joyal, C. C. (2018). Controversies in the definition of paraphilia. *The Journal of Sexual Medicine*, *15*(10), 1378-1380.

Joyal, C. C., & Carpentier, J. (2017). The prevalence of paraphilic interests and behaviors, in the general population: A provincial survey. *The Journal of Sex Research*, *54*(2), 161-171.

Joyal, C.C., Cossette, A., & Lapierre, V. (2014). What exactly is an unusual sexual fantasy? *Journal of Sexual Medicine*, *12*, 328-340. https://doi.org/10.111/jsm12734

Kafka, M. (2012). Axis I psychiatric disorders, paraphilic sexual offending and implications for pharmacological treatment. *The Israel Journal of Psychiatry and Related Sciences*, *49*(4), 255.

Kafka, M. P., & Hennen, J. (2002). A DSM-IV Axis I comorbidity study of males (n = 120) with paraphilias and paraphilia-related disorders. *Sexual Abuse: A Journal of Research and Treatment*, *14*(4), 349-366.

Krueger, R. B., & Kaplan, M. S. (2001). The paraphilic and hypersexual disorders: An overview. *Journal of Psychiatric Practice®*, *7*(6), 391-403.

Kuhle, L. F., & Beier, K. M. (2014). Estimating risk in undetected pedophiles/hebephiles from the community (Prevention Project Dunkelfeld). *In 13th Conference of the International Association for the Treatment of Sexual Offenders*. Porto, Portugal.

Långström, N., & Seto, M. C. (2006). Exhibitionistic and voyeuristic behavior in a Swedish national population survey. *Archives of Sexual Behavior, 35*(4), 427-435.

Malone, L. (2014). *You're 16. You're a pedophile. You don't want to hurt anyone. What do you do now?* https://medium.com/matter/youre-16-youre-a-pedophile-you-dont-want-to-hurt-anyone-what-do-you-do-now-e11ce4b88bdb#.jgkgylsug

Merrick, W. A. (2016). Changes in DSM-5 diagnostic criteria for paraphilic disorders. *Archives of Sexual Behavior, 45*(8), 2173-2179.

Moser, C., & Kleinplatz, P. J. (2006). DSM-IV-TR and the paraphilias: An argument for removal. *Journal of Psychology & Human Sexuality, 17*(3-4), 91-109.

Moulden, H. M., Chaimowitz, G., Mamak, M., & Hawes, J. (2014). Understanding how sexual offenders compare across psychiatric and correctional settings: Examination of Canadian mentally ill sexual offenders. *Journal of Sexual Aggression, 20*(2), 172-181.

Pope, K. S., & Feldman-Summers, S. (1992). National survey of psychologists' sexual and physical abuse history and their evaluation of training and competence in these areas. *Professional Psychology: Research and Practice, 23*(5), 353.

Saleh, F. M., & Guidry, L. L. (2003). Psychosocial and biological treatment considerations for the paraphilic and nonparaphilic sex offender. *Journal of the American Academy of Psychiatry Law, 31*(94), 486-493.

Seto, M. C., Cantor, J. M., & Blanchard, R. (2006). Child pornography offenses are a valid diagnostic indicator of pedophilia. *Journal of Abnormal Psychology, 115*(3), 610.

Singh, M. M., Parsekar, S. S., & Nair, S. N. (2014). An epidemiological overview of child sexual abuse. *Journal of Family Medicine and Primary Care, 3*(4), 430.

Smith, D. M. (2015). Dangerous diagnoses, risky assumptions, and the failed experiment of sexually violent predator commitment. *Oklahoma Law Review, 67*, 619.

Stern, P. (2010). Paraphilic coercive disorder in the DSM: The right diagnosis for the right reasons. *Archives of Sexual Behavior, 39*(6), 1443-1447.

Thibaut, F. (2012). Pharmacological treatment of paraphilias. *Israel Journal of Psychiatry and Related Sciences, 49*(4), 297-305.

Wakefield, J. C. (2012). The DSM-5's proposed new categories of sexual disorder: The problem of false positives in sexual diagnosis. *Clinical Social Work Journal, 40*(2), 213-223.

Wollert, R. (2011). Paraphilic coercive disorder does not belong in DSM-5 for statistical, historical, conceptual, and practical reasons. *Archives of Sexual Behavior, 40*(6), 1097-1098.

Wright, S. (2014). Kinky parents and child custody: The effect of the DSM-5 differentiation between the paraphilias and paraphilic disorders. *Archives of Sexual Behavior, 43*(7), 1257.

20 File Length Cases

The first session with a client generally begins with a formal intake session. These sessions tend to last 60-90 minutes and most often are given structure by an intake form. The intake form provides structure for gleaning information about your client's current symptoms as well as the history of past symptoms. The intake interview also provides an opportunity to begin to understand some of the relational dynamics that your client experiences, as well as work history, legal issues and so on. A thorough intake will provide the clinician with enough information to make a symptom timeline, an initial diagnosis, justify that diagnosis and to create a list of client problems and concerns. A rich intake will support the development of a hypothesis about the cause of those problems and will supply needed information for developing a treatment plan.

The following cases, John and Seo-Yeon, are written in the format of a formal intake form. These cases will offer an opportunity to make a diagnosis using information in the form that you are likely to encounter in the field, and to use that information to make a diagnosis and justification, a case conceptualization, and to develop a treatment plan. This format will provide you with a great deal of information that you will need to organize and analyze. Carefully consider whether a single diagnosis is sufficient or if a dual diagnosis is more appropriate. Remember to list questions you may have for follow-up that would clarify your diagnoses.

Adult Intake Form: Case 1: John King

Name: K. (Last) John (First) Lane (MI)

Your Birth Date: 01 / 13 / 1970 Age: 30

Gender: ☒ Male ☐ Female ☐ Transgender

Local Address:

436 Olive Grove Drive
(Street and Number)

Anytown (City) VA (State) 22703 (Zip)

Home Phone: ____________ May I leave a message? ☒ Yes ☐ No

Cell Phone: 540.555.3545 May I leave a message? ☒ Yes ☐ No

E-mail: ____________ May I e-mail you? ☒ Yes ☐ No
*Please be aware that e-mail might not be confidential.

Person to contact in case of an emergency:

Polly K. (Name) mother (Relationship to client) same (Phone)

Primary Care doctor: Dr. Philips (Name) 540.555.6745 (Phone)

How did you learn about me: Dr. Philips referred me

What prompted you to seek therapy or an assessment?

John reports that he came to therapy because he has been out of work and has had to move back in with his parents.

Therapist's observations here:
John has a strong smell of disinfectant on him. When I asked, John admits that he had already washed his hands several times that morning with Tilex ©. His hands were quite dry and chapped.

Sexual Preference: Men **Women** Both

Marital Status: ☒ **Never** Married ☐ Partnered ☐ Married ☐ Separated ☐ Divorced ☐ Widowed

Are you currently in a romantic relationship? ☐ Yes ☒ **No**

If yes, for how long?____________

If yes, on a scale of 1-10 (10 = great), how would you rate the quality of your romantic relationship? ______

Do you have children? ☒ **No** ☐ Yes

If yes, how many?: _____ Ages: ____________________________

Have you had previous psychotherapy? ☒ **No** ☐ Yes

If yes, why? ____Feelings of depression ____________________________

If yes, when?_______1997, 2005, 2007____________________________

Are you currently taking prescribed psychiatric medications (antidepressants or others)? ☐ Yes ☒ **No**

If Yes, please list names and doses: ____________________________

If No, have you been previously prescribed psychiatric medication? ☒ Yes ☐ **No**

If Yes, please list names and dates: __"Luvox, can't remember when, and Celexa, (can't remember)"

How do you feel about your future? "I don't have a job and my parents have to help me out a lot financially. I look like a clown . . . I'll never get a woman to be interested in me, I'll be alone forever. I don't see things changing for me anytime soon."

Are you having current suicidal thoughts? ☐ Frequently ☐ Sometimes ☒ **Rarely** ☐ Never

If yes, have you recently done anything to hurt yourself? ☐ Yes ☒ **No**

Have you had suicidal thoughts in the past? ☐ Frequently ☒ **Sometimes** ☐ Rarely ☐ Never

If you checked any box other than "never," when did you have these thoughts? "I first had suicidal thoughts when I was in high school, I've had those thoughts on and off since then. I don't think I have ever come close to really hurting myself and I don't have a plan, but it does feel like my parents would be better off without me."

Did you ever act on these feelings? ☐ Yes ☒ **No**

Are you having current homicidal thoughts (i.e., thoughts of hurting someone else)?
☐ Yes ☒ **No**

Have you previously had homicidal thoughts? ☐ Yes ☒ **No**

If yes, when?________________________________

HEALTH INFORMATION

How is your physical health currently? (please circle)

☐ Poor ☐ Unsatisfactory ☒ **Satisfactory** ☐ Good ☐ Very good

Date of last physical examination ____________________

Please list any chronic health problems or concerns (e.g., asthma, hypertension, diabetes, headaches, stomach pain, seizures etc.):

__________John denies any health issues__________

Any Allergies? ☒ **No** ☐ Yes If yes, please list:____________________

Medications:__**none**____________________

Hours per night you normally sleep __3______

Are you having any problems with your sleep habits? ☐ No ☒ **Yes**

If yes, check where applicable: ☒ **Sleeping too little** ☐ Sleeping too much ☒ **Can't fall asleep** ☒ **Can't stay asleep**

Do you exercise regularly? ☒ **No** ☐ Yes

If yes, how many times per week do you exercise? ______ For how long? ________

If yes, what do you do?________________________

Are you having any difficulty with appetite or eating habits? ☐ No ☒ **Yes**

If yes, check where applicable: ☒ **Eating less** ☐ Eating more ☐ Binging ☐ Purging

Have you experienced significant weight change in the last 2 months? ☒ **No** ☐ Yes

Do you regularly use alcohol? ☒ **No** ☐ Yes

If yes, what is your frequency?

☐ Once a month ☐ Once a week ☐ Daily ☐ Daily, three or more ☐ Intoxicated daily

How often do you engage in recreational drug use? ☐ Daily ☐ Weekly ☐ Monthly ☐ Rarely ☒ **Never**

If you checked any box other than "never," which drugs do you use?

____

Do you smoke? ☒ **No** ☐ Yes

If yes, how many cigarettes per day?________________

Do you drink caffeinated drinks? ☐ No ☒ **Yes**

If yes, # of sodas per day_2-3_____ cups of coffee per day__1-2_____

Have you ever had a head injury? ☒ **No** ☐ Yes

If yes, when and what happened?____________________________________

In the last year, have you experienced any significant life changes or stressors?

____

____

Can you describe your early home experiences?

"When I was about 5 my mom got pregnant. Everyone was really excited, but mom was kind of sick and had to go to the hospital several times. My dad and I tried to keep the house really clean and quiet because she was on edge a lot. I remember that sometimes when I would go into her room she would be crying. It was kind of scary. Then one day she lost the baby. My dad said that it wasn't my fault. He said that the baby was sick and there was nothing I could do to make it better. But ever since that time I have had a fear that I could make my parents sick or that if I wasn't careful that something bad could happen to them. I've had a lot of habits to try to keep them safe over the years: praying, counting, even tapping but I don't ever really feel safe that my parents will be ok. I know that is crazy sounding, scientifically I know this is nonsense, but in my head it feels real."

"When I started high school that was the first time I remember feeling really down, sometimes so much that I couldn't concentrate. The first time was after my first girlfriend moved away. I really cared about her a lot and I could trust her with my feelings. Once she left I felt really isolated and alone. I didn't want to go to school and even flunked a couple of classes. But the depression didn't get really bad until a couple of years ago. I started having trouble getting to work and that kind of thing. Then, suddenly I was living with my parents after having been independent because I couldn't support myself. I feel like a complete failure."

*Note: For each of the following, note which symptoms you experience. For those you mark "yes" use a rating scale to indicate the degree to which the symptom interferes with your daily living or well-being. Where possible provide a description of what is happening:

Are you now experiencing: *Rating Scale 1-10 (10 = worst)

Depressed Mood or Sadness **yes** no 7

"I feel down a lot, most every day, actually. Sometimes it is hard for me to get out of bed. When I'm in bed, though, I just lay there staring into space. I feel pretty useless. Last month I lost my job because I kept calling in sick. I just couldn't make myself get up and go to work even though I generally like my work a lot."

Hopelessness **yes** no 6

"I don't feel like there is much hope of any of this changing but I am willing to try counseling one more time."

Guilt/Shame	**yes**	no	6
Lack of Interest	**yes**	no	3
Irritability/Anger	yes	**no**	____
Mood Swings	yes	**no**	____
Rapid Speech	yes	**no**	____
Racing Thoughts	yes	**no**	____
Anxiety	**yes**	no	6

"I can't keep from worrying that something really bad is going to happen if I make one wrong move. The trouble is I don't know what the wrong thing is, so I try to do everything perfectly."

Constant Worry **yes** no 6

"Like I was saying, I worry a lot about causing accidents when I drive, so I don't drive. I worry about getting sick so I wash my hands and scrub the kitchen all the time. I worry that there will be some kind of bad weather so I have to constantly follow the weather updates, checking over and over that nothing is coming that I don't expect. I hate it when my parents decide to go out when rain or snow is expected, that makes me really nervous."

Panic Attacks	yes	**no**	_____
Phobias	yes	**no**	_____
Lack of Appetite	**yes**	no	4
Excess Appetite	yes	**no**	_____
Sleep Disturbances	**yes**	no	4

"I have a hard time falling asleep so I stay up really late trying to get tired enough to sleep. When I finally do fall asleep, I keep waking up with worries about the weather and if the kitchen is still dirty. I wonder if I got it clean enough. I worry that my parents will get up before me and use the sink and get sick if it is not clean enough. Sometimes I get up at 3 in the morning and clean the sink just to be sure."

Hallucinations	yes	**no**	_____
Paranoia	yes	**no**	_____
Poor Concentration	**yes**	no	5

"I have a hard time concentrating because I don't sleep and I'm so distracted."

Alcohol/Substance Abuse	yes	**no**	_____
Frequent Body Complaints (e.g., headaches)	yes	**no**	_____
Eating Disorder	yes	**no**	_____
Body Image Problems	yes	**no**	_____
Repetitive Thoughts (e.g., Obsessions)	**yes**	no	8

"Like I said, I have lots of repeated thoughts about things being dirty or unsafe. I worry that something bad will happen to me or my parents."

Repetitive Behaviors (e.g., counting)	**yes**	no	9

"All day long I am either washing my hands, washing the kitchen or checking the weather over and over again. I know it is crazy but it is the only way I can feel calm. But it never helps for long and I have to do it over and over again. I feel like I am losing my mind."

Poor Impulse Control (e.g., ↑ spending)	yes	**no**	____
Self-Mutilation	yes	**no**	____
Hx of Sexual Abuse	yes	**no**	____
Hx of Physical Abuse	yes	**no**	____
Hx of Emotional Abuse	yes	**no**	____

Have you experienced in the past: ***Rating Scale 1-10 (10 = worst)**

Depressed Mood or Sadness	**yes**	no	7

"I started having depressed feelings when I was in high school and have experienced them on and off ever since. I think this is what is keeping me from getting to work since I can't even get out of bed. I've had to move in with my parents."

Irritability/Anger	yes	**no**	____
Mood Swings	yes	**no**	____
Rapid Speech	yes	**no**	____
Racing Thoughts	yes	**no**	____
Anxiety	**yes**	no	4

"I've always worried about my parents and that something bad would happen to them. It seems like I would be too old for that but really that is what I feel now, too."

Constant Worry	**yes**	no	8
Panic Attacks	yes	**no**	____
Phobias	yes	**no**	____
Sleep Disturbances	**yes**	no	6
Hallucinations	yes	**no**	____
Paranoia	yes	**no**	____

Poor Concentration	**yes**	no	6
Alcohol/Substance Abuse	yes	**no**	_____
Frequent Body Complaints (e.g., Headaches)	yes	**no**	_____
Eating Disorder	yes	**no**	_____
Body Image Problems	yes	**no**	_____
Repetitive Thoughts (e.g., Obsessions)	**yes**	no	8

"I've had times when I have had other kinds of thoughts, too, like worries that I have hurt someone and don't know it. I would stay awake at night worrying that maybe I had accidently cut or hit someone and that they were hurt and bleeding and couldn't get help. It was an awful feeling."

Repetitive Behaviors (e.g., counting) **yes** no 8

"I have had behaviors like counting, tapping, and even praying for hours at a time, but none of it really helps with the fears."

Poor Impulse Control (e.g., ↑ spending)	yes	**no**	_____
Self-Mutilation	yes	**no**	_____
Sexual Abuse	yes	**no**	_____
Physical Abuse	yes	**no**	_____
Emotional Abuse	yes	**no**	_____

OCCUPATIONAL, EDUCATIONAL, LEGAL INFORMATION:

Are you employed? ☒ **No** ☐ Yes

If yes, who is your current employer/position? ______________________________

If yes, are you happy at your current position? ______________________________

Please list any work-related stressors, if any: ______________________________

Do you have financial concerns? ☐ No ☒ **Yes**

If yes, please explain: "I lost my job because I couldn't get out of bed and get to work. I depend on my parents for most of my support right now."

Can you describe your past work-related experiences?
"I am a photographer and I have had a couple of really good jobs that I liked a lot. I miss working."

Highest level of education: **B.A. Photography & Graphic Arts**

Do you have any legal concerns? ☒ **No** ☐ Yes

If yes, please explain: ____________

FAMILY HISTORY:

Are your parents:

☒ **Still together**
☐ Divorced, when____________
☐ Remarried
☐ Unmarried
☐ Deceased, if yes whom____________ age at death______

Number of siblings: 2 Ages: 22 and 27

Do you have good family support? ☒ **No** ☐ Yes From whom? "Parents are supportive, sisters think I need to grow up."

FAMILY MENTAL HEALTH HISTORY:
Has anyone in your family (either immediate family members or relatives) experienced difficulties with the following? (circle any that apply and list family member, e.g., Sibling, Parent, Uncle etc.):

Difficulty		Family Member(s)
Depression	**yes**/no	mother/grandmother
Bipolar Disorder	yes/**no**	
Anxiety Disorders	**yes**/no	father
Panic Attacks	yes/**no**	
Schizophrenia	yes/**no**	

Alcohol/Substance Abuse	yes/**no**	
Eating Disorders	**yes**/no	younger sister
Learning Disabilities	yes/**no**	
Trauma History	yes/**no**	
Suicide Attempts	yes/**no**	
Psychiatric Hospitalizations	**yes**/no	grandmother

OTHER INFORMATION:

What role, if any, do religion and/or spirituality play in your life?

"My parents attend the Episcopal church but I don't really go. I just don't feel God or any special force in my life. I feel alone in the universe."

Are you satisfied with your social situation/interpersonal relationships? ☒ **No** ☐ Yes

If no, explain why:

"I am lonely and I would like to have a girlfriend to hang out with and eventually have a family but right now I can't even seem to get motivated to get together with friends."

What do you consider to be your strengths?

"I am artistic, good at languages, and I am able to connect with others pretty well."

What do you like most about yourself?

"Right now there isn't much that I like about myself except that I know that I like to help other people. I learned Spanish so that I could help the Spanish speaking community."

What are effective coping strategies you use when stressed?

"I like to draw. Sometimes I draw storms and it calms me down a little."

What are your overall goals for therapy?

"I want to stop this crazy cleaning and watching the weather. I don't want to be plagued by worries about the weather and I don't want to feel so blue all the time. It would be great to find a girlfriend."

What do you feel you need to work on first?

"I need to get back to work so I can move out of my parent's house."

Source: Intake Form format created by Amanda Williams.

Adult Intake Form: Case 2: Seo-Yeon

Intake

Name: ___L.________________ Seo-Yeon ________________ Grace __________
(Last) (First) (MI)

Your Birth Date: __04__ / __30__ / 1967______ Age: __48___

Gender: ☐ Male ☒ **Female** ☐ Transgender

Local Address:
__2123 Oak Hill Drive____________________________
(Street and Number)
_____Anytown___________ VA _________ 22703 __________________
(City) (State) Zip

Home Phone: ________________________ May I leave a message? ☒ **Yes** ☐ No

Cell Phone: ___555.621.3214______________ May I leave a message? ☒ **Yes** ☐ No

E-mail: ______________________________ May I e-mail you? ☐Yes ☒ **No**
*Please be aware that e-mail might not be confidential.

Person to contact in case of an emergency:

_Ye-eun L._______________ mother _____________ same ____________
(Name) (Relationship to client) (Phone)

Primary Care doctor:____Dr. Kim__________________________ 540.555.6745
(Name) (Phone)

How did you learn about me? ____Dr. Kim referred me____________________

What prompted you to seek therapy or an assessment?

I seem to feel sad all the time. There doesn't seem to be any end to it. I've tried most everything and all I can think of to do is to come see a counselor.

Therapist's observations here:
Ms. Kim sits stiffly in her chair, speaking very softly, almost too softly to hear her. Her shoulders are slumped and she stares into her hands as she talks. She does not make eye contact and punctuates her conversation with quiet tears.

Sexual Preference: **Men** Women Both

Marital Status: ☒ **Never** Married ☐ Partnered ☐ Married ☐ Separated ☐ Divorced ☐ Widowed

Are you currently in a romantic relationship? ☒ **Yes** ☐ No

If yes, for how long?________________

If yes, on a scale of 1-10 (10 = great), how would you rate the quality of your romantic relationship? ______

Do you have children? ☒ **No** ☐ Yes

If yes, how many?: _____ Ages: ________________________

Have you had previous psychotherapy? ☒ **No** ☐ Yes

If yes, why?____

If yes, when?____

Are you currently taking prescribed psychiatric medications (antidepressants or others)? ☐ Yes ☒ **No**

If Yes, please list names and doses: _______________________________

If No, have you been previously prescribed psychiatric medication? ☐ Yes ☒ **No**

If Yes, please list names and dates: _______________________________

How do you feel about your future? "I'm unsure about what the future has in store for me. I don't have any reason to believe I will ever feel any different than I do now."

Are you having current suicidal thoughts? ☒ **Frequently** ☐ Sometimes ☐ Rarely ☐ Never

If yes, have you recently done anything to hurt yourself? ☐ Yes ☒ **No**

Have you had suicidal thoughts in the past? ☐ Frequently ☒ **Sometimes** ☐ Rarely ☐ Never

If you checked any box other than "never," when did you have these thoughts? "Sometimes I think I just can't stand these feelings any more. I imagine ways of killing myself like taking a lot of pills or drinking myself to death. I could jump in front of a train or something. But then I think about my parents finding me or what it would be like for the train conductor and I just can't do it."

Did you ever act on these feelings? ☐ Yes ☒ **No**

Are you having current homicidal thoughts (i.e., thoughts of hurting someone else)? ☐ Yes ☒ **No**

Have you previously had homicidal thoughts? ☐ Yes ☒ **No**

If yes, when?____

HEALTH INFORMATION

How is your physical health currently? (please circle)

☐ Poor ☐ Unsatisfactory ☐ Satisfactory ☒ **Good** ☐ Very good

Date of last physical examination __________________________

Please list any chronic health problems or concerns (e.g., asthma, hypertension, diabetes, headaches, stomach pain, seizures etc.):

________________ Seo-yeon reports frequent headaches and occasional stomach problems such as nausea, but a recent medical exam did not reveal any medical cause for her symptoms.

Any Allergies? ☒ **No** ☐ Yes If yes, please list:__________________________________

Medications: **none**

Hours per night you normally sleep 3-5

Are you having any problems with your sleep habits? ☐ No ☒ **Yes**

If yes, check where applicable: ☒ **Sleeping too little** ☐ Sleeping too much ☒ **Can't fall asleep** ☒ **Can't stay asleep**

Do you exercise regularly? ☒ **No** ☐ Yes

If yes, how many times per week do you exercise? ______ For how long? ______________

If yes, what do you do?____

Are you having any difficulty with appetite or eating habits? ☐ No ☒ **Yes**

If yes, check where applicable: ☒ **Eating less** ☐ Eating more ☐ Bingeing ☐ Purging

Have you experienced significant weight change in the last 2 months? ☐ No ☒ **Yes**

Do you regularly use alcohol? ☒ **No** ☐ Yes

If yes, what is your frequency?

☐ Once a month ☐ Once a week ☐ Daily ☐ Daily, three or more ☐ Intoxicated daily

How often do you engage in recreational drug use? ☐ Daily ☐ Weekly ☐ Monthly ☐ Rarely ☒ **Never**

If you checked any box other than "never," which drugs do you use?

____

Do you smoke? ☒ **No** ☐ Yes

If yes, how many cigarettes per day?________________

Do you drink caffeinated drinks? ☐ No ☒ **Yes**

If yes, # of sodas per day 2-3 cups of coffee per day 2-4

Have you ever had a head injury? ☒ **No** ☐ Yes

If yes, when and what happened?____________________________________

In the last year, have you experienced any significant life changes or stressors?

____

____

Can you describe your early home experiences?

"My parents came to the States when I was just a kid but I started out speaking Korean, so I had to learn English when I started school. My parents never really got used to Americans and we stayed mostly to ourselves. There was a Korean Baptist church on the other side of town and my parents would socialize with other Koreans. They encouraged me to hang out with other Korean kids but I always felt awkward, kind of half way in the culture and half way out."

"My sister and brother were born here and they never spoke Korean, though they can understand it when my parents speak it. I got along well with them, but I was more like a parent to them than an older sister, since I was often asked to care for them while my mother and father worked."

*Note: For each of the following, note which symptoms you experience and then for those you mark "yes" use rating scale to rate the degree to which the symptom interferes with your daily living or well-being. Where possible provide a description of what is happening:

Are you now experiencing: *Rating Scale 1-10 (10 = worst)

Depressed Mood or Sadness **yes** no 6

"I can't really put my finger on my feelings of sadness but they are there. They are something that I wake up with and something that settles in with me and follows me through the day. The only time I can escape them is when I sleep, so I sleep a lot."

Hopelessness **yes** no 4

"I don't feel like there is much hope of any of this changing but I am willing to try counseling."

Guilt/Shame **yes** no 6

"No one in my family has ever seen a counselor before. In fact I can't remember a time when anyone in the family has ever shared their feelings with an outsider. I feel very ashamed of these depressed feelings, of not being able to snap out of this and of coming to counseling."

Lack of Interest **yes** no 7

"I love to go birding, especially in the spring when the song birds are returning. But this year I can't find any joy in it. I used to love to paint birds in the winter and think about their return, but I can't get up the energy to set up my paints or to think of cleaning up again, it all seems like too much effort."

Irritability/Anger	**yes**	no	3
Mood Swings	yes	**no**	____
Rapid Speech	yes	**no**	____
Racing Thoughts	yes	**no**	____
Anxiety	yes	**no**	____
Constant Worry	yes	**no**	____
Panic Attacks	yes	**no**	____
Phobias	yes	**no**	____
Lack of Appetite	**yes**	no	4
Excess Appetite	yes	**no**	____
Sleep Disturbances	**yes**	no	6

"I have a lot of trouble getting to sleep and sometimes wake in the early morning hours and have to read for a while before I am sleepy enough to get back to sleep. It was better when I started my job as a traffic controller or I couldn't have gotten that job. But now it is becoming a problem again."

Hallucinations	yes	**no**	____
Paranoia	yes	**no**	____
Poor Concentration	**yes**	no	5

"I have heard from both my coworkers and my mother that I don't seem to have the concentration that I once had."

Alcohol/Substance Abuse	yes	**no**	____
Frequent Body Complaints (e.g., headaches)	yes	**no**	____
Eating Disorder	yes	**no**	____

Body Image Problems	yes	**no**	______
Repetitive Thoughts (e.g., Obsessions)	yes	**no**	______
Repetitive Behaviors (e.g., counting)	yes	**no**	______
Poor Impulse Control (e.g., ↑ spending)	yes	**no**	______
Self-Mutilation	yes	**no**	______
Hx of Sexual Abuse	yes	**no**	______
Hx of Physical Abuse	yes	**no**	______
Hx of Emotional Abuse	yes	**no**	______

Have you experienced in the past: ***Rating Scale 1-10 (10 = worst)**

Depressed Mood or Sadness **yes** no 7

"My first experience of depression was in college. My grades dropped and I considered taking a semester off, but decided to push through. I slept a lot then, too, and missed some classes, I remember that. The rest is a little hazy."

Irritability/Anger	yes	**no**	______
Mood Swings	yes	**no**	______
Rapid Speech	yes	**no**	______
Racing Thoughts	yes	**no**	______
Anxiety	**yes**	no	4

"I've had periods in which I worried a bit about money and about being able to pay for school. Sometimes I would be so distracted by these worries I could think of little else."

Constant Worry	**yes**	no	8
Panic Attacks	yes	**no**	______
Phobias	**yes**	no	6

"I had an intense fear of shots as a kid but I guess I got over that when I was a teen."

Sleep Disturbances	**yes**	no	6

"I have never slept well, since the time I was a small child. At first my parents thought it was the time change from Korea to the U.S., because that is when it started, but since that time I have had great difficulty getting to sleep. I remember seeing a lot of different doctors about it when I was a child."

Hallucinations	yes	**no**	____
Paranoia	yes	**no**	____
Poor Concentration	**yes**	no	6
Alcohol/Substance Abuse	yes	**no**	____
Frequent Body Complaints (e.g., headaches)	yes	**no**	____
Eating Disorder	yes	**no**	____
Body Image Problems	yes	**no**	____
Repetitive Thoughts (e.g., Obsessions)	yes	**no**	____
Repetitive Behaviors (e.g., counting)	**yes**	no	8
Poor Impulse Control (e.g., ↑ spending)	yes	**no**	____
Self-Mutilation	yes	**no**	____
Sexual Abuse	yes	**no**	____
Physical Abuse	yes	**no**	____
Emotional Abuse	yes	**no**	____

OCCUPATIONAL, EDUCATIONAL, LEGAL INFORMATION:

Are you employed? ☐ No ☒ **Yes**

If yes, who is your current employer/position? ________Air Traffic Control____

If yes, are you happy at your current position? ________no__________________

Please list any work-related stressors, if any: " This is a high stress job and if I make a mistake people's jobs are at risk"

Do you have financial concerns? ☒ **No** ☐ Yes

If yes, please explain: ______

Can you describe your past work-related experiences?
"I have worked for air traffic control for 5 years."

Highest level of education: **B.A.**

Do you have any legal concerns? ☒ **No** ☐ Yes

If yes, please explain: ______

FAMILY HISTORY:

Are your parents:

- ☒ **Still together**
- ☐ Divorced, when ______
- ☐ Remarried
- ☐ Unmarried
- ☐ Deceased, if yes whom ______ age at death ______

Number of siblings: 2 Ages: 27 and 31

Do you have good family support? ☐ No ☒ **Yes** From whom "Our family is very close and I feel supported by them."

FAMILY MENTAL HEALTH HISTORY:

Has anyone in your family (either immediate family members or relatives) experienced difficulties with the following? (circle any that apply and list family member, e.g., Sibling, Parent, Uncle etc.):

Difficulty Family Member(s)
Depression **yes**/no mother/grandmother
Bipolar Disorder yes/**no** ______
Anxiety Disorders **yes**/no father

Panic Attacks yes/**no** ______________________________
Schizophrenia yes/**no** ______________________________
Alcohol/Substance Abuse yes/**no** ______________________________
Eating Disorders **yes**/no ____younger sister______
Learning Disabilities yes/**no** ______________________________
Trauma History yes/**no** ______________________________
Suicide Attempts yes/**no** ______________________________
Psychiatric Hospitalizations yes/**no** ______________________________

OTHER INFORMATION:

What role, if any, do religion and/or spirituality play in your life?
"I still attend the Korean Baptist Church with my parents but I attend more out of respect for their wishes than from my own desires and beliefs. I don't know what I believe about God."

Are you satisfied with your social situation/interpersonal relationships? ☒ **No** ☐ Yes
If no, explain why:
"I would like to have more friends outside of work and church but I can't seem to meet anyone. It is hard for me to get out and meet people. I guess I am shy."

What do you consider to be your strengths?

"I am loyal, smart and kind."

What do you like most about yourself?

"That is a hard question to answer. I guess I am someone that I would want to be friends with because I am honest and you can count on me."

What are effective coping strategies you use when stressed?

"Normally, I like to paint birds and go out birding. One day I would like to take a vacation and go on an extended birding trip."

What are your overall goals for therapy?

"I want to get past this depression and start living my life."

What do you feel you need to work on first?

"I need to understand why I am so down."

Source: Intake Form format created by Amanda Williams.

Appendix

CHAPTER 5

BOX 5.04

Answer Key: Definitional Cases

Austin: 299.00 F84.0) Autism Spectrum Disorder (not enough information to determine intellectual impairment) (Diagnostic table available on pages 50–51 of the DSM 5.)

Gurveer: 307 (F98.4) Stereotypic Movement Disorder, With Self-Injurious Behavior, Associated with Lesch-Nyhan Syndrome (Diagnostic table located on page 77 of the DSM 5.)

Nakita: 314.01 (F90.2) ADHD, Combined Presentation (pg. 59)

Mehdi 314.01 (F90.1) ADHD, Predominantly Hyperactive/Impulsive Type (pg. 59)

Ryan: 307.23 (F95.2) Tourette's Disorder (pg. 81)

Felicity: 307.22 (F95.1) Persistent (Chronic) Motor or Vocal Tic Disorder, with vocal tics only (pg. 81)

Lina: 307.21 (F95.0) Provisional Tic Disorder (pg. 81)

Answer Key: Narrative Diagnosis

Rose: F90.2 Attention-deficit/hyperactivity disorder, combined presentation, mild (Diagnostic table found on pp. 59–61 of the DSM 5)

Jackson: F84.0 Autism spectrum disorder, without accompanying intellectual impairment, with accompanying language impairment (Diagnostic table located on pp. 50–51 of the DSM 5)

Pierce: F80.89 Social (pragmatic) communication disorder (Diagnostic table can be found on pp. 47–48 of the DSM 5)

CHAPTER 6

BOX 6.06

Answer Key: Cases in Schizophrenia & Related Disorders

Sunil: F23 Brief psychotic disorder, with marked stressor (Diagnostic table found on p. 94 of the DSM 5)

Elias: F22 Delusional disorder, erotomanic type, first episode, currently in acute episode (Diagnostic table found on pp. 90–91 of the DSM 5)

Julius: F20.81 Schizophreniform disorder, With good prognostic features (Diagnostic table found on pp. 96–97 of the DSM 5)

Heather: F20.81 Schizophreniform disorder, without good prognostic features, provisional* (Diagnostic table found on pp. 96–97 of the DSM 5)

Note that Heather's diagnosis must be provisional until she has resolved her symptoms, unless the symptoms continue past 6 months when another dx, schizophrenia, must be applied

Winston: F23 Brief psychotic disorder, without marked stressor (Diagnostic table found on p. 94 of the DSM 5)

Deidre: F25.1 Schizoaffective disorder, depressive type, multiple episodes, currently in partial remission* (Diagnostic table found on pp. 105–106 of the DSM 5)

*Note: DSM 5 asks the diagnostician to withhold specifiers until after a year-long duration of the disorder, thus no specifiers are offered here.

**Diagnoses are being offered without severity specifiers since the severity assessment is not available in these case studies.

CHAPTER 7

BOX 7.07

Select Answers: Mood Disorders Definitional Cases

Episodes:

Aleksander: Major depressive episode, with melancholic features (p. 151)

Alejandro: Hypomanic Episode (p. 124)

Elena: Major depressive episode, with atypical features (p. 151)

Ivan: Major depressive episode, with seasonal pattern (p. 153)

Disorders of Mood: Select Definitional Cases

Becky: F32.81 Premenstrual dysphoric disorder (Diagnostic table found on pp. 171–172 of the DSM 5)

Aafreen: Bipolar I disorder (not enough information to provide diagnostic coding or specifiers) (Diagnostic table on DSM 5 pp. 123–127)

Franklin: F34.81 Disruptive mood dysregulation disorder (Diagnostic table found in DSM 5 p. 156)

Tim: F34.1 Persistent depressive disorder (not enough information to complete specifiers) (Diagnostic table found in DSM 5 pp. 168–169)

BOX 7.08

Select Answers: Mood Disorders Narrative Cases

Lidia: F34.0 Cyclothymic disorder, with anxious distress, mild (Diagnostic table found on pp. 139–140 of the DSM 5)

Arturo: F34.1 Persistent depressive disorder, late onset, with pure dysthymic syndrome, mild (Diagnostic table found on pp. 168–169 of the DSM 5)

Amanda: F34.0 Cyclothymic disorder (Diagnostic table found on pp. 139–140 of the DSM 5)

Jeremy: F32.0 Major depressive disorder, with anxious distress, mild (Diagnostic table found on pp. 160–162 & 184 of the DSM 5)

Dale: F31.74 Bi-polar I disorder, in full remission, most recent episode manic, mild, with anxious distress, mild

Hannah: F34.1 Persistent depressive disorder, early onset, moderate (Diagnostic table found on pp. 168–169 of the DSM 5)

Donna: F32.0 Major depressive disorder, mild, with peripartum onset (Diagnostic table found on pp. 160–162 & 186 of the DSM 5)

CHAPTER 8

BOX 8.10

Case	Diagnosis
Levi	F94.0 Selective mutism (Diagnostic table found on p. 195 of the DSM 5)
Ann	F93.0 Separation anxiety disorder (Diagnostic table found on p. 190-191 of the DSM 5)
Jamal	F40.218 Specific phobia, animal type (Diagnostic table found in DSM 5 pp. 197-198)
Fanta	F.41.1 Generalized anxiety disorder (Diagnostic table found on p. 222 of the DSM 5)

Narrative Cases in Anxiety: Select Diagnoses

Case	Diagnosis
Philip	F40.232 Specific phobia, other medical care (doctors/hospitals)
Esther	F40.00 Agoraphobia (Diagnostic table found on pp. 217-218 of the DSM 5)
Leroy	F41.1 Generalized anxiety disorder (Diagnostic table found on p. 222 of the DSM 5)
Bethany	F94.0 Selective mutism (Diagnostic table found on p. 195 of the DSM 5)
Mim	F41.0 Panic disorder (Diagnostic table found on p. 208 of the DSM 5)

CHAPTER 9

BOX 9.06

Answer key for Box 9.03**: Try This**

Cynthia: compulsion

Arron: non-pathological consuming interest

Lupita: obsession

Jimmy: social phobia

Daisy: obsession

Alissa's daughter: compulsion

Ellen: obsession

Octavio: non-pathological fear

Wes: compulsion

Bo: generalized anxiety disorder

BOX 9.07

Select Answers: Definitional Cases in Obsessive-Compulsive and Related Disorders

DX: Eastman: F45.22 Body dismorphic disorder, with absent insight/delusional beliefs

(Diagnostic table found in DSM 5 pp. 242-243)

DX: Todd: F63.3 F63.2 Trichotillomania (Diagnostic table found in DSM 5 p. 251)

DX: Dan: F42.2 F42 Obsessive-compulsive disorder, with fair insight (Diagnostic table found in the DSM 5 on p. 237)

DX: Connor: F42.4 L98.1 Excoriation (skin picking) disorder (Diagnostic table found in DSM 5 on p. 254)

DX: Emily: F42.3 F42 Hoarding disorder, with excessive acquisition, with absent insight

(Diagnostic table found in DSM 5 on p. 247)

BOX 9.08

Select Answers: Narrative Cases in Obsessive-Compulsive and Related Disorders

DX: Devin: F42 Obsessive-compulsive disorder, with good insight (Diagnostic table found on pp. 237-238 of the DSM 5)

DX: Addie: F63.2 Trichotillomania (Diagnostic table found on p. 251 of the DSM 5)

DX: Marta: F42 Obsessive-compulsive disorder, with poor insight, tic-related (Diagnostic table found on pp. 237-238 of the DSM 5)

DX: Martin: L98.1 Excoriation (skin picking) disorder (Diagnostic table found in DSM 5 on p. 254)

DX: Cara: F42 Hoarding disorder, with excessive acquisition, with absent insight (Diagnostic table found in DSM 5 on p. 247)

DX: Manny: F45.22 Body dysmorphic disorder, with absent insight/delusional beliefs

(Diagnostic table found on pp. 242-243 of the DSM 5)

Select Answers: Sleep-Wake Disorders

Abby: F51.11 Hypersomnolence disorder, subacute (not enough information to provide severity specifier) (Diagnostic table found in DSM 5 pp. 368–369)

Gurkiran: F51.11 Hypersomnolence disorder, with major depressive disorder (not enough information to provide duration or severity specifiers) (Diagnostic table found in DSM 5 pp. 368–369)

Vanessa: G47.24 Circadian rhythm sleep-wake disorder, non 24-hour sleep-wake type (not enough information to provide all specifiers) (Diagnostic table found in DSM 5 p. 420)

Ava: F51.01 Insomnia disorder, with non-sleep disorder mental comorbidity (not enough information to provide all specifiers) (Diagnostic table found in DSM 5 pp. 362–363)

CHAPTER 11

BOX 11.04

Answer Key: Definitional Cases Trauma & Stress-Related Disorders: Select Answers

Theo: F43.0 Acute stress disorder (Diagnostic table found in DSM 5 pp. 280–281)

Bellamy: F43.24 Adjustment disorder, with disturbance of conduct (Diagnostic table found in DSM 5 pp. 286–287)

Galina: F94.2 Disinhibited social engagement disorder (Found in DSM 5 pp. 268–269)

Answer Key: Narrative Cases Dissociative & Trauma Disorders

Marcel: F43.10 Posttraumatic stress disorder, with dissociative symptoms (Diagnostic table found on pp. 271–274 of the DSM 5)

Eddie: Reactive attachment disorder (Diagnostic table found on 265–266)

Simon: F43.24 Adjustment disorder with disturbance of conduct (Diagnostic table found on pp. 286–287 of the DSM 5)

Alice: F43.22 Adjustment disorder with anxiety (Diagnostic table found on pp. 286–287 of the DSM 5).

CHAPTER 12

BOX 12.04

Answer Key: Definitional Cases in Dissociative Disorders: Select Answers

Takumi: F44.81 Dissociative identity disorder (Diagnostic table found in DSM 5 p. 292)

Charlotte: F48.1 Depersonalization/derealization disorder (Diagnostic table found in DSM 5 p. 302)

Alisha: F44.0 Dissociative amnesia

Answer Key: Narrative Cases Dissociative & Trauma Disorders: Select Answers

Serge: F48.1 Depersonalization/derealization disorder

Bridget: F44.1 Dissociative amnesia, with dissociative fugue (Diagnostic table found on p. 298 of the DSM 5)

CHAPTER 13

BOX 13.07

Answer Key: Definitional Cases in Somatic Symptom & Related Disorders: Select Answers

Alex: F45.1 Somatic symptom disorder (Diagnostic table found in DSM 5 p. 311)

Jessica: F68.10 Factitious disorder, recurrent episodes (Diagnostic table found in DSM 5 pp. 324–325)

Chloe: F45.21 Illness anxiety disorder, care-seeking type (Diagnostic table found in DSM 5 p. 315)

Answer Key: Narrative Cases in Somatic Symptom Disorders: Select Answers

Edmund F45.1 Somatic symptom disorder, with predominant pain, moderate (Diagnostic table found on p. 311 of the DSM 5)

Brooklyn: F68.A Factitious disorder imposed on another, recurrent episodes (Diagnostic table found on pp. 324–325 of the DSM 5, code revised 10.01.18)

Willow: F44.4 Conversion disorder, with speech symptom, without psychological stressor (Diagnostic table found on pp. 318–319 of the DSM 5)

Charlotte: F54 Psychological factors affecting other medical conditions, extreme (Diagnostic table found on p. 322 of the DSM 5)

CHAPTER 14

BOX 14.03

Select Answers: Cases: Feeding and Eating Related Disorders

Definitional Cases

Sadie: F50.2 Bulimia nervosa (not enough information for specifiers) (Diagnostic table found in DSM 5 p. 345)

Keith: F50.81 Binge eating disorder, moderate (Diagnostic table found in DSM 5 p. 350)

Bethany: F50.01 Anorexia nervosa, restricting, moderate (Diagnostic table found in DSM 5 pp. 338–339)

Bobby: F98.3 Pica (child) (pp. 329–330)

Trish: F50.8 Avoidant/Restrictive food intake disorder

Narrative Cases

Katrina: F50.01 Anorexia nervosa, restricting type, severe

Gina: F50.81 Binge-eating disorder, moderate (Diagnostic Table on p. 350 of the DSM 5)

Behir: F50.8 Avoidant/Restrictive food intake disorder

Mindy: F50.2 Bulimia nervosa, in partial remission, mild (Diagnostic table found in DSM 5 p. 345)

Darian: F98.3 Pica (child) (p. 329–330)

Anna-Jane: F50.02 Anorexia nervosa, binge-eating/purging type, mild

Kelly: F50.89 Pica (adult) (Diagnostic table found on pp. 329-330 of the DSM 5)

Felicity: F50.81 Binge-eating disorder, mild (Diagnostic table found in DSM 5 p. 350)

CHAPTER 15

BOX 15.03

Select Answers Definitional Cases: Sexual Dysfunctions

DX: Christian: F52.4 Premature ejaculation (not enough information to provide specifiers) (Diagnostic table found in DSM 5 pp. 443–444)

DX: Tunde: F52.32 Delayed ejaculation, acquired, generalized (not enough evidence for severity specifier) (Diagnostic table found in DSM 5 p. 424)

DX: Timothy: F52.0 Male hypoactive sexual desire disorder, acquired (not enough information to provide all specifiers) (Diagnostic table found in DSM 5 pp. 440–441)

DX: Victoria: F52.31 Female orgasmic disorder, lifelong, generalized (not enough information for severity specifier) (Diagnostic table found in DSM 5 pp. 429–430)

BOX 15.04

Select Answers: Narrative Cases in Sexual Dysfunctions

Dx: Jennifer: F52.6 Genito-pelvic pain/penetration disorder, lifelong, severe (Diagnostic table found in DSM 5 p. 437)

Dx: Logan: F52.4 Premature (early) ejaculation, lifelong, generalized, moderate (Diagnostic table found in DSM 5 pp. 443–444)

Dx: Matteo: F52.21 Erectile disorder, acquired, situational

CHAPTER 16

BOX 16.05

Select Answers: Disruptive, Impulse & Conduct

Differential Diagnosis

Cooper: Kleptomania

Mike: No Diagnosis

Pim: Pyromania

Sheela: Conduct disorder

Definitional Cases

Jackson: F91.3 Oppositional Defiant Disorder

Lena: F63.1 Pyromania

Ethan: F63.81 Intermittent explosive disorder

Anika: F63.2 Kleptomania

Eric: Conduct disorder (not enough information to provide diagnostic code or specifiers) (Diagnostic table found in DSM 5 pp. 469-471)

Narrative Cases

Jude: F 63.81 Intermittent explosive disorder (Diagnostic table found on p. 466 of the DSM 5)

Kris: F63.1 Pyromania

Crystal: F 91.3 Oppositional defiant disorder, mild (Diagnostic table found on pp. 462-463 of the DSM 5).

Bruce: F91.1 Conduct disorder, childhood-onset type, with limited prosocial emotions, lack of remorse or guilt, severe (Diagnostic table found on pp. 469-471 of the DSM 5)

Felicia: F63.2 Kleptomania

CHAPTER 17

BOX 17.09

Select Answers: Definitional Cases for Substance-Related & Addictive Disorders

David: Opioid Intoxication (not enough information to apply an ICD-10 code and specifiers) (Diagnostic table found in DSM 5 pp. 546–547)

Holly: Alcohol use disorder (not enough information to apply specifiers or coding) (Diagnostic table found in DSM 5 pp. 490–491)

Desmond: Cannabis use disorder (not enough information to apply specifiers or coding) (Diagnostic table found in DSM 5 pp. 509–510)

Libby: Phencyclidine intoxication (not enough information to apply specifiers or coding) (Diagnostic table found in DSM 5 pp. 527–528)

Anar: Inhalant use disorder (not enough information to apply specifiers or coding) (Diagnostic table found in DSM 5 pp. 533–534)

Answer Key: Narrative Cases Substance-Related Disorders

Ann: F10.10 Alcohol use disorder, mild; F40.10 Social Anxiety Disorder

Shelby: F16.20 Phencyclidine use disorder, moderate

Sawyer: F18.20 Inhalant intoxication, moderate (Diagnostic criteria found on page 538 of the DSM 5)

Ingrid: F43.81 Posttraumatic Stress Disorder; F13.10 Sedative use disorder, mild

**Find all revised codes in the 2018 DSM 5 Supplement here:* https://psychiatryonline.org/pb-assets/dsm/update/DSM5Update_October2018.pdf

CHAPTER 18

BOX 18.08

Answer Key: Cases in Personality Disorders

Box 18.08	Definitional Cases Answer Key: Alternate answers will be available in the back of the final text
Cyndi	DX: **F60.6 Avoidant personality disorder**
Art	DX: **F60.81 Narcissistic personality disorder**
Ernesto	DX: **F60.1 Schizoid personality disorder**
	Narrative Cases
Anoushka	DX: **F60.7 Dependent personality disorder**
Eric	DX: **F60.0 Paranoid personality disorder**
Irenka	DX: **F60.2 Antisocial personality disorder**
Wainwright	DX: **F60.3 Borderline personality disorder**

CHAPTER 19

BOX 19.07

Select Answers: Paraphilias

Answers: Definitional Cases in Paraphilia

DX: Kenneth: F65.1 Transvestic disorder (Diagnostic table found on pp. 702–703 of the DSM 5)

DX: Andrew: F65.51 Sexual Masochism (Diagnostic table found on p. 694 of the DSM 5)

DX: Donna: F65.4 Pedophilic disorder (Diagnostic table found on pp. 697–698 of the DSM 5)

DX: Suresh: F65.0 Fetishistic disorder, body part (feet) (Diagnostic table found on pg. 700 of the DSM 5)

DX: Clarke: F65.3 Voyeuristic disorder (Diagnostic table found on pg. 686 of the DSM 5)

DX: Phillipa: F65.52 Sexual sadism disorder (Diagnostic table found on p. 695 of the DSM 5)

DX: Brian: F65.81 Frotteuristic disorder (Diagnostic table found on pp. 691–692 of the DSM 5)

DX: Melinda: F65.0 Fetishistic disorder, objects (Diagnostic table found on p. 700 of the DSM 5)

DX: Todd: F65.2 Exhibitionistic disorder (Diagnostic table found on p. 689 of the DSM 5)

Index

ABA. *See* applied behavior analysis
acceptance-based model of 216
acquired immunodeficiency syndrome (AIDS) 52
acrocyanosis 384
acute stress disorder (ASD) 303
acute trauma 301
adaptive information processing model 257
addictive disorders. *See* substance use disorders (SUDs)
ADHD 447
ADHD. *See* attention deficit hyperactivity disorder
adjustment disorder 303
adolescents, substance use 472
adulthood, intermittent explosive disorder 448
adverse childhood experiences (ACE) 307, 474
aggressive and sexual obsessions 246
aggressive obsessions 253
aggressive themes 253
aging 370
agoraphobia 211
alcohol 392, 419
amenorrhea 384
American Counseling Association 5
American Psychiatric Association (APA) 1, 5, 18, 305, 538
AN. *See* anorexia nervosa
anchoring bias 9
androgen deprivation therapy (ADT) 548
andropause 418
anergic depression 163
anorexia 387, 397, 400
anorexia nervosa (AN) 383
anorexia nervosa (AN) 387
anorexia trumps bulimia 401
anosognosia 359
ANP. *See* apparently normal part
anticonvulsants 176
anti-psychiatric movement 11
antipsychotics 176
antisocial personality disorder (ASPD) 436, 441
anxiety 95, 203, 205, 419
  biofeedback 223
  cognitive-behavioral therapy for 221
  definitional cases 223–224
  differential diagnosis 217–220
  imagery 222
  mindfulness 222
  mindfulness-based stress reduction 221
  narrative cases in 224–232
  pivot points 225
  response prevention 222
  selective mutism 207
  separation anxiety disorder 206
  social anxiety disorder (SAD) 209
  specific phobias 209
  theoretical approaches to 204–206
  treatment of 220–223
  worry outcome monitoring 222
anxious 204
APA. *See* American Psychiatric Association
apparently normal part (ANP) 342
appetitive function 397
applied behavior analysis (ABA) 106
APS. *See* attenuated psychosis syndrome
AS. *See* Asperger syndrome
ASD. *See* autism spectrum disorder
asexuality 424
Asperger syndrome (AS) 89, 92, 93
attentional bias 214
attention deficit hyperactivity disorder (ADHD) 42, 91, 165, 540
  comorbidities 101
  etiology 101
  evidence-based practices for 103–105
  misdiagnosis of 102
  oppositional defiant disorder and 102
  overdiagnosis, relative age effects and 103
  psychosocial interventions for 105
  sleep disturbance and 102
  stimulants 104
  sudden unexplained deaths 104
  treatment-emergent psychosis 104
attenuated psychosis syndrome (APS) 127
augmentative communication 94
autism diagnosis 96, 97
autism severity specifiers 92
autism spectrum disorder (ASD)
  anxiety and 95
  applied behavior analysis 106
  communication delays and obstacles 94
  compensatory medications 105
  complicated etiology of 98
  early signs and symptoms 92
  evidence-based interventions 105

autism spectrum disorder (ASD) (*Continued*)
  instrumental *vs.* expressive relationship 93
  neurological differences 98
  obsessive-compulsive disorder 95, 96
  pain sensitivity 95
  prevalence rates of 98
  questions about cognition and 93
  race and social class impact on 100
  schizophrenia and 136
  sensory sensitivity and food selectivity in 95
  social engagement 94
  specifiers 92
  treatment interventions for 105–106
  vaccines 99
autism spectrum disorder (ASD) 42, 87, 91, 273, 399, 441
autistic psychopaths 97
autonomic nervous system (ANS) 444
availability bias 9
avoidant/restrictive food intake disorder 386

BDD. *See* body dysmorphic disorder
BED. *See* binge eating disorder
behavioral interventions 105
  for phobia 220
benzodiazepines 282
bias 49, 50
bigorexia 384
binge eating disorder (BED) 388
binging episodes 387
biofeedback 223
bipolar depression 172
  vs. unipolar depression 172
bipolar disorder (BPD) 167, 170–175
  circadian rhythms and treatments for 177
  cognitive behavioral therapy 178
  discerning mood episodes 170–175
  psychotherapy for 178
  sleep constitutes hypersomnia and insomnia 172
  vs. borderline personality structures 173
bipolar I disorder (BPD I) 157
bipolar I disorder (BPD I) 132, 160
bipolar II disorder (BPD II) 157
bipolar II disorder (BPD II) 160
bipolarity, in children and adolescents 164–166
Bipolar-Schizophrenia Network on Intermediate Phenotypes (B-SNIP) 132
body 71
body dysmorphic disorder (BDD) 240, 241
borderline personality disorder (BPD) 503, 505
  deliberate self-harm 517
  differential diagnosis of 519
  early trauma 518
  etiology theories 522–526
  false-positives in 521
  history of 516
  misdiagnosis danger 520
  skilled diagnostician 519–522
  SUDs 518
borderline personality structures (BPS)
  vs. bipolar disorders 173
BPD. *See* bipolar disorder
bradycardia 384
brief limited intermittent psychotic symptoms (BLIPS) 125
brief psychotic disorder 124
brief strategic family therapy (BSFT) 485
Briquet's syndrome 356
British Psychological Society 4, 5
bulimia 397
bulimia nervosa (BN) 387

callous-unemotional trait 440
  conduct disorder 443
careful planning 74
CAS. *See* cognitive-attentional syndrome
case conceptualization 67, 79
  clinical hypothesis and 65–70
catastrophizes 81
caution in crisis, transition and personality concerns 43
CBT. *See* cognitive behavioral therapy
central sensitivity syndrome 359
childhood sexual assault (CSA) 537
chronic fatigue 371
circadian rhythm 177, 270, 273
circadian rhythm disorders (CRD) 270
  subtypes and specifiers 270
client identities 67
client resonance 44
clinical hypothesis 67
  and case conceptualization 65–70
clinical significance 37–47
cluster A: 504
cluster B: 505
cluster C: 506
cluster complaints 50
cluster related symptoms 24
cognitive-attentional syndrome (CAS) 205
cognitive-behavioral analysis system of psychotherapy (CBASP) 179
cognitive behavioral therapy (CBT) 138, 178, 179, 213, 256, 316, 451, 550
cognitive-behavioral therapy (CBT) 221
cognitive behavioral therapy for insomnia (CBT-I) 279

cognitive-behavioral treatment plan 81–82
cognitive bias 214
cognitive models 250
cognitive processes 9
cognitive shifts 392
command hallucinations 125
comorbid disorders 36
comorbid mood disorders 478
compassion fatigue 163
compensation neurosis 356
compensatory behavior 384, 388
complex post-traumatic stress disorder 307
complex post-traumatic stress disorder (CPTSD) 521
complex trauma 315
compulsion 240, 245, 247
conceptualization 79
  approaches to 69
conduct disorder (CD) 436, 439, 440
  callous-unemotional 443
  cultural considerations 445
  definitional cases 451–453
  gender differences 446
  narrative cases 453–456
  treatment for 450–451
confirmation bias 9
congenital disorders 418
consultation 46
contact contamination 246
contamination 245
contemplative approach to conceptualizing client difficulties and strengths 70–73
  body 71
  mind 72
  speech 71
contributing factors 44
conversion disorder 361, 362
co-occurring disorders 36
coupolepause 418
Course and Outcome of Bipolar Youth (COBY) 165
Covid-19 pandemic 163, 247, 275, 309, 360, 477
CRD. *See* circadian rhythm disorders
culturally informed responding 38
cultural norms 121
culture 121
culture-related diagnostic issues 8
cyberchondria 359, 361
cyclothymia 161

daily microaggressions 8
DD. *See* delusional disorder
deaffectualization 336
deliberate self-harm (DSH) 517
delusional disorder (DD) 122, 123
delusions 120, 125
dependent personality disorder 507
depersonalization 301, 306, 336, 338, 344
depression 154, 179, 422, 446
  diagnosis in children and adolescents 166–170
depressive disorder 135
depressive episode 154
depressive type 135
derealization 301, 306, 336, 338, 344
desomatization 336
detox 479
detoxification 464, 479
developmental psychopathology 442–444
developmental trauma. *See* complex post-traumatic stress disorder
diabetes 2
diabulimia 384
diagnosis 65, 80–81
  cluster related symptoms 24
  diagnostic notation 30
  diagnostic principles 28
  eight steps 24
  identify potential diagnoses 25
  identify presenting problems, symptoms and observations 23
  locate the diagnosis 28
Diagnostic and Statistical Manual of Mental Disorders (DSM 5) 1
  changing structure of 12–15
  criticisms of 4–11
  culture-related diagnostic issues 8
  early editions 12
  importance of mastering 12
  inter-rater reliability 6
  lack of clarity 10
  minimizing risk 12
  organizational structure of 15
  pedophilic sexual orientation 10
  poor wording choices 10
  purpose of 1
  social trends and diagnostics 11–12
  validity questions 7–10
diagnostic bias 9
diagnostic concerns and matching diagnoses 29
diagnostic deferral 32
diagnostic genogram 46
diagnostic inflation 38
diagnostic notation 30
diagnostic principles 28, 37–47, 39
  caution in crisis, transition and personality concerns 43

diagnostic principles (*Continued*)
client resonance 44
clinical significance 37–47
contributing factors 44
culturally informed responding 38
horses and zebras or principle of commonality 40
Law of Parsimony 42
life span development 38
Occam's Razor 42
principle of predominance 42
unaccounted for symptoms 43
warranted concern 37
diagnostic process 50–51
cluster complaints 50
key information 50
potential diagnoses 50
diagnostic table 15, 55
dialectical behavioral therapy (DBT) 402, 512, 526
diathesis stress model 130
diathesis stress models 444
DID. *See* dissociative identity disorder
differential diagnosis 39, 52
difficult situations 43
discussion 17
disinhibited social engagement disorder (DSED) 302
disorder, disruptive mood dysregulation disorder (DMDD) 103
disorganized attachment 334
disorganized speech 125
disorganized thinking 122, 125
disruptions in sleep 274
disruptive impulse-control and conduct disorders. *See* conduct disorder (CD)
disruptive mood dysregulation disorder (DMDD) 161, 166, 167
dissatisfaction with sleep 271
dissociation 301, 306, 333, 334, 336
as emotion modulation 335
dissociative amnesia 339
dissociative disorders 299
definitional cases in 318–320
narrative cases in 320–324
pivot points 319
dissociative identity disorder (DID) 338
competing theories of 341
cultural considerations 344
definitional cases in 348–349
ethical considerations 343
factitious disorder 346
history 340–344
narrative cases in 349–350
pivot points 347
schizophrenia 346
sociocognitive model 342
structural dissociation theory 342
DMDD. *See* disruptive mood dysregulation disorder
documentation of diagnostic process 54
dopamine 129
Dottie's concerns and symptoms 25
double bind 129
double depression 162, 163
dream anxiety 273
drift 273
DSED. *See* disinhibited social engagement disorder
DSM 5. *See* Diagnostic and Statistical Manual of Mental Disorders
DSM III 14
DSM IV-TR 15
dual-diagnosis 35
dunkelfeld 543
dysthymia 162

eating disorders (EDs)
anorexia nervosa 387
avoidant/restrictive food intake disorder 386
binge eating disorder 388
body-positive moment 397
bulimia nervosa 387
cognition 392
compensatory behavior 388
cultural influences and 395
definitional cases 402–403
eating and gender transition 394
media 396
medical complications associated with 391
mental health 392
narrative cases 403–407
neurological and genetic factors 397
night eating syndrome 389
orthorexia nervosa 390
PANDAS 397
persons with autism spectrum disorders 398
pica 385, 386
purging disorder 390
race, ethnicity and gender 393
rigid eating patterns 398
rumination disorder 386
scope of practice 398
substance use disorders 392
suicide and deliberate self harm 393
theories of etiology 394–398
eating disorders (EDs) 383
echolalia 89, 94, 125

echopraxia 125
edema 384
EDs. *See* eating disorders
EE. *See* expressed emotion
EFT. *See* emotional freedom technique
EMDR. *See* eye movement desensitizationand reprocessing
emotional freedom technique (EFT) 317
endocrine systems 391
energy 71
episode of mood 152
ERP. *See* exposure and ritual prevention
excoriation disorder (ExD) 242
ExD. *See* excoriation disorder
exhibitionistic disorder 542
existential treatment plan 83
experiential avoidance 205
exposure and ritual prevention (ERP) 256
expressed emotion (EE) 179, 181
eye movement desensitization and reprocessing (EMDR) 256, 317

factitious disorder 346, 363, 367
  differential diagnosis of 369
factitious disorder imposed on another (FDIA) 363
false belief 81
false memory syndrome 336
family-focused therapy (FFT) 179
family systems 394
family therapy 402
fatosphere 384
faulty information processing 81
FDIA. *See* factitious disorder imposed on another
fear 203, 205, 217
female athlete triad 384
FFT. *See* family-focused therapy
fibromyalgia 371
food neophobia 384
frotteuristic disorder 542
FSS. *See* functional somatic syndromes
functional family therapy (FFT) 485
functional neurological symptom disorder 361
functional somatic syndromes (FSS) 356, 359

GAD. *See* generalized anxiety disorder
gender dysphoria 548
"gender paradox" 446
generalized anxiety disorder (GAD)
  acceptance-based model of 216
  attentional bias 214
  metacognitive model 216
  relationship to depression 212
  role of avoidance in 214
  theories and models 214–217
  vs. illness anxiety disorder 219
  vs. obsessive compulsive disorder 219
  vs. somatic symptom disorder 219
generalized anxiety disorder (GAD) 211–213, 274
general personality disorder (GPD) 504
genitourinary syndrome of menopause (GSM) 418
glutamate 129
grief 175
grossly disorganized behavior 121, 125
GSM. *See* genitourinary syndrome of menopause

hallucinations 120, 125
health anxiety 359
high functioning autism (HFA) 89
historical trauma 311
histrionic personality 506
HIV. *See* human immunodeficiency virus
hoarding disorder 241
homogeneity 87
homophobia 311
homosexuality 10
horizons of possibility 73
human immunodeficiency virus (HIV) 52
hyperphasia 384
hypersomnia 172, 271, 273
hypochondriasis 356, 360
hypomania 154
hypomanic episode 154
hypothalamus-pituitary-adrenal system 444
hypothesis 67
hysteria 356

IAD. *See* illness anxiety disorder
iatrogenic 337
IFS. *See* internal family systems
illness anxiety disorder (IAD) 52, 219, 220, 360
  differential diagnosis of 366
illness behavior 359
imagery 222
independent psychosis (IPD) 136
inference 56
infertility 418
insomnia 172, 271, 273, 274
  cognitive behavioral therapy for 279
  differential diagnosis of 282–283
  stress and learning 271
instrumental *vs.* expressive relationship 93

integrated interpersonal lens 84–85
integrated interpersonal treatment plan 85–86
"intense sexual arousal" 538
intermittent explosive disorder (IED) 436, 439
  diagnosis of 444
  in adulthood 448
International Classification of Diagnoses (ICD) 3, 30
International Society of Trauma and Dissociation 346
interpersonal therapy with social rhythm therapy (IPSRT) 178
inter-rater reliability 6
intoxication 464, 471
intrusive thoughts 252
IPD. *See* independent psychosis
IPSRT. *See* interpersonal therapy with social rhythm therapy

justification 30, 49, 80–81
  purpose of 49, 50
  steps 51–54
  writing 54–62
kleptomania 441
  diagnosis of 448
knowledge 74

LAAM 479
la belle indifference 361
lanugo 384
Law of Parsimony 42
learning theories 250
least restrictive care (LRC) 480
lesbian, gay, bisexual and transgender (LGBT) issues 4
life span development 38
lifestyle medicine 371
lithium 176

major depressive disorder (MDD) 2, 154, 162
malingering 369
mania 153
manic episodes 153, 164
marasmus 384
MBCT. *See* mindfulness-based cognitive therapy
MDD. *See* major depressive disorder
measles, mumps and rubella (MMR) vaccines 99
measurable goals 76
medically unexplained symptoms (MUS) 356
melancholia 163
menopause 418
mental contamination 246
mental disorder 6
mental health
  constructivist nature of 2–3
  disorders 2
  non-Western approaches 4
mental illness
  alternative frameworks for understanding 3–4
  constructivist nature of 2–3
mentalization 89, 525
mentalization-based therapy (MBT) 527
metabolic systems 391
metacognitive model (MCC) 216
metaworry 205
microaggressions 8, 311
mind 72
mindfulness 222
mindfulness-based cognitive therapy (MBCT) 179
mirror neurons 98
misdiagnosis 38, 52
mixed features specifier 154
MMR vaccines. *See* measles, mumps and rubella vaccines
monosymptomatic hypochondriacal psychosis 356
mood congruency 156
mood disorders 164, 174, 274
  bipolar disorder. *See* bipolar disorder
  definitional cases 180, 184–185
  grief 175
  narrative cases in 186–193
  pivot points 182
  psychotherapy and treatment of 177–180
  sexual dysfunction 175
  treatment of 175–177
mood episode 152, 153
  discerning 171
moral injury 301, 309
MPD. *See* multiple personality disorder
multicultural competence 11
multidimensional family therapy (MDFT) 485
multiple diagnosis 35
Multiple Family Group Treatment (MFT) 526
multiple personality disorder (MPD) 340
Munchausen's syndrome 356
muscle dysmorphia 384

narcissism 443
narcissistic personality disorder 506
narrative auditory hallucinations 125
narrative therapy lens 83–84
narrative treatment plan 84
National Epidemiologic Survey on Alcohol and Related Conditions (NESARC) 516
National Institutes of Health (NIH) 165

National Institutes of Mental Health (NIMH) 131
NES. *See* night eating syndrome
neurodevelopmental dimension 88–91
  attention deficit hyperactivity disorder 91
  social (pragmatic) communication disorder (SPCD) 88
  stereotypic movements 90
  tic disorders 90
neurodevelopmental disorders 87
  attention deficit hyperactivity disorder. *See* attention deficit hyperactivity disorder
  autism spectrum disorder. *See* autism spectrum disorder
  definitional cases in 106–108
  narrative cases in 108–110
  pivot points 107
neurodiversity 89
neurological shifts 391
neurotypical 89
night eating syndrome (NES) 389
nightmare disorder 270
nihilistic delusions 120
NIMH. *See* National Institutes of Mental Health
non-medical use 104
non-pathological mood states
  charette 159
  ennui 159
  flow 157
  protracted irritation and dissatisfaction 160
non-verbal communication 94
nosophobia 360

obesity 384
observations 23
obsession 240, 245
obsessive compulsive dimension 240
obsessive compulsive disorder (OCD) 95, 96, 219, 239, 242–248
  aggressive and sexual obsessions 246
  biological contributions 248
  checking 244
  cognitive models 250
  compulsions 247
  contamination 245, 246
  Covid-19 pandemic 247
  culture and 248
  definitional cases 257–259
  differential diagnosis in children 253
  etiological theories of 248–251
  family accommodation 251
  learning theories 250
  narrative cases in 259–262
  obsessional themes in 243
  obsessive thoughts of 244
  PANDAS 250
  pivot points 258
  religiosity 246
  scrupulosity 246
  symmetry obsessions 246
  treatment of 255–257
obsessive compulsive personality disorder (OCPD) 507, 543
obsessive compulsive related disorders (OCRD) 240–242
  body dysmorphic disorder (BDD) 240, 241
  definitional cases 257–259
  excoriation disorder (ExD) 242
  hoarding disorder 241
  narrative cases in 259–262
  pivot points 258
  skin picking disorder 242
  treatment of 255–257
  trichotillomania 242
Occam's Razor 42
ODD. *See* oppositional defiant disorder
oligomenorrhea 384
oppositional defiant disorder (ODD)
  vs. disruptive mood dysregulation disorder 168, 169, 170
oppositional defiant disorder (ODD) 102, 436
  ADHD 447
  and depression 446
  children behavior 447
  complex trauma 446
  diagnosis of 444
  lifetime prevalence 436
orthorexia 384
orthorexia nervosa (ON) 390
outcome goals 74
overt racism 311

pain sensitivity 95
panic
  disorder 210, 211
panic attack specifier 210
PANS. *See* pediatric acute-onset neuropsychiatric syndrome
paraphilia disorders
  accurate diagnosis 545–546
  clinician self-awareness 545
  definitional cases 550–552
  dimension 538–543
  DSM 5 539
  exhibitionistic disorder 542
  frotteuristic disorder 542
  gender dysphoria 548
  narrative cases 552–558
  normal sexual fantasies 542

paraphilia disorders (*Continued*)
  pedophilic disorder 542–543
  pharmacological interventions 548–549
  psychotherapy 550
  sexual masochism disorder 542
  sexual sadism disorder 542
  shared criteria 540
  shared traits 540–541
  transvestic disorder 542, 548
  voyeuristic disorder 541
parasympathetic nervous system 335
parent management training (PMT) 450
PBD. *See* pediatric bipolar disorders
PD. *See* purging disorder
PDD. *See* persistent depressive disorder; pre-menstrual dysphoric disorder
pediatric acute-onset neuropsychiatric syndrome (PANS) 250
pediatric autoimmune neuropsychiatric disorders associated with streptococcus (PANDAS) 250
pediatric bipolar disorders (PBD) 164
pedophilia OCD 252
pedophilic disorder 542–543
pedophilic sexual orientation 10
peer-based recovery 485
perinatal depression, psychosis and 135
perseveration 89
persistent depressive disorder (PDD) 162
personal diagnostic skill 49
personality disorders
  alternative framework 507
  borderline personality 505, 516–519
  children and teens 513
  classification of 503
  cluster A: 504
  cluster B: 505
  cluster C: 506
  clusters 508
  continuum 504–507
  culture, gender 515
  definitional cases 527–528
  dependent personality 507
  dialectical behavioral therapy 526
  DSM 5 503
  histrionic personality 506
  multiaxial system 510
  Multiple Family Group Treatment 526
  narcissistic personality 506
  narrative cases 529–532
  obsessive compulsive personality 507
  schizoid personality 505
  schizotypal personality 505
  transference focused therapy 527
phallometry 543
phobia, behavioral interventions for 220
phrasing 76
physical aspects 71
pica 385, 386
pivot tables 28
play therapy 317
polytrauma clinical triad 301
polyvagal model 335
positive stress 300, 301
post-traumatic growth (PTG) 301, 312
post-traumatic model (PTM) 341, 451
post-traumatic play 301
post-traumatic stress disorder (PTSD)
  body-based interventions 317
  child abuse experiences 310
  comorbidity in 313
  complex 307
  Covid-19 pandemic 309
  development of 310
  diagnosis 306–308
  dissociative subtypes 307
  history of 304
  in the DSM 5 305
  pharmacological interventions 317
  play therapy 317
  populations and 308–313
  post-traumatic growth 312
  promoting 316
  psychotherapy 316
  specifiers and subtypes of 306
  trauma resilience 312
  treatments 316–318
  war-related 308
post-traumatic stress disorder (PTSD) 275, 446, 474, 521, 543
post-traumatic stress (PTS) 306
potential diagnoses 50
  identify 25
  matching symptoms to 54
potential diagnostic dimensions 27
pre-menstrual dysphoric disorder (PDD) 163
premonitory urge 89
presenting problem 23
primary mental health disorder (PMHD) 470
principle of predominance 42
prioritize problems 66
pro-ana 385
problematic sleep 271
problems 65, 66
professional ethics 13
pro-mia 385

prosody 89, 125
psychoanalytic conceptualizations 128
Psychodynamic Diagnostic Manual (PDM-2) 3
psychoeducation 138
psychological factors affecting other medical conditions (PFMC) 362
psychopathy 442
psychosis 131, 153, 156, 344
  and perinatal depression 135
psychosomatic illness 356
psychotherapy 138, 316, 347, 550
psychotic episodes 176
PTM. *See* post-traumatic model
purging disorder (PD) 390
pyromania 441
  diagnosis of 448
race-based trauma 301
racism 8, 9
RAD. *See* reactive attachment disorder
rapid eye movement (REM) 273, 274
reactive attachment disorder (RAD) 300, 303
recovered memory 336, 346
refeeding 401
refeeding syndrome 385, 401
relative age effects 89
relaxation techniques 281
religiosity 246
REM. *See* rapid eye movement
repression 336, 337
Research Domain Criteria (RDoC) 3
response prevention 222
restoring sleep 177
retarded depression. *See* anergic depression
risperidone 105
role impairment 163
rule out 33
rumination disorder 386
Russell's sign 385

SAD. *See* social anxiety disorder
schizoaffective disorder 126, 127, 135
  vs. unipolar or bipolar psychosis 173
schizoid personality disorders 505
schizophrenia 126, 346
  and autism spectrum disorder 136
schizophrenia continuum 122–128
  attenuated psychosis syndrome 127
  brief psychotic disorder 124
  delusional disorder 122
  schizoaffective disorder 126
  schizophrenia 126
  schizophreniform disorder 124
  schizotypal personality disorder 127
schizophrenia spectrum
  cases in 138–144
  cultural and normative beliefs and experiences 121
  diagnostic nosologies 131–132
  diathesis stress model 130
  differential diagnosis 132–137
  disorganized thinking 122
  features of 120–122
  grossly disorganized behavior 121
  negative symptoms 121, 122
  pivot points 140
  positive symptoms 121
  sociocultural considerations 130
  treatment interventions for 137–138
schizophreniform disorder 124
schizophrenogenic mother 128
schizotypal personality disorder 122, 127, 505
Scholastic Assessment Test (SAT) 435
scrupulosity 246
selective eating 385
selective mutism 207
selective serotonin reuptake inhibitors (SSRIs) 165, 317, 548
self-psychology 395
separation anxiety disorder 206
serotonergic system (SS) 444
serotonin and norepinephrine reuptake inhibitors (SNRI) 317
sex therapy 427
sexual desire 537
sexual disorders 315
sexual dysfunctions 175, 417
  asexual identities 424
  biopsychosocial model for 417–423
  cancer treatments 419
  changes in DSM 5 416–417
  chronic and acute trauma 422
  definitional cases in 428–429
  differential diagnosis 426
  disorders 416
  infertility 418
  medical conditions 421
  medical conditions and relationship 417
  medications and side effects 418, 419
  menopause and andropause 418
  narrative cases in 429–431
  pivot points 425
  psychological sources of 419
  screening and outside referrals 424
  side effects in men and women 421
  sociocultural factors 422

sexual dysfunctions (*Continued*)
  substances 419
  substance use 423
sexual health 415
sexually-themed obsessive thoughts 252
sexually violent predator (SVP) commitment laws 546–548
sexual masochism disorder 542
sexual obsessions 253
sexual sadism disorder 542
shift work 273
SIP. *See* substance-induced psychosis
situational depression 301
skill and intervention planning 74
skin picking disorder 242
sleep 274
sleep disorders 272
sleep disruption 274, 282
sleep disturbance 272, 273, 274, 275
  and attention deficit hyperactivity disorder 102
sleep hygiene 273
  and psychoeducation 281
sleeplessness 271
sleep rhythms 270
sleep-wake disorders
  autism spectrum disorders 273
  circadian rhythm disorders 270
  definitional cases 286–288
  diagnostic discernment 278
  generalized anxiety disorder 274
  hypersomnia 271
  insomnia. *See* insomnia
  intersection with mental health disorders 276
  mood disorders 274
  narrative cases 288–294
  nightmare disorder 270
  pivot points 284
  sleep disturbance 273
  suicidality 274
  treatment 279–282
slow-wave sleep 273
small t traumas 301
social anxiety disorder (SAD) 135, 209, 218
  agoraphobia 211
  culture and prevalence of 210
  panic attack specifier 210
  panic disorder 210
  vs. selective mutism 219
social engagement 94
socially deviant behavior 6
social or occupational impairment 153
social phobia 217
social (pragmatic) communication disorder (SPCD) 88
Society of Humanistic Psychology 4
sociocognitive model (SCM) 342
somatic delusions 120
somatic symptom
  aging and 370
  culture and 371
somatic symptom continuum of disorders 358–364
  conversion disorder 361, 362
  Covid-19 360
  factitious disorder 363
  illness anxiety disorder 360
  psychological factors affecting other medical conditions 362
  somatic symptom disorder. *See* somatic symptom disorder
somatic symptom disorder (SSD) 219, 220, 355
  cases for diagnosis 372
  changes in the DSM 5 357–358
  complications in diagnosing 366
  definitional cases 373–375
  differential diagnosis of 366
  in childhood and adolescence 365–366
  narrative cases in 375–378
somatization 356
  by proxy 356, 370
specific phobias 209, 217
specifiers 16, 56, 92
speech 71
  client's communication style 72
  energy 71
  use of language 72
SSD. *See* somatic symptom disorder
SSRIs. *See* selective serotonin reuptake inhibitors
stabilizing mood 176
stabilizing sleep 274
stereo-typed memory bias 9
stereotypic movements 89, 90
  vs. tics 91
stimulant diversion 104
stress 300, 420
stressor-related disorders
  narrative cases in 320–324
strong goal, elements of 78
structural dissociation 337
structural dissociation theory 342
subgoals 74
substance-induced mood disorder (SIMD) 478
substance-induced persisting disorder 464
substance-induced psychosis (SIP) 135, 136, 478, 484
substance use 174, 275
substance use disorders (SUDs)

addiction conversation 468
addiction treatment 479–486
biological models 465
borderline personality disorder 518
cognitive-behavioral model 465
co-occurring disorders 481
cultural and theoretical shifts 462–469
definitional cases 486–488
diagnostic language 466
diagnostic process 469–472
DSM criteria 468
dual diagnosis 477–478
family treatment 485
impaired control 470
moral model 465
narrative cases 488–493
outpatient treatment 484
pharmaceutical interventions 479
pharmacological criteria 471
racial and ethnic minority groups 475
residential care 480
risky use 471
social impairment 470
sociocultural models 466
special populations 472–477
treatment of 461
substance use disorders (SUDs) 315, 392
sub-threshold 35
sudden unexplained deaths 104
suicidality 274, 313
suicide 157
suicide obsessions 253
suppression 337
suprachiasmatic nucleus 270
symmetry obsessions 246
symptoms 23
symptom timeline 46
synesthesia 137
systematic desensitization 427
systems of managed care 35

theoretical grounding 68
theory of mind 89, 93
thinspiration 385
thought-action fusion likelihood (TAF-L) 250
thought-action fusion (TAF) model 250
thought broadcasting 121, 125
thought insertion 125
thought suppression 205
thought withdrawal 125
tic disorders 89, 90
timelines, treatment plan 75
TKS. *See* taijin kyofusho
tolerable stress 302
tolerance 464
toxic stress 302
transference focused therapy (TFT) 527
transvestic disorder 542, 548
trauma 300, 302, 315
narrative cases in 320–324
pivot points 319
trauma continuum 300, 302
disorders of 300–304
trauma disorders 299
traumagenic 337
trauma resilience 302, 312, 316
treatment-emergent psychosis 104
treatment plan 73–79
existential 83
integrated interpersonal 85–86
measurable goals 76
narrative 84
outcome goals 74
structure 74
subgoals 74
timelines 75
writing achievable goals 77
trichotillomania (TTM) 242
type II trauma 300
type I trauma 300

ultradian cycling 166
unaccounted for symptoms 43
unconscious processes 50
unipolar depression 172
vs. bipolar depression 172
unipolar mood disorders 170–175
cognitive behavioral therapy 178
psychotherapy for 178
unipolar or bipolar psychosis
vs. schizoaffective disorder 173
unwanted sexual experiences (USE) 538
up-coding 35
use of language 72

vertical split 395
vital exhaustion 163
voyeuristic disorder 541

warranted concern 37
war-related PTSD 308
women, substance use 473
World Health Organization (WHO) 3, 157
worry 205
worry outcome monitoring 222
writing achievable goals 77
writing up justification 54–62
  benefits of 56
  diagnostic table 55

Z codes 18
zeitgebers (time giver) 181, 273
zeitstorers (time disturber) 181, 273